1997 Medical and Health Annual

Encyclopædia Britannica, Inc.

Chicago • Auckland • London • Madrid • Manila • Paris • Rome
Seoul • Sydney • Tokyo • Toronto

1997 Medical and Health Annual

Library of Congress Catalog Card Number: 77-649875
International Standard Book Number: 0-85229-632-0 International Standard Serial Number: 0363-0366

Foreword: A Look Back

Twenty years ago Encyclopædia Britannica, Inc., introduced a brand new yearbook. "We have tried to produce a book that is both informative and interesting in a field of universal concern. . . . We support the modern view that the person informed in medical matters is likely to be healthier . . . [and] better equipped to maintain health," wrote Charles E. Swanson, then president of Britannica, in the foreword to the 1977 *Medical and Health Annual.*

That now well-established yearbook has evolved in many important ways. It still aims to convey to a lay audience the challenge and excitement in the ever-expanding fields of medicine and health—and to do so with authority. It remains "a book by experts, for laymen . . . intended to inform, not to prescribe." More than anything else, however, the *Annual* has attempted to reflect the sweeping changes that have occurred over the past 20 years—stunning advances in the understanding, diagnosis, prevention, and treatment of human illness; unqualified breakthroughs, as well as disappointing setbacks; unanticipated—and sometimes dire—disease outbreaks; newly recognized threats to health; and even shifts in the very notion of what constitutes "health." Always our goal has been to reflect the "real world" of medicine and health, to present the "big picture" by having our expert contributors put medical news in perspective—something the daily news media seldom do.

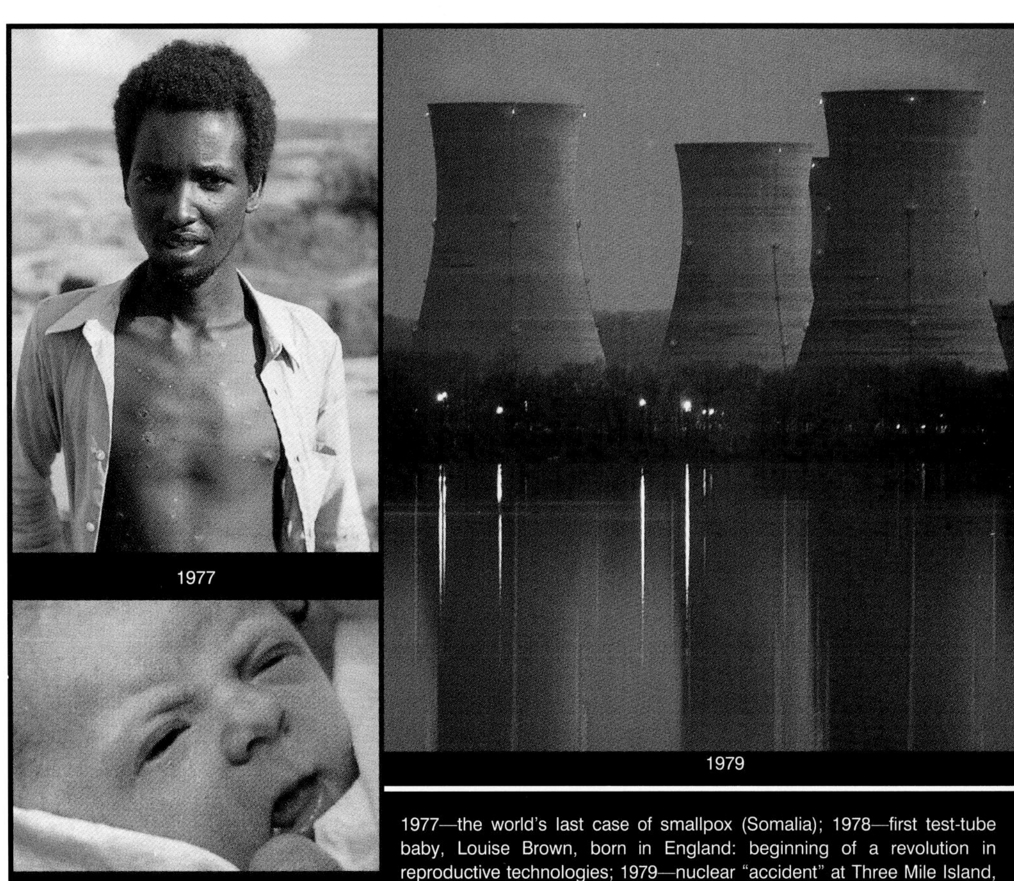

1977

1978

1979

1977—the world's last case of smallpox (Somalia); 1978—first test-tube baby, Louise Brown, born in England: beginning of a revolution in reproductive technologies; 1979—nuclear "accident" at Three Mile Island, Pennsylvania.

(Top) Centers for Disease Control and Prevention; (right) Robin Moyer—Black Star; (above) Hulton Getty

To mark the 20th anniversary of the *Medical and Health Annual,* the editors decided to take a look back—to highlight in words and pictures some of the major happenings in medicine and health over the last two decades. We solicited the help of our two medical advisers, Drummond Rennie (deputy editor of the *Journal of the American Medical Association*) in the U.S. and Stephen Lock (editor emeritus of the *British Medical Journal*) in the U.K.

Quite naively, we assumed that to come up with our 20-year "progress report" we could simply look through the past 19 years' *Annual*s and select, say, three to five developments per calendar year. How wrong we were! It soon became apparent that the task we had set about to accomplish was neither easy nor straightforward. As Dr. Rennie discovered, "It's no trivial matter to assess when a discovery becomes published or ripe, or has become popular, or has held up long enough for us to know it won't collapse, as so many discoveries have, under the weight of counterevidence, or later events (didn't we say good-bye to malaria in the '70s?). A major advance, for example, is medicine's realization that violence is a public health matter—or that one aspect of violence, abuse in the home, is a medical issue. But when did those things happen? When did the tide of research reach 'enough'?"

(Top row, left to right) Trippett—Sipa; © Dan McCoy—Rainbow/PNI; © Phototake/PNI; Alon Reininger—Contact Press Images; (second row, left) Greg Mellis—Copley News Service; (right) Karen Wollins; (bottom row, left to right) © Annie Griffiths Belt; Calais—VSO/Gamma Liaison; Gary Hershorn—Reuters

1981—AIDS pandemic begins; 1982—Jarvik-7 artificial heart implanted in a human patient; 1990—Human Genome Project launched; 1991—U.S. establishes an Office of Alternative Medicine to study unconventional therapies; 1992—U.S. surgeon general declares violence a public health emergency; 1993—food labels introduced; 1994—obesity reaches epidemic proportions in industrialized parts of the world; 1995—Ebola outbreak, Zaire; 1996—new starring role for Christopher Reeve: advocate for people with disabilities.

Dr. Lock found that attempting to pin a discovery or advance in medicine to a particular year was exceedingly tough, to say the least. "What should the year commemorate?" he wondered. "Is it the discovery, first-ever documentation, or when some survey showed there was a problem (or a solution)?" Almost always, he noted, "an actual discovery is some years in the making before anything comes into prominence (such as laser surgery)."

Some things *could* be tied to a specific year—*e.g.*, production of the first genetically engineered drug, human insulin (1978); the first AIDS cases (1981); official declaration of the eradication of smallpox (1980)—the last case having been detected in 1977; approval of the immunosuppressant cyclosporine for preventing transplant rejections (1983); routine testing of blood for HIV (1985); Chernobyl nuclear disaster (1986); the antidepressant fluoxetine (Prozac) first marketed (1987); aspirin shown to protect against heart disease in men (1988) and women (1991); the first "assisted suicide" involving retired pathologist Jack Kevorkian (1990); passage of the Americans with Disabilities Act (1990); the first gene therapy undertaken in a human patient (1991); breast cancer genes, *BRCA1* and *BRCA2*, discovered (1994); polio officially eradicated from the Western Hemisphere (1994); and frightening outbreaks of cholera in Latin America (1991), hantavirus in the American Southwest (1993), plague in India (1994), and Ebola virus in Zaire (1995).

Then there was the Human Genome Project, which many scientists consider the most ambitious scientific research project of the 20th century. While the year 1990 was the date that the project was officially launched, the actual plan to identify the estimated 50,000–100,000 human genes first had to be conceived, proposed, approved, and, most important, funded. Goals had to be set; specific institutions and laboratories had to be enlisted; officials and scientists had to be recruited. Moreover, it was only because amazing new tools and technologies had been developed (over many years) that such an undertaking could even be considered. Thus, embarking on the Human Genome Project in 1990 represented the culmination of decades of earlier work and breakthroughs; at the same time, it was only the first step in a process sure to produce a revolution in scientific knowledge.

On these three pages we present a few of the milestones that made it onto our lists. By no means do we suggest that our humble selections represent the "top" events in 20 years of medicine and health. Enough said.

—*The Editors*

CONTENTS

Features

42

62

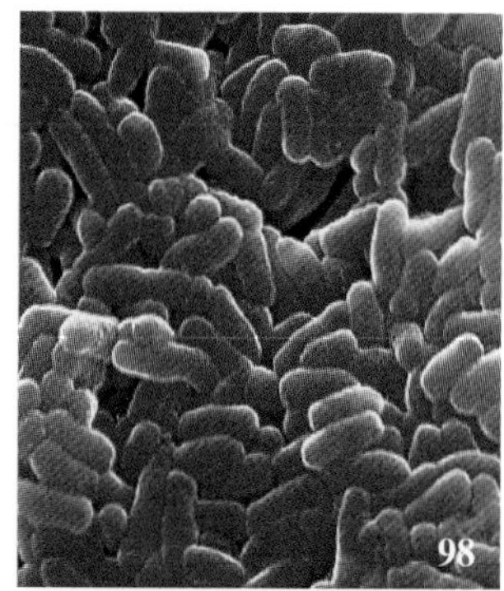
98

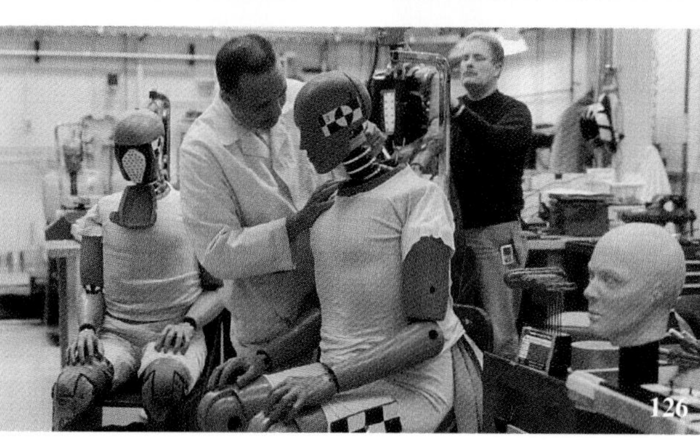
126

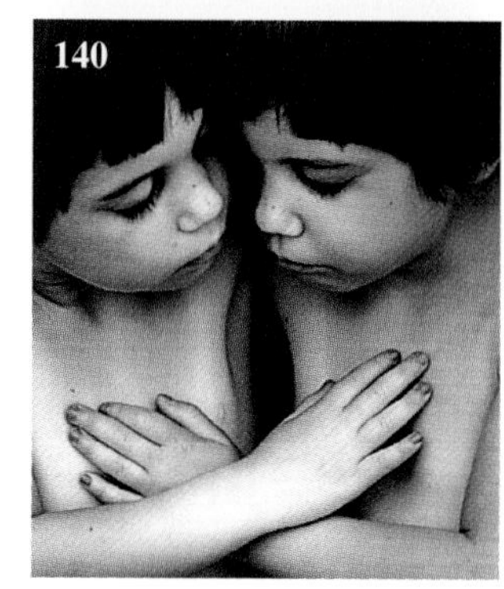
140

220

298

308

342

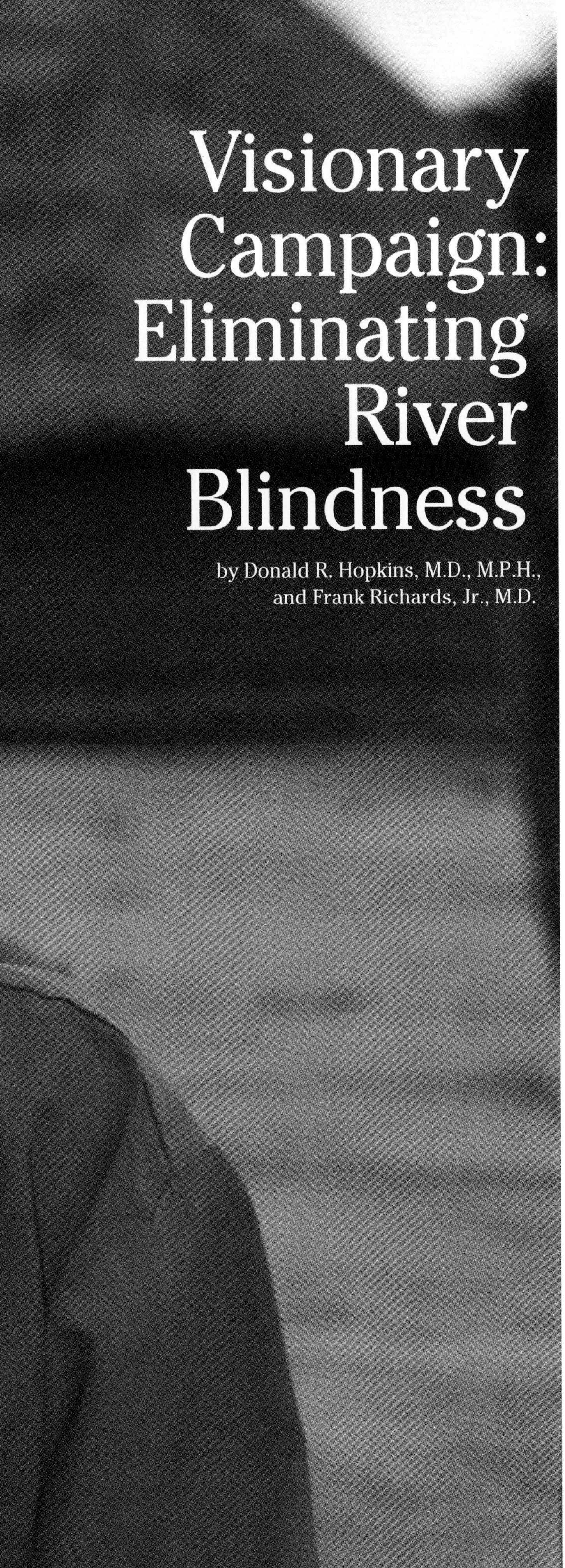

Visionary Campaign: Eliminating River Blindness

by Donald R. Hopkins, M.D., M.P.H., and Frank Richards, Jr., M.D.

Nearness to large rivers eats the eye.
—a West African proverb

Virtually all evidence suggests that the tropical malady onchocerciasis (often called river blindness) originated in Africa and spread to Arabia and Latin America with the slave trade. It was not until the last century, however, that a British surgeon, John O'Neill, first described the immature microfilariae of the parasite, associating them with skin lesions that he observed in patients in the Gold Coast (now Ghana) in 1875. The adult worms were first noted 18 years later. (*See* River Blindness: Milestones, page 22.) Named *Filaria volvulus* in 1893, the parasite was reclassified to the genus *Onchocerca* in 1910. The Guatemalan physician Rodolfo Robles recognized the adult worms and skin lesions in patients in 1915, suspecting that they

Donald R. Hopkins, M.D., M.P.H., *is Senior Consultant, Global 2000, The Carter Center, Atlanta, Georgia, and Director, Global 2000 River Blindness Program.*
Frank Richards, Jr., M.D., *is Deputy Director, Global 2000 River Blindness Program, The Carter Center, detailed from the Centers for Disease Control and Prevention, Atlanta, Georgia.*

Blinded by onchocerciasis (river blindness), Séguéla, Côte d'Ivoire, Africa.

Chris Brown—Saba

Impossible Hope?

by Jimmy Carter

In September 1994 my wife, Rosalynn, and I visited Nia, a village of about 500 people in southern Chad, near the geographic center of Africa. Nearly all of the inhabitants were infected with the parasite that causes river blindness (onchocerciasis), which was the reason for our visit. Although the disease had long been known in this part of Chad, its prevalence had been made much worse in Nia after a small dam was built nearby in 1966. The purpose of the dam was to help the villagers grow more rice. Unfortunately, it also dramatically increased the number of breeding sites for the blackflies that transmit onchocerciasis to humans. Of the many affected people we saw that morning, one stood out: a 24-year-old mother, Christine, who already was blind from the disease. As she spoke to us, with a shy smile and sightless eyes, she held her young son Tidum, whose name means "impossible hope."

We were accompanied to Nia by a physician, Roy Vagelos, who was then the president of Merck & Co., Inc., which in 1987 had made the momentous decision to donate, in perpetuity, as much of the drug Mectizan as was needed for treating river blindness in all the affected areas of the less developed world. Mectizan (ivermectin), which Merck discovered in 1975, virtually eliminates the terrible symptoms of onchocerciasis and prevents sight loss.

The nonprofit Carter Center in Atlanta, Georgia, had been involved in the fight against river blindness since 1987, when Merck asked the center's senior health policy fellow, William Foege, to chair its Mectizan Expert Committee. In 1995 The Carter Center stepped up its efforts to control the disease by joining forces with the River Blindness Foundation (RBF), an organization that was founded in 1990 by John and Rebecca Moores of Houston, Texas, and that began its work in Latin America, Nigeria, Cameroon, and Uganda. John Moores was already an exceptionally generous supporter of The Carter Center and a member of its board of trustees. Although several other nongovernmental organizations (NGOs) also are helping to distribute Mectizan as part of their efforts toward providing broad primary health care in the less developed regions of the world, the RBF was the only one that was devoted exclusively to helping ensure that Mectizan reached the poor rural villages where it was needed. By 1995 local programs assisted by the RBF were distributing Mectizan to more than four million people.

were linked to disease of the eye; by 1917 he surmised that the biting blackflies that were found on coffee plantations at similar altitudes in his country were transmitting the disease.

For generations, if not centuries, some African societies may have associated prevalent blindness with the distinctively annoying riverine blackflies they encountered (as the West African proverb above suggests). The scientific proof of that association came only around 1938, when French doctors in Upper Volta (now Burkina Faso) first noted the relationship between onchocerciasis, mass blindness, and the abandonment of certain river valleys by local populations. A British physician confirmed the same phenomenon in northern Gold Coast in 1949.

From bite to blindness: a complex life cycle

People are infected by onchocerciasis when they are bitten by a blackfly of the

(Right) Adult worms of *Onchocerca volvulus;* female worms can measure up to 50 centimeters (20 inches). In humans, *O. volvulus* worms commonly reside in nodules that can be seen and felt beneath the skin. (Below) Larvae harbored by the *Simulium damnosum* blackfly, the most important vector of river blindness.

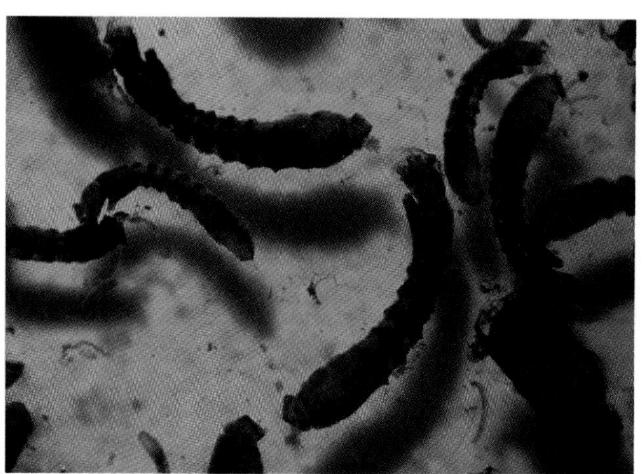

(Above) David Reed—Panos Pictures; (right) WHO

Merck & Co., Inc.

Jimmy and Rosalynn Carter and Roy Vagelos, president of Merck & Co., visit Nia, Chad, in 1994. Prior to Merck's donation of the drug Mectizan, most villagers were affected by river blindness.

In early 1996 The Carter Center assumed responsibility for the foundation's mission of global control of this terrible disease. Our new program, called the Global 2000 River Blindness Program of The Carter Center, is being directed by two eminent scientists, Donald Hopkins (a recipient of a 1995 John D. and Catherine T. MacArthur Foundation fellowship for his outstanding disease-eradication work) and Frank Richards, Jr., an international disease expert on loan from the Centers for Disease Control and Prevention.

The Carter Center has a history of battling "end of the road" diseases—those that are not well-known in the industrialized world but are devastating to the poorest people on Earth. Since 1986 we have led the fight against another parasitic affliction, dracunculiasis (guinea worm disease). That program, led by Hopkins, has helped reduce the number of guinea worm disease cases by 97% in a single decade. Now, by assuming the activities of the RBF and by working in close cooperation with the World Bank's new African Program for Onchocerciasis Control and other NGOs, we intend to help win this new public health battle.

Jimmy Carter, *the 39th president of the United States (1977–81), is founder of The Carter Center, Atlanta, Georgia, a nongovernmental, nonprofit organization that promotes peace and human rights; resolves conflicts; fosters democracy and development; and fights hunger, poverty, and disease throughout the world.*

genus *Simulium* that harbors one or more infectious (third-stage) *O. volvulus* larvae. The larva is deposited in the wound caused by the fly's bite and is transformed within four months into a fourth-stage larva; after about a year it molts a final time to reach the adult stage. Adult female *O. volvulus* worms measure 30–50 centimeters (12–20 inches) in length. Males are much smaller, measuring three–five centimeters (one–two inches). The adult worms can live as long as 12 years. Unique though poorly understood attractants bring the male and female worms together inside the human body, where they gather in groups of five or six, intertwined and encased in a fibrous capsule that forms a nodule. Nodules can often be felt under the skin. The uterus is the most prominent organ of the female worm, occupying some 80% of her internal space and enabling her to produce thousands of embryo offspring called microfilariae. Microfilariae (which are about the size of a period on a typewritten page) leave the nodule and migrate into the skin, eyes, and other organs. Persons with many fertilized female worms in their bodies may harbor as many as 200 million microfilariae. The microfilariae live 9–18 months, but they cannot develop into adult worms without first passing through the *Simulium* blackfly vector. In these insects the microfilar-

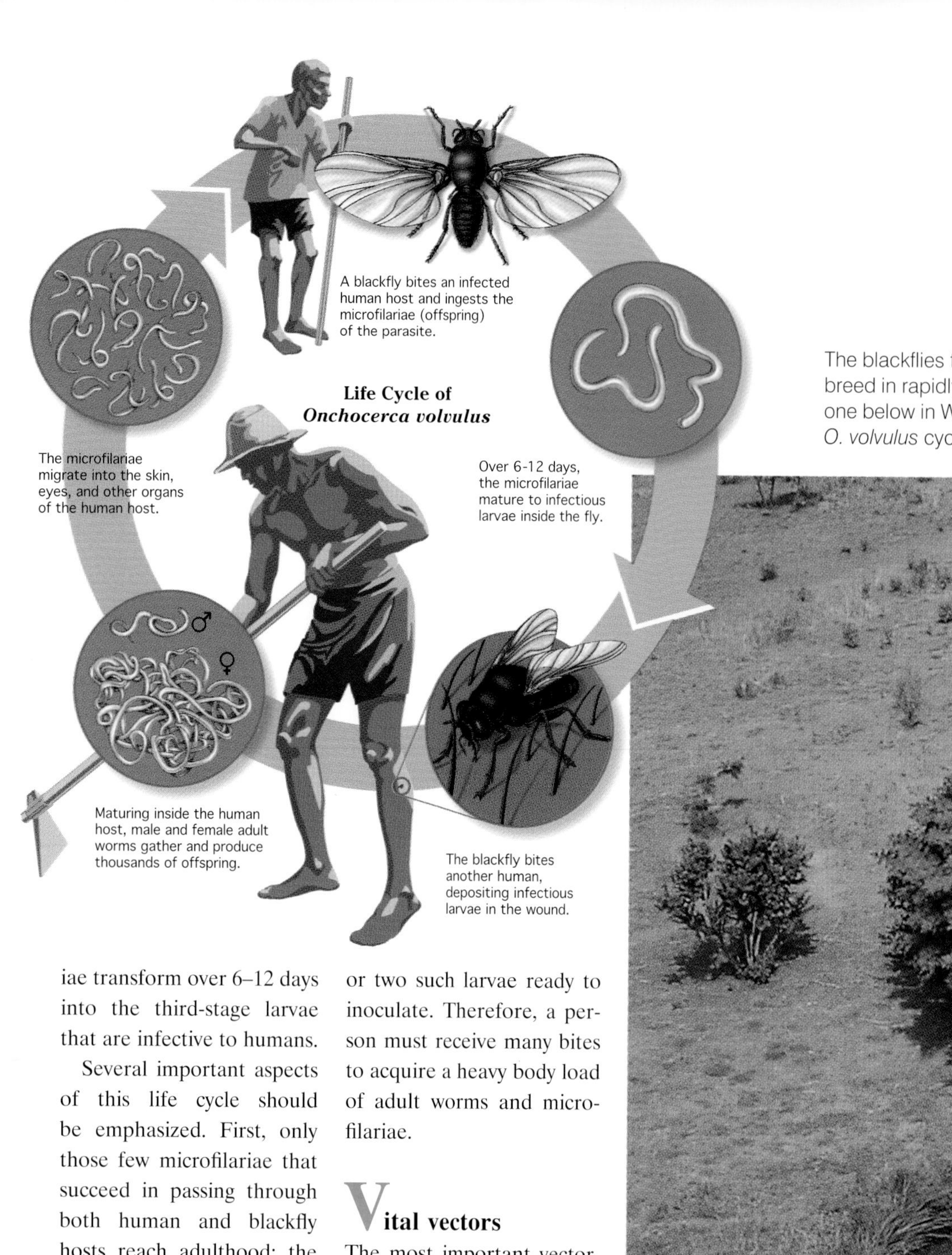
A blackfly bites an infected human host and ingests the microfilariae (offspring) of the parasite.
Life Cycle of
Onchocerca volvulus
The microfilariae migrate into the skin, eyes, and other organs of the human host.
Over 6-12 days, the microfilariae mature to infectious larvae inside the fly.
♂
♀
Maturing inside the human host, male and female adult worms gather and produce thousands of offspring.
The blackfly bites another human, depositing infectious larvae in the wound.

The blackflies that carry onchocerciasis breed in rapidly flowing rivers like the one below in West Africa. (Left) The *O. volvulus* cycle of destruction.

David Reed—Impact Photos

iae transform over 6–12 days into the third-stage larvae that are infective to humans.

Several important aspects of this life cycle should be emphasized. First, only those few microfilariae that succeed in passing through both human and blackfly hosts reach adulthood; the rest die by the thousands in the human body. Second, the blackfly must bite at least twice to transmit the infection: once to acquire microfilariae from an infected person and again to transmit the infectious larvae to someone else. Last, rarely do more than 5% of blackflies harbor infectious larvae at a given time, and most of these flies will have just one or two such larvae ready to inoculate. Therefore, a person must receive many bites to acquire a heavy body load of adult worms and microfilariae.

Vital vectors

The most important vector, or carrier, of onchocerciasis is *S. damnosum,* which is found widely throughout Africa and the Middle East. In East Africa *S. neavei* also transmits onchocerciasis. Major vectors in the Western Hemisphere are *S. ochraceum, S. metallicum, S. oyapockense, S. guianense,* and *S. exiguum*.

Blackflies breed in rapidly flowing streams and rivers,

and their numbers increase the closer one gets to these breeding sites. Thus, villagers living near rivers have a greater risk of being severely infected and acquiring heavy body loads of adult worms and microfilariae (hyperendemic onchocerciasis).

Farmers in the field

Onchocerciasis is a disease that primarily affects farmers and pastoral peoples, who, during a day of work in the fields, may suffer hundreds of blackfly bites. Each bite results in pinpoint-size bleeding sites on their skin, swelling, redness, and itching. In the words of Michael Richards, a public health worker who visited an endemic area in Venezuela: "There is an eerie sound in the community, and that is one of constant slapping as people try to keep the bugs off their skin. The movement of hands flaying away at backs, legs, and arms is ubiquitous and seemingly quite naturally accepted as a matter of daily living."

Dismal disease

The nodules caused by the adult worms are not painful;

they usually resemble lima beans in their size, shape (they are often flattened), and firm consistency. They can, however, be up to several centimeters in diameter. When located just beneath the skin, they are most common over bony prominences. In Africa it is typical for the nodules to occur mainly around the pelvis, whereas in Mexico and Guatemala nodules usually appear in the upper torso region or on the head. The terrible symptoms of onchocerciasis result from the inflammation provoked by dying microfilariae in the skin and eyes.

Skin reaction. Itching and skin rash (dermatitis) are the most common symptoms of people with onchocerciasis, who may be absolutely tormented by the itching over the lower trunk and thighs. Their constant and vigorous scratching can produce open and bleeding sores that may become secondarily infected. The initial skin rash usually appears as small raised bumps, similar to that caused by poison ivy. Both skin and regional lymph glands become tender and swollen. Over the years the inflammation in the skin results in changes in pigmentation. Uneven depigmentation over the shins gives the appearance of dark spots on a white background ("leopard skin"). In Yemen darkening of the skin from onchocerciasis on one arm or leg, with associated swelling, itching, bumps, and enlarged lymph glands, called *sowda,* is common. Skin may also appear prematurely aged, thick, scaly, and wrinkled ("lizard skin").

Eye damage. Microfilariae that enter the eyes may incite an inflammatory reaction that damages tissues there. Any part of the eye may be affected, but most commonly onchocerciasis causes corneal clouding, retinal damage, and optic nerve degeneration. The afflicted may complain of light sensitivity, inability to see at night, loss of peripheral vision, excessive tearing, or eye pain. Visual loss ranges from mild impairment to blindness.

There are considerable geographic variations in the severity of the eye disease. Blindness is most common among people dwelling in the African savannah, or tropical grassland (just south of the Sahara); it occurs much less frequently in those living in the forested areas of Africa and in the Americas.

Other manifestations? Some experts have suggested that onchocerciasis also causes other important health problems, such as epilepsy, wasting, and dwarfism. Studies are currently under way to determine whether these conditions might plausibly have a biological connection to onchocerciasis.

Diagnosis. Onchocerciasis is diagnosed by examination of a small sliver of skin from the patient, placed in a few drops of saline solution and viewed under a mi-

Jeremy Hartley—Panos Pictures

(Opposite bottom) A family hoes a field in Burkina Faso. In a single working day, rural African field-workers may be bitten hundreds of times by onchocerciasis-carrying blackflies. (Below) Dying microfilariae in the eyes and skin of onchocerciasis victims cause inflammation and many devastating symptoms: (top) severe ocular damage in a young woman (not all eye damage results in blindness); (center) swollen, thick, wrinkled "lizard skin" on a man's back; and (bottom) spotty "leopard skin" covering a victim's lower legs. (Right) A nodule containing adult *O. volvulus* worms is removed from a patient's head. The nodules themselves generally are not painful; they can vary in appearance but most often resemble lima beans in size and shape.

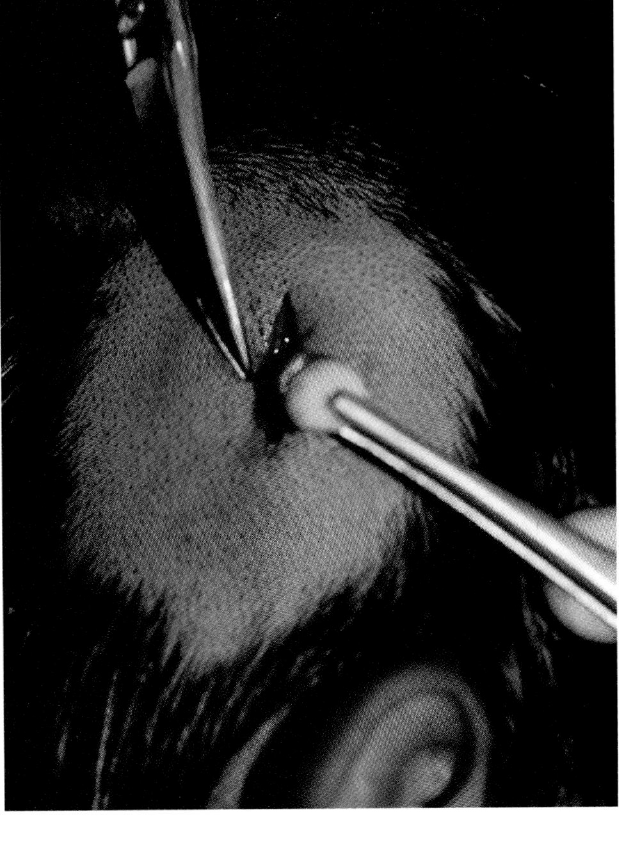

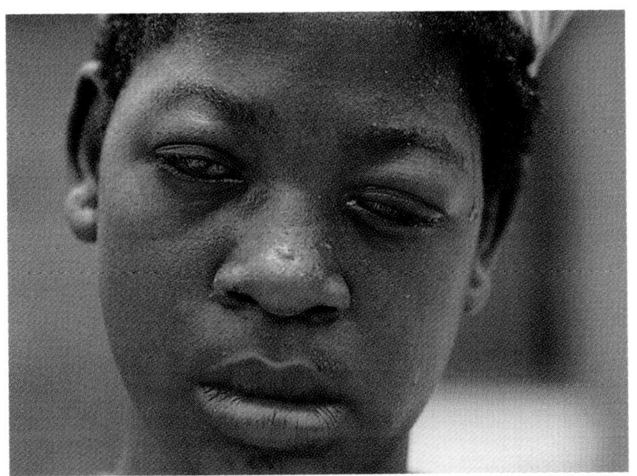

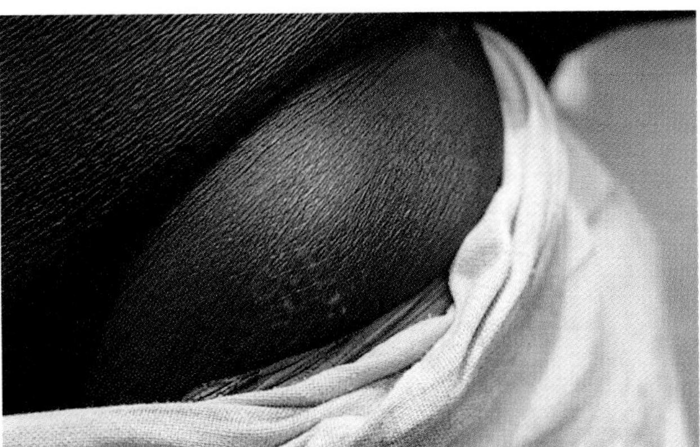

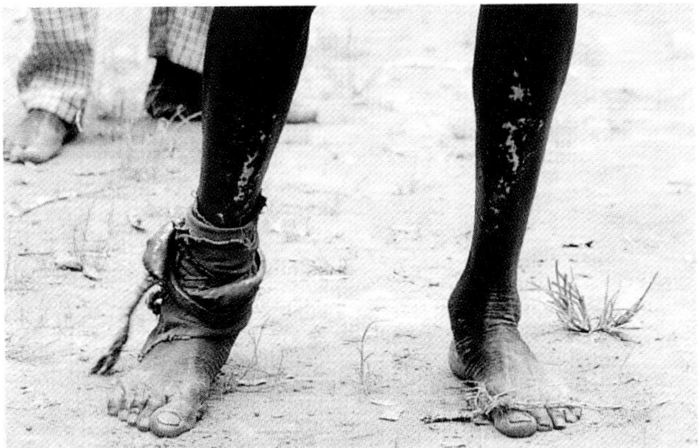

(Top left) David Reed—Impact Photos; (center) David Reed—Panos Pictures; (bottom) Bill Van Der Decker—Sygma; (top right) Frank Richards, Jr.

croscope. Microfilariae are then identified as they wiggle out of the specimen (within a few hours). Alternatively, the adult worms can be identified in a nodule that has been removed surgically. Some specialty laboratories can detect antibodies produced against *O. volvulus* proteins—the presence of which can indicate onchocercal infection.

Societies devastated

In 1995 the World Health Organization (WHO) estimated that 123 million people were at risk of contracting onchocerciasis and that between 17 million and 18 million persons were infected (of whom about 270,000 were blind and another 500,000 severely visually impaired). About 95% of infected persons are in Africa, where the disease is most severe along the major rivers in 27 countries in a belt spanning the northern and central part of the continent. The belt extends from the east in Ethiopia, The Sudan, and Uganda and continues westward through Zaire, the Central African Republic, Chad, and Cameroon to the West African countries of Niger, Mali, Burkina Faso, Nigeria, Senegal, Guinea, Sierra Leone, Liberia, Côte d'Ivoire (formerly Ivory Coast), Ghana, Togo, and Benin.

The forest strain of onchocerciasis (which, as pre-

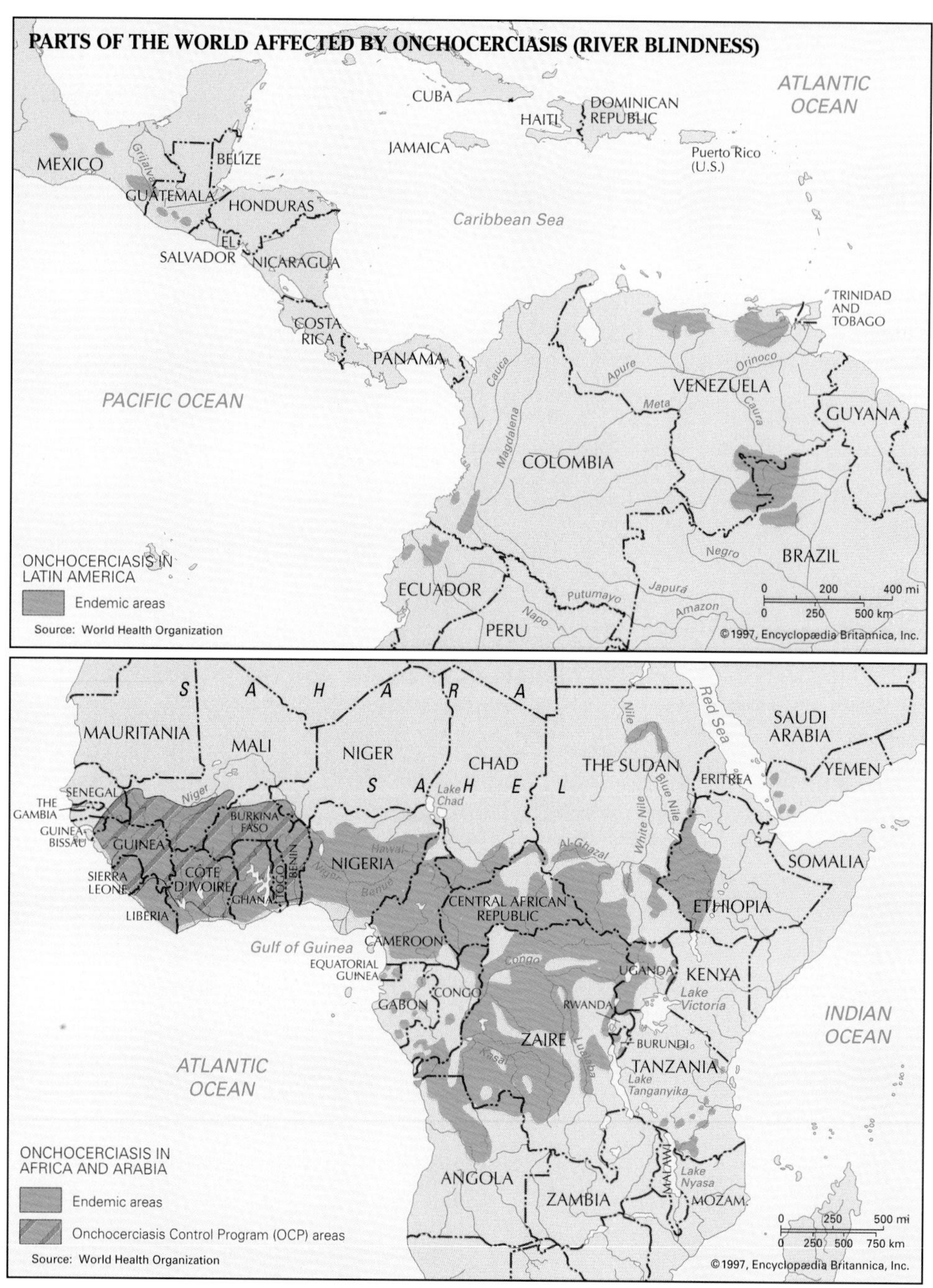

viously noted, is less likely to cause visual damage) occurs throughout most of the rain forest regions of Equatorial Guinea, Congo, and Gabon and extends into Angola, Burundi, Malawi, and Tanzania. Outside Africa, onchocerciasis occurs in Mexico, Guatemala, Ecuador, Colombia, Venezuela, and Brazil in the Americas and in Yemen in Asia. In all, 34 countries in the world are known to have endemic onchocerciasis.

In communities with severe (hyperendemic) onchocerciasis (of the savannah type), 15% of the population may be blind. This figure does not take into account the fact that the risk of visual loss increases with age. Therefore, up to 40% of adults in such areas may be visually impaired. In these often-isolated and largely agrarian communities, visual impairment is a major occupational and social handicap, and it reduces the life span of affected persons by an average of 10 years. The social and economic fabric of the community unravels in the face of decreased agricultural production; young children are forced to care for their parents; and adolescents, driven by the fear of becoming blind, leave home in search of a livelihood elsewhere. Ultimately, a village may become so impoverished that it is abandoned altogether.

Even in areas where the parasite is endemic but blinding onchocerciasis is rare, onchocercal skin disease occurs in up to 30% of the population. Recent studies have estimated that some eight million persons suffer from troublesome itching associated with dermal onchocerciasis, and this makes it difficult for them to concentrate, work, study, or interact socially. The unsightly skin changes cause psychological suffering in the affected person, who may also be socially ostracized within the community. The economic impact of onchocercal skin disease is currently the subject of intense research.

People uprooted

Several studies have pointed to an integral relationship between onchocerciasis and the settlement of farmland. In the Hawal valley in Nigeria, for example, the prevalence and severity of onchocerciasis infection is inversely proportional to the extent of land settlement.

In Burkina Faso, before the Onchocerciasis Control Program (OCP) began (*see* below), highly fertile river valleys where onchocerciasis was hyperendemic were largely deserted, but in unaffected river basins population densities exceeded 100 persons per square kilometer. Even when river basins with severe onchocerciasis were settled, the pattern of farming was affected by the disease. Compared with areas without onchocerciasis, farmers worked only fields near the village because the increasing impairment of their sight prevented them from ranging out to more distant cultivatable land. The result was fewer crops and reduced household incomes.

Attacking the problem

The first systematic efforts to control onchocerciasis involved large-scale surgical removal of onchocercal nodules by mobile teams that traveled through Guatemala and Mexico. These efforts began soon after Robles discovered the relationship between the disease and lesions of the eye in 1917.

Control measures in Africa began on a significant scale only in 1947–48, when DDT was used to eliminate the vector *S. neavei* from an area in Kenya and *S. damnosum* from part of the Congo River in Zaire near Léopoldville (now Kinshasa).

Two drugs, suramin and diethylcarbamazine (DEC), became available for treating onchocerciasis in 1947, but both have major drawbacks. Neither can be administered without the risk of serious side effects. Suramin is capable of killing the adult worms, but it has to be administered by injections given over several days or weeks. DEC is an oral drug but kills only the microfilariae. Those who take DEC become very ill with fever, rash, and swelling, and their eyes may become inflamed by the treatment. French colonial doctors began treating patients with these drugs in heavily affected areas of Upper Volta shortly before their British counterparts began doing so in northern Gold Coast in the early 1950s. By 1962 mobile teams were treating patients in parts of the newly independent nations of Upper Volta, Ivory Coast, and Mali.

A child guides a blinded elder through their West African village. This was formerly an all-too-familiar scene.

Concerted control

A giant leap in the attack on the disease was

David Reed—Panos Pictures

taken in 1968, when an international meeting sponsored by the U.S. Agency for International Development, the Organization for Coordination and Cooperation in the Control of Major Endemic Diseases in West Africa, and WHO convened in Tunis, the capital of Tunisia (in North Africa). That meeting resulted in a series of bold recommendations to establish the OCP, a targeted regional campaign to control onchocerciasis in most of West Africa. Then, in 1972, after World Bank president Robert S. McNamara and his wife, Margaret, witnessed the devastating socioeconomic effects of onchocerciasis in Upper Volta, the bank committed significant funds to the cause. At the time, the decision to launch the OCP—at an expected cost of about $120 million, starting in 1973 and lasting over a period of 20 years—was unprecedented in the field of public health.

By 1974 the OCP had begun in Benin, Upper Volta, Ivory Coast, Ghana, Mali, Niger, and Togo. Operations were extended to parts of four adjacent countries (Guinea, Guinea-Bissau, Senegal, and Sierra Leone) in 1986, to prevent reinvasion of the core area by blackflies.

As its main strategy, the OCP called for aerial larviciding, supplemented by hand spraying of blackfly breeding sites, covering a vast area (*see* map, page 19). The spraying had to be maintained for at least 20 years—the only way to ensure that the life span of the adult worms in humans who were already infected would be exceeded.

The chemical temephos (Abate), which is not harmful to the environment or to humans, was used for the larviciding until 1980, when the blackflies developed resistance to it. After that, several other "environmentally friendly" compounds were used in rotation. During recent years sophisticated technology has aided the OCP's effort. Satellite readings of river-flow rates have been entered into computers in order to determine the optimal timing and targets for larvicides. Other research has applied computer modeling of the parasitic transmission, and molecular genetics has been used to distinguish subspecies of blackflies.

West African success story

After 20 years onchocerciasis is no longer a serious problem in the original OCP area. When the program began, infection rates in the most severely affected country, Burkina Faso, were as

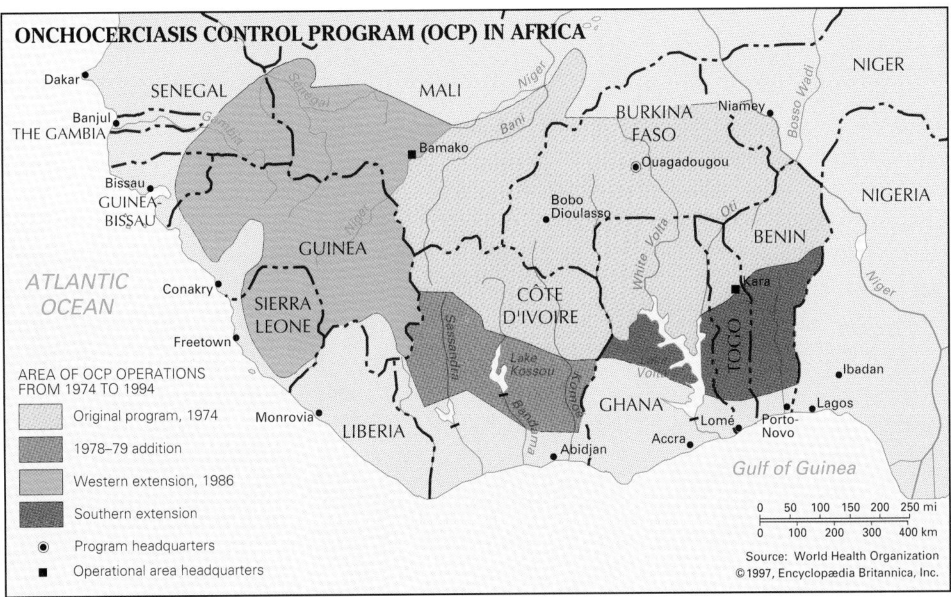

River blindness can uproot entire villages. (Left) A fertile river valley in Burkina Faso abandoned by inhabitants who feared becoming blind. (Below) A West African village resettled following the successful Onchocerciasis Control Program.

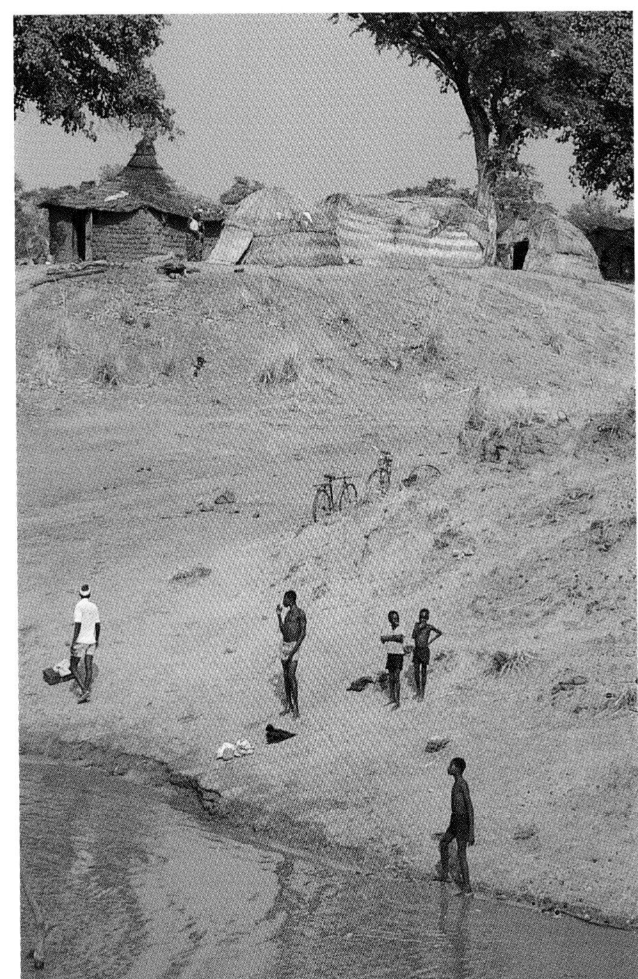

high as 80–90%; the highest rates in 1995 were less than 2%. Currently, some 30 million persons at risk in the 11 countries covered by the OCP are being protected, and blindness resulting from onchocerciasis has been prevented in an estimated 125,000 to 200,000 persons. About 10 million children born since the OCP began are free of onchocerciasis entirely. Further, some 25 million hectares (62 million acres) of land along West African rivers are now available for resettlement—enough to support 17 million persons.

At the end of 1995, the total cost of the OCP was approaching $500 million, a sum that was provided by 22 donor nations. The World Bank estimates that the annual rate of return on this investment—owing to the program's salutary effects on agricultural output—is almost 20%. Current projections suggest a final investment of $571 million for the OCP over the nearly 40-year economic life of the project. Most important, however, is the projection that $3.7 billion will have been generated in terms of increased labor and agricultural productivity in the recipient nations.

The rest of the world

It was not practical to replicate the OCP for the 87% of the population affected by onchocerciasis who live outside the targeted area in Africa. Airborne larviciding of forested zones is not only expensive but exceedingly difficult, unlike larviciding of the savannah that characterized the OCP area. Furthermore, the risk of blindness, which provided most of the economic justification for the OCP, was considerably lower in many of the other parts of the world where onchocerciasis has been endemic.

Photographs, David Reed—Panos Pictures

A golf course, cured dogs, and help for 85 million people. Help for these other areas came in 1987 with the introduction of a completely new pharmaceutical agent. In 1975 while screening for microbes in soil samples collected from around the world, researchers at Merck & Co., Inc., discovered ivermectin. They had been searching for a new anthelmintic—a substance capable of destroying or expelling parasitic worms—for veterinary use. The specific soil sample containing the substance had been obtained from a golf course in Japan. Ivermectin rapidly became a commercial success for treating veterinary parasites (*e.g.,* heartworm in dogs), and a research program subsequently demonstrated its potential for safely treating onchocerciasis in humans.

Ivermectin kills *Onchocerca* microfilariae (but not the adult worms) with almost no serious side effects, and its effect lasts for about a year after a single oral dose. After its extraordinary efficacy and safety in humans was confirmed in trials that began in 1981, Merck officials were aware that the persons who needed ivermectin the most could not afford to buy it. Merck's president, physician Roy Vagelos, announced in October 1987 that the pharmaceutical company would donate the drug, whose trade name is Mectizan—in whatever amounts were needed and for however long it was

(Top and right) David Reed—Panos Pictures; (bottom) David Reed—Impact Photos

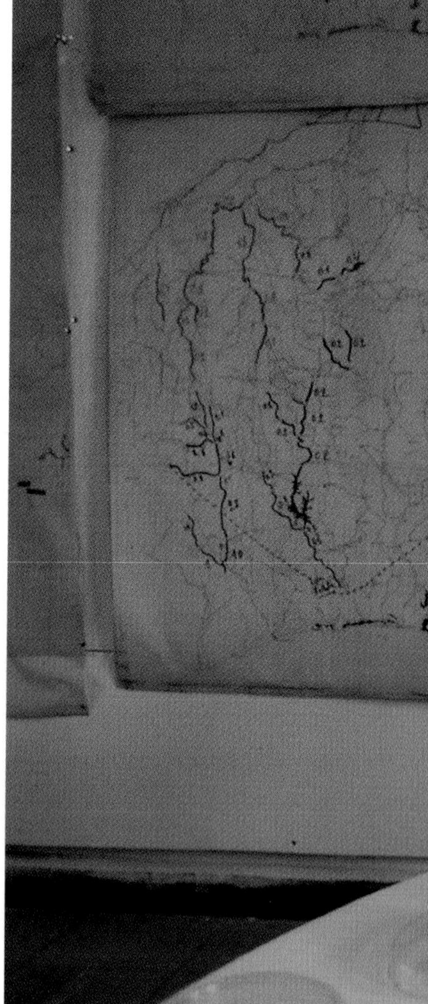

The Onchocerciasis Control Program (OCP), targeting a large area of West Africa, began in 1973. (Left) One of the OCP's main strategies was the aerial larvaciding of blackfly breeding sites. (Left bottom) OCP workers search for blackfly larvae in an infested riverbed. (Below) A scientist working in a research laboratory examines blackflies under a microscope; the map behind him shows the entire OCP area. By 1993 river blindness was no longer a serious threat to the health and well-being of most West Africans.

needed, at no charge—for both treating and preventing onchocerciasis. Merck also established an independent group of distinguished international scientists, the Mectizan Expert Committee, to evaluate applications and requests for supplies of Mectizan and oversee the distribution of the highly efficacious medicine.

Corporate generosity and NGO resourcefulness. This unprecedented corporate generosity presented a challenge to national and international health workers. Most of the affected countries had no established public health systems, or infrastructures, capable of distributing the orally administered drug. Even though the drug itself was free and had to be taken only once or twice a year, it was a formidable task to dispense ivermectin to millions of persons at risk in remote villages. In 1988–89 only about 500,000 persons were treated with the drug, and in 1990 there were 1.3 million—relatively small numbers, considering the huge number of persons who could benefit. By 1995, however, over 10 million were being reached in most of the affected countries of Africa and Latin America.

How was the distribution problem solved? Most programs for community-based distribution of Mectizan are assisted by nongovernmental organizations (NGOs), voluntary humanitarian aid agencies that are without political ties. The NGOs that have participated in public health missions throughout the world have repeatedly demonstrated their flexibility, creativity, and rapid responsiveness.

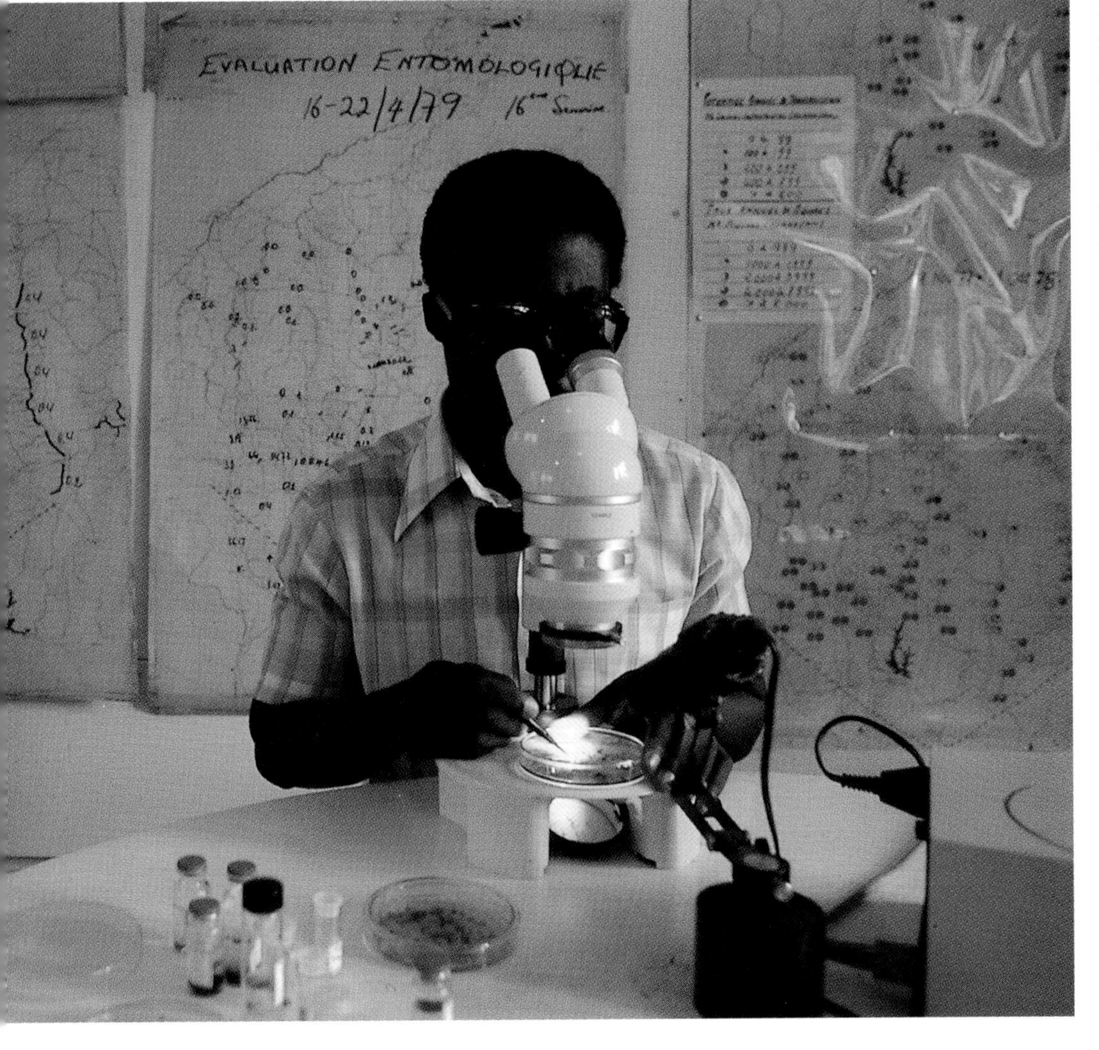

In November 1992 Merck, along with 10 key NGOs (Africare, Christoffel Blindenmission, Helen Keller International, Interchurch Medical Assistance, Inc., International Eye Foundation, Lions SightFirst Program, Organisation de la Prévention de Cécité, River Blindness Foundation, Sight Savers International, and World Vision International), established a secretariat at WHO headquarters in Geneva. Similar coalitions of NGOs devoted to onchocerciasis control on a national basis also have been established. These agencies not only have enabled remote villages to receive the anthelmintic medication but have taken advantage of the situation to help develop broader health care services for the people in the affected areas.

Of the NGOs involved, the River Blindness Foundation (RBF) was unique in that it was established (in 1990) expressly to help distribute Mectizan, and it remains solely committed to eliminating onchocerciasis from the world. In addition to facilitating Mectizan delivery in all six affected countries of the Americas, the RBF established similar programs in three highly endemic African countries (Cameroon, Nigeria, and Uganda) and provided grants to a few other NGOs for similar work in six other African countries. In 1996 the RBF was absorbed into The Carter Center.

The last stretch

By 1994 NGOs were reaching about 15% of the target population outside the OCP area. In conjunction with Merck officials, the governments of some affected countries, and a few international organizations, including the World Bank, a number of NGOs then began to develop another regional program for the remaining areas in Africa. This program, the African Program for Onchocerciasis Control (APOC), was launched in December 1995. The main goal of APOC is to reach the remaining 50 million to 60 million persons at risk for potentially blinding onchocerciasis and/or severe skin disease in 16 countries between 1996 and 2007.

Adapted from information obtained from the Global 2000 River Blindness Program

Nigerians Protected

Number of persons at risk for onchocerciasis treated with Mectizan

1989	1990	1991	1992	1993	1994	1995
49,556	50,688	71,205	571,132	1,140,177	2,356,244	4,237,892

Unlike the OCP, APOC will use annual or semiannual community-based distribution of Mectizan as its primary control strategy. The strategy also entails rapidly determining the severity and distribution of onchocerciasis in remote areas and communities by testing a carefully selected sample of the populations and communities, using new microcomputer-based mapping techniques and noninvasive, field-based diagnostic methods. Once the at-risk communities have been identified, Mectizan is offered to all healthy persons in those communities who are over five years of age and not pregnant or nursing infants under one week of age. With WHO as the executing agency, an estimated

River Blindness: Milestones

- **1875** (*Gold Coast*) John O'Neill describes microfilarial skin disease
- **1893** (*Gold Coast*) G.F. Leuckhart finds adult parasites in skin nodules
- **1915** (*Guatemala*) Rodolfo Robles first recognizes the disease

Rodolfo Robles contributed to the early understanding of river blindness.

- **1920** J. Montpellier and A. Lacroix link microfilariae and adult worms
- **1926** (*Sierra Leone*) Donald Blacklock discovers *Simulium damnosum* vector
- **1932** (*Belgian Congo*) J. Hissette finds *S. neavei* vector and, for the first time, links onchocerciasis to blindness in Africa
- **1938** (*Upper Volta*) French doctors link onchocerciasis to mass blindness and abandonment of river valleys
- **1949** (*Gold Coast*) B.B. Waddy confirms the above findings
- **1947** (*Kenya*) *S. neavei* is eliminated from focus area by DDT
- **1948** (*Congo River*) DDT is successful against *S. damnosum*
- **1947** Suramin is discovered effective against adult worms; diethylcarbamazine is found effective against microfilariae (both with side effects)
- **1974** Regional Onchocerciasis Control Program (OCP) begins in West Africa
- **1975** Researchers at Merck & Co., Inc., discover ivermectin; later they learn of its effectiveness against *Onchocerca volvulus* microfilariae and that only one oral dose a year is needed
- **1987** Merck donates ivermectin (Mectizan) for onchocerciasis control and establishes Mectizan Expert Committee
- **1995** The African Program for Onchocerciasis Control (APOC) is launched
- **2007** Global control of onchocerciasis is anticipated

(Bottom) Department of Onchocerciasis, Malaria Division, Ministry of Health, Guatemala; (below) River Blindness Foundation

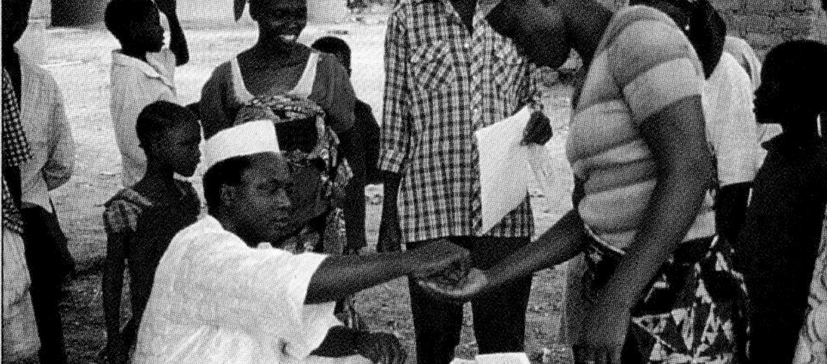

Community-based distribution of Mectizan. A single oral dose virtually eliminates river blindness symptoms for up to a year.

W. Imbert—WHO

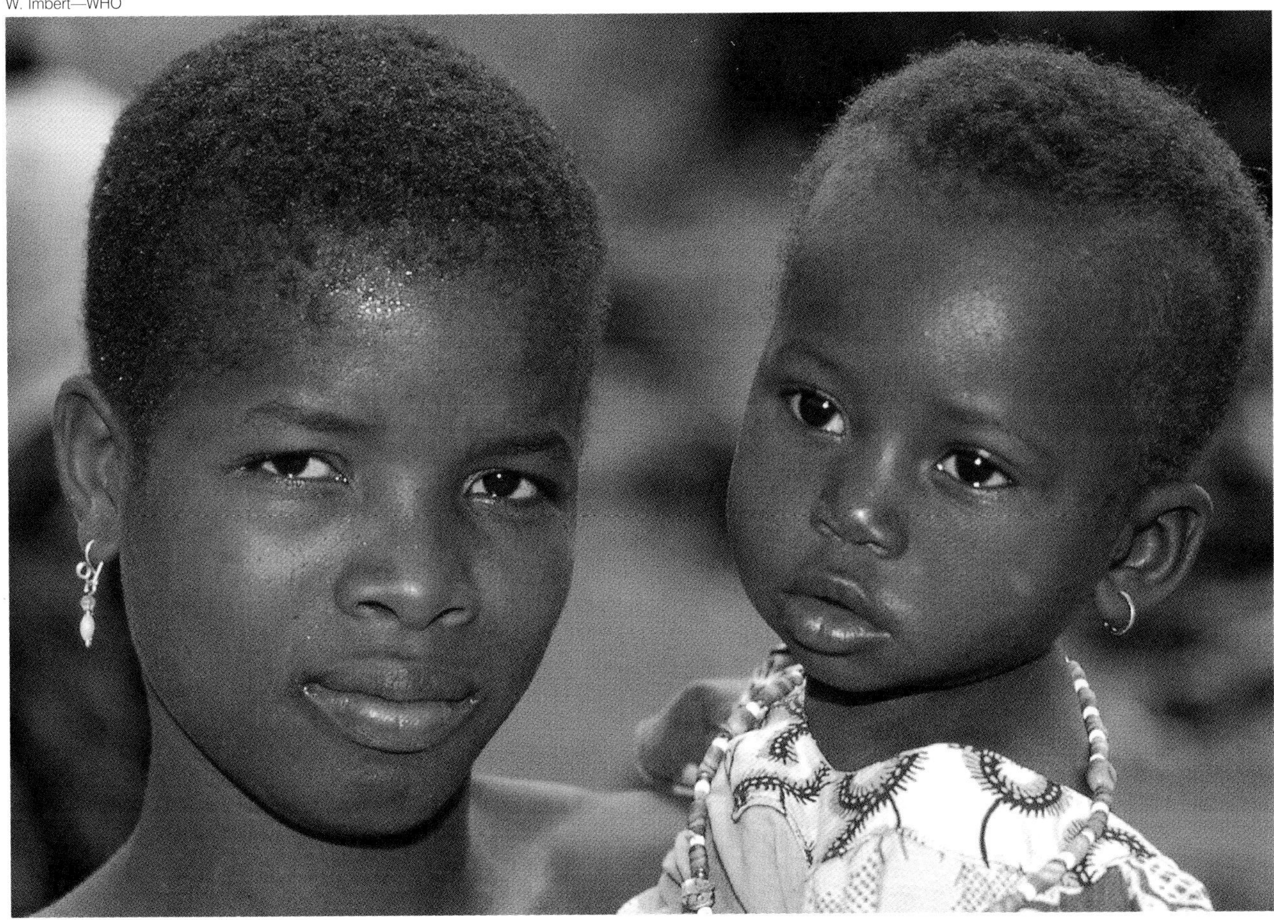

Freed from the specter of river blindness, this mother and daughter—and millions of other Africans—can look forward to a healthy, productive future.

$124 million will be required for the new program over the next 12 years. Up to 75% of the program's costs will be funded through the World Bank and the remainder by the affected countries and various other partners. Merck will provide about 410 million tablets of Mectizan, valued at hundreds of millions of dollars.

Onchocerciasis into oblivion

The OCP in West Africa will end in 2002. Mectizan treatments of selected populations in the OCP area began soon after the drug became available in 1987. About two million persons were being treated annually by 1995, and distribution of Mectizan in the OCP area will continue after larviciding ends. APOC, which is taking community-based treatment with Mectizan to the rest of Africa, will continue through 2007, the same year that onchocerciasis is targeted to be eliminated as a public health problem in the Americas.

In addition to preventing disease, broad use of Mectizan may also reduce transmission of onchocerciasis by preventing infection of blackflies. However, mathematical models of onchocerciasis confirm that a drug that would kill the adult worms (a macrofilaricide) before the end of their normal life span would greatly reduce the time required for continuing mass treatment with Mectizan, and it would make total eradication of the disease possible. What is needed is an inexpensive macrofilaricide that could be administered orally, infrequently, and with few or no serious side effects. Researchers are investigating the potential suitability of Mectizan and a few other drugs such as CGP 6140 (Amocarzine) as a practical macrofilaricide. If such studies succeed, onchocerciasis could soon follow smallpox and dracunculiasis (guinea worm disease) into oblivion.

In the meantime, the model of sustainable community-based distribution of Mectizan to control onchocerciasis can be adapted for the use of other needed drugs to control other widespread diseases of the less developed world. One example is the highly effective drug praziquantel to treat schistosomiasis, which remains a major scourge of the tropics. MHA

The High Life: Health and Sickness at High Altitude

by Peter H. Hackett, M.D., and David R. Shlim, M.D.

Early travelers to the high mountains—in China, South America, or the Himalayas—sometimes noticed that they or their healthy companions became suddenly and mysteriously ill. Since the advent of modern travel, tens of millions of adventure-seeking tourists have flocked to the high-mountain regions of the world. In the Rocky Mountains of Colorado, a study conducted in 1989 showed that as many as 20% of tourists become ill. An even more recent study, conducted by physician Benjamin Honigman and colleagues at the Colorado Altitude Research Institute and published in the *Annals of Internal Medicine* in 1993, found that acute mountain sickness occurs in as many as 25% of visitors to resort communities located at even moderate altitudes (elevations of 1,920 to 2,960 meters [one meter is about 3.28 feet]). Thus, one need not be an accomplished climber to succumb; even the casual tourist can be affected.

***Peter H. Hackett, M.D.**, is Affiliate Associate Professor of Medicine, University of Washington School of Medicine, Seattle; Director, Denali Medical Research, Anchorage, Alaska; Emergency Physician, Grand Junction, Colorado; and a Mt. Everest summiter.*

***David R. Shlim, M.D.**, is Medical Director, The Canadian International Water and Energy Consultants Clinic; Medical Adviser, The Himalayan Rescue Association, Kathmandu, Nepal; and Chairman, Medicine for Adventure Travel, Jackson Hole, Wyoming.*

Climbers on Hillary Step, a treacherous passage on Mt. Everest's Southeast Ridge that leads to the magisterial summit.

Ned Gillette—Adventure Photo

Overview of altitude illness

The mysterious malady referred to above is part of the spectrum of high-altitude illness. Caused by the lack of oxygen in the air, high-altitude illness predominantly affects two organ systems of the body—the brain and

the lungs. The brain form of the illness is called acute mountain sickness (AMS); the lung form is called high-altitude pulmonary edema (HAPE). The symptoms of AMS are headache, nausea, vomiting, dizziness, lethargy, and insomnia. This is by far the most common of the altitude illnesses, usually lasting for a day or two and resolving spontaneously as a person acclimatizes to the high elevation. Although uncomfortable, feeling much like a hangover or the flu, it is not dangerous. Some travelers, however, go on to develop a severe form of the illness known as high-altitude cerebral edema (HACE). The latter can produce severe mental disturbances, coma, and death if not properly recognized and treated.

Moonrise over a Himalayan peak: transcendent beauty and natural grandeur that may entice trekkers to risk their lives.

Those who develop the lung form of altitude illness notice increasing shortness of breath while exercising and eventually feel breathless at rest. If they neither get treatment nor descend, their lungs gradually fill with fluid, and the HAPE sufferers literally drown in their own bodily fluids. What researchers have been trying to figure out for at least a century is what is causing these severe changes. Furthermore, why do some people succumb to illness while others do not?

The study of sick sojourners

One of these authors, Peter Hackett, became interested in these questions in 1974, when he traveled to the base of Mt. Everest, in Nepal, as the trip physician accompanying a trekking group. Intrigued by a disease that can kill some individuals while it leaves others who are breathing the very same air unharmed, he remained in Nepal for the next several years and established a rescue post in the yak-herding village of Pheriche, at an elevation of 4,270 meters, en route to Everest Base Camp (which sits at 5,500 meters). There Hackett carried out the first surveys of high-altitude illness in a nonmilitary, nonmountaineer tourist population.

The surveys proved that AMS was indeed a serious problem among trekkers in Nepal. Over half of the trekkers had symptoms, and as many as one in 20

© Gordon Wiltsie

had cerebral or pulmonary edema (swelling due to fluid retention). Several people died each year because they (or their companions) failed to recognize that their symptoms were caused by the high altitude; instead, they blamed them on the flu, smoky teahouses, dehydration, or too much sun—until it was too late to descend. Hackett published his findings in collaboration with physician Drummond Rennie, a veteran climber and high-altitude researcher who had previously done studies on Mt. Logan in the Yukon Territory and on the massive Mt. Dhaulagiri in Nepal.

Subsequently, a group of investigators studied 100 subjects in Kathmandu, Nepal, at the low elevation of 1,324 meters, and again at the Pheriche aid post. What they found was that people who developed symptoms of AMS were retaining fluid in their bodies as they ascended, developing mild edema of the skin, lungs, and brain. People who felt fine despite the high altitude generally breathed more and actually lost water through their kidneys as they ascended. This increased urine flow, or diuresis, proved to be a healthy sign. It was known that people automatically increased their rate and depth of breathing as they ascended, but it was not known that some people did this better than others—and had fewer physical problems as a result. Subsequent studies confirmed the importance of increased breathing at high altitudes and also verified the relationship between breathing and fluid balance (although the mechanism responsible for the latter is still unknown). Nonetheless, this knowledge suggested that if a drug could be found that caused people to increase their breathing as they ascended to moderately high elevations, perhaps many cases of AMS could be avoided.

In fact, such a drug had already been studied and found to work at high elevations, although the way that it prevented AMS was not known. The drug, acetazolamide (Diamox), a type of diuretic that is particularly useful in treating the eye disease glaucoma, blocks an enzyme reaction in the kidneys. When this enzyme (carbonic anhydrase) is blocked, bicarbonate is excreted in the urine, and the blood becomes less alkalotic, which therefore increases the acidity of the bodily fluids. The brain interprets the acidified blood as a need to breathe more. Thus, when acetazolamide

The World's Pinnacles

Mountain name[1] and location	Height: Feet	Height: Meters	Year first climbed
AFRICA			
Kilimanjaro (Kibo peak), *Tanzania*	19,340	5,895	1889
Mt. Kenya (Batian peak), *Kenya*	17,058	5,199	1899
Margherita, *Ruwenzori Range, Zaire-Uganda*	16,795	5,119	1906
Ras Dashen, *Simen Mountains, Ethiopia*	15,157	4,620	1841
Meru, *Tanzania*	14,978	4,565	...
AMERICA, NORTH			
McKinley (Denali), *Alaska Range, Alaska, United States*	20,320	6,194	1913
Logan, *St. Elias Mountains, Yukon, Canada*	19,524	5,951	1925
Citlaltépetl (Orizaba), *Cordillera Neo-Volcánica, Mexico*	18,406	5,610	1848
St. Elias, *St. Elias Mountains, Alaska, United States-Canada*	18,009	5,489	1897
Popocatépetl, *Cordillera Neo-Volcánica, Mexico*	17,930	5,465	1519
AMERICA, SOUTH			
Aconcagua, *Andes, Argentina-Chile*	22,831	6,959	1897
Ojos del Salado, *Andes, Argentina-Chile*	22,615	6,893	1937
Bonete, *Andes, Argentina*	22,546	6,872	1913
Tupungato, *Andes, Argentina-Chile*	22,310	6,800	1897
Pissis, *Andes, Argentina*	22,241	6,779	1937
ANTARCTICA			
Vinson Massif, *Sentinel Range, Ellsworth Mountains*	16,066	4,897	1966
Tyree, *Sentinel Range, Ellsworth Mountains*	15,919	4,852	1967
Shinn, *Sentinel Range, Ellsworth Mountains*	15,751	4,801	1966
Kirkpatrick, *Queen Alexandra Range*	14,856	4,528	...
Markham, *Queen Elizabeth Range*	14,272	4,350	...
ASIA			
Everest (Chomolungma), *Himalayas, Nepal-Tibet, China*	29,028	8,848	1953
K2 (Godwin Austen) (Chogori), *Karakoram Range, Pakistan-Xinjiang, China*	28,251	8,611	1954
Kanchenjunga I (Gangchhendzonga), *Himalayas, Nepal-India*	28,169	8,586	1955
Lhotse I, *Himalayas, Nepal-Tibet, China*	27,940	8,516	1956
Makalu I, *Himalayas, Nepal-Tibet, China*	27,766	8,463	1955
EUROPE			
Mont Blanc, *Alps, France-Italy*	15,771	4,807	1786
Dufourspitze (Monte Rosa), *Alps, Switzerland-Italy*	15,203	4,634	1855
Dom (Mischabel), *Alps, Switzerland*	14,911	4,545	1858
Weisshorn, *Alps, Switzerland*	14,780	4,505	1861
Matterhorn, *Alps, Switzerland-Italy*	14,692	4,478	1865
OCEANIA			
Jaya (Sukarno, Carstensz), *Sudirman Range, Indonesia*	16,500	5,030	1962
Pilimsit (Idenburg), *Sudirman Range, Indonesia*	15,750	4,800	1962
Trikora (Wilhelmina), *Jayawijaya Mountains, Indonesia*	15,580	4,750	1912
Mandala (Juliana), *Jayawijaya Mountains, Indonesia*	15,420	4,700	1959
Wisnumurti (Jan Pieterszoon Coen), *Jayawijaya Mountains, Indonesia*	15,080	4,595	...
CAUCASUS			
Elbrus, *Caucasus, Russia*	18,510	5,642	1874
Dykh-Tau, *Caucasus, Russia*	17,073	5,204	1888
Koshtan-Tau, *Caucasus, Russia*	16,900	5,151	1889
Shkhara, Caucasus, *Russia-Georgia*	16,627	5,068	1888
Dzhangi-Tau, Caucasus, *Russia-Georgia*	16,594	5,058	1903

[1] "I" in the name of a peak refers to the highest in a group of numbered peaks of the same name.

(Top, bottom left and right) David R. Shlim; (center) © Gordon Wiltsie

In the mid-1970s an aid post to treat and study altitude sickness was established at Pheriche, Nepal, a yak-herding village en route to Everest Base Camp. (Above) A comatose patient with acute mountain sickness (AMS) is carried from the clinic. (Right) Helicopter rescue of AMS victim at 4,270 meters (14,000 feet). (Far right) Namkha Sherpa and Ang Rita Sherpa, workers at the Pheriche aid post for more than 20 years, have undoubtedly seen more altitude sickness than anyone else on Earth. (Below) Author Peter Hackett, who started the clinic, gives oxygen to an unconscious climber.

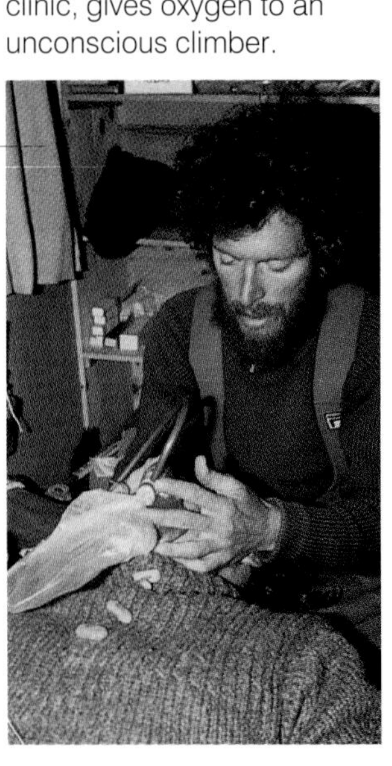

was taken before and during ascent to a high altitude, it increased climbers' respiration and urination and prevented or ameliorated the symptoms of AMS.

The brain at risk?

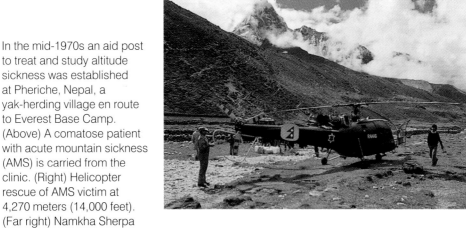

The brain is the keeper of consciousness and initiator of commands to all other organs. The human anatomy has protected it in a rigid, bony, strong but inflexible vault. Being rigid, the skull allows no room for expansion; thus, any swelling inside it has the effect of compressing the brain itself. The brain is nourished constantly with blood from the heart that carries life-sustaining oxygen and glucose. Anything that interrupts that flow results in immediate loss of consciousness.

The brain is also protected internally by a modification to the brain capillary wall called the blood-brain barrier (*see* diagram, page 29). Unlike other capillaries, the brain capillary consists of a continuous wall of crescent-shaped endothelial cells that overlap in "tight junctions" to minimize formation of open pores. Surrounding the endothelial cells are additional protective layers: a basement membrane and partial coating of glial cells. Substances leaving the blood plasma must penetrate several membrane layers before entering the extracellular brain fluid. Differences in the permeability among molecules effectively allow the blood-brain barrier to act as a selective filter.

When high-altitude sojourners experienced such symptoms as headache, dizziness, appetite loss, nausea, and even change in consciousness, it was clear that these physiological disturbances were neurological in origin. Some experts opined that the hypoxia (low oxygen) interfered with energy production—in particular, production of adenosine triphosphate (ATP) in brain cells. ATP is present in all cell types and permits a finely adjusted use of energy. Without adequate ATP, brain cells could no longer work properly, researchers concluded.

Only in the last decade has it become clear that ATP in the brain is not adversely affected by the degree of hypoxia that occurs at high altitude and that when ATP is depleted, unconsciousness is immediate.

Therefore, another mechanism must be responsible for AMS. A likely candidate was the "transmission system" of the brain, which is composed of chemicals called neurotransmitters. It is the effect of hypoxia on neurotransmitters, for example, that causes muddled thinking and slow reaction times at altitudes of about 5,500 meters or more. But these symptoms are quite different from those of mountain sickness.

The clues to understanding AMS came from the very sickest climbers, those who developed HACE. Their symptoms pointed to brain swelling as a likely cause of the more mild AMS as well. In what may be the most important medical research paper on the subject (published in 1969), Inder Singh, an Indian military physician, described the effects experienced by thousands of Indian soldiers who were rushed from a relatively low altitude to a very high one when the Chinese attacked their border in the Himalayas. Singh measured the pressure of the soldiers' cerebrospinal fluid by doing spinal taps; he found that it was higher when the soldiers were severely ill. He also did a biopsy of the brain of a soldier, which showed marked edema. Since the symptoms of these soldiers with cerebral edema were essentially exaggerated symptoms of AMS, Singh logically assumed AMS to be due to increased intracranial pressure resulting from swelling of the brain. It was because of his studies, as well as autopsies conducted by other researchers on trekkers and climbers who had died as a result of severe brain swelling, that the extreme form of AMS came to be known as high-altitude cerebral edema.

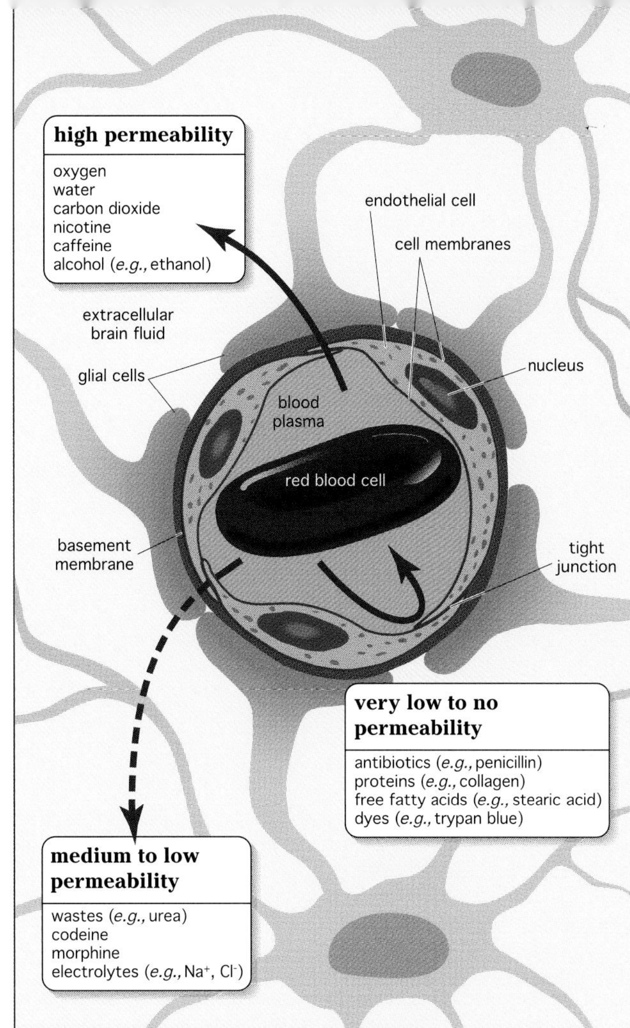

The permeability of the blood-brain barrier to various substances depends upon factors such as the molecular size, degree of electrical charge, and relative solubility of the substance in question.

Still, important questions remained unanswered: What exactly causes cerebral edema? Is it really a physiological extension of AMS? Why are some susceptible and others not?

Until recently there were no sensitive ways to view the brain inside the skull of a living human in order to determine the degree of swelling that might or might not be present. With the advent of computed tomography (CT) scanning and magnetic resonance imaging (MRI) in the 1970s and '80s, researchers could finally obtain brain images of persons who became ill at high altitudes. The location of the edema in the brain could give clues to its cause, and the comparison of brain images across a range of illness could help explain the relationship of AMS to HACE. Unfortunately, however, CT and MRI machines were expensive and cumbersome and thus, for practical reasons, could not be taken up onto a mountain.

From 1981 to 1989, Hackett was working on Denali in Alaska. (Denali, meaning "the Great One," is the ancient Athabascan Indian name for Mt. McKinley, at 6,194 meters the highest mountain in North America.) Hackett frequently treated victims of severe altitude sickness on the mountain. His patients were then evacuated from Denali to a hospital in Anchorage.

Knowing how important it was to try to answer the questions about the relationship of AMS to HACE, Hackett managed to obtain highly revealing MRI scans of the brains of these victims, many of whom were unconscious at the time. What he found was totally unexpected: plasma was leaking from the brain's blood vessels and forming pools between the brain cells—particularly in an area of the white matter known as the corpus callosum (consisting of fibers that unite the two cerebral hemispheres). The brain cells themselves did not appear swollen. This exact image had never before been seen in any condition. With descent, the plasma, which is mostly water, apparently stopped leaking and was reabsorbed into the blood circulation, which explained why the severe symptoms were completely reversible. Hackett and his colleagues studied a total of nine HACE victims, and the findings were present in seven of them. The paper reporting these findings will be published in a major medical journal in 1996; the researchers' conclusion—that the blood-brain barrier is the culprit in HACE—is likely to prove controversial. There are many hypotheses as to what may cause the brain's blood vessels to leak at high altitudes. Further studies in humans, as well as in not-yet-developed models using animals that are susceptible to edema of the white matter, should help resolve this question in the next few years.

If patients with AMS had early HACE, then perhaps abnormalities would be seen on their brain scans as well. Benjamin Levine, an American cardiologist and exercise physiologist, and a group of Japanese researchers found such evidence by doing CT and MRI scans of the brains of a few subjects with moderately severe AMS. Their studies were carried out in a laboratory chamber that simulated high altitude and in climbers in the Japanese Alps, near Matsumoto. Since they were not as ill as the Denali climbers, the changes were not as marked. Studies by several other groups of researchers have found some degree of brain swelling in essentially all who have ascended to elevations of 2,750–3,660 meters or higher, but the fact remains that only some of them become ill. Thus, the ability to accommodate swelling of the brain may be an important factor determining susceptibility to AMS.

Some other intriguing observations that support the concept of altered intracranial dynamics in AMS were made by coauthor David Shlim in Kathmandu. As already noted, Kathmandu is at an elevation of 1,324 meters, so AMS is not a risk in the city. From Kathmandu, however, as many as 70,000 trekkers annually, many of whom are inexperienced, head out on expeditions that can rapidly take them as high as 5,500 to 5,790 meters, which makes altitude sickness a significant risk. When overeager tourists get too ill to continue their climb, they are often evacuated to Kathmandu, where Shlim and his colleagues at the Canadian International Water and Energy Consultants (CIWEC) Clinic are usually consulted. For years it has been the rule that any illness that occurs at a high elevation should be considered altitude sickness until proved otherwise. Only in recent years has the "proved otherwise" gained attention. Shlim was away from the CIWEC Clinic

© Pat Morrow

when he first saw a patient who had what turned out to be something other than altitude sickness.

The woman from Sweden

A 69-year-old Swedish woman traveled to Lhasa, Tibet (at 3,650 meters). Within 24 hours of arrival, she developed paralysis of her right side. Shlim was visiting Lhasa at the same time and happened to be at the same hotel. He was called upon to examine her because the hotel staff feared she was suffering from AMS. He found that she had virtually complete paralysis of her right arm and leg, but her face was not paralyzed, and her mental functioning was entirely intact. The immediate assumption had been stroke, but this pattern did not make sense in terms of a classic stroke, which consists of a sudden "bleed" (hemorrhage) or blood clot in the brain. In such instances there is usually an alteration of consciousness, as well as a recognizable drooping of the facial muscles.

On the other hand, the woman from Sweden was clearly not suffering from AMS. Arrangements were made for her to be evacuated by air to Hong Kong. There she underwent a CT scan, which revealed a large meningioma (benign brain tumor) in her left frontal lobe. Her right-sided paralysis was accounted for by the fact that the nerves from the brain cross over in the spinal cord. The tumor likely had been growing for years without previously drawing attention to itself. Why did it suddenly become symptomatic within a day of flying to a high altitude? And what did the Swedish woman's case demonstrate about how the brain reacts at high altitude?

Shlim puzzled over the case for months. The following year at an international conference on mountain medicine in Davos, Switzerland, he mentioned it to some other doctors. Heleen Meijer, a Dutch physician who works with an international air rescue company in Amsterdam, overheard the conversation and approached Shlim, saying, "I had a case just like that last year in Peru." She then told of a woman in her 20s who had developed severe neurological symptoms and seizures after ascending to 4,270 meters. Even after she descended, her symptoms persisted. In Lima, at sea level, a brain scan showed a large meningioma. After doctors in Europe were consulted, it was decided to operate in Lima, as a prolonged air journey at a cabin pressure of 2,440 meters was considered risky.

Meijer and Shlim decided to collaborate on a paper presenting these two cases. Amazingly, while the manuscript was in preparation, Meijer encountered a third case. The three cases

(Top) David R. Shlim; (bottom) Peter H. Hackett

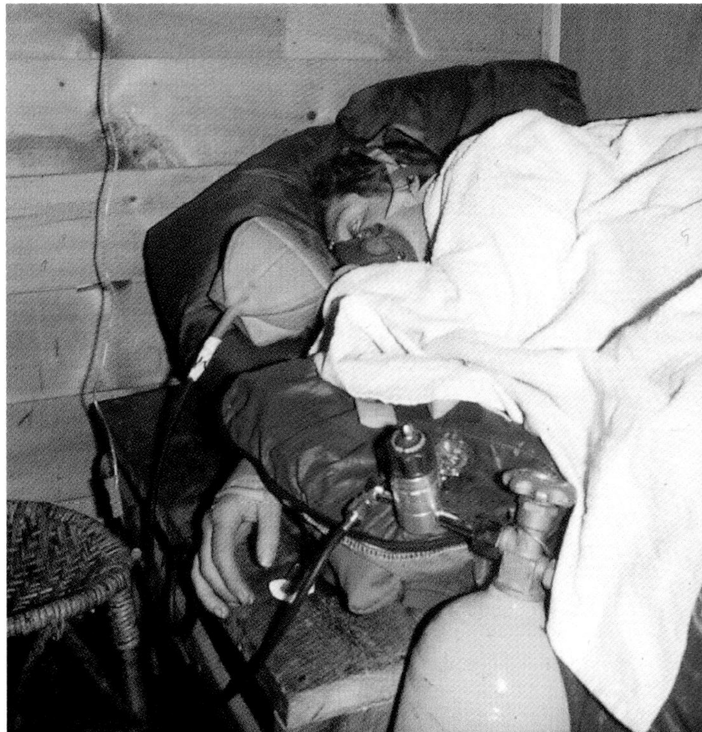

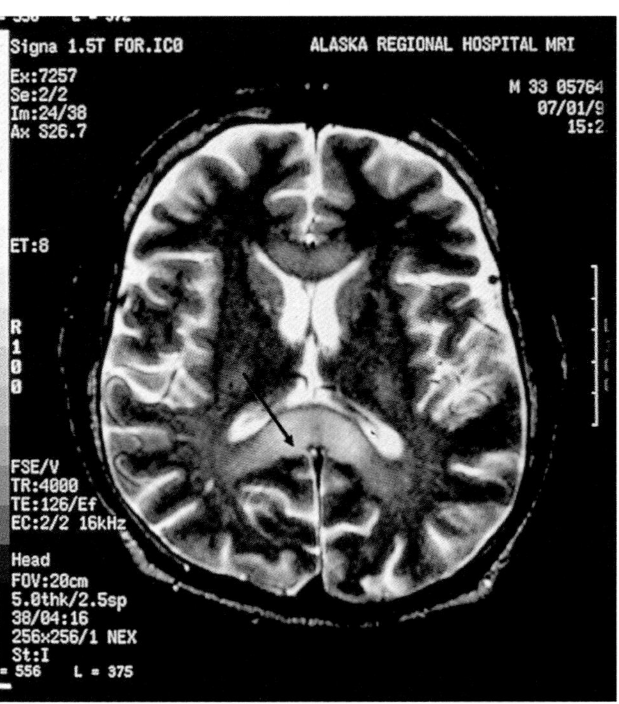

(Opposite page) Rescue of a climber stricken with high-altitude cerebral edema (HACE) on Mt. Aconcagua in the Central Andes. (Top) Patient with severe HACE symptoms at the Pheriche aid post; thanks to prompt recognition and treatment of her condition, she survived. (Above) Magnetic resonance imaging reveals an accumulation of fluid just below the brain's ventricles—a finding that helped illuminate the mechanisms of HACE.

suggested that brain tumors can react at high altitude, suddenly becoming symptomatic. The tumors may have swelled abruptly owing to their large independent blood supply, but it was more likely that the rest of the brain swelled, crushing itself against the immobile tumor taking up space within the skull. Undoubtedly, more such cases will be reported in the future.

Given this new understanding of brain swelling at high altitudes, might new approaches to prevention and treatment of altitude sickness in tourists follow? When extra oxygen is available via oxygen tanks or descent, the leaks in the brain quickly stop, and blood flow to the brain is decreased, which reduces pressure within the skull.

Drugs that promote fluid loss also help reduce altitude sickness, since they tend to help dry out the brain. These include acetazolamide, as well as furosemide (Lasix), a diuretic used in treating high blood pressure, congestive heart failure, and other conditions in which it is desirable to rid the body of excess fluid. In addition, the potent steroid dexamethasone had been used with success in shrinking brain swelling associated with brain tumors and abscesses; dexamethasone, therefore, was an obvious drug to investigate in altitude sickness. When dexamethasone was used in persons in coma, the results were not very impressive; however, when the drug was given to people with more moderate symptoms, there was a dramatic improvement. Dexamethasone is now used very successfully for treating moderately severe AMS and HACE and can also be used for prevention when necessary. Exactly how dexamethasone prevents leaking of the blood-brain barrier in HACE (as well as in other types of brain swelling) is still a mystery, and further studies are ongoing. This research will benefit many patients at sea level and is an excellent example of how high-altitude investigations may benefit other fields of medicine.

Dreaded breathlessness

Lung problems at high altitudes have fascinated medical scientists ever since people began to explore high mountains. Inconsistent, subtle, and occasionally rapidly fatal, the syndrome known as HAPE has always hovered like a dark cloud over climbing expeditions. For years its effects were misattributed to heart failure, pneumonia, or exhaustion. Only in the latter half of this century was HAPE proved to be a disease of the lungs caused by sudden exposure to high altitude and not a form of heart failure induced by exertion at altitude.

The U.S. physician Charles Houston, a noted researcher and mountaineer who did studies in the Himalayas from the 1930s through the early '50s, was living in Aspen, Colorado, in December 1958, when two young cross-country skiers headed over a 3,660-meter pass near Aspen over the Christmas holidays. One of them developed severe breathlessness and was evacuated back to Aspen. Houston examined him and noted that the 19-year-old's heart was fine but his lungs were filled with fluid. He correctly attributed the problem to high-altitude hypoxia. When his groundbreaking findings were reported in *The New England Journal of Medicine* in 1960, this unique problem was brought to the attention of the world.

Almost two decades ago, researchers working on Denali set out to determine what kind of fluid was actually flowing into the lungs in cases of HAPE. This information was critical in helping to sort out competing hypotheses. Some researchers thought that arterial spasm, or clamping down of blood vessels, caused selective high pressure in capillary vessels, resulting in a thin, protein-free fluid (or transudate) leaking into the lungs. Others thought that there might be direct damage to the vessels of the lungs that caused them to leak a thick, protein-rich fluid (or exudate). But how could this fluid be obtained for analysis during an actual episode of HAPE?

To answer that question, Hackett teamed up with Robert Schoene, a pulmonary specialist. In Alaska they ascended to the research camp on Denali, armed with a fiber-optic bronchoscope. The idea was to find people suffering from HAPE and, before instituting lifesaving treatment, thread the scope down into their lungs and extract a sample of the fluid that had accumulated there. Since the bronchoscopy procedure would take just a few

The CIWEC Clinic, Kathmandu, Nepal, where thousands of ailing trekkers are treated annually; snake charmers in the foreground.

David R. Shlim

minutes, and the life-giving oxygen would be readily at hand, the experiment seemed justified. In fact, all of the participants tolerated the procedure well. The results showed that their lung fluid contained large proteins from the blood, much too large to pass through intact capillary vessels. In order for the leakage of such large proteins to occur, significant holes would have to be present. What might cause these large holes to appear and how they could heal themselves so rapidly with descent remained unexplained. That chapter has yet to be written.

Lofty research

Nonetheless, understanding of HAPE has advanced significantly in the last few years. Advances in technology have allowed researchers to look at the pulmonary blood flow of climbers without having to do an invasive procedure. Doppler flow devices can bounce innocuous sound waves through the chest and measure changes in pressure in the pulmonary arteries. It had been known since the 1960s that people suffering from HAPE have greatly increased pressure in the pulmonary arteries; in fact, this seemed to be the sine qua non of the illness. Normally, the right ventricle of the heart pumps blood to the lungs with a pressure of around 20–25 millimeters of mercury. At high altitudes that pressure steadily increases; at 4,270 to 4,570 meters, the pulmonary-artery pressure (PAP) can be up to 40 millimeters of mercury, and it can be much higher in those with pulmonary edema. What would happen if one could reduce PAP in HAPE victims?

Such an experiment was first successfully performed in the late 1980s at another high-altitude research post, this time perched precariously on the very sum-

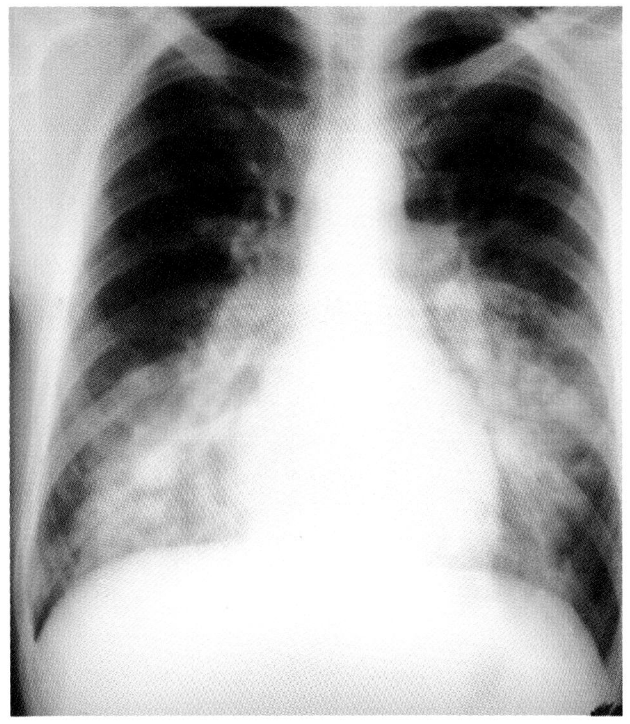

X-ray shows fluid in the lungs of a climber with high-altitude pulmonary edema (HAPE), a baffling syndrome that has yet to be fully elucidated.

Peter H. Hackett

Adapted from P. Hackett and R. Roch, "High Altitude Medicine," in *Wilderness Medicine,* Paul Auerbach, ed. (St. Louis: Mosby, 1995)

Not in Peak Health: Studies of Altitude Illness in Tourists and Soldiers

Study group	Number at risk each year	Sleeping altitude	Maximum altitude reached	Average rate of ascent[1] (in days)	Acute mountain sickness (% affected)	HAPE[2] or HACE[3] (% affected)
Visitors to western U.S. states	30 million	~2,000 m ~2,500 m ~3,000 m	3,500 m	1-2	18-20 22 27-42	0.01
Mt. Everest trekkers	10,000	3,000-5,200 m	5,500 m	1-2 (flown to height) 10-13 (climbed to height)	47 23	1.6 0.05
Mt. McKinley climbers	800	3,000-5,300 m	6,194 m	3-7	30	2-3
Mt. Rainier climbers	6,000	3,000 m	4,392 m	1-2	67	...
Indian soldiers	...	3,000-5,500 m	5,500 m	1-2	...	2.3-15.5

[1]Number of days traveling from low altitude to sleeping altitude. [2]High-altitude pulmonary edema. [3]High-altitude cerebral edema.

mit of Monte Rosa (Dufourspitze) on the Swiss-Italian border, at a height of 4,634 meters. The research team was headed by Oswald Oelz, an Austrian physician and accomplished mountain climber, and worked out of a small cabin, the Capanna Regina Margherita, whose back porch overhangs a 1,525-meter nearly vertical face of the mountain!

The researchers were helicoptered to the hut with their equipment. Then a group of climbers, chosen because they had experienced HAPE previously, ascended rapidly to the hut, part way via aerial tram and the rest of the way on foot. As anticipated, they became sick. Some of the group were treated with nifedipine (a drug that dilates blood vessels, including the pulmonary artery, and therefore can lower PAP). The other group received a placebo. The group treated with nifedipine had a marked reduction in PAP, which coincided with clinical improvement. The placebo group stayed ill and required conventional therapy (oxygen and rest) for recovery.

The following year the same researchers evaluated nifedipine as a potential prophylactic medication—determining whether it would prevent HAPE. They gave HAPE-susceptible subjects nifedipine before their rapid ascent to the Capanna Regina Margherita. The nifedipine drastically reduced their pulmonary edema (compared with that of a control group not taking nifedipine), and persons prone to the illness now use the medication for prevention.

Back in the U.S., Hackett and his group were pursuing the same idea of lowering the pulmonary artery pressure to treat HAPE. On Denali they confirmed the value of nifedipine in ill climbers, showing that it caused a drop in PAP and an increase in oxygenation. They also showed that hydralazine, another vasodilator, worked in the same way, as did supplemental oxygen. In 1989 they moved their laboratory to a ski resort in Colorado, where they investigated the role of the sympathetic nervous system in HAPE. (The sympathetic nervous system is the part of the autonomic nervous system that, among other things, helps the body prepare to react in situations of stress.) The hypothesis was

Important questions about altitude sickness have been answered at this research outpost on Denali (Mt. McKinley), in Alaska. (Opposite page) Pulmonary specialist Robert Schoene (right) removes fluid from the lungs of a Denali climber suffering from HAPE.

that if increased sympathetic tone was partly responsible for the elevated PAP, then giving a drug to relax the sympathetic tone might be helpful. They had no trouble finding skiers with HAPE and discovered that phentolamine, an agent that blocks the alpha receptors of the sympathetic nervous system, was especially effective at reducing PAP—even more effective than nifedipine.

This line of work was extended in the past year on Monte Rosa by Urs Scherrer and a team of researchers from Switzerland and Germany. This group experimented with nitric oxide in HAPE. Nitric oxide is a chemical that appears to be important in many of the body's functions. In the lungs it is a potent dilator of the pulmonary arterial vessels (and has been used to reduce PAP in neonates). Because it can be inhaled, nitric oxide goes directly into the alveoli that are filled with air, in contrast to alveoli that may be fluid-filled owing to edema. From air-filled alveoli it easily reaches the adjacent blood vessels and causes them to dilate, which takes the blood flow away from the edematous, or flooded, areas and into the dry areas of the lungs. The result is an improvement in oxygen

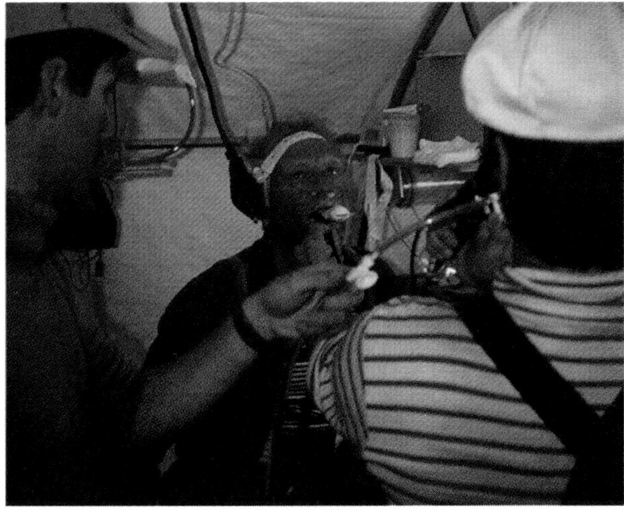

exchange from the air to the blood, as well as a decrease in PAP. With the use of radionuclide lung scanning on Monte Rosa, researchers were able to show that the blood did indeed shift from the areas of edema to the drier areas, improving the condition of climbers with HAPE. All of these investigations confirmed the important role of pulmonary hypertension in the pathogenesis of HAPE. Since PAP can rapidly change with descent from high altitudes or administration of oxygen or drugs, this might also help explain why the syndrome is so rapidly reversible. But there was still another unexplained factor.

Measurements on Denali showed that while all those with HAPE had high PAP, so did a number of climbers without HAPE. Even more curious was the fact that HAPE victims who descended the mountain were found to have very high PAP again on reascending but this time had no edema! The conclusion was that high PAP is essential for HAPE to develop, but there must be another important factor (or factors) directly affecting the blood vessel permeability. What this other contributor is remains a mystery.

Functioning at extreme altitude

The highest point on Earth is the summit of Mt. Everest (*see* "Climbing the World's Highest Peak," page 36), at an altitude of 8,848 meters. If a person was flown to the peak by helicopter (which is not presently possible) and stepped onto the summit without supplemental oxygen, he or she would rapidly lose consciousness and die in minutes. Yet mountain climbers have succeeded in reaching the summit without supplemental oxygen, first in 1978 and many times since then. How is that possible?

When Reinhold Messner of Italy and Peter Habeler of Austria first contemplated climbing Everest without supplemental bottled oxygen, many doctors told them that they would either die or suffer permanent brain damage in the process. The doctors' fears were based on extrapolations of measurements of oxygen in the blood and physical performance from lower altitudes. They foresaw a distinct incompatibility for healthy human functioning at 8,848 meters. Thus, the mountaineering pioneers headed off into territory where medical angels feared to tread.

In fact, Messner and Habeler successfully reached the summit on May 8, 1978, and suffered no apparent brain damage. Their success presented a quandary for scientists who were already planning a medical and mountaineering "first": an expedition to Mt. Everest that would take place in the late summer of 1981

(continued on page 39)

Photographs, Peter H. Hackett

(Top) Hulton Getty; (bottom) © Alfred Gregory—Royal Geographic Society

(Left) Members of the famed 1924 British expedition up the world's highest mountain, photographed by Capt. John Noel. Standing (far left) are Andrew Irvine and George Mallory, who disappeared very close to the summit, never to be seen again. Several months into the climb, Mallory wrote, "We expect no mercy from Everest . . . but yet it will be well for her that she deign to take notice of the little group that approaches stealthily over her glaciers." (Below) May 29, 1953: Edmund Hillary (left) and Tenzing Norgay just before they became the first climbers ever to conquer Everest.

Climbing the World's Highest Peak

by David R. Shlim, M.D., and Elizabeth Hawley

Mountaineering, *also called* MOUNTAIN CLIMBING, *the sport of attaining, or attempting to attain, high points in mountainous regions, primarily for the pleasure of the climb. . . . Climbing mountains embodies the thrills produced by testing one's courage, resourcefulness, cunning, strength, ability, and stamina to the utmost in a situation of inherent risk. . . . For most climbers, the pleasures of mountaineering lie not only in the "conquest" of a peak but also in the physical and spiritual satisfactions brought about through intense personal effort, ever-increasing proficiency, and contact with natural grandeur.*

—Encyclopædia Britannica

When the mountain that was to be named Everest was confirmed as the world's highest peak by Indian surveyors in 1852, further exploration was prevented by the political situation. Mt. Everest (Chomolungma in Tibetan) is situated on the Nepal-Tibet border, and both countries were off limits to foreigners. In the early 1920s, Great Britain alone was granted permission to explore the northern approaches to the mountain via Tibet. On the third British expedition, in 1924, climbers came to within 305 meters (1,000 feet) of the summit (8,848 meters [29,028 feet]) and may have even succeeded a few days later, when George Mallory and Andrew Irvine disappeared very close to the summit.

When Nepal opened to foreign visitors in 1950, the southern approach to the mountain became the focus of expeditions. On May 29, 1953, two men who were part of a large British-led military-style expedition ascended to the top of Everest and returned to tell about it. Edmund Hillary, a beekeeper from New Zealand (who was knighted in July of that year), and Tenzing Norgay, a Sherpa mountaineer and devout Buddhist, were celebrated around the world for this stunning feat. By May 1978, 59 people had stood on the summit of Everest, all of whom had used supplemental bottled oxygen

during the ascent. The use of oxygen necessitates a large expedition (to haul all the required gear). Each bottle weighs at least 7½ kilograms (16½ pounds) and lasts for only a few hours. Thus, large loads have to be carried to the highest camp so that oxygen is available to the final summit attempters.

In May 1978 Reinhold Messner and Peter Habeler climbed to the summit of Everest without using supplemental oxygen. They did, however, follow in the footsteps and use the tents of a much larger expedition. Then, in 1980, Messner stunned the mountaineering world and forever changed expectations in Himalayan mountaineering. After acclimatizing for six weeks at his base camp in Tibet, he set off totally alone, with only a small backpack and no oxygen. He reached the summit after spending only two nights en route and then returned unharmed to his base camp after an additional night on the descent.

This climb paved the way for other rapid ascents throughout the Himalayas with only lightweight equipment. In fact, by mid-1996, 57 people had climbed Everest without supplemental oxygen. The most rapid climb was in 1988 by the French mountaineer Marc Batard, who traveled from the base camp (at 5,500 meters) to the summit in 22 hours 29 minutes. This remarkable feat is the equivalent of climbing a 40-story building every hour for 22½ hours straight, with only one-half to one-third the normal oxygen available at sea level.

As success on Everest became commonplace, nations and corporations no longer cared to bear the high costs of such ventures. Instead, mountaineers who wished to climb Mt. Everest offered to take wealthy clients to the top for a substantial fee. That sum would cover the "peak permit" (currently $120,000 for a 12-person expedition on the South Col route in Nepal) and the expensive logistic support (transportation of supplies, Sherpa porters, oxygen, food, tents, and climbing gear). So, for a mere $35,000 to $65,000, any highly motivated person can attempt to climb to the highest point on Earth.

And climb they have. By early 1996 the number of summiters was 615, which included 32 women; multiple ascents by the same climbers brought that number to 748. Exactly 40 years after Hillary and Tenzing struggled to the summit, 40 people stood on the top of Everest on the same day (May 10, 1993)! The record for the most ascents belongs to Ang Rita, a Sherpa mountaineer who climbed Everest nine times between 1983 and 1996—each time without using supplemental oxygen. Junko Tabei of Japan was the first woman to climb Everest (in 1975). The oldest person to make it to the top of Everest was a 60-year-old Venezuelan man. The youngest was a 17-year-old French youth who accompanied his father to the summit. The youngest female to succeed on Everest was a 19-year-old from India.

What has enabled so many to reach the pinnacle of Mt. Everest? An intimate knowledge of the mountain and its conditions. Those who know the mountain best are the Sherpa guides, who have vast experience with weather conditions and the complex logistic factors that contribute to a successful climb. In Nepal on the standard South Col route, Sherpa porters now break the trail, fix the dangerous route through the Khumbu Icefall, set up camps, and carry up all the supplies. The guides and their clients ascend only to levels to which they can acclimatize, while Sherpas perform the back-breaking work of carrying loads and stocking camps. When it is time for the final summit push, the climbers ascend to camps that are already completely stocked with food, fuel, and oxygen. If they time the ascent correctly in terms of weather and snow conditions, success will be mainly dependent on the willpower of the climber to put one foot in front of the other until he or she reaches the top.

Some mountaineers, including Hillary, lament the fact that ascending Mt. Everest has become a guided outing with little sense of adventure. True as that may be, there are still many unbeaten paths up Everest—hazardous and difficult routes that would deter all but the best mountaineers—and some routes that have never been attempted. In that regard, Everest is just like other great peaks, including the Matterhorn and Mt. Blanc, whose ascents once were incredible feats of daring but now, largely, are guided climbs on certain routes.

Still, no one who has stood on Everest's summit takes its grandeur for granted. All are painfully aware that one of every 40 climbers who have tried to climb Everest has died in the attempt, and 21 of the successful summiters died while trying to make their way back down the mountain.

Deadliest day

Late in the evening on May 9, 1996, two major guided parties—led by adventure travel companies based in the United States and New Zealand—left their highest camp on Mt. Everest, at 7,900 meters, and headed for the summit. They were the first groups up the mountain that season, and the going was slow. Because ropes had to be fixed across difficult sections for the climbers, many reached the summit on the following day well past 1 PM, the usual cutoff time that will allow summiters enough time to get back to their camp before dark. As the exhausted climbers started back down the Southeast Ridge, a sudden storm, with hurricane winds, snow, and arctic temperatures, struck full force. Climbers and guides were separated, which meant that every climber was on his or her own in a total survival situation. Would their own inner resources give them sufficient stamina for getting back down the mountain?

By 5 the following morning, 21 of the 31 people who had climbed the day before still had not returned to camp. Many of the climbers had reached the flat South Col during the night only to become disoriented and lost just a few hundred meters from the tents. A brief clearing in the storm allowed most of them to find their tents; then stronger climbers went back out into the wind to search for the missing. The world's most experienced Everest guide, Rob Hall of New Zealand, who had just climbed Everest for his fifth time, was stranded near the summit, having stayed behind the day before to help an exhausted client. Unable to rescue himself, Hall awaited the help of Sherpa climbers battling their way through the fierce winds to reach him. Later in the day he was informed by radio that the Sherpas had had to turn back. Then Hall, in a new twist on the satellite technology that is changing the face of Everest climbing, was able to phone his wife, Jan Arnold, seven months pregnant with their first child, at home in New Zealand. "Don't worry about me," he reassured her before turning off his radio. A few hours later he was dead.

Four others died as well: Hall's client Doug Hansen of the U.S.; another client, Yasuko Namba of Japan; New Zealand guide Andrew Harris; and Scott Fischer, head of the U.S. tour company Mountain Madness. Three Indian mountaineers died on the northern side of Mt. Everest during the same storm, and a Taiwanese climber died earlier in the day in a non-storm-related accident below the South Col. May 10 thus became the deadliest day in Everest's history. More than anything else, that fateful day in May burst the euphoric bubble of guided Everest climbs and proved how marginal existence can be at extreme altitude when the weather changes.

***Elizabeth Hawley** is an American writer living in Nepal. She has been the main chronicler of Himalayan mountaineering for more than 32 years.*

Deavers—Ft. Worth Star/Sipa

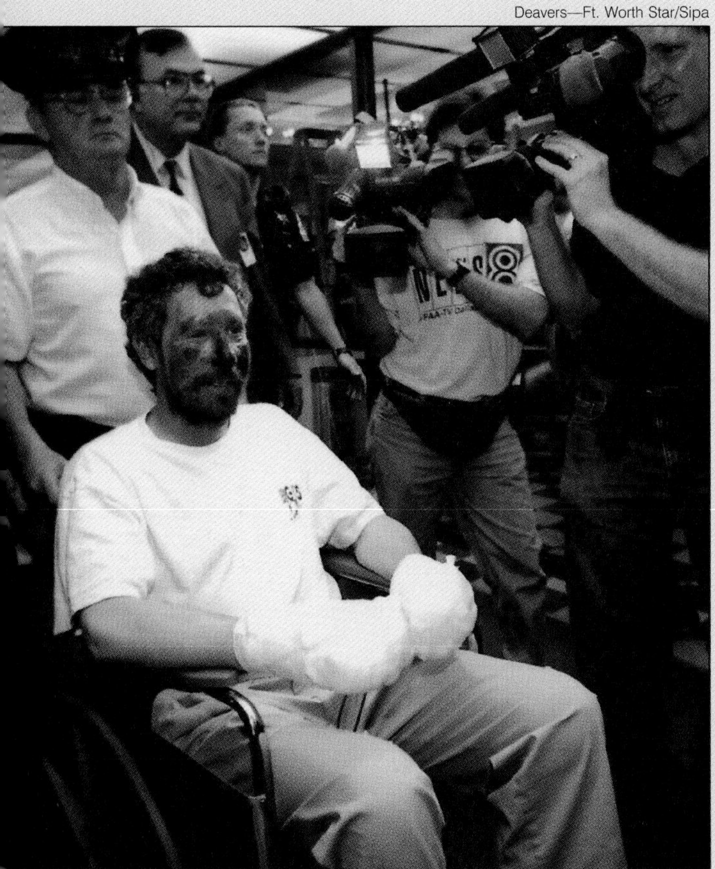

Seaborn Weathers of Dallas, Texas, was one of the survivors of the deadliest day on Mt. Everest—May 10, 1996—when a sudden storm took the lives of eight climbers.

(continued from page 35)
and would focus entirely on the medical aspects of high-altitude climbing. The expedition team (called the American Medical Research Expedition to Everest, or AMREE) now had to design experiments that would determine how the two prior mountaineers had succeeded where science dictated they should have failed.

They first looked at the factors that went into a successful "summit day" on Mt. Everest. Weather was the most important factor. High winds or snow would have made the climbing extremely dangerous and finding a route nearly impossible. May 8, 1978, was a clear, sunny day, marked by a high barometric pressure. Was that a clue? There was only one way to find out: carry the appropriate instruments to the summit and get the appropriate readings.

AMREE ascends

AMREE was in every way committed to science. The climbers even carried an exercise bicycle as high as 7,925 meters, but it was then demolished in high winds.

One of the climbing doctors, pathologist Chris Pizzo, made it to the summit wearing monitoring equipment that measured his breathing and heart rates; at the top he captured a sample of his expired breath to be carried down and later analyzed in the United States. Also, for the first time, atmospheric measurements were made from the summit. The combination of these measurements revealed that the atmospheric pressure over Everest was higher than predicted. This was due to two factors. First of all, the day the AMREE climbers reached the summit was one of unusually high pressure. Second, barometric pressure varies with latitude, and at 28° N the pressure on Mt. Everest is higher than at the same altitude farther from the Equator. In fact, calculations reveal that if Everest was at the latitude of Denali (63° N), reaching the summit without oxygen would be truly impossible.

In addition, the season of the year makes a substantial difference to a human trying to survive at such an altitude. The variation between summer and winter would account for a 25% or more difference in maximal oxygen consumption (the ability to do maximal physical work). Thus, it was found that very small changes in barometric pressure, resulting in tiny oxygen-level changes, make a huge difference physiologically, which indicates that Everest's altitude is indeed at the very edge of survival.

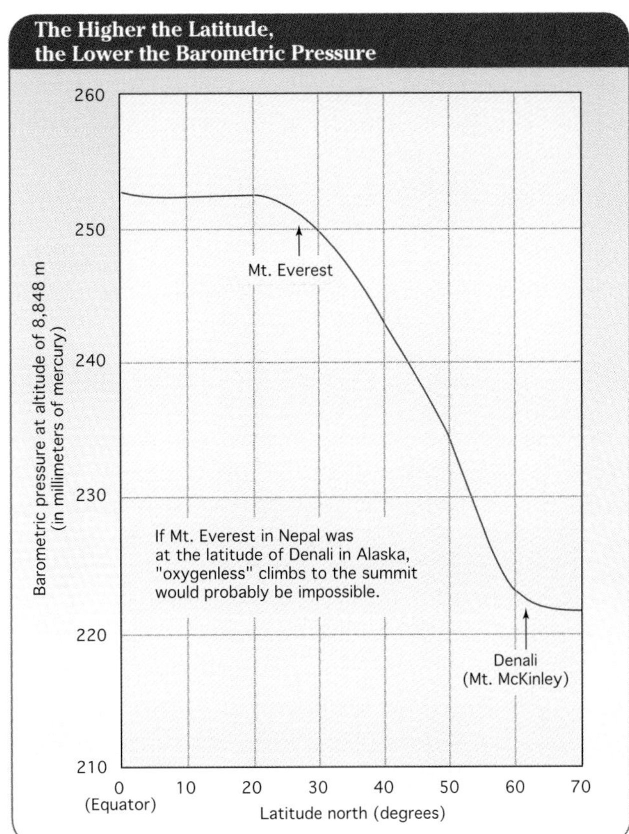

Barometric pressure at high altitude decreases with increasing distance from the Equator.

Adapted from J.B. West, " 'Oxygenless' Climbs and Barometric Pressure," *American Alpine Journal,* vol. 226, no. 58 (1984), pp. 126–133, © American Alpine Club

For many years it was thought that an increase in red blood cells was an important adaptation to high altitude. There is, however, a danger in having too many red cells, especially in conjunction with dehydration, a combination that can easily occur as one reaches a high elevation; pumping the thickened blood through small vessels then becomes extremely difficult for the heart. This knowledge has led some physicians to withdraw quantities of blood from mountain climbers with high hematocrits (a measure of red blood cell concentration, indicating thickened blood) in order to thin the blood and improve its flow. When this was done in the AMREE climbers, exercise performance was not impaired, and brain functioning improved slightly.

A safer alternative—and the next logical step—was to see if the exceedingly high hematocrits could be avoided by assiduous attention to rehydration, but there were many obstacles. First of all, the mountain environment, although covered with millions of tons of snow, is basically a desert in that the snow is frozen solid and yields no readily drinkable water. For a few sips of water, snow and ice must be chopped from the mountainside and then balanced in a small pot over a tiny mountain stove. Because the yield of a hunk of ice is so small, repeated trips outside the tent to get more are needed. At 8,000 meters, the very effort of putting on boots and crawling out of the tent can be utterly exhausting—

AMERICAN MEDICAL RESEARCH EXPEDITION TO EVEREST
1981

Yong Tenzing Sherpa

taking four or five times as long to accomplish as it would under more obliging circumstances. Furthermore, hunger and thirst are dulled, and drinking becomes an intellectual goal to be achieved rather than a natural craving to be satisfied. Both the AMREE data and those from a later medical mission, Operation Everest II, indicated that paying special attention to hydration helped prevent thickening of the blood and improved performance. Despite the grueling effort, self-imposed rehydration is now the state of the art in high-altitude climbing.

Scientific surprises

So-called Operation Everest II, a decompression chamber experiment in which eight men were kept at the equivalent pressure of Everest for 40 days, was carried out at the U.S. Army Research Institute of Environmental Medicine, Natick, Massachusetts, in 1985. The chamber, constructed of thick steel to withstand the pressure gradients, was divided into two "rooms," one living quarters and the other for physiological studies, with an air lock between them. Food was passed into the chamber through small air locks. Conditions were, to say the least, cramped and stressful!

Physician Chris Pizzo, a member of the first-ever medical research expedition up Everest, collects samples of expired air from his lungs on the summit.

A remarkable and poignant incident occurred during the experiment. One of the investigators who was studying the performance of a subject on an exercise bicycle at a simulated altitude of 8,000 meters fell unconscious when someone stepped on his oxygen hose. The subject just continued cycling, without any supplemental oxygen, since he had been fully acclimatized over a long time; the unacclimatized investigators, however, required oxygen every time they entered the chamber.

A surprising finding from AMREE, which was validated by Operation Everest II, was the huge respiratory effort a climber must expend merely to stay functional at summit level without supplemental oxygen. On Everest, Pizzo was breathing at a rate of 90 times per minute, over five times the normal respiratory rate at sea level. As a result, the carbon dioxide (CO_2) in his system dropped to lower levels than had ever before been measured in an athlete. The CO_2 in his blood was more than five times lower than normal. Despite this incredible breathing effort, the pressure of oxygen in his blood was so low that at sea level such a value would be practically incompatible with life. Clearly, anyone who sets foot on the summit of Everest without supplemental oxygen has reached the limit of human functioning. MHA

x²+y² √487300165

Contemplating Creativity

by Andrea Gellin Shindler

Illustration by Paul Cozzolino

What is creativity? Or, as psychologist Mihaly Csikszentmihalyi asked in his best-selling book *Flow: The Psychology of Optimal Experience* (1990), "*Where* is creativity?"

Creativity has long been a field that fascinates. Today this field is being explored by psychologists, neuroscientists, educators, artists, dancers, athletes, musicians, and many, many others. Some of the research issues currently being investigated by this interdisciplinary group are: the role of insight—the "sparks" that set off creative thinking; whether endeavors must be "unique" in order to be "creative"; whether there are accessibility and control of the creative process in the conscious awareness; whether all people are capable of creativity; whether the unconscious mind is involved in creative thinking; how the individual creator, the evaluators who judge the quality of the new work, and the domain that defines the creative product interact; whether creative potential in a given individual can be identified at an early age; and whether an array of sociological constraints inhibit or limit creativity.

Csikszentmihalyi, professor of psychology at the University of Chicago, defines creativity as "the ability to produce something that changes the existing patterns and thoughts in a domain." Domain refers to the symbol system in which the individual works, whether it be in art, science, mathematics, or other areas of human endeavor. Csikszentmihalyi, whose most recent book is *Creativity: Flow and the Psychology of Discovery and Invention* (1996), is one of the leaders who have contributed to an emerging scientific "picture" of creativity. That picture includes the following observations:

- A creative person regularly solves problems or fashions products in one or more domains.
- Beyond a certain point, there is rarely a correlation between measured IQ and creativity.
- Creative output is a predictable occurrence, not a one-time "accident."
- A creative tendency in one field does not predict similar tendencies in other fields.
- Most creative insights come about gradually, not with a burst of insight (Charles Darwin's theory of evolution and Albert Einstein's theory of relativity emerged over years of observation and thought).
- Personality traits of creative people include independence, self-confidence, unconventionality, alertness, ambition, commitment to work, willingness to confront hostility, inquisitiveness, a high degree of self-organization, and the ability to work effectively for long periods without sleep.
- Creative individuals are risk takers who confront problems with an unusual combination of intellectual strengths that allows them to investigate an area in a new way or to define a new area of study.
- Cognitive style, the way one thinks, rather than native intelligence seems to set creative individuals apart from their peers.
- Intrinsic factors (the passion for pursuing a particular activity for the sake of the *activity itself*) rather than extrinsic factors (rewards such as fame, fortune, status, or prizes) motivate creative individuals.
- Parental support of creative young people in their formative years tends to be either very strong or lacking.
- Creative people often have special mentors.
- Creative people have an aesthetic sensibility that distinguishes "good" problems (those to be pursued with vigor) from "unimportant" problems (ones that can be ignored).

Strengths, weaknesses, and intelligences

The work comes out of the unconscious, that is certain. You recognize if it is good

***Andrea Gellin Shindler** is Founder and Executive Director of the Foundation for Human Potential, a Chicago-based not-for-profit organization that has an ongoing association with the School of the Art Institute of Chicago and is dedicated to exploring issues concerning creativity and learning. She has conceived and directed three internationally attended symposia—"Art and the Brain" (1988), "Music and the Brain" (1992), and "Sports, Dance, Movement and the Brain" (1995)—and is currently organizing another symposium in this series, scheduled for 1997. She is also Visiting Instructor, Department of Neurological Sciences, Rush Medical College, Chicago.*

or not. . . . If you have a preconception, any notion of where you are going, you will never get anywhere.
—Spanish artist Joan Miró (1893–1983)

Joan Miró with lithograph.

Howard Gardner, professor of education at Harvard University and adjunct professor of neurology at Boston University School of Medicine, has a unique interdisciplinary perspective on creativity. His work, which spans the fields of education, psychology, neurology, and the arts, led him to formulate his pioneering "theory of multiple intelligences," presented in *Frames of Mind* (1983). The essence of his theory is that all people possess strengths and weaknesses and that by capitalizing on their strengths, they may function maximally. Gardner, an outspoken critic of IQ tests and standardized measures of educational achievement (such as the Scholastic Aptitude Test), compiled a preliminary list of seven intelligences for research purposes. He recently added an eighth. These intelligences are:

1. *linguistic:* the ability to understand and communicate through the written or spoken word (most fully realized by poets)

2. *logical-mathematical:* the ability to understand and solve problems in mathematics, logic, and science (nuclear physicists and architects fall into this category)

3. *spatial:* the ability to form a mental model of a spatial world and to maneuver and operate by using that model (sailors, engineers, surgeons, sculptors, and painters are a few examples)

4. *musical:* the ability to understand and combine sounds in harmonious and expressive ways (Wolfgang Amadeus Mozart, Leonard Bernstein, the Beatles, and John Coltrane are extraordinary examples of this intelligence)

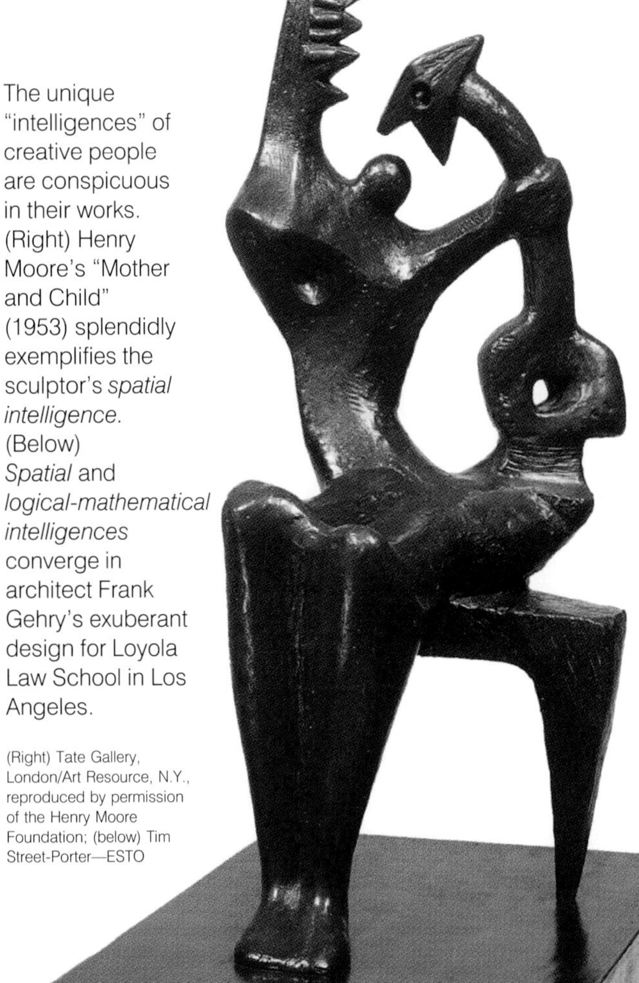

The unique "intelligences" of creative people are conspicuous in their works. (Right) Henry Moore's "Mother and Child" (1953) splendidly exemplifies the sculptor's *spatial intelligence.* (Below) *Spatial* and *logical-mathematical intelligences* converge in architect Frank Gehry's exuberant design for Loyola Law School in Los Angeles.

(Right) Tate Gallery, London/Art Resource, N.Y., reproduced by permission of the Henry Moore Foundation; (below) Tim Street-Porter—ESTO

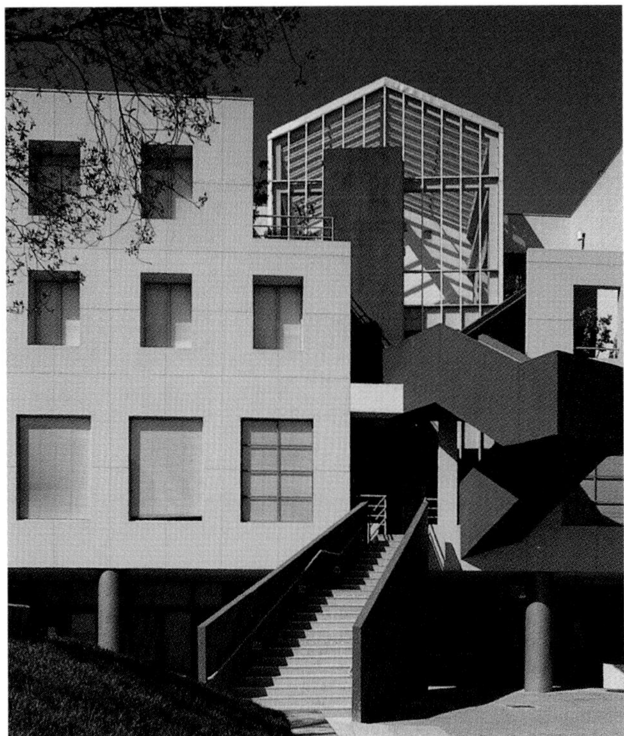

5. *bodily-kinesthetic:* the ability to use one's whole body or parts of it in a creative, therapeutic, or otherwise communicative way (exhibited by dancers, athletes, surgeons, and craftspeople, to name a few)

6. *interpersonal:* one of two "personal" intelligences—so-called people skills—the ability to understand others, what motivates them, and how to interact effectively with them (successful salespeople, politicians, teachers, clinicians, and religious lead-

(Top) UPI/Corbis-Bettmann; (bottom left) Susumu Takahashi—Reuters; (bottom right) Jane Burton—Bruce Coleman Inc.

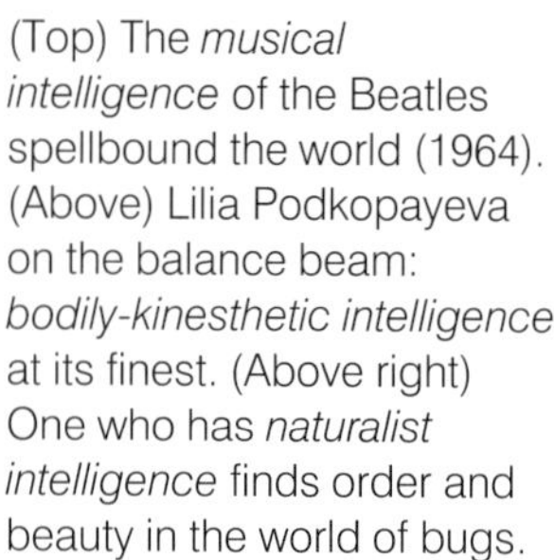

(Top) The *musical intelligence* of the Beatles spellbound the world (1964). (Above) Lilia Podkopayeva on the balance beam: *bodily-kinesthetic intelligence* at its finest. (Above right) One who has *naturalist intelligence* finds order and beauty in the world of bugs.

ers demonstrate high levels of this intelligence)

7. *intrapersonal:* represented by an acute self-awareness that facilitates one's communication with others (Sigmund Freud, innovator of psychoanalysis, was the prime model for this intelligence)

8. *naturalist:* the ability to discriminate fine patterns in the natural world and to appreciate flora and fauna (Charles Darwin, Edward O. Wilson, and John J. Audubon are extraordinary examples of this intelligence)

One of the questions that especially intrigues Gardner is how residual strengths and new abilities can be realized after brain damage:

> *Damage to the brain continues to be one of the principal human afflictions. It is crucial to understand the effects of brain damage on artistic, musical, and kinesthetic capacities and, especially, to understand the important roles that the arts can assume in the treatment and rehabilitation of brain injury. Artistic and other forms of expression may assume an even more critical communicative role when other avenues are blocked or impaired.*

In 1967 the Harvard University Graduate School of Education received a grant to investigate the role of the arts in education. Because at the time there was virtually no meaningful or valid information on the topic, the program "Harvard Project Zero" was launched. Dean Theodore Sizer appointed philosopher Nelson Goodman to lead the project. Goodman then recruited Gardner, among others, to work with him. Gardner's involvement with Harvard Project Zero has continued for over two decades; during most of this time he has served as the project's codirector, along with David Perkins, a specialist in artificial intelligence.

In the course of studying artistic development in children, Gardner became interested in studying deterioration of artistic ability following brain damage. Through collaboration with the neurologist Norman Geschwind at the Boston Veterans Administration Hospital (now the Department of Veterans Affairs Medical Center), Gardner found that both populations, children and artists with brain damage, had distinct abilities, though some were stronger than others. This finding enabled him to challenge long-standing theories about intelligence: "In going into neuropsychology, I was interested chiefly in the question of whether all artistic-symbolic capacities hung together, or could, as the evidence from studies of brain-damaged individuals suggests, be modularized, *i.e.,* break down separately." Finding that children often develop competency in some areas but not in others and that brain-damaged persons may suffer a loss of many capacities while others remain intact led to his groundbreaking "multiple intelligences" scheme.

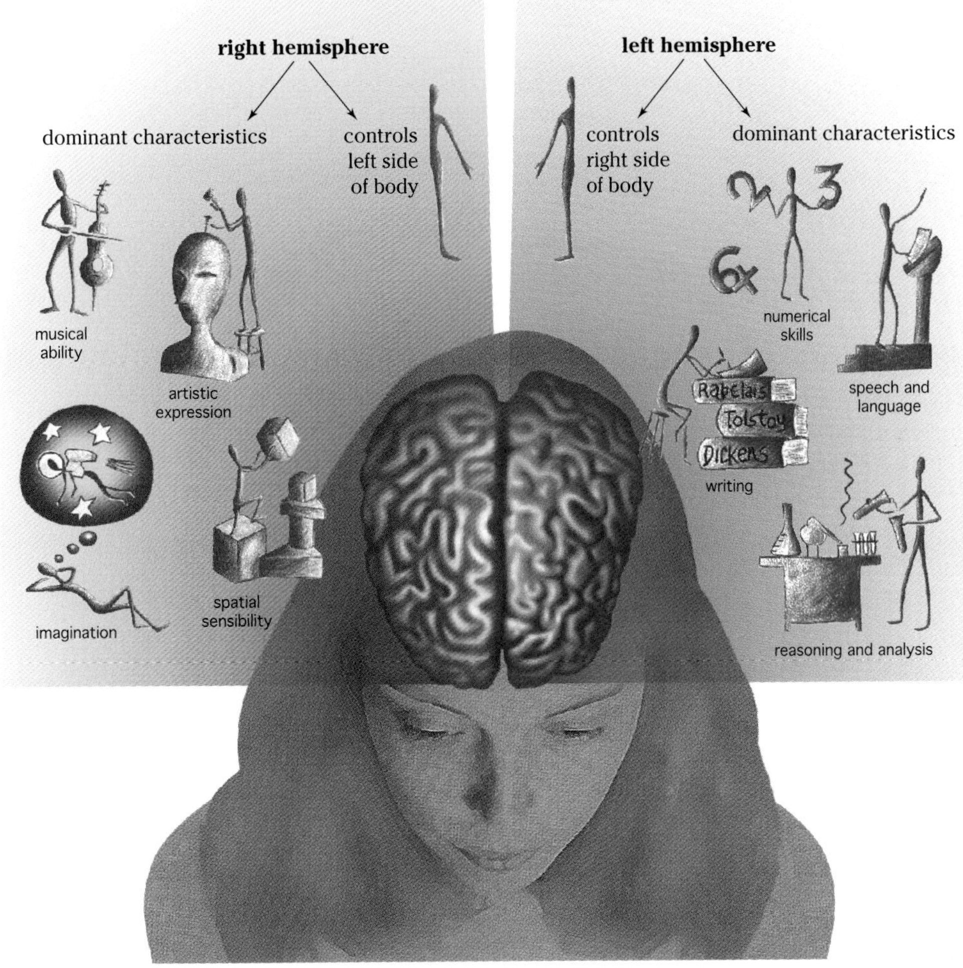

Deep in the brain

The experience that furnishes the material for artistic expression is no longer familiar. It is a strange something that derives its existence from the hinterland of man's mind.... Every creative person is a duality or a synthesis of contradictory aptitudes.

—Swiss psychologist and psychiatrist Carl Gustav Jung (1875–1961)

Other scientific researchers have been more interested in pursuing the role of brain function in their studies of human creativity. The late Geschwind and his colleague neurologist Albert Galaburda showed that individuals gifted in both math and music (that is, extraordinarily skilled in these areas, though not necessarily creative in the sense of true innovation or actually changing the nature of thinking in the domain) often have larger than usual right-hemisphere structures and smaller left-hemisphere structures in the brain. Studies of brain-damaged individuals suggest the importance of an intact right hemisphere for potentially creative activity.

C.G. Jung at work.

UPI/Corbis-Bettmann

Basic neurology teaches that certain areas of the brain govern specific functions. For example, speech is localized to the left hemisphere in most right-handed people. Each side of the brain controls the opposite side of the body.

While potentially creative work in the visual arts can continue despite left-hemisphere damage, right-hemisphere damage compromises creativity. For example, the painter with an injury to the right side of the brain has a tendency to neglect the left side of the canvas or to draw incomplete or distorted figures.

Failure of information to transfer from one hemisphere of the brain to the other is typical of the "split brain." Neurosurgeon Joseph Bogen, at the University of Southern California, has said, "If learning can proceed simultaneously but independently and differently in each hemisphere, so may problem solving. . . . [But] even in the best brains, a complicated task learned with one hand transfers only incompletely to the other." The Israeli-born violinist Itzhak Perlman, a right-handed virtuoso, concurs: "It's not hard remembering what it was like to start playing the fiddle. You just change hands and try to play that way, and the [difficulty of the] whole experience comes back to you." In other words, one may be able to play with the other hand, but the virtuosity is not there.

Neuroscientists have learned that various areas of the brain work in concert to accomplish most human activities. The question is whether the brain is the *sole* mediator of human behavior. Many investigators consider it reductionistic to assume that all behavior can be explained on the basis of biology.

Dan McCoy—Rainbow

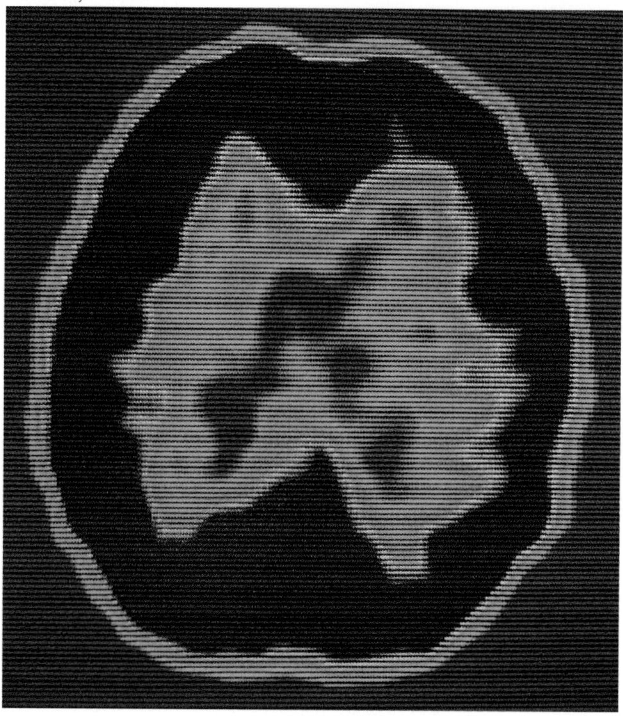

(Left) Positron emission tomography reveals metabolic activity in the brain. Such studies may help neuroscientists figure out what makes creative people "tick." (Right, far right, and below) Some innovators doing what they do best: Sarah Chang concertizing at age 15, having begun her career at 4, when her violinist father handed her her first instrument; Michael Jordan leaping high for the Chicago Bulls, with teammate Dennis Rodman ever ready for a rebound; Mikhail Baryshnikov (in white) performing in *Signals* with his White Oak Dance Project.

Maximizing human potential

Many elements deeper in the brain centers must discharge only in very special activities, and, if these activities are not exercised—especially during maturational stages when the neurons seem to be particularly dependent on use—the neuron types involved may regress, leaving profound functional deficiencies in the integrative machinery.

—American psychobiologist Roger Sperry (1913–94)

Much of the understanding that neuroscientists have of the brain comes from studying individuals with brain damage. Today it is possible to study the brain's role in creativity by taking advantage of new imaging technologies to view the functioning brains of creative people during activity. Among the technologies that can pinpoint idiosyncratic differences in brain function and structure are positron emission tomography, or PET (a diagnostic technique in which images reflect and characterize the metabolic activity of tissues), and the very new and exciting technique called functional magnetic resonance imaging, or fMRI (a noninvasive way to record brain activity as it is occurring while the subject is performing various mental operations). Such studies are likely to provide useful clues concerning the particular influence, if any, of the brain on the given abilities. Although

(Below) Keith Bernstein—FSP/Gamma Liaison; (right) Nathaniel S. Butler—NBA Photos

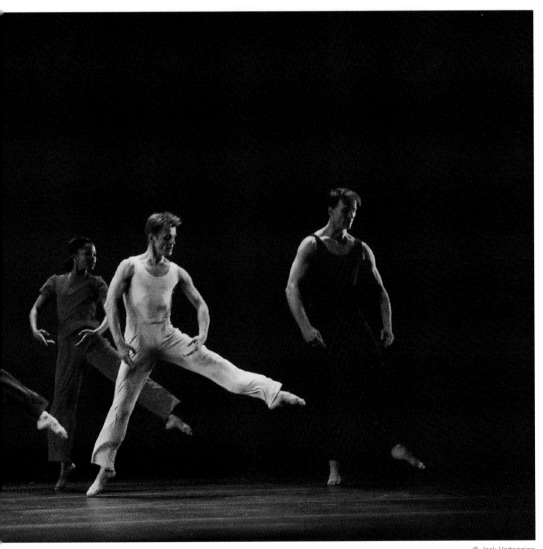

they have not yet been done, imaging studies of the brain at work in extraordinary achievers like basketball player Michael Jordan; violinist Sarah Chang, who made her professional debut at age eight; or ballet dancer Mikhail Baryshnikov might one day help scientists learn exactly what makes these individuals—and others—so outstanding at what they do.

Research on the plasticity of the brain—the brain's ability to learn despite a neurological impairment or to relearn following brain damage—is highlighting the capacity of the brain to reorganize its circuitry in response to new experience. This concept is being specifically addressed by neuroscientists studying language acquisition.

As already noted, the most striking examples of the relationship of brain functioning, learning, and creativity are seen in the behavior of

© Jack Vartoogian

(Below, right, far right, and opposite page, center right)
From J.L. Cummings and J.M. Zarit, "Probable Alzheimer's Disease in an Artist," *Journal of the American Medical Association,* vol. 258, no. 19, pp. 2731–34, Nov. 20, 1987, copyright 1987, American Medical Association

of the tragedy of Ravel's illness was that although he could still listen to and enjoy music, play scales on the piano, perceive pitch, rhythm, tempo, and pace, and detect any errors that were made when his own compositions were played, he could not read a score and then play or sing it himself. In the end, while he alluded to composing melodies in his mind,

he articulated an inability to either write them down or play them. To a friend he confided, "I will never write my *Jeanne d'Arc;* this opera is here, in my head, I hear it, but I will never write it. It's over, I can no longer write my music."

Studies by the late neuropsychologist Justine Sergent, a research scientist at McGill University, Montreal, and a speaker at the symposium,

individuals who have sustained damage to different parts of the nervous system. This localization approach seeks to attribute behavior to specific areas of the brain. Gardner has written, "If one could see how skills broke down, in what combination they occurred and recurred, which ones could be spared or destroyed in isolation, one might receive just those insights into the organization of skills which seem beyond reach in the intact artist."

In 1988 a symposium entitled "Art and the Brain" was held at the Art Institute of Chicago. The conference included an exhibit of works by artists who had experienced brain damage. Study of this artwork yielded a number of intriguing insights—among them, that changes in artistic ability in an individual with Alzheimer's disease were commensurate with the functional deterioration associated with progression of the dementia, that artistic ability can emerge poststroke, that profound changes in artistic style may occur during the growth of a brain tumor, and that precocious drawing ability may be evident in autistic children. The jurors of the art exhibit, art professionals and neuroscientists, differed in their subjective evaluations of the works by this small group of artists, but they were unanimous in affirming that all of them demonstrated remarkable talent and ability, despite, in most cases, having extensive brain damage. (*See* selections from the "Art and the Brain" exhibit, pages 50–52.)

To further understand the relationship of the brain to creative endeavors, the Foundation for Human Potential was established in 1990. The foundation's mission is to sponsor educational symposia that bring together leading researchers and educators who have an abiding interest in maximizing human potential.

Mozartian minds

Moving from the visual arts to music allows for a consideration of other questions about the brain's involvement in creative processes. When the Foundation for Human Potential presented the symposium "Music and the Brain" in 1992, one of the topics explored was the neurological illness that affected the French musician Maurice Ravel (1875–1937) and eventually obliterated his ability to compose. Part

(Opposite page and below) Windmill series by a Dutch artist with Alzheimer's disease. A relentless decline in cognitive function is obvious. (Left) Landscape by Carol Frankel, who suffered a brain hemorrhage that left her unable to speak and partially paralyzed. Despite her disabilities, she began painting prolifically, which suggested that her brain injury may have stimulated previously unrealized abilities. (Bottom) Three works by Reynold Brown, a left-handed cinematic illustrator who had a right-hemisphere stroke: (left) prestroke drawing of actor James Cagney in the 1957 movie *Man of a Thousand Faces;* poststroke Brown tended to neglect the left side of his drawings (center); "Three Faces" (right), drawn about 10 years after his brain damage, shows considerable recovery of artistic skills.

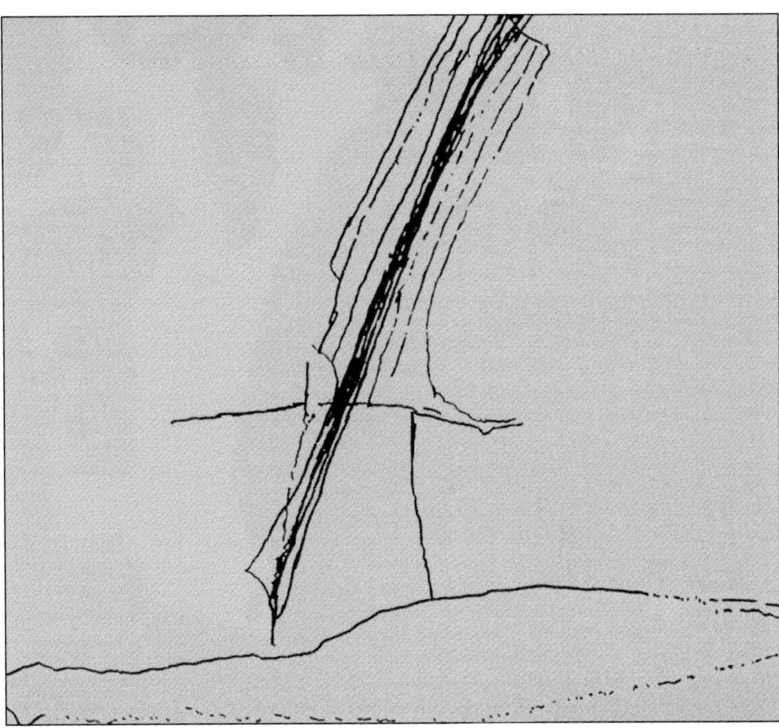

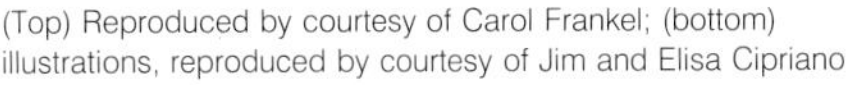

(Top) Reproduced by courtesy of Carol Frankel; (bottom) illustrations, reproduced by courtesy of Jim and Elisa Cipriano

From Lorna Selfe, *Nadia, a Case of Extraordinary Drawing Ability in an Autistic Child,* (London and New York, Academic Press: 1977); reproduced by courtesy of Lorna Selfe showed that several other composers suffered brain damage with *no* adverse effects upon their musical composition. These included the Russian composer and director of the Moscow Conservatory Vissarion Shebalin (1902–63) and the English composer Benjamin Britten (1913–76). The American composer George Gershwin (1898–1937) suffered a brain tumor, but because the course of his disease was so rapid, no obvious impairment of thinking was evident until days before his death.

At the "Music and the Brain" symposium, Tony DeBlois, a blind and autistic pianist then 18 years old, gave remarkable performances of classical music and jazz. Despite significant cognitive deficits, DeBlois regularly performs solo and plays with a jazz ensemble. In 1992 he received the Panasonic Young Soloists Award from Very Special Arts, an affiliate of the John F. Kennedy Center for the Performing Arts, Washington, D.C.

DeBlois is a prime example of a "musical savant"—one who is mentally retarded but shows unusual musical skills at an early age. These individuals are most often male, may have congenital blindness or very poor vision, and typically have significant language deficits, including difficulty in verbal communication. Professionals who have studied musical savants such as DeBlois believe that music becomes a "language" that offers them a way of understanding and relating to the world.

How do accomplished musicians *without* brain damage explain their own abilities? The Pulitzer Prize-winning composer Shulamit Ran responded very pensively to this author's question: "How do you compose music?" "I just do it. I can't explain it," she said. Ran's response echoes a comment of the English sculptor Henry Moore (1898–1986) about his own work: "It is a mistake for a sculptor . . . to speak or write

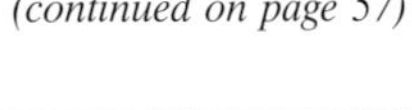
(continued on page 57)

(Left) Neurological illness obliterated Maurice Ravel's capacity to compose; even so, he could still appreciate the music he listened to. (Below) Benjamin Britten had a cerebral embolism that had no obvious impact on his ability to compose.

(Below) A rapidly growing brain tumor took the life of George Gershwin at age 38 but did not curtail his creative output until days before his death. (Bottom) Tony DeBlois, blind and autistic, is an award-winning classical and jazz concert pianist.

(Left) Drawing by Nadia, an autistic child with profound developmental impairments. Perplexingly, as her autism improved, her precocious drawing skills declined.

(Top) Archive Photos/Popperfoto; (center) photographs, Corbis-Bettmann; (above) Henry Grossman—Life Magazine © Time Inc.

Creativity with a Capital C

by Ellen Bernstein

"Good style, great energy, nice moves, but way too many four-letter words" was Homer Hans Bryant's comment after attending his first rap concert at the Royal Theatre in Victoria, British Columbia, several years ago. What truly moved him was not so much the rappers on stage but the youthful audience so totally caught up in the experience. The music kept jumping and rhyming in his head as he traveled home to Chicago, where he is founder, artistic director, and choreographer of a blossoming ballet company.

Months later the hypnotic rhythm of rap was still beating in Bryant's brain. Rap, he thought, might be a way to introduce countless kids to the discipline and beauty of ballet. The "rap muse" had beckoned, and Bryant set about creating. Before long he had conceived, choreographed, and written original lyrics for a five-part *Rap Ballet: A Musical Message About Dance, Discipline, and Determination,* which may be one of the most effervescent works of art to grace the contemporary stage.

Bodies by Bryant

Launched in 1990, the Bryant Ballet is a multiethnic, multicultural professional ballet company and training school; its mission is to give young people from all backgrounds the opportunity to realize their potential through ballet. The environment in which Bryant's protégés learn to dance is nurturing, supportive, and, above all, disciplined. From day one every Bryant Ballet pupil learns that "the fun of studying ballet is in the discipline, and the discipline is in the fun!" The students do not just learn pliés and pas de deux; they can take classes in tap, mime, jazz, and ballroom dance; on a day that this author was visiting the studio, Bryant was teaching an intermediate ballet class to students on minitrampolines.

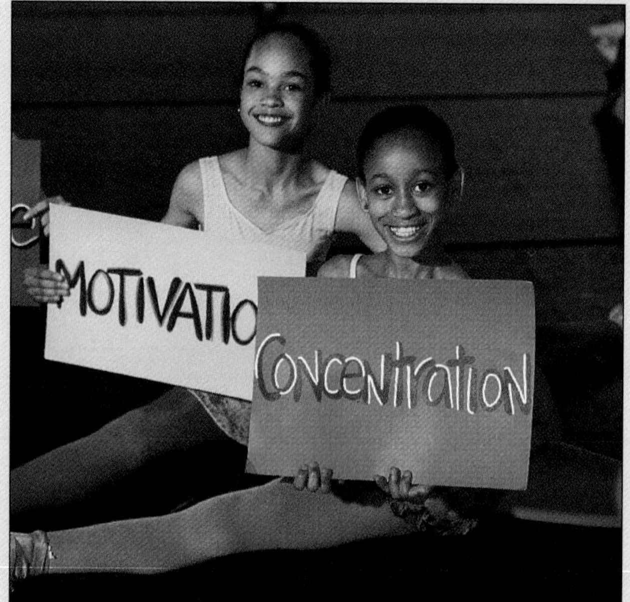

Young Chicago dancers perform in *Rap Ballet: A Musical Message About Dance, Discipline, and Determination,* conceived and choreographed by Homer Hans Bryant (below). Bryant has inspired youngsters from every walk of life with his effervescent approach to dance. For his young male protégés, he has a special message: "Boys in ballet are here to stay!"

A guiding principle of the Bryant Ballet is that few are born with a "ballet body." Rather, bodies are developed. And no one is better at developing them than Bryant. He has both the anatomic knowledge (of every joint and muscle in the body) and the willingness to work with students at every level and every stage of development to help them achieve professional ballet technique and refinement. It should not be surprising that not all of his pupils are able-bodied; his school offers a Wheelchair Ballet program that has had some

(Opposite page, top and center) Joshua B. Dreyfus; (bottom) Thomas Fezzey; (below) Joshua B. Dreyfus

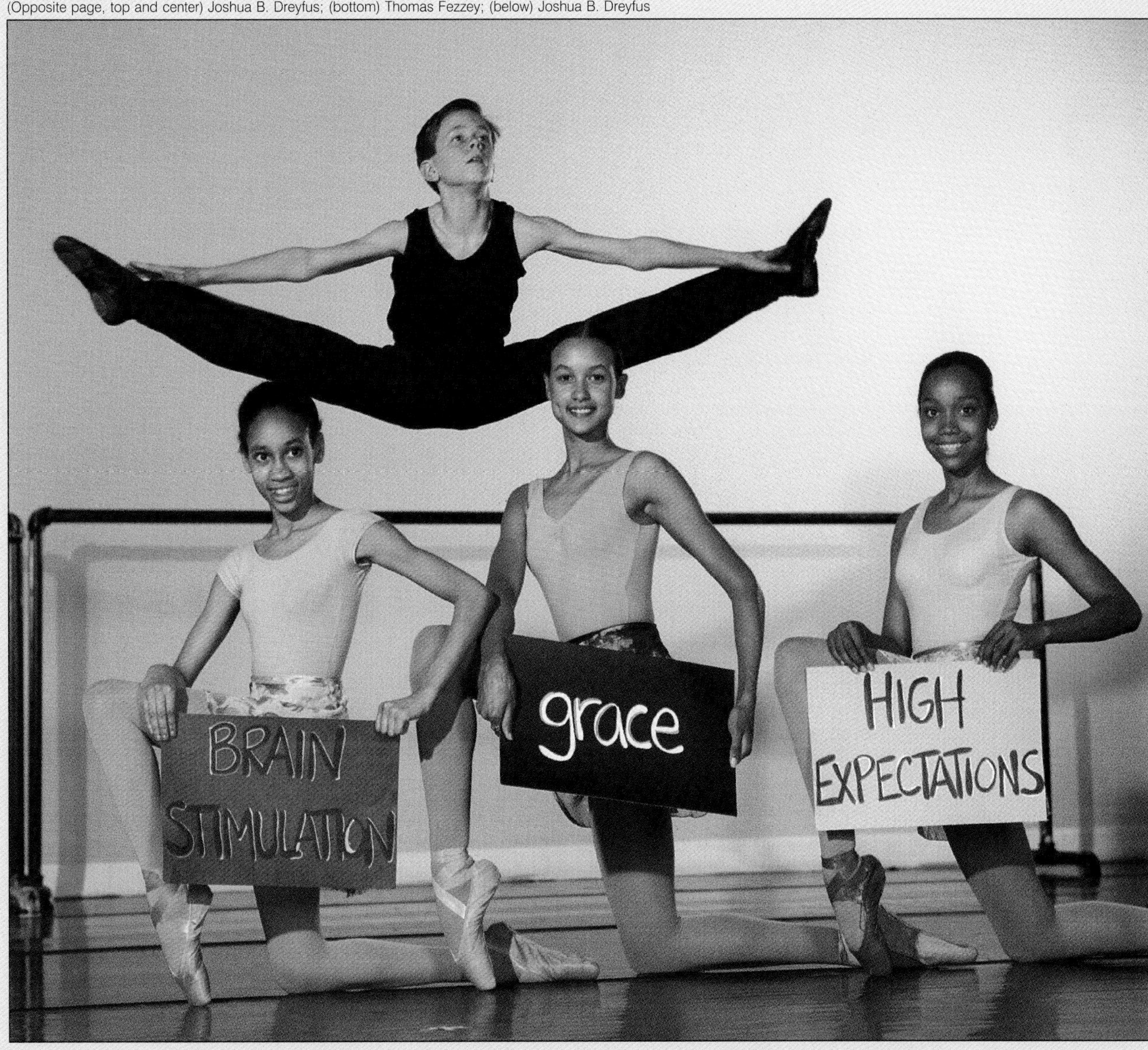

remarkable graduates, several of whom participated in the 1996 Paralympics in Atlanta, Georgia.

Bryant himself has studied and performed with the best—George Balanchine, Jerome Robbins, Ted Shawn, Arthur Mitchell, Alvin Ailey, and Maria Tallchief, to name a few. He has been a principal with the Dance Theatre of Harlem, performed for the royal families of England and Norway, and danced in the movie *The Wiz* and a Metropolitan Opera of New York production of *Porgy and Bess.*

In addition to dancing, Bryant has another all-consuming devotion—his daughter, Alexandra, who was born with cerebral palsy. He has spent the last 14 years helping her "be the best person she can be." Though "Alex" has profound physical impairments, her father often dreams that one day she too might dance, and that thought makes him nurture and inspire his students even more.

A whole lot of men-tal-ness

The creator of *Rap Ballet* included a role for himself—the onstage "guru of rap," who steps and moves and preaches his message of motivation, coordination, concentration, brain stimulation, and high expectations, never missing a beat. In perfect syncopation the hip-hopping guru chants:

Ballet is a form of art with style and grace/ Danced by every color of the human race. . . .

When you study ballet you gain grace and poise/ It's the perfect harmony to help girls and boys. . . .

When you study ballet it's like taking a test/ It involves a whole lot of men-tal-ness. . . .

Ballet puts your body in touch with your mind/ It's just about the greatest discipline of all times. . . .

Joshua B. Dreyfus

I liked the ballet dance. I liked the part when Homer did the split. . . . I thought the rap ballet was going to be stupid because I thought ballet was just people jumping around. . . . But like Homer said it takes all lot of practice.

The Rap baley was a good Rap baley because nobody messed up.

I like how the group standed on their Tippy Toe.

Ballet puts your body in touch with your mind/ And the rap beat keeps you stepping on time. . . .

When you study ballet you become very smart/ Because the body-mind is the instrument of our art. . . .

Boys in ballet

Bryant knew from the start that attracting boys to ballet would be no easy feat. Where there is a will, however, there is a way. His *Rap Ballet* contains a special "rap" for boys:

Boys in ballet are here to stay/ And we get better day after day. . . .

Boys in ballet is a whole different trip/ It's like being in the army and that's a sure tip. . . .

The desire to dance must come from deep down inside/ Boys in ballet should study with a great sense of pride. . . .

Boys in ballet must learn to think fast/ Especially in a pas de deux class/ Working together is a must/ Based upon composure, skill, and trust.

Bravo!

The *Rap Ballet*'s success has been nothing short of sensational. The exhilarating 45-minute work has been performed no fewer than 300 times and has hooked first-time ballet audiences from every walk of life. In the past several years, Bryant has taken his *Rap Ballet* to elementary schools throughout Chicago. Captivated schoolkids have not been reticent about the performances.

I can't say I was into Ballet But when I seen your act I could not believe My eyes I enjoyed watching Ballet for the first time I believe that Ballet was Boaring nothing real exciting to talk about. But I talk, talk about your performance.

Teachers, too, have evaluated the performances. At Ravenswood School, where more than 600 students were entertained and inspired by Bryant's opus, a special education teacher commented that "blending classical dance with current dance provided a window through which our students could appreciate the beauty of both." An art teacher at the same school said, "Every child was enthralled from K through 8." Yet another teacher said, "The *Rap Ballet* showed our kids what is possible." Ravenswood's principal, Jay Donova, raved: "The children loved it. All the girls want to be ballerinas." Asked what he thought the educational value of the program had been, Donova said, "STUDY, STUDY, STUDY!"

About such responses the *Rap Ballet*'s guru could not be more jubilant.

(continued from page 53)
very often about his job. It releases tension needed for his work."

Cellist Yo-Yo Ma, speaking about his own musical performances, has said:

> *The desirable state of mind is to be "in-phase," with an open channel between the conscious and the unconscious. If you plan a performance ahead of time, it will be stilted. You have to go with the flow and you come from within it. You own it. You're part of it. Then, you're like a computer scan. Your conscious mind can take over, but it better be empty of the things you have to do. I feel that creativity comes when the mind is unbelievably aware, slightly asleep, slightly out of focus, so you can actually focus on something, see everything very clearly.*

Courtesy of Yo-Yo Ma

Cellist "slightly asleep."

Ma likens his ideal performing state to "being nearly asleep and having ideas that keep you awake so much that you want to stay up and write them down." His comments fit particularly well with the notion of "flow states" theorized by Csikszentmihalyi. Flow states are self-reported periods of high achievement, when the individual is completely immersed in an activity and feels euphoric.

Bodies and minds in motion

> *A basketball player perfects skill, constantly challenging himself in the sport, gaining exhilaration from the activity itself.*
>
> —concept suggested by Csikszentmihalyi

Another symposium presented by the Foundation for Human Potential in April 1995 brought together researchers from the neurosciences and many other disciplines, as well as leaders from the worlds of dance and athletics. The "Sports, Dance, Movement and the Brain" symposium was indeed a unique gathering—one that may spawn a new field of interdisciplinary investigation. In fact, studies of bodily-kinesthetic ability are already under way, focusing on instances of outstanding human achievement in the face of cognitive disability, impoverished environment, or advanced age, among other circumstances.

After some three decades as a principal dancer with the New York City Ballet, Jacques d'Amboise, once the protégé of the late ballet master George Balanchine, is recognized for his athletic prowess and dramatic interpretation of roles. His achievements have earned him high recognition, and his awards have included a fellowship from the John D. and Catherine T. MacArthur Foundation (1990) and the Kennedy Center Honors (1995)—not to mention the fact that d'Amboise had more works choreographed for him by Balanchine than did any other male dancer.

D'Amboise is one of the leaders in the field of arts education today. "I had been dancing for 30 years before I felt I knew the depth and scope of dance: its historical and cultural roots, its enriching and transforming aspects, its force as a preeminent tool for communication," he says.

While still with the New York City Ballet, d'Amboise acted on his belief that the arts have a unique power to engage children and motivate them toward excellence. He founded the National Dance Institute (NDI) in 1976. The NDI's mission is to break down cultural and elitist stereotypes of the arts and make the arts accessible to everyone, especially children, regardless of their socioeconomic background or physical and emotional challenges. Most NDI dancers are from poor neighborhoods (as was d'Amboise), and they represent a broad range of ethnic minorities. The NDI program fosters self-confidence and a sense of direction. Studies to validate the NDI's approach to teaching dance and excellence are currently under way.

D'Amboise's students have included blind and deaf children thought to be incapable of dancing. His special teaching technique harnesses other sensory systems to compensate for the senses that are impaired. His philosophy is that the arts should be an integral part of every child's education and that dance, in particular, provides children with a unique perspective for learning that inspires hard work, discipline, and perseverance. "We're not just teaching dance. We're teaching excellence," he says.

When he started the NDI, he "wanted to pay something back since I never paid for a dance lesson. . . . Children need to participate in something that has magic in it." D'Amboise's energy and genuine dedication to children have earned him the title "Pied Piper of Dance."

As keynote speaker of the "Sports, Dance, Movement and the Brain" symposium, d'Amboise presented "An Encounter with Dance"—a lecture and demonstration dance class with schoolchildren who had no prior dance experience. In keeping with his notion that "if you can control your body, you can control your life," he gently admonished one child who continued to step after the music stopped: "*You* control your leg. Don't let *your leg* control you!" (It worked!) And what a big smile another young dancer displayed at his early success when the instructor exclaimed, "Baryshnikov!"

Exceptional style

As was noted above in the case of DeBlois, retarded individuals can be exceptional, showing a unique sparing of one ability against a background of marked deficits in most other areas of human functioning. In personal correspondence with this author, the neurologist and well-known author Oliver Sacks has described an autistic boy with unique bodily-kinesthetic ability:

> *[He] gives an impression of clumsiness but picks up some motor skills, it seems, almost instantly. . . . Most striking was seeing him mime, sing, and dance, during which time his movements and gestures become fluid and normal. He takes on the voice, the style, the identity of a young Elvis and seems to gain access to all the appropriate emotions while so doing—emotions to which he has so little access at other times. When his song-and-dance "performance" is over, he is back to his awkward . . . autistic self . . . incapable of direct address.*

Sacks has written literally volumes, profiling fascinating individuals who have major brain impairment but are at the same time uniquely talented. Indeed, Sacks seems to believe that every mind has untapped potential.

The myth of creativity and "madness"

Unfortunately, many myths associated with creativity have fallen hard on the artistic community, suggesting that mental illness, emotional disturbance, and even suicide are common among great artists. Psychologist and writer Kay Redfield Jamison, professor of psychiatry at Johns Hopkins University School of Medicine, Baltimore, Maryland, has explored the connection between creativity and psychiatric illness in numerous papers, articles, and one of her books, *Touched with*

Exposing children to the magic of dance is Jacques d'Amboise's mission. (Below) Leading students through a pas de deux; (right) nurturing the talents of visually impaired dancers.

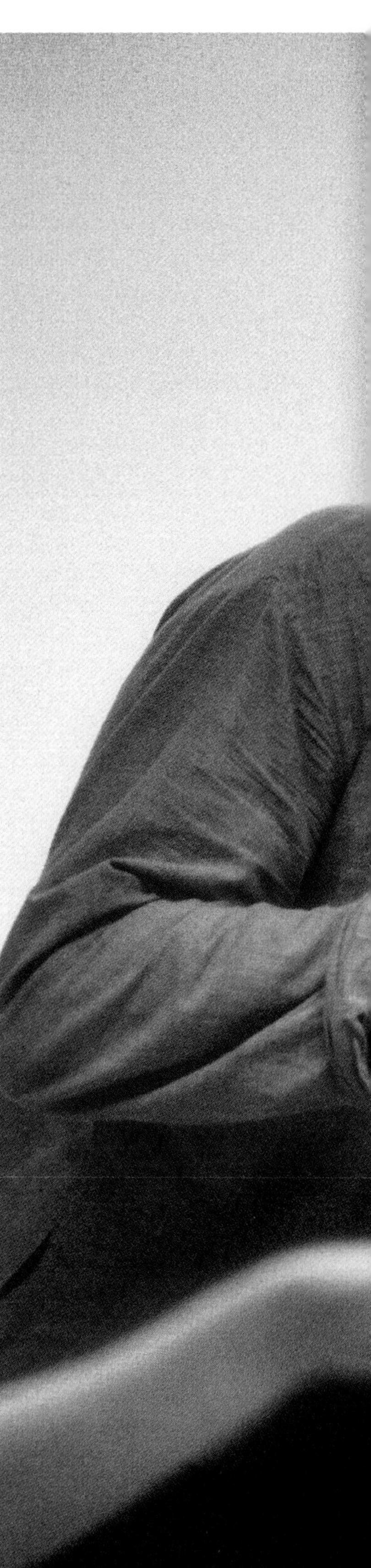

Photographs, © Lynn Johnson

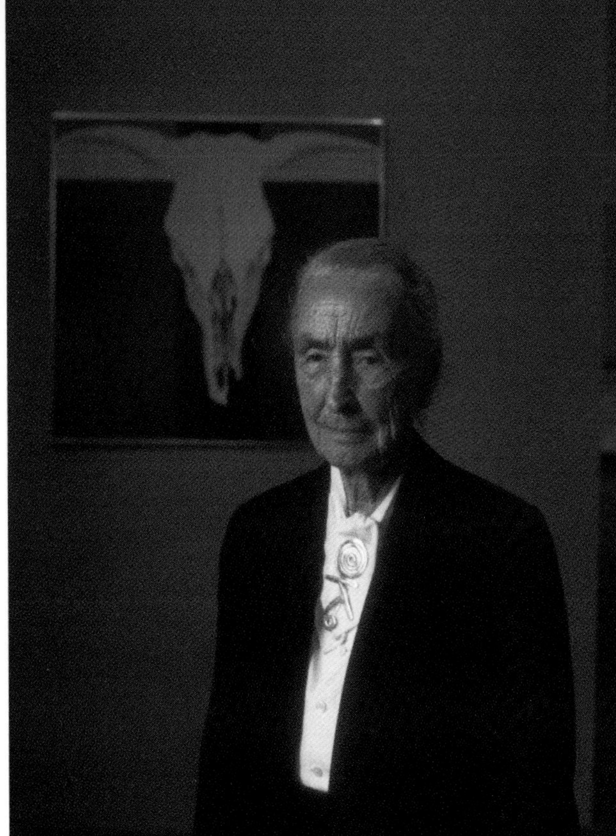

Georgia O'Keeffe is one of many well-known artists who suffered from an affective (mood) disorder. Mental illness, however, is *not* a predictor of either brilliance or creativity.

Fire: Manic-Depressive Illness and the Artistic Temperament (1993). In the February 1995 issue of *Scientific American,* Jamison wrote:

> *Many people have long shared [Edgar Allan] Poe's suspicion that genius and insanity are entwined. Indeed, history holds countless examples of "that fine madness." Scores of influential 18th- and 19th-century poets, notably William Blake, Lord Byron and Alfred, Lord Tennyson, wrote about the extreme mood swings they endured. Modern American poets John Berryman, Randall Jarrell, Robert Lowell, Sylvia Plath, Theodore Roethke, Delmore Schwartz and Anne Sexton were all hospitalized for either mania or depression during their lives. And many painters and composers, among them Vincent van Gogh, Georgia O'Keeffe, Charles Mingus and Robert Schumann, have been similarly afflicted.*

In that article Jamison went on to point out, however, that "most manic-depressives do not possess extraordinary imagination, and most accomplished artists do not suffer from recurring mood swings.... It would be wrong to label anyone who is unusually accomplished, energetic, intense, moody or eccentric as manic-depressive."

Psychiatrist Arnold M. Ludwig at the University of Kentucky also has studied art and madness extensively. He is the author of *The Price of Greatness: Resolving the Creativity and Madness Controversy* (1995). Writing in the March 1996 issue of the *Harvard Mental Health Letter,* Ludwig stressed that "most people who suffer from mental illness or mood disorders show little evidence of creativity." Indeed, it is unlikely that mental illness could be routinely advantageous to the creative process, because the concentration required for creative endeavors is likely to be hampered by symptoms of the illness, which would make "flow" difficult to achieve. Furthermore, the treatments available for manic-depressive illness and other major mood disorders—primarily psychoactive medications—can compromise the aspects of thought and temperament that are presumed to be necessary for the creative process. The high rate of mental illness among artists does not mean that emotional turmoil is a *source* of creativity, Ludwig emphasizes. Jamison acknowledges that hypomania—a hallmark of manic-depressive illness, characterized by unusually sharp thinking, unrepressed fluency, grandiose moods, and increased productivity—may in some cases contribute to artistic achievement. But she also thinks that generalizations linking art and "madness" are inappropriate. They "[trivialize] a very serious medical condition and, to some degree, [discredit] individuality in the arts as well."

Emotion's untapped role

> *Don't aim at success—the more you aim at it and make it a target, the more you are going to miss it. For success, like happiness, cannot be pursued; it must ensue . . . as the unintended side-effect of one's personal dedication to a course greater than oneself.*
>
> —Austrian psychiatrist and neurologist Viktor E. Frankl, *Man's Search for Meaning* (in the preface to the 1963 edition)

To date, few studies have assessed the role of emotion in creativity. Psychologist Daniel Goleman, who writes regularly on behavior and brain sciences for the *New York Times,* suggests in his book *Emotional Intelligence* (1995) that emotion is indeed a ripe topic for accelerated neurological investigation. One who has pioneered in this largely untapped area of exploration is Antonio R. Damasio, a neurologist at the University of Iowa College of Medicine. Damasio's book *Descartes' Error: Emotion, Reason, and the Human Brain* (1994) holds that reason is inseparable from emotion—in fact, he contends, emotions are *essential* to rational thinking.

Miles to go

> *To conceive is nothing, to express is all.*
>
> —French neurologist Théophile Alajouanine (1890–1980)

(Opposite page) © Dennis Brack—Black Star/PNI; (below) © Hiroji Kubota—Magnum Photos; (bottom) Lawrence Migdale—Tony Stone Images

Key questions about what constitutes creativity are beginning to be asked. Now innovative research must be designed to find the answers.

In this Decade of the Brain (1990–99), it is important to focus on and ultimately to understand the truly positive aspects of human nature, of which all forms of expression—artistic, musical, scientific, mathematical, philosophical, and bodily-kinesthetic—are included. While understanding of the brain is accumulating rapidly and cutting-edge research on human creative potential is already under way, interdisciplinary research is only in its infancy. The initial questions are beginning to be asked, and now research must be designed to seek vital answers.

Why is this work so important? The acceleration of interdisciplinary investigations in all fields of human endeavor could yield nothing less than the fullest possible realization of human creative potential. MHA

Photograph by Dennis Marsico

Marie McNeill, 101, enjoys the serenity of her front porch on a Georgia summer day.

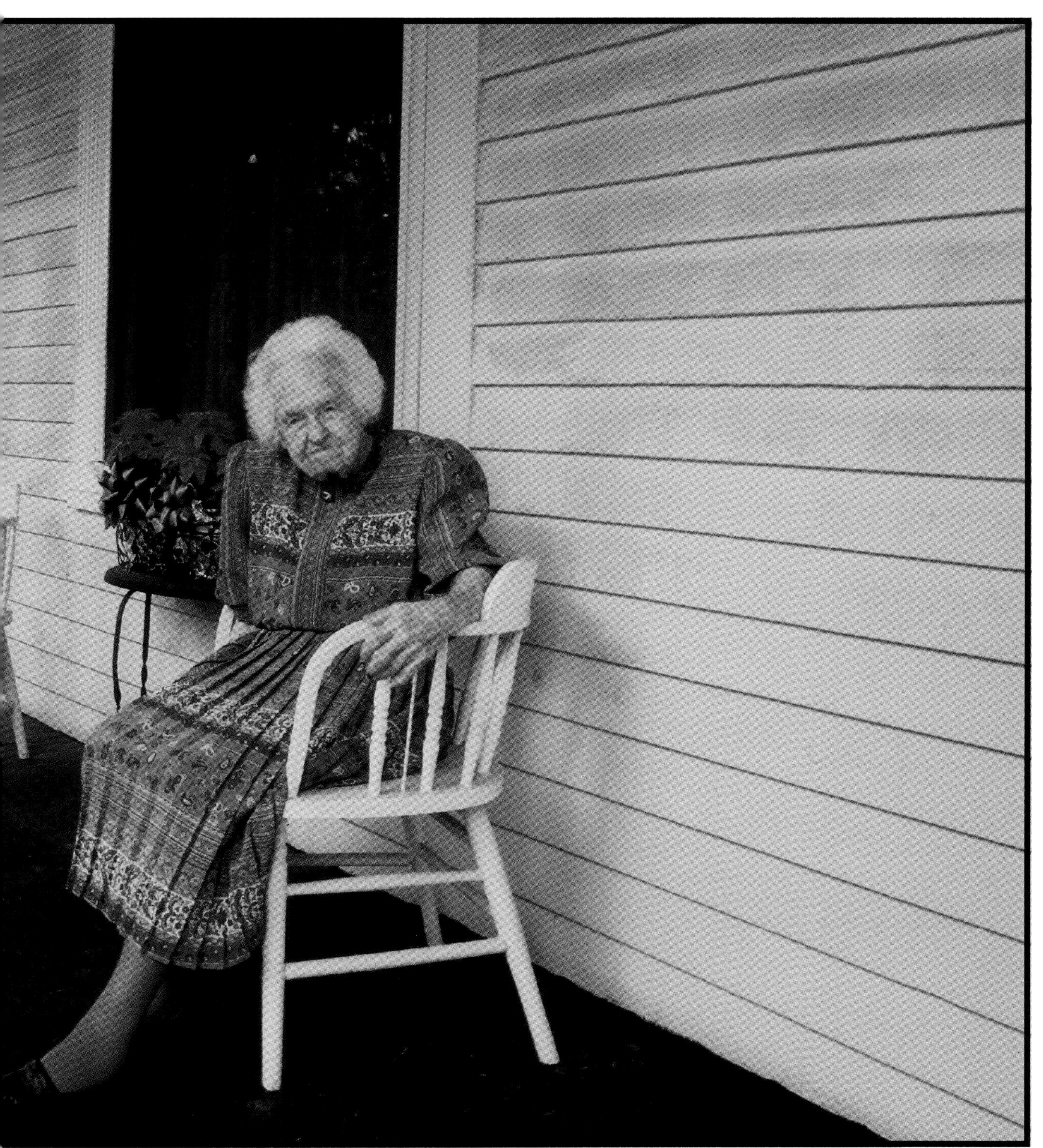

Who Will Survive to 105?

by Leonard W. Poon, Ph.D., Martha H. Bramlett, R.N., Ph.D., Philip A. Holtsberg, J.D., M.B.A., Mary Ann Johnson, Ph.D., and Peter Martin, Ph.D.

Once you've lived to 100 you've really got it made, because very few people die over 100.
—George Burns (1896–1996)

The truth, of course, is that only a very few people *live* to be 100, which accounts for the fact that not many die at 101. That only a relatively small number of individuals survive to this ripe age accounts for the fascination that these "oldest old" hold. Belle Boone Beard, a pioneer centenarian researcher at Sweet Briar (Virginia) College, called 100 "the magic number." Ninety years is old, Beard allowed, but "100 is news." Prior to her death in 1984, Beard spent some 40 years collecting case histories, "recipes" for longevity, biographical sketches, and other data from and about people who had lived to be 100 or more. This collection, the world's largest assemblage of information on centenarians, now resides at the University of Georgia.

A few scientists regard centenarians as nothing more than biological accidents. They believe that studying 100-year-olds will yield little insight into the mechanisms of human aging. In the tradition of their predecessor Beard, however, the researchers at the University of Georgia's Gerontology Center, along with a growing number of other investigators, view centenarian research as an important area of specialization within the discipline of gerontology. It is their hope that the study of these very long-lived individuals will shed light on the process of aging. Beyond that, they hope their work will offer clues to how to reach the limits of the human life span and, perhaps most important, how to make these later years as vital, productive, and enjoyable as possible.

The authors of this report are scientists participating in the Georgia Centenarian Study, a long-term investigation of the factors that contribute to longevity. In the

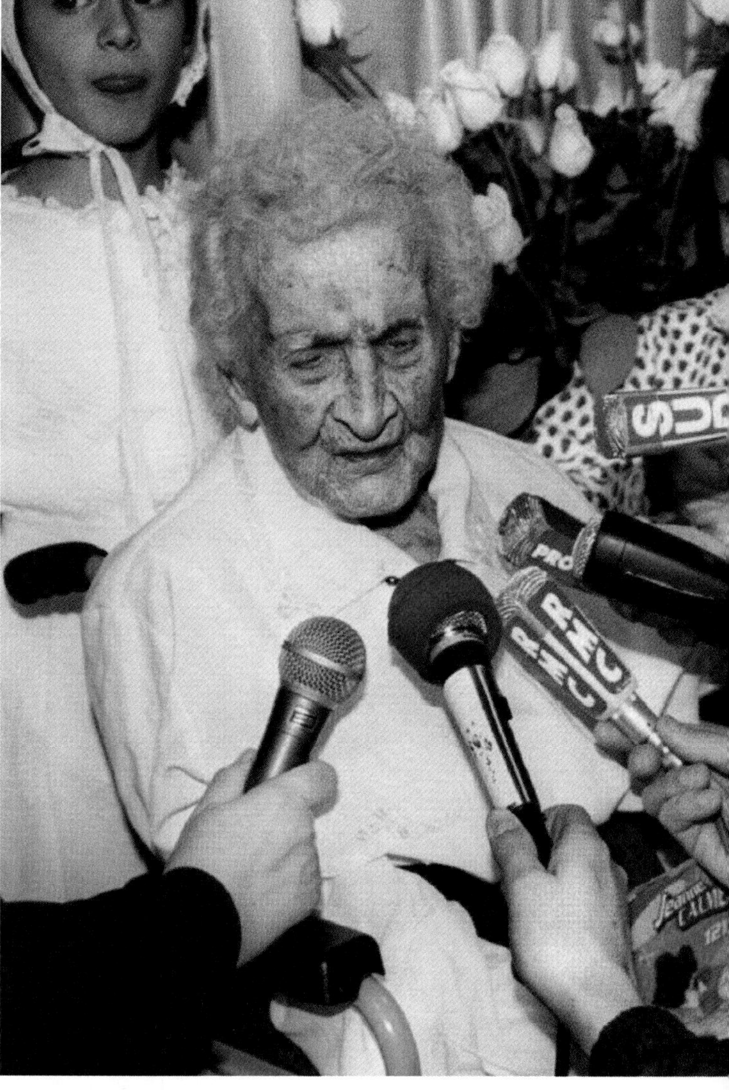

Jeanne Calment, the world's oldest person, talks with reporters two days before her 121st birthday. Born in Arles, France, in 1875, she met Vincent Van Gogh at age 14, was still riding a bicycle at age 100, and quit smoking only a few years ago.

Leonard W. Poon, Ph.D., *is Professor of Psychology; Chair, Faculty of Gerontology; and Director, University of Georgia Gerontology Center, Athens; he is also a Fellow of the American Psychological Association, American Psychological Society, and Gerontological Society of America.*

Martha H. Bramlett, R.N., Ph.D., *is Adjunct Faculty Member and Research Scientist, University of Georgia Gerontology Center, and Data Acquisition Manager, Georgia Centenarian Study.*

Philip A. Holtsberg, J.D., M.B.A., *is a Graduate Student in Psychology, University of Georgia.*

Mary Ann Johnson, Ph.D., *is Professor of Foods and Nutrition, University of Georgia.*

Peter Martin, Ph.D., *is Professor of Human Development and Family Studies, Iowa State University, Ames, and Senior Research Scientist, University of Georgia Gerontology Center.*

Jean Paul Pelissier—Reuters

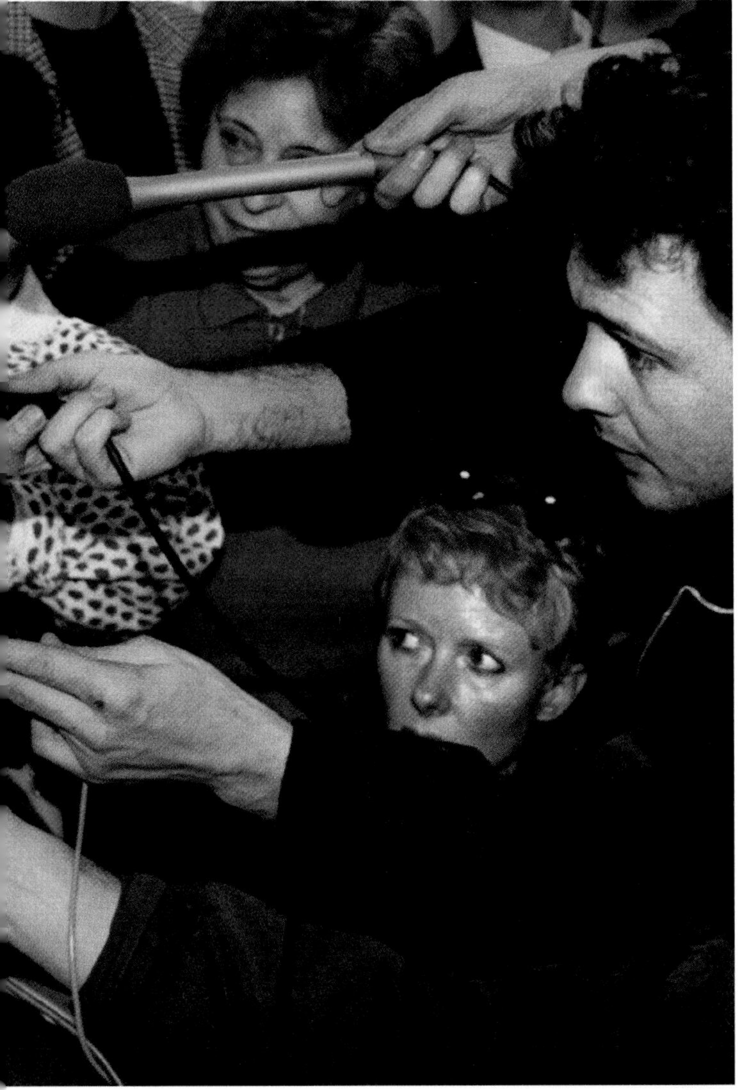

(Left) A carpet weaver in Azerbaijan and a Wisconsin nursing home resident (below, pictured with her daughter) have something in common—both have reached 100. (Bottom left) Belle Boone Beard, who devoted her career to the study of centenarians. (Bottom right) The Spanish explorer Juan Ponce de León, who set out in 1513 to find the fabled fountain of youth—but discovered Florida instead!

following they briefly review the history of centenarian research, summarize preliminary findings from their own work, and speculate on what the future might hold for the study of centenarians.

Search for Shangri-La

The notion that aging and death might be postponed or even avoided has existed throughout human history, inspiring myth and literature and prompting all manner

(Top) Tass/Sovfoto/Eastfoto; (center) Mitch Kezar—Tony Stone Images; (bottom left) Belle Boone Beard Gerontology Center of Lynchburg College, Lynchburg, Va.; (bottom right) The Granger Collection, N.Y.

(Opposite page) Retired lawyer Tom Lane of San Diego, California; (above) Lovada Brooks of Chillicothe, Ohio. Centenarians come from many disparate walks of life and differ widely in education level, occupational history, and socioeconomic circumstances. Nonetheless, scientists are certain that they must share some important characteristics—biological as well as psychological—and researchers around the world are attempting to identify these common traits.

of experimentation. The ancient Greeks, for example, invented the myth of the Hyperboreans, a perpetually youthful people who lived in a land of sunshine and abundance. Stories of remarkable longevity abound in the Old Testament—Adam is said to have lived 930 years, Noah 950 years, and Methuselah 969. In the 20th century the English novelist James Hilton captured the popular imagination with *Lost Horizon* (1933), a story about the discovery of Shangri-La, the land of eternal youth.

The promise of such imaginary realms inspired explorers like Juan Ponce de León, seeker after the legendary fountain of youth, to embark on dangerous travels, jeopardizing the very lives they hoped to prolong. Likewise, the prospect of longevity has, from time to time, prompted people to adopt highly ascetic or abstemious lifestyles. Some contemporary scientists, having observed that laboratory rodents live longer than normal when their caloric intake is drastically curtailed, are now experimenting with reduced-calorie diets in hopes of obtaining the same benefits for themselves.

Thus, the quest for a means to arrest aging continues. Today's studies, however, focus on scientific variables associated with longevity—dietary regimens, hormone levels, personality traits—rather than on magic elixirs or lands where time stands still.

Separating fact from fiction

Scientific studies of longevity have always been hampered by the difficulty of verifying the age of extremely elderly individuals. *Human Longevity: Its Facts and Its Fictions* (1879), by William J. Thoms, the deputy librarian of the British House of Lords, represents one of the first rigorous efforts to evaluate claims of unusual life spans. Subsequent research has repeatedly demonstrated that reports of extraordinary longevity are often based on miscalculation or simple exaggeration.

Even today, at the end of the 20th century, authorities cannot prove that all those in the U.S. claiming to be centenarians have actually lived that long, as these individuals were born before the government instituted a system for the certification of births and deaths. In the state of Georgia, for example, official birth records started to be compiled only in the 1920s. Since home births were the norm in rural agricultural areas until well into the 20th century, the only records for many people were those in the family Bible, which in many cases has long since disappeared. Census data may not be helpful, as remote rural areas were sometimes missed by census takers. Even when reliable census information is available, a centenarian may be unsure where the family was living at the time the census was conducted.

Sometimes, too, ages have been intentionally altered. Families or individuals may exaggerate age out of pride or a desire for prestige. An individual's age may have been changed earlier—for example, to avoid military service—with the result that family members no longer remember the true birth date.

Some families have altered existing records over

time, presumably in an effort to attain accuracy but, in fact, only to confuse the issue further. Members of one Georgia family preparing to celebrate their mother's 100th birthday found, on examining the family Bible, that her age had been changed several times. No one still living was sure which of the numerous birth dates was correct. In such situations the only documentation of date of birth is the centenarian's word.

Even official demographic data must be viewed skeptically. For example, the U.S. Bureau of the Census has reported the number of centenarians over the past five decades as follows:

- 1950—4,447
- 1960—10,369
- 1970—106,000
- 1980—32,194
- 1990—35,808

(The inflated figure for 1970 was due to poor design of the census questionnaire, which resulted in individuals' checking the wrong boxes.)

Independent demographers, on the other hand, have asserted that more accurate estimates for the period are considerably lower:

- 1950—2,300
- 1960—3,300
- 1970—4,800
- 1980—15,000

Because demographers do not have the kind of reliable data needed to develop population models and estimate trends in death rates, it is impossible for them to predict with any accuracy the exact number of centenarians who will be alive after the year 2000. The projections, like the estimates of past numbers, cover a broad range—anywhere from 85,000 to 138,000.

Jacques M. Chenet—Gamma Liaison

Their "first hundred years" was the subject of sisters Sarah (left) and Elizabeth Delany's memoir, *Having Our Say.*

U.S. Centenarians: Past, Present, Future

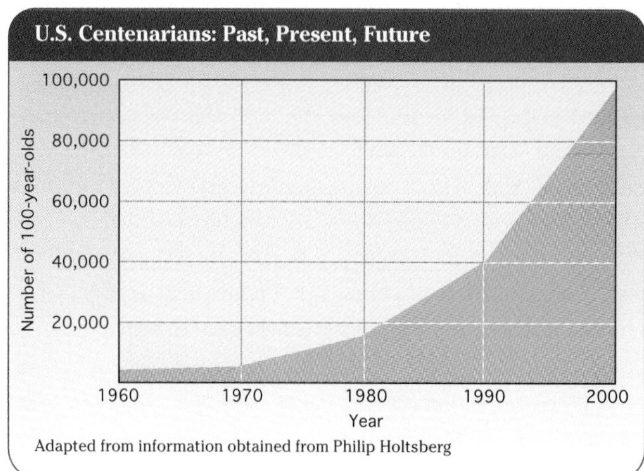

Adapted from information obtained from Philip Holtsberg

Demographers also have difficulty calculating a person's odds of becoming a centenarian, although the chances clearly have improved since 1900. For babies born in the United States in 1980, approximately one in 50 girls and one in 200 boys will live to the age of 100; in 1900 the comparable figures were one in 2,500 and one in 5,000, respectively.

Most researchers would agree that throughout history the number of genuine centenarians has been substantially fewer than the number claiming that status. Fortunately for those who study longevity, age verification is less problematic in countries that have maintained accurate birth records for some time—Sweden and France, for example. Comparing findings across cultures, while taking into account environmental differences, will be an important element in future research on aging.

Centenarian research: an ancient pursuit

Throughout the course of history, the scientific and cultural climate of the day has determined what questions have been asked about aging and how the answers have been sought. In contrast to today's scientific reports, with detailed observations and measurement of physical, mental, and social functioning, the earliest literature on aging consisted of philosophical musings on the thoughts and habits virtuous long-lived people ought to possess.

Next came autobiographical accounts in which the presumed secrets of a long life were revealed. The life story of the Italian nobleman Luigi Cornaro (1467–1565) is of this genre. In it Cornaro reveals how, after 40 years of living a life of excess, he adopted a lifestyle of temperance and moderation (especially with respect to diet), to which he attributed his long and happy life. Such accounts are still being written and enjoyed today. A more recent representative is *Having Our Say: The Delany Sisters' First 100 Years,* a memoir by two African-American women born at the end of the 19th century. This popular book made the best-seller lists in 1995 and was subsequently adapted for the stage. According to one of these crusty seniors, remaining single was an important factor in her longevity—there was no man around to "worry her to death"!

Compilations of demographic and anecdotal information became popular in the 19th century. One of the earliest examples is James Easton's ambitious 1799 book entitled *Human Longevity: Recording the Name, Age, Place of Residence and Year of the Decease of 1,712 Persons Who Attained a Century & Upwards from A.D. 66 to 1799, Comprising a Period of 1,733 Years: With Anecdotes of the Most Remarkable.* Among the notable historical figures included in this work were Attila, king of the Huns (lived to the age of 124), who "led to the altar of Hymen, [his] second wife, one of the most beautiful princesses of the age, and the next day died of excess."

Another similar kind of compilation, *Remarkable Aged Persons* (*c.* 1800) by G. Smeeton, can be found in the Raymond Pearl Collection of Books and Papers Pertaining to Longevity (at Dartmouth College, Hanover, New Hampshire). The volume is a scrapbook of newspaper clippings, handwritten notes, and illustrations of individuals who had reportedly lived to be 100. Some of the obituaries date to the early 1700s.

Until about the mid-20th century, inquiries into longevity were limited to anecdotal observations and accounts that were never subjected to systematic scientific scrutiny. A major advance in aging research occurred in the 1950s and '60s, when investigators began using statistical methods to analyze data collected from and about alleged centenarians. Although most of these studies did not follow rigorous scientific protocols—and therefore are not considered thoroughly reliable—they were notable in that they sought to discover consistent links between longevity and specific, measurable variables. Among the variables studied were physical health (measured by assessing the function of major organ systems or collecting autopsy findings), social supports, personality characteristics (*e.g.,* ambition, optimism), and self-reported longevity secrets. By the 1970s the ranks of researchers into aging included specialists from the biomedical, economic, political, social, and psychological sciences.

The Georgia Centenarian Study: who and how

Collectively, the centenarian studies conducted to date suggest that extreme longevity cannot be attributed to any *single* factor but rather is a result of the complex interplay of many disparate factors. Most authorities would agree that these factors may be different for different people and may have both direct and indirect effects on longevity. The goal of the Georgia Centenarian Study (GCS) is to develop and test hypotheses about exactly how biological, psychological, and social factors combine to contribute to successful aging in these very long-lived individuals.

The GCS started in 1988. It is unique not only in being

Approaching 100: Two Poems

by Cecilia Payne Grove

The Hospital (1983)

It's mighty bad to go through an operation at 93
You must have to grit your teeth and pray,
They came with pills each day
No matter what you say.
Then the shots puncture your skin
Until you feel like it's a sin.

Then the devilish bed pan comes
To haunt you 'til the set of sun.
What a relief when two strong men come
To take you home again on the ambulance run.
Well, I just missed heaven, they say,
Thank you, Lord, for another day.

Age (1986)

Age is a quality of mind
If you have left your dreams behind,
If hope is lost
If you no longer look ahead
If ambition's fires are dead—
Then you are old.

Cecilia Payne Grove was born in 1889. She started writing poetry when she was a young woman.

Tim Boxer—Archive Photos

U.S. composer and ragtime virtuoso James Hubert ("Eubie") Blake, 1883–1983.

the largest U.S. centenarian study but also in having an unusual research design. In addition to persons 100 and older, the GCS also includes two comparison groups—one in their 60s and one in their 80s. Moreover, all of the participants, regardless of age, share two important characteristics: they live independently or semi-independently, and they are cognitively intact (*i.e.,* unimpaired in their ability to think and reason).

The research team includes members from various academic backgrounds, among them education, demography, human development, neurology, nursing, nutrition, psychiatry, psychology, and sociology. All of the investigators are faculty members at the University of Georgia, the Medical College of Georgia, or Iowa State University.

The initial group of participants consisted of 264 Georgians equally distributed among the three age groups. The researchers decided to focus on 60-year-olds and 80-year-olds because the members of these groups have an important factor in common: they share the influence of two different and distinctive historical eras—the Great Depression and World War II—on crucial periods of their development. The composition of each group was designed to mirror the male-female ratio and racial distribution of Georgians in their respective age groups.

(Below) Harrison Funk—Archive Photos/PNI; (bottom) Archive Photos/PNI

The selection process was as follows. A sample population was constructed by the University of Georgia Survey Research Center; selected members of the sample were then contacted by phone. Those who agreed to participate were contacted personally by GCS staff, and arrangements were made for them to travel to various sites around the state—the university, churches, senior centers, etc.—for interviews and testing.

Recruiting centenarians was a slightly more difficult matter. Names were obtained from a variety of sources, including the office of the Georgia secretary of state, local social agencies, religious organizations, television stations and newspapers, and personal contacts of the GCS staff. Interviews and testing were carried out on a one-to-one basis in the centenarians' homes. Because the life expectancy for a 100-year-old is estimated to be only about two years, the study has had to continually recruit new centenarian volunteers so that data could be obtained over time. To date, more than 150 centenari-

Cigar-brandishing comedian George Burns, 1896–1996.

Self-taught artist Anna Mary Robertson Moses, better known as "Grandma Moses," 1860–1961, began her career as a painter in her late 70s.

ans have participated. The researchers emphasize that the centenarians in the study represent the best-functioning members of their age cohort and that their findings may not, therefore, be applicable to all who have reached 100.

"Recipe" for longevity?

Although the GCS is projected to run for 10 years, and all of the data are not yet in, the investigators have reached certain preliminary conclusions. Some of these were predictable, others quite surprising.

First, as might be expected, age is a strong predictor of differences between the three groups of participants with respect to health, mobility, vision, hearing, and economic resources. Compared with the subjects in their 60s and 80s, the centenarians on average are less affluent—many are below the poverty level—and have less education. While all of the centenarians in the study are "community-dwelling" (as opposed to being in custodial institutions), on average their hearing and vision are substantially worse and their mobility more restricted compared with those of the participants in the two younger groups.

There is, nonetheless, considerable variability in functioning, and some of the oldest subjects far surpass their younger counterparts. One centenarian can still thread a needle without her glasses, and a 104-year-old continues to teach exercise classes. Another, though confined mainly to a wheelchair, writes poetry, and still another, who is totally blind, continues to manage her own finances.

(Above and below) Mary Sims Elliott, an early participant in the Georgia Centenarian Study, pictured at four different stages of life.

Photographs, courtesy of Mary Sims Elliott

Accepting limitations. One of the most striking preliminary findings of the GCS is the paradoxical disparity between the realities of old age, with its increasing restrictions on functioning, and its perception by the centenarians as a generally satisfying time of life. More than half of the Georgia centenarians rate their eyesight as poor, and more than 40% use hearing aids. Members of this group report substantial difficulties in traveling, shopping, cooking, and doing housework; fewer than 10% can go places without assistance, and many require supportive services in order to continue to live independently. At the same time, 60% rate their health as good or excellent, and only about one in three feels that health problems or medical conditions greatly limit his or her activities; an equal number state that their health does not interfere at all. The majority describe their financial situation as no worse than anyone else's and, on balance, say that they experience a great sense of satisfaction with life.

What accounts for this sanguine outlook? The Georgia scientists speculate that the centenarians may compare their present situations with life in earlier, harder times. They grew up in a world without automobiles or labor-saving appliances. Telephones were a novelty, houses were not air-conditioned, and many families drew their water from a well. By comparison, life today seems easy to them.

Another possibility is that the coexistence of restrictions and satisfaction seems paradoxical only from the point of view of the investigators, who are predominantly young and middle-aged individuals. In other words, the idea that decrements in functioning detract from the pleasures of life comes from people who are not centenarians and may not understand what it takes to survive for 100 years.

This latter view is borne out by the GCS finding that many centenarians measure their abilities and expectations by their own standards. Thus, one of them might say, "For someone my age, my health is pretty good." They may even adjust their thinking about what activities are necessary or crucial for a good life. As one 105-year-old woman put it:

> *I feel fine except that I don't hear very well and I don't see very well, . . . I am so old I better be glad with what I have.*

A question of genes. Another unexpected finding has been a failure to confirm genetics—*i.e.,* a family history

(Below) Walker Montgomery; (right) courtesy of Bernice Smith

Georgia Centenarian Study participant Jennie V. Williams, 105.

of longevity—as the important influence some other investigations, including research in Hungary and the Scandinavian countries, have found it to be. Among the GCS centenarians, parental longevity is not associated with having reached 100. The researchers do not rule out a genetic influence; rather, they feel that the role of heredity needs to be investigated in a much larger population of centenarians.

A strong constitution. Their medical histories show the Georgia centenarians to be remarkably healthy individuals. One out of seven reports no current illness; one in four takes no prescription medications (compared with an average of 4.5 prescription drugs taken by urban-dwelling seniors in one recent U.S. study) and requires no more medical services than the younger groups. These findings are consistent with those of a Japanese researcher, the psychiatrist Akira Homma at the Tokyo Metropolitan Institute of Gerontology, who has observed that centenarians are persons who have "congenitally strong constitutions" and a high degree of resistance to infectious diseases.

No dietary secrets. The GCS data do not support the widespread popular belief that consuming—or avoiding—certain foods promotes longevity. The Georgia centenarians eat a wide variety of foods and do not abstain from alcoholic beverages. In general, the diets of these seniors are typical of those of many older adults in the southeastern U.S. They continue to eat the same foods they have eaten all their lives. Of course, many others who ate the very same diet never reached the age of 100! This latter observation simply underscores the difficulty of determining the part played by diet in successful aging.

Among all study participants—regardless of age—low income, poor mental health, and minority-group status are predictors of poor eating patterns and inadequate nutrient intake. As a group, however, the centenarians tend to consume about the same number of calories as the 60- and 80-year-olds, although the sources are slightly different. The centenarians, for example, consume less yogurt and 2% milk and fewer carbonated beverages, salads, and salad dressings than the two younger groups—probably because foods like yogurt, soft drinks, and sal-

Georgian Jessie Champion, 107, harvests the first squash of the 1995 season.

ads have increased in popularity in recent decades but never constituted a significant part of the diet of their generation. Likewise, the 100-year-olds consume more milk and butter than their younger counterparts, again because these foods are a traditional component of their diet and because they have made fewer dietary changes based on recent recommendations that Americans reduce their intake of these products. The centenarians typically eat a wide variety of vegetables and have higher intakes of vitamin A and carotenoids than persons in the other age groups. Almost half of the participants in each of the three age groups take vitamin or mineral supplements.

The faith factor. While many of the centenarians describe their religious beliefs as a source of strength and comfort, religious and spiritual life and participation in church activities are equally important for all three age

(Below and opposite page) Dennis Marsico

(Above and opposite) Marie McNeill at home with her daughter and her memories.

groups in the GCS. Because religion is such an integral part of daily life for many in the South, it is hard to tell if the association of religious participation and longevity reflects local cultural practices or suggests a cause-and-effect relationship.

Personality: is it protective? Despite the widespread belief that centenarians must have unique personality characteristics, little research has been conducted on the relationship between personality and longevity. The GCS investigators embrace three accepted tenets of gerontological research regarding personality: (1) they expect as much variation among the centenarians as between centenarians and younger comparison groups; (2) they assume that many people with personality traits similar to those of the 100-year-olds have *not* lived to be 100; and (3) they understand that there is no way to know which of the younger GCS participants will live to reach 100. These caveats temper any sweeping conclusions that the investigators might draw from their data.

Nonetheless, the researchers have found that two traits stand out among the Georgia centenarians—dominance and suspiciousness. Compared with the younger groups, the centenarians overall are more determined to have their own way, even despite physical limitations that might prevent them from imposing their will on others. One 100-year-old woman being filmed for a television interview gave very precise instructions to the cameraman on how to photograph her. She even had a family member retrieve a favorite photograph of herself to show him how to capture her from the most flattering angle. Centenarians also may maintain tight control of their immediate environment, determining the placement of furniture and possessions or firmly determining their daily schedules.

The Georgia centenarians display a high level of suspiciousness. Often they will refuse to be interviewed unless the interviewer is referred by someone they know and trust. Even then, the individual may ask the interviewer extensive questions regarding how the information will be used. These attributes may have been shaped by experience, by unique historical events, and by personal losses, as well as by internal survival mechanisms.

Because they have lived longer, the centenarians have experienced a greater variety of events and physiological changes than those in the younger groups. They are likely to have outlived spouses, other relatives, peers, and even their own children. Most have been retired for more years than many adults have worked. Simply to have survived these vicissitudes, centenarians must possess a repertoire of coping strategies—of which dominance and suspiciousness may be two.

The GCS team found that centenarians are just as likely as younger people to use cognitive modes of coping—that is, introspection, contemplation, and resolution of problems in their minds. Some of the Georgia centenarians write poetry to help them cope with physical pain or other everyday challenges. (*See* "Approaching 100: Two Poems," page 69.)

IQ versus common sense. While it would seem obvious that a person must be intelligent simply to overcome the

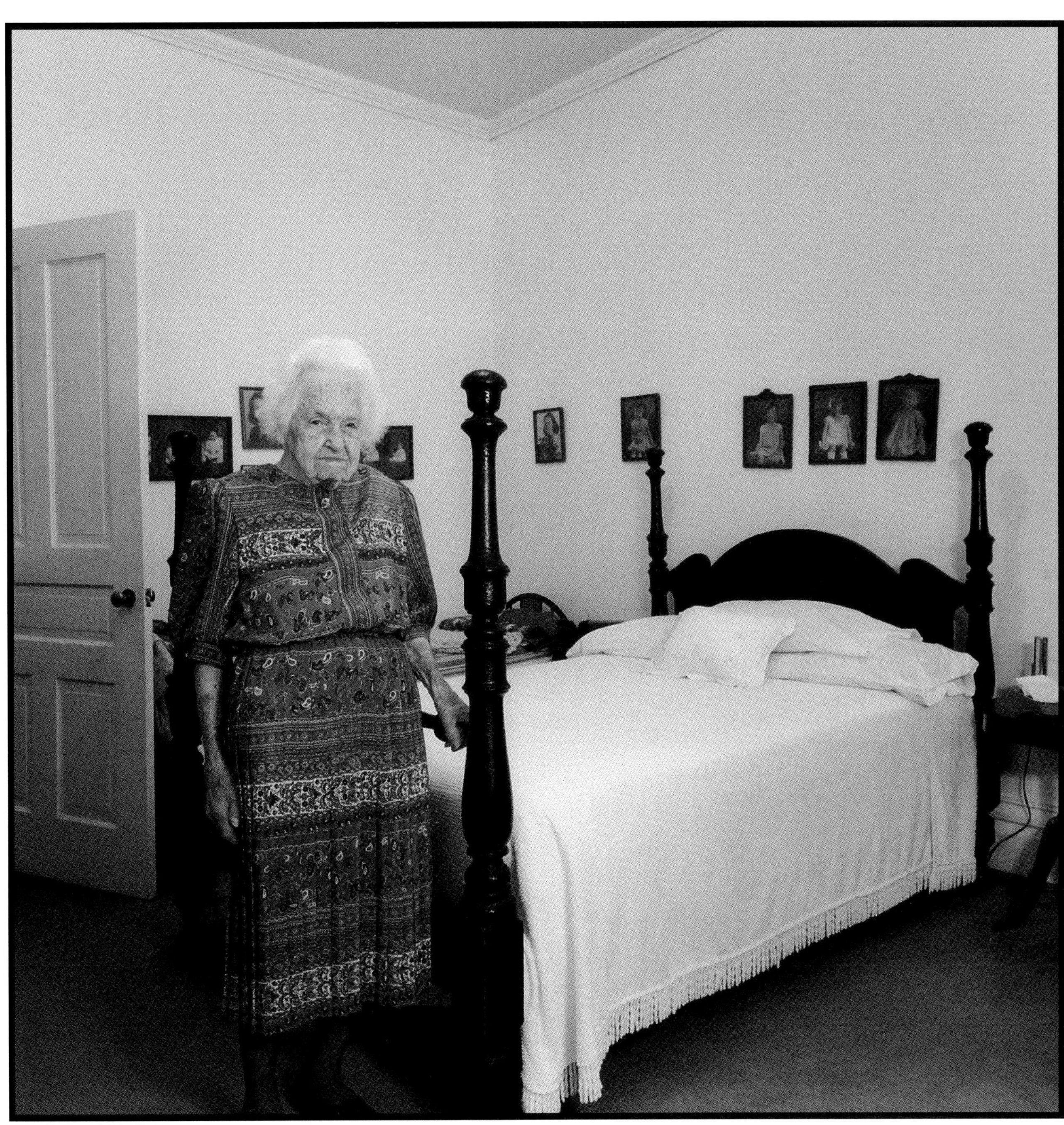

many obstacles that prevent most people from reaching extreme old age, not all centenarians perform at a high level on tests of intelligence and cognitive ability. Some do perform as well as or better than some of the younger GCS participants in such tasks as absorbing new information, thinking abstractly, defining words, and processing spatial data; this finding is surprising, given that they have been out of a formal learning environment for more than 70 to 80 years. The cognitive performance of the centenarians as a group is poorer than that of the younger participants, however. Of course, some individual centenarians do excel. One at age 104 could still converse and write in French even though she had had few opportunities to use the language since she learned it in school some 75 years earlier. Nonetheless, other centenarians have difficulty with cognitive tasks like the simple arithmetic necessary to purchase groceries or pay household bills.

The oldest old perform relatively well on tests of ability to solve everyday problems, perhaps because they are more familiar with practical dilemmas than with abstractions or because such questions seem more relevant than, say, an exercise that calls for rearranging a set of blocks. They demonstrate this resourcefulness in everyday life. One woman, although totally blind, was able to manage her own money by keeping bills of different denominations in different-sized envelopes. A man whose arthritis made fully independent living impossible slept at night in a retirement home. In the morning he used a battery operated cart to travel to his own home, where he carried out everyday activities, including preparing his own meals. Some authorities postulate that practical problem solving may be a more accurate measure of survival skills than tests of isolated intellectual processes. Certainly, the two individuals just described are a testimony to this theory.

Why some people survive to 105—or even to a mere 100—while others meet their end at relatively youthful ages of, say, 70 or 80 continues to intrigue scientists who study aging.

A science still in its infancy

As the life histories of two Georgia centenarians, Sarah

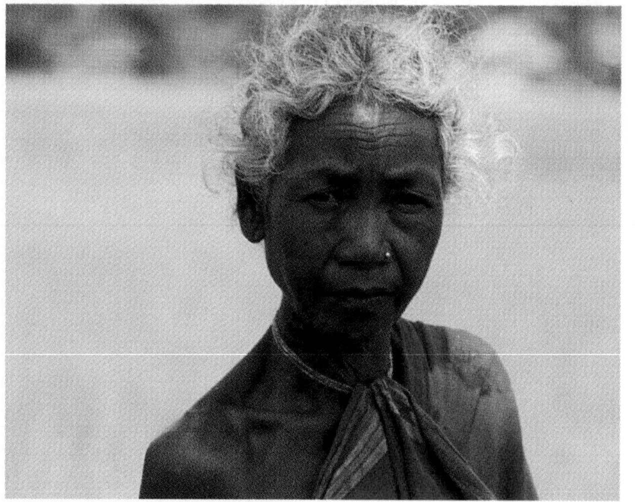

(Top left) Harvey Lloyd—Peter Arnold, Inc.; (top center) Bruno P. Zehnder—Peter Arnold, Inc.; (top right, center left, bottom three photos) © Wolfgang Kaehler; (center) John Kay Paul—Peter Arnold, Inc.; (center right) Judy Griesedieck—Black Star and Esther (*see* below), amply demonstrate, the GCS researchers have found that there are few similarities in the day-to-day experiences of these remarkable survivors. They come from many different walks of life and have different educational levels, work experience, religious beliefs, and financial resources. For people who aspire to long life, this is perhaps the "good news."

The "bad news," if there is any, is that so far there is no easy answer to the question, What does a person have to do to live to be 100? As the GCS data show, the Georgia centenarians eat a varied diet, with more vegetables and vitamin A than are consumed by the comparison groups—but then others who ate a similar diet died much earlier. The researchers also note that the centenarians are generally more determined to have their way than are members of the younger groups—but this does not mean that all who reach 100 have this characteristic, nor does it mean that younger individuals with this characteristic will live to be 100. And so the story goes for each variable they examined.

If there is an answer to the question of how to reach 100, it is that achieving this milestone is based on a combination of advantageous circumstances, including—but not limited to—a genetic makeup that predisposes to long survival, positive attitude toward life, ability to cope with stress in positive ways, health-promoting behaviors to reduce risk of illness, sufficient common sense to deal with everyday problems, and the good fortune to avoid infectious diseases and serious injuries. While the Georgia scientists accept the assumption that not one or two but many factors contribute to extreme longevity, they hope that by continuing to follow individuals who are successfully reaching very old age, they can begin to identify the major variables associated with aging well and gain a better understanding of the interplay between them. MHA

A Tale of Two Centenarians

Sarah, an African-American woman, was born in July 1888 on a small Georgia farm. She was the oldest of six daughters. Education was an important goal of her family. Five of the sisters—including Sarah—went on to attain teacher's certificates. Their education required a great deal of sacrifice and support on the part of their parents. This legacy of education was passed on to Sarah's children and grandchildren, who each received a college education.

Sarah was married at the age of 20 to a teacher who was 23 years her senior. Her husband died at the age of 103. Sarah worked for 39 years in the public-school system as an elementary-school teacher. After retirement at age 59, she discovered that she needed to occupy her time and returned to work for nine more years in a part-time position as a kindergarten teacher. During her working and semiretirement years as a teacher, Sarah participated in many conferences, some as far away as New York and Ohio. She became active in an organization called Senior Citizens at the age of 66 and remained active until 99, when, she said, she began to feel too tired to keep up with the activities.

* * *

Esther was another African-American who lived not far from Sarah. According to government records, she was born in May 1888.

Esther lived in a weather-beaten house on a dirt road in the poorest section of town. She was one of 10 children born to a tenant farmer. She told of the beatings she received as a child from her father and said that her mother attempted to intercede. Esther liked to attend school and had wanted to be a teacher. For economic reasons, however, she was forced to leave school at the age of 15 and began to work on the farm. She spent her leisure time going to shows and dances and considered that time period the best years of her life.

Esther married for the first time at the age of 20. She worked intermittently as a cook or housekeeper. Her only son was born when she was 21. When she was 35 her husband, who was 37, died of a stroke. Four years later, at the age of 39, she married for a second time. Her second husband frequently got in trouble with the law and finally was sent to prison for petty thievery. When Esther was 41, her 19-year-old son was stabbed to death. The next year her second husband was released from prison, but he was unable to settle down or hold a steady job, and finally he left Esther, who never heard from him again.

Esther stated that it was at this time that she "saw the light." She became very involved with her church and was able to maintain her biweekly church meeting attendance. About the age of 42, she began working regularly as a cook, housekeeper, and nanny.

She lived out her entire life in the same 260-square kilometer (100-square mile) region of Georgia. Her closest living relative was a niece who lived nearby but whom she never visited.

Esther acknowledged that she had a difficult life, yet she also believed that she had made her life "right with God." Esther stated that her life had become "good" because of her strong religious convictions.

An Active Mind, a Bunch of Push-ups... Strategies for Aging Gracefully

The editors of the *Medical and Health Annual,* who are in various decades of life, were curious: How do others approach growing old? Do they have personal anti-aging strategies? They wrote to some well-known people, asking, "What are YOU doing to ensure your own health and vitality in old age?" They requested spontaneous and candid responses. Here is what they got:

Mortimer Adler with bust of himself and framed swim trunks. The trunks are a stand-in for the bachelor's degree that Columbia University, New York City, refused to give him in 1923 because he failed to attend gym classes and never took a required swimming test.

Courtesy of Mortimer and Caroline Adler

A philosopher, author, editor, and teacher, ***Mortimer J. Adler,*** *93, wrote the first of his more than 45 books in 1927. He served as director of the Institute for Philosophical Research in Chicago for 43 years, was chairman of the board of editors of Encyclopædia Britannica, Inc., from 1974 to 1995, and was editor in chief of the 1990 edition of the* Great Books of the Western World, *published by Encyclopædia Britannica. His most recent book is* Adler's Philosophical Dictionary *(1995). Among his most popular books are:* How to Read a Book *(with Charles Van Doren, 1972),* Aristotle for Everybody: Difficult Thought Made Easy *(1978), and the two volumes of his autobiography,* Philosopher at Large *(1977) and* A Second Look in the Rearview Mirror *(1992).*

"Do whatever is honorable as well as expedient in order to succeed, and if not completely honorable, at least *appear* to be virtuous in doing it!" So I told my friends and colleagues at my 80th birthday party. I proceeded to offer them my 10 rules and recommendations for achieving both success and happiness in old age. I believe those are worth reiterating:

1. With regard to health, vigor, and vitality: never exercise. As for dieting, eat only the most delicious calories.
2. With regard to marriage: if at first you don't succeed, try again.
3. Never work more than seven days a week or 12 hours a day, and sometimes a little less. To grow younger with the years, work harder as you get older.
4. Never take money for work you would not do if you did not need the money.
5. If you have the inclination and ability, the best way to spend time is to write books; the next best is to edit them; and if you cannot do either, then sell them.
6. Never write more than one book a year, because it doesn't pay; but edit as many as possible, and sell them by the hundred thousands.
7. Have a secretary who thinks she understands what you are up to as well as you do.
8. Surround yourself with friends and associates with whom you can be almost as honest as you are with yourself.

9. Get over the folly of thinking that there is any conflict between high living and high thinking; asceticism is for the birds.

10. Never give up; never say die; always say "If I die," *NOT* "When I die."

(Left) Courtesy of Bailey Seminars, Inc.; (right) Sigrid Estrada

Covert Bailey, *64, is a health and fitness expert, the host of the Public Broadcasting Service television series "Fit or Fat," and the author of national best-selling books—among them,* The Fit-or-Fat Target Diet *(1984),* Fit-or-Fat Target Recipes *(with Lea Bishop, 1985),* The Fit-or-Fat Woman *(with Lea Bishop, 1989),* The New Fit or Fat *(1991), and* Smart Exercise: Burning Fat, Getting Fit *(1994).*

Fitness is my antiaging strategy. I am still in training just the way I was when I was 24. What am I training for? The mountains to be climbed, the rivers to be paddled, the square dance that lasts all night.

Readers of the New York Times *depend on **Marian Burros'** two weekly columns, "Eating Well" and "Plain and Simple," for inspiring recipes and thoughtful appraisals of whatever nutrition issues are making news. Burros, who cites her age as "somewhere between 40 and death," has written many cookbooks, the latest of which is* Eating Well Is the Best Revenge: Everyday Strategies for Delicious, Healthful Food in 30 Minutes or Less *(1995).*

Eating lots of vegetables, grains, and fruits with small amounts of chicken and fish and very little red meat.

Exercising five to six times a week—sometimes working out on a Nordic Track, sometimes bicycling, sometimes walking, and in-line skating whenever weather permits.

Taking calcium, vitamin E, and one-a-day supplements.

Sounds perfect? So, how come I'm not sylphlike? Too much cheating, perhaps.

(Below) Claudio Vazquez; (bottom) courtesy of Henry J. Heimlich

***Jean Carper,** 64, is an exponent of the "you-are-what-you-eat" philosophy. She writes a column for* USA Weekend *and is author of 19 books, including* Food—Your Miracle Medicine: How Food Can Prevent and Cure over 100 Symptoms and Problems *(1993) and* Stop Aging Now!: The Ultimate Plan for Staying Young and Reversing the Aging Process *(1995).*

I eat sardines and drink lots of real tea (not herbal), as my grandmother told me to. I also eat nuts, berries, fruits, and greens, as our Stone Age ancestors did. I stay away from meat and cigarette smoke. I take vitamin-mineral and antioxidant supplements. I work out at the gym and play tennis. I keep my mind active, reading and writing about all the new medical research on aging. I thank my mother, age 91, for her good genes.

***Henry J. Heimlich, M.D., Sc.D.,** 76, president of the Heimlich Institute, Cincinnati, Ohio, is inventor of the Heimlich Chest Drain Valve, the Heimlich MicroTrach (for rehabilitating emphysema patients), and the Heimlich Esophagus Replacement Operation. He is currently researching cures for cancer and AIDS and serving as head of "A Caring World," a campaign that relies on TV, computers, and economic interdependence to promote universal peace and health. But he is best known for his Heimlich maneuver, which saves choking victims by dislodging objects from the windpipe and resuscitates drowning victims by expelling water from the lungs. Heimlich's name appears in most standard dictionaries, and he is credited with having saved more lives than anyone else in the world.*

I stay young by being more productive than ever before. I've developed an oxygen system that rehabilitates emphysema patients, as well as a promising treatment for AIDS. The Heimlich maneuver not only saves choking persons, but I recently proved it is also the first step for saving drowning victims.

To remain healthy I ski, swim, play tennis, sail, and am primarily a vegetarian. My father did none of these; he claimed his good health was due to eating at regular hours: "I noticed that soldiers ate at the same time every day and were always healthy." Dad lived to 100.

(Left) Baylor College of Medicine; (right) Archive Photos/Consolidated News

M. Joycelyn Elders, M.D., *63, served a tempestuous 15 months as U.S. surgeon general in 1993–94. Today the outspoken pediatrician teaches at the University of Arkansas College of Medicine and cares for youngsters at Arkansas Children's Hospital in Little Rock.*

I am so pleased to be growing older that I don't give any thought at all to trying to stay around, which, of course, is not possible anyway. What is important to me is not just to age but to "sage" by helping youngsters as they go along on their trek of growing older. To consciously "sage," I listen carefully to those wise people that I have the opportunity to know, and I live in the moment. Keeping active is a part of "saging," and to do this a person needs to stay as fit as possible. Using our minds and bodies keeps us from losing them, so I use all my faculties the best I can, as much as I can, and as often as I can.

"Master surgeon" ***Michael E. DeBakey, M.D.,*** *is chancellor emeritus and distinguished service professor at Baylor College of Medicine and director of the DeBakey Heart Center in Houston, Texas. An innovator in the field of cardiovascular medicine, he performed the world's first successful coronary bypass operation. The octogenarian is also the coauthor of several books, including* The Living Heart *(1977),* The Living Heart Diet *(1984),* The Living Heart Guide to Eating Out *(1993), and* The Living Heart Brand Name Shopper's Guide *(1992).*

Although we cannot absolutely ensure lifelong health and vitality, we can do a great deal to avoid known risks for illness. I have always tried to do this by eating a moderate diet, with emphasis on seasonal fruits and vegetables; exercising regularly by walking, climbing stairs, and otherwise incorporating physical activity in my daily routine; pursuing a vigorous schedule of daily activities; and avoiding smoking, excessive alcohol, and other drugs.

To lead a fulfilled life, and thus further enhance health and vitality, one should also choose a career that will be gratifying and fulfilling, be actively engaged in new and exciting endeavors, and associate with stimulating, vibrant people. Old age is often more a state of mind than one of physiology. An active mind, like an active body, staves off senescence.

George Lundberg as proud father of the bride.

A virologist and head of viral oncology at the Pasteur Institute in Paris, **Luc Montagnier, D.Med.,** *64, led the research team that isolated the AIDS virus in 1983 and remains a prominent AIDS researcher. In his spare time Montagnier enjoys playing Mozart's piano sonatas, listening to music, and swimming.*

Having observed many AIDS patients in the final stage of their disease, I have been struck by the similarities between their physical appearance and behavior and those of elderly people. Aging is often closely associated with long-term chronic diseases (Alzheimer's, Parkinson's, atherosclerosis, cancers). A common denominator of all of these diseases is the alteration of proteins by oxidation. Oxidative stress, characterized by a predominance of oxidative molecules (free radicals) over antioxidants, is a common feature of these diseases and of aging.

I am therefore taking a combination of antioxidants, such as vitamins C and E, beta-carotene, and selenium every day. There will probably be better combinations available in the future for AIDS patients and aging people. Still, I feel extremely well and strong with this treatment!

A pathologist by training, **George D. Lundberg, M.D.,** *63, is the editor of the* Journal of the American Medical Association *and an adjunct professor of health policy at Harvard University.*

Unfortunately, one cannot "ensure" one's own health and vitality in old age. One cannot even ensure that one will have an old age. But, these caveats aside, I make the following efforts:

- Work a 60–70-hour workweek and have no plans to cut back.
- Cultivate active contact with people of all ages, especially the young.
- Get regular, vigorous exercise and regular sleep.
- Limit intake of salt and of fat and calories to prevent weight gain.
- Take extra folate, calcium, and vitamin E to limit atherosclerosis.
- Use no tobacco, sleeping pills, or tranquilizers and avoid excessive use of alcohol.
- Maintain an active family, intellectual, cultural, athletic, and sex life.
- Travel a lot and adapt quickly to new time zones, cultures, and people.
- Approach many problems as exciting challenges and opportunities.
- Shift gears emotionally, physically, geographically, and personally, quickly and often.
- Never shelter myself from "ordinary" or "unusual" people, places, cultures, or conveyances.
- Maintain an inquisitive attitude.
- Find humor wherever and whenever possible.

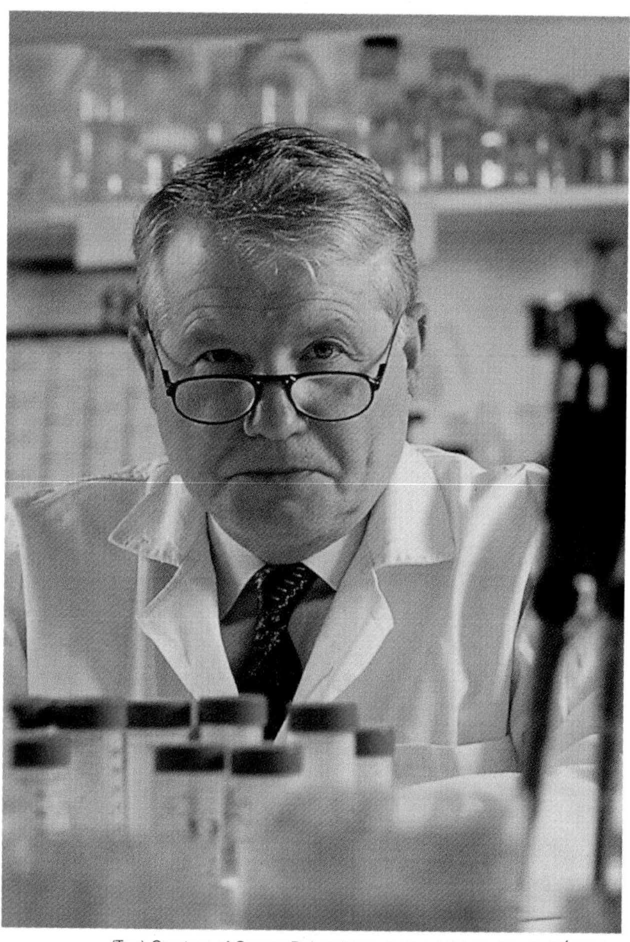

(Top) Courtesy of George D. Lundberg; (bottom) Patrick Allard—RÉA/Saba

© Jerry Bauer

***Sherwin B. Nuland, M.D.**, 65, is a scholar, author, and editor who teaches surgery and the history of medicine at Yale University. His 1988 book* Doctors: The Biography of Medicine *was reissued in paperback in 1995. His most recent,* How We Die: Reflections on Life's Final Chapter *(1994), won the National Book Award for nonfiction. Despite the bleakness of the title, one reviewer described the work as "life-enhancing in the most profound sense."*

I think of my life as a continuity from childhood and incorporate all of my life experiences into what I am now. I have always believed, along with Sigmund Freud, that what really counts is the combination of work and love. To me, love does not mean love for mankind generally but for my own family and a relatively small circle of friends whose lives have meaning in mine. As for work—work is a combination of curiosity and creativity. I'm convinced of the importance of not allowing anything to dampen one's curiosity and of following its urgings wherever they may lead. Curiosity leads to formulations of thought as understanding increases and then to creativity that arises from that thought.

Love and work are available to all of us. The trick is to recognize that they are independent of age or of any other condition in which we may find ourselves, including poverty. I don't think of myself as being at any particular age but only as being always much less completed and mature than I would like to be. Perhaps if I maintain my curiosity, I can come closer to my goal, which is by its very nature unattainable. I think of myself as a work in progress (as much of a cliché as that may be). When I die, I would like my final hour of consciousness to be filled with regrets about all of the things I have not been able to do and satisfaction with those that I have been fortunate enough to complete.

P.S. Oh yes, I do a bunch of push-ups each morning and play tennis as much as I can. But these are for the body, which is secondary in my view, although (along with the Roman writer Juvenal) I do believe in the concept of *mens sana in corpore sano* ("a healthy mind in a healthy body"). MHA

Faith and Flu Shots

by Caswell A. Evans, Jr., D.D.S., M.P.H.

There is nothing incongruous about worship and wellness.

Photograph by Joel DeGrand

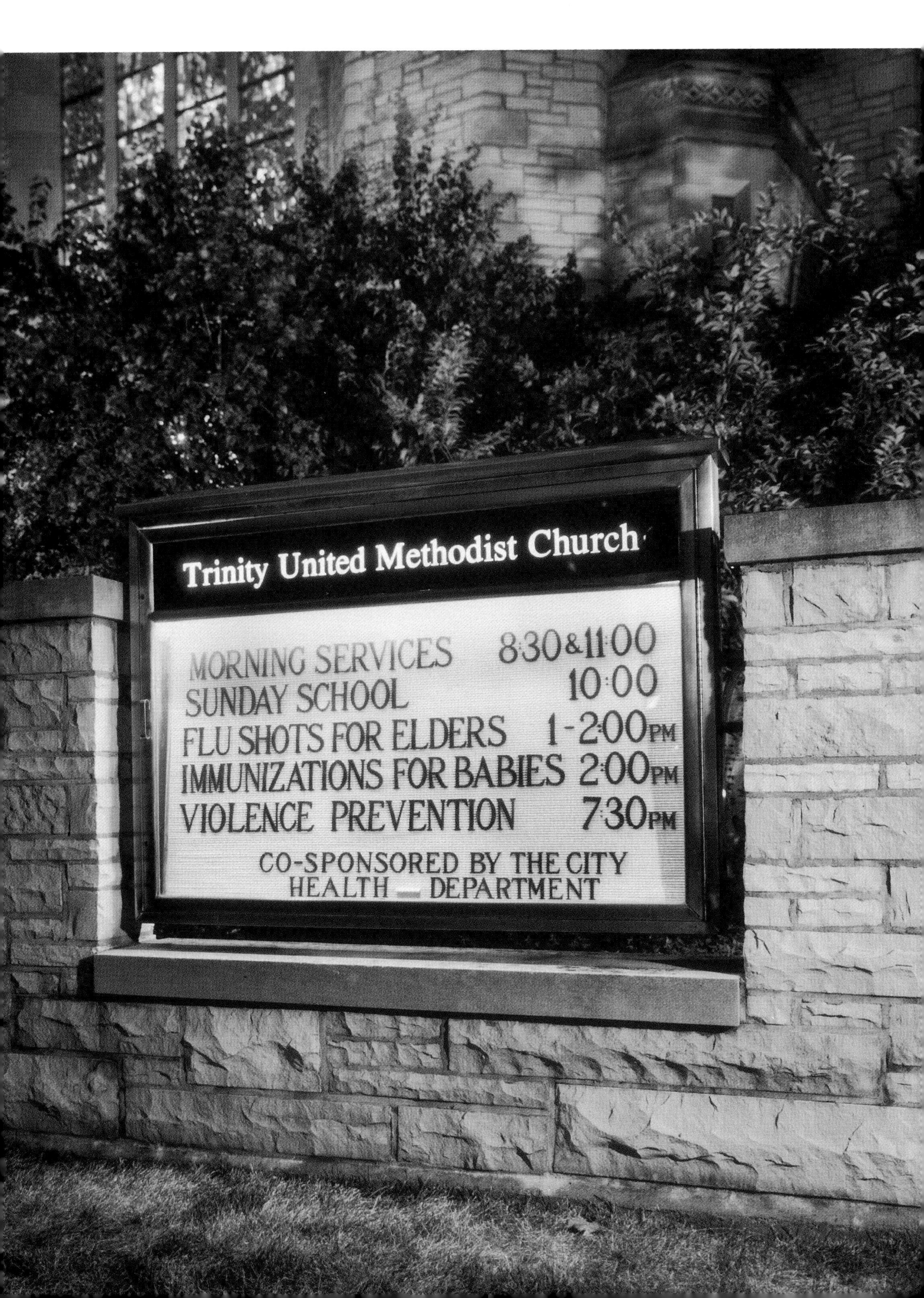
Trinity United Methodist Church
MORNING SERVICES 8:30 & 11:00
SUNDAY SCHOOL 10:00
FLU SHOTS FOR ELDERS 1-2:00 PM
IMMUNIZATIONS FOR BABIES 2:00 PM
VIOLENCE PREVENTION 7:30 PM
CO-SPONSORED BY THE CITY
HEALTH DEPARTMENT

Do not be wise in your own eyes; fear the Lord and shun evil. This will bring health to your body and nourishment to your bones.
—Jewish poem, Proverbs 3:7–8

With faith in God you can climb the highest hill. With faith in God, you can conquer every ill.
—Christian song, by Juanita Griffey Hines

Praise unto God Who hath delivered me here safe and in health.
—Islamic prayer, Muhammad's words on entering the village of Mina

Jim Zuckerman—Westlight

Public health and faith. The terms seem incompatible within the same context. In fact, as the health care situation in the United States becomes ever more critical, public health and faith are becoming passionate partners. "Not a single faith fails to address the issues of illness and wellness, of disease and healing, of caring and curing," states Martin E. Marty, professor of the history of religion at the University of Chicago and senior scholar in residence at the Chicago-based Park Ridge Center for the Study of Health, Faith, and Ethics. In fact, says Marty, "most faiths were born as . . . efforts to heal." Indeed, there is a growing national movement to bring the rich spirituality that faith groups inspire into the public health domain.

What is public health?

Before proceeding to explore the exciting partnerships forming between public health and faith communities, it is important to appreciate what public health is. While "medical care" implies services provided by a physician that are targeted to treat and cure the illness of an individual, public health aims to prevent disease within the population as a whole—so that individuals within the community do not become ill in the first place. The Institute of Medicine of the U.S. National Research Council has defined public health's mission as one of fulfilling society's interest in ensuring conditions in which people can be healthy.

New solutions

Gradually, society has come to realize that treatment of disease alone is insufficient to meet the needs of the people and that the cost of treating disease has spiraled out of all control. It has been projected that by the year 2000, health care costs in the U.S. will have reached $1.5 trillion, while between 50 million and 60 million people could be uninsured or underinsured.

Too many deaths. How do Americans die? Consider the 10 leading causes of death in the United States, listed

***Caswell A. Evans, Jr., D.D.S., M.P.H.,** is Assistant Director of Health Services and Director, Public Health Programs and Services, County of Los Angeles Department of Health Services; Adjunct Professor, School of Public Health and School of Dentistry, University of California, Los Angeles; and Immediate Past President, American Public Health Association.*

(Top) Cathy Melloan—Tony Stone Images;
(center) Alan Levenson—Tony Stone Images; (bottom) Lois Ellen Frank—Westlight

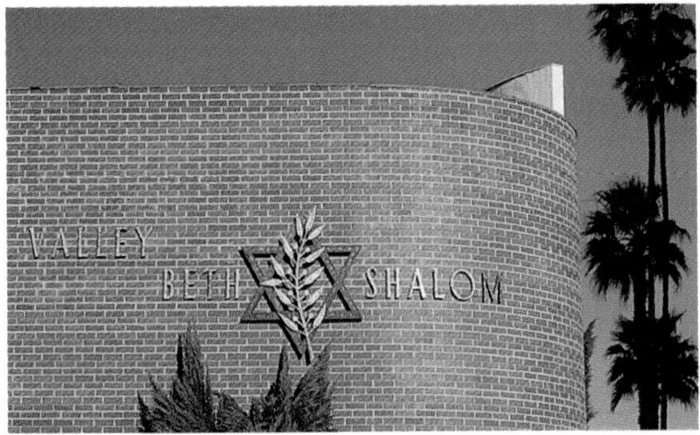

Houses of worship are among the most trusted institutions in the U.S., and they have an enormous capacity to promote the health of their congregations. (Opposite page) A Greek Orthodox church in Seattle, Washington; (top) an Evangelical Lutheran church in rural Iowa; (above) Valley Beth Shalom, a Jewish synagogue in Encino, California; (right) San Francisco de Assisi, a Catholic church in Taos, New Mexico.

in decreasing order of occurrence (from the *Monthly Vital Statistics Report,* Oct. 23, 1995):

- heart disease: 734,000 deaths annually
- cancer: 537,000 deaths
- cerebrovascular disease: 154,000 deaths
- chronic obstructive pulmonary disease: 102,000 deaths
- injuries: 90,000 deaths
- pneumonia and influenza: 82,000 deaths
- diabetes mellitus: 55,000 deaths
- AIDS/HIV: 42,000 deaths
- suicide: 32,000 deaths
- liver disease and cirrhosis: 26,000 deaths

This list identifies the *ultimate* causes of death—that is, the medical diagnoses that are stated on death certificates.

Real causes. Personal lifestyle has a lot to do with the 10 ultimate causes of death. Annually nearly half of all U.S. deaths are behavior-related: tobacco use leads to 400,000 deaths; poor diet and sedentary lifestyle, 300,000; alcohol consumption, 100,000; infections, 90,000; toxic agents, 60,000; firearms, 35,000; sexual behavior, 30,000; motor vehicles, 25,000; and illicit drug use, 20,000.

With all its sophistication, medicine today is capable of treating most illnesses. Unfortunately, however, there are no medications or medical procedures for achieving more wholesome lifestyles or effecting the kinds of behavior changes that will lead people to better health. This is where public health and faith community partnerships come in.

Capacities of congregations

Religious houses of worship—whether churches, chapels, cathedrals, tabernacles, synagogues, temples, pagodas, mosques, meetinghouses, or storefronts—are among the most trusted institutions in U.S. society. Faith communities reach out to all sectors of the surrounding community and to all cultures. And they communicate in all languages. Even the portions of the

(Top) Rick Falco—Black Star; (bottom) Donna DeCesare—Impact Visuals

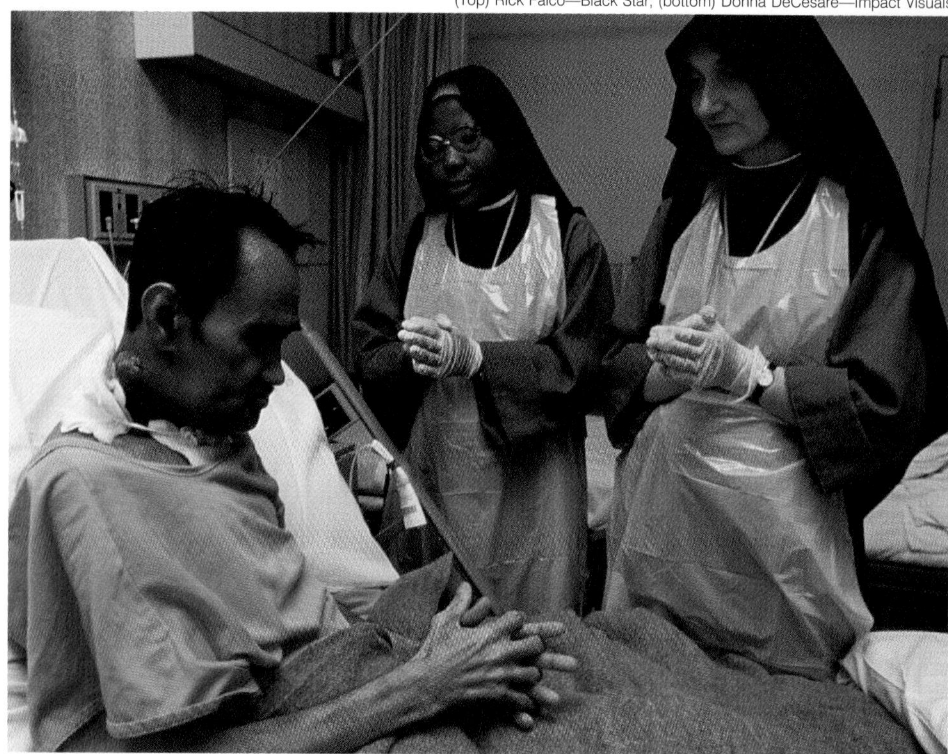

(Left) Nuns of the French Order of Fraternité Notre Dame offer solace to an AIDS patient in a hospital in New York City's East Harlem; they also dispense food to the city's homeless, work with drug addicts, and plan to start a program for unwed mothers and their children. (Below) A young Salvadoran immigrant has a checkup at a clinic run by the Lutheran Church in Freeport, Long Island, New York. (Opposite page) A weight-loss program at the First Baptist Church in Houston, Texas, inspires dieters not to be led into temptation.

community often described as "hard to reach" (by census takers, government bodies, and standard health care providers) are touched by the faith community. Advocating social justice for the poor and sponsoring health-outreach programs are among the most vital capacities of any congregation. And reach out they can! The National Council of Churches has identified 220 religious groups in the 50 states, with 346,100 congregations comprising nearly 143 million members.

Faith's fortes

It is the shared interests of healthy body, mind, and spirit that make public health's partnership with the faith community so natural and productive.

The Old Testament abounds with divine regulations intended not only to test the obedience of the Israelites but (interpreted with today's hindsight) to protect their health. About one-third of the teachings in the Gospels are about healing. With their allegiance to the New Testament, many Christian groups have responded to Christ's model by building and staffing hospitals for the sick and providing shelters for the homeless, soup kitchens for the hungry, and prayer support groups for the wayward. The Catholic Health Association of the United States, for example, has over 600 member hospitals. These institutions provide care for Catholics and non-Catholics.

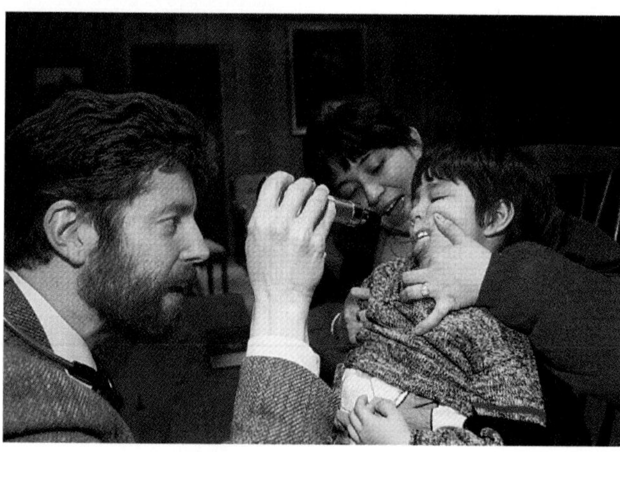

Particular Christian denominations—Mormons, Seventh-day Adventists, and Pentecostals among them—center their evangelical mission on the "well-being" of the faithful. The most familiar "prescription"—abstinence from alcohol—has very obvious health implications, given the statistics cited above.

Jewish values have had an important impact upon American medicine. In *Health and Medicine in the Jewish Tradition,* one in a series of publications edited by the Park Ridge Center, Rabbi David M. Feldman of Teaneck, New Jersey, writes, "Major contributions to the theory and practice of medicine in all its individual and communal aspects continue to be made by modern heirs to Jewish tradition and Jewish history."

Judaism has long supported health-related volunteerism, and Jewish hospitals, like Christian institutions, serve people of all creeds.

Racial and ethnic minorities have often been the subjects of medical (as well as social and economic) discrimination. Not surprisingly, African-American churches provide physical as well as spiritual healing to their congregations. African-Americans have inherited many traditional African remedies; their "prescriptions" for health often include forms of herbalism and spiritualism combined with Western medicine.

Believers in Islam likewise view health as one expression of their religion. In *Health and Medicine in the Islamic Tradition,* the late scholar Fazlur Rahman wrote, "After faith, the art and practice of medicine is the most meritorious service in God's sight." Modern medical practice, especially the establishment of hospitals, clinics, and pharmacies, would not be what it is today without the vital contributions from the Islamic world.

Creative coalitions

Religious-order hospitals and long-term-care facilities are well-known, widespread, and highly respected. Today increasingly innovative health initiatives are extending the reach of religious institutions. They are promoting health in ways that

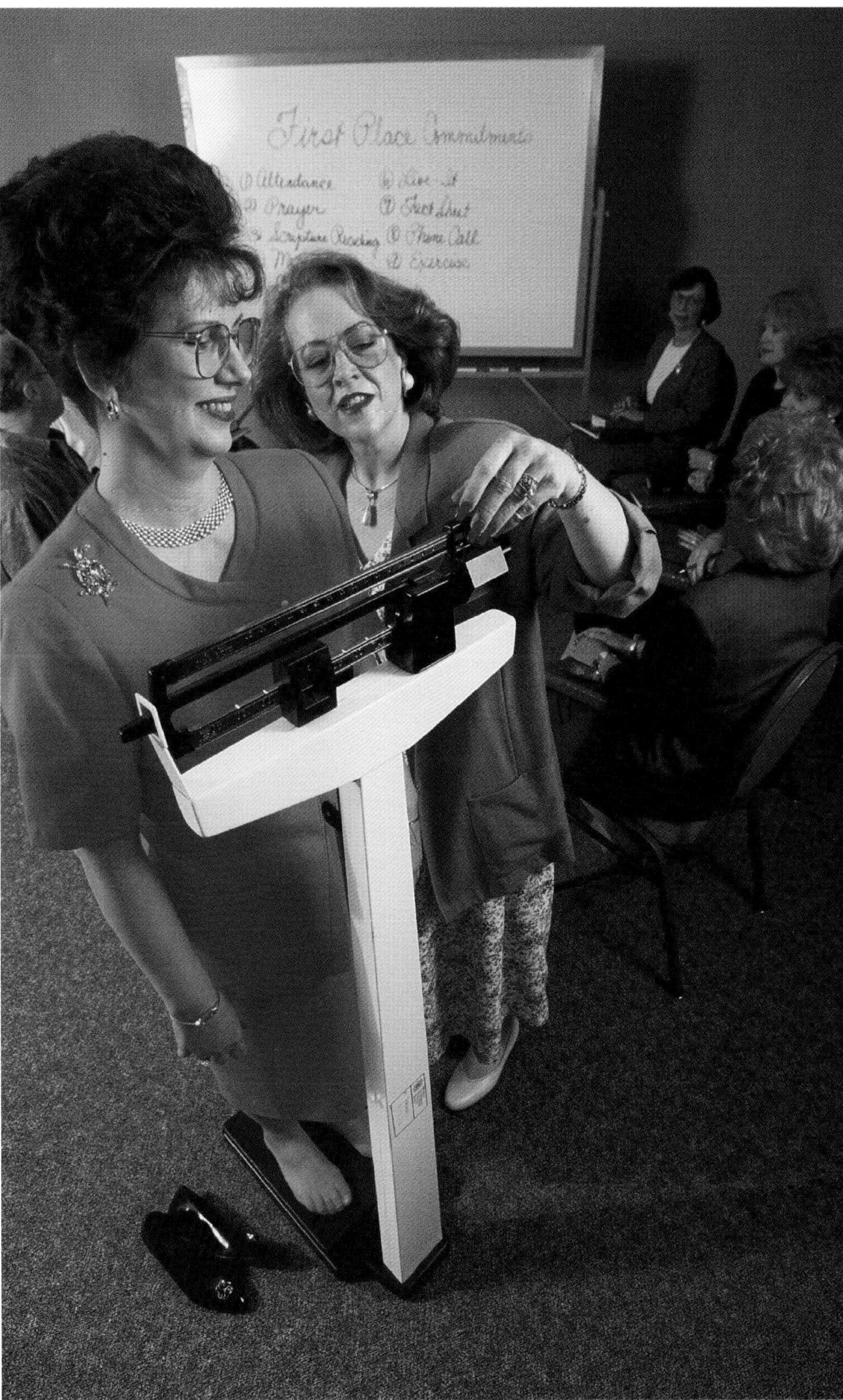

Paul S. Howell—Gamma Liaison

(Top left) Jack Kurtz—Impact Visuals;
(bottom left) © Jose Azel—Aurora/PNI; (right) Lynn Johnson—Aurora

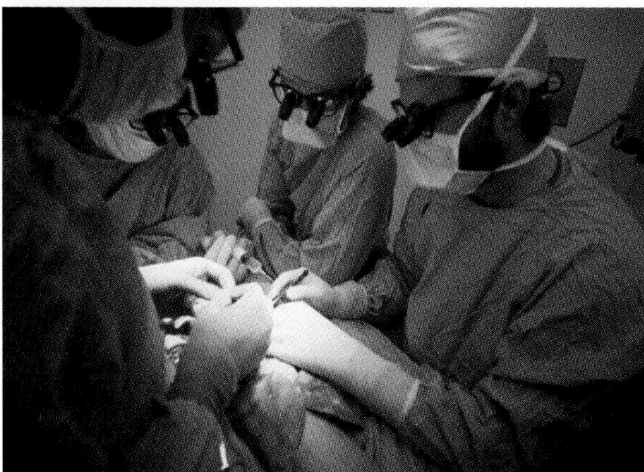

(Left) Adherents of Islam celebrate the end of Ramadan at a mosque in the Hudson Valley of New York state; the Islamic faith encompasses all aspects of life, of which health is a vital part. (Below left) Surgeons perform microsurgery at a Jewish hospital in Louisville, Kentucky, where an interdenominational staff serves patients of all creeds. (Below) A Sunday morning service in a Baptist church in Atlanta, Georgia; some of the most successful public health programs in the U.S. are those that reach out to African-American congregations.

are generating considerable excitement.

An example can be found in the Health Ministries Association Inc. (HMA), established in 1989 as an interfaith, not-for-profit organization to promote "whole-person health." As its founders realized, it is natural for people to turn to their congregation for fellowship and support. That "health is more than the absence of disease" and that "healing and authentic community are essential for every human being" are precepts that are central to the HMA's philosophy.

The work of this unique group is carried out by laypersons, clergy, and health professionals, especially the parish nurse. The parish-nursing movement began in the Midwest under the leadership of Granger Westberg, a Lutheran minister. Parish nurses are usually registered nurses, whose services are far-reaching. They conduct blood pressure screenings, organize health fairs, link people to local health departments and Red Cross agencies, assist in volunteer recruitment, coordinate transportation for the immobile who otherwise might not receive health services, immunize children and give flu shots to the elderly, visit shut-ins and new parents, offer training in cardiopulmonary resuscitation, arrange for hospice care, teach first aid and nutrition, provide spiritual support for those who are grieving, re-

fer substance abusers to special treatment programs, and conduct counseling for the codependent, the depressed, and those with eating disorders. Not surprisingly, parish nursing in its myriad permutations is expected to flourish throughout this century and into the next.

Shots for kids

Lack of childhood immunization is one of the major failings of the U.S. medical system. As a result, youngsters are needlessly susceptible to infectious diseases that easily can be prevented.

HOPE *worldwide* is a not-for-profit organization that sponsors the HOPE for Kids program, a model faith-health partnership in the U.S. This nationwide program has developed a large volunteer corps, including many teenagers, and has made a major commitment to ensuring full immunization of all U.S. children by the age of two. Among its supporters is the International Churches of Christ.

African-American churches: benefits for the brethren

Recently, the Centers for Disease Control and Prevention, Atlanta, Georgia, joined forces with the Congress of National Black Churches. The congress represents 8 different denominations, 65,000 congregations, and 19 million people, many of whom live in the inner-city and rural U.S. This partnership focuses on problems in the communities it serves: lack of immunization, teenage pregnancy, single-parent families, violence, and the epidemic of HIV/AIDS. These are tough problems that require inspired solutions.

"Churches as an Avenue to High Blood Pressure Control" is a program sponsored by the National Institutes of Health that was developed to reach minority groups. High blood pressure (hypertension) is particularly threatening to minority populations—especially African-Americans. Almost one in three African-Americans has hypertension (140/90 millimeters of mercury or higher) but either does not know it or is not being treated for it.

Religious institutions are especially well positioned to support high blood pressure control programs by offering screening, education, and encouragement of church members to comply with treatment. Because churches provide services in a familiar, nonthreatening setting, they can often succeed where traditional medical practice fails.

Innovation is the key

The Park Ridge Center for the Study of Health, Faith, and Ethics was founded in 1985 on the premise

"Wellness Sunday" at Chicago's St. Margaret Mary parish: after mass churchgoers attend a health fair, where they learn preventive health strategies and get professional advice. (Below) A parishioner has her blood pressure checked by a parish nurse; (right) another attendee consults podiatrist Robert Cohen about her sore feet.

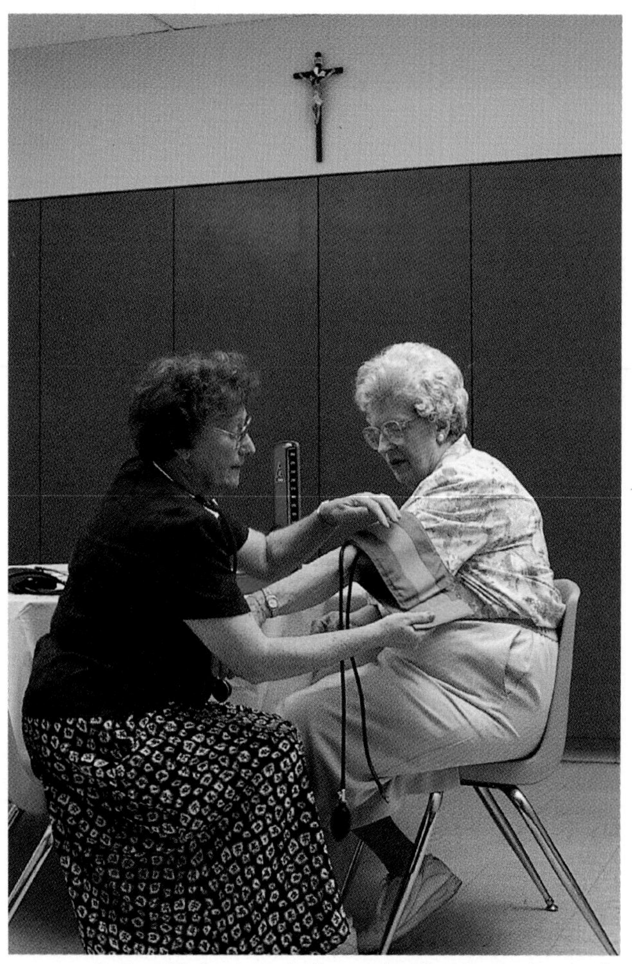

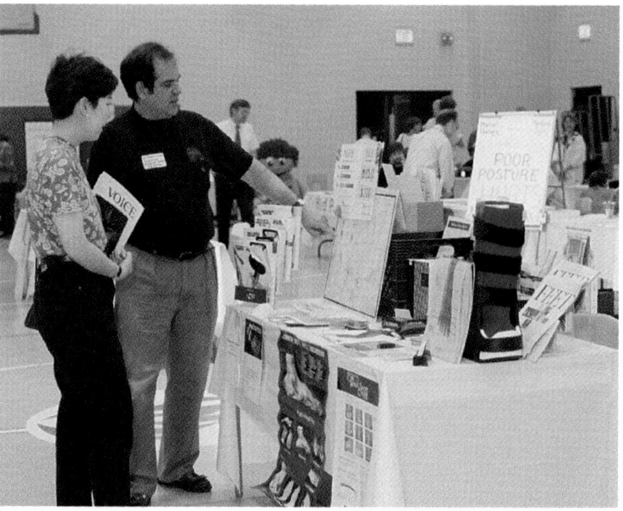

Courtesy of St. Francis Hospital Congregational Nurse Program, Evanston, Ill.; photographs, Cathy Melloan

Courtesy of HOPE for Kids

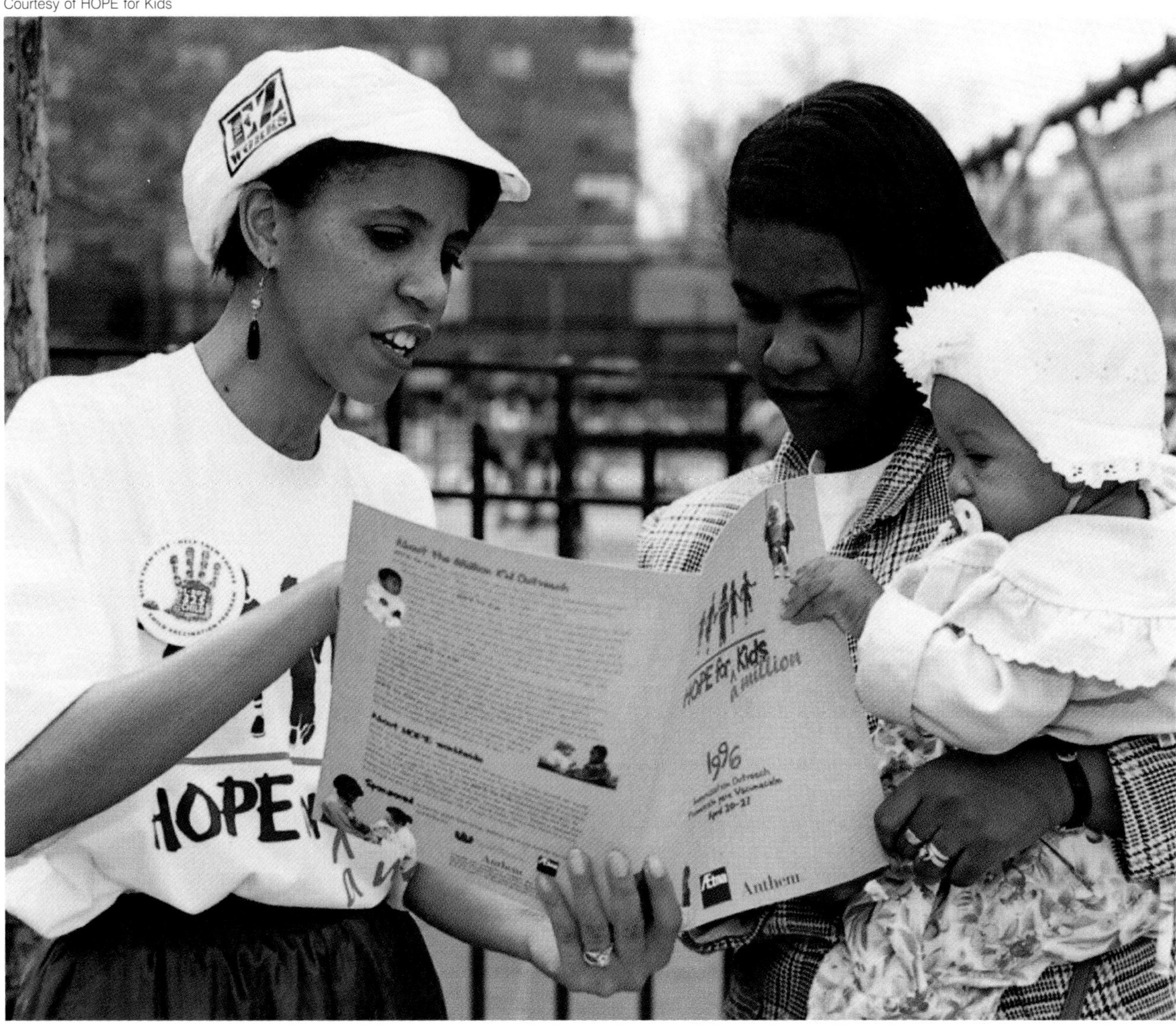

A volunteer with HOPE for Kids, a model faith-health outreach program, educates a mother about the importance of getting her youngster immunized.

that studies of health and bioethics cannot be complete unless they take into account basic human belief systems. The center focuses its work upon both the religious and the secular expressions of faith in all issues of health and health care.

The Carter Center in Atlanta was founded in 1982 by former president Jimmy Carter and his wife, Rosalynn. In 1989 The Carter Center cosponsored "The Church's Challenge in Health Conference" with the Wheat Ridge Foundation (now Wheat Ridge Ministries), a Lutheran charitable organization. At that conference religious leaders representing many faiths were challenged by well-known health leaders to respond to the overwhelming scientific evidence that health promotion reduces premature death.

Following that meeting, The Carter Center initiated the Interfaith Health Program, whose mission is to encourage faith groups to improve the individual and collective health of their members. By gathering examples of effective church and health collaborations, Interfaith Health acts as a broker between those with experience and those seeking experience. Information on effective faith-public health models is shared through the publication *What if Every Congregation . . . ?: A Sampling of Congregation and Community Health Promotion Models,* which is accessible in a variety of ways, including via the Internet (http://www.interaccess.com/ihpnet/models.htm).

The American Public Health Association, Inc. (APHA), the largest organization of its kind in the world, representing over 50,000 health professionals, is aware of the potential for expanding public health

Courtesy of Dennis Fey

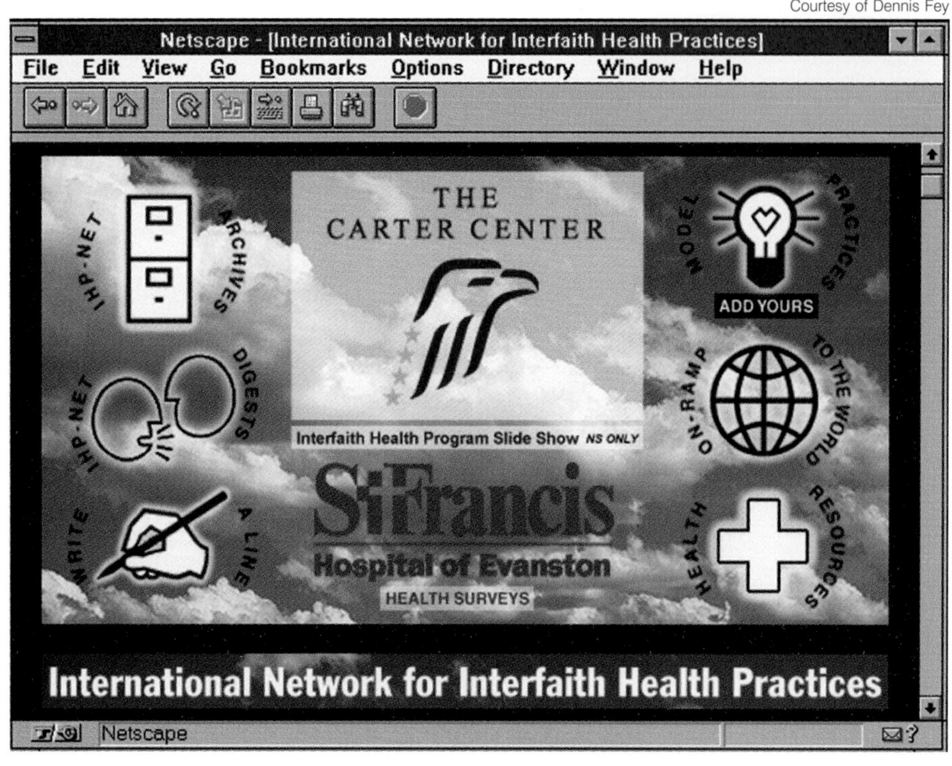

practice through collaboration with faith communities. In early 1996 APHA formally recognized the newly formed Caucus on Public Health and the Faith Community. Perhaps its most important guiding principle is that health, wholeness, and well-being are human rights.

Poverty in perspective

There is little question that poverty is a reliable predictor of health. Simply put, people who are poor are more likely than others to get sick. Consequently, faith and commu-

(Above) The Carter Center of Atlanta, Georgia, and St. Francis Hospital of Evanston, Illinois, jointly maintain a Web site that is a veritable gold mine of information about successful faith-health partnerships. One such partnership is Bethel New Life on Chicago's West Side, which has earned a national reputation for its community revitalization efforts. Beth-Anne Life Center (far right) is helping Bethel New Life fulfill its mission of "weaving a healthy sustainable community." This new facility houses the Molade Child Development Center (right top), where children from the community learn and thrive while their parents are at work; (right bottom) two seniors in the Adult Day Care program make progress on a joint quilt.

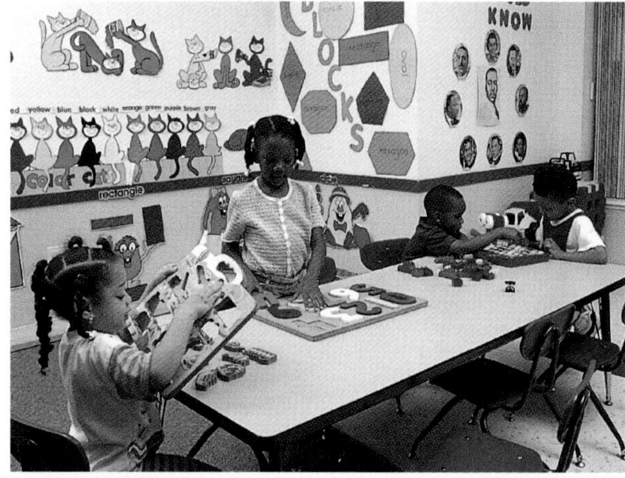

Courtesy of Bethel New Life, Inc.; photographs, Cathy Melloan

nity projects that can change a community's *economic* status can also have a profound effect upon its *health* status.

As an example, consider Bethel New Life, Inc., a comprehensive community development organization serving a low-income, largely African-American community on Chicago's West Side. The organization grew out of volunteer efforts by members of Bethel Lutheran Church, and the church remains a constant source of encouragement and sustenance. Bethel New Life, however, has burgeoned into a dynamic separate entity that has succeeded in offering "hope in hard times." In the process, it has developed a national reputation for its innovative initiatives.

Perhaps most significant, Bethel New Life contributes to the community's socioeconomic improvement. It helps people get decent and affordable housing and employment in living-wage jobs. It works to strengthen families and bring about safety in the community. Everyone in the community has access to a full range of primary care and preventive health services. For example, in fiscal 1995 some 8,000 mothers and young children received comprehensive medical and nutritional care. In that same year, plans were completed for the construction of a publicly funded $2.5 million Family Wellness Center. One of Bethel's unique family-strengthening initiatives is known as "self help/sweat equity." This program enables people in the community to acquire their own residences through their physical labors and volunteer work, which serve as equity toward a down payment on a home. Another program, Lead Outreach and Advocacy, aims to identify children with high lead levels, make sure they have access to health care, and reduce or eliminate lead in buildings and in the environment of the community.

Bethel New Life's success is based upon the premise that grass-roots, community-based initiatives must be the foundation of any sustainable effort. People and dollars have made the difference. For its outstanding achievements, Bethel New Life received a Healthier Communities Award from the Healthcare Forum in 1995. Bethel's motto is: "God's people weaving together a healthier community."

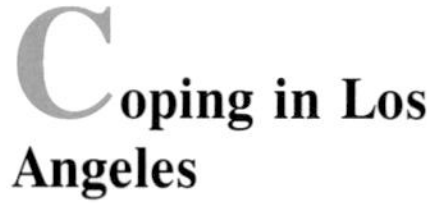

Coping in Los Angeles

Approximately 2.7 million persons in Los Angeles county do not have health insurance and have little access to health care. In 1994 a coalition known as the County of Los Angeles Health and Faith Project was formed among the Greater Hollywood Health Partnership, the Southern Area Clergy Council, and the Public Health Programs and Services branch of the County Department of Health Services. This coalition represents approximately 90 congregations and a broad cross-section of the community; many of the congregations are in geographic areas

(Top) Mark Sandlin; (center) Los Angeles Mammography Promotion in Churches Program; photograph, Kathryn Pitkin; (bottom) County of Los Angeles Health and Faith Project

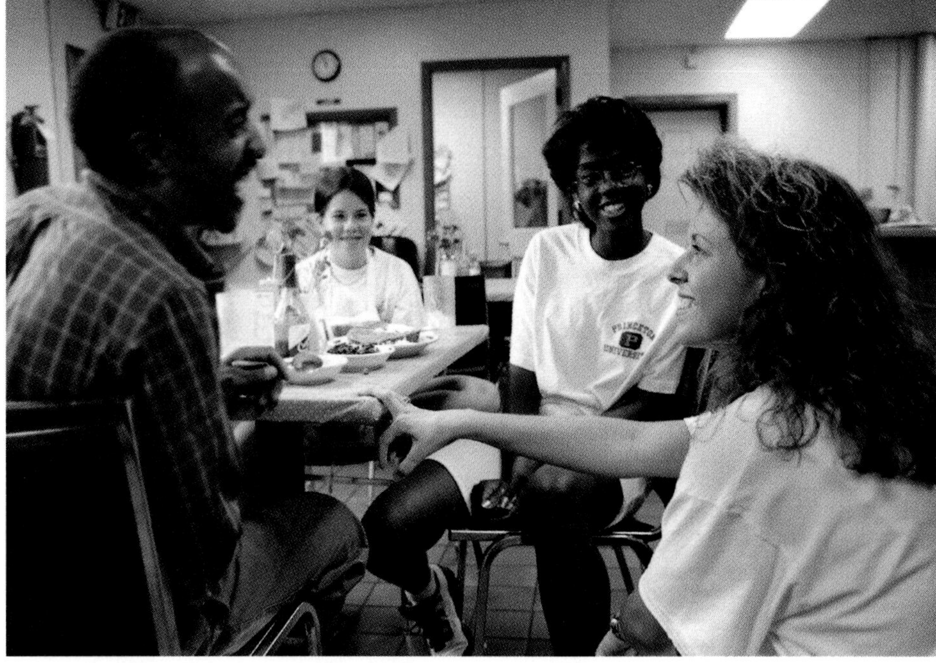

known for higher-than-average rates of poverty. The goal of the project is simply stated: to improve the overall health of county residents. The project works as follows:

- Congregations form "health cabinets" that direct and oversee the program, with a spiritual leader at the helm.
- The very specific needs of the congregation and community are identified.
- Distinct ways that health suffers but can be improved are identified.
- Appropriate prevention projects are developed.
- Congregations work in partnership with already-established health organizations within the community.

The Health and Faith Project is also assisting congregations in conducting research, making sure people in the community are aware of existing resources, establishing referral mechanisms so that people get the services they need when they need them, and providing educational seminars that train participants in effective fund-raising, grant writing, and other ways to obtain the financial support that is essential to sustaining the health and faith partnership.

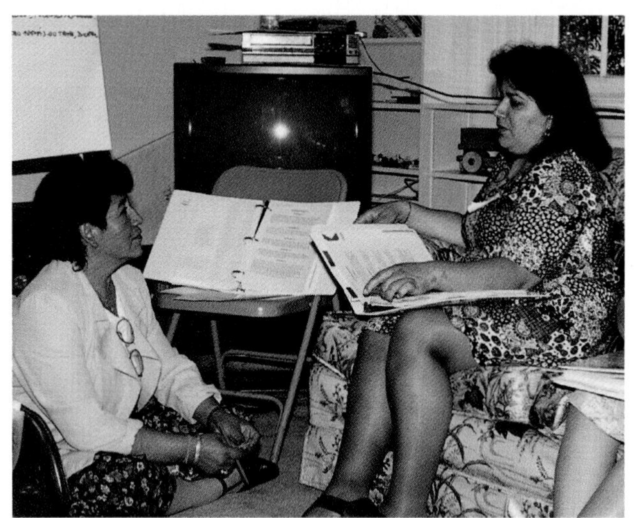

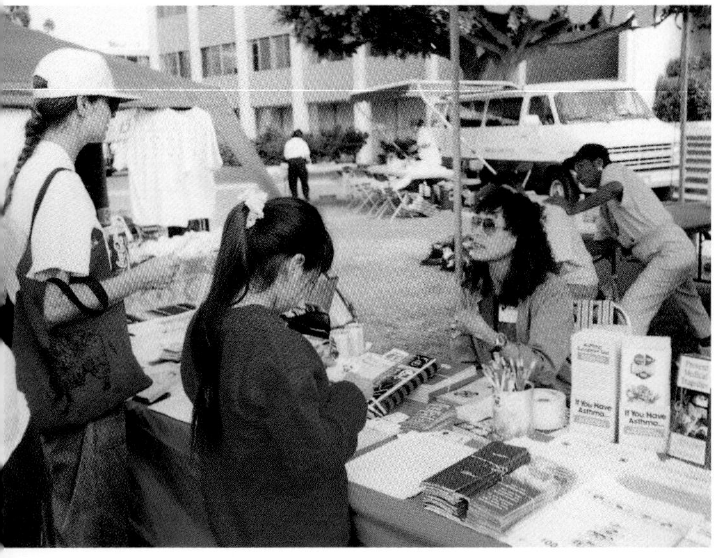

(Top) Café 458 in Atlanta, Georgia, offers its homeless patrons a lot more than home-cooked meals; free counseling and a recovery program for substance abusers are also on the menu. (Above) Women are trained as telephone counselors for the Los Angeles Mammography Promotion in Churches Program. (Left) Kateri Circle, an American Indian religious organization, holds a "pow wow health fair" in Los Angeles.

In a related initiative, the Los Angeles Mammography Promotion in Churches Program reaches women of diverse economic and racial/ethnic backgrounds, aged 50–80, through their places of worship. Begun in 1995, the program, dedicated to the fight against breast cancer, has enrolled more than 1,500 women from 45 different churches in the Los Angeles area. Thanks to this project, these women will receive regular screening mammograms—and follow-up care, if needed. The project is coordinated by the RAND Corporation, a nonprofit organization known nationally for health policy research.

Yet another Los Angeles-based program is directed at gangs. The Southern Area Clergy Council, a coalition of 75 African-American churches, was established to cope with gang problems and violence in African-American neighborhoods in southern Los Angeles. The council's "Keeping It Good in the Hood" project does a lot more than prevent violence; it helps young people get jobs and receive entrepreneurial training, sponsors community health education such as lead-poisoning awareness, offers a year-round sports league, runs substance-abuse programs, trains young people to do construction work, and promotes and encourages academic excellence. Financial support comes from the 75 churches, grants, and various local businesses. "We [came] to the conclusion that if we [were] going to make our communities a better place, *we* [had] to make it better because we're the ones that live here," said the Rev. Romie Lilly, former executive director of the Southern Area Clergy Council.

Eating and breathing in Atlanta

What are some other faith-health programs doing? Café 458 in Atlanta is a unique eatery that not only serves good meals to homeless men but offers its diners counseling, free legal services, and alcohol- and drug-recovery treatment. The café seats 50 at a time, and reservations are required.

A Seventh-day Adventist church in the heart of Atlanta recently joined with a local public health clinic to help smokers quit. Volunteers from the church adapted an eight-session "Breathe Free" curriculum. Over the last 25 years, more than 15 million people nationally have stopped smoking as a result of similar "Breathe Free" programs. Now a great many Georgians are being added to that number.

Pondering the future

Collaboration and cooperation are the keys to resolving society's most pressing problems. New methods and strategies must continually be sought. Coalitions formed by public health and faith communities are taking a major leap forward. The U.S. Constitution guarantees separation of church and state for the mutual benefit of each. The public health and faith community partnerships that are emerging do not violate that principle. Rather they build on tandem values to achieve the goal of improved health.

Former president Carter has put the concept nicely in a nutshell:

Truvail Bass

A red ribbon at the center of a stained-glass window created by Stephen Thomas of the Rollins School of Public Health at Emory University, Atlanta, Georgia, poignantly conveys its AIDS-awareness message.

> *Wouldn't it be wonderful . . . if [Baptists, Catholics, Jews, and Muslims got together] and made sure that every single child in the neighborhood was immunized . . . ? that there was no hungry person . . . ? that every person had a basic medical exam? that every woman who became pregnant would get prenatal care? that every elderly person was contacted daily? Suppose these congregations convinced parents and children to fight the presence of guns. Suppose they made a commitment to provide the kinds of alternatives needed to reduce the violence that afflicts the poorest among us. These are very exciting and very redemptive options.*

Are they possible? Carter, as well as those Americans who have been touched by the faith-health movement, believes the answer is a resounding "yes." MHA

The Global Challenge of Tuberculosis

by Donald A. Enarson, M.D.

At age 23, Betty, who grew up on a midsize Canadian farm, had seen little of life because, since age 18, she had suffered from tuberculosis and had spent more time in the hospital than out of it. Betty knew very well what tuberculosis was—an aunt and two cousins had died of it. At the outset of her disease, she was merely very tired, but then she lost her appetite and started to lose weight. At the same time, she began to have spasms of coughing and then noticed the sweats at night. Finally, she coughed blood, and she knew without question what was wrong with her. When she went to the doctor, he told her she had to enter the hospital, where she would have to lie completely still in bed for months on end in order to "chase the cure," the only hope of overcoming the disease. She was in a hospital ward with 60 other women, most of them young, where she stayed for 24 months. She watched as many of her newfound friends in the hospital declined and died, but some, like her, slowly improved and finally became well enough to go home. Twelve months after she became better, the hope that she might be one of the few who would overcome this disease was dashed when the old cough and loss of appetite returned, and she had no choice but to return to the hospital.

This living on an emotional roller coaster was characteristic of Betty's disease—denial, followed by despair, followed by hope, alternating with despair. Only the few (one in four) would find a permanent cure. But even the lucky ones' lives were overshadowed by the shameful fact that they had "weak lungs" (the word tuberculosis *was never used because of the shame associated with it). Unfortunately, Betty was not one of the lucky ones; before her 25th birthday she died.*

(text continues on page 100)

Patient in a tuberculosis hospital today, Phnom Penh, Cambodia.

Mark Henley—Impact Photos

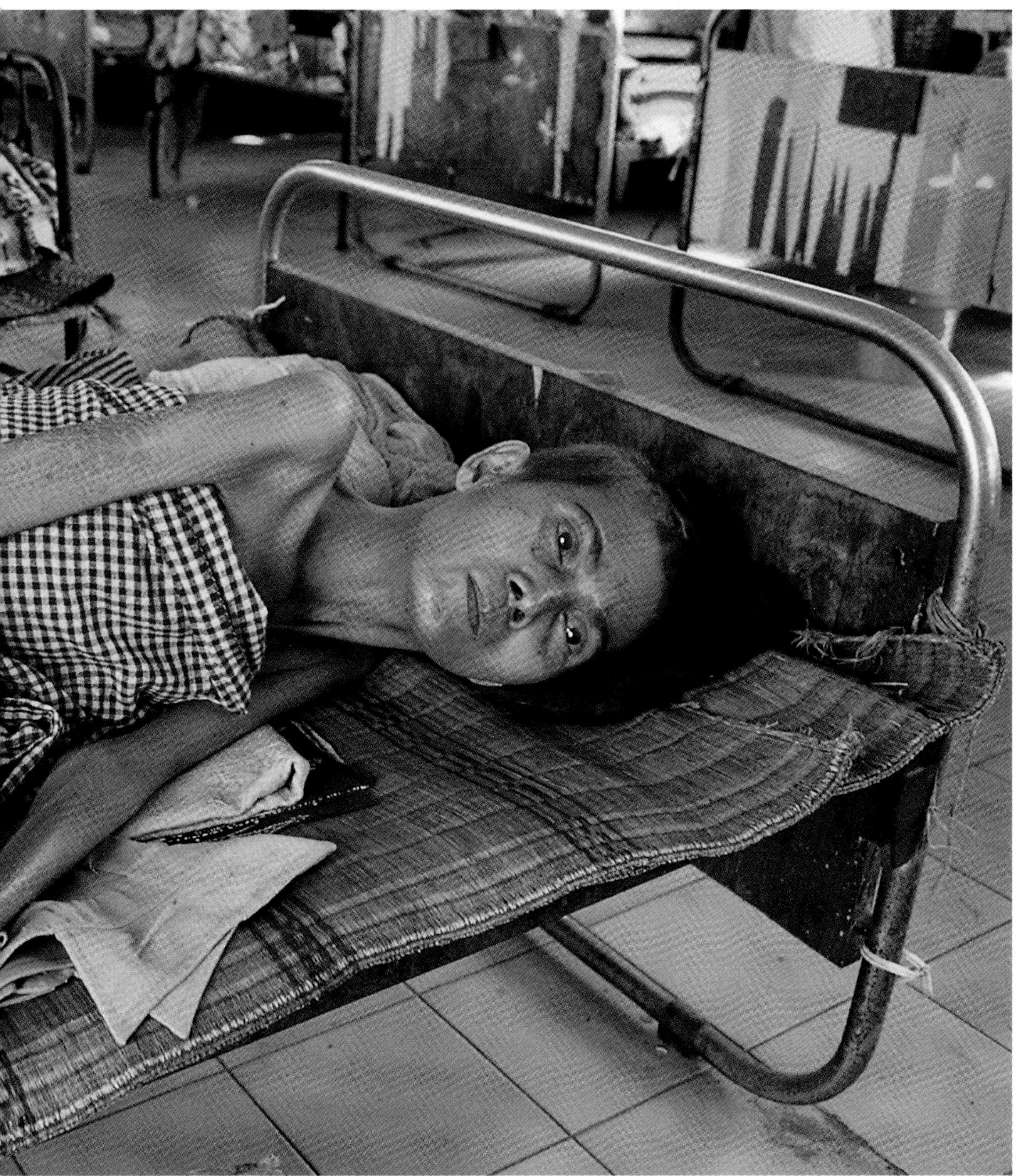

With death from consumption near, Marguerite (Greta Garbo) is reunited with her true love, Armand (Robert Taylor), in the 1937 cinematic masterpiece *Camille,* based on the novel and subsequent play by Alexandre Dumas *fils*. In the 19th and early 20th centuries, tuberculosis was often portrayed as a romantic illness that struck young people of a delicate and sensitive nature in the prime of life.

Everett Collection

The preceding true case history characterizes tuberculosis (TB) before the development of antibiotics. Betty got sick in 1931; her family was hardworking but lived a comfortable rural life. In her lifetime it was typical that every year each village or town in the industrialized world lost many of its young people in the prime of life to this cruel disease. With the miracle of antibiotics and the slow realization that TB could be permanently cured, society began to assume that the disease had more or less disappeared—that it was found only in poor communities that were unable to provide modern care.

TB's enigmatic visage

Tuberculosis is a strange disease: it is infectious but chronic; it is caused by a bacillus but also by poverty; it reflects what is currently happening and what happened decades ago; it is exogenous and yet endogenous. It would be fair to say that tuberculosis is so complex that it is a collection of conditions rather than a single one; its visage changes with different settings.

So began the summary statement following a recently held conference attended by tuberculosis experts from around the world. Those medical scientists were singularly determined to begin the work of finally eliminating the millennia-old foe TB from the face of the globe.

TB has an epidemic cycle; its prevalence in a given community slowly declines, even if nothing is done about it. Though the disease has been around for millennia, it is clear that in some communities (for example, the Inuit of the Arctic), TB was unknown until the 19th century. It is quite likely that it was introduced by Europeans during the time of the search for the Northwest Passage. Over several decades TB reached its peak incidence in the Inuit people, and only recently has it declined to fairly low levels.

The reason for the decline is the unique two-stage process of transmission, each stage of which is inefficient. Even when TB is common, most (in one study, five out of six) individuals who are exposed to the bacterium, or bacillus, that is responsible for the disease, *Mycobacterium tuberculosis,* do not become infected; even if they do become infected, most (again, five out of six) do not develop the disease but merely harbor the infection within their bodies. It

Donald A. Enarson, M.D., *is Professor of Medicine, University of Alberta, Edmonton, and Director of Scientific Activities, International Union Against Tuberculosis and Lung Disease, Paris.*

is the human immune system that prevents the bacteria from escaping the areas where they become "walled off." This fact has given medical scientists hope that the disease might eventually be eliminated from human society. When TB is very common, most new cases are in newly infected individuals. At low levels, however, most cases of illness (*i.e.,* "active" TB) arise in individuals who were infected years before and continue to carry the bacilli in their bodies; these people develop the disease when their immune systems fail to keep the bacilli contained (for example, if they develop other diseases like cancer or certain viral illnesses or if their immune systems simply become less efficient as a natural part of aging).

Not everyone who gets TB will die of it if left untreated. Indeed, over a period of five years, typically about half of those with TB die; one-quarter overcome the infection through their own immune defenses and are "cured"; the remaining quarter of patients live but remain sick and spread infection to those around them; it was this latter group that fueled the continuing epidemic in the first half of the century.

Miracle of the '40s

The development of antibiotics in the 1940s had an immediate effect; it saved the lives of those who would have died. Treatment with a combination of medications rapidly stopped TB's infectiousness in active cases; it also prevented the transmission of the bacteria to other people, which left the subsequent generation uninfected. (The first effective anti-TB medication available was streptomycin; that was followed by para-aminosalicylic acid and then by isoniazid.) In industrialized countries today, almost all the people who harbor the tubercle bacillus were born before 1940. By contrast, in less developed countries where adequate treatment has only recently become widely available, younger generations are still becoming infected.

The permanent cure of treated TB cases was further advanced in the mid-1960s by the introduction of the antibiotic rifampin into the treatment regimen. To be successful, treatment must include several drugs that are able to kill the bacteria.

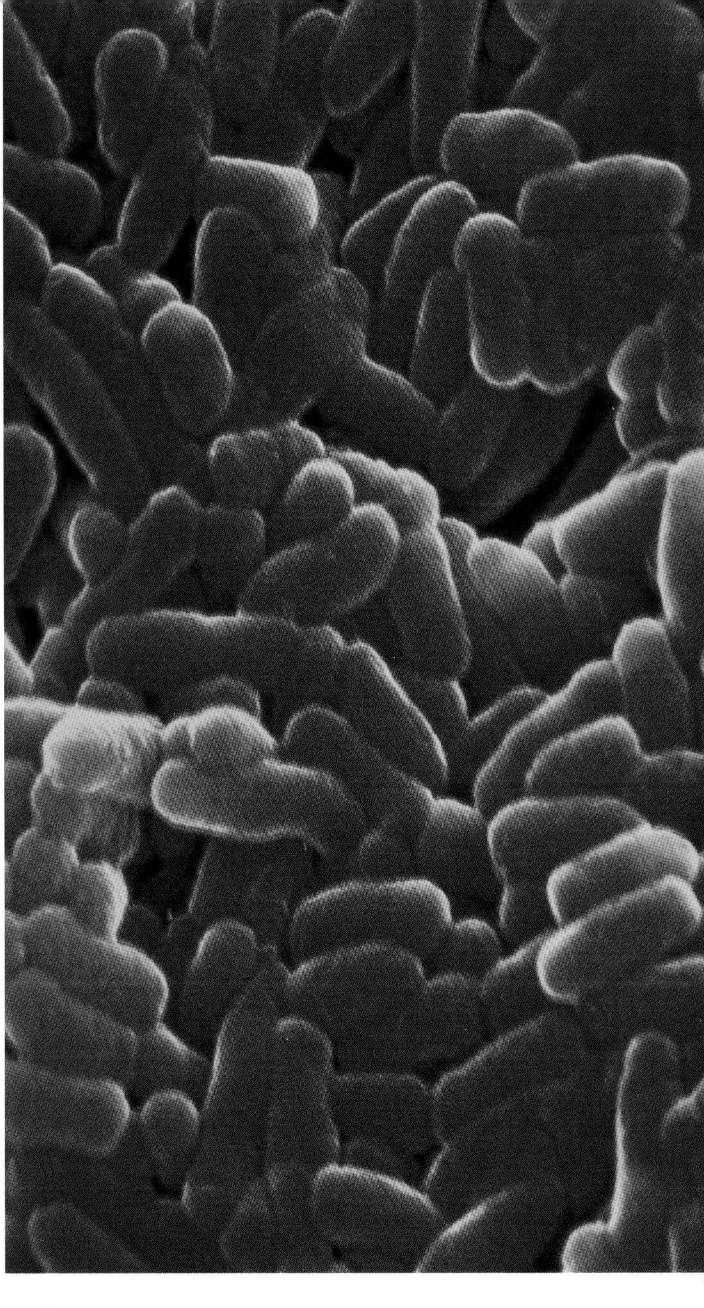

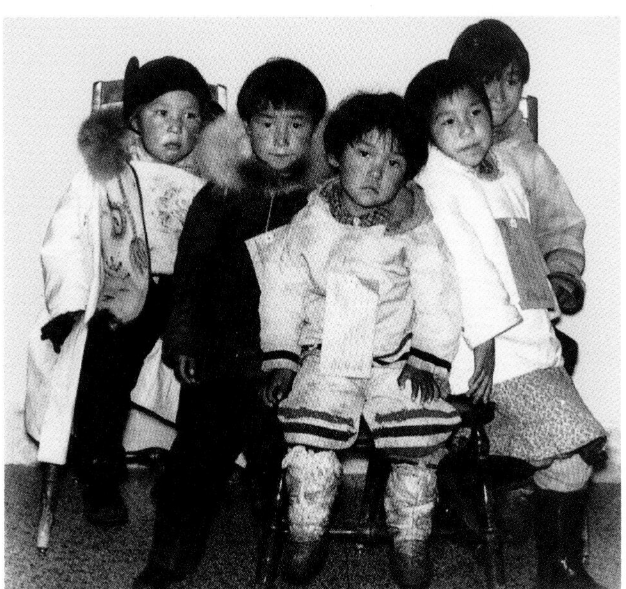

(Above) The cause of TB in humans: rodlike bacilli of *Mycobacterium tuberculosis* (magnified about 15,000 times). (Left) Inuit children at the Mountain Sanitorium, in Hamilton, Ontario, in the 1950s. Before the 19th century, TB was completely unknown in the Inuit people.

(Top) CNRI/Science Source/Photo Researchers; (bottom) Chedoke-McMaster Hospital Archives

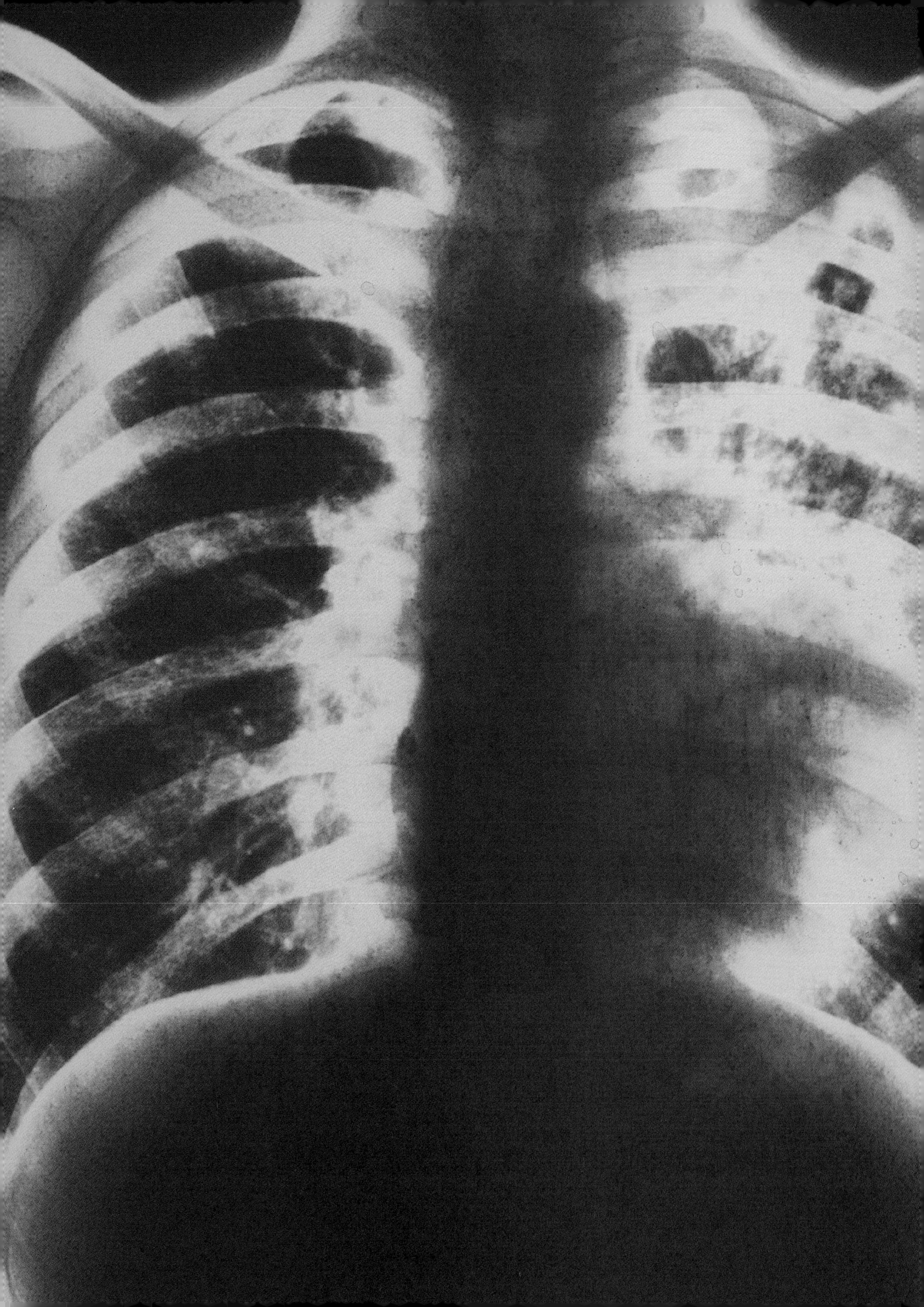

The drugs must be taken long enough to ensure that all bacteria, including those that lie dormant for long periods, are killed. A multidrug approach is crucial so that none of the small number of bacteria that may have a natural resistance to the effects of individual antibiotics are allowed to survive and multiply.

Treatment with rifampin and other drugs usually lasts for six to eight months. Antituberculous drugs taken by mouth are well absorbed in the intestines and widely distributed throughout the body. Rifampin and other anti-TB drugs work much like other antibiotics—that is, they either directly kill bacteria or prevent them from multiplying. Other drugs in the modern anti-TB regimen are ethambutol, isoniazid, pyrazinamide, and streptomycin (which must be given by intramuscular injection).

Vaccines

Vaccination with bacteria similar to those usually causing TB (bacteria taken from tuberculosis in cattle and rendered relatively harmless through laboratory techniques), called bacillus Calmette-Guérin (BCG), has been used in humans since 1921 and is currently the most widely administered vaccine in the world. Why, then, has TB not been eliminated?

BCG vaccination works primarily by preventing the spread of *M. tuberculosis* throughout the body at the time of first exposure; it has been clearly shown to prevent cases of active TB from occurring at that stage (including life-threatening disease in small children). It does not, however, reduce the number of infectious TB cases among those—mainly adults—in whom large numbers of bacteria are already present in the lungs and who are the major source of transmission in the community.

(Opposite page) Science Source/Photo Researchers; (top) Illinois Masonic Medical Center, Chicago; photograph, Cathy Melloan; (bottom) Peter Chartrand—Gamma Liaison

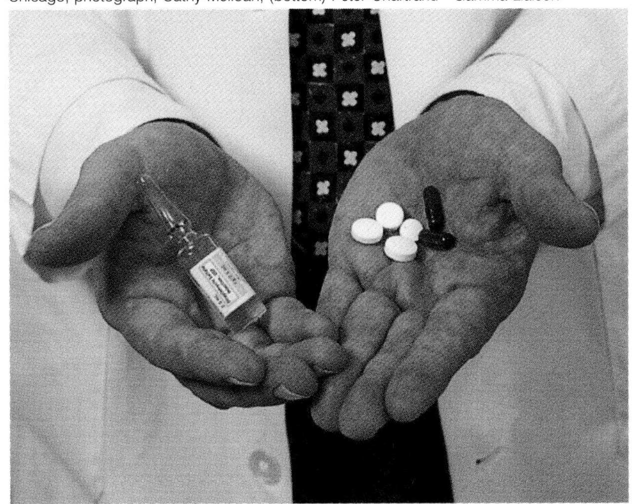

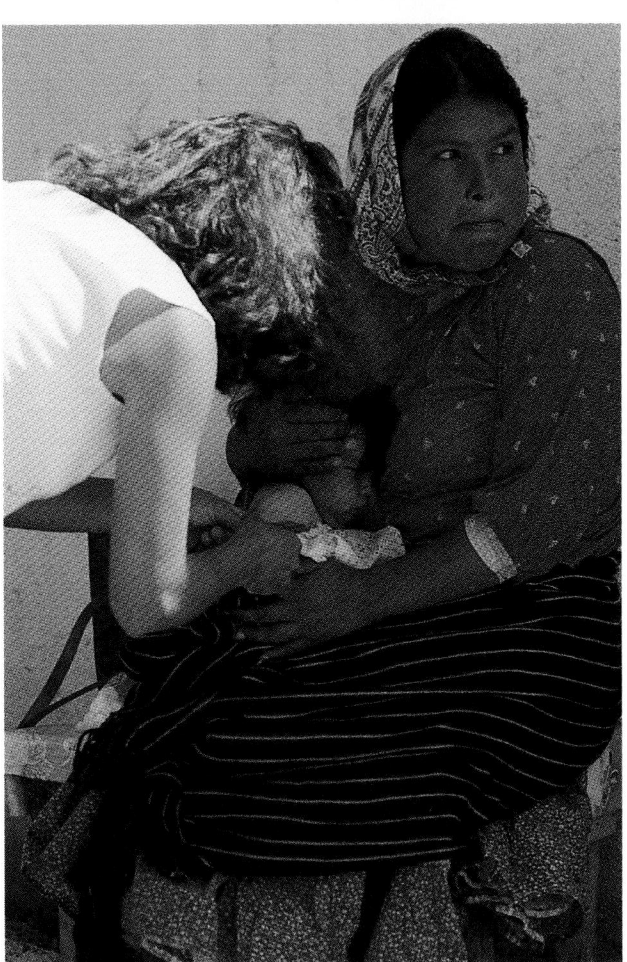

(Opposite) Chest X-ray reveals TB in a patient's left lung. (Top) Multidrug regimens are crucial in the battle against TB; rifampin, isoniazid, ethambutol, pyrazinamide, and streptomycin (in the ampoule) are among the weapons. (Above) A Mexican child is vaccinated with bacillus Calmette-Guérin (BCG). BCG prevents the spread of *M. tuberculosis* in the body at the time of first exposure and may protect children from developing life-threatening disease.

Prevention through treatment

For many diseases, prevention and cure are quite different things. This is not true for TB, where treatment of contagious individuals is the only means to prevent infection of susceptible community members. This approach to prevention, known in the medical community as a "case-management package," consists of:

- prolonged antibiotic treatment using a combination of medications
- detection of active cases (requiring laboratory examination of sputum samples obtained from patients who go of their own accord to the health service)
- well-run health services that have well-operating information and supply systems that carefully protect against the development of resistance to the strongest antibiotic drugs

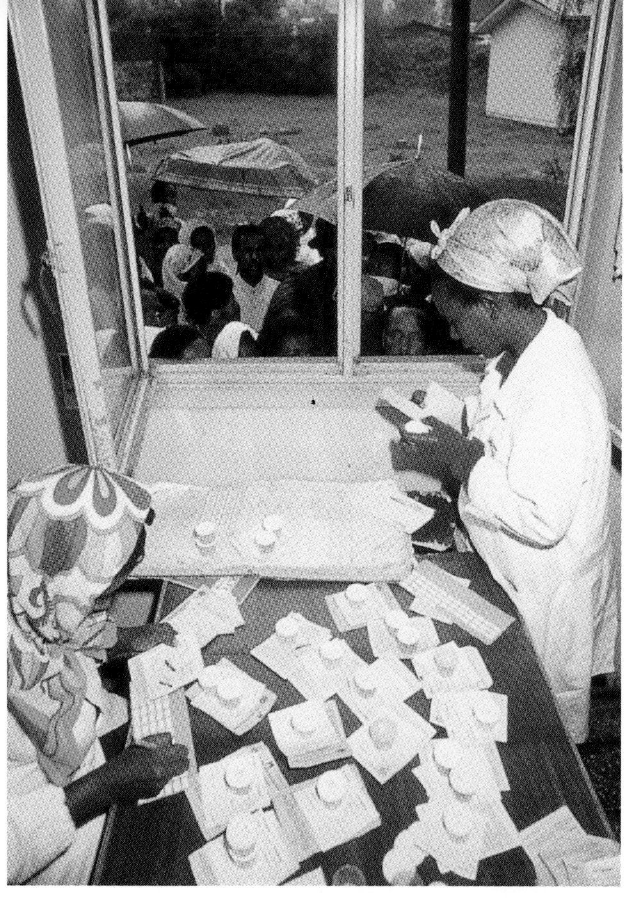

Two facets of tuberculosis control: (left) sputum samples are collected for laboratory examination at a clinic in Ethiopia; (below) in Accra, Ghana, antituberculous drugs are dispensed to an infected patient. The World Bank has found that the funding of TB-control programs in low-income countries is one of the wisest investments in global health that can be made.

- the use of directly observed therapy (*i.e.,* patients go to the health service to receive and take their multidrug regimens, or health care workers go to them)
- combined preparations and treatment based upon patients' individual susceptibility patterns

Such a multipronged approach stops the spread of *M. tuberculosis* infection in its tracks; in many industrialized countries, there is now an entire generation of the population free from TB infection.

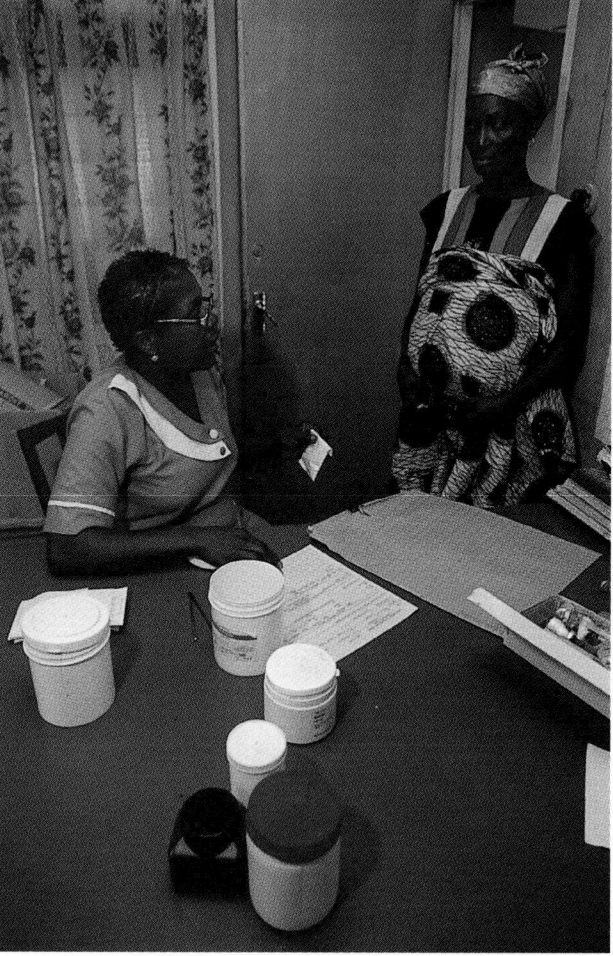

(Top) F. MacDougall—WHO; (bottom) Liba Taylor—Panos Pictures

Global emergency

Although it was possible to achieve these good results in most industrialized countries by 1970, the situation in low-income countries was quite different. By 1990 the World Health Organization (WHO) estimated that of the nearly eight million people diagnosed with TB every year (approximately three million of whom died as a result of their disease), over 90% resided in less developed nations. TB was the most common cause of death from a single organism in persons between ages 15 and 49 years worldwide. By 1980 treatment of TB had been introduced into many low-income countries, but this occurred in a haphazard manner, having the effect of actually increasing the number of infectious cases by preventing patients from dying but failing to cure them. This resulted in large numbers of chronic cases as sources of infection and "epidemics" of TB spreading in communities. In addition, the incorrect use of the antibiotics had resulted in most of these cases being resistant to the medications.

This picture began to change in 1978 when the governments of Tanzania and Switzerland invited the International Union Against Tuberculosis and Lung Disease, based in Paris, to advise them on the development of national tuberculosis programs. Collaboration resulted in a model for such programs, which was shown by a recent World Bank analysis to be among the most cost-effective of any health intervention in low-income countries—indeed, so cost-effective as to achieve results similar to

(Top) The Research Institute of Tuberculosis, Japan Anti-Tuberculosis Association; (bottom) M. Raviglione—WHO

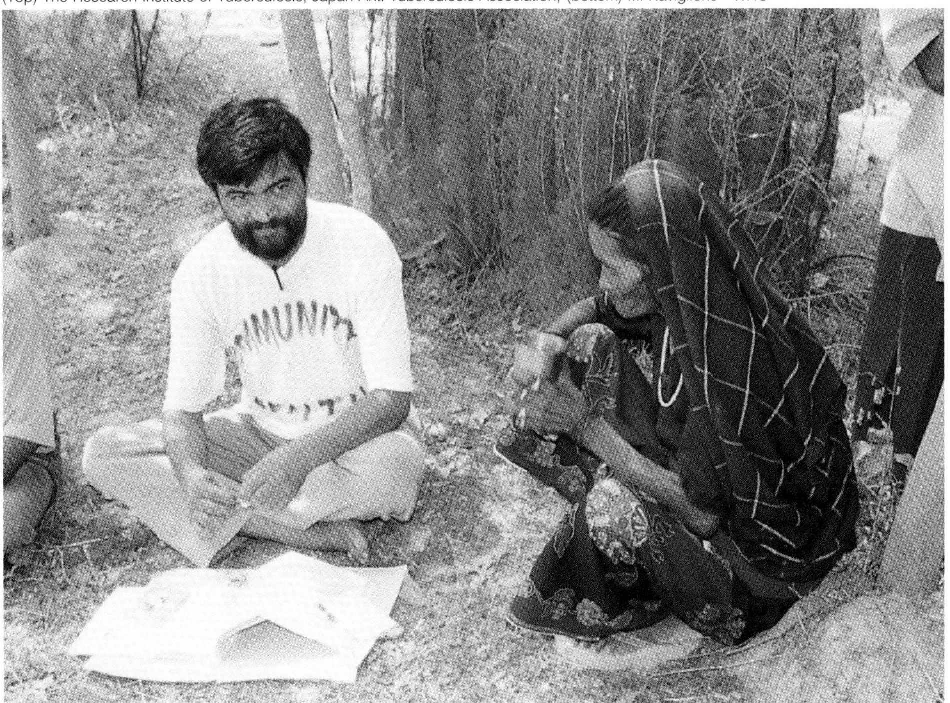

Directly observed therapy virtually ensures that patients will be cured. This dynamic approach to treatment often means that public health workers must go out in the field to find their patients. (Right) A health care worker (in T-shirt) waits to see that a woman in rural Nepal takes her full course of anti-TB drugs. (Below) A patient in a clinic in the Central Asian republic of Kyrgyzstan swallows pills that a staff member dispenses.

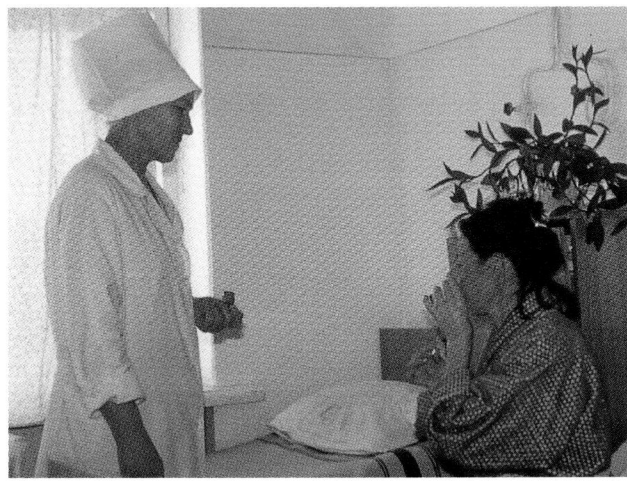

those previously seen in industrialized countries. (The World Bank's findings were summarized in the 1993 publication *Investing in Health.*) This model was adopted by WHO as the basis of its strategy in the fight against TB and implemented in a large proportion of less developed countries—most notably in Africa and Central and South America. Subsequently, such model programs were extended to a large number of low-income areas of China and India, where perhaps the largest portion of TB-infected individuals live today. Still, in 1993 WHO declared TB to be a "global emergency" that only the most concerted vigilance could surmount, and in 1996 the organization reaffirmed that gloomy outlook, noting that more people died of TB in 1995 than in any other year in history!

Deficiencies in the treatment process

The use of antibiotics as a basis for prevention is ultimately limited in its application. The development of drug resistance compromises the care of patients and is virtually always caused by the incorrect use of antibiotics—usually resulting from an error on the part of the physician caring for the patient or as the result of a badly run program that administers the drugs improperly to TB patients. Only a small number of existing medications—those mentioned above—are effective against *M. tuberculosis,* and there does not appear to be any likely prospect that this will change within the next few years.

As previously noted, poor management of treatment programs has actually increased the number of resistant, infectious cases in the community today. What does this mean for the future? Clearly, the current situation is alarming; new infections will develop, resulting in disease with bacteria that do not respond to available antibiotics. The need to continue efficient application of the interventions over a number of decades—that is, for the remaining lifetime of the last generation heavily infected with TB bacteria—represents a huge challenge. This is particularly true as TB becomes increasingly a disease of segments of the population who lack access to proper TB care or who do not participate in services provided for the mainstream of the population, either because of their poverty or for other reasons such as homelessness, mental illness, or drug addiction. The possibility that TB will break out of such restricted circles and once again affect the whole population (particularly in the face of adverse socioeconomic conditions) is not so remote; in fact, this proclivity has been characteristic of this menacing illness's history.

Is an end in sight?

In spite of its long history, there is little doubt that it is theoretically possible to eliminate tuberculosis from the world. Great strides in this direction have already been made by means of the strategy described above. Without doubt, if this effort could be maintained for the lifetime of those born before antibiotics were introduced and who harbor the TB bacteria, the current world community could be free of the disease. With the potential for transmission of the bacteria halted within this group, in the future TB could be introduced only from outside. This is likely to occur in some remote and isolated societies. Most societies today, however, are not isolated; the entire globe and its people are becoming increasingly accessible. Already, in many countries (such as Switzerland and Canada), more than half of all TB cases are among persons who were born in another country, acquired the infection there, and then settled in the new country and eventually developed their disease. For this reason, there cannot be a TB-control strategy focused on isolated areas. There must be a global approach.

What are the roadblocks that will be encountered on the way to this goal? There are several. Certainly, the already-noted resistance of the bacteria to the medications and the concentration of TB in marginalized and inaccessible subgroups of society will toughen the course. Governments and official agencies also constitute an obstacle because of the decline in priority that they have accorded the disease. Even in the United States, funds set aside by the government to combat the disease are drying up. This is in spite of the alarm engendered by the recent and dramatic resurgence of TB, along with the emergence of resistant forms of the disease.

There must be continual reminders of the need for a vigilant global strategy. Such a reminder came Sept. 14–15, 1995, in Washington, D.C., where the British journal *The Lancet* sponsored an international conference, "The Challenge of Tubercu-

A clinic near Calcutta offers TB checkups. India's TB death rates are among the world's highest, yet little effort has been made to control the disease.

Robert Nickelsberg—Gamma Liaison

losis," which was attended by leading TB specialists from around the world. The final statement from the conference outlined a "research and policy agenda that we hope will be seen as a benchmark by which to judge future developments in tuberculosis prevention and control," noted Richard Horton, *The Lancet*'s editor and an organizer of the meeting. Despite the four impediments that stand in the way of progress: (1) national governments, (2) science policy makers, (3) the market, and (4) national health infrastructures, Horton emphasized that "still, there are reasons to be cautiously optimistic."

In addition to the commitment required for finishing the job at hand—global control through careful case management—the development of new tools will be necessary to deal with the limitations inherent in the case-management approach to the elimination of TB. In a perfect world, one of the most useful tools to prevent the development of infectious TB would be an effective vaccine. A second useful tool to hasten the elimination of the disease would be an easy-to-administer, reliable test that could identify which persons among those already infected were most likely to develop disease. This would make preventive chemotherapy with isoniazid or another drug a feasible intervention at the community level. The best way to identify infected persons in the community (inactive cases) is still tuberculin skin testing using the so-called Mantoux method. In the November–December 1995 issue of *Public Health Reports,* investigators from the Bureau of Tuberculosis Control of the New York State Department of Health pointed out, "In this age of high technology diagnostic techniques and sophisticated laboratory analysis, the basic test to determine the TB infection status of any person has not changed substantially in the last century." They emphasized that the skin test is a "tool" only, "but it is not diagnostic." A third tool that would enhance efforts at elimination would be the development of new, more powerful antituberculous drugs that would destroy *M. tuberculosis,* even if given for a very short duration (say, 6 to 10 days, instead of 6 to 8 months).

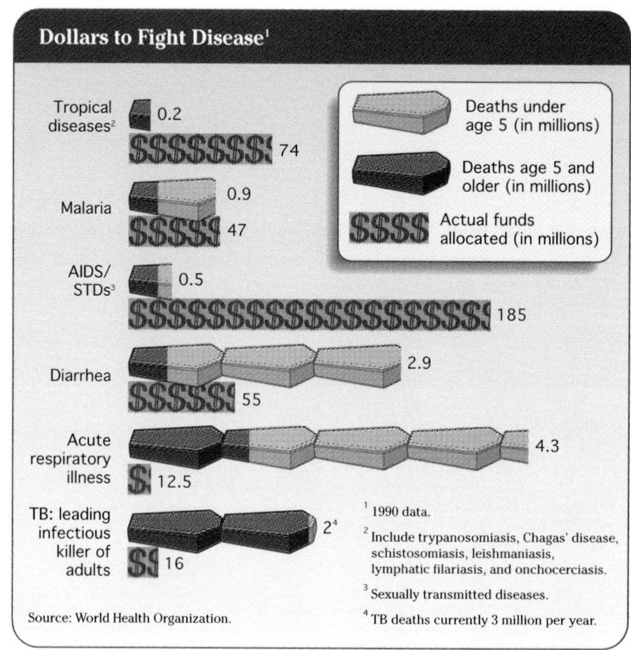

The future: foolish to ponder?

It is often said that only a fool would try to predict the future. On the other hand, the global human community needs to consider the possibilities if it is to move forward in a logical manner. Future trends will reflect a number of separate factors. It is already clear that over the past five decades the rate of TB cases has declined; this has been documented in all major regions of the world. This is partly due to the natural tendency of the disease to decline, coupled with the impact of efficiently implemented case management in areas such as North America, northern Europe, and the northern countries of the Far East, where TB reached its highest levels in the pre-antibiotic era. However, if TB is to decline in absolute numbers as well as in rates, it will be necessary to maintain the decline at a higher rate than the one at which the population is growing. This is especially true in less developed countries, where the majority of infected individuals reside and where the rate of population growth is also greatest. (WHO predicts 10.2 million TB cases in the year 2000 and as many as 3.5 million deaths annually during the current decade.)

The second important future factor that will affect TB is economic. It goes without saying that the presence of TB is one of the most sensitive indicators of poverty, so much so that it could be considered the "shadow" of economic deprivation. The worrisome decline in social conditions affecting the poor has gone hand in hand with a shocking decline in health services for the world's poorest people, which can only ensure TB's spread.

Along with these general trends, in certain areas of the world the spread of HIV infection has led to frightening rises in TB cases. This has been most evident so far in countries in central Africa, where each year TB

Impoverished living conditions and inadequate prevention measures in Phnom Pehn are contributing to a surge of new active TB cases in Cambodia.

Giovanni Diffidenti—FSP/Gamma Liaison

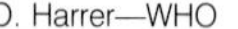

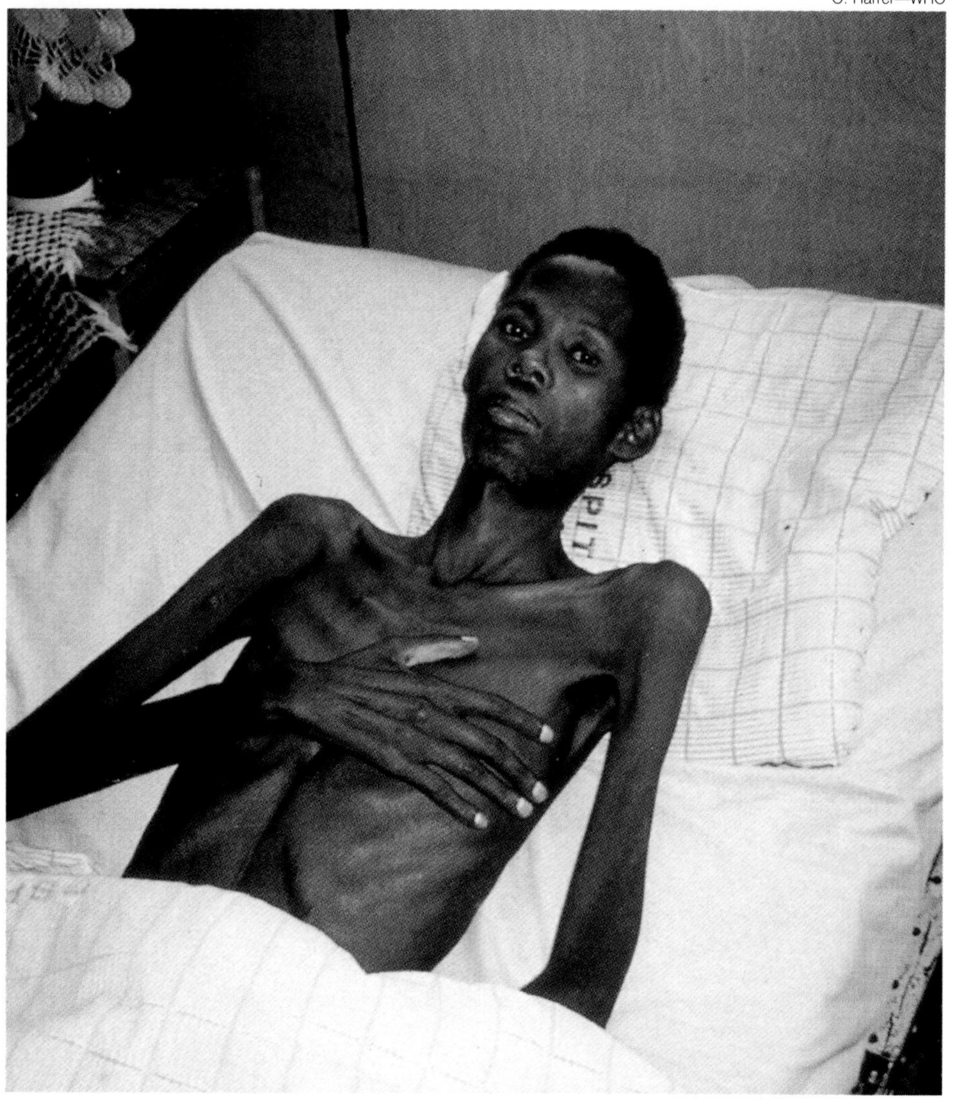

An AIDS patient with TB in Tanzanía. The rapid spread of HIV infection in Africa and many other parts of the world has led to an alarming rise in TB incidence.

kills a vast number of people in the general, heterosexual population. The same trend is expected to become obvious in the near future on the Indian subcontinent and in some countries of Southeast Asia, most notably Thailand. This HIV/AIDS–TB trend will clearly contribute to a TB resurgence. Current WHO predictions, however, suggest that at the beginning of the next century, the great majority of active TB will not be the result of coinfection with HIV.

Finally, the world is beginning to see the effects of poor medical management in the form of many drug-resistant TB cases. This is true in major metropolitan areas in North America. It is also true in many less developed countries in many parts of the world.

Consider Ahmed, a 35-year-old merchant from The Sudan, who became ill in 1990—first feeling tired and having a cough, then experiencing fever and weight loss, and finally, after six weeks, coughing up blood. As a result of these symptoms, he went to a local chest clinic, where he was diagnosed as having TB and given treatment that was to be taken for 12 months. Though he took the drugs irregularly, at the end of his treatment his symptoms had subsided. After several months of improvement, however, they returned. Because he had the financial resources, he decided to go to Saudi Arabia for treatment. There he was given a new and likely more appropriate combination of medications with instructions to take the drugs daily for six months. After completion of the treatment, his symptoms returned as they had before. Once again, he sought help at the chest clinic where he had been treated originally; his continuing TB was documented by laboratory tests, and he was given the most powerful form of treatment available at that time—isoniazid, rifampin, pyrazinamide, and ethambutol—but by then he had developed resistance to all of these medications. Once again, the story repeated itself.

Seven years after he originally became sick, Ahmed sought the advice of this author at a TB program based in a large hospital in the capital of The Sudan, Khartoum. I questioned him about his previous treatment and how he had taken his medications. "Did you need to go to the clinic every day to receive the medication?" I asked. "No," he answered. "I took all the pills at home." I questioned him further: "Did you take your medications regularly, and did you always take them as the doctor advised?" "No," he replied, "I sometimes missed taking them, and occasionally I took some of them and not others."

WHO/Ministry of Health, Peru

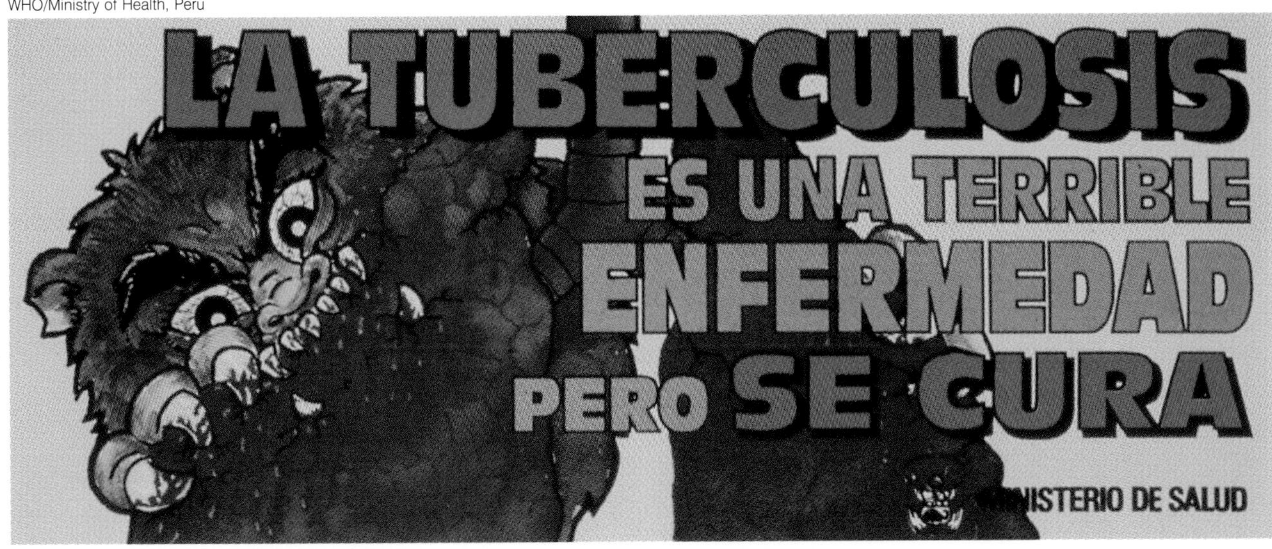

Public health posters from Peru proclaim that tuberculosis is terrible but that it is also curable.

Ahmed's story is typical of those of patients who have mid-level incomes and therefore access to treatment in the private sector. Unfortunately, such treatment tends not to be standardized, especially when it comes to TB. The fact that Ahmed had not taken his drugs regularly and correctly has now converted his disease into a condition that has virtually no chance of being cured. Furthermore, it will be a prolonged illness, putting his young wife and four children at risk. They are almost sure to become infected and may themselves develop active, debilitating, and possibly drug-resistant TB.

What is the lesson of Ahmed's case? Medical science, in essence, has "progressed" to the point where a dreaded infectious disease is, once again, without cure, much as it was before 1940!

Collaborative programs of the International Union Against Tuberculosis and Lung Disease have demonstrated over the past decade that tuberculosis can be controlled even in the midst of poverty, war, and HIV. It has also been shown that international collaboration is required for the implementation of successful programs. The World Bank has proclaimed that funds directed to the global anti-TB effort are funds wisely invested. These are the facts; it remains to be seen if the global community has the wisdom to pursue its goal vigorously and finally rid humanity of this ancient foe. MHA

Culver Pictures

TB in the U.S.
The Cost of Complacency

by Lee B. Reichman, M.D., M.P.H.

Allan Tannenbaum—Sygma

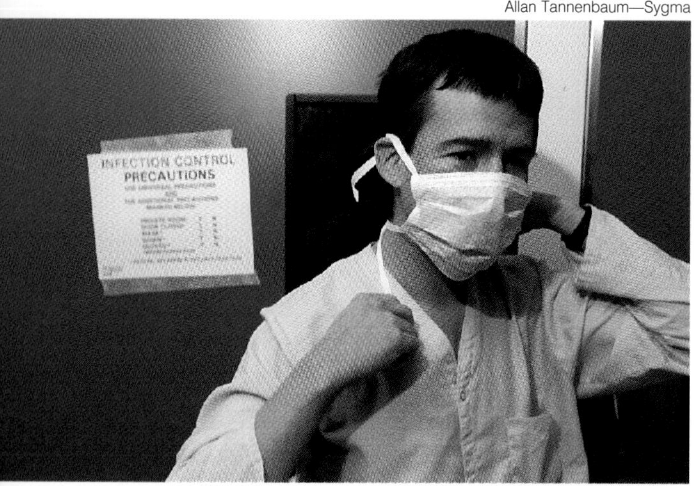

An upsurge in TB incidence in the late 1980s reflected a lapse in previously successful efforts to control the disease.

Public health is purchasable. Any community can determine its own death rate.
—Hermann M. Biggs, general medical officer of the New York City Department of Health in the 1890s

Tuberculosis (TB) is a disease with a long history, having been recognized for more than 5,000 years. Although the illness is fully treatable and preventable today, the World Health Organization estimates that one-third of the world's population is infected—about 1.9 billion people. TB is the leading cause of adult deaths from a single infectious organism, taking some three million lives per year.

The fact that a well-recognized treatable and preventable disease continues to exact such an enormous toll should be a matter of profound embarrassment to public health authorities and policy makers around the globe. Even more embarrassing is the recent resurgence of TB in the United States after several decades of successful control. In 1984, 22,201 new TB cases were recorded in the U.S., the lowest number since reporting was initiated in 1953. Yet by 1992, the number had jumped to 26,673.

Understanding the "curve of concern"

Although the U.S. incidence of TB rose steadily every year after 1984, it was not until seven years later that resources that had been diverted to other programs were finally restored to tuberculosis control. The renewed effort produced a dramatic reversal in TB rates, which, in turn, has led to a call to scale back TB-control efforts. This sequence of events exemplifies the frustrating but predictable phenomenon that this author calls the "U-shaped curve of concern": as soon as a public health emergency has been alleviated, policy makers repeal the relief measures and thus ensure a recurrence of the crisis within a few years.

In 1995, with 22,812 reported cases, the U.S. achieved its third consecutive year of reduction in TB cases. The reason for the decrease is apparent: an unprecedented appropriation of attention and funds, which enabled a reestablishment of the public health infrastructure that had functioned so effectively to control and prevent TB in the 1960s. Similarly, the chief factor underlying the un-

TB over Time

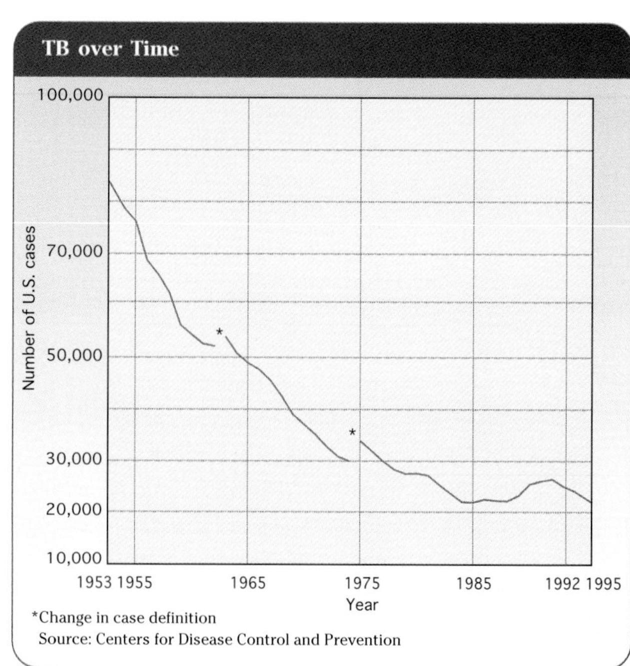

*Change in case definition
Source: Centers for Disease Control and Prevention

Lee B. Reichman, M.D., M.P.H., *is Professor of Medicine, Department of Medicine and Community Health, University of Medicine and Dentistry of New Jersey–New Jersey Medical School, and Executive Director, National Tuberculosis Center, Newark.*

(Overleaf) Tuberculosis sanatorium, Saranac Lake, New York, c. 1870

Brown Brothers

To prevent the introduction of new TB cases into the U.S. at the turn of the century, infected immigrants were turned away from Ellis Island, New York.

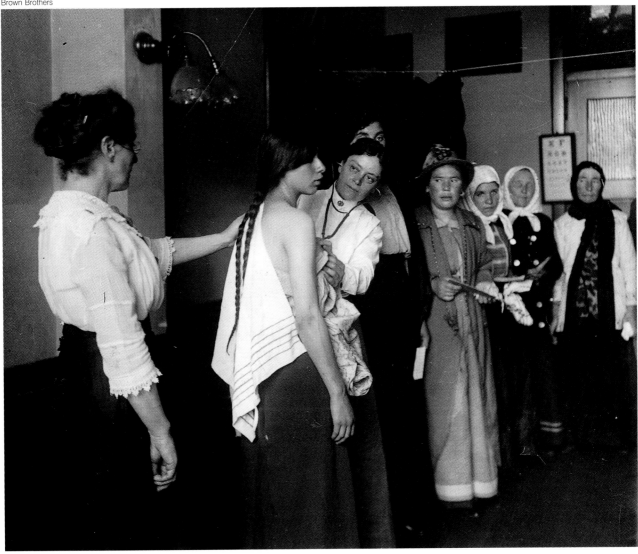

precedented resurgence of the disease during the 1980s and early 1990s is equally obvious: the erosion of many state-level TB-control programs under block-grant funding in the 1970s.

 look back

In order to fully understand the developments of the 1980s and '90s, it is necessary to know something of the history of the anti-TB effort. When the U.S. initiated its organized war against TB in the late 1880s, the disease was the leading cause of death in Americans. The germ theory of disease was a recent discovery, but even though the tubercle bacillus, the organism that causes TB, had been identified and its mode of transmission was understood, no cure was known.

The strategy at that time was to isolate TB patients in sanatoriums, a measure that at least halted the spread of the disease. Some recovered at the sanatorium, but many died. Health departments in large cities launched intensive efforts to identify all those infected with TB, and laws were passed to prevent immigrants with symptoms of the disease from entering the country.

During the first half of the 20th century, TB remained the number one cause of death in the U.S. The National Association for the Study and Prevention of Tuberculosis, established in 1904 and later renamed the American Lung Association, was the first national voluntary health agency dedicated to fighting a single disease and the first to combine the efforts of physicians and laypeople. The organization launched the Christmas Seal campaign to raise money for TB programs. Prevention and control of TB, prior to the advent of specific anti-

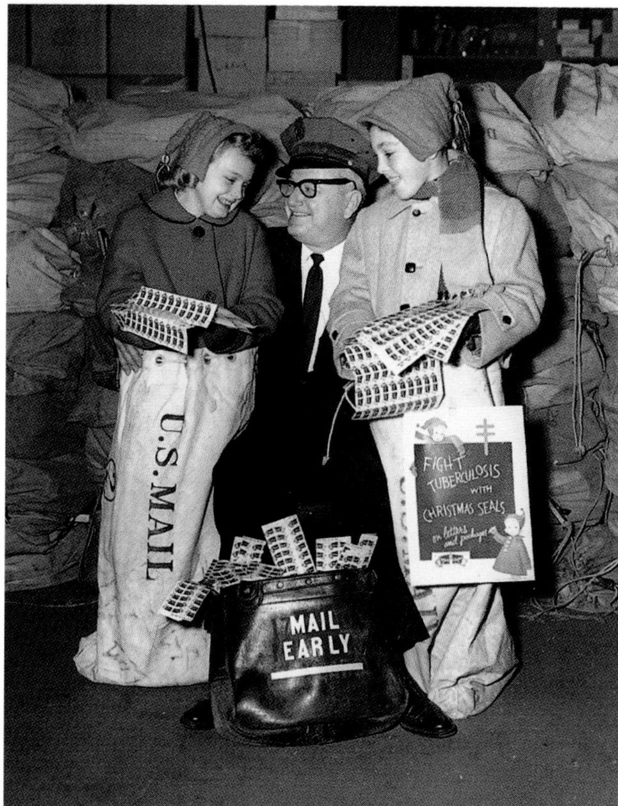

Photographs, American Lung Association of Metropolitan Chicago

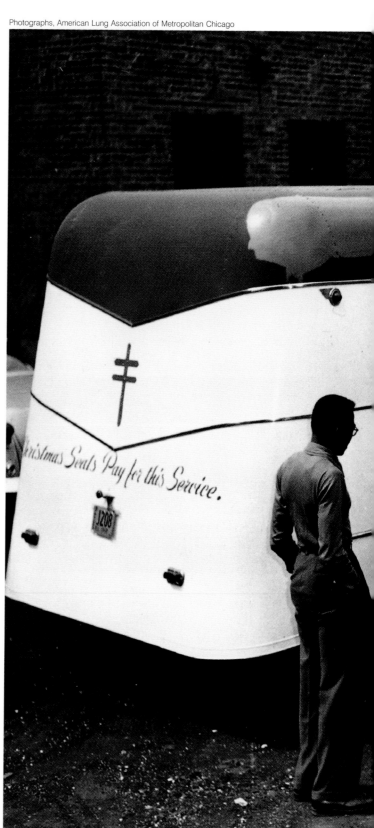

During the 1940s and '50s, both public and private resources were mobilized against TB. (Above) The Christmas Seal campaign, launched by the American Lung Association, raised money and consciousness. (Right) Free chest X-rays helped identify those in the community who were infected.

TB drugs in the late 1940s, consisted largely of education, consciousness-raising, and the removal of thousands of persons with infectious disease to thousands of sanatoriums in communities throughout the country. The only "treatment" for TB was bed rest and fresh air.

In 1944 Congress established the Division of Tuberculosis Control within the Public Health Service to screen all Americans for the illness. The public was urged to take advantage of mobile units offering free chest X-rays at convenient locations; all children who attended public schools were screened for the disease at school.

The first drug capable of destroying the tubercle bacillus, the antibiotic streptomycin, was introduced in 1946. For the first time, then, tuberculosis was a curable illness.

Targeting TB for extinction

At the Arden House Conference, a historic public health meeting convened in New York state in 1959, a panel of leading U.S. medical experts recommended that the nation focus its efforts on community-based outpatient treatment, an approach made possible by the availability of effective drug therapy. The sanatori-

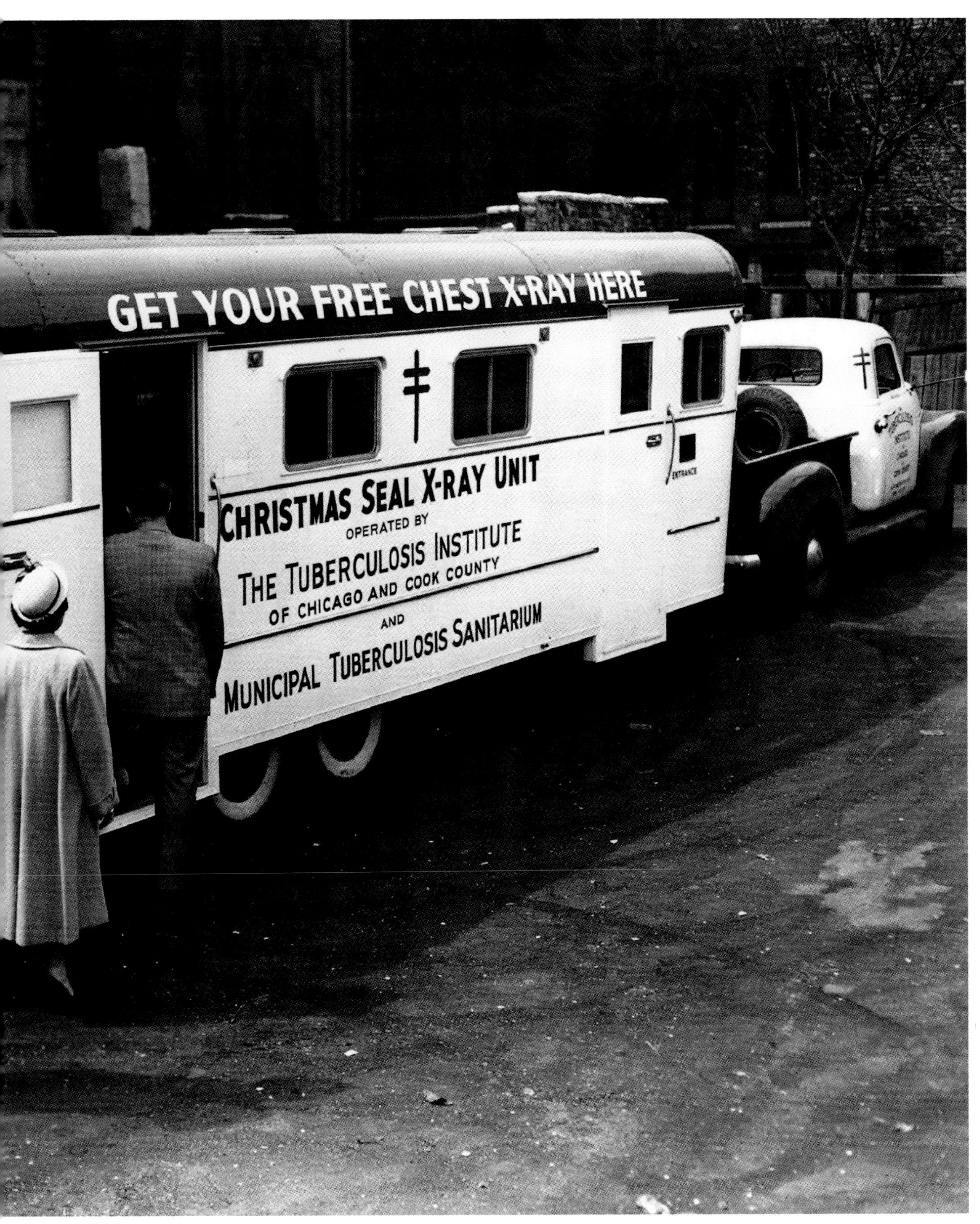
GET YOUR FREE CHEST X-RAY HERE
CHRISTMAS SEAL X-RAY UNIT
OPERATED BY
THE TUBERCULOSIS INSTITUTE
OF CHICAGO AND COOK COUNTY
AND
MUNICIPAL TUBERCULOSIS SANITARIUM

ums were phased out, and outpatient clinics were established to provide the bulk of care for TB patients following a brief initial hospitalization.

To help state health officials cope with the logistic and financial demands of implementing this new strategy, the federal government instituted "targeted" TB project grants. These grants provided moneys to be devoted solely to the efforts that are a necessary part of any successful offensive against TB. These include:

- educating health professionals about appropriate diagnostic tests
- educating the public to recognize the symptoms of TB
- providing free or low-cost screening for persons at risk
- sending health workers into the community to identify those who are ill and notify contacts to whom they may have transmitted the disease
- providing affordable anti-TB drugs
- monitoring the progress of each patient's treatment
- initiating legal measures to confine infected individuals who refuse treatment

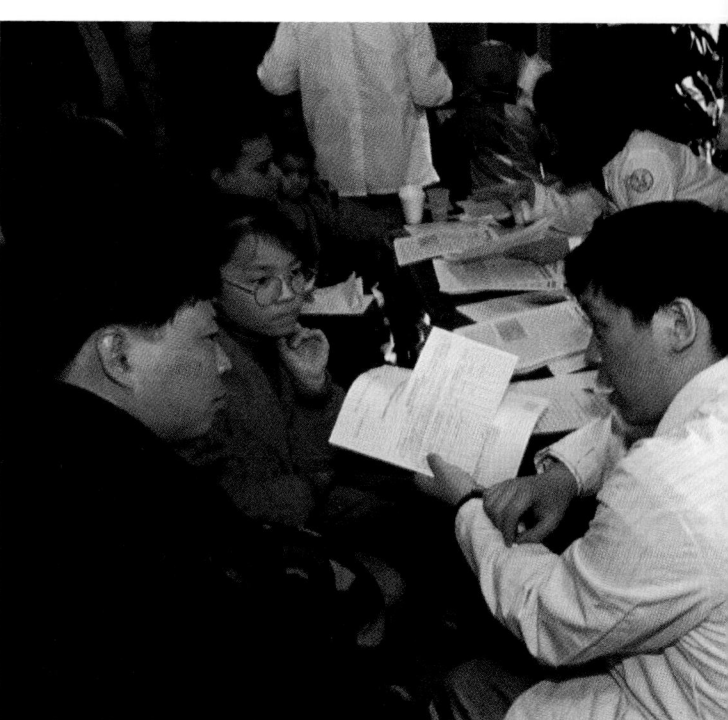

(Top) Jon Levy—Gamma Liaison; (bottom) Mark Ludak—Impact Visuals

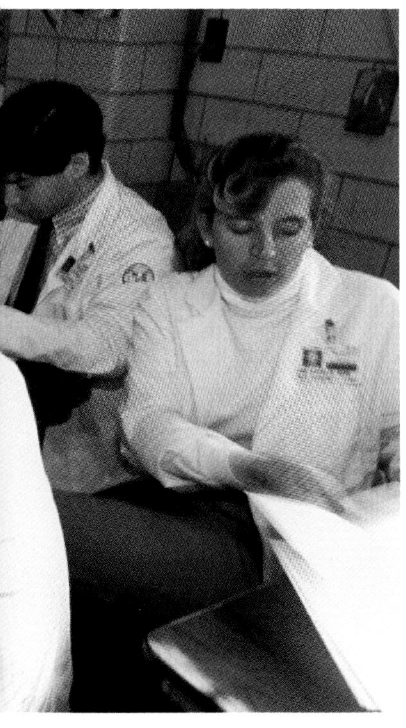

Low-income populations, the medically underserved, and immigrants from countries where TB is prevalent are at greater-than-average risk of infection. (Above) In 1993, in response to the resurgence of the disease in New York City, free TB testing is offered to residents of a lower Manhattan housing project. (Left) As part of the effort to halt the spread of TB in San Francisco, a city health worker goes into the community to identify and counsel those who are ill.

- maintaining laboratories that watch for the development of drug-resistant TB strains
- searching for faster diagnostic tests and better drugs

Under targeted funding, each jurisdiction receiving federal grants for TB control is required to spend the money for that purpose. The TB allocations may not be diverted to other programs—even to other public health programs.

Targeted funding was in operation from 1961 through 1969. After 1970, however, it was gradually replaced with block grants to the states, nontargeted appropriations that gave state and local authorities wide discretion in spending. It was then that some two decades of progress toward controlling TB ground to a halt.

Unheeded warning

In April 1972, at a hearing before the House Subcommittee on Public Health and Environment, several physicians on the front line in the war against TB predicted dire consequences if block grants supplanted targeted funding. One of these experts cautioned that there would surely be a reversal in the downward trends of TB incidence. Another predicted that "this funding error" would inevitably be recognized as a mistake but too late and "with a loss of all that has been gained to this point in time."

However prescient, these warnings fell on deaf ears. Congress enacted block grants, and states had the freedom to act as they saw fit, even if that involved curtailing or dismantling their own TB education and control programs. With each passing year, the impact of the block-grant approach on TB control became more apparent. By 1982 the rate of decline in new TB cases had slowed perceptibly.

A dire prediction fulfilled

By the end of 1984, just as had been anticipated, the U.S. incidence of TB had actually begun to rise, marking the start of a resurgence unparalleled in any other industrialized nation in modern times. From 1985 to 1992, new TB cases rose almost 20% nationwide. Among children under 15, new cases increased 35%.

Certain populations and geographic areas became focal points of the epidemic. Localized outbreaks occurred among prison inmates, migrant workers, and hospital patients. Transmission from patients to health care workers was documented.

Cities, with their dense populations, were harder hit than rural and suburban areas. New York City experienced a 30% increase in the TB rate from 1988 to 1992. About 60% of the country's cases of multidrug-resistant TB were reported among New Yorkers. In the Harlem neighborhood the TB case rate of more than 200 per 100,000 people was higher than that in many less developed countries.

Contributing to the weakened condition of state and local health departments in general, and of TB-control programs in particular, were a variety of social circumstances, including:

- the emergence of HIV, which accelerates the course of TB
- the rise in substance abuse, another independent risk factor for TB
- the increase in homelessness, which results in increased efficiency of TB transmission
- the surge in immigration from parts of the world with a high prevalence of TB

But while the AIDS epidemic and other events of the 1980s played a part in TB's comeback, they did not cause it. TB is a preventable and treatable disease, even in immunocompromised individuals or in people like the homeless, who lack access to regular medical care. Had the public health infrastructure established in the 1960s been left in place and supported to an appropriate level, the resurgence of the 1980s would not have occurred.

The next challenge

The emergence of strains of TB that are resistant to most or all of the standard anti-

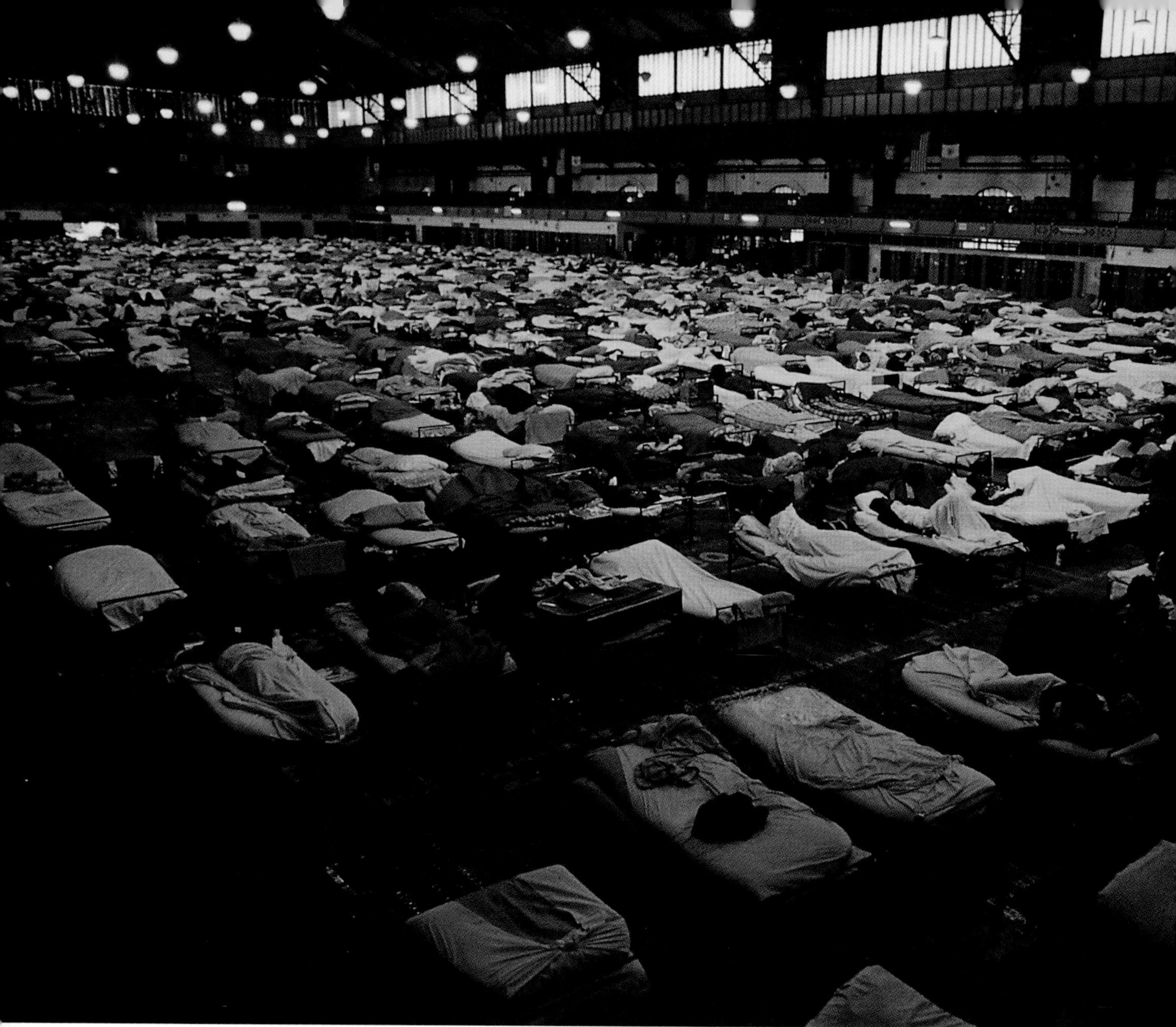

TB drugs is another health threat whose origin can be traced to the dismantling of proven, effective TB-control programs. Studies have demonstrated conclusively that improper use of anti-TB drugs promotes the development of multidrug-resistant TB strains. Improper drug use, in turn, can usually be attributed to lack of education—of caregivers as well as patients—and inadequate monitoring of treatment.

Patients who are not well informed or closely supervised may fail to take their medication regularly. Or, upon experiencing an improvement in symptoms, they may simply stop taking the drugs. When treatment is erratic or incomplete, the underlying infection persists. Some TB-causing organisms are killed, but those that are resistant to the medications survive and multiply unchecked, producing a new population of drug-resistant microbes.

The problem of compliance—that is, adherence to a treatment regimen—is compounded in TB by the fact that the therapy typically involves the concurrent use of two or more drugs and must be followed for at least six months. (At one time the course of therapy was as long as two years.)

Improper prescribing contributes to inappropriate drug treatment and thus to the development of drug resistance. As the incidence of TB declined in the U.S., the medical establishment came to view it as a disease to be consigned to the history books. Most physicians trained in the 1970s and '80s had little experience in diagnosing and treating TB and were unfamiliar with basic principles of TB prevention. When the U.S. Centers for Disease Control and Prevention (CDC) conducted a survey of physicians in 1993 to determine their knowledge of TB treatment and diagnosis, two-thirds of those questioned misinterpreted the results of the tuberculin skin test (a common tool for di-

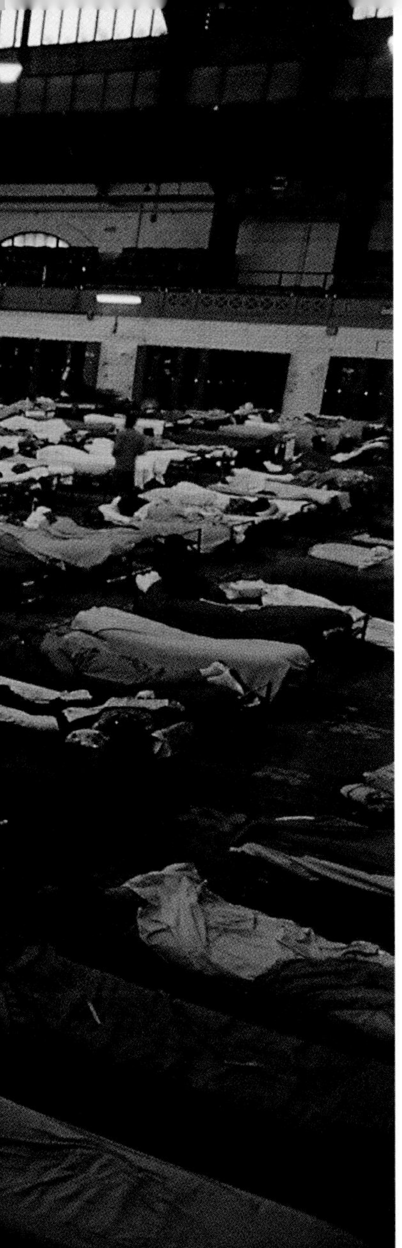

Social factors have contributed to TB's U.S. comeback. (Left) The homeless seek refuge in crowded urban shelters. (Below) The number of immigrants from Asia and other regions where the disease is still common has grown. (Bottom) A rise in substance abuse has coincided with the rapid spread of HIV.

(Left) Jon Levy—Gamma Liaison; (right and above) Mark Peterson—Saba

agnosing TB); asked how they would treat a case of TB, more than 40% failed to choose a treatment plan that accorded with published guidelines.

Ensuring that physicians know how to diagnose and treat TB depends on education. Ensuring patient compliance requires resources—personnel, educational materials, and, of course, funds. In the 1960s the New York City Department of Health employed lay investigators who helped public health nurses contact noncompliant patients by phone or, if necessary, sought them out in person. Although expensive, such intensive measures are extremely cost-effective in the long run.

Renewed commitment

As mentioned above, in 1990–91, after many years of pressure from the public health community, and confronted with a continuing rise in new TB cases, the fed-

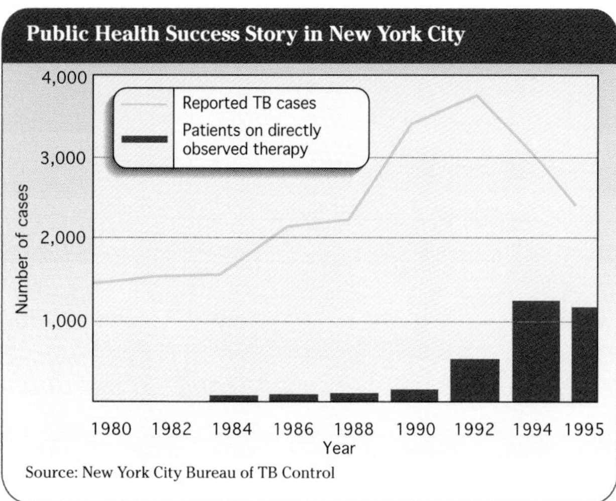

Source: New York City Bureau of TB Control

eral government put an end to block grants and restored targeted funding for TB control. The CDC and leading public health authorities credit the progress against TB in the U.S. since 1993 to the renewed commitment to targeted funding. This positive impact of dollars on disease is ample validation for the unprecedented expenditure of resources. In New York City, where $40 million has been spent for TB programs, TB incidence has declined steadily and substantially since 1993, an accomplishment considered by many as one of the great public health successes of the 20th century.

The restoration of targeted funding has allowed state and city health departments to adopt the procedure known as directly observed therapy (DOT) as the standard of care in the U.S. With DOT, health workers actually observe patients taking each and every dose of their medication. The objective is to ensure that patients complete a full treatment regimen. DOT may be carried out in a variety of settings—some patients may report to a clinic, some may receive treatment at a drug rehabilitation center, and others may be visited by an outreach worker at home, school, or work, or even in a parking lot or on a street corner. Successful programs, like the one in operation for many years in Baltimore, Maryland, may

(Below) A physician examines a man with drug-resistant TB who is also HIV-positive. In 1990–91 the growing threat of multidrug-resistant disease prompted renewed commitment to TB control, including intensive efforts to ensure that all patients complete their treatment. One of the most effective strategies is directly observed therapy, or DOT. (Right) Outreach workers from the New Jersey Medical School National Tuberculosis Center spend their days in Newark and its surrounding communities making sure that patients take their medications.

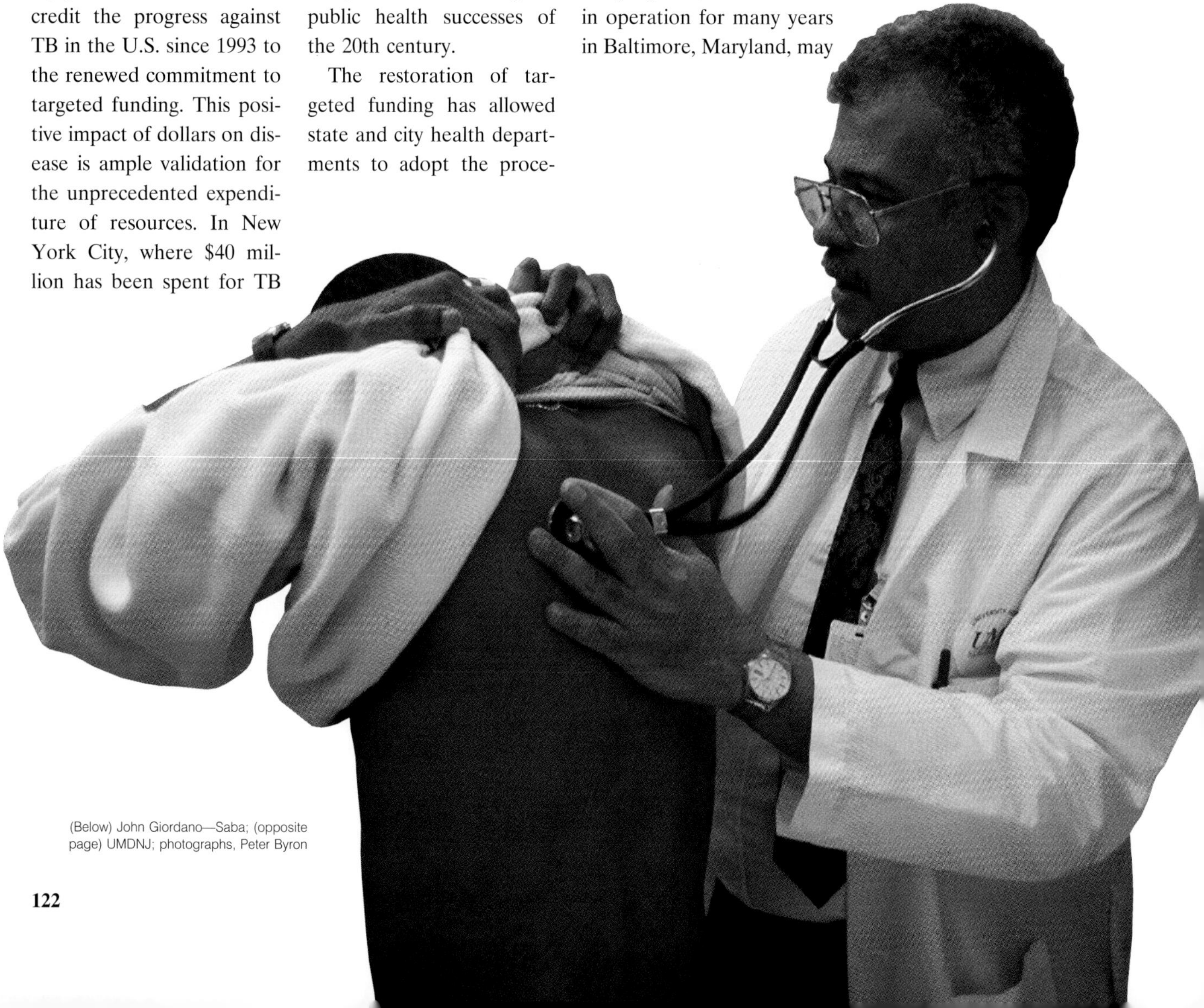

(Below) John Giordano—Saba; (opposite page) UMDNJ; photographs, Peter Byron

(Below) © Yoav Levy—Phototake; (right) Ann Purcell and Carl Purcell—Words & Pictures/PNI; (bottom) courtesy of Gen-Probe Incorporated

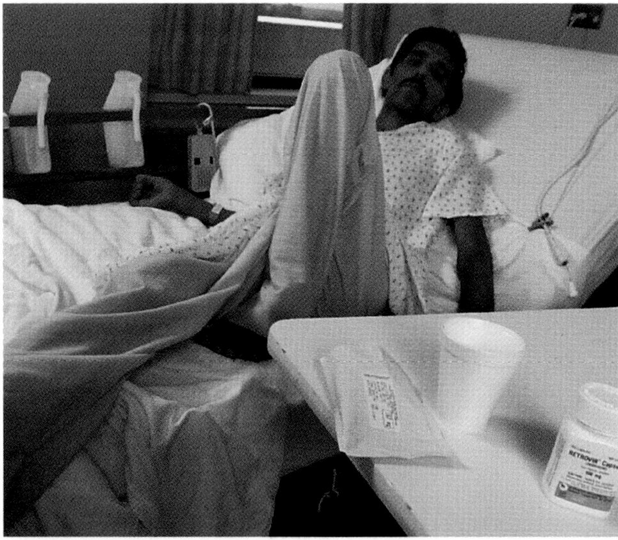

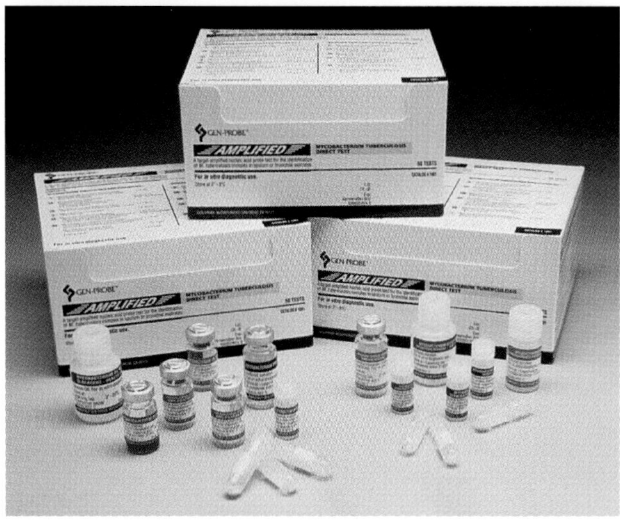

also include legal measures such as involuntary hospitalization when absolutely necessary to achieve compliance.

Beyond implementation of DOT, the new resources made available in 1990–91 have been used to initiate studies of new anti-TB drugs, to assess educational programs for enhancing physician and patient compliance, and to develop more rapid and specific diagnostic measures. A new diagnostic test approved in 1996 enables laboratories to detect the TB organism in sputum samples in four to five hours—a vast improvement over conventional methods, which can take as long as eight weeks.

Whose problem?

Even though more than 15 million Americans remain TB-infected in 1996, many policy makers continue to express the view that this disease is not their concern. "My constituents don't get TB," is a common retort when they are asked why they do not support sustained appropriations for TB control.

Despite elected officials' persistence in denying the problem, nonpartisan investigative bodies, many of them appointed by those very same officials, have sounded an alarm. "The threat of TB reminds us of the importance of maintaining a strong public health infrastructure," cautioned *The Continuing Challenge of Tuberculosis,* a document issued in 1993 by the U.S. Office of Technology Assessment.

The potential costs of an ongoing TB epidemic were highlighted by the General Accounting Office (GAO) in its report *Tuberculosis Cases in Five Cities* (1995). The GAO forecast that total expenditures for TB prevention and control could reach $1.5 billion by 1999. According to GAO estimates, inpatient hospitalization expenditures could increase by 126%, and the costs of local TB-control programs could grow 101%.

Breaking a vicious circle

Infectious diseases respect neither race, class, wealth, nor national boundaries. TB transmission occurs just as easily on commercial airline flights (even in first class),

After many years of neglect, TB diagnosis and treatment are receiving much-needed scientific attention. A diagnostic test (far left, bottom) approved in 1996 yields results in hours rather than the weeks required by conventional methods. Also needed is a new appreciation of TB's potential to affect all levels of society. (Far left, top) Patient with AIDS and TB; (left) affluent travelers; (below) the contagious disease unit in a U.S. prison.

in the workplace, and in affluent suburban high schools as in homeless shelters, prisons, and crowded immigrant households.

Although thc number of new TB cases reported in the U.S. has declined for three successive years, it remains higher than when the resurgence started. Not surprisingly, success in reducing TB incidence has generated another movement to eliminate targeted TB programs. Public health professionals are united in their determination to ensure that this time the lessons of history are not forgotten. MHA

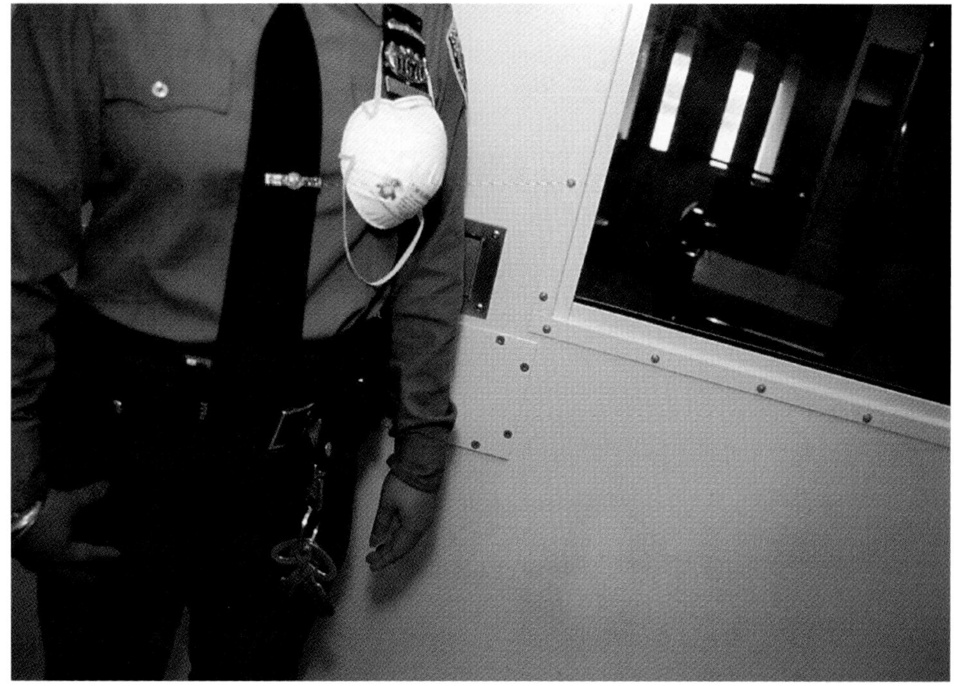

Jim Tynan—Impact Visuals

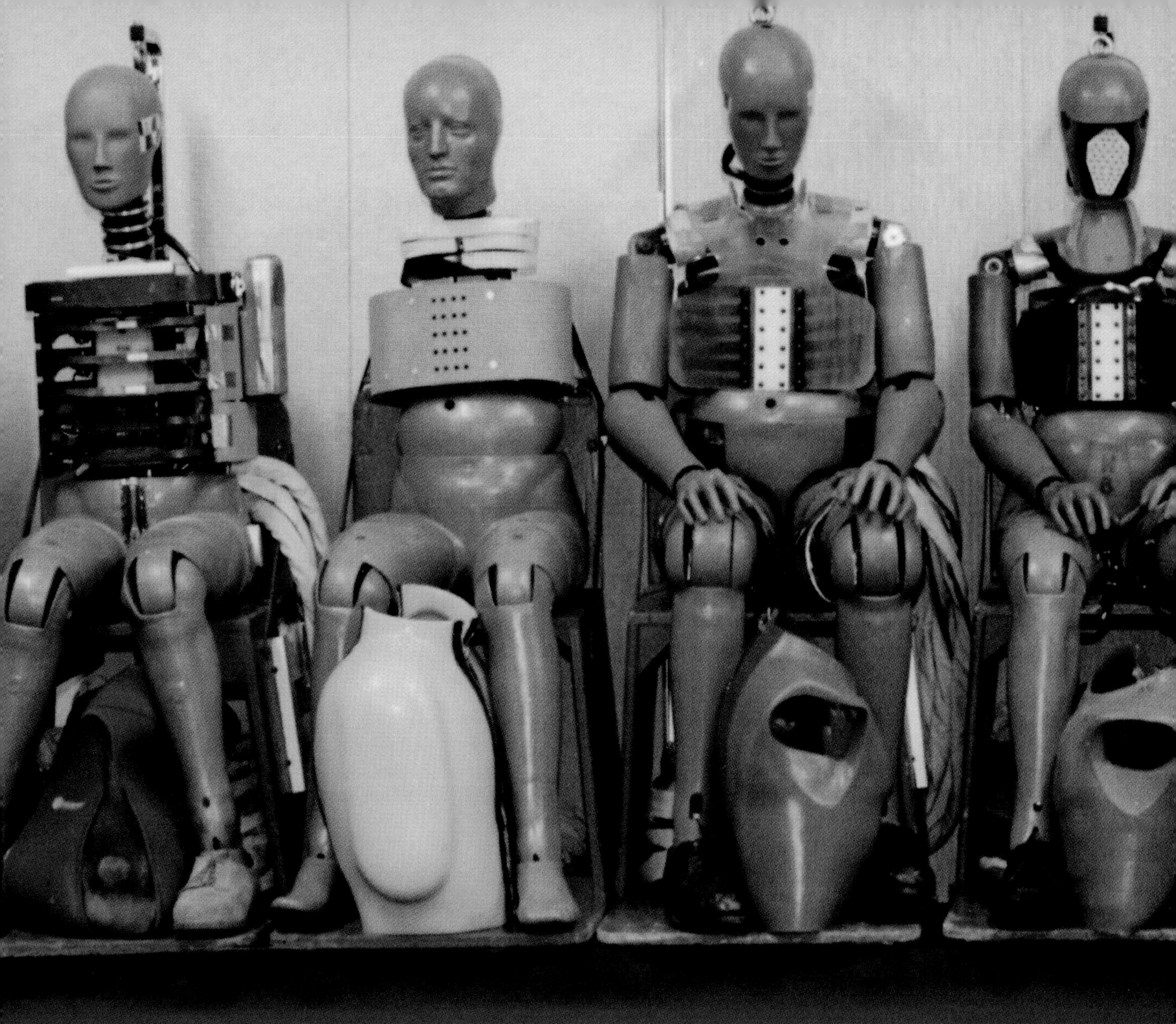

A Crash Course in Traffic Safety

by Leonard Evans, D.Phil.

Public health and welfare gains are closely related to industrialization. A cornerstone of industrialization is the use of motor vehicles for the economic transport of people and goods. Motorization is further intensified by a near universal human desire to enjoy the freedom and mobility afforded by owning a *personal* vehicle, a desire that transcends just about all national, ethnic, and cultural barriers. An unintended and undesired consequence of motorization is the deaths and other harm that result from crashes.

Professionals from many disciplines have been devising and refining ways to reduce harm from traffic crashes. A distinct discipline called "automotive medicine" has evolved to provide a focus to these efforts. The Association for the Advancement of Automotive Medicine (AAAM),

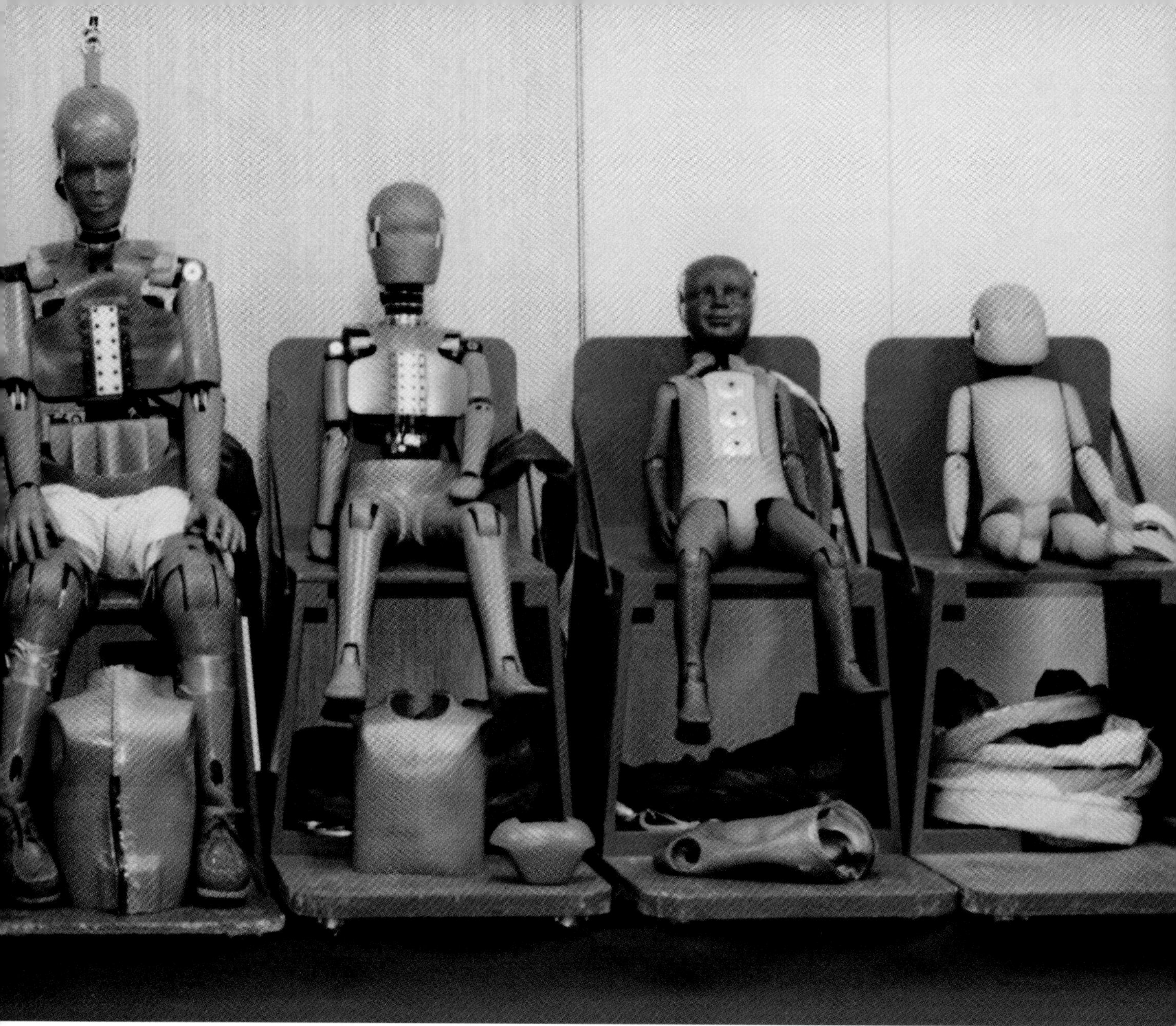

founded in 1957, is an international multidisciplinary organization. Approximately half of its members are physicians; many of the remainder are professionals in disciplines such as engineering and psychology. The AAAM's members comprise institutions around the world—governmental agencies, automobile manufacturers, and insurers among them—with a commitment to reducing harm from traffic crashes. The AAAM maintains the Abbreviated Injury Scale, which is used internationally. First published in 1971, the scale enables the systematic accumulation of data on injuries resulting from vastly different types of crashes that occur all over the world.

Another important organization is the International Association for Accident and Traffic Medicine, which is affiliated with the World Health Organization. These international organizations, together with others, play a crucial role in disseminating knowledge that enables all motorized jurisdictions to have the best and most current information about interventions that are successful in reducing traffic injuries.

Death on the road: a look at the trends

The main patterns associated with traffic deaths are particularly well illustrated by data from the United States, because (1) the U.S. motorized earlier than other countries, (2) it has the

Family of instrumented anthropomorphic test devices—better known as crash-test dummies—used by General Motors in the 1980s and '90s to design safer motor vehicles.

General Motors Corporation

***Leonard Evans, D.Phil.**, is Principal Research Scientist, Safety Research Department, General Motors Research & Development Center, Warren, Michigan, and the author of* Traffic Safety and the Driver *(1991, reprinted 1996), a classic in the field of driving and traffic safety.*

world's largest number of vehicles, and (3) it has collected large quantities of reliable data over a long period. In the early decades of the 20th century, few people were killed on U.S. roads for the obvious reason that there were few motorized vehicles (Figure 1). As vehicle ownership increased rapidly, so did traffic deaths, peaking in 1972 at close to 55,000 and declining later to a present rate of about 40,000 per year.

The number of traffic deaths per year shows little in the way of a pattern. If, however, one examines the number of traffic deaths for the same distance traveled, a clear trend emerges (Figure 2). Ever since 1921, when data were first collected on the total distance traveled by all vehicles, the number of traffic deaths for the same distance of travel has edged downward, with an average decrease of about 3.5% per year. The 1994 rate of 11 traffic deaths per billion kilometers (620 million miles) of travel is more than 90% below the 1921 rate of 150 traffic deaths per billion kilometers. If the 1921 rate were to apply today, the calculated number of traffic fatalities would exceed half a million. The downward trend in the number of deaths for the same distance traveled is observed in all countries for which data are available. Indeed, the downward trend seen in most countries is even greater than that observed for the U.S. (Figure 3).

The number of traffic deaths for the same distance traveled can be measured only after a nation has initiated a procedure to estimate the distance all vehicles are driven. A useful measure that is universally available is the number of traffic deaths per thousand registered ve-

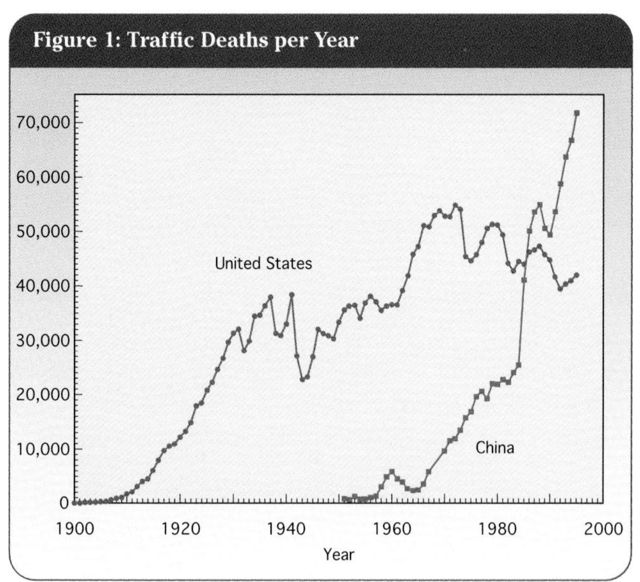

Rush hour in Beijing: as China modernizes and vast numbers of vehicles jam its roadways, an increase in traffic fatalities is virtually guaranteed.

© Jeffrey Aaronson—NETWORK ASPEN

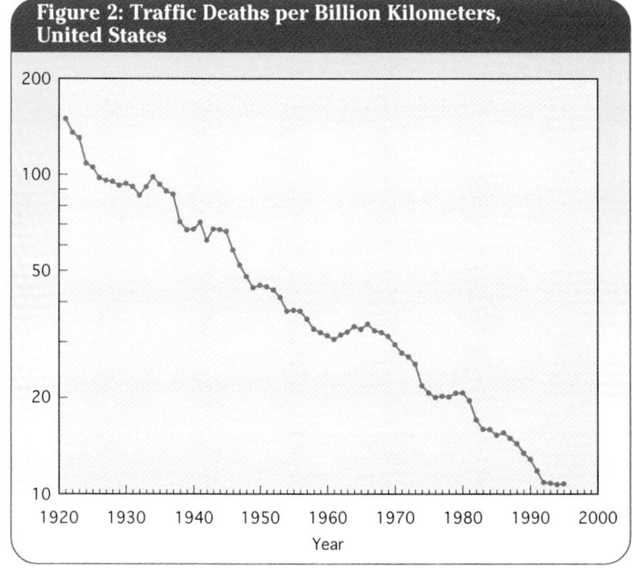

Figure 2: Traffic Deaths per Billion Kilometers, United States

hicles. Nearly all nations routinely register motor vehicles. The number of deaths per thousand vehicles varies greatly among countries—by a factor of more than 100 (*see* Table, page 130). In general, the higher the degree of motorization, the lower the number of traffic fatalities per thousand vehicles. Another key factor that influences fatality rates is the difference between rural and urban driving. Fatality risk tends to be lower in urban areas, where speeds are lower. In 1994 the states of Rhode Island, Massachusetts, and Connecticut had 0.09, 0.11, and 0.12 deaths per thousand vehicles, respectively, whereas Mississippi and Arkansas had 0.39.

While the number of deaths per thousand vehicles for China, the world's most populous nation, is substantially higher than that for more motorized countries, that rate is dropping much faster than in the U.S. and other highly industrialized countries (Figure 4). Although China's rate of deaths on the road is dropping, the dramatic growth of vehicle ownership in China (Figure 5)—and other countries that are rapidly industrializing—will inexorably increase the number of casualties.

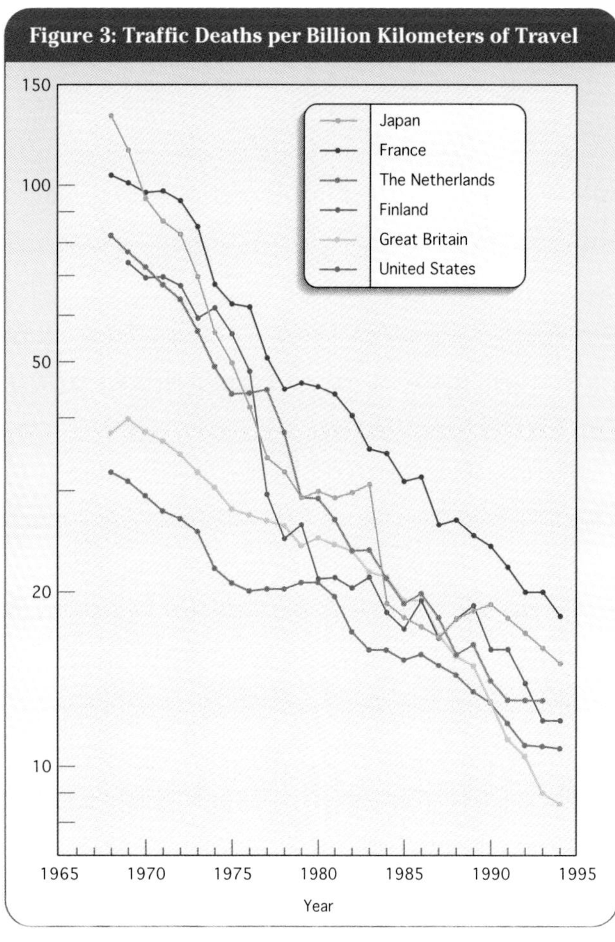

Figure 3: Traffic Deaths per Billion Kilometers of Travel

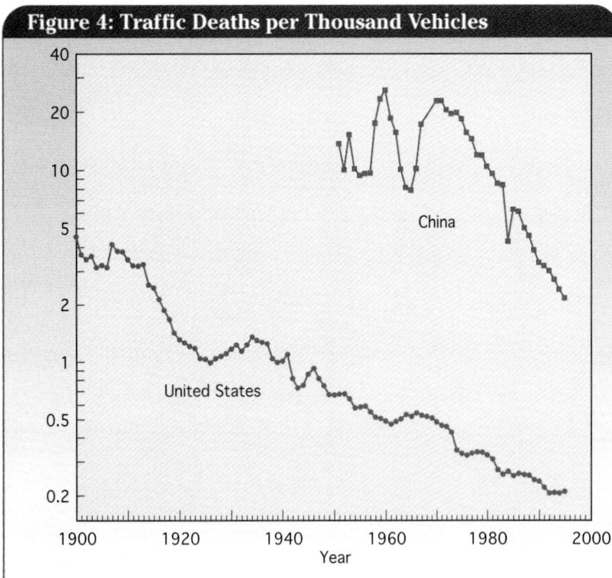

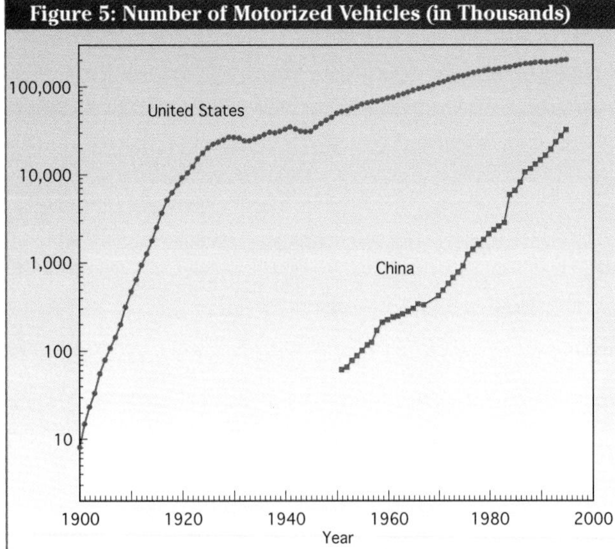

Traffic Deaths Around the World

Country	Vehicles per 1,000 people	Deaths per 1,000 vehicles	Deaths per million population	Deaths per year	Data year
United States	763	0.21	159	41,798	1995
Japan	647	0.13	85	10,649	1994
Australia	591	0.17	99	1,742	1992
France	568	0.26	148	8,533	1994
Norway	510	0.13	65	283	1994
Sweden	446	0.16	73	632	1993
Great Britain	415	0.16	65	3,650	1994
Spain	361	0.34	121	5,615	1994
Ireland	300	0.41	122	431	1993
Israel	251	0.39	99	539	1994
Thailand	219	1.17	257	15,176	1994
Saudi Arabia	167	1.44	241	4,077	1994
Brazil	89	1.89	169	25,000	1991
Morocco	43	2.99	129	3,359	1993
Algeria	33	4.23	140	3,678	1993
China	27	2.20	60	71,494	1995
India	25	2.75	67	59,300	1993
Kenya	15	7.13	108	2,516	1993
Lesotho	13	13.74	172	326	1993
Ethiopia	1	17.20	23	1,169	1990

Many ingredients in the safety pie

Why do motor vehicle fatality rates decline and vary so much from country to country? This question is somewhat akin to asking why average human longevity keeps increasing but varies so greatly from country to country. Many factors affect longevity, including availability of and advancements in surgery, drugs, preventive medicine, sanitation, nutrition, hygiene, etc. Likewise, many factors affect traffic safety.

Trauma care. As medical science has advanced, the same traffic crash has become less likely to result in death. Indeed, it is often said that if a crash victim today can be transported alive to a modern, well-equipped emergency trauma center, the probability of survival is extremely high. This places a high value on rapid transportation from the crash site to the hospital. Here the infrastructure of vehicular transportation contributes in a fairly direct way to reducing the severity of the harm from the crashes. The importance of getting the injured to a hospital with a minimum of delay has led a few jurisdictions to devote substantial resources to supporting helicopter ambulances.

Roadway engineering. On rural two-lane roads, vehicles traveling in opposite directions pass each other only a few meters apart. Even if speed limits are obeyed, the combined relative speed may still far exceed 160 kilometers (100 miles) per hour. A head-on crash at such a speed is likely to prove fatal. Many crashes occur because drivers pass other vehicles improperly or because they lose control of their vehicles on curves. On freeways, where there is physical separation of traffic traveling in opposite directions, the only vehicles permitted to drive close to each other are traveling in the same direction at similar speeds. Fixed objects, such as trees, are far removed from the path of freeway travelers. Risk of side impact at intersections is eliminated because intersections have been replaced by under- and overpasses.

The roadway engineering improvements typified by the difference between freeways and rural two-lane roads constitute one of the most effective engineering countermeasures available. In the U.S., fatality risk on interstate rural freeways is 80% lower than on rural two-lane roads. Such benefits, however, involve trade-offs. Freeways are expensive undertakings that are inappropriate when traffic

(Right) Orderly versus chaotic traffic in two major metropolises: (top) a four-level freeway interchange in Los Angeles and (bottom) street scene in Delhi, India's third largest city. There is no question that modern, well-planned roadways reduce the risk of traffic injuries.

(Top) Baron Wolman—Tony Stone Images; (bottom) © Dilip Mehta—Contact Press Images/PNI

(Below) From an 1889 London newspaper; (right) adapted from information obtained from General Motors Corporation

(Left) A car crash in London, 1889; in the earliest days of automobiles, crashes were often the consequence of mechanical failures of key vehicular components, like wheels or brakes. (Below) A so-called first collision occurs when a car hits an outside barrier. The driver is injured during the "second collision," in which he or she is thrust against the steering column and windshield—in this case, unprotected by a safety belt—and the moving car becomes stationary.

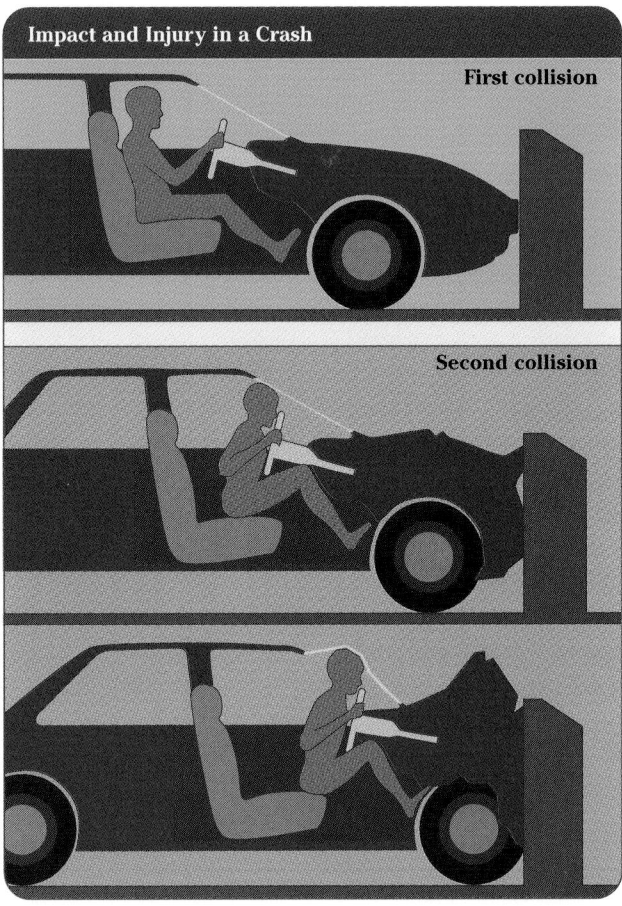

volumes are light or when resources are scarce. Other arguments against building freeways have to do with their social and aesthetic impact on neighborhoods and the urban landscape. Better roads generate more traffic and stimulate urban sprawl, which can place a burden on financial and environmental resources. While the additional travel that freeways stimulate generates additional travel risk, this effect is inconsequential compared with the risk reduction resulting from replacing rural two-lane roadways with freeways.

Vehicle engineering. In the earliest days of the automobile industry, crashes often resulted from the mechanical failure of such key components as wheels, tires, or brakes. As the reliability of those components increased, the safety focus shifted toward fundamental understanding of mechanisms that cause injuries and toward technologies aimed at protecting occupants of vehicles when crashes occur.

Trauma surgeons distinguish between penetrating and blunt trauma. Penetrating trauma occurs when small objects exert sufficient localized force to penetrate the human body, an obvious example being a bullet. Blunt trauma occurs when an object of larger area exerts sufficient force on the body to damage its structure; this occurs, for example, when someone falls from a building. Nearly all traffic injuries, whether involving vehicle occupants or pedestrians, involve blunt trauma. Consider a vehicle traveling at, say, 48 kilometers (30 miles) per hour and crashing into a perfectly rigid horizontal barrier. A motorist who is not wearing a safety belt would, in accordance with the laws of elementary physics, continue to travel at 48 kilometers per hour until he or she was stopped by a force. Such a force occurs when the motorist is thrust against the interior of the now-stationary vehicle; it is this so-called second collision that causes injuries, not the first collision of the vehicle striking the barrier. A person falling from a fourth-floor window would strike the ground at a similar speed and be subject to similar injury forces. While evolution has provided humans with a protective fear of heights, no corresponding fear exists for the relatively new experience of traveling at speeds faster than can be produced by muscle power.

Increasing survival odds in a crash

Theoretically, the best protection would be for the driver to slow down from the initial speed to zero speed at a constant deceleration, using the entire distance between the driver's body and the barrier. For this to happen, the vehicle structure in front of the driver would have to crumple until it had shrunk to zero thickness. The engine and other rigid components make it impossible to achieve this ideal goal.

The practical goal that automotive designers seek is

for the vehicle structure to crumple in such a way as to provide as much "ride-down" distance as feasible and for the driver to travel this distance at as constant a deceleration as possible. Computer techniques that tax even today's fastest supercomputers contribute to approaching this vehicle structure design goal. While the structure outside the occupant compartment is carefully designed to crumple in a crash, the occupant compartment itself is a strong safety cage designed to reduce the risk that it will crush and to help prevent outside objects from intruding.

Modern vehicles incorporate hundreds of innovations aimed at increasing safety. Some are required by governmental regulations. U.S. regulations focus mainly on how vehicle systems perform under test conditions but generally leave decisions regarding how to achieve the required performance level to the design engineers. European regulations are more likely to prescribe specific engineering design details. Most of the rest of the world has adopted one or the other set of standards (or some combination) in order to keep regulations from becoming hopelessly complicated on a global scale and in order to facilitate international trade.

The engineering of safety designs and compliance with governmental regulations are facilitated by the use of instrumented anthropomorphic figures, better known as crash-test dummies. In the most common crash test, dummies with the height and weight of typical motorists are seated in a prototype vehicle that is propelled on a track at a speed of 30 miles per hour into a solid barrier. Engineers have a particular interest in the forces on the head, chest, and legs. In addition to the readings that are taken from many instruments, high-speed films are made so that the detailed movement of the different parts of the dummies and different aspects of the vehicle structure can be studied.

The engineering changes that have contributed to the largest reductions in motorist fatality risk are collapsible steering columns, lap/shoulder safety belts, and airbags. When a driver's chest hits the steering wheel with a high force, the collapsible steering column allows the steering wheel to move forward. This simple device is estimated to reduce overall driver fatality risk in a crash by about 6%.

By far, the most effective occupant protection device is the standard lap/shoulder safety belt. This device not only reduces the likelihood and severity of impact with the interior of the vehicle but also is highly effective at preventing ejection from the vehicle. Ejection quadruples the risk of death in a crash; about one in four unbelted drivers killed is ejected from his or her vehicle.

Attention to Detail: General Motors' "Safety Cage"

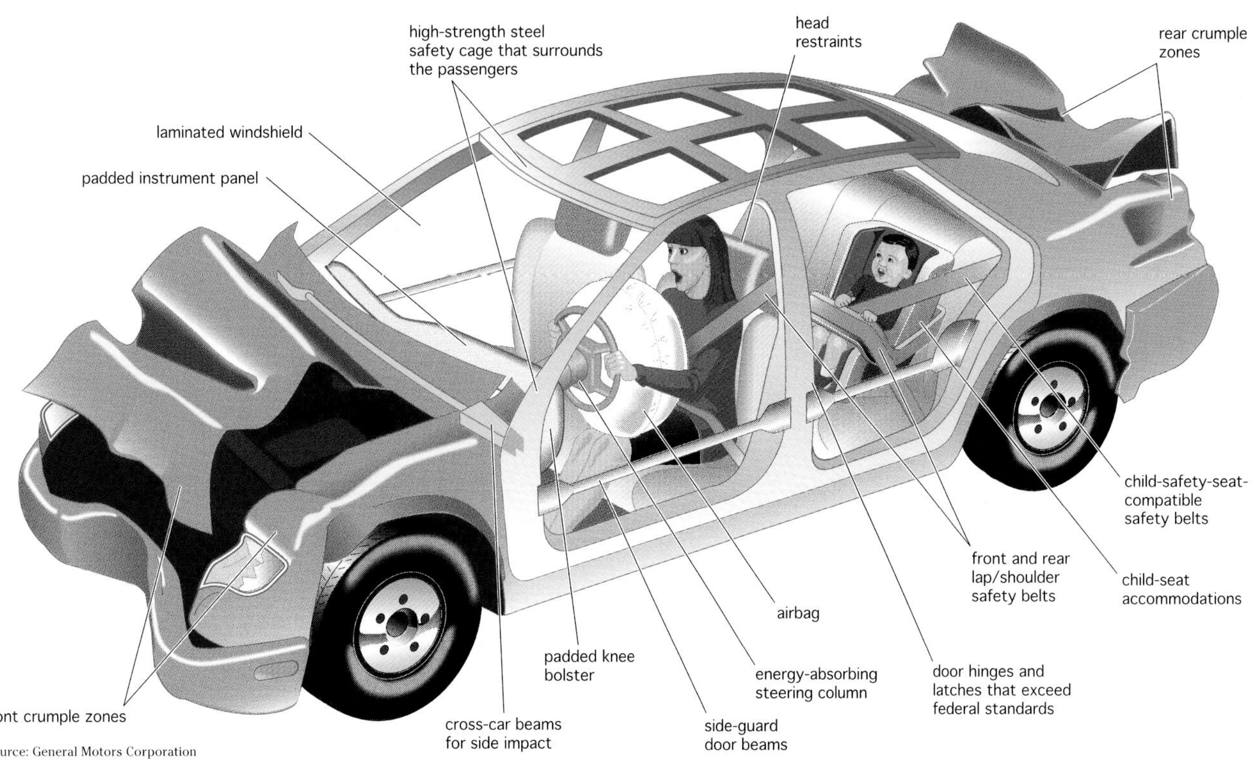

Source: General Motors Corporation

The effectiveness of the lap/shoulder belt is enhanced by airbags. A bag placed in front of the occupant inflates rapidly when sensors detect a frontal crash of a severity exceeding a preset limit (usually equivalent to striking a barrier at a speed in the range 10 to 20 kilometers [6 to 12 miles] per hour). The occupant's body rides down the crash in contact with the airbag, which spreads the impact forces over a large area and reduces belt forces on the occupant. The combination of lap/shoulder belt and airbag reduces motorist fatality risk in a crash by 47%. The safety belt alone reduces risk by 42%. No vehicle manufacturers offer airbags as complete occupant protection devices; rather, they are supplementary devices designed to enhance the performance of the primary device, the lap/shoulder belt.

Increased size and weight of a vehicle increase protection. Doubling the weight reduces occupant risk by about 50%. Even when a crash involves only one vehicle—and in the U.S. 45% of drivers who are killed are killed in single-vehicle crashes—the driver of a heavier vehicle would be safer than the driver of a lighter vehicle.

Two-wheeled and two-footed risks. Riders of two-wheeled vehicles (*e.g.,* motorcycles, motor scooters, mopeds, or bicycles) are at a dramatically higher risk than occupants of even the smallest four-wheel vehicle. Wearing a helmet reduces fatality risk for a motorcyclist by 28%. An unhelmeted motorcyclist, however, is about 22 times as likely to be killed as is an average car driver; wearing a helmet reduces this risk to 18 times that of the car driver. Riders of two-wheeled ve-

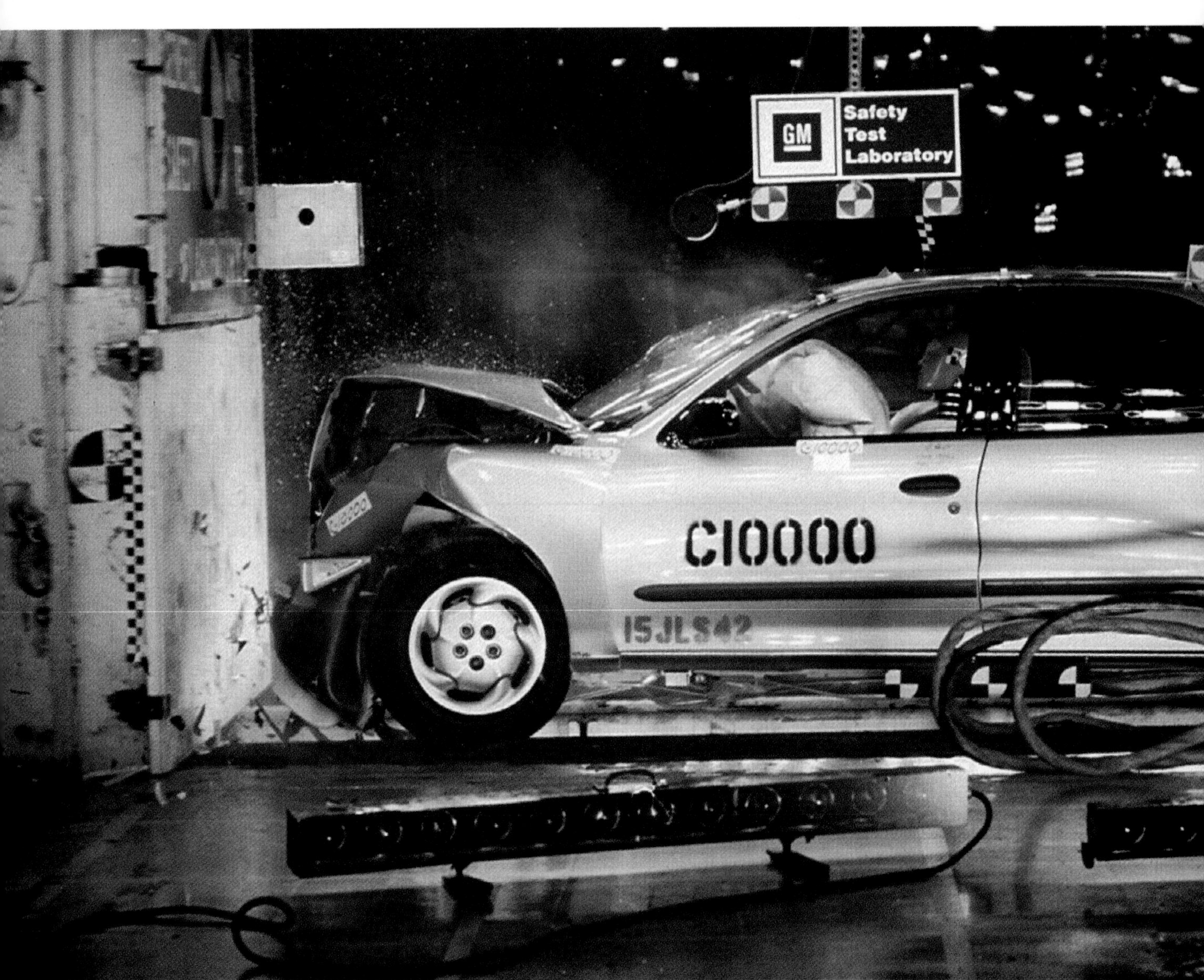

(Right) A properly worn lap/shoulder belt provides a high level of occupant protection in crashes. (Below) With an instrumented dummy in the driver's seat, a 1995 Chevrolet Cavalier hits a concrete barrier at 30 miles (48 kilometers) per hour. GM has been carrying out "crashworthiness" tests of its cars at its Milford (Michigan) Proving Ground since 1934. (Below right) Dummies at the Milford facility are groomed for testing.

hicles (whether engine- or human-powered) and pedestrians constitute a particularly vulnerable group of road users. This group accounts for a large proportion of all traffic deaths in countries in early stages of motorization.

While much attention has been devoted to modifying vehicle design to better protect pedestrians in crashes, the opportunity is intrinsically less than for protecting vehicle occupants. The main way to prevent harm to pedestrians and drivers is to somehow change the way thcy both bchave.

Humans in the driver's seat

Any discussion of the behavior of the driver (or other road user) must begin by making the clearest possible distinction between two deceptively similar but fundamentally different concepts. The first is driver performance (what the driver is capable of doing), and the second is driver behavior (what the driver actually does).

Many studies have identified errors made by drivers as being a contributory factor in over 95% of traffic crashes. Such findings have generated suggestions that the first priority for better safety is to impart higher levels of skill and knowledge about driving—in other words, to improve levels of driver performance. While driver training, especially that of motorcyclists, has reduced crash rates in some instances, it has not been found to do so generally (although it may provide other benefits). There are a number of reasons why crash risk is not determined mainly by driver capability.

Young, male, and overinvolved. Young male drivers (adolescents and young men in their 20s) have the highest crash rates everywhere in the world. Yet this is the very age group that has the best visual acuity, swiftest reaction times, and fastest cognitive processing skills. Males, rather than females, generally tend to be more knowledgeable about and interested in driving and automobiles. Race-car drivers have higher on-the-road crash rates than average drivers, which makes

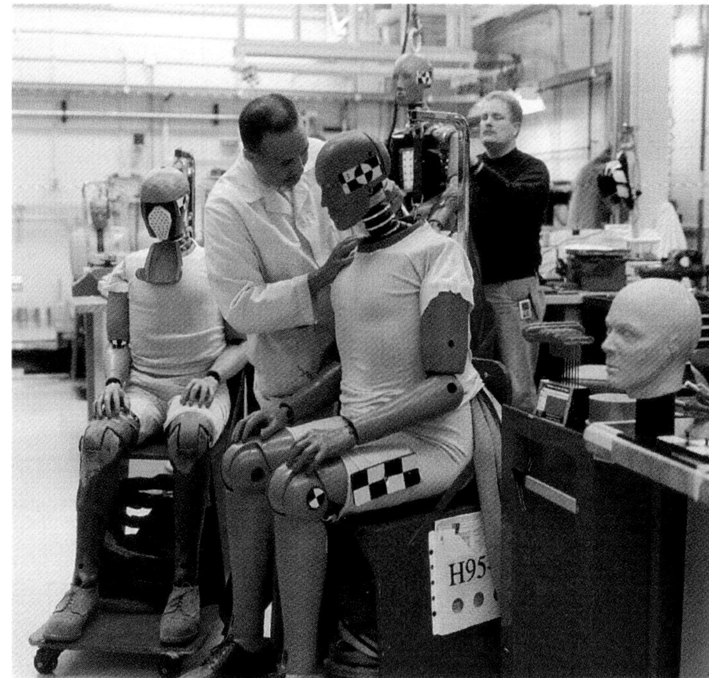

(Left and above) General Motors Corporation

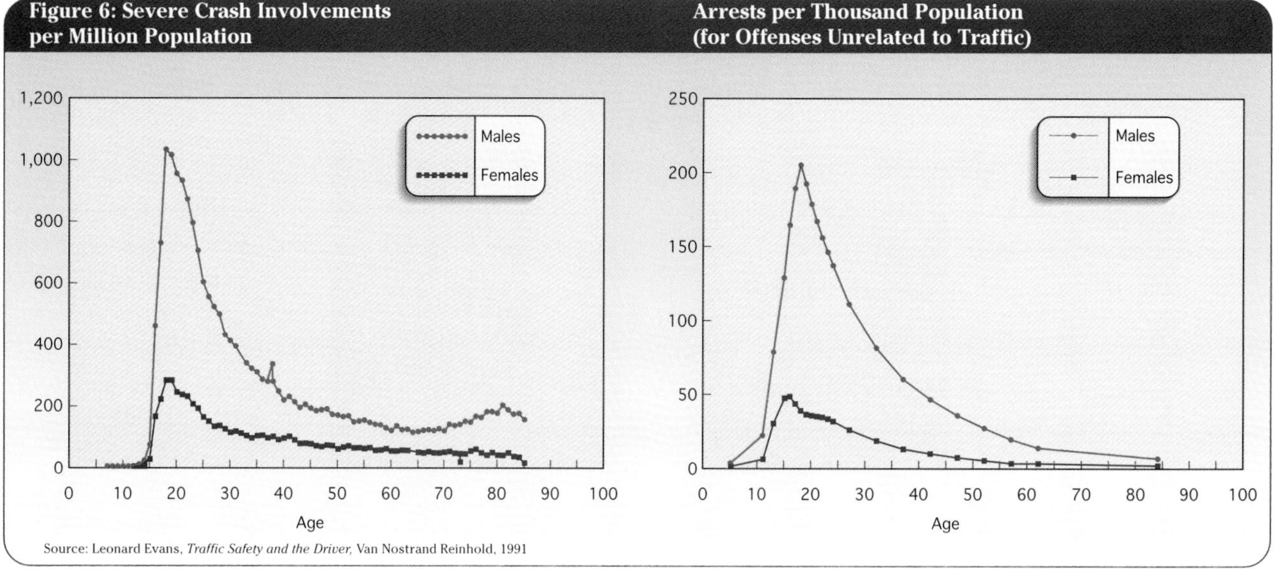

it clear that it is not lack of skill that leads to crashes.

A comparison of gender and age in severe single-vehicle crashes and in crimes unrelated to traffic offenses (for example, burglary) shows that there are remarkable similarities (Figure 6). No one would suggest that the lower arrest rate for 40-year-olds compared with 20-year-olds occurs because 40-year-olds have learned how not to commit burglaries! A parallel caution should be taken in interpreting lower crash rates for 40-year-old drivers; this does not mean that 40-year-olds have simply learned how not to crash. Increases in male drivers' skills and knowledge do not appear to be the major factors in the large decline in crash rates with increasing age. Important though skill and knowledge are, of greater importance is driver behavior.

Behavior is paramount. The average driver has a crash (usually involving minor property damage) about once per decade. When crashes occur, drivers tend to dismiss them as "unpredictable," "unpreventable," "bad luck," or "the other person's fault." The more appropriate interpretation of "once per decade" is that average driving produces one crash per driver every 10 years. Yet that knowledge is unlikely to affect anyone's behavior. Every time a trip is completed safely, it reinforces the driver's incorrect notion that average driving is safe driving. Thus, individual experience is a false teacher.

How many people would fly on commercial aircraft if the pilot's method of learning how to avoid crashes was to experience them? Air safety requires that pilots follow procedures that are based on expert analyses of the experience of many. Traffic laws attempt to do the same for ground vehicles. There are, however, major differences—the main one being that ground vehicle drivers frequently violate rules of the road.

Vehicles are used for purposes that go beyond mere transportation. Competitiveness, a sense of power and control, and other hedonistic objectives—the pursuit of sensual pleasure for its own sake—are all important. Speed and acceleration appear to produce pleasurable excitement even when the driver has no specific destination and there is no reason for haste. While most drivers are motivated to some extent by nontransportation factors, as they mature their hedonistic motives play a lesser role. This undoubtedly is one reason why the crash risk for male 40-year-olds is so much lower than that for male 20-year-olds. It is plausible that as a nation's degree of motorization increases, a similar evolution occurs in crash rates. Drivers in newly motorized countries—usually the first generation to drive—are likely to approach the activity as a novelty that imparts a sense of excitement and adventure. By contrast, in long-motorized countries automobiles play an essential part in most people's daily lives and thus lack the gloss of novelty.

Very basic personality factors influence behavior in traffic. A comparison of male and female pedestrian deaths produces a remarkably consistent picture. At all ages (including babies less than one year old!), the male rate exceeds the female rate. This supports the idea of an intrinsic gender difference, one that is likely linked to the hormone testosterone. Such an interpretation receives additional support from the fact that risk-taking behaviors and involvement in traffic crashes are different for males and females. This has been seen in all jurisdictions that collect such data.

Slower is safer. A dominant factor affecting traffic fatality risk is speed. Research indicates that the risk of crashing increases approximately in proportion to travel speed, injury risk increases in proportion to the travel speed squared, and fatality risk increases in proportion to the travel speed to the fourth power. In 1974, following the Arab oil embargo (imposed in the fall of 1973), speed limits on the U.S. rural interstate system were reduced from 70 to 55 miles per hour. As a result, the average travel speed dropped from 63.4 to 57.6 miles per hour. Such a change would be expected to lead to a 32% decrease in fatality risk—remarkably close to the 34% decline that was actually observed (Figure 7).

Buckled up? It has already been noted that behavior is a crucial factor in the protection of drivers and passengers. Indeed, the most effective occupant protection device, the safety belt, works only when fastened. Mandatory safety-belt-wearing laws have been introduced in most countries, though compliance rates and the level and type of enforcement vary greatly. The safety-belt-wearing law that has been evaluated most thoroughly is that in the United Kingdom. Fatality rates for front-seat occupants declined by about 20% after safety-belt wearing became compulsory in 1983.

Sober and safer. Drunk driving is a major traffic-safety problem in all countries in which alcohol is consumed, often accounting for close to half of all fatalities. In many cases reducing the availability of alcohol has led to reduced traffic deaths. When all U.S. states increased the minimum drinking age to 21 (from a previous minimum of 18 to 20 in various states), a 13% reduction in fatal crashes involving those targeted by the law changes followed. Random breath testing by police is aimed at enforcing drunk-driving laws. In the Australian state of New South Wales, breath tests are administered to about one-third of all drivers each year, and many drivers are tested more than once. While many consider such measures extreme, the New South Wales intervention has decreased overall fatalities by about 19% (Figure 8).

Figure 7: Speed Limits and Deaths on the U.S. Rural Interstate System (Deaths per Billion Kilometers)

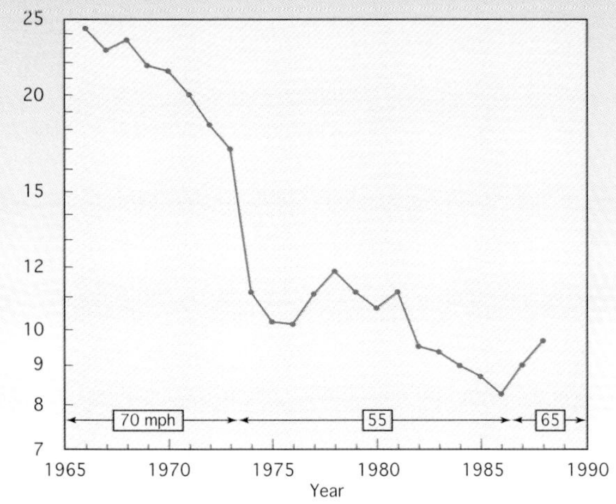

Source: Leonard Evans, *Traffic Safety and the Driver*, Van Nostrand Reinhold, 1991

Lincoln Journal Star—AP/Wide World

Research has shown that the risk of crashing increases with speed; nonetheless, some U.S. states, including Nebraska (above), have raised highway speed limits.

Behavior can change. In driving behavior, as in most human activities, social norms play a central role. People drive in a way that they think would win the approval of those whose approval they desire. In the U.S. a profound change in social norms regarding drunk driving has

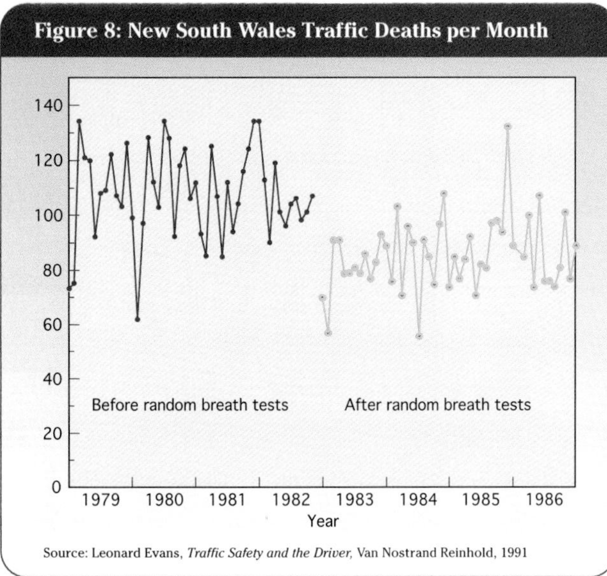

Figure 8: New South Wales Traffic Deaths per Month

Source: Leonard Evans, *Traffic Safety and the Driver*, Van Nostrand Reinhold, 1991

(Right) In the Australian state of New South Wales, random breath testing for alcohol consumption has been shown to save lives. (Below) A stunt from the movie *Lethal Weapon* (1987). Many find Hollywood's claim that such portrayals have no effect on driving behavior to be both implausible and ingenuous. (Far right) A truck-jeep collision in Florida left the drivers of both vehicles hospitalized in critical condition.

occurred. Drunk drivers are no longer considered the comical characters they once were. In the 1980s attitudes toward drinking altered radically. Drunken behavior has ceased to be an amusement to society at large. This change in attitude has contributed to reductions in drunk driving.

While the fictional portrayal of drunk driving as a harmless activity has become uncommon, the same cannot be said for the portrayal of illegal and life-threatening driving in general, which is often presented as heroic or humorous in television programs and motion pictures specifically aimed at young people. The possibility that such behavior may lead to tragic consequences is rarely addressed. Claims that fictional portrayals do not influence behavior ring hollow when one considers the billions of dollars that are spent on television advertising aimed at young consumers. These expenditures are predicated on the belief

(Top) Greg Lovett—© The Palm Beach Post; (center) Michael Henderson, M.D./New South Wales Police Service; (bottom) Everett Collection

that they *do* influence behavior. Surely the programs themselves have an even more profound influence on viewers. Shaming the entertainment industry into desisting from some current practices would, at least in this author's view, save the lives of many young people.

Driving in the 21st century

Worldwide, over half a million people are killed annually in traffic crashes. The number of injuries is about 70 times greater. Victims are predominantly young, and about 65% are male. As motorization increases, so will these totals. A large number of interventions have proved to be effective in reducing casualties. These can be divided into practices that reduce harm when crashes occur (occupant protection) and ways of avoiding crashes. A crucial difference between the two is that when the crash is avoided, all harm is prevented. On the other hand, when the occupant is protected, the prevented fatality is almost certainly converted to some other level of injury, most likely a severe injury.

The overall problem of harm that results from the use of motor vehicles is somewhat analogous to the morbidity and mortality that are caused by disease. It is as unrealistic to hope for a "magic bullet" to eliminate harm from all traffic crashes as it is to hope for a panacea for all disease. Reduction of risk occurs one step at a time—by a percentage or so for every safety advance. The goal is for each country to be aware of the considerable body of scientific evidence now available on the effectiveness of a large number of interventions and then to choose the ones that are most pertinent to its own circumstances, needs, and budget. Automotive medicine will become even more vital in the 21st century as more and more countries motorize. MHA

Identical Twins:

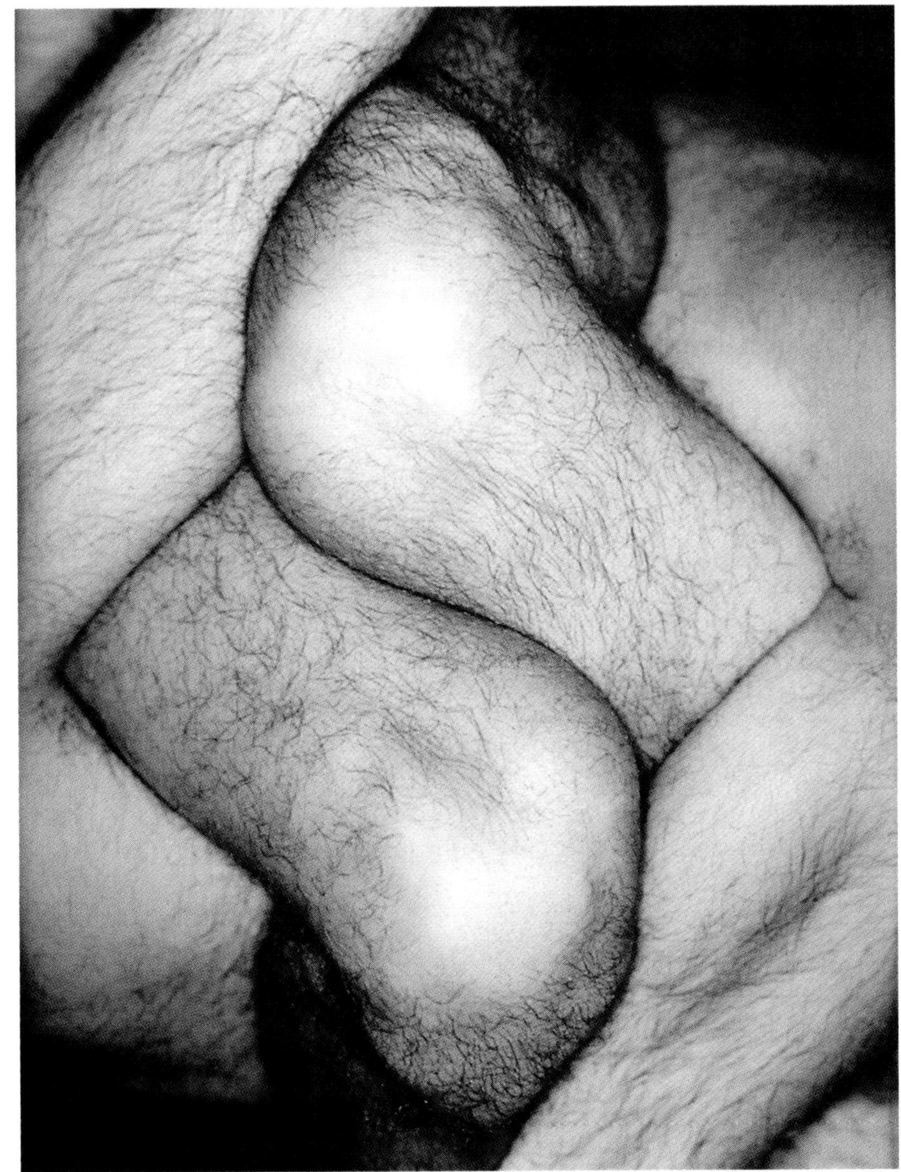

Double Takes

by David Teplica, M.D., M.F.A.

(Opposite) "Refusion" (the Dworkin twins), 1991; (above) "Untitled" (the Dworkin twins), 1995.

David Teplica has two careers—plastic surgery and photography—and one all-consuming obsession: identical twins. After earning his medical degree from Dartmouth Medical School, Hanover, New Hampshire, in 1985, Teplica began his surgical residency at the University of Chicago Pritzker School of Medicine. Between general surgical training and a residency in plastic and reconstructive surgery, he attended the School of the Art Institute of Chicago and received a master of fine arts degree. His scientific and artistic careers have burgeoned simultaneously. He presently has a full-time plastic surgery practice—and he photographs twins every chance he gets.

Whether he is removing a basal-cell carcinoma, doing delicate skin grafts on a burn patient, repairing a broken nose, or performing a cosmetic rhytidectomy (facelift), Teplica the plastic surgeon must pay exquisite attention to detail. The same is true when Teplica the photographer focuses his camera lens on the faces, knees, toes, pores, or intertwined bodies of identical twins.

His twin picture taking began in earnest in 1989, when he and an 11-member research team traveled to Twinsburg, Ohio, for the annual Twins Days Festival, a three-day extravaganza that attracts close to 3,000 sets of twins each August. That first visit to Twinsburg was "a fascinating and very odd experience," says Teplica. He remembers that he was constantly doing double takes. While some members of his team took detailed medical histories from more than 100 volunteer identical-twin pairs and others carried out skin examinations, Teplica photographed. His pictures, enlarged to lifesize, revealed stunning similarities, subtle dissimilarities, and some quite unanticipated things like identical twins' skin cancers arising at the same time in precisely the same body locations.

Over the years Teplica, in collaboration with the Center for Study of Multiple Birth in Chicago, has compiled an unprecedented archive of clinical photographs. "It's amazing to look at these scientific images and see things like two 12-year-old girls whose acne has erupted on exactly the same spot on the nose," he comments.

The more he photographs twins, the more his fascination grows. In addition to his clinical photographic studies, Teplica the artist has created many thousands of black-and-white images, capturing his identical-twin subjects in some quite dramatic poses. A selection of those images is presented on these pages. What amazes Teplica most about identical twins is that they seem to "yearn for individuality but are inexorably bound in their identical relationship . . . that they are not only physically identical but psychologically meshed in ways that we as single individuals can't begin to fathom." MHA

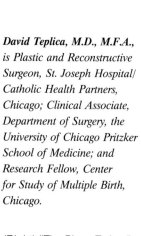

David Teplica, M.D., M.F.A., is Plastic and Reconstructive Surgeon, St. Joseph Hospital/ Catholic Health Partners, Chicago; Clinical Associate, Department of Surgery, the University of Chicago Pritzker School of Medicine; and Research Fellow, Center for Study of Multiple Birth, Chicago.

(Right) "The Place Twins," 1995; (opposite) "Untitled" (the Acosta twins), 1996.

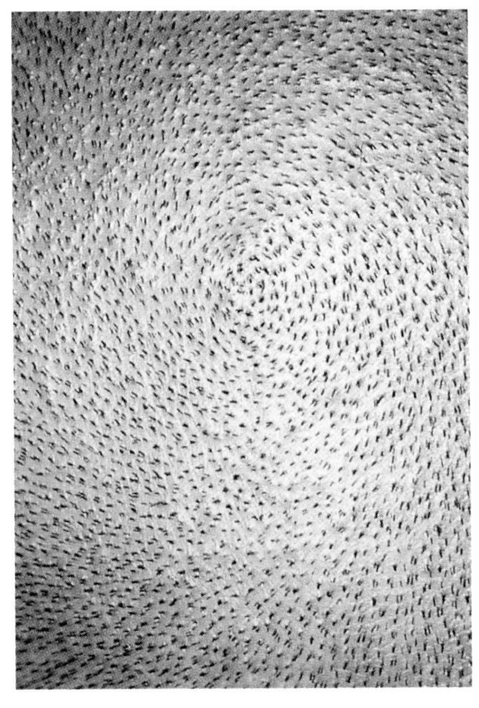

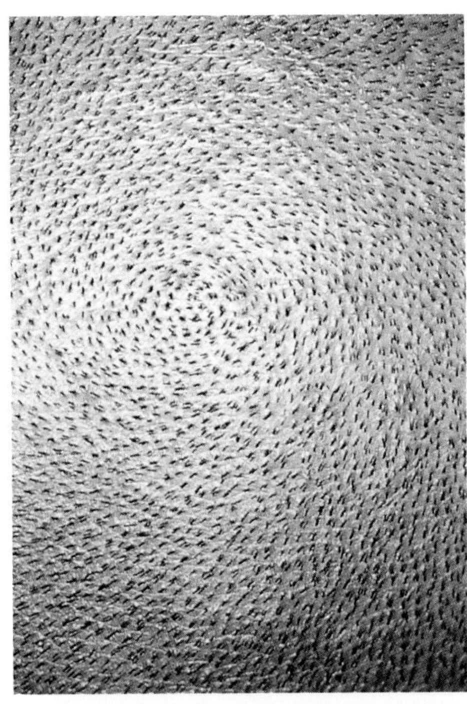

(Opposite) "Difference" (the Payto twins), 1990; (left) "Vertex/Vortex" (the Dworkin twins), 1990; (below) "The Reed Twins," 1990.

"Untitled" (the Sternberg twins), 1990.

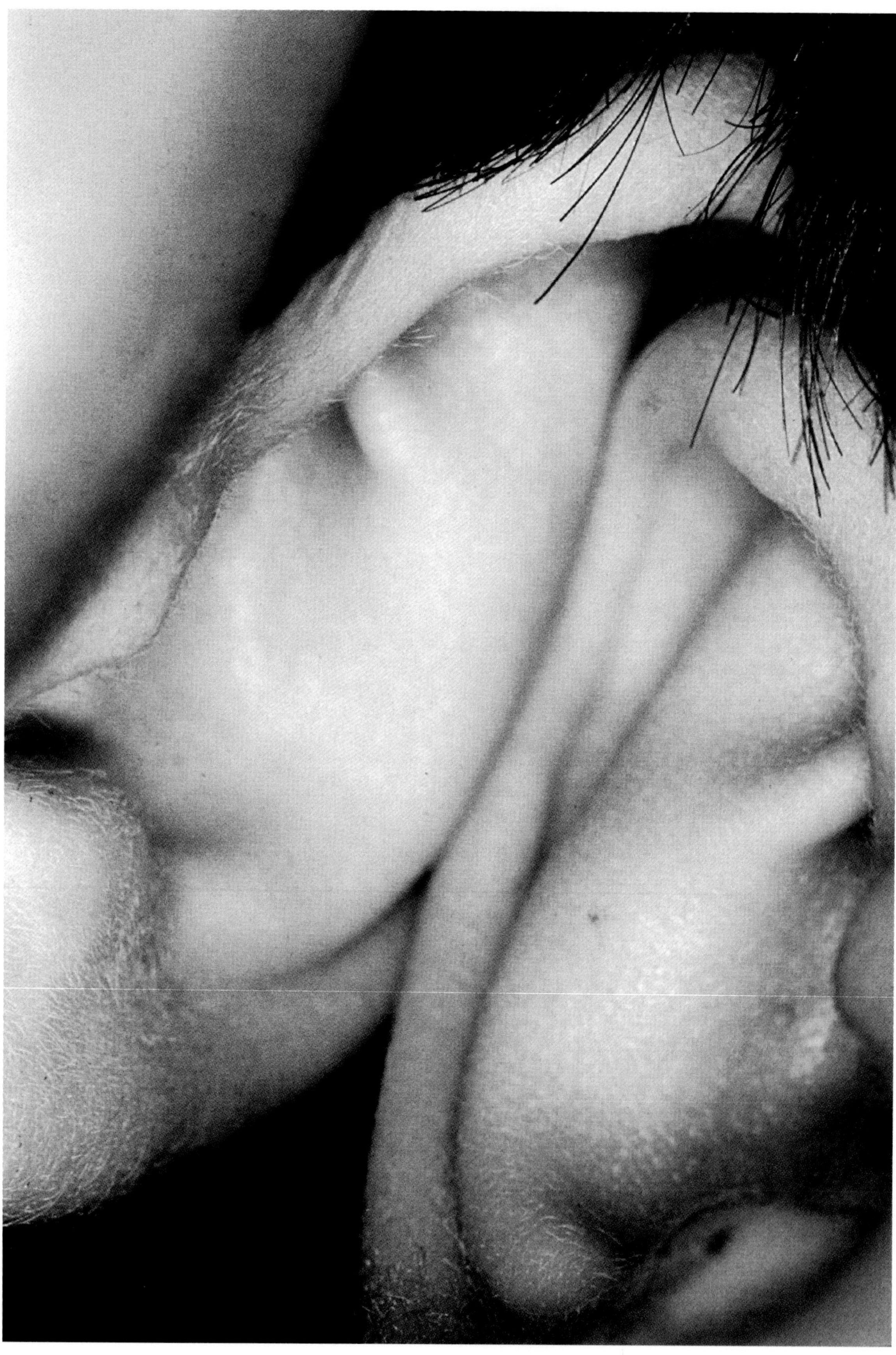

"Kiss/Bite" (the Dworkin twins), 1990.

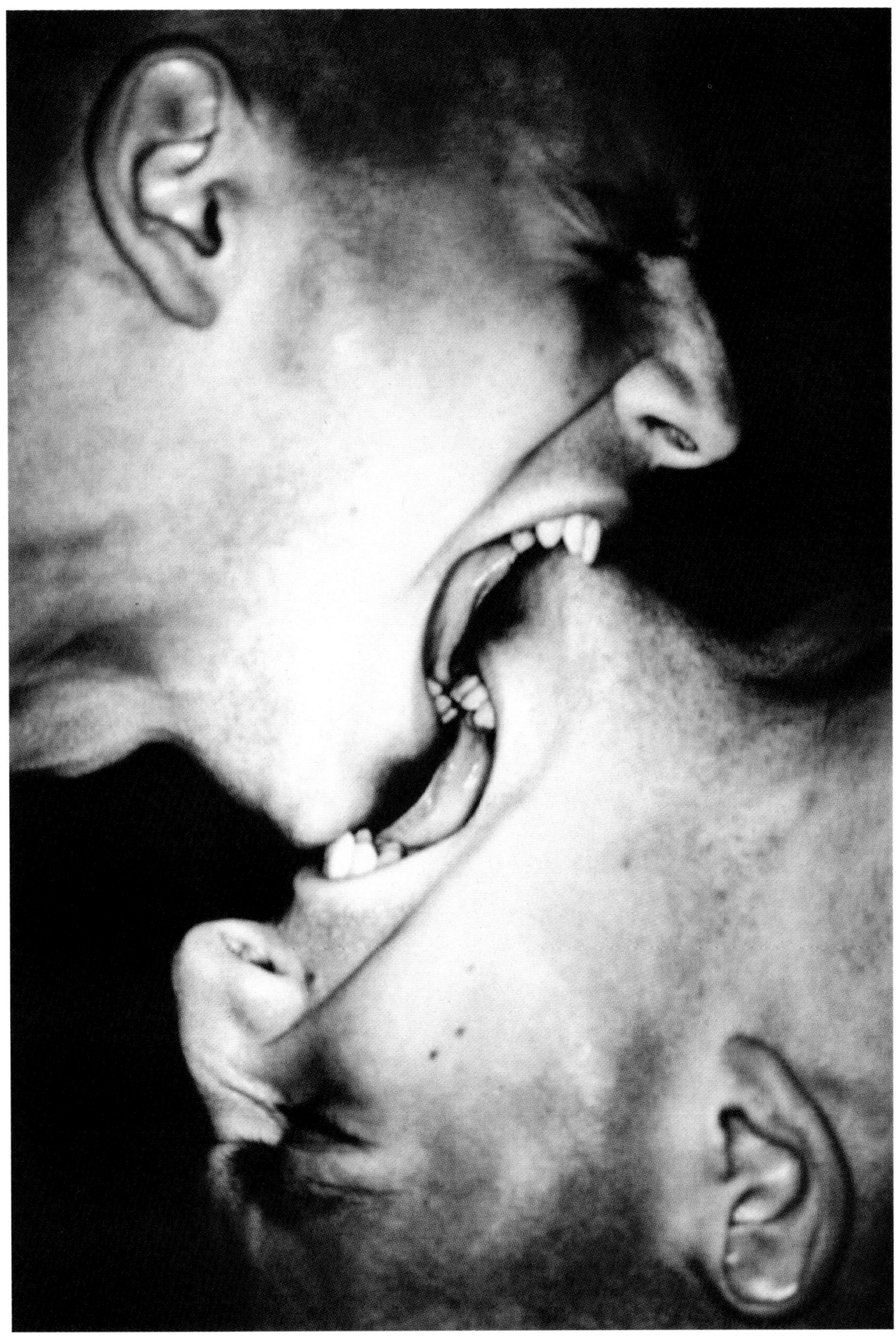

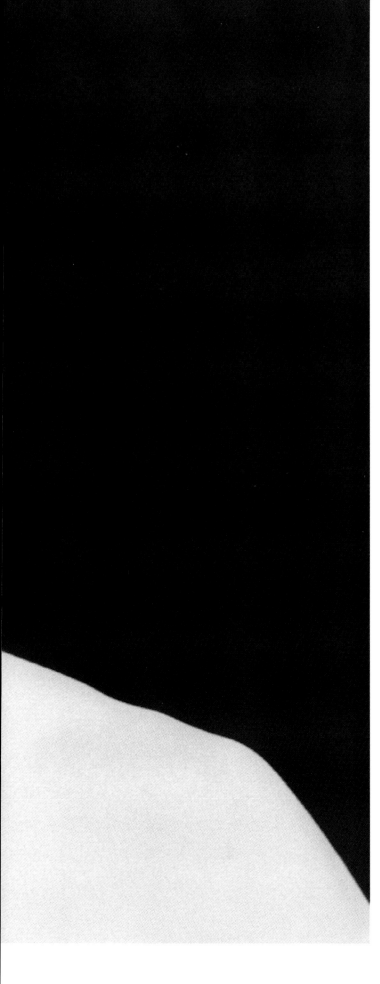

(Left) "Untitled" (the Derma twins), 1994; (below top) "Untitled" (the Lorkowski twins), 1990; (below bottom) "Identity" (the Dworkin twins), 1990.

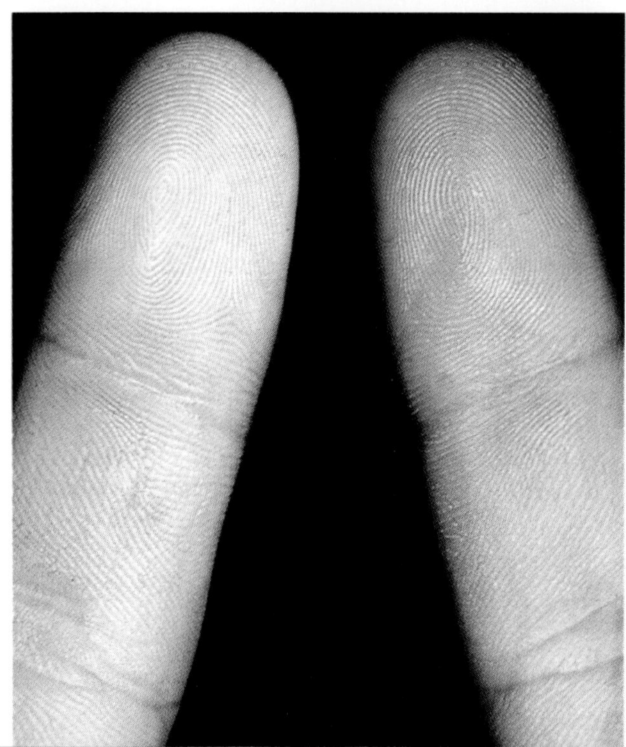

(Right) "Untitled" (the Place twins), 1995; (below) "The Schell Twins," 1991; (opposite) "Untitled" (the Dworkin twins), 1995.

The Bookshelf

Because the editors of the *Medical and Health Annual* suspect that its readers are people who appreciate a good book, they have selected and reviewed 24 recent medicine- and health-related books from among the hundreds that have been published in the past year or so—volumes that they think will appeal to anyone with a lively curiosity about medicine, health, or the biological and psychological sciences. The list includes some titles that have attracted wide audiences, as well as others less noted. Some are practical guides; some are scholarly, philosophical, or historical works; and there is even a best-selling novel that confronts a sociomedical issue. An extract from the text precedes each review.

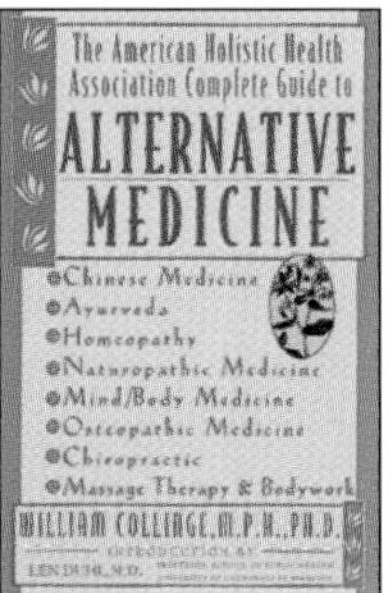

The American Holistic Health Association Complete Guide to Alternative Medicine
William Collinge, M.P.H., Ph.D.
New York: Warner Books, 1996.
361 pp., notes, index. $24.95

We now know that at least a third of Americans use some form of alternative medicine. On their own, people are choosing to integrate other traditions with their regular allopathic care [rendered by conventional physicians and surgeons]. *By voting with their feet, they are choosing a new paradigm of health care that could be called* integrative medicine.

Alternative medicine, once considered the preserve of eccentrics and faddists, has steadily gained respectability. It has earned a place in the ranks of the healing and curing arts on the basis of positive results, often where more conventional treatments have failed. The high level of public curiosity about alternative medicine is motivated by numerous currents in contemporary American society, among them: a growing interest in natural substances and concern about the overprescription of synthetic drugs, a desire for a more mutually respectful relationship between patient and health care provider, and a search for therapies that are holistic (involving the whole person—physical, emotional, mental, and spiritual) and in which the patient plays an active part in the healing process.

This comprehensive guide from the American Holistic Health Association, a professional organization incorporated in 1989, was written for those seeking sound information about the different kinds of nontraditional medicine practiced in the United States. It profiles eight major alternative approaches: Chinese medicine, Ayurveda (an ancient system of medicine that originated in India), naturopathic medicine, homeopathy, mind/body medicine, osteopathic medicine, chiropractic, and massage therapy. In addition to analyzing the effectiveness of each of these types of alternative medicine in a practical and objective way, Collinge, a specialist in behavioral medicine and supervisor of a cancer support center in California, discusses costs, insurance coverage, and other important practical concerns. This is a book whose time has come; it provides readers the facts they need to become informed health care consumers.

Between the Heartbeats: Poetry and Prose by Nurses
Cortney Davis and Judy Schaefer, eds.
Iowa City: University of Iowa Press, 1995.
225 pp. $27.95

tries a nose-dive, kamikaze,
when the intern flings open the isolette.

The kid almost hits the floor. I can see the headline:
DOC DUMPS TOT. Nice save, nurse.

Why thanks. Young physician: "We have to change
the tube." His voice trembles, six weeks

out of school, I tell him: "Keep it to a handshake,
you'll be OK." Our team resuscitated

this Baby Random, birthweight
one pound, eyelids still fused. Mother's

a junkie with HIV. Never named him.
Where I work we bring back terminal preemies,

No Fetus Can Beat Us. *That's our motto. . . .*

—from "Baby Random" by Belle Waring

The brief biographical sketches of the contributors to this anthology are, in their own way, every bit as intriguing as the writings themselves. These poets and storytellers, all of whom are nurses, feel that they simply *must* write. It is the only way they can deal with their feelings about what they see and do every day, about their own personal limits and the limits of their profession. "What nurse has never needed healing?" one of them asks.

As a part of their training, nurses learn to be keen observers of patients; those finely honed observational skills stand them in good stead as writers. This talented group has created vivid pictures of their work and their patients. There are memoirs of nurse's training in a quaint past when novices—all women in those days—wore black cotton stockings. Poems describe the care of the very elderly, the wounded, women in labor, the deranged. There is a remarkable piece written from the point of view of a patient on a respirator.

The authors, men and women of many generations and diverse backgrounds and training, include professional writers as well as those whose work is published here for the first time. What they have in common is that each is the kind of caregiver any patient would welcome into the sickroom.

Breakthrough: The Race to Find the Breast Cancer Gene
Kevin Davies, Ph.D., and Michael White. New York: John Wiley & Sons, Inc., 1996.
310 pp., glossary, notes, appendix, index. $24.95

The structure of BRCA1 *is just about the worst possible in terms of devising a simple screening test for women at high risk of breast cancer.* BRCA1 *is five to ten times the size of most human genes, and the fact that the first handful of mutations in affected families were different and spread throughout the gene, rather than clustered in one place, suggested that the development of a test would be difficult. It took only a few weeks after the cloning of* BRCA1 *for that suggestion to be confirmed.*

Breast cancer is a complex disease; the riddle of its origins has occupied some of the most innovative scientific minds of the late 20th century. Over a period of nearly 20 years, Mary-Claire King, at the time a researcher at the University of California, Berkeley, was consumed with the search for genetic influences in breast cancer. Specifically, King and her colleagues were convinced of the existence of a gene that confers susceptibility to the disease.

In 1990 they succeeded in mapping such a gene, subsequently named *BRCA1,* to chromosome 17, but disappointingly, King and her team lost the race to isolate the gene itself. (The winners were a group led by Mark Skolnick at the University of Utah Medical Center.) Kevin Davies, the editor of *Nature Genetics,* and science writer Michael White describe in detail the collaborative effort that culminated with the discovery of the *BRCA1* gene and the fierce competition between the rival groups of investigators seeking to be the first to determine its exact location.

As Davies and White take pains to emphasize, the end of the "race" to find the gene is by no means the end of the breast cancer story. If anything, the recently acquired knowledge had added to the unsolved issues surrounding the disease—especially the difficult questions posed by the possibility of genetic screening for women at high risk. Who would pay for such screening? Could the results be kept confidential? What would be the psychological consequences for families? Many women at risk for breast cancer, the authors point out, would prefer not to know that they will eventually develop "a disease . . . for which there is presently no successful treatment and about which they can do little." Davies and White deplore both the politicization of medical research and its domination by the profit-oriented, and they advocate a scientific climate in which researchers are free to pursue work that may not show instantaneous results but that could, in the longer term, produce tomorrow's breakthroughs.

The Case of the Frozen Addicts
J. William Langston, M.D., and Jon Palfreman. New York: Pantheon, 1995.
309 pp., illustrations, index. $25.00

"Er, Dr. Langston, one of our inmates has developed a medical problem which he thinks you might be able to help with." . . .

"What is the name of this prisoner?"

"It's a Mr. Vincent Mason."

There was something vaguely familiar about the name, but Langston couldn't place it. "What has all this to do with me?" he replied.

"Mr. Mason was arrested for manufacturing PCP. He had set up a designer-drug operation down here. . . ."

"You don't mean he's the guy who made the bad heroin."

In 1817 the British surgeon James Parkinson wrote the classic clinical description of a neurological disorder that would eventually be named for him ("An Essay on the Shaking Palsy"). Parkinson's disease ravages the nerve cells that produce dopamine, a chemical that transmits nerve impulses vital to normal motor function. Patients experience a progressive loss of voluntary control over their movements and, in advanced cases, may become "frozen"—unable to speak or even to blink their eyes. An estimated 500,000 to one million persons in the U.S. alone are said to suffer from Parkinson's, most of them aged 60 and over. The cause—whether viral, genetic, environmental, or some combination of these factors—remains unknown.

In 1982 more than 100 U.S. drug abusers injected so-called designer drugs (compounds created to mimic addictive substances) tainted with a chemical called MPTP; the result was a minor epidemic of Parkinson's-like symptoms in a largely youthful population. Six of those individuals became patients of California neurologist William Langston and thus changed the course of his life and theirs. Langston had a busy clinical practice, but his chance involvement with these highly atypical Parkinson's sufferers redirected his energies toward his chief scientific interest, neurobehavioral research. With coauthor Jon Palfreman, Langston chronicles an eventful decade in

Parkinson's research and the fates of the unfortunate addicts who, albeit unintentionally, made a major contribution to the understanding of a devastating disease.

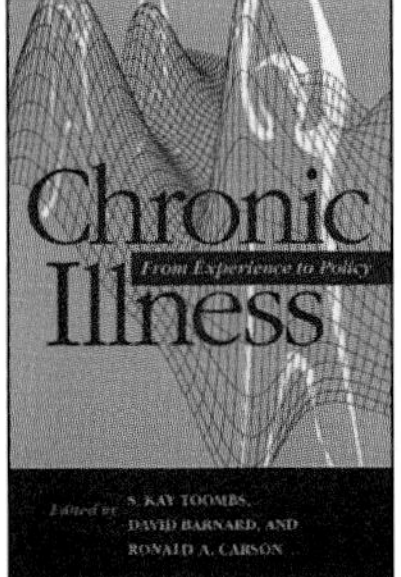

Chronic Illness: From Experience to Policy
S. Kay Toombs, David Barnard, and Ronald A. Carson, eds. Bloomington: Indiana University Press, 1995.
221 pp., bibliography, notes, index.
$27.95

Because chronic illness is illness that extends into the future, it defines the present from the future and in light of the pain, the disability, and ultimately the death that it portends. One crucial concern, therefore, is the . . . function of hope. Individuals suffering from chronic illness . . . cannot by mere exercise of will or professional ministration change . . . their condition. To try only breeds despair. Defenders of the mainstream model of autonomy often forget this compelling point. By underscoring . . . choice in a circumstance in which some of the most meaningful options are simply unavailable, they recommend what seems either absurd or cruel.

What does a child with cerebral palsy have in common with a stroke patient, a person with multiple sclerosis, and a survivor of disabling burns? All will live the rest of their lives in the unrelenting grip of a condition that inevitably delineates their interactions with others.

This book opens with two personal accounts of life with chronic illness, the first by one of the editors (S. Kay Toombs), who was diagnosed some 20 years ago with multiple sclerosis, and the second by the mother of a developmentally disabled child. Both of these narratives compellingly convey the acute self-consciousness and pervasive sense of isolation experienced by those singled out by disability. Three essays that follow concentrate on the importance—for health care workers in particular and for society in general—of understanding the "lived experience" of these individuals. The second half of the text consists of philosophical explorations of such issues as the relevance of autonomy in the context of chronic illness and the meaning of hope.

A chapter that draws a distinction between *respect*—which can be a negative, distance-producing attitude—and the more positive attitude of *regard* relies chiefly on autobiographical stories and poems that evoke the interior lives of the disabled. Another chapter explores an existential paradox—how those with chronic conditions must try to overcome the limitations imposed on them by the illness while at the same time accepting those limitations in order to avoid squandering precious energy. Although it may seem to be intended largely for health care providers, this thought-provoking volume has much that will interest a wider lay audience.

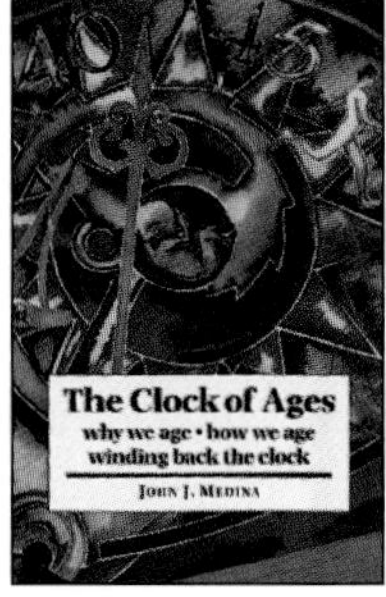

The Clock Of Ages: Why We Age—How We Age—Winding Back the Clock
John J. Medina. Cambridge: Cambridge University Press, 1996.
332 pp., illustrations, bibliography, index.
$24.95

We seem to share these mysterious biological clocks with every other living thing, and we know just as little about theirs as we do about our own. As is true for our own experience, we have found no external method to predict an individual animal's life span. The word to describe the life spans of living things is 'diversity.' For example, the golden splendor beetle . . . has a life span that can stretch more than four decades. . . . In California, there exist sequoia pines that started growing when the Egyptians were first building their pyramids. In the same state, a creosote plant nicknamed King Clone has been estimated to have been on the planet for nearly 12,000 years.

In what may be the most reader-friendly book to date about growing old, John Medina, a molecular biologist and member of the faculty of the University of Washington School of Medicine, explores the aging process in an unconventional but fascinating way. Beginning with the premise that death is not a mandatory requirement for every living thing (many organisms are capable of multiplying endlessly and never "die" in the technical sense), Medina suggests that human beings may not be as "mortal" as scientists have always assumed.

From this unique—and some would say optimistic—perspective, Medina attempts to humanize aging and death. He offers a thorough explanation of the natural process of programmed cell death (apoptosis), followed by a description of the part played by the immune system in aging and death. Despite the widely accepted notion that death can be studied scientifically, Medina is forced to concede that it is an elusive event. In fact, each death carries with it such a multitude of intricate system failures that scientific clarity is an impossibility. Medina therefore chooses to focus on the body systems individually in explaining why cells and tissues die and speculating on ways the deterioration can be slowed or even stopped. He likens the body to a well-built house, in which some structural elements—a window pane, for example—may be short-lived, while other parts—the hearth, say, or the foundation—remain intact much longer.

Each section of the book begins with a description of the untimely death of a well-known person—among them, the film star Rudolph Valentino (died of peritonitis at 31), the poet John Keats (tuberculosis, 26), and the Wild West outlaw Billy the Kid (shot down, 21). The choice of individuals immortalized in youth is deliberate. Medina believes that people should neither seek nor glorify eternal youth; instead, their goal should be to gain a full understanding of aging itself.

The Cure of Childhood Leukemia: Into the Age of Miracles
John Laszlo, M.D. New Brunswick, N.J.: Rutgers University Press, 1995.
287 pp., illustrations, bibliography, index. $29.95

> *Howard Skipper, Ph.D., calls himself a "mouse doctor" and confesses to puzzlement at being included here among the "real doctors" he so admires. As he looks back on his life as a biochemist in cancer research, he frets that "it has always seemed to take me inordinately long to recognize principles which in retrospect were really quite simple." His colleagues in cancer research, though, would laugh at these demurrals. They know that his work on leukemia in mice provided an essential model for treating human patients.*

It is not very often that scientists can assert unequivocally that they have developed a cure for what was previously a fatal form of cancer. John Laszlo, currently an officer of the American Cancer Society, provides a neat summary of the history of leukemia in general—*e.g.,* the earliest recognition of this cancer of the blood-forming organs and the subsequent elucidation of its types—and the treatment of childhood leukemia in particular. He then introduces nine researchers and clinicians whose work was especially important in finding a cure. Their personal stories combine to create a vivid and detailed picture of the world of biomedical research, with its serendipitous discoveries and dogged persistence in the face of failures and setbacks.

Among the scientists whose accounts form the core of the book are two physicians who experimented with early variants of chemotherapy, two chemists who searched for more effective drugs (and subsequently became Nobel laureates), and two innovative clinicians who combined existing drugs to produce "cures." Were the long years of study, hard work, late nights, and inevitable disappointments worth it? As if in answer to this question, Lazlo ends with memoirs by patients who, as youngsters, endured the rigors of treatment and triumphed—the "lucky ones," he calls them.

> *The other day while I was picking peas I started thinking about something that happened a couple of months ago when I gave a speech to some medical students about what it was like to be a patient. At the end of the speech, one of the students asked me an incredible question. He said, if I knew that I would be OK, that I wouldn't be sick again, and if I could choose, would I choose to have been sick, to have gone through the experience I had gone through, as awful as it had been. I looked at him, stunned. That was a secret. I had never said it out loud. Of course, I would never choose to have cancer—that's just silly—but you don't get to choose, and the secret he had guessed was that there were things about having had cancer that I liked.*

Alice Trillin is a producer of television programs for children. She is also a cancer survivor. In 1979, when she heard that a friend's 12-year-old son had been diagnosed with a rare form of lung cancer, she sat down and composed a letter to the boy, Bruno, in which she shared some of the feelings and experiences she remembered from her own lung cancer treatment three years earlier. Though there is little doubt that Bruno appreciated Trillin's words of encouragement, he did not get around to sending her a reply until 1995, explaining that he had been extremely busy in the interim, what with going to high school and then college (Harvard), traveling around the world, and climbing mountains.

A couple of years ago, Trillin found a copy of her letter just as she and her husband, the writer Calvin Trillin, were about to leave for a stint as volunteer counselors at the Hole in the Wall Gang Camp, a camp for children with cancer. Later that summer, when she read her letter to some young campers, they urged her to publish it.

Illustrated with whimsical drawings by cartoonist Edward Koren, the text of *Dear Bruno* shines in its simplicity. Probably because of the youthful age of her correspondent, Trillin adopted a disarmingly matter-of-fact tone, even about such fearful topics as radiation treatment and its unpleasant side effects. Temporarily unable to swallow as a result of the treatment, she subsisted on banana milkshakes and tells of the difficulty of explaining to her two young daughters why she was allowed to have dessert even though she had not eaten dinner. Trillin's description of what she terms the "ripeness" that comes from coping with a life-threatening illness reminds her readers that even the most painful and frightening experiences can lead to personal growth. As Trillin explained to Bruno, "I am a different person now."

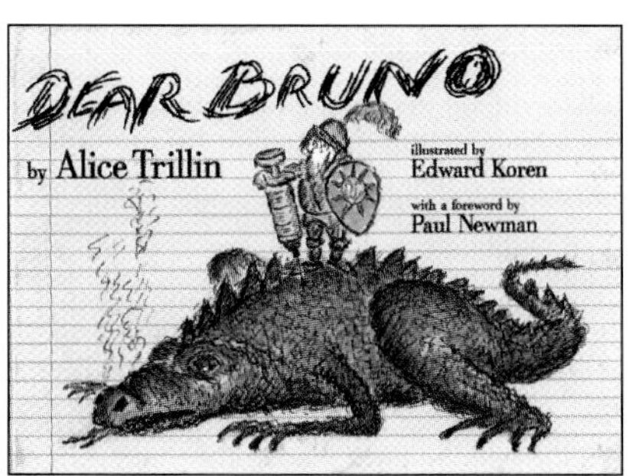

Dear Bruno
Alice Trillin.
New York:
The New Press,
1996.
32 pp., illustrations. $12.00

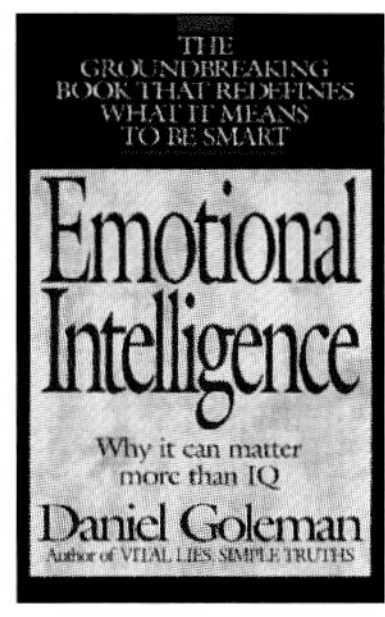

Emotional Intelligence
Daniel Goleman.
New York: Bantam Books, 1995.
352 pp., illustrations, notes, appendixes, index. $23.95

The emotional mind is far quicker than the rational mind, springing into action without pausing even a moment to consider what it is doing. Its quickness precludes the deliberate, analytic reflection that is the hallmark of the thinking mind. In evolution this quickness most likely revolved around that most basic decision, what to pay attention to, and, once vigilant while, say, confronting another animal, making split-second decisions like, Do I eat this, or does it eat me?

In this groundbreaking work that quickly achieved best-seller status, Daniel Goleman, a psychologist and contributing writer on behavioral sciences to the *New York Times,* questions the widely held view that IQ (intelligence quotient) alone is a measure or predictor of lifelong achievement or happiness. His thesis is that "emotional maturity" is ultimately more crucial to success. A term coined by Yale psychology professor Peter Salovey, *emotional intelligence* is the ability to respond to stressful situations—which often arise too suddenly for rational thought—with emotional wisdom. Characteristics of this special type of intelligence include acute self-knowledge and the finely honed abilities to express and manage feelings and to empathize with others.

Goleman peppers what could have been an academic, clinical treatise with real-life examples, many of which show how emotional intelligence can be used in creative and subtle ways to improve people's lives. His arguments throughout are compelling in their simplicity. Even complex structures and functions of the brain are deftly explained. He expresses concern for what he considers to be a worldwide crisis: a generation of children who are growing up without the family support necessary to develop a high level of emotional maturity. Goleman offers solutions to what he sees as today's chief societal ill—violence—which he considers to be, at least in part, a consequence of emotional immaturity. The author's reason for writing the book was to identify the factors that are contributing to a growing emotional malaise and to provide alternatives for coming generations. "Shouldn't we be teaching these most essential skills for life to every child—now more than ever? And if not now, when?" he asks.

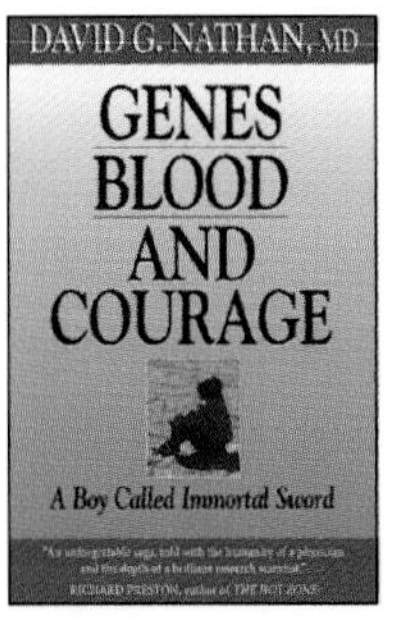

Genes, Blood, and Courage: A Boy Called Immortal Sword
David G. Nathan. Cambridge, Mass.: Belknap Press of Harvard University Press, 1995.
276 pp., illustrations, glossary, bibliography, index. $24.95

There is something about determination in a patient that changes the results of a procedure. Every doctor who has to use a difficult treatment or manage very ill patients has seen the effects of a patient's attitude and confidence on the outcome. We don't understand mind-body connections very well because they are so difficult to study with acceptably quantitative methods. We know, however, that confidence and will often seem to make an enormous difference.

David Nathan, a researcher and clinician specializing in inherited diseases of children, has written an engrossing book about a particular type of anemia known as thalassemia. Similar to sickle-cell anemia, thalassemia is a genetic disorder of the red blood cells; it is also called "Mediterranean anemia" because it is most prevalent in people of Mediterranean ancestry. Ironically, both thalassemia and sickle-cell anemia have a beneficial side effect: they confer protection against malaria on those who inherit the gene from one parent. When a child receives the gene for thalassemia from both parents, however, the disease is generally fatal before the youngster reaches puberty.

In telling the story of Dayem Saif, a Middle Eastern boy desperately ill with the disease, Nathan also describes many of the tremendous advances in medical genetics over the past 20 years. The author comes across as both an astute clinician and a remarkably compassionate human being. His patient, whose name means "immortal sword" in Arabic, is no less unusual. At age six, when he became Nathan's patient at Children's Hospital in Boston, Saif was no larger than a two-year-old, was suffering from early signs of heart failure, and had deformities of the face and skull—all hallmarks of severe thalassemia. He was also an engaging, strong-willed, and intelligent child, and the lasting bond that formed between this patient and his doctor makes this story all the more poignant. Thanks to Nathan's persistence and Saif's life-affirming outlook, the youngster lived to achieve an adulthood no one could have predicted for him.

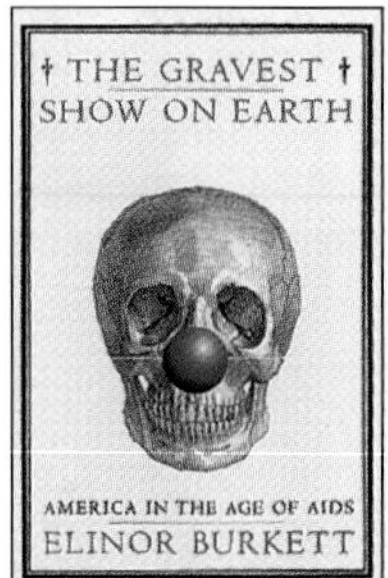

The Gravest Show on Earth: America in the Age of AIDS
Elinor Burkett.
Boston: Houghton Mifflin, 1995.
399 pp., bibliography, notes, index.
$24.95

I began to see AIDS as a lens through which the flaws of the nation were magnified. It revealed America's need to blame someone rather than to accept tragedy and cope with the truth of our relative powerlessness against nature. It shone a light on Americans' need to define themselves by membership in victim groups, competing for most-victimized status and the financial and psychic benefits that carried. AIDS provided a glimpse of a society more comfortable with fairy-tale villains—human or viral—than the reality of sluggish scientific progress and the complex interaction between behavior and infectious agents.

Elinor Burkett, an investigative reporter with a background in history, has written a stinging indictment of the U.S.'s response to the AIDS epidemic. Burkett exposes the greed and opportunism of the medical-industrial complex, the media, AIDS activists, and a host of other interest groups, each single-mindedly pursuing its own agenda.

When Burkett began reporting on AIDS for the *Miami* (Fla.) *Herald* in 1988, it seemed that a cure, or possibly even a vaccine, was just around the corner. Instead, as research foundered, the years dragged on, and the death toll mounted, the author began to see the epidemic and the way it was being handled as a metaphor for much that was wrong with the country—most notably and ominously, its unwillingness to confront hard, unpleasant, or inconvenient truths.

Starting with a clearly articulated description of what is known about the pathogenesis of HIV/AIDS, Burkett goes on to disclose questionable conduct by some researchers, condemn exploitation of the disease by Hollywood, and cite numerous miscalculations and blunders on the part of gay and lesbian organizations and other AIDS activists. Despite her uncompromisingly critical stance, the author is not without compassion. It is about those dying of AIDS in the prime of life that she writes most movingly, ending her story with the account of a memorial service for a gay activist.

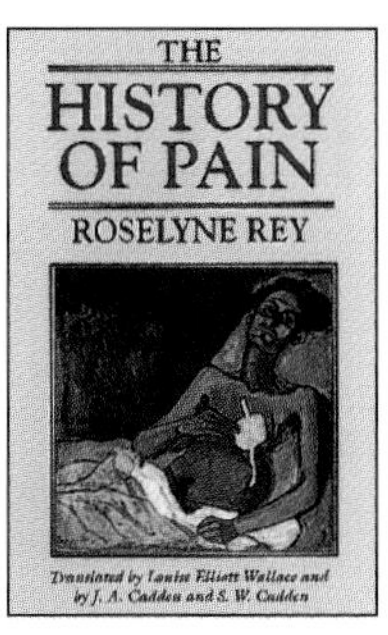

The History of Pain
Roselyne Rey. Translated from the French by Louise Elliott Wallace, J.A. Cadden, and S.W. Cadden.
Cambridge, Mass.: Harvard University Press, 1995.
394 pp., glossary, bibliography, notes, index. $39.95

Why, then, are individuals still suffering and why are we so powerless when it comes to certain intractable pains? Doesn't the time lapse between technical progress and the proposed treatments seem striking? The history of the relationship between pain-related knowledge and pain-relieving practices reveals that it has often been governed by differing rhythms and logic. . . . If the opening of the 19th century enjoyed a major leap forward with the discovery of morphine and its close with the advent of aspirin, our own century has yet to have produced anything of such revolutionary moment.

The observation of the 19th-century English poet Francis Thompson, "For we are born in other's pain,/And perish in our own," is a philosophical reminder that human life exists between the brackets of stimuli that are perceived as unpleasant at best, agonizing and intolerable at worst. To regard pain as a discrete entity with a linear history, as Roselyne Rey does in this scholarly work, offers another way of understanding it.

The author, a Parisian historian of medicine, begins by looking at the poetic portrayal of pain in *The Iliad.* Physicians in Homer's time conceived a sophisticated way of classifying pain; duration, intensity, and quality of pain were among the organizing principles. Searching for an appropriate way to define pain—was it a symptom or a sickness?—led to early explorations of human perceptions and sensibilities. Early Christians saw pain as having both cleansing and redeeming powers; thus, it was spiritually justified as a "necessary evil." Renaissance physicians devoted themselves to the relief of pain with anodynes (painkilling substances). Advances in the study of anatomy and the refinements in the preparation and use of medicines in the 18th century shed new light on the physiology of pain; the belief that all knowledge originated in sensation led physicians of the Enlightenment to regard pain as a distinct sixth sense.

The major focus of the book is contained in three long chapters: "Pain in the Age of Enlightenment," "The 19th Century: The Great Discoveries," and "Communication Strategies: The Approach to Pain During the First Half of the 20th Century." Rey's ambitious goals are to clarify the various scientific theories of pain that have held sway over the centuries, to elucidate the physiological mechanisms, and to chronicle the ongoing search for appropriate remedies. Readers will be rewarded by this fascinating history of a subject that continues to elude full understanding.

I'll Not Go Quietly: Mary Fisher Speaks Out
Mary Fisher. New York: Scribner, 1995.
219 pp., illustrations, notes, index. $20.00

My Name Is Mary: A Memoir
Mary Fisher. New York: Scribner, 1996.
288 pp., illustrations, notes, index. $24.00

I was asked to speak this evening under the title "Ignorance Is the Enemy." The assumption embedded in this title is that, if we knew more about AIDS, we would do more about AIDS. And I may as well tell you at the beginning that I am not sure this is true. . . .

I discovered nearly three years ago that I am also on the road to AIDS. I am no longer a spectator; I'm a traveler. When I asked others on the road to AIDS how I could help, they said, "Tell your story to those we can't reach. Go to the suburbs and to the families; go to the straight communities and to the women. Tell them, show them, that this is their disease."

At the 1992 Republican national convention in Houston, Texas, artist and socialite Mary Fisher delivered an electrifying speech describing her reaction to the news that she was HIV-positive. Overnight, this upper-class white mother of two became a nationally known figure and a powerful confounder of the AIDS stereotype. She also developed into an eloquent advocate for the HIV-positive community. *I'll Not Go Quietly* consists mainly of selections from speeches Fisher delivered around the U.S. in 1993 and 1994 to audiences ranging from church congregations to panels of medical experts and government officials.

My Name Is Mary is a revealing self-portrait in which Fisher describes her transformation from a gently reared child of affluence and prominent Republican Party functionary to a zealot, crusading for justice and compassion for people infected with HIV. She demanded that the nation acknowledge AIDS for what it is: an inevitably fatal disease that respects neither age, sexual orientation, color, nor socioeconomic class. She raised money and consciousness simply by telling her story.

This memoir is hardly a "little-rich-girl" fairy tale. The child of an alcoholic mother, deserted by her father, Fisher herself wrestled with alcoholism, drug dependency, a weight problem, and lack of self-esteem. Two divorces and many therapies later, she stepped forward to enlighten all Americans not only about HIV but about how to deal with adversity.

Infinite Jest: A Novel
David Foster Wallace.
Boston: Little, Brown and Co., 1996.
1,079 pp., notes and errata. $29.95

> *Ennet House Drug and Alcohol Recovery House was founded in the Year of the Whopper by a nail-tough old chronic drug addict and alcoholic who had spent the bulk of his adult life under the supervision of the Massachusetts Department of Corrections before discovering the fellowship of Alcoholics Anonymous . . . and undergoing a sudden experience of total self-surrender and spiritual awakening in the shower during his fourth month of continuous AA sobriety. This recovered addict/alcoholic—who in his new humility so valued AA's tradition of anonymity that he refused even to use his first name, and was known in Boston AA simply as the Guy Who Didn't Even Use His First Name—opened Ennet House within a year of his parole, determined to pass on to other chronic drug addicts and alcoholics what had been so freely given to him in the E-Tier shower.*

David Foster Wallace draws much of his knowledge of drug and alcohol addiction from the experiences of friends who allowed him to sit in on their Alcoholics Anonymous meetings. In this, his second novel, he has woven into one of the most omnibus plots since Thomas Pynchon's *Gravity's Rainbow* (1973) a keen understanding of the nature and consequences of addiction. While many of Wallace's characters suffer from fairly conventional forms of substance abuse and some are merely addicted to their own neuroses, several others develop a bizarre habit—they become hooked on a movie called *Infinite Jest,* which they watch over and over, powerless to tear themselves away.

Wallace presents a futuristic vision of a world in which advertising has gone berserk. Companies purchase the rights to entire calendar years and name them for products—*e.g.,* the Year of Glad (as in Glad Wrap) and the Year of Dairy Products from the American Heartland. Much of the novel's action takes place during the Year of the Depend Adult Undergarment (an aid for the incontinent), which corresponds to the 18th year in the life of Hal Incandenza. A member of his school's tennis elite and a superior student, Incandenza is also a habitual marijuana user. Wallace vividly chronicles his senior-year transformation into a full-blown drug addict.

By the end of the book, it becomes clear to the reader that everyone in the story is addicted to something and that, in fact, addiction is an integral part of life. Accordingly, the author of this tour de force refrains from passing judgment on Incandenza—or any of his other flamboyantly wayward characters.

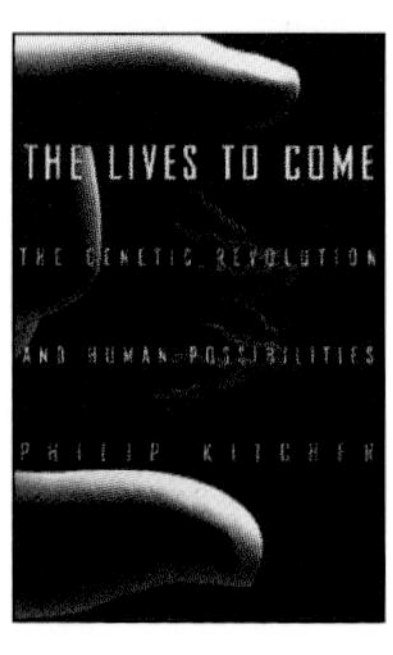

The Lives to Come: The Genetic Revolution and Human Possibilities
Philip Kitcher.
New York: Simon & Schuster, 1996.
381 pp., illustrations, glossary, notes, index. $25.00

> *Our lives are the products of many lotteries, and only one of them shuffles and distributes pieces of DNA. Behind the often acrimonious controversy about the value of molecular genetics is a deep disagreement about the implications of this fact, a disagreement dividing pragmatists from idealists. Their dispute intertwines two large classes of questions. What is the extent of our obligation to aid people whose initial circumstances greatly reduce the quality of the lives they can expect to lead? What are the practical possibilities for meeting this obligation, specifically for fighting the environmental causes of pinched and painful lives?*

The complex science of molecular genetics demands just the kind of step-by-step explanation that Philip Kitcher, presidential professor of philosophy at the University of California, San Diego, offers. His concise history of modern genetics begins with James Watson and Francis Crick's landmark description of the structure of DNA, published in a paper in the journal *Nature* in 1953. It then goes on to look at how the essential genetic material functions. Kitcher elaborates upon the mapping, sequencing, and cloning of disease-causing genes—monumental achievements of the past decade that have led to the development of tests to determine whether a given individual has inherited a mutation.

Described in detail is the centerpiece of the molecular revolution, the Human Genome Project, an ambitious international collaboration involving geneticists in Europe, North America, and Japan. Science of this magnitude does not operate in an ethical vacuum, and Kitcher examines some of the many bioethical dilemmas raised by the project. Will society condone the altering of genes to eliminate undesirable behavior traits such as violence? Should pregnancies be terminated when genetic testing indicates a defect? Who will reap the benefits of molecular medicine, society at large or only the privileged? Kitcher emphasizes that these are questions that must be confronted; many are already subjects of passionate debate. Finally, he insists that an active social conscience must guide the molecular revolution at every step to ensure that its medical and biological benefits are universally shared.

Mapping Fate: A Memoir of Family, Risk, and Genetic Research
Alice Wexler.
New York: Times Books, 1995.
294 pp., illustrations, notes. $23.00

I had never heard of Huntington's chorea until that afternoon in our father's apartment, and at first I did not want to learn too much, as if knowledge of the symptoms would bring them on. Mom's experience was not unusual. One morning in May, a policeman had seen her weaving her way across a parking lot in downtown Los Angeles, heading for jury duty in the Federal Building. "Hey, lady," he had called out, "aren't you ashamed of being drunk so early in the morning?" But she had not been drinking—in fact, she drank very little—and she must have known instantly what the words really meant.

Into this powerful and elegantly written story of her own family's experience with Huntington's disease, or HD (formerly known as Huntington's chorea), Alice Wexler weaves the story of the scientific search for HD's causes, for ways to test people who might be at risk, and for a possible cure. A hereditary neurological disorder, the disease usually appears in the fifth or sixth decade of life and is characterized by increasingly severe involuntary movements of the limbs and body, accompanied by unremitting cognitive deterioration. It is inevitably fatal, and so far no treatment—much less a cure—has been found.

Wexler's mother, Lenore Sabin Wexler, was diagnosed with HD in 1968. *Mapping Fate* records the family's private anguish and also tells of their resolutely courageous desire to do something beyond the family. The author's father, psychoanalyst Milton Wexler, organized the Hereditary Disease Foundation to facilitate research that might unlock the genetic secrets of HD. The author's younger sister, Nancy, a professor of neuropsychology at Columbia University College of Physicians and Surgeons, New York City, became director of a congressional commission on the disorder in 1976 and eventually a key participant in the genetic studies of HD.

The gene responsible for Huntington's disease was found in 1993. Studies are now under way to document how this gene does its damage. In telling the family's story, Alice Wexler not only honors her mother, to whose memory the book is dedicated, but also offers encouragement to other families whose lives continue to be blighted by the disease.

Our Stolen Future: Are We Threatening Our Fertility, Intelligence, and Survival? —A Scientific Detective Story
Theo Colborn, Dianne Dumanoski, and John Peterson Myers.
New York: Dutton, 1996.
306 pp., illustrations, notes, appendix, index. $24.95

Persistence is viewed as a virtue in people. In chemicals, it is the mark of a troublemaker. The synthetic chemical industry helped bring convenience and comfort to American homes, but at the same time, it unleashed dozens of chemicals, including PCBs, that became notorious for combining the devilish properties of extreme stability, volatility, and a particular affinity for fat.

Besides PCBs, this lot includes the pesticides DDT, chlordane, lindane, aldrin, dieldrin, endrin. toxaphene, heptachlor, and the ubiquitous contaminant dioxin, which is produced in many chemical processes and during the burning of fossil fuels and trash. They ride through the food web on particles of fat or vanish into vapors that gallop on the winds to distant lands.

When the synthetic hormone diethylstilbestrol (DES) and the pesticide DDT became available in 1938, it seemed that a new era of healthier pregnancies and more abundant crops was opening. What may have opened instead was a Pandora's box. By the 1950s some species of animals exposed to the "miraculous" new chemicals were beginning to exhibit developmental deformities and bizarre changes in reproductive behavior. It became clear in subsequent decades that the daughters of women who took DES to prevent miscarriages were unusually susceptible to vaginal cancer and that worldwide the populations of birds and other animals exposed to DDT were on the decline.

The subject of this book is the connection between the widespread use of synthetic chemicals and an emergent ecological crisis. In addition to DES and DDT, a number of other chemicals are linked to impaired reproduction in animals as diverse as beluga whales, lake trout, otters, and bald eagles, all of which have failed to thrive in recent decades.

The authors contend that similar warning signs may be appearing in the human population. For example, several studies have shown significant declines in human sperm counts; while these findings are still being debated, the authors argue that damage to reproductive and immune systems among all animals could soon be a reality. They cite the destruction of the ozone layer as further evidence of the scientific community's failure to predict the deleterious effects of the chemicals it continues to develop. Though some of its conclusions may call for cooler scientific scrutiny than is offered here, this book has been hailed as a worthy successor to Rachel Carson's classic *Silent Spring*.

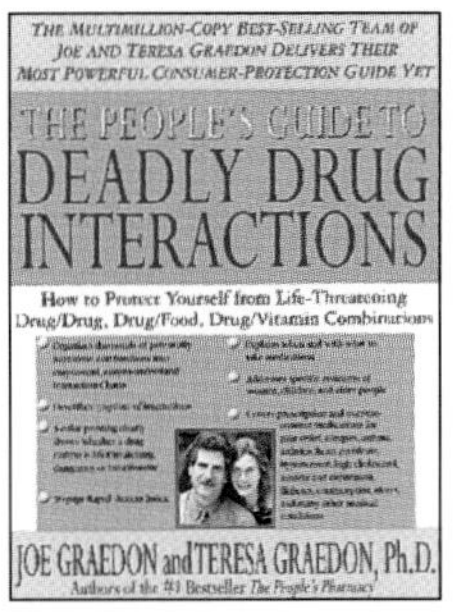

The People's Guide to Deadly Drug Interactions: How to Protect Yourself from Life-Threatening Drug/Drug, Drug/Food, Drug/Vitamin Combinations
Joe Graedon and Teresa Graedon, Ph.D.
New York: St. Martin's Press, 1995.
434 pp., illustrations, index. $25.95

When people drop dead of an apparent heart attack, it may be hard for the doctor to determine whether a medication or combination of medications could have contributed, especially if the drug is . . . seemingly benign. . . . Even if a doctor suspects that a patient's symptoms might be related to a combination of medicines, there is no simple way to alert others to this possibility. Getting a written report into the medical literature where other physicians can read it can take years.

Like their many earlier books and their syndicated newspaper column, "The People's Pharmacy," the Graedons' latest volume was prepared with the consumer in mind. Its purpose is to inform readers about the hundreds of interactions—many of them dangerous and some lethal—that can occur when specific drugs are taken with other agents or substances. The book's opening statement is the boldface caveat "This book is not intended as a substitute for the medical advice of physicians." Throughout the volume consumers are encouraged to have meaningful dialogues with their doctors and pharmacists about all the medications they are taking. The authors caution that one should never discontinue a medication or alter a dosage without medical advice, nor should anyone assume that if an interaction is not included in the book, it cannot occur.

The first half of the book describes in detail potentially hazardous interactions. Each chapter includes useful tables and drug lists, as well as a complete list of references at the end. The reader will learn, for example, what happens when ibuprofen, an over-the-counter nonsteroidal anti-inflammatory drug, or NSAID, used to treat arthritis and other painful inflammatory conditions, is taken along with a prescription blood thinner like warfarin. The book explains why vitamin/mineral supplements should be shunned by those taking the common antibiotic tetracycline. It also examines the surprising number of interactions that can occur as a result of taking certain drugs and consuming such presumably healthful foods as oatmeal or brussels sprouts.

The volume's second half puts this information into easy-to-consult chart form. Interactions are characterized by their level of hazard—"life-threatening," "dangerous," or merely "troublesome"—and warning symptoms are summarized. Joe and Teresa Graedon are highly respected pharmacology experts. Their newest guide is one that readers are likely to consult again and again.

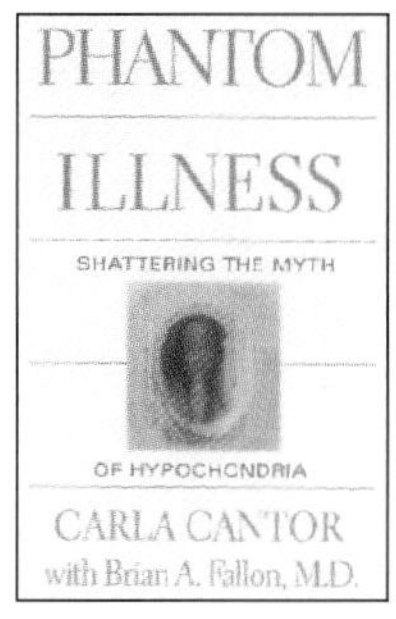

Phantom Illness: Shattering the Myth of Hypochondria
Carla Cantor, with Brian Fallon, M.D.
Boston: Houghton Mifflin, 1996.
351 pp., notes, appendix, index. $22.95

I didn't think I had the answers, yet I knew that what I had learned from my own experience and that of others could be prescriptive in its own way, without step-by-step solutions. After three years of studying and contemplating hypochondria in its various guises, I have become something of an expert on it. Still, I have trouble pinning the malady down: each time I put my finger on some tangible, universal truth, it slips away from me.

Is hypochondria a real illness? A state of mind? A bid for attention? Whatever it is, can anything be done to treat it? These are questions posed and answered by Carla Cantor, a journalist who suffers from the perplexing condition.

Indeed, hypochondria (morbid preoccupation with one's own health) has puzzled the medical profession for over 2,000 years. The 2nd-century Greek physician Galen was the first to use the term *hypochondriasis*—a condition he attributed to the production of excess bile by the spleen, an organ lying below the cartilage of the lower ribs. (*Hypo* means "below or under"; *chondros* means "cartilage.") This and other early ideas about hypochondria's physical origins have given way to psychological explanations. As Cantor points out, better understanding of the condition has enabled helpful treatments to be developed. Today many patients benefit from a combination of psychotherapy and psychoactive medication.

Cantor describes the disabling symptoms she knows all too well. First and foremost is the patient's fear of having or getting a terrible—and often unspecified—illness. Hypochondria sufferers typically experience pain and other physical manifestations that send them from doctor to doctor, and often from specialist to specialist, to have test after test. Even normal results fail to convince them that they are well. They continue to believe they are afflicted by some dread disease.

In addition to describing the many forms that hypochondria can take and pointing out its costs to society, Cantor offers case histories of individuals who have endured contempt and dismissal for their "imaginary ailments." Her message is that hypochondria is a treatable illness; in shattering the myths that surround it, she offers reassurance to others who may have hidden their fears, believing that nothing could be done.

Sleep Thieves:
An Eye-Opening Exploration into the Science and Mysteries of Sleep
Stanley Coren.
New York: The Free Press, 1996.
304 pp., bibliography, notes, index.
$24.00

Today, my favorite aid to sleep comes from trying to recall poems from various sources, such as Alice in Wonderland *or the writings of Carl Sandburg or even old nursery rhymes. I know the beginnings of most of them, but somehow I seldom make it through them far enough to determine if I know the whole poem. I simply start wandering through one of those poems and begin to doze off. A typical one to put me to sleep might be that famous child's poem by Eugene Field. Now how did that go? Wynken, Blynken and Nod one night / Set sail in a wooden shoe / Sailed on a river of crystal light / Into a sea of dew.*

In this thoughtful study of sleep in general and the effects of sleep deprivation on the many life situations that require alertness and sound judgment, Stanley Coren suggests that people need to reevaluate the amount of sleep they really get. Coren, a professor of psychology at the University of British Columbia, provides compelling evidence that today's society is becoming increasingly sleep-deprived. The author has sprinkled his text with folklore about sleep and is intent on correcting common misapprehensions about an activity "that plays a vital part in our health and our efficiency." In particular, he explodes the myth perpetuated by Thomas Edison, the inventor of the lightbulb, that too much sleep makes a person "dull and indolent."

Since the advent of electric light, Coren argues, people have tried to ignore the fact that to function properly, everyone needs sleep. And although many individuals claim that they can function at maximum potential on less, 8–10 hours of sleep is the minimum needed by the average human being. Coren is firm on this point, despite some research done in the last 20 years suggesting that less sleep is acceptable—or even better. His own studies have convinced him that most Americans get far less than they should, with negative—sometimes serious—consequences. He goes so far as to link sleep deprivation to the human errors that triggered such disasters as the *Exxon Valdez* oil spill and the explosion of the nuclear reactor at Chernobyl.

Having discussed sleep from physiological and evolutionary perspectives, Coren provides tips on how to recognize sleep deprivation at all stages of life and how to alleviate it. His chapters on sleepy children, sleepy parents, and sleepy teenagers offer practical help for fatigued families. In addition, his descriptions of many sleep-related disorders provide anyone who has trouble sleeping with a better idea of what might be causing the problem.

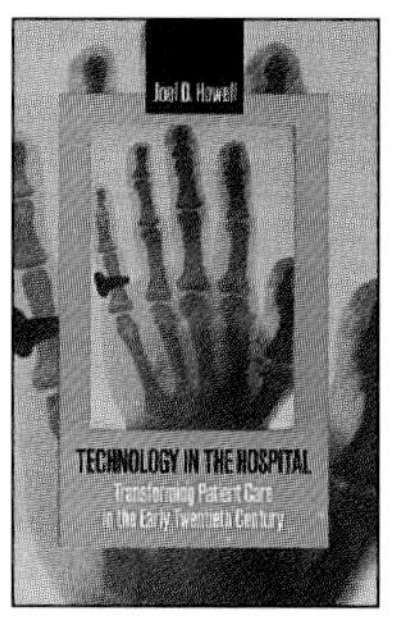

Technology in the Hospital:
Transforming Patient Care in the Early Twentieth Century
Joel D. Howell. Baltimore:
Johns Hopkins University Press, 1995.
341 pp., illustrations, notes, appendix, index. $47.50

For whatever reason, early in the twentieth century there was an astonishing increase in the number of operations performed in hospitals. The most commonly performed operation at the Pennsylvania Hospital in 1895 was done 25 times; the most commonly performed operation in 1925 was done 1,356 times. The total number of operations went from 870 in 1900 to 4,180 in 1925. These raw figures start to suggest the overall transformation that took place in the hospital. The impact of this new activity was felt at every level: housekeeping, nursing, cooking, accounting.

Better stethoscopes and advanced sterilizing techniques, new methods for analyzing blood and urine, and electrocardiograms and X-rays were among the many innovations that transformed the early-20th-century hospital from a holding area for the hopelessly ill to a place where patients could reasonably expect to be cured. Joel Howell, a physician and medical historian, chronicles both the dramatic and the subtle aspects of this transformation as it occurred in hospitals in the United States. In the course of his research, he reviewed the records of more than 2,000 patients treated between 1900 and 1925 at the Pennsylvania Hospital in Philadelphia and New York Hospital, New York City.

Two major chapters are devoted to the medical revolution brought about by Wilhelm Röntgen's discovery of X-rays in 1895. "It is difficult to overestimate the profound impact the invention of the x ray had on the broadest possible scope of humankind," writes Howell. In addition to describing how X-rays provided the first *noninvasive* way to examine internal structures of the body, the author considers the new rays' *invasive* potential. Indeed, the public at large tended to view X-rays as a major threat to privacy.

Technology also created disparities in hospital-based patient care. As the author points out, "All technologies did not follow the same trajectory." Consequently, it took several decades for medicine to "catch up with itself" and for procedures such as urinalysis and blood counts to become as sophisticated as, say, techniques for repairing fractures.

Howell clearly connects early advances in technology with changes in the doctor-patient relationship. For better or worse, that relationship continues to alter as medicine continues to be transformed by technology. *Technology in the Hospital* is a scrupulously researched and illuminating history that will be appreciated by almost anyone interested in the evolution of modern medicine. The author is currently preparing a "sequel" on technology in early-20th-century British hospitals.

Time on Fire: My Comedy of Terrors
Evan Handler.
Boston: Little, Brown and Co., 1996.
279 pp., notes. $21.95

There is little chance that I could ever give an accurate, visceral impression of what the chemotherapy treatment for acute leukemia felt like physically. But believe me, if the body had any sense of its own, it would not allow what was about to happen to begin. Death be damned, no body would allow itself to be punctured and poisoned, to be reduced to a state of heinous malfunction without an egocentric personality running the show. The body knows that the universe is just as accepting of its death as of its life. Only the frightened person steering the ship believes that the Earth needs them alive as desperately as they need Her to live.

And that's what makes chemotherapy possible.

In 1985 when Evan Handler, then a 24-year-old actor, learned that he had acute myelogenous leukemia, he had little hope of being cured. Untreated patients usually died quickly, and the chemotherapy available to Handler was painful and potentially toxic. Over the next five years, he rode the physical and emotional roller coaster of life with a grave illness. Handler's story, which is sometimes funny and often deeply distressing, tells of his less-than-satisfactory treatment at a major New York City cancer center. His account of his experiences as a patient invites the reader to share in his rage. Why, he demands, are doctors, technicians, and nurses so unresponsive?

The exemplary treatment he later receives at another hospital in another city is in stark contrast to his initial experiences, and Handler makes a point of detailing the differences between the two institutions and their staffs. Handler survives his illness, enlisting an army of therapists, gurus, mystics, friends, relatives, and lovers. One of his most significant discoveries was that he could exercise his right to disagree with doctors and regulations. Seven years after a successful bone marrow transplant, the author finds that, happily, he takes life for granted once again.

An Unquiet Mind:
A Memoir of Moods and Madness
Kay Redfield Jamison.
New York: Alfred A. Knopf, 1995.
224 pp. $22.00

Doctors, of course, need first to heal themselves; but they also need accessible, competent treatment that allows them to heal. The medical and administrative system that harbors them must be one that encourages treatment . . . but also one that does not tolerate incompetence. . . . Doctors, as my chairman is fond of pointing out, are there to treat patients; patients never should have to pay—either literally or medically—for the problems and sufferings of their doctors. I strongly agree with him about this; so it was not without a sense of dread that I waited for his response to my telling him that I was being treated for manic-depressive illness, and that I needed to discuss the issue of my hospital privileges with him. I watched his face for some indication of how he felt. Suddenly, he reached across the table, put his hand on mine, and smiled. "Kay, dear," he said, "I know *you have manic-depressive illness." He paused, and then laughed. "If we got rid of all of the manic-depressives on the medical school faculty, not only would we have a much smaller faculty, it would also be a far more boring one."*

In this firsthand account of manic-depressive illness (also known as bipolar disorder), psychologist Kay Redfield Jamison vividly describes her long struggle with an ailment that is characterized by spectacular mood swings. Her story is sometimes grim and terrifying, sometimes ecstatic and deeply personal, but never sentimental.

Jamison, a professor of psychiatry at the Johns Hopkins University School of Medicine, Baltimore, Md., has had an indisputably distinguished career. She has come to grips with her own illness by making it her professional specialty. Her previous book, *Touched with Fire: Manic-Depressive Illness and the Artistic Temperament* (1993), examined the lives of artists who suffered from either bipolar disorder or severe depression—Virginia Woolf, Lord Byron, Herman Melville, and Robert Schumann among them. Perhaps what makes *An Unquiet Mind* so compelling is that she wrote it largely as a "confession" to her professional colleagues. Because her illness has been well controlled for many years with the mood-stabilizing medication lithium and psychiatric treatment, she had not previously revealed to those she works with that she suffers from a serious mental disorder. In the book, she recounts at what cost her achievements have come and writes compellingly of the professional dilemma she has long faced: should she treat patients when she herself is "ill"?

Jamison's disorder has evoked periods of hypermanic activity and acute intellectual clarity, but these invariably gave way to periods of profound, toxic depression. She has been hospitalized, attempted suicide, and taken many different psychoactive drugs, sometimes to overdose. For years she fought taking lithium, contending that she did not want to compromise the energy and inspiration that accompanied her disorder, even if it meant not being in control of her emotions. Now she says without hesitation that lithium restored her sanity and saved her life.

—books selected and reviews prepared by Jean S. Gottlieb, freelance editor and historian of science, Fort Myers Beach, Fla., and Chicago, and Medical and Health Annual *editors Ellen Bernstein, Sara Brant, and Linda Tomchuck*

Recent Developments from the World of Medicine

AIDS Update

The past year was marked by important developments in understanding of the pathogenesis of HIV (the process by which the virus causes illness) and improved strategies for combating infection. In sharp contrast to these positive steps were reports of the rapid and relentless spread of the disease in large parts of the world. In June 1996 the United Nations Joint Program on HIV-AIDS issued new data showing that the number of persons ill with symptoms of AIDS rose by 25% between 1994 and 1995. According to the program's estimates, 21 million adults worldwide are infected with HIV, and 7,500 new infections occur each day. The virus was reported to be spreading especially rapidly in India, which had emerged as the country with the largest number of infected persons—over three million. At the same time, the infection rate was apparently stabilizing in countries like Uganda and Thailand in response to AIDS-awareness campaigns. Even with a decline in incidence, however, Thailand still faces an epidemic of huge proportions—an estimated one million of its 60 million inhabitants are HIV-infected.

U.S. toll: half a million cases and counting

By the end of 1995, reported cases of AIDS in the United States had surpassed 500,000. The death toll stood at approximately 300,000, or nearly two-thirds of all those who had become ill. Although homosexual and bisexual men account for fewer than 50% of new AIDS cases each year, they still represent the country's largest single group of AIDS patients. Injecting drug users constitute the next largest group. Of 74,000 new cases of AIDS reported in 1995, 35% were associated with the use of intravenous drugs. Although the annual increase in the number of cases has slowed somewhat in recent years among drug users themselves, a steady increase continues among their heterosexual contacts.

The Centers for Disease Control and Prevention (CDC) estimated that in the U.S. alone, nearly 42,000 persons died from AIDS in 1994, the most recent year for which complete data were available. HIV infection was the leading cause of death among men aged 25 to 44 and the third leading cause for women in this age group. The disproportionate impact of the epidemic on African-Americans was reflected in the mortality figures: the death rate from HIV infection was almost four times higher for black men than for white men and nine times higher for black women than for white women.

The first HIV test for home use was approved by the Food and Drug Administration (FDA) in May 1996. AIDS advocates had varying reactions. Some applauded the FDA for taking a step that might encourage people to learn their HIV status; others were opposed to the concept of home testing because the results are made available by phone, and those who receive the news that they are infected do not have the benefit of face-to-face counseling. Distribution of the test kits was initially limited to over-the-counter sales in Texas and phone sales through a toll-free number in Texas and Florida. The test was to become available in pharmacies throughout the U.S. in early 1997 and was expected to sell for $40–$50. Given the cost of the kit and the fact that results can be learned only over the telephone, some authorities doubted that adolescents, drug users, and others at high risk would make much use of the procedure. They predicted that the market for the kit would be found largely among the "worried well."

Spread of subtypes

Epidemiologists have been following with particular interest the distinct pattern of spread of different strains, or subtypes, of HIV in Thailand. Individual isolates of HIV are grouped into types and subtypes on the basis of genetic differences and similarities. Two major types of HIV are known: type M (main) viruses, which includes at least eight subtypes, and type O (other) viruses, which have only recently been recognized and thus far are found only in Africa. Subtype B is the predominant type-M strain circulating in North America and Europe. Subtype E is found primarily in Thailand and other Southeast Asian countries. Subtype B also circulates in Thailand but is spreading principally among injecting drug users. Most of the HIV vaccines under development are based on subtype B; therefore, if the other subtypes achieve worldwide distribution, the entire vaccine strategy may have to be rethought.

The sharp distinction between the heterosexual spread of subtype E viruses and the spread by needle sharing of subtype B viruses in Thailand prompted speculation that one strain

(Below) In Thailand, where the extremely high rate of HIV infection seems to be stabilizing, a "sex worker" undergoes a weekly test for HIV. (Below right) The first home blood-collection kit for diagnosing HIV infection was approved in May 1996 and was expected to be available in U.S. pharmacies by early 1997.

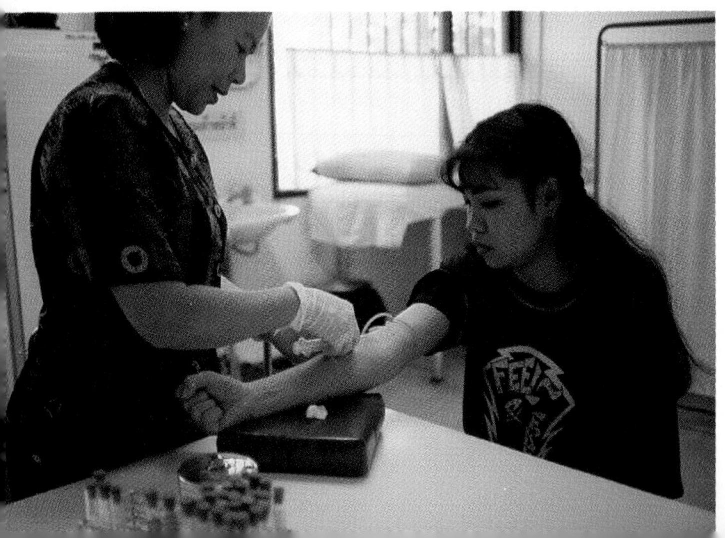

is more easily spread by sexual contact than the other. In laboratory studies at the Harvard School of Public Health, investigators showed that subtype E isolates are better able than subtype B isolates to infect specialized immune cells that line the genital tract. If confirmed, these results could suggest a virological basis for the dramatic spread of subtype E among heterosexuals in Southeast Asia. Subtype B isolates are nevertheless fully transmissible by heterosexual contact, as is demonstrated by the spread of this subtype among the sexual partners of injecting drug users in the U.S.

An even safer blood supply

Rigorous screening of blood donors has been in effect in the U.S. since the mid-1980s. These measures have been quite effective, reducing to a tiny percentage the donated units of blood that test positive for HIV (approximately 0.008%, or 8 out of 100,000 donations). Blood found to be infected is either discarded or used for research purposes.

HIV infection is usually diagnosed by a blood test that identifies antibodies to the virus. In most individuals HIV antibodies become evident three to four weeks after infection. Prior to that time, however, during the so-called window period, HIV infection cannot be discovered by standard antibody tests. Infection can be diagnosed during the window period by detecting the presence of viral particles in the blood. A test capable of detecting one component of the viral particle, the protein known as the p24 antigen, received FDA approval in March 1996, and as a consequence, U.S. blood banks revised their screening procedures.

The CDC has estimated that of the 12 million blood donations made annually in the U.S., approximately 18 to 27 come from donors in the window period. Prior to the approval of the new blood test, the chance of receiving a transfusion of HIV-infected blood was estimated to be about one in 500,000. Use of the p24 antigen assay is expected to reduce the risk of transfusion-related infection to around one in a million.

Viral load: a window on progression

During the past year scientists have made critical discoveries concerning the relationship between the number of virus particles, or virions, circulating in the blood of infected individuals and the rate at which AIDS develops. In the past, efforts to quantify the amount, or titer, of HIV in the blood relied on assays that were imprecise and relatively insensitive. Such assays depended on scientists' being able to grow HIV in the laboratory or to detect proteins like the p24 antigen, which make up the virion core. Although these tests were useful for addressing specific research questions in the context of clinical trials, they had limited application to the day-to-day management of patients with HIV infection.

By applying techniques from molecular biology to the quantification of HIV, scientists have developed assays based on detection of the virus's RNA—its genetic material. (Like all retroviruses, HIV carries its genetic information in the form of RNA rather than DNA.) Several different RNA assays have been adapted for commercial use and are now widely available.

Because each particle of HIV contains two nearly identical RNA molecules, measurement of the amount of viral RNA in the blood or plasma (the fluid portion of blood) provides an accurate estimate of the number of circulating virus particles. The titer of circulating virus is often referred to as the "viral load." AIDS experts point out, however, that plasma titers of virus provide only an estimate of the total amount of virus in the body of an infected person; most HIV resides in the lymphoid tissues (*i.e.,* the lymph nodes, ducts, and vessels).

RNA assays can provide important information on patients' prognosis and response to treatment. Several different groups of investigators have shown that the quantity of HIV RNA in plasma is directly related to the stage of disease. High titers of viral RNA (100,000–1,000,000 RNA molecules, or "copies," per milliliter) are found in plasma during initial, or primary, HIV infection, but lower levels (fewer than 10,000 copies per milliliter) are seen as the infected person develops an effective immune response to the virus. Replication of HIV does not cease completely at this time, but it is brought under control by the immune system, which leads to the temporary establishment of a steady state, or equilibrium, between the body and the virus. It is the eventual depletion by HIV of T-helper cells, also known as CD4+ lymphocytes (which, along with monocytes, are the immune system cells targeted by the virus), that leads to immunodeficiency and AIDS. As the immune system deteriorates, the rate of virus production increases, and the plasma levels of HIV RNA rise. Thus, the lowest levels of virus are found in relatively healthy patients with normal CD4+ lymphocyte counts. Slightly higher levels are found in patients with lower CD4+ counts and mild symptoms of HIV infection, and the highest levels of virus are found in patients with nearly depleted CD4+ lymphocytes and AIDS. (Healthy people have from 800 to 1,200 CD4+ lymphocytes per cubic millimeter of blood. A CD4+ count of 200 or less is diagnostic of AIDS.)

A study by scientists at the University of Pittsburgh, Pa., conducted as part of the Multicenter AIDS Cohort Study (MACS), provided evidence for the usefulness of plasma HIV RNA levels as a means of predicting the course of HIV infection. Using stored blood samples obtained 5–10 years earlier, when the subjects—all HIV-infected homosexual men with no symptoms of AIDS—enrolled in the MACS, the Pittsburgh team determined plasma HIV RNA levels. When the researchers analyzed the relationship of viral load to the risk of death from AIDS in the intervening years, they found that the death rate was highest among individuals with the highest HIV RNA levels when they entered the investigation (*see* diagram, page 166). The findings were particularly striking for patients with relatively normal CD4+ counts, in whom viral load was a much better predictor of outcome than was CD4+ count. Similar results in patients with moderately advanced HIV infection were reported by investigators from the AIDS Clinical Trials Group (ACTG). Both studies were sponsored by the U.S. National Institutes of Health (NIH).

The results of these studies can be explained by work conducted by investigators at the Aaron Diamond AIDS Research Center in New York City and the University of Alabama at Birmingham. In 1995 these groups reported that the amount of HIV in the blood of an infected person at any given time

(Opposite page, left) Peter Barker—Panos Pictures; (right) Ron Edmonds—AP/Wide World is the result of a dynamic equilibrium between the production of virus in lymphoid tissues and the continuous clearance of the virus from the body by the immune system. These same investigators also demonstrated that virus production is tightly coupled to destruction of CD4+ lymphocytes. Further work by the New York City scientists has provided evidence that the quantity of viral RNA in the blood of an infected individual is related to the rate of virus production in that individual. Since the rate of CD4+ lymphocyte destruction is also proportional to the rate of virus production, measurements of plasma HIV RNA levels in fact provide a reliable estimate of the rate at which the immune system is being depleted.

Equally significant were the results of three studies conducted by the Adult ACTG and a fourth by the Department of Veterans Affairs, which explored the relationship between treatment-induced changes in HIV RNA levels and clinical benefits (*i.e.,* reduced occurrence of opportunistic infections; improved survival). Each of these studies demonstrated that a reduction in viral load in response to treatment correlated with a reduced risk of disease progression. Moreover, the degree of benefit of a particular treatment was strongly associated with the extent to which viral load was reduced. These studies imply that maximum benefits of treatment will be obtained by maximal suppression of HIV replication.

These findings also suggest that monitoring the effect of treatment on plasma HIV RNA levels might be a useful way of individualizing therapies for HIV infection, much as monitoring blood sugar levels in a person with diabetes helps the physician determine the appropriate insulin dose for that particular patient. The first test for measurement of HIV RNA levels was approved by the FDA in June 1996. It is likely that in the future the agency will rely on changes in plasma HIV RNA levels, as well as changes in CD4+ counts, as evidence that new anti-HIV drugs have potential clinical benefit. Thus, HIV RNA assays could replace the more costly and time-consuming clinical end points trials, which judge the effectiveness of therapies in terms of disease progression and patient survival.

Viral Load and Risk of Death[1]

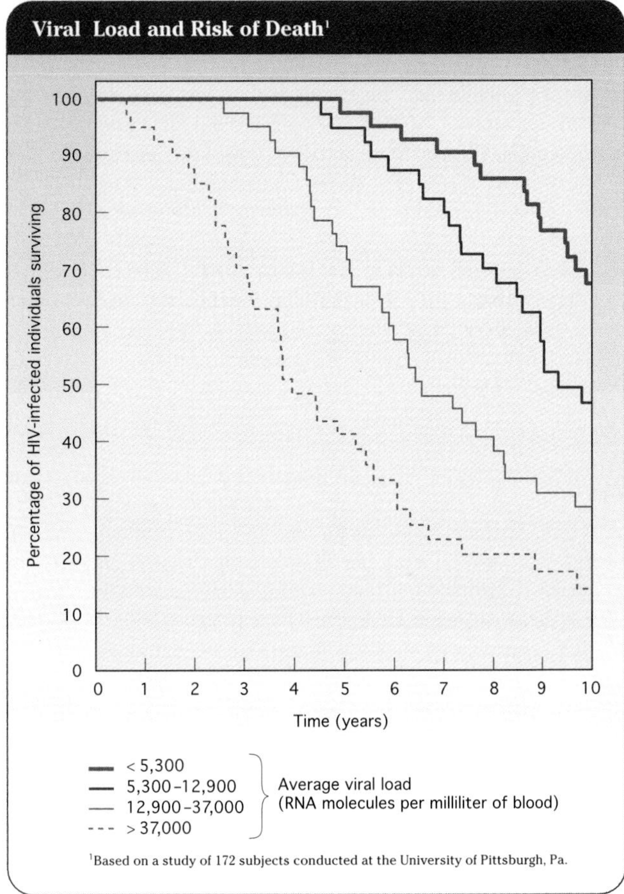

[1]Based on a study of 172 subjects conducted at the University of Pittsburgh, Pa.

A crucial role for coreceptors

Revelations about how HIV enters and infects cells have shed new light on the disease process. As mentioned above, HIV selectively infects two types of immune system cells, CD4+ lymphocytes and monocytes. The virus identifies its targets by recognizing a specific receptor molecule, known as CD4, which is found on the surface of both of these kinds of cells. The attachment of virus particles to these "host" cells is mediated by a protein in the outer coat, or envelope, of the virus, which binds tightly to CD4. Once the virus is bound to the receptor, secondary interactions occur between the virus and the host cell, which lead to fusion of the cellular and viral membranes. Fusion is necessary for the core of the virus, which contains the RNA, to enter the cell and begin the process of infection.

For many years investigators had suspected that in addition to CD4, another receptor—or possibly more than one—must play a part in the fusion process. In the spring of 1996, several research teams demonstrated that at least two such coreceptors do indeed exist. The first coreceptor, discovered by investigators from the National Institute of Allergy and Infectious Diseases in Bethesda, Md., was given the name fusin because of its role in promoting fusion of infected CD4+ lymphocytes (which express HIV envelope protein on their surface) with neighboring, uninfected CD4+ lymphocytes. Although fusin's normal role in the body is unknown, its molecular structure closely resembles that of the interleukin-8 receptor. (Interleukins are a class of cytokines, proteins released by cells of the immune system to regulate immune responses.)

While fusin appears to be essential for the entry of certain strains of HIV into CD4+ lymphocytes, it does not mediate the entry of other strains into CD4+ lymphocytes or monocytes. Since monocytes are believed to be the first cells in the body to come into contact with HIV and serve as an important reservoir of virus in the central nervous system, understanding how HIV gains access to these cells is of considerable importance. In a pair of articles in the June 1996 issue of *Nature,* two teams of scientists in the U.S. reported that they had identified a second coreceptor for HIV, one that mediates the entry of the virus into monocytes. The normal function of this molecule, named CC-CKR-5, is to serve as a receptor for a special class of cytokines called chemokines. Chemokines are small messenger molecules secreted by immune cells to attract different types of white blood cells to sites of inflammation. Certain chemokines are known to inhibit infection by some strains of HIV. It now seems likely that these inhibitory chemokines block HIV infection by competing for CC-CKR-5, thereby preventing HIV from binding

Mike Greenlar—The New York Times

Thanks to new drug regimens, prolonged survival now seems a possibility for New York City artist Frank Moore and thousands of other Americans living with AIDS.

to the receptor. Since these chemokines are small molecules that are easily synthesized, the discovery of their interaction with CC-CKR-5 could open the way for the development of an entirely new class of anti-HIV drugs.

Combination therapy: benefits confirmed

In 1995–96 patients, physicians, and AIDS researchers were buoyed by the results of several major clinical trials and the approval of five new drugs for the treatment of HIV infection. The largest of the clinical trials, ACTG protocol 175, compared the effectiveness of a single anti-HIV drug, either zidovudine (AZT) or didanosine (ddI), versus combinations of AZT plus ddI or AZT plus zalcitabine (ddC). More than 2,400 patients were followed for as long as three years. The study found that treatment with either ddI alone or with one of the combination regimens led to a significant reduction in the rate of disease progression and to improved patient survival as compared with treatment with AZT alone. Although the study did not definitively determine whether combination therapy is superior to treatment with ddI alone, the findings favored early use of combination therapy.

Similar results were obtained in trials by European and Australian investigators (the Delta trial) and by the U.S.-based Community Programs for Clinical Research on AIDS (the CPCRA NuCombo study). Both demonstrated that combination therapy delayed the onset of AIDS and improved survival when compared with AZT alone as initial therapy for HIV infection. ACTG 152, a trial involving HIV-infected children, also found that either ddI alone or a combination of ddI with AZT significantly delayed progression to AIDS or death.

As a result of these studies, the treatment of HIV infection has changed significantly. In the view of most experts, a combination of AZT plus other HIV inhibitors is now recommended in place of AZT alone for the treatment of HIV infection. These data also provide important evidence that for those who are infected but asymptomatic, early initiation of anti-HIV therapy can prolong survival.

New anti-HIV drugs

Armed with new evidence of the clinical benefits of treatment, the FDA moved swiftly to approve new drugs for the treatment of HIV infection. In November 1995 accelerated approval was granted for lamivudine (3TC; Epivir), a nucleoside analog (the category that also includes AZT and ddI) that acts by inhibiting the reverse transcriptase enzyme of HIV. (Reverse transcriptase is required for the synthesis of DNA from viral RNA, a crucial early step in the infection process.) Patients treated with a combination of AZT and 3TC had sustained decreases in viral load and substantial increases in CD4+ lymphocyte counts. The FDA set a precedent by approving 3TC "for the treatment of HIV infection" rather than limiting use of the drug to a specific group of patients (for example, those with CD4+ counts under 500), thus allowing clinicians to determine the best time to initiate treatment. Lamivudine was also approved for the treatment of pediatric HIV infection.

Nevirapine (Viramune) was granted accelerated approval in June 1996. Unlike AZT, ddI, and 3TC, nevirapine is a nonnucleoside reverse transcriptase inhibitor; it acts by blocking HIV reverse transcriptase, but it does so by a completely different mechanism from the nucleoside analogs. In a study by Boehringer Ingelheim Pharmaceuticals, Inc., manufacturer of the drug, 60% of those who received the three-drug combination AZT-ddI-nevirapine had undetectable plasma HIV RNA levels for the duration of the 52-week study. By comparison, viral RNA was undetectable in only 30% of patients who received the two-drug combination of AZT plus ddI.

Saquinavir (Invirase), a member of the newer class of antiretroviral drugs known as protease inhibitors, was granted accelerated approval in November 1995. Protease inhibitors prevent viral replication by blocking the action of HIV protease, an enzyme required for the maturation of new virus particles. Drugs that inhibit this enzyme lead to the production of noninfectious virus. An ACTG study showed that patients who received saquinavir in combination with AZT plus ddC experienced greater reductions in plasma HIV RNA levels compared with patients who received two-drug combinations consisting of either AZT plus ddC or AZT plus saquinavir. Although saquinavir has few side effects, its anti-HIV activity is limited by very poor absorption when taken orally. Attempts are under way to enhance the absorption of the drug by altering its formulation. Despite this limitation, a recently concluded trial conducted in Europe and Canada found that the combination of saquinavir plus ddC slowed progression to AIDS or death compared with treatment with either drug alone.

Ritonavir (Norvir) and indinavir (Crixivan), two other protease inhibitors recently approved for clinical use, have substantially greater anti-HIV activity than saquinavir. Even when given individually, these drugs can produce 100-fold reductions in the amount of circulating HIV. By comparison, the combination of AZT plus 3TC reduces viral load only 80-fold. When ritonavir and indinavir are given singly, however, their activity is ultimately limited by the emergence of drug-resistant HIV variants. Resistance can be delayed or prevented by use of the protease inhibitors in combination with nucleoside analogs. In a study of the three-drug combination of indinavir plus AZT and 3TC, plasma HIV RNA levels were suppressed below the limit of detection in 90% of patients for at least six months. The longevity of this dramatic treatment effect remains to be determined, as the study is ongoing.

The benefits of protease inhibitor therapy were proved in a clinical trial of ritonavir. In this study, sponsored by the drug's manufacturer, Abbott Laboratories, more than 1,000 patients with advanced HIV disease (CD4+ counts below 100) were randomly assigned to receive either ritonavir or a placebo in addition to any treatment they were already receiving. After just six months, a significant difference between the two groups emerged; patients receiving ritonavir developed AIDS-related complications at half the rate of the placebo group. Moreover, the death rate in the ritonavir group was 50% that of the placebo group. Consequently, the study was halted and all patients offered ritonavir. The drug was approved swiftly by the FDA, just 72 days after the application was filed by the company. Approval of indinavir followed quickly, in a record 42 days after filing. The breathless pace left indinavir's manufacturer, Merck & Co., Inc., unprepared to cope with the demand, and the company had to restrict U.S. distribution of the drug to a single mail-order pharmacy until new production facilities could be brought into operation.

A growing role for specialists

The availability of nine approved drugs for treatment of HIV infection, along with new tools for monitoring the response to treatment, creates new challenges for practitioners who treat HIV-infected individuals. Experience gained during the development of the protease inhibitors suggests that the most effective way to prevent the emergence of drug resistance is to treat patients with a combination of drugs at their maximally tolerated doses. This strategy dovetails with the results of clinical trials data supporting the early use of combination therapy. The watchword in AIDS treatment these days is "hit early, hit hard."

A corollary of the growing complexity of AIDS therapies is that HIV infection is no longer a disease that can be adequately treated in a primary-care setting. Until fairly recently, many health policy experts believed that HIV-infected individuals could be cared for by generalists during the early phases of the illness, reserving referral to AIDS specialists for those with complicated, late-stage disease. As multidrug regimens become the standard of care for patients in early-stage disease, generalists will be less able to cope with the intricacies of HIV treatment, and earlier referral to specialists will be necessary.

The benefits to patients of care by practitioners knowledgeable in the treatment of HIV was demonstrated in a study conducted by the Group Health Cooperative of Puget Sound, a health maintenance organization in Washington state. The researchers found that HIV-infected patients cared for by physicians experienced in the treatment of AIDS survived longer than did those treated by less experienced physicians. Physicians with little or no experience in the management of HIV infection were less likely to prescribe potentially life-prolonging therapies, such as prophylaxis against pneumocystic pneumonia (PCP; the most common type of pneumonia in patients with AIDS), even though such treatment is recommended by the Public Health Service. Studies such as this may have a profound impact on the current debate about health care delivery in the U.S.

Building a better clinical trial

An inevitable consequence of the rapid approval of new drugs for treatment of HIV infection is confusion among both physicians and patients about how best to use the available therapies. This situation has led to a call for additional clinical trials to determine which drugs, or combinations of drugs, will produce the greatest clinical benefit over the long term. At one end of the spectrum are those researchers and clinicians who would be satisfied only with a large trial, relatively simple in design, in which all possible drug combinations would be tested in a very large number of patients over many years; the regimens would be judged on the basis of which treatment leads to the longest survival.

At the other end are the many experts who feel that such trials are deceptive in their simplicity and yield little useful data. Since no single drug combination will be best for all patients, these experts advocate smaller, focused studies. The goal of such trials would be to develop treatment principles based on an understanding of the disease process. The principles delineated by such trials, the proponents argue, could be applied to new treatments as they are developed. By contrast, the results of a large, simple trial very likely would be out of date by the time such a study could be completed, owing to the rapid pace of new drug development.

Kaposi's sarcoma: viral culprit

AIDS patients frequently develop an otherwise rare tumor known as Kaposi's sarcoma (KS), which is manifested by characteristic violet-colored skin patches or nodules. In the early 1980s the discovery of unusual clusters of KS cases among homosexual men in New York City and Los Angeles was one of the first clues to the existence of AIDS. Classic KS is a slowly progressing disease typically seen only in elderly men of Mediterranean heritage, although a more aggressive form of KS was recognized in parts of Africa many years ago. (KS also occurs sometimes in organ-transplant recipients who are taking immunosuppressants.) AIDS-associated KS resembles the aggressive form of the disease.

Early in the AIDS epidemic, it was noted that KS develops almost exclusively in homosexual and bisexual men; it is extraordinarily rare in HIV-infected women and in those

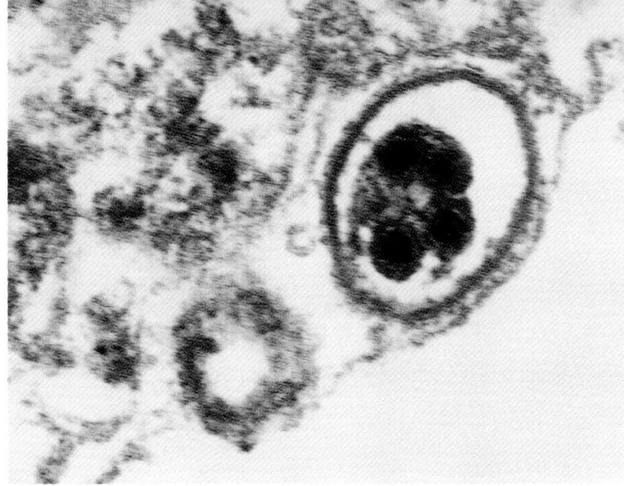

The first photograph of the virus believed to cause Kaposi's sarcoma. Scientists now hope to learn how the newly identified virus leads to this rare form of skin cancer that occurs fairly commonly in AIDS patients.

who have acquired the virus via transfusion or intravenous drug use. This epidemiological pattern triggered speculation that a sexually transmitted agent, possibly an unknown virus, might be the cause of KS. Other investigators proposed that proteins or hormones produced by HIV-infected cells were responsible.

The recent discovery of a new virus in the tissues of KS lesions provides evidence in support of a viral cause for KS. In December 1994 a team from the Columbia University College of Physicians and Surgeons, New York City, demonstrated the presence of unique, nonhuman gene sequences in DNA extracted from KS specimens. The genes resembled those found in viruses belonging to the herpesvirus family but were different enough from known herpesvirus sequences to suggest that the genes belonged to a novel member of the family, which was given the name KS-associated herpesvirus, or human herpesvirus 8 (HHV-8). In February 1996 scientists at the University of California, San Francisco, announced that they had grown HHV-8 in the laboratory and had been successful in photographing the organism. It resembles the Epstein-Barr virus, which causes mononucleosis and is associated with certain cancers of the lymph nodes.

Researchers have detected antibodies to HHV-8 in nearly all AIDS patients with KS lesions, as well as in many patients with classical KS. This finding provides support for the idea that KS, like many other complications of AIDS, is an opportunistic infection—that is, one caused by an organism that is normally kept in check by the immune system. Several groups are now seeking to determine exactly how HHV-8 infection leads to the development of KS.

Preventing complications

Opportunistic infections are the principal cause of illness and death in patients with advanced HIV infection. Although treatment is available for many AIDS-associated opportunistic infections, in most cases lifelong drug therapy is needed to keep them from recurring. Prevention of these infections is therefore a major goal.

The benefits of prophylactic antibiotics in preventing several of the most serious opportunistic infections have been demonstrated in numerous clinical trials. Among the disorders for which successful prophylaxis exists are PCP, disseminated infection due to *Mycobacterium avium* complex (MAC), and infection of the retina of the eye by cytomegalovirus (CMV), which often leads to blindness. Routine prophylaxis to prevent PCP and MAC are now considered the standard of care for patients with advanced HIV infection. Because of the high cost and serious potential toxicity of currently available drugs, routine prophylaxis against CMV retinitis is more controversial. Studies are under way to identify patients at greatest risk for developing CMV retinitis, in whom the benefits of prophylaxis would outweigh the risks.

An inevitable consequence of the growing number of infections for which prophylaxis is available is the ever-increasing number of pills that people with AIDS take on a daily basis. It is not uncommon for patients to require treatment with 9 or 10 medications per day. And as the number of medications increases, so too does the possibility of side effects and adverse drug interactions. Balancing the need for each medication against these potential risks is a constant challenge for physicians caring for AIDS patients.

Report card on U.S. AIDS research

In the spring of 1996, the Office of AIDS Research released the results of a yearlong review of the NIH AIDS research program, conducted by over 100 members of the AIDS and general scientific research communities under the leadership of Arnold Levine, a molecular biologist at Princeton University. The report was generally laudatory of the NIH efforts, noting the many advances in the understanding of HIV and the treatment of AIDS that have come from the work of investigators funded by the NIH.

At the same time, the reviewers pointed out several areas for future improvement. These included implementation of a plan that would coordinate public and private AIDS vaccine research, development of a comprehensive scientific agenda for the prevention of HIV infection, integration of adult clinical trials programs into a single network, and restructure of federally funded drug-development efforts.

—*Daniel R. Kuritzkes, M.D.*

At the XI International Conference on AIDS in Vancouver, B.C., an activist waves a banner resembling the Canadian flag but bearing the universal symbol of AIDS awareness instead of the red maple leaf.

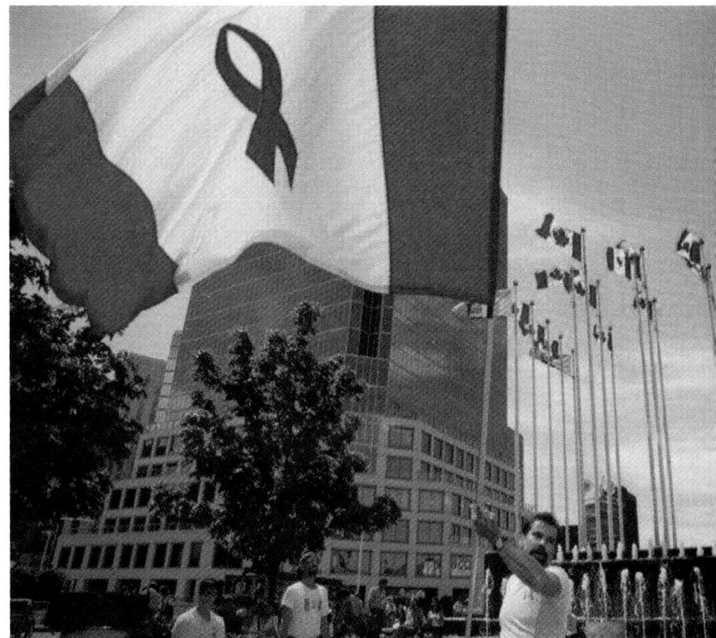

(Top) Don Ganem, UCSF; (right) Kim Stallknecht—AFP

NEWS CAP

Believing in Magic

On Feb. 2, 1996, wearing his familiar bright yellow number 32 Los Angeles Lakers jersey and luminous smile, Earvin ("Magic") Johnson, Jr., began the second act of his extraordinary life, ending a retirement that had begun a little more than four years earlier with the shocking announcement that he was HIV-positive. He left the court—reluctantly—during the 1991–92 season, afraid that he would no longer be up to the rigors of the game. Admitting that he had probably contracted HIV as the result of his own promiscuous lifestyle, Johnson became a spokesperson for AIDS awareness. He immersed himself in marriage and fatherhood, became part owner of the Lakers, and opened a multiplex movie theater in South Central Los Angeles, bringing jobs and hope to a neighborhood that had been ravaged during the riots of 1992. Always a fierce competitor, he threw himself into battle with his disease, taking the anti-AIDS drug zidovudine (AZT) for a time and adding 13.6 kg (30 lb) of muscle through weight lifting.

Allsport

When Johnson attempted a comeback during the 1992–93 season, a number of NBA players protested because they feared on-court contact with an HIV-positive player. Again Magic withdrew, while the sports world awkwardly addressed AIDS. Currently, any professional basketball player who sustains a cut is required to leave the court and be bandaged—even though the chance of contracting AIDS through incidental contact in a game is one in 85 million, according to the Centers for Disease Control and Prevention.

In the meantime, Johnson's helper-T-cell (CD4+) count reportedly remained above 500 (800–1,200 CD4+ cells per cubic millimeter of blood is normal; 200 or fewer is diagnostic of AIDS). Finally, in the winter of 1996, Johnson rejoined the Lakers as a player, determined to have his three-year-old son, Earvin III, see him play. This time he returned with not only the blessing of his doctors but also the support of some of the very players who had spoken out against his first comeback.

One athlete for whom Johnson's example had special meaning was one-time World Boxing Organization heavyweight champion Tommy Morrison, who was himself diagnosed as HIV-positive. After a mandatory prefight blood test in February 1996 revealed the presence of the disease, the 27-year-old U.S. fighter announced his retirement, citing promiscuity as the probable cause of his contracting HIV. I "blew it with irresponsible, irrational, and immature decisions . . . that one day will cost me my life," said Morrison.

After a season in which Johnson showed flashes of his old brilliance but that was also marked by personal frustrations, he, too, announced his retirement—again. Although he averaged 14.6 points, 6.9 assists, and 5.7 rebounds per game, Magic, at age 36, had some problems fitting in with his new "Generation X" teammates—both on and off the court. The low point of his season came on April 15, when he learned of his three-game suspension after the most un-Magic-like act of shoving a referee while disputing a foul call against him. Unhappy at not being able to operate in his accustomed point-guard position and disenchanted by the Lakers' first-round ouster from the play-offs, Johnson decided it was time (once and for all?) to let his jersey adorn the rafters of L.A.'s Great Western Forum.

—*Jeff Wallenfeldt*

Patrick Allard—RÉA/Saba

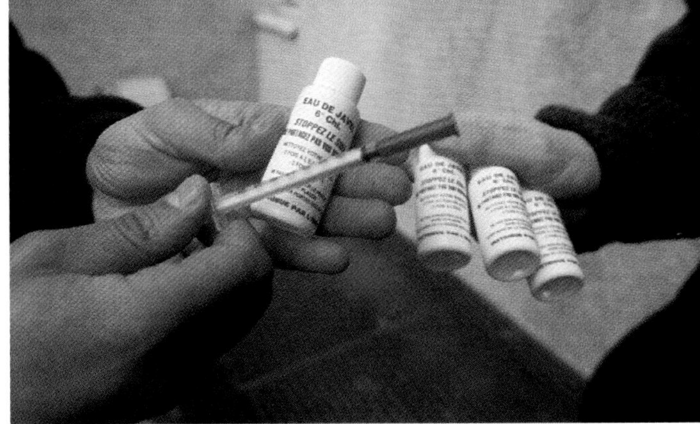

Bottles of household bleach are distributed along with sterile syringes at a Paris needle-exchange facility. Considerable research supports the effectiveness of needle-exchange programs in reducing the spread of HIV.

Needle Exchange—It Works

In 1981, when the first cases of a mysterious immune deficiency syndrome were reported among homosexual men in New York City and Los Angeles, it was believed that the new disease—subsequently named AIDS—might be limited to the homosexual population. That the causative organism was bloodborne soon became apparent, however, as did the fact that other groups were also at risk. One of these was injecting drug users (IDUs).

Today, a decade and a half after the start of the AIDS epidemic, HIV infection among drug users has been reported in 80 countries around the globe. In some locales as many as 40–80% of IDUs are infected with HIV. The virus can spread rapidly in this population. In Edinburgh, for example, in a single year the rate of HIV seroprevalence (*i.e.,* the proportion of those who have a positive blood test for antibodies to HIV) among IDUs went from zero to more than 40%. Nonetheless, some communities have continued to report stable, low levels of seroprevalence among intravenous drug abusers. Clearly, the spread of the virus, even in this high-risk group, is not inevitable.

Clean needles: part of the solution

Prior to injecting a drug, the user typically draws blood into the syringe to determine if a vein has been located. It is this practice that makes multiperson use of drug-injection equipment a relatively efficient mechanism for the transmission of bloodborne viruses.

How can the spread of HIV (and similarly transmitted viruses) be prevented in those who inject drugs? Outreach programs can inform drug users of their risks and thus promote changes in behavior. Drug-treatment programs, and in particular methadone maintenance for heroin addiction, can enable some drug users to stop injecting. Pharmacies can be allowed to sell sterile injection equipment to drug users, which thereby increases the chances that "clean" equipment will be available when drug injection occurs. Household bleach can be used to disinfect previously used injection equipment (although studies conducted in New York City and Baltimore, Md., in the early 1990s indicated that it is difficult to disinfect used injection equipment adequately in nonmedical settings).

Syringe-exchange programs, in which drug users are given sterile injection equipment in return for used, "dirty" equipment, offer several potential advantages as a method for reducing HIV transmission. First, they make sterile equipment available at very low cost, the price being simply the drug user's expenses in returning the used equipment. Second, they ensure proper disposal of HIV-contaminated needles and syringes. Third, they enable drug injectors to obtain clean water and "cookers" (containers in which drugs are heated and dissolved). Bloodborne viruses can potentially be transmitted through the sharing of these items even when needles and syringes are not shared. Finally, the setting of the syringe exchange provides an opportunity for encounters between drug injectors and health workers, where the drug users may receive health-related information, condoms, and referrals for social and medical services.

Despite these potential advantages, syringe-exchange programs are controversial. Opponents claim that such programs will lead to an increase in the number of people injecting drugs and that they condone illicit drug use. Particularly heated debate surrounds the question of whether federal funds should be used to support syringe exchanges—the government, in effect, helping people to commit an illegal act while at the same time potentially protecting the public health. Can syringe-exchange programs effectively reduce HIV transmission? Do they contribute to increased rates of illicit drug use? After more than a decade of research in the U.S. and Western Europe, it should now be possible to assess scientifically how well these programs meet their stated goals.

An incentive to inject?

In 1993 when AIDS researcher Peter Lurie and his colleagues at the University of California, San Francisco, interviewed experienced drug users about whether the presence of a syringe exchange would influence people to start injecting drugs, the most common response was laughter at the silliness of the question. To date, not a single study has produced evidence that the easy availability of sterile equipment leads to increases in illicit drug use.

Most of the research that has followed syringe-exchange participants over time has found that these individuals generally do not change their levels of drug use (a few studies have shown small decreases). Apparently, access to sterile equipment does not encourage IDUs to inject more often. Nor does it provide an inducement to new users. If the opportunity to obtain clean syringes acted as an incentive to noninjectors, it could be expected that relatively large numbers of new IDUs would take advantage of exchange programs. In fact, most programs have reported very few new users participating; typically, fewer than 3% of participants say that they began injecting within the previous year.

Pioneering syringe-exchange programs have been in operation in Amsterdam since 1984 and thus provide an excellent opportunity for evaluating the impact of syringe exchanges on rates of illicit drug injection. The city also has a good system for maintaining contact between health workers and drug users, so there is relatively complete information about the population of illicit drug users. Since 1984 the average mean age of IDUs in Amsterdam has been rising at a rate of approximately six months per year. Because people just starting to use intravenous drugs are typically young—usually under 20—if there were a large number of new injectors, the mean age of the drug-injecting population should be decreasing over time. That the reverse is happening in Amsterdam is relatively strong evidence that the presence of syringe exchanges is not associated with an increase in the numbers of new drug injectors. Many of the syringe exchanges in Amsterdam are operated in conjunction with programs that provide methadone to persons who have smoked heroin as well as those who formerly were intravenous heroin users. Despite the fact that the former heroin smokers go for treatment to the very sites where clean syringes are being distributed, there has been no evidence of smokers' shifting to drug injection or of former injectors' relapsing.

Less sharing, lower risk

More than 20 studies have assessed whether drug injectors who participate in syringe-exchange programs change the drug-related practices that put them at risk for HIV infection. In almost all of these studies, the syringe-exchange participants report substantial reductions in such behaviors. Most participants say that prior to using the exchanges, they injected drugs very frequently and shared injection equipment fairly often. While their rates of drug injection remained steady once they had access to sterile equipment, sharing decreased by about half. No study has found a complete elimination of sharing, however, and little evidence of adoption of safer sexual practices has been seen.

Reports of behavior change among persons at risk for HIV infection must always be treated with some skepticism. The individuals may be deceiving themselves about the extent of their risk behavior, or they may be trying to impress an interviewer with their efforts to avoid HIV infection. Nonetheless, the self-reports of reduced injection-risk behaviors are quite consistent with the large amounts of sterile equipment obtained by participants in syringe exchanges and the equally sizable amounts of used equipment returned.

Measuring success

HIV incidence—the rate of new infections—is the ultimate yardstick for assessing the effectiveness of syringe-exchange programs. While there have been no strictly scientific controlled trials of these programs, there have been enough studies of HIV incidence among program participants to make some risk assessment possible. As is true when evaluating HIV incidence in other populations, it is useful to compare HIV incidence among syringe-exchange participants with the prevalence of HIV infection among all drug injectors in the local community. HIV prevalence—the proportion of people in a given population who are infected with the virus—is one of the strongest determinants of incidence. Once people have become infected with HIV, they are probably capable of transmitting the virus to others for the rest of their lives. In an area of high HIV prevalence, where a substantial percentage of drug injectors are already infected, an uninfected individual would need to share drug-injection equipment with a comparatively small number of others before he or she encountered someone who potentially could transmit the virus.

HIV incidence among syringe-exchange participants has been studied in communities with low, moderate, and high prevalence. Areas with low HIV prevalence (under 5% of drug injectors infected)—including Lund, Sweden; Glasgow, Scotland; locations in England and Wales; Sydney, Australia; Kathmandu, Nepal; Toronto, Ont.; Vancouver, B.C.; Tacoma, Wash.; and Portland, Ore.—have yielded fairly consistent data. In all except Vancouver, HIV incidence among syringe-exchange participants was quite low, typically less than one new HIV infection per 100 person-years at risk. (A "person-year" denotes a research subject followed for a single year; if two subjects are followed for six months each, this would also generate one person-year of data.)

HIV-incidence studies have been conducted in two areas with a moderate prevalence (10–30% of IDUs infected), London and Montreal. In London HIV incidence among syringe-exchange participants was low, between one and two per 100 person-years at risk. In Montreal, on the other hand, the rate was quite high—about five per 100 person-years at risk.

Four studies of HIV incidence in exchange-program participants have been conducted in areas with a high prevalence of infection (over 30%) among IDUs, including Amsterdam; Chicago; New Haven, Conn.; and New York City. The HIV-incidence rates among program participants in these studies have ranged from low (1.5 per 100 person-years at risk in New York) to moderate (4 per 100 person-years in Amsterdam).

In almost all of these studies, there is a pattern of relatively low rates of new HIV infection among the syringe-exchange participants. The Vancouver and Montreal findings demonstrate, however, that the presence of syringe-exchange programs does not guarantee a low rate of new HIV infections. Research is continuing in these cities in an attempt to better understand the factors contributing to the limited success of their syringe-exchange programs. A partial explanation may be that these programs placed fairly strict limits on the number of syringes that could be exchanged per visit. Even though the participants had access to sterile injection equipment, they may not have had clean equipment on hand at all times. Having a sufficient supply of sterile injection equipment is particularly problematic for intravenous cocaine users—injections may be frequent (as often as every 15 to 20 minutes), needles and syringes often become dull, bent, or clogged, and it may be difficult to keep track of which syringe belongs to whom.

Some caveats

None of the studies of HIV incidence among syringe-exchange participants was a randomized clinical trial in which some injectors were assigned on a random basis to participate in a syringe-exchange program, while others were scheduled to attend some other form of HIV-prevention program. A randomized trial of syringe exchange would be enormously difficult and expensive to conduct, and there is no agreement on what the appropriate comparison program should be. In the absence of such a study, it cannot be concluded that syringe exchanges are responsible in themselves for low rates of new HIV infection. Still, it is possible to draw relatively firm conclusions about the potential for syringe-exchange pro-

(Opposite page) Russ Carmack—Tacoma News Tribune

grams to result in reduced HIV-risk behavior and lower rates of infection with bloodborne viruses. Such conclusions must be based on consistency of findings across different studies, however, rather than on the results of any single study.

The Tacoma program: persuasive example

Tacoma has had a syringe exchange since 1988. The program operates from two fixed outdoor sites and the local public health department pharmacy. It also operates a van; program participants can arrange a meeting with the van by phone. The Tacoma exchange does not place any limits on the number of syringes that can be exchanged per visit. Half or more of the drug users in the area have used its services, and one-fifth to one-third are regular participants. Since the exchange is the primary HIV-prevention program in Tacoma, any risk reduction among IDUs can safely be attributed primarily to the exchange program.

Two risk-behavior interview studies have been conducted in connection with the Tacoma exchange. One study asked participants about "unsafe" injections (*i.e.,* with previously used equipment) prior to and while using the exchange. This number fell by almost half, although the frequency of drug injections did not change. In a second study, exchange participants were compared with IDUs who did not use the exchange. More than twice as many nonparticipants reported unsafe injections in the month prior to the interview. The HIV-infection rate was also higher in the nonparticipants—8%, compared with 2% among participants.

Because Pierce county, of which Tacoma is the county seat, is part of the Centers for Disease Control and Prevention hepatitis surveillance system, it has among the most reliable hepatitis data in the U.S. Hepatitis B and C are spread by the sharing of drug-injection equipment (as well as by unprotected sex) and are therefore relatively good indicators of risk behavior. Prior to the implementation of the syringe exchange, Pierce county was experiencing a high rate of new hepatitis B cases among IDUs. The rate of new hepatitis infections among drug users fell sharply beginning several months after the syringe exchange opened. A "case-control" study of new hepatitis B and hepatitis C infections was conducted; drug injectors who had recently become infected with one of these viruses ("cases") were compared with drug injectors who had remained uninfected ("controls"). This study showed that use of the syringe exchange had a strong protective effect against becoming infected with these common bloodborne viruses.

HIV rates also have been studied among IDUs in Tacoma. The percentage of drug injectors who are infected has remained low and stable for an extended time period, which indicates that relatively few new HIV infections are occurring in this population. A study among syringe-exchange users found a very low rate of new HIV infections (fewer than 0.5 per 100 person-years at risk).

Acting on the evidence

In 1988 the U.S. Congress enacted a ban on the use of federal funds for syringe-exchange programs until scientific research could demonstrate that these programs effectively reduce disease risk without encouraging drug use. Many public health authorities feel that sufficient documentation now exists. The availability of sterile equipment reduces drug-related risk behavior and transmission of bloodborne viruses and has not resulted in any detectable increase in illicit drug use. In 1995 even the National Academy of Sciences recommended that the ban on federal funding be lifted.

Further studies are needed to learn more about how syringe exchanges can be made more effective and how they can be integrated with other efforts to prevent disease transmission among drug users. Perhaps equally important—and certainly equally challenging—is the need for the development of a broad public health perspective on the nonmedical use of psychoactive drugs. Just as violence has recently been recognized in the U.S. as a public health problem—and not simply a law-enforcement issue—the time has now come to seek public health solutions for drug abuse and the harms it inflicts on society.

—Don C. Des Jarlais, Ph.D.

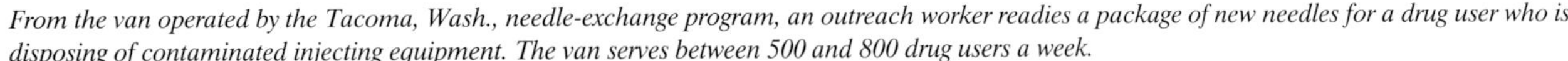

From the van operated by the Tacoma, Wash., needle-exchange program, an outreach worker readies a package of new needles for a drug user who is disposing of contaminated injecting equipment. The van serves between 500 and 800 drug users a week.

NEWS CAP

Visible Woman: View Her Byte by Byte

The Visible Man, the cyberspace cadaver who inhabits the Internet, now has a female counterpart. The Visible Woman made her on-line debut in late 1995, one year after her mate.

Both digital bodies are part of the U.S. National Library of Medicine's $1.4 million Visible Human Project, which was undertaken to aid and enhance medical research and education. The virtual cadavers, which represent average, normal male and female bodies, are also expected to be useful in countless other ways, including the designing of artificial joints and the safety testing of new products for human use.

The actual female cadaver was that of an unidentified Maryland woman who died at age 59 of a cardiopulmonary obstruction. Like her male counterpart, she had bequeathed her body to science. Both cadavers were "assembled" in Denver at the Center for Human Simulation at the University of Colorado Health Sciences Center by principal investigators Victor M. Spitzer and David G. Whitlock. The female cadaver was placed in a gelatin and frozen at −107° C (−160° F). Her body was then X-rayed, scanned by means of computed tomography and magnetic resonance imaging, and then cut into more than 5,000 0.3-mm (0.01-in) slices. Finally, the digitized photographic images and radiological data were fed into a computer to create a three-dimensional picture. While the visible male was cut into one-millimeter slices, the thinner cross-sections of the visible female allow for much higher image resolution.

The Visible Woman takes up 40 gigabytes of computer storage space, 25 gigabytes more than her male counterpart. Selected full-scale, full-color images of the Visible Man and his distaff partner can be viewed by anyone who has access to the Internet; *all* of the Visible Human image files can be viewed in scaled-down versions. Anyone interested can check the National Library of Medicine's home page: http://www.nlm.nih.gov.

—*James Hennelly*

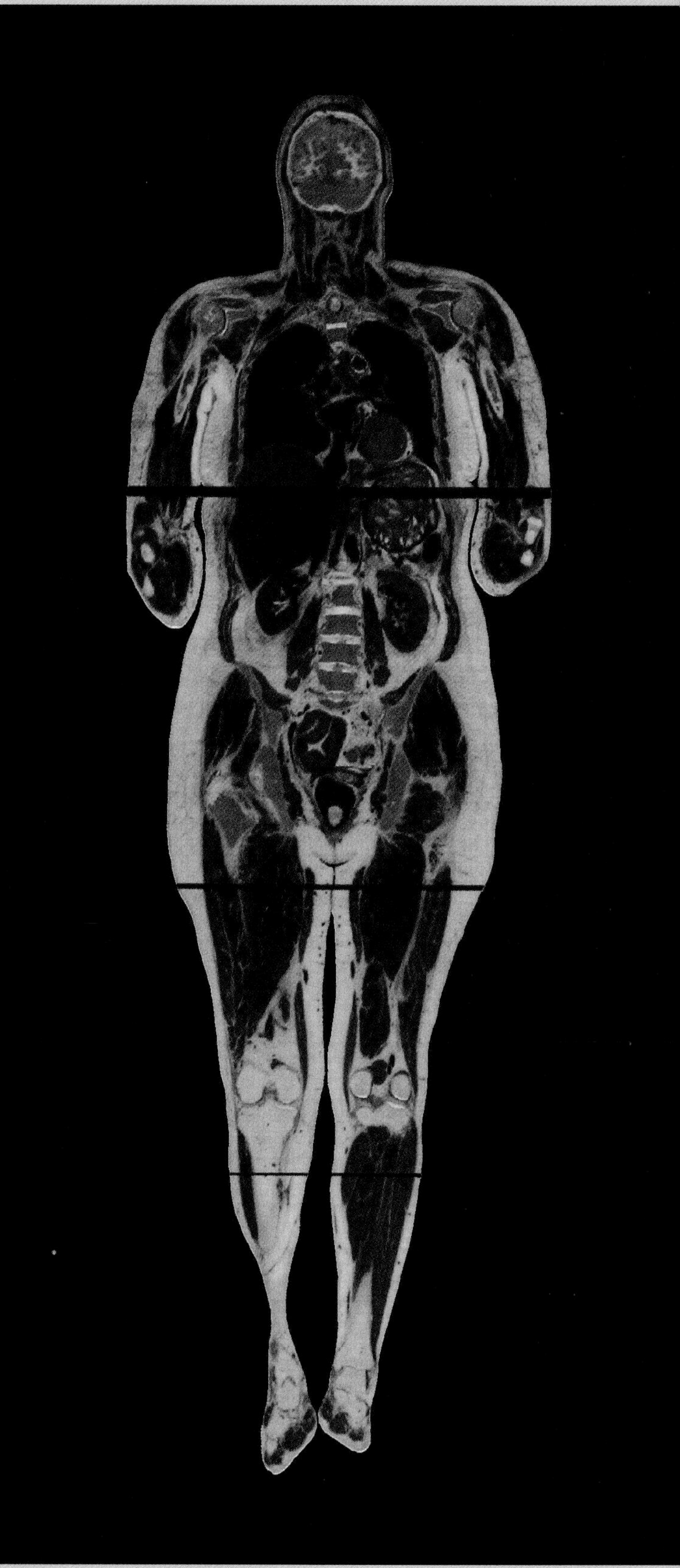

The Visible Woman (left) has joined her male counterpart (right) on the World Wide Web. Anyone with ample megabytes of storage space can browse the entire Visible Human database.

Center for Human Simulation, University of Colorado Health Sciences Center

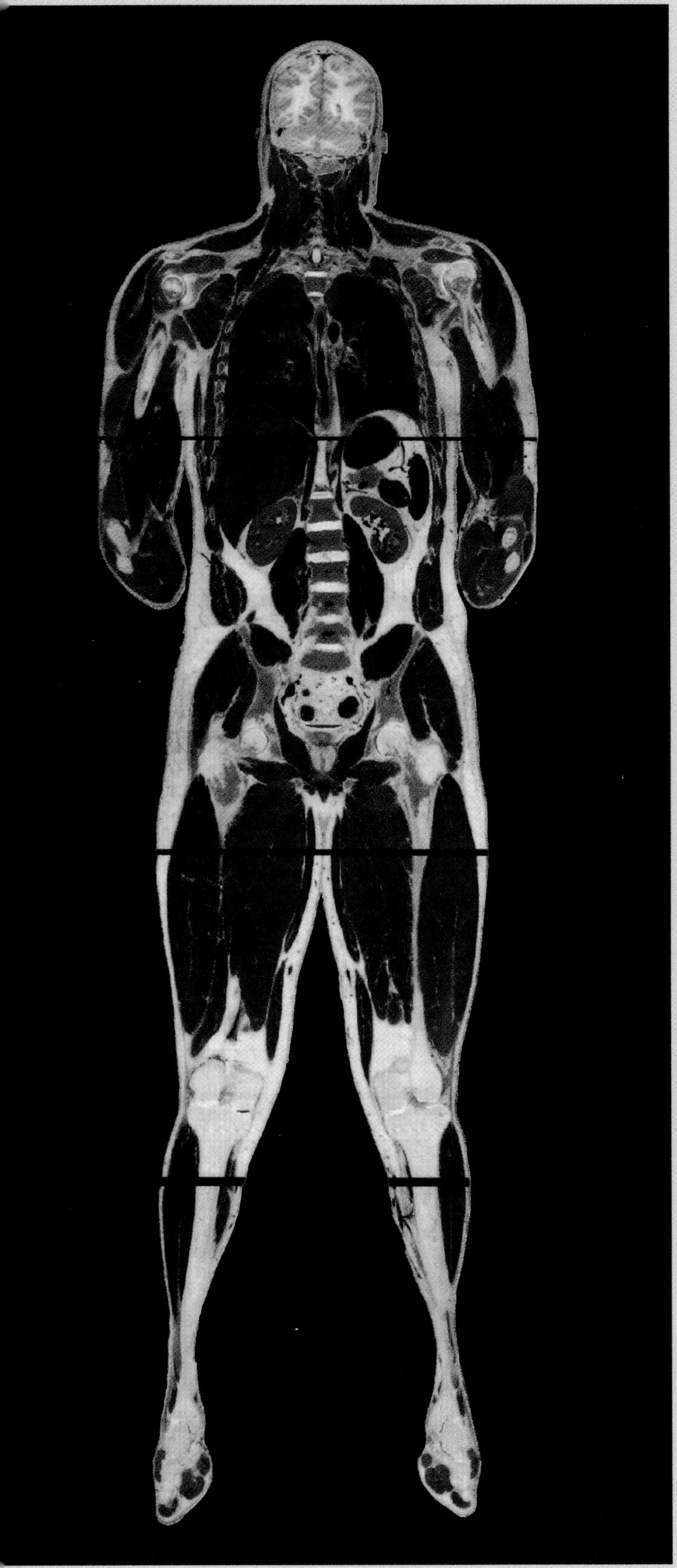

NEWS CAP

Jaws V: A Cutting-Edge Discovery

Anatomists, who long have been without a major find into which to sink their teeth, now have something exciting to chew on, thanks to the discovery of a new muscle in the human jaw. Early in 1996 Gwendolyn F. Dunn and Gary D. Hack of the Dental School of the University of Maryland at Baltimore discovered a fifth mastication muscle, which they called "sphenomandibularis." Extending from behind the eye socket to the lower jaw, the muscle was previously thought to be an extension of the temporalis muscle but now has been shown to be independent and to have its own blood and nerve supply.

Dunn, an orthodontist, and Hack, an assistant professor of dentistry, had been investigating the muscles involved in the chewing process. The muscle revealed itself to them only because they deviated from the standard dissection method. Rather than approaching the jaw from the side of the head, they angled the scalpel in from the front. Then, eureka!

The existence of the previously unappreciated muscle was confirmed, first by neuroradiologist Michael Rothman, using magnetic resonance imaging, then by *The Dissectible Human,* an interactive computerized three-dimensional atlas of the human body produced by Engineering Animation, Inc., and the C.V. Mosby Co. and derived from the National Library of Medicine's Visible Human Project. The latter enabled the two scientists to repeat their seminal cut on a digitized head visible on a computer screen.

—Jeff Wallenfeldt

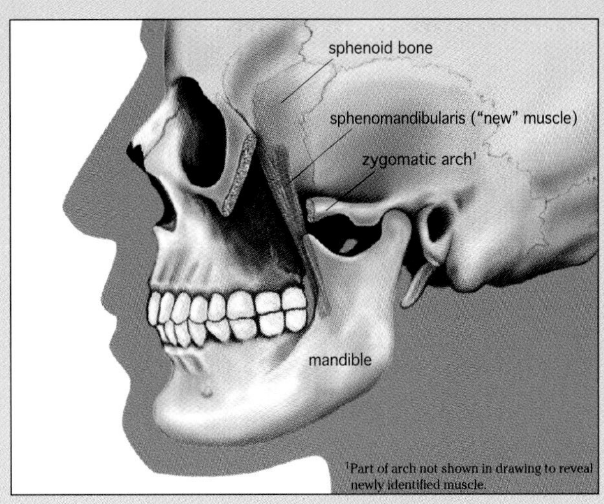

[1]Part of arch not shown in drawing to reveal newly identified muscle.

Reproduced with permission of the Anti-Cancer Council of Victoria

Australia's magnificent beaches and glorious climate are powerful inducements to spending leisure time outdoors—precisely what these two fair-skinned youngsters are doing. Unfortunately, only one is protected; the other industrious playmate is exposed to the sun's harmful midday rays.

Australians Get Smart About the Sun

> *The white races may have spread all over the globe, but they are biologically suited only to the high latitudes and should either stay there or adapt their lifestyle so that their skin believes it still lives in the Shetlands.*
>
> —Tony Smith, associate editor, *British Medical Journal*

Australia has the unenviable reputation of being the skin cancer capital of the world. It is an example of the old maxim that to be among the biggest is not necessarily to be among the best. About two of three people who live their life in Australia will be treated for at least one skin cancer; almost 1% of the population is treated for skin cancer each year. There is no other cancer statistic like that for any cancer anywhere else in the world.

Skin cancer types

There are three major types of skin cancer: basal cell carcinoma, squamous cell carcinoma, and melanoma (also known as malignant melanoma). The most common and least dangerous, basal cell carcinoma, accounts for about 80% of all skin cancer lesions removed. Melanoma is the least common, making up around 3% of treated skin cancers. On the other hand, melanoma is the most lethal of the three, being responsible for 80% of skin cancer deaths. Squamous cell carcinoma, which accounts for 15–20% of the cancers treated, is responsible for 20% of skin cancer deaths.

History, climate, and fashion

What led to this major public health problem in Australia? History is part of the answer. Just over 200 years ago (in 1788), the British colonized Australia, settling first in New South Wales. The motives behind this decision are a matter of some controversy, but the traditional explanation is that Great Britain sought to relieve the burden upon its overcrowded prisons. At first using the country as a repository for its unwanted classes, the British commenced a migration pattern that continued for almost the next two centuries. Other Europeans also migrated to Australia during that time. Owing to this settlement history, until recent decades the immigrant Australian population was predominantly British or continental European in ancestry—and, consequently, fair-skinned.

These white immigrants from the north and their descendants lived in a country just south of the Equator that is hot and sunny for many months of the year. Over the years Australians developed a great tradition of outdoor sport and recreational activities that encouraged people to spend long periods in the sun.

The final component that led to Australia's skin cancer epidemic was the fashion for a suntan—a trend that started in the early decades of the 20th century in Europe and North America and that Australians took up with great gusto. This was accompanied by changes in attitudes about exposing the body in public. Eventually, people intentionally exposed large areas of their skin to sunlight in an attempt to acquire the "bronzed-Aussie" look.

Cause for alarm

In the 1950s and '60s, medical practitioners in Australia became aware that more and more of their patients were requiring treatment for skin cancer. By the 1970s, when it was clear that something needed to be done, public and professional health education programs had been launched in Queensland in earnest. By the early '80s such programs were being developed throughout the country. Today skin cancer warning messages reach virtually everyone in Australia.

The first public education programs in Queensland were initiated by medical professionals, who carried out this work over and above their normal patient care duties. The medical community then combined forces with cancer councils (charitable nongovernmental agencies charged with developing cancer control programs) in each state and coordinated through the Australian Cancer Society. In some states specific melanoma research and treatment centers—for example, the Sydney Melanoma Unit in New South Wales and the Queensland Melanoma Project—were established. They became involved in both professional and public education programs at the very early stages of the skin cancer epidemic and remain active today.

In 1985 the Australasian College of Dermatologists collaborated with the Australian Cancer Society to establish a nationally coordinated skin cancer control program. Each year, at the beginning of summer, a National Skin Cancer Awareness Week is held. The themes of these weeks and the associated resources, which are different every year, then become incorporated into the continuing programs of the state cancer councils.

In the 1990s the state and federal governments became increasingly active in addressing the skin cancer problem, as did many commercial enterprises such as those manufacturing sunscreens, clothing, hats, and other sun-protective products. Polls suggest that the coordinated campaign has been quite successful in educating the public. According to recent surveys, over 95% have heard of melanoma, over 90% recognize that skin cancer can be a dangerous disease, and at least 60% believe that they personally are at risk of developing one of the cancers.

Two forms of attack

Two major approaches to skin cancer control are possible: primary prevention and early detection. Primary-prevention programs are those that aim to reach people before they develop skin cancer. More than anything else, they attempt to change people's attitudes about suntans in a way that encourages increased sun protection. This is the long-term approach to skin cancer control, and it can take decades before any effect on skin cancer incidence is apparent.

Early-detection programs constitute the short-term approach. They aim to reach people who have already developed skin cancer. If skin cancers can be detected at a very early stage, all types can be easily cured. Moreover, the extent of treatment required is less; the cost to the patient and the community is reduced; and overall skin cancer death rates can be curtailed in a relatively short period of time.

Both approaches are taken in Australia. Because it is difficult to do one without the other, a balance between the two is sought. The nature of specific programs required for each of these approaches is also varied. Public education is the major approach to primary prevention. It can be reinforced by timely advice from medical professionals; physicians and nurses, for example, can stress the benefits of wearing hats and long-legged and long-sleeved clothing, using sunscreens with an adequate sun protection factor (SPF), and so forth.

Last but not least

A third component of campaigns against skin cancer is not an educational one. It is the approach known as structural change—*i.e.,* altering some aspect of the political, social, economic, or physical structure of a society in such a way that a desired change in the behavior of the population results. Forms of structural change for skin cancer control in Australia have included the development of a federal standard for testing and labeling of sunscreens; products that comply with the standard are not subject to a sales tax. Local government agencies have taken it upon themselves to provide protection from the sun (some form of shade) in outdoor public spaces. Through legislation, the government encourages the phaseout of the manufacture, use, and release of substances that deplete atmospheric ozone, notably chlorofluorocarbons and halons. Presently, standards are being developed for the manufacture of sun-protective clothing fabrics.

Primary prevention: a natural

Australia has adopted the approach that natural protection is the best protection. This means encouraging people to wear hats and protective clothing, to seek shade when outdoors, and to avoid the sun around the middle of the day if possible. Sunscreens are recommended in addition to natural protection, not as a substitute for it. Judicious use of products with an SPF of 15 or above is recommended regardless of skin type. Sunscreens reflect or absorb ultraviolet light through chemical agents and are ranked in the laboratory by their protective power; a sunscreen with an SPF of 15 requires 15 times the dose of ultraviolet light in the laboratory that unprotected skin would require before reddening. These numbers, however, are of limited value. Sunscreens with especially high numbers can be misleading, as a sunscreen with an SPF of 30 does not necessarily double the effect of an SPF 15 sunscreen in reducing the risk of skin cancer in the long term. That is the reason the cancer societies in Australia recommend that people choose a product with an SPF of at least 15 but do not specify any particular number above that.

Children, adolescents, and those responsible for the care of young people have been the major target of campaigns stressing the need to cover up. The popular cartoon characters Sid Seagull and his son Sam have been promoting the "Slip! Slop! Slap!" message since the 1980s: Slip! (on a shirt), Slop! (on a sunscreen), Slap! (on a hat). The prevention message is widely broadcast in the media, taught in schools, and incorporated in sport sponsorship programs—to reach all young people who are likely to be exposed to a lot of sunlight.

Children are the primary target of Australia's ambitious skin cancer prevention efforts. Well-covered kids plant trees for shade (below) and troop off to school in SunSmart uniforms (bottom left). (Bottom right) A young man has his skin checked for abnormalities. Early detection of cancerous lesions is the best way to ensure a cure.

Curricular resources were developed for primary schools. School councils established guidelines, set standards for provision of shade on school grounds, encouraged exemplary behavior among teachers, scheduled sporting activities at times other than the middle of the day, and made rules such as "no hat, no play." Tree planting for the sake of shade has been a popular activity undertaken not only in schools but wherever people congregate out of doors. (A recent study in Great Britain showed that a tree with a dense canopy provides the equivalent protection of an SPF 15 sunscreen.)

In the past decade health-promotion foundations, which receive a large amount of money from a tax on tobacco products, have supported Australia's hard-hitting sun-protection programs. The funds enable extensive sponsorship of popular sporting events. The "SunSmart" program, promoted through the cancer councils, enlists lifeguards, cricketers, tennis players, and other heroes to young people to set an example by taking care while still having fun in the sun.

Adults are also targets of primary-prevention campaigns—particularly those who participate in sports and people who work outside. Unions and employers have worked together to provide sun protection for outdoor workers. Measures include scheduling work times away from the middle of the day, providing canopies as well as hats and other protective clothing, and encouraging liberal use of sunscreen.

The primary-prevention programs are most active during the summer months, but they would not have the impact they do if the activities were suspended during the rest of the year. Moreover, winter skiing and other sports are popular activities, especially in the Australian Alps, where exposure to sunlight can be intense. In the north of Australia, there are sunny periods for most of the year. There, especially, skin cancer education campaigns must continue year-round.

Early detection: spotting potential cancer

Early-detection programs rely on education—teaching both the public and medical professionals to recognize skin abnormalities that could be early-stage skin cancer. People are taught to watch for telltale lesions, new moles, or irregular spots that do not heal or are discolored. Individuals with any of these abnormal signs are directed to seek early attention from a medical practitioner. The programs do not condone self-diagnosis; rather the public is taught to recognize when it is appropriate to seek medical attention.

(continued on page 180)

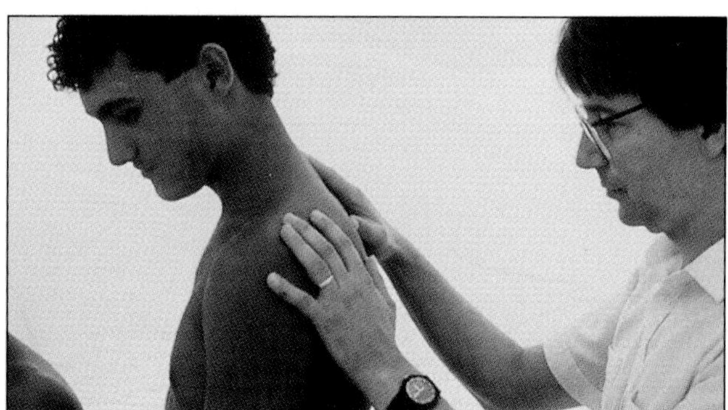

(Top) Reproduced with permission of the Anti-Cancer Council of Victoria; (bottom left and right) courtesy, New South Wales Cancer Council

NEWS CAP

Breast Cancer Genes: Insights and Issues

In the past year researchers have discovered a great deal about the contribution of genetic defects to breast cancer, the second most common cancer of women worldwide and the most common in the United States and most other developed countries. In 1994 investigators identified *BRCA1,* the first gene associated with an increased susceptibility to breast cancer. Defects, or mutations, in *BRCA1* are responsible for about half of all familial cases, which represent 5–10% of all breast cancer cases. A woman who inherits a flawed copy of *BRCA1* from either parent has an 85% chance of developing breast cancer during her lifetime and a 45–50% chance of developing ovarian cancer. About half of the breast cancer cases in these women will occur before age 50.

Researchers have now identified more than 100 different mutations of *BRCA1*—although not all are associated with tumor development—dashing hopes for a simple screening test. It was reported in the October 1995 issue of *Nature Genetics* that a single mutation *does* occur repeatedly in one population, Ashkenazic Jews (those of Eastern and Central European origin). Approximately 1% of this population is believed to carry one copy of this particular defect. But even for women in this group, which includes most U.S. Jews, screening will not provide all the answers. For example, a woman who tests positive for the mutation will not necessarily develop the disease; conversely, a negative test result is not a guarantee that breast cancer will not occur. Despite these uncertainties, and despite strong concerns about the psychological consequences of such screening and the potential misuse of results, one clinic in the U.S. was offering a test for this specific mutation. Most medical authorities believe, however, that such testing should be conducted only in a research setting.

Another and possibly a key piece to solving the breast cancer puzzle was added when researchers at the University of Texas Health Science Center in San Antonio reported in *Science,* Nov. 3, 1995, that *BRCA1* may play a part in sporadic (nonfamilial) breast and ovarian cancers—which account for the great majority of cases. The gene is not mutated in these cancers, and it appears to function normally, instructing cells in breast and ovarian tissue to produce the BRCA1 protein. The protein, however, is not in its normal location in the cells.

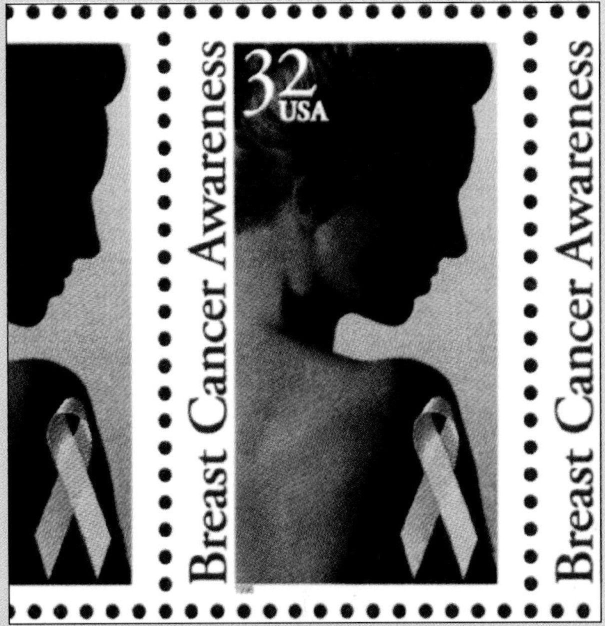

On June 15, 1996, the U.S. Postal Service issued a stamp to focus public attention on breast cancer—a disease that strikes one in nine women. Education and awareness can reduce the toll.

Papers published in March 1996 (in *Nature Genetics*) shed more light on the function of both the gene and its protein. In one experiment researchers showed that the insertion of normal copies of the *BRCA1* gene into laboratory cultures of breast and ovarian cancer cells slowed the growth of the cells. The gene failed to halt growth in cells from other kinds of cancer. In another study scientists determined that the BRCA1 protein is probably a growth inhibitor belonging to a family of proteins called granins. Researchers were hopeful that these findings would lead to more effective treatments.

Several studies have focused on the role played by the second breast cancer susceptibility gene, *BRCA2,* which was located in December 1995. Reports published in May 1996 (*Nature Genetics*) indicated that *BRCA2,* like *BRCA1,* has many mutations. Different *BRCA2* mutations appear to be present in different ethnic groups, and *BRCA2* may be linked to prostate, pancreatic, and ovarian cancer as well as breast cancer. *BRCA2* was also found to play a part in a majority of familial male breast cancer cases.

—*M.J. Friedrich*

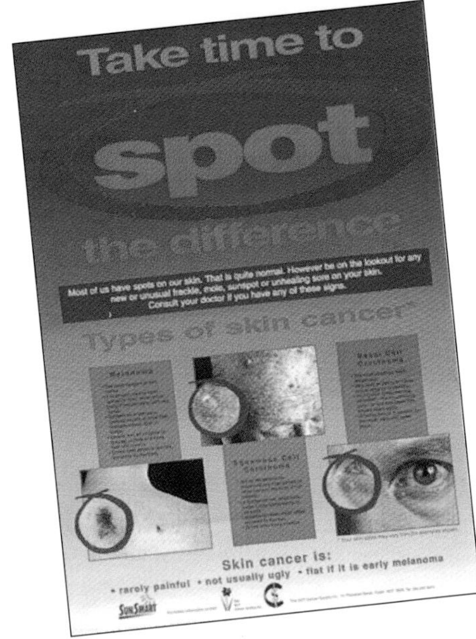

(continued from page 178)

Public education materials are delivered through many networks, including the electronic and print media. They are also distributed in pharmacies, doctors' offices, sporting clubs, elderly citizens' clubs, and other places that serve the public. In a recent National Skin Cancer Awareness Week promotion, for example, hairdressers were encouraged to comment on any unusual-looking spots on their clients' heads or necks and provide printed materials to help the customers decide whether they ought to see a medical practitioner.

Public education programs encourage people to seek medical attention if they notice a skin abnormality. It is vital, therefore, that medical professionals be prepared to deal correctly with a suspicious spot.

So-called opportunistic screening has been widely encouraged among health professionals. This means that physicians take the opportunity to look at their patients' skin (particularly that of elderly patients) when they come in for some other medical problem. Skin cancer death rates are highest in older people, whose lesions tend to occur on easily examined areas of the body such as the head, neck, hands, forearms, legs, and upper back.

Primary care practitioners are well-prepared in most instances. They have viewed slide and video teaching materials, attended lectures and seminars, or participated in other interactive skin cancer awareness programs. Extensive educational materials are available. Undergraduate medical students are specially targeted for skin cancer awareness as well.

Has Australia licked the skin cancer problem?

Public awareness of the dangers of skin cancer in Australia is high, and most people know that it is a serious disease. The terms *Slip! Slop! Slap!* and *SunSmart* are widely recognized. Behavioral research has shown that attitudes and beliefs about suntans have changed substantially in the country. A deep suntan is now considered to be unfashionable. A comprehensive survey of women's fashion magazines showed that over a 10-year period (the early 1980s through the early '90s) there was a major reduction in the use of models with deep suntans. This included not only models promoting swimwear and other products that have to do with being outdoors but *all* models. Also noted was an increase in the proportion of pale-complected models wearing hats for protection. On the favorable side, then, Australians are increasingly wearing hats and other protective clothing, using sunscreen, avoiding the sun toward the middle of the day, and, consequently, not getting sunburned.

As yet, however, there has been no demonstrable reduction in the incidence of skin cancer, but for epidemiological reasons this would not be expected for at least several decades. If the skin cancer control programs continue and current behavior patterns persist, however, a clear reduction in skin cancer in the Australian population will almost certainly result.

(Left) Two posters and a street sign deliver strong sun-protection messages. Australia has gone all out to shed its reputation as "skin cancer capital" of the world. Hard-hitting public health campaigns are now reaching Aussies nationwide. Fast-fading suntans are just one sign that sun-related attitudes and behaviors are indeed changing.

Photographs reproduced with permission of the Anti-Cancer Council of Victoria

An encouraging note is that the death rates due to melanoma have begun to level off, especially in younger groups. A much greater proportion of skin cancers of all types are being detected at and treated in the early, curable stage. Unfortunately, the successes seen in younger adults have not extended to the elderly, men in particular. The death rate from skin cancer in men aged 60 and over continues to rise. Examination of the characteristics of Australians who have died from squamous cell carcinoma reveals that this population is predominantly elderly and has one or more other major illnesses such as heart or lung disease. Therefore, merely sponsoring sun-protection programs is unlikely to make a difference among members of this older group, who have many other health problems that would overshadow their efforts to detect skin cancer.

Although public education will continue to reinforce sun protection, new and innovative tactics must be introduced. As examples, sunscreens could be made readily available in all places where people are likely to get caught without them. Many people enjoy vacations on Australia's glorious beaches. Hotels that cater to vacationers, therefore, could include sunscreen along with the toiletries (shampoo, soap, hand cream, shower caps, etc.) that are already supplied in most rooms. In addition, more canopies need to be erected in sun-exposed public places. The fashion industry could concentrate on designing and manufacturing more clothing that is attractive and reasonably priced and at the same time provides good-quality sun protection. Finally, further research is needed to determine whether mass population screenings for the detection of undiagnosed skin cancers would be of value. (Until good-quality data are available, health authorities in Australia will not recommend screenings for people who do not have any obvious abnormality.) All of the above activities would enable Australians to continue to enjoy their wonderful climate without paying the price of skin cancer.

—Robin Marks, M.B.B.S., M.P.H.

NEWS CAP

A Billionaire's Gift to Research

Jon M. Huntsman stood helplessly by and watched his mother die painfully from breast cancer; then his father suffered an agonizing death from prostate cancer. Finally, Huntsman himself was diagnosed with cancer—first of the prostate gland, then of the mouth. Although he responded well to treatment of both cancers, he could not help asking, "Why me?" And he backed his question with more than $150 million.

Huntsman, a Mormon and a self-made billionaire, is intent on learning why some families suffer again and again from the unmerciful disease. He dares to hope that his contribution to cancer research might prevent his 26 grandchildren—and countless other people—from becoming cancer's victims.

Huntsman's initial contribution established the Huntsman Cancer Institute at the University of Utah. The philanthropist's donation of about $100 million to date will be disbursed over the next 5 to 10 years and is earmarked for the recruitment of no fewer than 40 exceptional cancer researchers. This generous gift is the largest of its kind ever made by an individual to medical research. A further pledge of about $50 million also will go to the institute. The latter will include funds solicited by Huntsman from the pharmaceutical company Glaxo Wellcome, the Church of Jesus Christ of Latter-day Saints, and other sources.

The institute is directed by the world-renowned geneticist and molecular biologist Raymond White. White, who has been making cancer research breakthroughs for decades, relying largely on the Mormon church's unique genealogical library, anticipates that the Huntsman Cancer Institute will help "make cancer tomorrow what smallpox is today: a disease of the past." Exactly what the philanthropist has in mind!

—Katherine I. Gordon

Terry Newfarmer

Philanthropist Jon Huntsman and geneticist Raymond White (center, right and left) admire a model of the Huntsman Cancer Institute, a facility that will be directed by White and staffed by some of the world's finest cancer researchers. They are joined by the benefactor's son Jon Jr. and wife, Karen.

Angiography: At the Heart of Cardiac Research

Diseases of the heart and blood vessels constitute one of the major human health problems of modern times. In the more technologically advanced countries of the world—*e.g.,* the United States, the United Kingdom, and most other Western European countries, Russia, Japan, and Australia—cardiovascular disease continues to be the primary cause of death. In the U.S. alone, an estimated 1.5 million heart attacks (myocardial infarctions) occur annually, resulting in some 500,000 deaths.

Prevention, in the form of adoption of a healthy lifestyle, remains the single most important solution to the problem. Eating a low-fat, or "prudent," diet, maintaining a healthy weight, being physically active, and not smoking or consuming more than moderate amounts of alcohol are all measures that will lower individual risk.

For those who already have cardiovascular disease, some cardiologists may prescribe a radically modified diet and other lifestyle changes; in most cases, however, cardiovascular specialists rely on drugs and interventional devices to lessen the arterial buildup that causes heart attacks. Annually, more than 400,000 U.S. heart patients undergo intervention with an angioplasty device (a small balloon that is threaded into an obstructed artery and inflated to clear a blockage), and new technologies to open arteries and keep them open, such as the coronary stent, are constantly being developed. At the forefront of current research are several new drugs, called platelet inhibitors, which are used to prevent blood coagulation following angioplasty. Research facilities that assess the safety and effectiveness of these and other new cardiovascular procedures are crucial links in the chain of steps taken to get experimental drugs and devices approved for routine use. One such facility, the angiography core laboratory, is a highly specialized environment for evaluating cardiac interventions. This report offers a "behind-the-scenes" look at the work performed by "core labs" and elucidates some of the ways that new technologies lead to better treatments for the countless people worldwide afflicted with cardiovascular disease.

Seeking the FDA's seal of approval

In the United States, before new drugs and medical devices can be used to prevent, reduce, or cure disease, their safety and effectiveness in humans must be demonstrated to the Food and Drug Administration (FDA), the government agency that regulates and approves the use of all new medical treatments. After undergoing thorough testing in animals to determine safety, a drug or device receives approval from the FDA to be tested in humans.

The initial human studies (called Phase 1 clinical trials) often involve healthy volunteers and are administered in order to verify that the experimental treatment does not harm the body. After adequate safety has been determined, the Phase 2 clinical trial begins. Phase 2 trials are used to determine the appropriate dose for effectively treating the disorder (in the case of a drug) and to provide more information about a drug or device. Phase 2 trials may also test the effectiveness of the new treatment against an already approved and clinically accepted treatment. During the Phase 2 research process, extremely comprehensive medical information is gathered on patients in many different hospitals. This process is necessary so that enough eligible patients can be recruited to complete a clinical study. Each patient who is then enrolled undergoes both the initial tests and subsequent follow-up examinations. Patient randomization (the process of randomly assigning a patient to either the treatment or the control group) and patient/investigator blinding (the development of a procedure to ensure that the people who analyze the data collected for a Phase 2 trial, as well as the patients themselves, do not know what drug a patient received) enable a Phase 2 trial to be conducted in an unbiased and clinically approved fashion.

Phase 3 clinical trials generally involve large numbers of patients and are used to determine the effectiveness of a new drug or device when it is compared with a standard treatment for the disease or ailment under investigation. In drug tests the dose that worked best in the Phase 2 trials is usually the one used in Phase 3. The Phase 3 investigation is narrowed in its focus, involving close observation of specific indicators to determine whether a treatment was a success or a failure.

An angioplasty device (shown here in two different sizes) is a small balloonlike instrument that can be inflated in an obstructed artery to clear a blockage. Angioplasty procedures are performed on more than 400,000 Americans every year.

Courtesy of The Cleveland Clinic Foundation

These include mortality (death) rate, recurrence of symptoms following treatment, and complications attributable to the new procedure.

After the completion of Phase 3, investigators can submit the data from all human investigations to the FDA. Once the clinical trial information has been received and thoroughly reviewed, the FDA may grant or deny approval for widespread use of the new treatment. It may also defer approval until more data have been collected. The FDA's review of all the data collected during all three phases of clinical trials takes, on average, roughly two years. It requires about eight years for a new drug to go from the initial discovery, through animal and then human testing, to approval by the FDA.

Hope for heart patients

Clinical trials pave the way for new procedures that reduce the risk of a heart attack. Of the more than 400,000 U.S. patients who undergo angioplasty every year, close to half experience a significant improvement in heart function as a result of the procedure. In trials to test new cardiovascular drugs or devices, patients usually undergo periodic heart catheterizations, blood tests, electrocardiograms, physical exams, chest X-rays, and other tests to determine the extent and severity of disease. Most patients are admitted to a study because they have some amount of disease in one or more of their coronary arteries. In coronary artery disease fatty deposits (termed *lesions, plaques,* or *stenoses*) collect on the inner surface of the artery. Like clogs in a drainpipe, these lesions inhibit the flow of blood to the heart muscle. A heart attack usually occurs when a lesion suddenly ruptures and a blood clot, or thrombus, forms inside the artery. This clot slows or stops the flow of blood to the heart muscle, which begins to die from lack of oxygen. The larger the area of oxygen-deprived heart muscle, the larger and more severe the heart attack. With the use of new "artery-expanding" procedures, the risk of a patient's experiencing a heart attack can be significantly reduced.

Core labs: critical coordinators

The results of many of the medical tests used to determine the extent of a patient's coronary artery disease require interpretation by trained professionals. For example, in clinical trials of thrombolytics (drugs that dissolve blood clots in coronary arteries), a coronary angiogram (an X-ray motion picture of the heart's circulation) is taken to determine whether the blood clot was dissolved by the drugs and whether the blood flow has returned to normal. Upon reviewing the angiogram, a physician must decide if normal flow has been reestablished. Not all hospitals and cardiologists, however, use the same method to characterize normal flow. Also, the physician reviewing the angiogram may have a bias, which could change the outcome of the analysis. In order to improve the accuracy and consistency of data collected from angiograms in clinical studies, facilities have been established whose sole purpose is to perform such analyses. These facilities, angiography core laboratories (the term *core* reflecting their centralized and uniform analysis function), are sent all the angiograms produced in a given clinical study. The functions of the core lab are:

- to provide unbiased interpretations of the results of drug or device treatment methods used for coronary artery disease and recorded by angiograms
- to maximize accuracy and reproducibility of study results by using uniform analysis techniques (standard definitions, protocols, and operating procedures), providing consistent training programs for technical staff, and utilizing computer-assisted technology
- to provide quality assurance of angiograms by establishing appropriate procedures for the collection of data
- to ensure that each hospital involved in the study complies with the established procedures for the collection of data

Core labs are contract research facilities. In other words, the government, a drug company, or a medical device manufacturer that sponsors a cardiovascular research project will award a contract to a particular lab for angiographic analyses. Since there are many hospitals involved in a clinical trial, the study's sponsor will usually bring the physicians, nurses, and other personnel from the designated hospitals and core lab facility together to confer at regular intervals throughout the course of the trial. The core lab works in conjunction with a designated nurse coordinator at each hospital. This nurse handles all patient recruitment, testing, and follow-up and completes a case report form on each patient, which details all pertinent medical information.

The most important component of analysis in studies of coronary artery disease is the angiogram itself. Cardiologists obtain these medical images by inserting a catheter into the femoral artery of the leg or brachial artery of the arm and threading the catheter tip to the opening (ostium) of one of the coronary arteries. An iodine-based dye is injected through the catheter and into the artery. When X-rays pass through the heart, the dye absorbs the radiation and produces a silhouette of the artery's interior. This silhouette, acquired while the heart is beating, is projected on video monitors in the catheterization lab so that the cardiologist can see the artery on which she or he is planning to intervene.

An angiographer's most basic tool is a clear understanding of the heart's anatomy. The human heart has its own mini-circulation system. Surrounding the heart are two small arteries that branch out from the aorta at the base of the aortic valve. One artery, called the left main coronary artery, divides into two major branches, the left circumflex and the left anterior descending arteries. The other artery is the right coronary artery. The left coronary artery provides circulation to the pumping chambers of the left side of the heart—the left atrium and left ventricle—while the right coronary artery provides circulation to the right atrium and right ventricle. Since the angiographer's job is to correctly identify the portion of artery that has been damaged by disease and then to measure the diseased area to determine what factors might make an intervention difficult, close scrutiny of the coronary anatomy must be performed in every case.

Angiography, like photography, relies on good equipment and technique for good results. Lens quality, exposure, image composition, focus, film, and development are all important for acquiring adequate angiograms. If the angiogram's quality

Photographs courtesy of The Cleveland Clinic Foundation

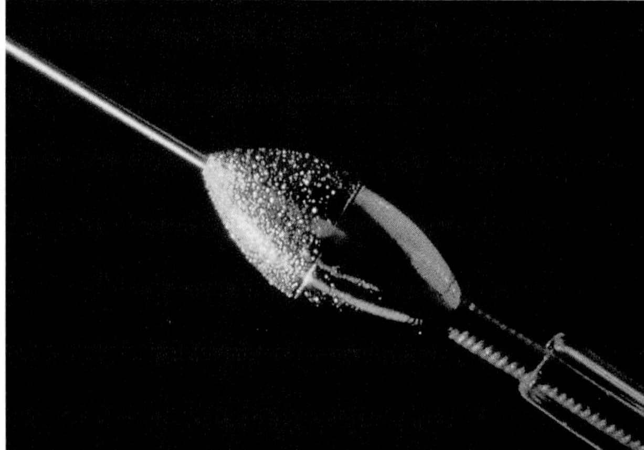

(Top) A "directional" coronary atherectomy device utilizes a small rotating knife to slice strips of plaque from the area of disease. (Above) A "rotational" atherectomy device employs a spinning burr to tunnel through plaque buildup on artery walls.

is good, the core lab's analysis is likely to be reliable; if the angiogram is poor, the analysis is compromised.

Prior to the 1990s, angiograms were routinely recorded on rolls of 35-mm film (called cinefilm) that had been placed in a cinematic camera attached to the X-ray system in a catheterization lab. The cardiologist performing the catheterization was able to obtain a permanent record of the procedure by exposing to cinefilm the series of X-ray images taken during the procedure. A technician would unload and develop the film, which was available for review by the cardiologist or surgeon several hours later. Today angiograms are also recorded on computer disks, which enables instant review of the intervention.

Cineprojectors allow the cardiologist to review angiograms recorded on cinefilm. The image produced by a cineprojector can be displayed on a projection screen for visual examination or sent to a computer through an optical digitizer (a machine that converts film images into digital images) for computer-assisted analysis.

Recently, the compact disc has become the standard medium for the distribution of angiograms that have been digitally acquired. Digital angiograms are produced by catheterization laboratories using high-speed disk drives. The advantages of this method are not only the instant playback of the angiogram for review but also the reduced costs to hospitals resulting from elimination of film development and storage. Most core labs now have the equipment to analyze the digital images archived on compact disc.

The nuts and bolts of coronary interventions

Interventional cardiologists who perform the procedures that are later analyzed by the lab use special tools to "intervene" in the natural progression of heart disease. These cardiologists thread small devices through a catheter to the site of narrowing in the coronary artery. All devices work by enlarging the lumen, or artery diameter, and restoring blood flow. Some of the interventions that rely on such devices are:

- *Balloon angioplasty:* In balloon angioplasty a very small "balloon" is passed through the catheter and threaded to the site of disease. The balloon is then inflated, which compresses the fatty deposits against the sides of the artery. After a successful procedure, blood can more readily flow to feed the heart muscle. If the procedure is performed while a heart attack is occurring, the angioplasty balloon can be used to break up the blood clot, open the artery, restore blood flow, and thereby stop the attack.
- *Atherectomy:* Atheroma is another name for coronary disease. Several atherectomy devices work by removing plaque from the artery to widen the stenosis (narrowing caused by disease). The "directional" coronary atherectomy device uses a small rotating knife to slice strips of plaque from the artery wall, while the "rotational" atherectomy device uses a spinning burr to tunnel a larger opening through the plaque. Various new laser devices use an intense beam of light to vaporize the plaque.
- *Stenting:* In coronary stenting a small tubelike metal or plastic structure is inserted into the coronary artery and expanded with an angioplasty balloon at the point of artery disease (some stents are self-expanding). The expanded stent, which looks like a cylindrical cage, implants itself in the artery walls and thereby holds the artery open. The stent remains in the artery for the life of the patient.

Quantifying the data

Sophisticated workstations allow the lab's technologists to perform specialized analytic procedures, collectively called quantitative coronary angiography and quantitative left-ventriculography. The core lab technologist performs quantitative coronary angiography (assessment of the artery and disease) by first digitizing selected frames from angiograms recorded on cinefilm. The frames selected for analysis include a pair from the film taken before the intervention, a pair from the film taken following the procedure, and a pair from the recatheterization film (which is usually taken six months after the original procedure). These paired images are taken from angles of the artery that are then matched with the postinterventional and follow-up acquisitions so that each of the three provides approximately the same view of the artery.

The catheter tip is used to "calibrate" the frame. Since the catheter tip is a known dimension, it can be used to determine the actual size of the artery. On each side of the catheter tip, there is a rapid change from dark to light, which outlines the borders of the catheter. A computer analyzes the area in and around the catheter tip and places points where the most rapid changes in gray scale occur. The computer places several points along each edge of the catheter and then connects the points to produce an outline following the catheter's contour. This process is called "contour edge-detection" and is the core of quantitative analysis technology.

Stenosis and restenosis. The next step is to analyze the artery itself. Using the same procedure as above, the computer detects the edges of the artery's diseased region. The areas of the artery that are free from disease are then tagged as "normal" and used by the computer as reference segments. The tightest point in the diseased segment is tagged and named the "minimum lesion diameter." Using these values, the diameter of the diseased segment is compared with the average diameter of the normal segments. A simple formula is then used to calculate the diameter and area of the stenosis, which is represented as a percentage. The larger the percentage, the greater the extent of disease. The same measurement processes are then performed on the postinterventional and follow-up images. The postinterventional analysis determines whether the procedure was successful. If the disease that remains after intervention is less than 50% of the diameter of a normal segment, the procedure is considered to have been a success. Images from the follow-up angiogram are analyzed to determine if there was recurrence of the lesion (restenosis) during the six months after initial intervention. Generally, if the lesion from a successful intervention is greater than 50% of the diameter of a normal segment after six months, it is considered restenosed. In clinical drug and device trials, the restenosis rate from one group of patients is compared with the restenosis rate of another group on a different therapy. (The restenosis rate is defined as the percentage of the study population that experiences restenosis.) The lower the percentage, the better the therapy at reducing restenosis. Stents are currently very popular interventional devices because they have low complication and restenosis rates.

Measuring the capacity of the vital left ventricle. "Quantitative left-ventriculography" is used to measure the left ventricle's capacity to pump blood. Oxygen-rich blood enters the left atrium from the pulmonary veins of the lungs. The atrium pumps this blood into the left ventricle, where it is then pumped into the aorta and distributed throughout the body. After a heart attack it is common for a part of the muscle surrounding the left ventricle to be damaged. One method used to determine the extent of damage is the left-ventriculogram, which is similar to coronary angiography. A catheter is placed in the left ventricle and contrast dye is injected. Motion picture X-rays are then taken of the heart while it pumps. The dye outlines the left ventricle and reveals its ability to contract and pump blood. Heart muscle damaged by a heart attack will not contract effectively, and there will be a reduction in the amount of blood pumped out to the body.

Photographs courtesy of The Cleveland Clinic Foundation

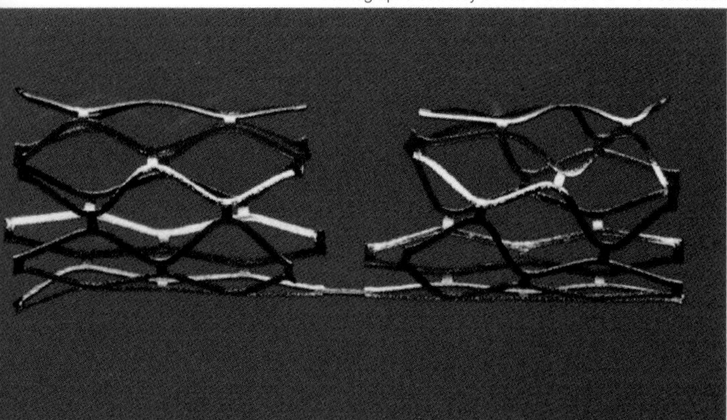

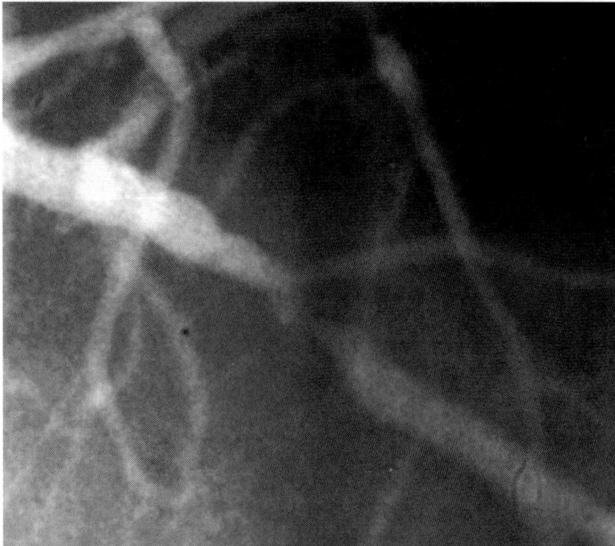

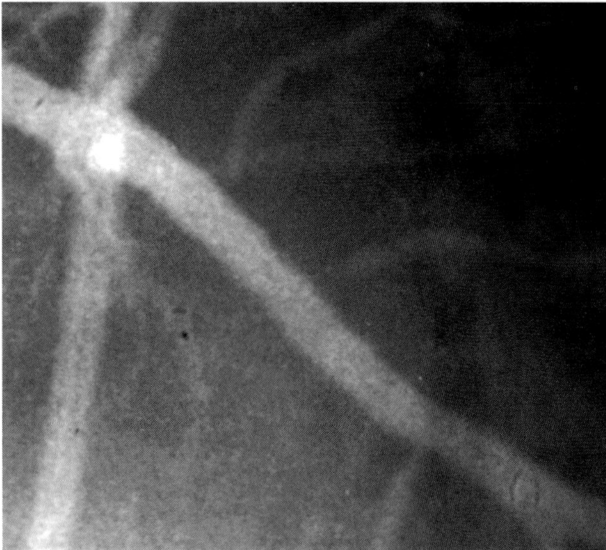

(Top) A coronary stent, a wire or plastic mesh tube that is expanded with an angioplasty balloon, is embedded into an artery wall to prevent restenosis (the recurrence of narrowing). Cineframes show the left circumflex coronary artery before (center) and after (above) a stent has been placed at the site of disease.

When performing quantitative left-ventriculography, a core lab technologist will select two frames from the left-ventriculogram for analysis. The first frame is taken at end-diastole, when the ventricle's cardiac muscle is relaxed and the ventricle is filled to capacity with blood. The dye injected into the ventricle outlines the edge of the heart muscle, which the technologist traces. The second frame is selected at end-systole, when the muscle of the ventricle has contracted completely. These two ventriculographic silhouettes are then compared to determine the extent of the damage to the heart muscle. The area of heart muscle that has been damaged by a heart attack does not pump or contract as normal heart muscle would. This damaged region is called the "infarct zone," and its lack of contractility can be measured by examining the same digital silhouettes described above. By analyzing the distance between the silhouettes, the computer can determine the amount of motion and strength of the ventricle compared with that of a normal heart. Recovery of the "infarct zone" can be determined by comparing the results of ventriculograms taken days or weeks apart. These time-sensitive comparisons have demonstrated the ability of thrombolytic drugs, if administered soon after the onset of a heart attack, to stop the attack and preserve cardiac muscle, enhancing the heart's ability to recover its function over time.

Accurate analysis

The analysis procedure developed by a core lab depends on what a particular clinical trial is studying. Thrombolytic drug and angioplasty trials require "thrombolysis in myocardial infarction grading," a standard procedure for determining blood flow through an obstructed area after a thrombolytic drug or balloon angioplasty has been administered.

The core lab at the Cleveland (Ohio) Clinic Foundation has established a routine process for analysis of thrombolytic drug trials. Since thrombolysis in myocardial infarction grading is a visual analysis and therefore subject to biases, two technologists perform detailed analyses of each film without knowing each other's results. Their independent findings are compared, and a third technologist adjudicates any disagreements between the two original reviewers. In this manner, observer variability is minimized, and accuracy of the analysis is enhanced. In a similar fashion, if quantitative left-ventriculography is required, the end-diastolic and end-systolic silhouettes are traced by one technologist and visually inspected by a second.

For device trials (such as those that involve stenting, balloon angioplasty, and atherectomy) and trials testing medications used in conjunction with such devices, quantitative coronary angiography is required. The films for these trials are sent to the core lab in pairs—the procedural and six-month follow-up angiograms. Because structural assessments (such as that of the curvature of the artery near the site of disease) are visual and therefore subject to observer variability and bias, each assessment is performed by two technologists, with adjudication by a third, similar to blood-flow grading, above. After the analyses have been reviewed and approved by the cardiologists affiliated with the lab, the films are returned to the hospitals, and the data are entered into comprehensive

Courtesy of The Cleveland Clinic Foundation

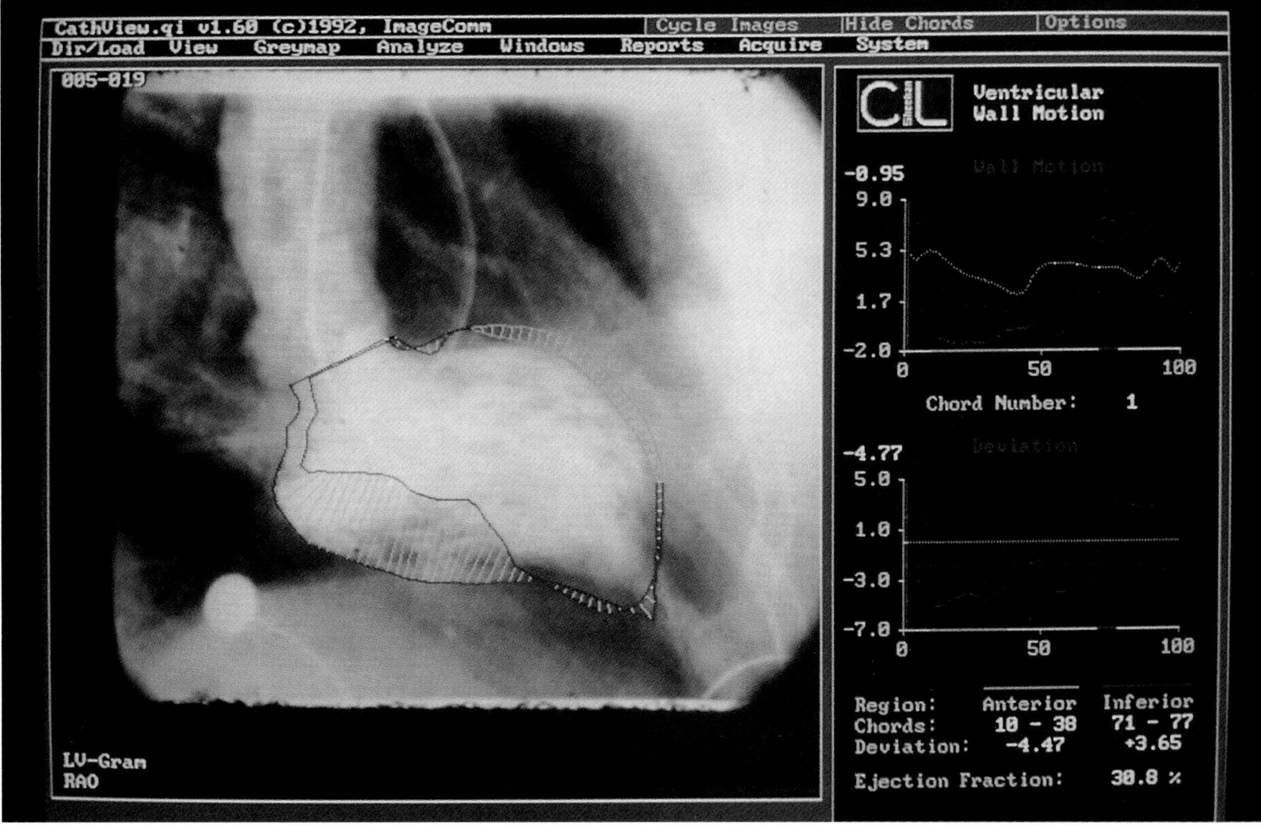

A computer screen used during the performance of quantitative left-ventriculography, which measures the pumping capacity of the left ventricle following a heart attack. Cutting-edge computer technology provides core labs with the necessary tools to do detailed analyses of the heart muscle.

databases. The data-entry process is tightly controlled and repeatedly checked for errors, while the databases are protected by high-security measures.

In many clinical trials the angiography core lab plays a pivotal role in the drug-approval process. The Cleveland Clinic core lab fulfilled this function during Phase 2 trials of the thrombolytic r-PA (reteplase), an analog of the naturally occurring clot-dissolving substance tissue plasminogen activator (t-PA). It was theorized that r-PA would have the ability to open blood vessels better than t-PA in the first 90 minutes after a coronary event. The core lab staff, blinded to which drug regimen each patient in the trial received, was able to confirm this hypothesis in an unbiased and consistent manner.

Room for improvement

Despite all its advantages, coronary angiography has inherent weaknesses. Since an angiogram is a two-dimensional picture of the artery's internal shape, it provides no information about the disease process in the vessel wall. Also, not all lesions can be viewed on an angiogram. Because they are silhouettes, angiograms can miss some complex lesions—*e.g.,* those that are broad in one plane and flat in another, those that are tortuous and fractured, and those in which plaque lines the vessel walls uniformly and concentrically. Many complex lesions appear normal when they are viewed in silhouette but demonstrate their true pathology when viewed in cross-section.

Because of the limitations of coronary angiography, an intravascular ultrasound device is often employed to give the cardiologist a view of a coronary artery's cross-section. The ultrasound probe, which is a very small transducer of sound waves, is passed through a catheter into the artery. As the probe passes along the interior of the artery, it returns an ultrasound cross-sectional image. Not only does the ultrasound procedure show lesions that angiography misses, but it also provides a picture of the disease progression in the wall of the vessel, which enables the amount of plaque in a lesion to be examined. Ultrasound enables visualization of other disease factors, such as calcium buildup in the artery and the presence of flaps of tissue and blood clots clinging to the vessel wall. Core labs utilize ultrasound analysis whenever this procedure is employed for research. Sometimes, to develop the most complete picture of the artery and its disease, both ultrasonic and angiographic analysis are employed.

Even though ultrasound is superior to angiography in many instances, it cannot be used to guide coronary interventions as they are being performed. The angiogram is still the best imaging modality for assisting the cardiologist in placing a stent in a coronary artery or performing balloon angioplasty. Since angiography continues to be used for diagnosing and intervening in coronary artery disease, the need for core lab analyses of coronary angiograms will continue for the foreseeable future.

—Darrell Debowey, M.S.

Stroke Update

"I'm sorry—it's a stroke. There's nothing to do but wait and see." Until recently, this is all that doctors could say to stroke patients and their families. Despite the fact that stroke is the third most common cause of death in the United States and one of the most common causes worldwide, effective stroke treatment has become possible only in the past several years. Because of the unique vulnerability of the brain and its limited ability to recover from injury, prevention traditionally has been the primary approach to stroke "treatment." And even as better therapies are being developed, medical scientists continue to seek more effective preventive strategies.

An "accident" in the brain

The term *stroke* describes the sudden onset of paralysis, numbness, loss of balance, inability to speak or slurring of speech, or other symptoms caused by brain dysfunction. Repeated small strokes may be relatively unobtrusive yet cause progressive loss of memory and other cognitive abilities—a syndrome called multi-infarct dementia, which may appear similar to Alzheimer's disease.

The usual medical term for a stroke, *cerebrovascular accident,* reflects the fact that strokes are the result of either obstruction or rupture of a blood vessel carrying blood to the brain (cerebrum). They are, therefore, usually divided into two major groups: ischemic (caused by blockage of a blood vessel) and hemorrhagic (caused by bleeding, or hemorrhage). These distinctions are important because they have a bearing on prevention and treatment.

Ischemic strokes are most frequently caused by sudden obstruction of blood flow, either by a blood clot or by a clump of the blood cells known as platelets. (The word *ischemia* means a deprivation of blood supply.) Both platelet clumping, or aggregation, and blood clotting are normal mechanisms that function to prevent blood from pouring out of broken or leaky blood vessels. In the case of strokes, however, these mechanisms are activated inappropriately or excessively. Any brain tissue "downstream" from the obstruction may be injured or killed by loss of its vital supply of oxygen and glucose, substances needed to maintain the life functions and structural integrity of the tissues. Only a few minutes of complete ischemia is enough to kill neurons (nerve cells).

Blood clots and platelet aggregates may form directly on the wall of a blood vessel injured by atherosclerosis, thus partially or completely blocking blood flow to nearby tissues. In some cases, the obstruction may break loose from the vessel wall and float downstream to be caught in a narrower vessel, which thus causes blockage in a brain area far removed from the place where the obstruction was formed. The development of such a mobile obstruction is called embolization, and the obstruction itself is called an embolus. Emboli may originate in blood vessels within the brain, in vessels of the neck, or even within the chambers of the heart.

A cerebral hemorrhage occurs when a blood vessel within the brain breaks, which allows blood to rush outward into the tissues of the brain. Large hemorrhages may cause abrupt increases in pressure within the skull or fatal shifts in the position of vital brain structures. Such hemorrhages are often the cause of sudden death in people with strokes.

Prevention

> *It is impossible to cure a severe attack of apoplexy and no easy matter to cure a mild one.*
>
> —Hippocrates

This statement, dating from the 5th century BC, is typical of the historical attitude toward the treatment of stroke (formerly known as apoplexy), although early practitioners did not understand why strokes were so devastating. With this limited knowledge, they chose to emphasize prevention over treatment. Today preventive strategies are becoming both more narrowly focused and more widely applied.

Preventive medicine is the science of altering risk factors for diseases. Its aim is to identify conditions that make a person or group of people especially vulnerable to a disease and then to change these conditions if possible. Some risk factors—race and family history, for example—cannot be changed, but others such as body weight, alcohol use, cigarette smoking, and environmental exposures can be altered to lower the risk for a certain disease to an individual.

A color-enhanced magnetic resonance imaging scan reveals an area of damaged tissue (dark blue) in the lower left cerebrum (at right in the image) of a stroke victim. Brain cells have only a limited capacity to recover from stroke-induced injury; much recent research has focused on developing therapies that will enhance this capacity.

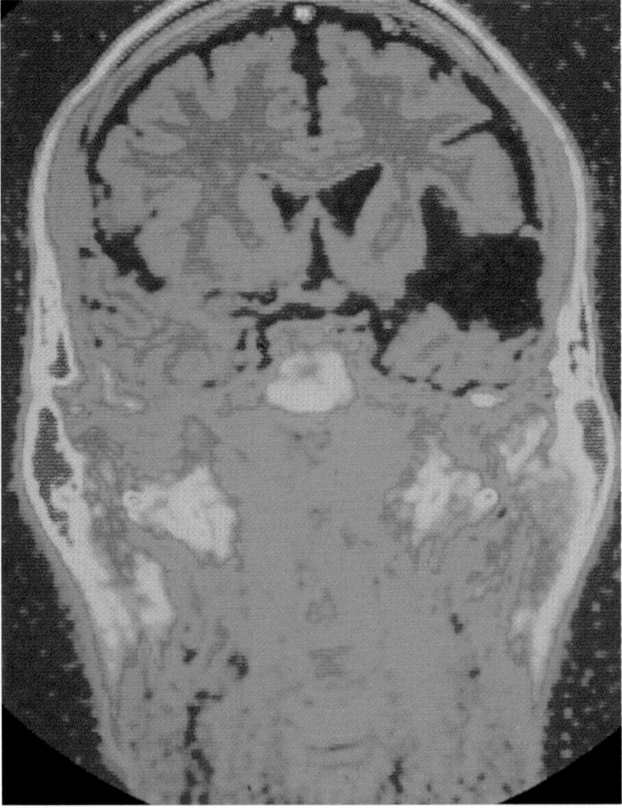

CNRI/Science Source/Photo Researchers

Assessing the risk factors. The most obvious risk factor for stroke is advancing age; it is largely a condition affecting older adults. Nevertheless, strokes can also occur in children and in young adults. In the latter, risk factors such as pregnancy, cocaine or amphetamine abuse, and migraine headaches or other medical disorders often contribute to the occurrence of stroke.

The other most important risk factor is inadequately treated hypertension (high blood pressure). Repeated studies have shown that lowering elevated blood pressure, even by small amounts, reduces the chance of stroke for people of all ages. Drug treatment is not always necessary. In some cases weight reduction and exercise may bring elevated blood pressure into the normal range. Better detection and treatment of hypertension is thought by some authorities to be the reason for the significant decline in stroke incidence in the industrialized countries since about 1950.

An elevated risk of stroke also is associated with an abnormal heart rhythm called atrial fibrillation, in which the atria of the heart contract so irregularly that blood clots tend to form on the atrial walls, break off, and travel through the bloodstream, ultimately sticking in and blocking arteries that supply blood to the brain. Atrial fibrillation is sometimes associated with other symptoms of heart disease or may occur in people with diseases of the heart valves.

Patients with other types of heart disease—for example, congestive heart failure and heart attack without atrial fibrillation—have about twice the rate of stroke as the rest of the population. This is not surprising, as much heart disease is really disease of the coronary arteries, the vessels that supply blood to the heart muscle. A person who has a stroke is more likely to die later of a heart attack than of another stroke.

Cigarette smoking roughly doubles an individual's risk of stroke, an effect that may be reversed within five years if smoking is stopped. Having diabetes mellitus also increases the risk of stroke, as it increases the likelihood of other vascular disorders such as coronary artery disease and disease of the arteries that carry blood to the limbs.

In the United States, African-Americans are at higher risk for stroke than other groups. The reasons are not entirely clear. A higher prevalence of hypertension, lower socioeconomic status, and a higher rate of diabetes may be involved, but these relationships have not been definitely proved. A large study now under way at Rush-Presbyterian-St. Luke's Medical Center in Chicago may eventually provide the answer. It has already been shown that whites and African-Americans differ in the types of strokes they have, which suggests that the causes may vary in these groups. Whites, for example, tend to have larger strokes caused by blockage or embolism involving the large arteries of the brain or neck, while African-Americans suffer from smaller but often multiple strokes caused by obstruction of tiny arteries that perforate the inner brain regions.

Many other factors increase an individual's risk of stroke, including a family history of stroke, the occurrence of a previous stroke, a high cholesterol level, heavy alcohol use, obesity, a sedentary lifestyle, abnormalities of blood clotting mechanisms, and the presence of certain abnormal blood factors called anticardiolipin antibodies.

The effect of all of these factors is additive. Some of them occurring together may even cause a risk that is greater than the sum of the individual risks. The combination of hypertension and smoking, for example, on a stroke-risk "scorecard" would yield a higher number than the sum of their separate scores. According to one estimate, some 375,000 strokes per year could be prevented in the United States by successful treatment of high blood pressure and atrial fibrillation, cessation of smoking, and reduction of heavy alcohol consumption.

National High Blood Pressure Education Program

Feeling fine is the primary cause of strokes.

Strokes result most often from high blood pressure. And high blood pressure has no symptoms. So it can sneak up on people who feel fine. People who have no idea they're at risk.

Fortunately, high blood pressure can often be prevented. Just watch your weight, limit your salt and alcohol intake, and exercise regularly. Then you won't just feel fine. You'll actually be fine.

What are you doing about your blood pressure?

High blood pressure is an insidious condition that often goes undiagnosed. Its prevalence in the African-American population accounts in part for this group's comparatively greater risk for stroke.

Modifying risk factors. Once the risk factors for a disease are known, those that can be changed are valid targets for efforts aimed at both individuals and identifiable population groups. Primary prevention—*i.e.,* efforts to keep a disorder from occurring in the first place (as opposed to those intended to prevent recurrences)—is the most direct technique and has enjoyed some success. For example, public health measures such as educational campaigns and free blood pressure screening have enabled the detection of hypertension in many people. The harder job of long-term, consistent, effective treatment of hypertension—drug therapy, diet modification, exercise programs—must then be undertaken on an individual basis; such efforts require strong personal motivation on the part of the patient and skilled medical care by committed health professionals.

Atrial fibrillation is readily detectable by an electrocardiogram or even in a simple physical exam by a physician feeling the patient's pulse. It can sometimes be stopped by medication or, in some cases, by electrical conversion of the heartbeat, using a stimulator. If atrial fibrillation cannot (or, for other reasons, should not) be altered, the anticoagulant drug warfarin may be used to reduce the risk of stroke. Warfarin has its own problems, however. Safe use requires frequent—sometimes weekly—blood tests and dosage adjustments. In addition, warfarin is sometimes associated with hemorrhages in various parts of the body, including the brain. The decision to use warfarin in an individual case may depend upon balancing the risk of stroke against the risk of a hemorrhage due to a fall (in an elderly patient, for example) or the difficulty of fine-tuning the dosage. Because of these potential problems, aspirin has been tried as an alternative to warfarin and has been found in some studies to reduce stroke risk. The ability of aspirin to reduce clumping of platelets has been exploited in stroke prevention as well (*see* below).

Secondary prevention. The newest methods of stroke prevention are those that have been developed for people with specific symptoms known to precede stroke and those in whom a stroke has already occurred. Over the past few years, new medical therapies have been devised, and the effectiveness of an older, surgical therapy has been proved and appropriate candidates for it defined.

Although many strokes occur without any prior warning, some are preceded by specific premonitory symptoms. It is now clear that appropriate treatment can reduce the subsequent risk of stroke in people who experience such symptoms. These warnings, called transient ischemic attacks, or TIAs, are like temporary strokes. They consist of transitory neurological symptoms of weakness, paralysis, numbness, impaired vision, or a variety of other symptoms that might be produced by a stroke. Unlike a stroke, however, the TIA lasts only minutes to hours, then dissipates.

Once a TIA has occurred, the individual's risk factors for stroke can be identified and treated. Some people with TIAs are found to have narrowing, or stenosis, of one or both of the carotid arteries, the vessels in the neck that carry blood to the brain. This condition can be treated by surgically cleaning out the area where atherosclerotic plaque has accumulated, narrowing the artery and serving as a nidus for platelet aggregation. The surgical procedure is called carotid endarterectomy. For years physicians debated whether these operations were useful, especially since strokes sometimes occurred as a direct result of the surgery itself. The answer was provided by two careful trials in which patients with TIAs or mild strokes and evidence of carotid stenosis were randomly assigned to treatment either with endarterectomy and medical treatment that included drugs to reduce the formation of clots or platelet clumps or with the medical treatment alone. These investigations—one conducted at centers in the U.S. and Canada, the other in Europe—showed that if the carotid artery is narrowed by at least 70%, surgical treatment prevents stroke better than medical treatment alone. Importantly, one of the studies, the North American Symptomatic Carotid Endarterectomy Trial, suggested that these positive results could be achieved only if the operation was done at a medical center with a record of performing the surgery successfully. A poor surgical record, in other words, might mean that any lowering of stroke risk from the operation could be outweighed by a high risk of stroke from the procedure itself.

The decision to perform endarterectomy is more problematic when patients have only a small amount of carotid stenosis or have more severe stenosis but no symptoms of cerebrovascular disease such as prior stroke or TIAs. A large trial is now under way to determine the effectiveness of the surgery in preventing stroke in these groups. The results of one multicenter trial of this approach, the Asymptomatic Carotid Atherosclerosis Study, published in May 1995, showed that in selected asymptomatic patients with carotid narrowing of 60% or more, surgery plus medical treatment was more effective than medical treatment alone in lowering the risk of a stroke in the short term (a little more than 2.5 years).

Drug treatments have also proved effective in preventing stroke in people who have already had a mild stroke or who are subject to TIAs. Both aspirin and a relatively new drug called ticlopidine are used in this way. Both belong to the category called platelet inhibitors, drugs that reduce aggregation of platelets. Once started, drug therapy may have to be continued indefinitely. Therefore, the cost, safety, and tolerability of these drugs have been important factors in determining which one to use in an individual case. Aspirin, for example, is very inexpensive, but it causes stomach irritation in some people, and others continue to have TIAs despite its use. Some studies have shown ticlopidine to be even more effective than aspirin, but it is costly and requires frequent (and even more costly) blood tests to monitor for potentially serious side effects. Tests of other drugs for this purpose are under way.

Treatment

Over the past several years, the nihilistic attitude toward treatment of an acute stroke has given way to increasingly aggressive treatment strategies. This change has come about as a direct result of animal studies of stroke and better understanding of why neurons die and how they recover from injury.

Unlike most other cells in the body, neurons that die are never replaced. Those that survive an injury have the capacity to reorganize their connections to each other to help compensate for the loss, and some neurological functions can be taken over by uninjured brain areas. When an ischemic stroke occurs, some neurons, deprived of blood flow, die. Others cease to function properly because their blood supply is reduced; although injured, these neurons are reparable. The strategy of emergency treatment for stroke is based on the possibility of enhancing the capacity of these neurons to recover from ischemic injury and on providing the most favorable environment within the brain for them to do so. For the best possible outcome, such interventions must be carried out quickly; the longer neurons are deprived of optimal blood flow, the greater the chance that injury will result in irreversible neuronal death.

Research on animals has revealed why neurons die when they are deprived of normal circulation and how some can be

CNRI/Science Source/Photo Researchers

helped to recover from nonfatal ischemia. This new understanding has enabled scientists to develop new treatments for acute stroke. Some physicians feel that treatment must begin within the first hour of a stroke to offer any hope of efficacy, and most trials of new therapies require treatment no later than six hours after the stroke begins. The sense of urgency behind these treatments is implied by the term sometimes used to describe them, *hyperacute therapy.*

Responding to cerebral ischemia. The first steps in responding to symptoms of a stroke are prompt recognition by the patient or family that an acute neurological change has occurred and immediate seeking of medical help. The next step is an accurate diagnosis by a physician.

If the stroke is due to an obstruction, thrombolytic agents (drugs that dissolve blood clots) may be used. Two of these "clot-busting" drugs, urokinase and streptokinase, have also been used successfully to treat coronary artery occlusion in heart attack. These drugs have been administered intravenously after stroke with some success. If they are delivered directly to the site of the clot by an arterial catheter—a thin flexible tube that is carefully threaded through the arterial system into the neck or head—90% of clots can be dissolved. Unwanted bleeding can occur in the brain or elsewhere, however, when these drugs are used, and in some circumstances reperfusing an injured brain area can actually cause further neuronal death. Clinical trials are under way to determine whether the benefits of such therapy outweigh the risks.

Another medical approach to breaking up clots involves the use of tissue plasminogen activator, or t-PA. This is a naturally occurring substance that helps dissolve tiny blood clots that act in regulating normal vascular function. When genetic engineering techniques are used to manufacture t-PA in the relatively large quantities needed for therapeutic use, the resulting product is called recombinant t-PA, or rt-PA. As with urokinase and streptokinase, hemorrhage is also a risk with t-PA therapy. The results of one large U.S. trial, published in December 1995, indicated that stroke victims treated with t-PA within three hours were 30% more likely than untreated patients to escape permanent brain damage. The study confirmed the risk of hemorrhage associated with t-PA therapy, however, and death rates in the treated and untreated groups were similar. The Food and Drug Administration approved t-PA for use in acute stroke in June 1996.

Much recent research has focused on the mechanisms by which reduced blood flow causes harm at the cellular level. Scientists have found that when ischemia occurs, larger-than-normal amounts of calcium pass through injured neuronal membranes, causing potentially fatal chemical reactions inside the cells. A group of drugs called calcium channel blockers (*e.g.,* nimodipine, nicardipine), which prevent transport of calcium into injured neurons, have been investigated as a therapy for stroke, but their efficacy has not yet been convincingly demonstrated.

The release of abnormally large amounts of chemicals from injured or dying neurons onto receptor sites, called *N*-methyl-D-aspartate (NMDA) receptors, on neighboring cells is thought to provoke the toxic influx of calcium. This process can be prevented by a class of drugs called NMDA antagonists (*e.g.,* lamotrigine, dextrorphan). Some animal tests suggest that these drugs may reduce the amount of cerebral tissue killed by ischemia, but tests in humans have not yet been completed. Other classes of drugs such as G(Ma) ganglioside and the anticoagulant heparin are also being investigated.

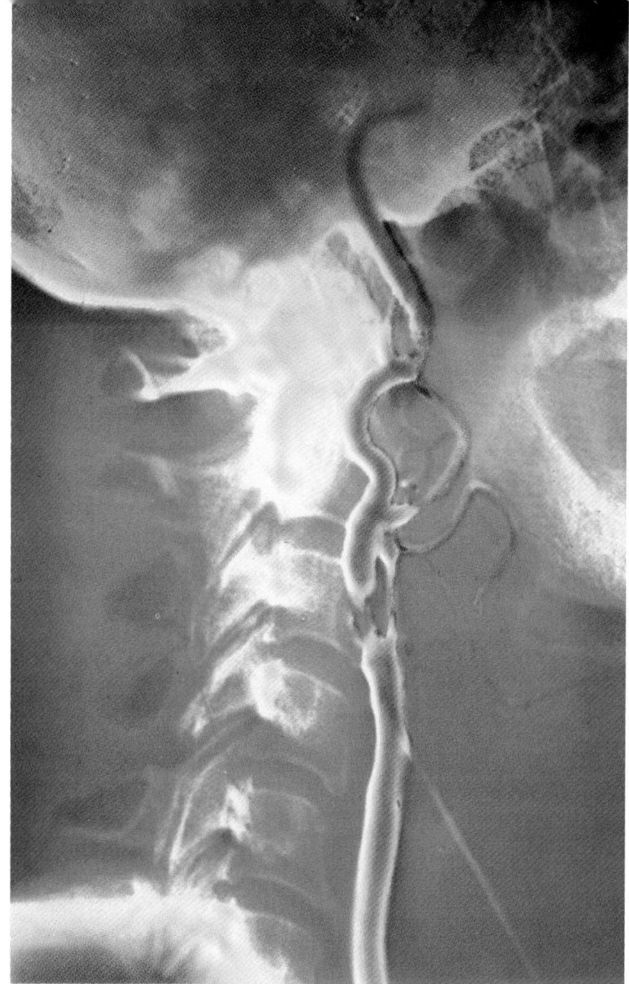

Interruption of blood flow in the carotid artery (shown in gold) is clearly visible on this angiogram. Surgery to remove atherosclerotic plaque blocking the vessel can sometimes prevent the occurrence of a stroke.

Treating intracerebral hemorrhage. As noted above, acute cerebral hemorrhage often proves fatal. Increased pressure inside the skull may prevent adequate blood flow to uninjured brain regions, or it may distort or displace vital areas of the brain. Occasionally, emergency surgical intervention is lifesaving; the surgeon removes the clotted blood and relieves the pressure inside the skull.

Appropriate care

The emerging emphasis on treatment of acute stroke has spawned the proliferation of specialized hospital units specifically for the acute and follow-up care of people with stroke. Usually but not always located at large university hospitals, these centers generally emphasize scrupulous attention to control of blood pressure and blood glucose levels and treatment for complications of stroke such as depression and infections. Most centers provide counseling for both patients and families. Despite their greater expense compared with community hospitals, specialized stroke-treatment centers shorten the time to discharge from the hospital and make available the most recent therapies, often in the context of investigational trials.

About half of those who survive a stroke have significant neurological disability, most commonly in the form of paralysis, speech problems, or sensory impairment. Early rehabilitation can maximize remaining neurological function and, if necessary, help patients learn to modify the way they carry out routine daily activities.

Depression is a common part of the recovery period after a stroke. Besides improving mood, prompt recognition and treatment of depression can often enable a person to take better advantage of rehabilitative help.

No more "wait and see"

Of all of the changes in approach to stroke, perhaps the most significant is that the occurrence of a stroke is now considered a medical emergency, equally as urgent and compelling as a heart attack. Symptoms suggestive of TIAs or stroke should prompt a rapid call to a physician or evaluation at an emergency medical facility. The "wait-and-see" attitude is a thing of the past.

—Donna C. Bergen, M.D.

Heart Smart: To Shovel or Not to Shovel?

- An apparently healthy 59-year-old cardiac surgeon—who had campaigned on local television and radio against smoking—dies of a heart attack while shoveling snow.
- A 70-year-old widower digs out after a snow storm one Sunday morning, suffers a heart attack, and dies.
- A 44-year-old supermarket cashier clears her driveway of snow so that she can get her children to school before she goes to work. She has a heart attack before she finishes. Her children never make it to school. Their mother spends the next two weeks in the coronary care unit, then several months at home in convalescence. Only after nearly six months is she able to return to work part time.

Stories like these are all too familiar. The names and faces change, but there is a common denominator: middle-aged or older men and women shovel heavy, wet snow, suffer acute cardiac symptoms, and collapse. In the United States every year, countless heart attacks result from this common chore, and roughly one-third of them are fatal.

Because snow shoveling is perceived as risky, many people who feel healthy and think they have no reason for concern still tackle this job with utmost care. They begin first thing in the morning, before the snow has hardened. They lift relatively small loads—weighing only 2–5 kg (4½–11 lb). Surprisingly, none of these precautions is guaranteed to help even the most careful shoveler avoid danger—and some "precautions" may actually increase the cardiovascular risk. Unfortunately, the harmful effects of snow shoveling are typically camouflaged until the damage has been done. In fact, shoveling snow may be one of the most strenuous activities that some people will ever put their heart through. Only recently have clinicians understood why shoveling poses such a danger.

Recent research shows that even for the physically fit, the simple act of shoveling snow puts profound stress on the heart in several different ways. This stress limits the flow of oxygen-rich blood to the heart at the very moment that the pumping demands on it are at their peak. For someone with a pre-existing heart condition, show shoveling increases the risk of a heart attack. For many millions of people who have "hidden" heart disease and live in snowy climes, shoveling may reveal their disease in a catastrophic way. Understanding why shoveling is dangerous can help the shoveler avoid a potentially hazardous situation.

Morning mayhem

When the alarm clock rings in the morning during the winter months, people in many parts of the land look out to see a crisp new blanket of snow. For most, it makes sense to clear paths and driveways before the day begins and members of the household must get to work, school, or some other destination. Such a timetable, however, may not make such obvious sense to the body's internal body clock ("circadian rhythm"), which governs the cardiovascular and other bodily systems.

When people wake in the morning, their bodies abruptly pick up the pace in order to adjust from the calm of sleep to the demands of upright activity. Heart rate, production of the hormone adrenaline, and blood pressure all rise. These normal responses generally pose no problems for those people with unobstructed arteries and healthy hearts. But for those with cardiac disease, the stress associated with waking in the morning may trigger acute complications, such as myocardial infarction (heart attack) or angina (chest pain). Several recent studies have shown that the risk of heart attack is greatest between 6 AM and noon—precisely the time period during which the middle-aged commuter or older retiree is likely to be out shoveling the sidewalk or driveway.

Bad news for the sedentary

Two important studies reported in *The New England Journal of Medicine* (Dec. 2, 1993)—one carried out by researchers in Berlin, the other by researchers in Boston—indicated that vigorous physical exertion transiently heightens the risk of a heart attack, particularly in those who have a sedentary lifestyle. Hard physical labor abruptly increases heart rate and blood pressure; the resulting greater-than-usual blood flow can dislodge arterial plaque (the fatty deposits that build up on artery walls). As this plaque is carried through the bloodstream, it reaches tight passages where vessel walls are thickened. Plaque can sometimes wedge in the vessel and block the flow of blood. Beyond the blockage, blood flow slows or even stops, which reduces the critical supply of oxygen needed to sustain body tissues. If such a blockage occurs in a coronary artery, the heart muscle becomes starved for oxygen, and most often a heart attack ensues.

These studies further indicated that even for people who exercise regularly—five or more times per week—and who then attempt taxing work like snow shoveling, the risk of having a heart attack directly following the activity is doubled. Worse, for the desk-bound executive or the "couch potato," the risk of having a heart attack following snow shoveling increases 107-fold!

Tom Dietrich—Tony Stone Images

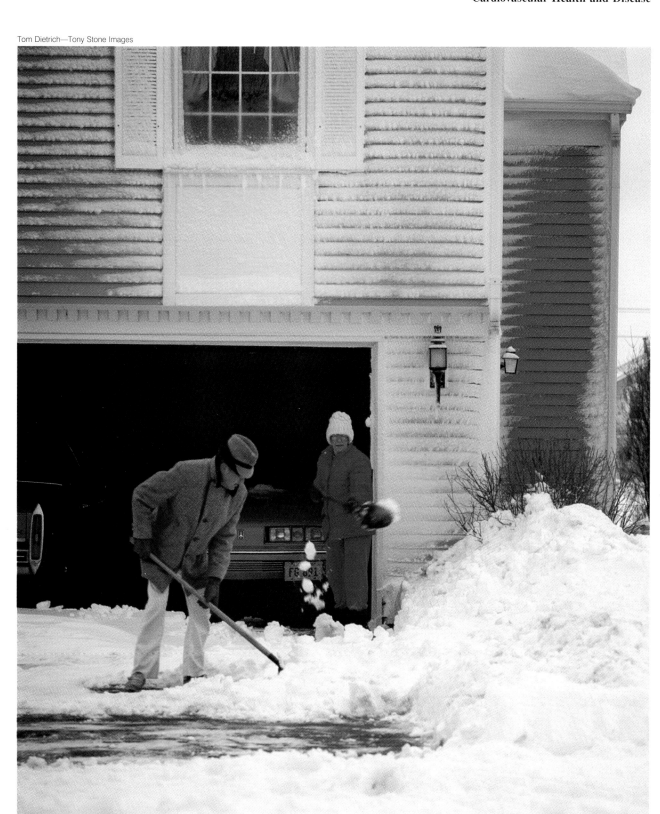

Countless heart attacks—about one-third of which are fatal—result from the common chore of shoveling snow on a cold winter morning. Middle-aged or older men and women who have silent heart disease are the most vulnerable, but even those who are younger and fit can succumb.

Lori Adamski Peek—Tony Stone Images

Snow shoveling is heart-taxing even for young healthy males who shovel at their own pace for a short stint of time on a mild day.

Shoveling takes a stress test

In a controlled study involving young healthy males (reported in the *Journal of the American Medical Association*, March 15, 1995), this author and his colleagues found that shoveling snow requires about the same energy expenditure as an active round of singles tennis or speed walking at eight kilometers (five miles) per hour. Although these are not *the* most energy-expending activities for many people, for the elderly or unfit they could represent a herculean effort.

The same study found that shoveling consumed a large share of energy—even for young healthy male subjects shoveling at their own pace for only 10 minutes at a time when the temperature was relatively mild, 2° C (35.6° F) with no wind chill. In fact, shoveling required two-thirds of the peak energy capacity of the test group, which was confirmed by treadmill testing.

One of the most surprising discoveries in the shoveling study was not the energy required for shoveling but the disproportionate impact of the activity on the heart. Shoveling snow put a far greater strain on the cardiovascular system than might be expected, stressing it more than any other activity that burned the same amount of energy. After only two minutes of shoveling, the heart rate of most subjects reached the upper limit commonly prescribed for aerobic exercise—85% of the maximum heart rate. Moreover, the stress on the heart continued to climb throughout the 10-minute activity, catapulting the test group's heart rates and blood pressures to dangerously high levels. In addition, pulses pounded at 175 beats per minute, more than twice the normal at-rest pulse. These data showed that shoveling snow resulted in heart stress equal to or higher than the most exhaustive treadmill exercise. And none of the test subjects faced the task of "shoveling out" under pressure—*e.g.,* to get to work, school, or elsewhere on time.

Why shoveling wreaks cardiac havoc

Research suggests that there is not one individual cause but a unique cascade of physiological stressors that place undue strain on the heart during snow shoveling. A beautiful 10-cm (4-in) snow cover on the average 3–12-m (10–40-ft) driveway can weigh as much as 3,600 kg (8,000 lb), which is equivalent to the combined weight of four midsize automobiles. While the snow is being removed, at least five physiological factors are contributing to excessive demands on the heart.

Tensed muscles. Snow shoveling is largely an isometric exercise. During isometric exercise, the body remains virtually still while muscles contract, or tense, against the weight being lifted. Demands on the heart often are not apparent during isometric exercise because it produces few warning signs of overexertion, such as sweating or deep breathing.

Isometric exercise, unlike aerobic exercise (*e.g.,* running or bicycling), requires little in the way of active rhythmic movements that stretch and expand muscles, dilate blood vessels, and help oxygen to flow throughout the body. In fact, research shows that tensed muscles during isometric exercise may actually restrict blood flow by reducing the volume of blood returning to the heart at the same time that blood pressure is rising.

This sudden imbalance—an increase in the demand on the heart accompanied by a decrease in blood supply—can bring on myocardial ischemia (insufficient oxygen delivery to the heart muscle). In persons with heart disease, ischemia can lead to life-threatening heart-rhythm irregularities. A doctor or emergency medical technician who is treating a patient with such irregularities has less than four minutes to normalize the heart rhythm by using electrical paddles on the chest to shock the patient's heart, a procedure known as defibrillation. Otherwise, the heart-rhythm irregularity (*i.e.*, ventricular tachycardia or fibrillation) will result in death.

In isometric exercise the amount of increase in blood pressure correlates directly with the strength of the muscles that are being exercised. Blood pressure does not increase as much when muscles are strong as when muscles are weak. As a result, when someone whose arm muscles have not been used to any great extent lifts even a relatively light load, that person will experience a more significant rise in blood pressure than someone who uses his or her arm muscles on a regular basis.

Taking a stand. A second, hidden risk factor in snow shoveling is standing upright for an extended period of time. When people exert themselves while in a standing position, gravity pulls blood to the lower body. In aerobic exercise this is not a problem because recurrent leg movements cause a continual contraction of veins in the leg, which forces blood back to the heart, where, by way of the lungs, it can be reoxygenated. But when someone stands to shovel snow, the heart must work harder to keep circulation moving upward toward it. Meanwhile, the isometric effect combined with gravity produces less blood volume per heartbeat. Blood flow to the heart is reduced at precisely the moment that the pumping demands upon it are at their peak.

Arms up. A third risk factor in snow shoveling is the amount of arm work involved. From a cardiovascular standpoint, arm exertion is much less efficient than leg work. In the process of lifting any given weight, heart rate and blood pressure will be greater when the arms are used than when the legs are used; this is partially due to the fact that arms have less muscle mass. Lifting the arms also works against gravity and thereby increases the effort required for performing the task.

The impact on the heart is even further increased when the shoveler is not in top physical shape. A large majority of people who exercise choose activities that strengthen primarily the legs, such as walking, jogging, or bicycling. The benefits of exercise are largely specific to the muscle groups that are worked in each activity. Even in the veteran distance runner, upper-body fitness may not be much better than in the nonexerciser. Thus, when the physically conditioned runner is called upon to perform even moderate upper-body work, the shock to the heart can be profound.

In fact, in their daily lives, few people rely on upper-body muscles. In the cardiac rehabilitation program at William Beaumont Hospital, Royal Oak, Mich., cardiologists and other health professionals frequently treat heart attack victims who work on assembly lines in Detroit's automobile factories. Their work—lifting or carrying parts, for instance, or moving machinery—typically places a heavy burden on their arms and shoulders; this is work that most are not sufficiently conditioned to do. Before these patients can return safely to their jobs, physiologists typically prescribe weight training, arm cranking, rowing, and other activities to strengthen the upper body and protect the heart.

Breathing matters. The stress placed on the cardiovascular system by snow shoveling includes a little-understood but fascinating physiological reaction to lifting a heavy weight: holding one's breath. No one knows exactly why people instinctively hold their breath when lifting heavy loads. Scientists do know, however, that when someone tries to force air from his or her lungs while holding the nostrils closed and keeping the mouth shut, the impact on the heart is severe. Pressure in the chest rises and hinders the return of blood to the heart, which causes an abrupt increase in blood pressure—the same kind of meteoric rise that can dislodge arterial plaque and lead to a heart attack. Once the shoveler has exhaled, blood pressure falls, which causes a compensatory increase in heart rate. This "seesaw" effect may be hazardous in persons with heart disease and may strain even the physically fit. In fact, professional weight lifters are taught to exhale on the most strenuous part of the lift to avoid heart strain.

Weather alert. Last of the heart risks posed by shoveling are effects of the cold. Exposure to cold air constricts blood vessels throughout the body, which increases the resistance to blood flow. At the same time, breathing cold air can cause a narrowing of the heart's blood vessels. Does that mean that the shoveler who tackles the job when the temperature is relatively mild—say, at or above freezing—is not at risk? Not

Tests carried out by physiologists in exercise laboratories have shown that snow shoveling results in heart stress equal to or greater than the most exhaustive treadmill exercise.

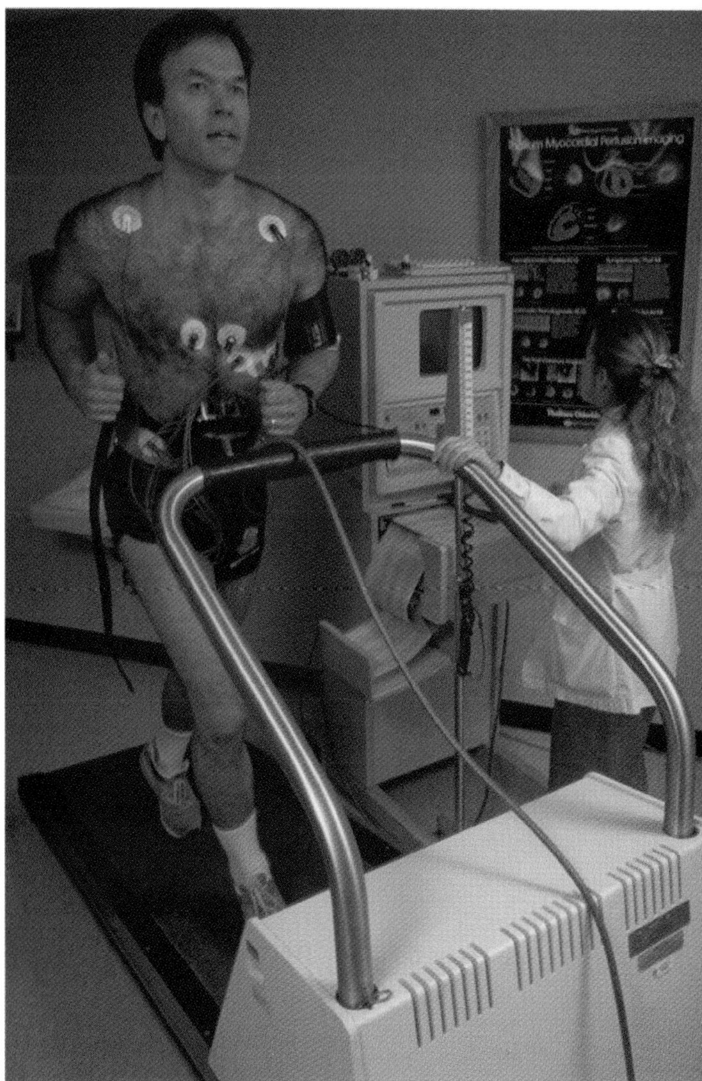

John Coletti—Stock, Boston/PNI

necessarily. Storms in milder temperatures, in which rain and snow may mix, result in especially heavy snow on the ground.

Researchers who conducted studies during five Minneapolis-St. Paul, Minn., winters found that cardiovascular deaths were linked more consistently to snowstorms per se than to severe cold weather. In fact, the most dramatic increase in heart-attack deaths came when snow was mixed with rain. Moreover, significantly, deaths rose not only on the day of the storm but also on the subsequent days when there was still heavy, wet snow to shovel.

Depending on the location, snowfalls of 10 or more centimeters may not be uncommon. In the U.S. snowfall amounts compiled over a 20-year period by the National Weather Service indicate average annual totals of 241.3 cm (95 in) in Flagstaff, Ariz., 152.4 cm (60 in) in Denver, Colo., 208.3 cm (82 in) in Erie, Pa., 94 cm (37 in) in Providence, R.I., and 101.6 cm (40 in) in Detroit. Residents of communities that normally get little snow often face the greatest difficulties. Though a snowfall that comes as a complete surprise may delight people because of its sheer novelty, it may also prove extremely hazardous to their hearts when they attempt to remove the pretty white covering from their walks and drives. In Sheffield, England, where snowfall is generally light, 35 cm (13.7 in) accumulated on Dec. 8, 1990. Physicians reported in the *British Medical Journal* (Feb. 23, 1991) that the following day five patients were admitted to the local coronary care unit with heart attacks. This was much greater than the average daily admission rate for myocardial infarction (one to two patients) in December, which led the physicians to conclude that Sheffield's residents would have been better off if they had let nature have its way and left the shovel in the shed.

NEWS CAP

Heart-Stopping News

The use of calcium channel blockers to control hypertension (high blood pressure) has been called into question. Evidence from several studies in 1995 and '96 suggested that those taking the class of drugs known as calcium channel blockers were at increased risk for heart attack, compared with patients taking the other types of commonly prescribed antihypertensive drugs—beta blockers and diuretics. The medication that raised the most concern was a fast-acting form of nifedepine (marketed under the brand names Procardia and Adalat), which goes to work immediately to lower blood pressure.

Although approved by the U.S. Food and Drug Administration (FDA) only as a treatment for angina (chest pain due to reduced blood flow to the heart muscle), fast-acting nifedepine had been prescribed for some people as a blood-pressure-lowering drug. In August 1995 the National Heart, Lung, and Blood Institute alerted physicians to avoid prescribing the drug for newly diagnosed cases of hypertension. Then in January 1996 the FDA recommended that the product carry a label warning against its use in high blood pressure.

Calcium channel blockers are available in fast-acting and slow-acting formulations. Although the recent studies questioned the safety of all calcium channel blockers, the slow-acting preparations, which effect a gradual rather than an instantaneous change in blood pressure, do not appear to carry the same level of risk.

Many authorities have emphasized that the evidence from these investigations is not conclusive. Long-term studies are under way to provide more definitive answers, but until the results are available, people who are taking calcium channel blockers for hypertension are advised not to discontinue treatment and to consult their physicians. Most experts are in agreement that the dangers of not controlling hypertension are greater than any possible risk posed by the drug.

—*M.J. Friedrich*

Who probably should *not* shovel snow

It cannot be emphasized enough that the *combination* of vigorous physical exertion and a diseased or susceptible heart puts the cardiovascular system in greatest jeopardy. Those at risk include both men and women over 40 years of age who have a history of heart disease, symptoms that suggest a cardiac disorder (*e.g.,* angina, palpitations, dizziness), or one or more of the major coronary risk factors (cigarette smoking, high blood pressure, elevated blood cholesterol, or a sedentary lifestyle).

Anyone who is not sure that he or she is free of heart disease should take precautions. William B. Kannel, former director of the Framingham (Mass.) Heart Study, points out that in 16% of all heart attacks "the first, the last, and the only symptom" of coronary distress is sudden cardiac death.

How can the cardiac stress of shoveling be reduced? Work should be paced and include frequent periods of rest. Before and after shoveling, the shoveler should refrain from consuming large meals, because digestion diverts blood flow from the muscles to the gut. Nor should the shoveler consume caffeine or alcohol or use tobacco, because these substances increase the heart's workload. While outside, the shoveler can avoid inhaling cold air by wearing a breathing mask or muffler. Further, protecting exposed parts of the body from cold, particularly when blowing winds lower the effective temperature, can reduce another snow-shoveling risk—frostbite.

There may be only one surefire solution to the cardiac problems that can result from snow shoveling: to put the shovel down. A heavy snowfall may be the perfect time to arrange for a snowplowing service, to put a hearty local teenager to work, or to find some alternative means of coping, like buying a pair of good waterproof boots!

—*Barry A. Franklin, Ph.D.*

Soy to the World

In the 1990s soyfoods have emerged in Western countries not only as a healthy vegetarian source of protein and other nutrients but as a possible contributor to the prevention of many chronic diseases. While most study results are still preliminary, soyfoods have been linked to a reduction in the rates of hormone-dependent cancers such as breast cancer, as well as to a reduced incidence of other malignancies, lower blood cholesterol levels, a decreased risk of osteoporosis, and relief of symptoms associated with menopause. Long enjoyed by vegetarians and other health-conscious individuals, tofu and other forms of soyfood are becoming more widely appreciated and are even being recommended by physicians.

Sacred crop

Ancestors of the modern-day soybean grew wild on the plains of eastern Asia over 3,000 years ago. Early Chinese farmers discovered the beans and eventually cultivated them. Soyfoods have played an important role in Chinese cuisine for many centuries. According to Chinese tradition, Emperor Shen Nung named them as one of five sacred crops. Soybean use spread gradually across northern China and then south to Korea and Southeast Asia. The Buddhist commitment to vegetarianism enhanced the importance of soyfoods in Asian cuisine. Buddhist missionaries took soyfoods with them—most likely in the form of tofu—when they journeyed to Japan in the 8th century AD.

The soybean, a staple of the Asian diet since ancient times, is one of the richest—and least expensive—sources of protein. Its virtues are just beginning to be appreciated in the West.

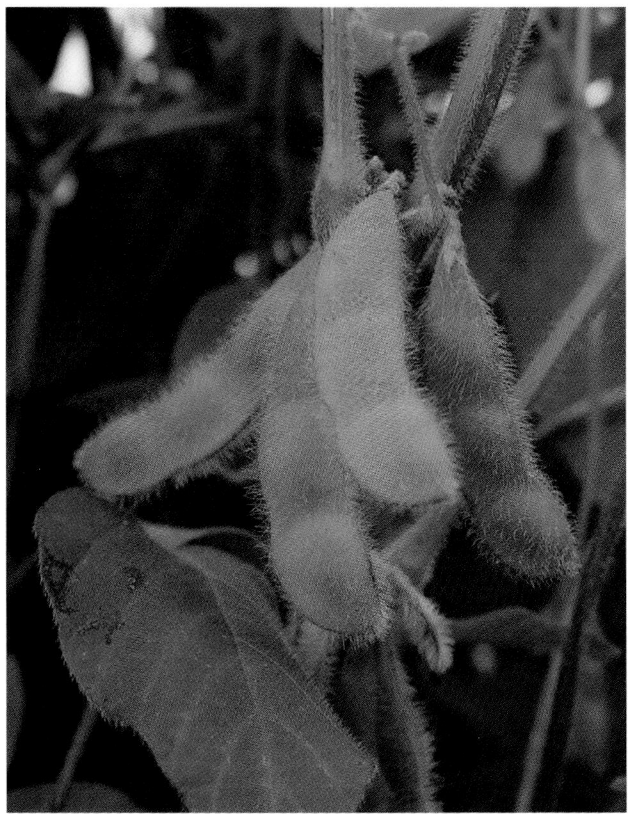

Thomas Hovland—Grant Heilman

Because soybeans, a leguminous plant food, yield more usable protein per hectare (2.5 ac) than any other food crop, they are a more easily and cheaply produced protein source than animal foods. In China, where arable land is in short supply, soybeans are an ideal food. Over time, inventive Asian cooks developed a great variety of foods from soybeans. Two staples remain: soymilk and tofu. In some Chinese cities factories still make early-morning home deliveries of soymilk, the liquid expressed from water-soaked soybeans. Tofu, the soft curd formed when a salt is added to soymilk, is made in over 30,000 small shops throughout Japan; the average Japanese citizen eats over 22.7 kg (50 lb) of tofu a year.

The means by which soyfoods arrived in the West are not clear. Some European traders and missionaries may have taken tofu home from Asia as early as the 16th century; later, people who emigrated from Asia to Europe and North America took traditional fare, including soy products, with them. Benjamin Franklin was one of several people to introduce soybeans to the U.S., sending them from London to be planted in Philadelphia in 1770. An early U.S. champion of the soybean was John Harvey Kellogg, the man who developed corn flakes and granola. Kellogg, a physician and advocate of vegetarianism, created a variety of meat and dairy substitutes to help Americans adopt a more plant-based diet.

Although the majority of soybeans are consumed in Asian countries, most are produced in the West. The United States grows half of the world's soybeans; they are the country's second most important crop (after corn). Approximately one-third of all U.S. soybeans are exported. More than 90% of what remains is fed to agricultural animals. Only the protein and starch portion of the bean goes into animal feed, however. The fat is removed and sold as vegetable oil. In fact, soybean oil (also called soya oil) is the most widely used cooking oil in the U.S., accounting for much of the fat used to make solid vegetable shortening and added to processed foods—the "partially hydrogenated vegetable oil" listed on so many labels.

Most Americans eat small amounts of soy protein, chiefly in the form of emulsifiers and thickeners added to food products. Soy protein is also added to ground meat as a commercial meat extender (to reduce the amount of meat in a given product and thereby lower costs). Over 54.4 million kg (100 million lb) of soy protein are fed to the U.S. armed forces and used in school lunch programs. Whole soybeans and the traditional soyfoods, however—including tofu, soymilk, tempeh, and miso—are used very little in Western cultures.

Varied and versatile

Soyfoods can be divided into four basic categories: (1) whole soybeans, (2) traditional soyfoods, (3) modern soy products, and (4) "second-generation" soyfoods.

Whole soybeans. Soybeans grow in small fuzzy pods, two to three round beans to a pod. They can be harvested while the pod and beans are 75% to 80% mature (still green). Green soybeans should be boiled in salted water, in or out of the pod, for about 15 to 20 minutes and then served hot (with the pod removed). Although they are common fare in Asia, green soybeans are difficult to find in Western countries. In U.S. cities, markets in Asian neighborhoods may have them, and frozen varieties are sometimes available.

Most soybeans are not harvested while green but are allowed to mature and dry on the vine. They usually are yellow, although black and brown varieties exist. Dried soybeans must be rehydrated in water (they need to be soaked overnight and then cooked in fresh water) before they can be consumed. Mature, cooked soybeans have a nutty, strong taste that stands up well to spicy sauces, especially in tomato-based dishes. Soybeans are available in natural foods stores and can be stored for several months in a tightly sealed container away from direct sunlight. Rehydrated beans also can be roasted to create a crunchy snack food.

Traditional soyfoods. While the preparation of traditional soyfoods is a household art in Asia, and techniques vary among cooks, these foods take certain basic forms. They include soymilk, tofu, okara, yuba, tempeh, miso, and soy sauce.

Soymilk. In China fresh soymilk is made daily and sold by street vendors and in cafés. It is usually served hot and sweetened or as a soup flavored with soy sauce and vegetables. In Western countries soymilk is sometimes available fresh but

Tofu is prepared in many ways in Japan—grilled, ground, sautéed, deep-fried—and eaten alone or in combination with vegetables and rice. (Below) A popular summer dish in Japan is hiyayakko*—chilled tofu served with chopped green onions and fish flakes. (Bottom) Tofu is manufactured in a Japanese factory.*

most often is sold in aseptic cartons (tightly sealed paper packages that can be stored, unopened, at room temperature). Once the carton has been opened, the soymilk must be refrigerated and used within five days. Soymilk can be used to replace cow's milk as a beverage, in baked goods and cream-type sauces, or over breakfast cereal.

Tofu. In Japan tofu is referred to as *o-tofu,* the prefix *o* meaning "honorable." While tofu is often the object of jokes in the West, this food is imbued with a sense of sacredness in Asia. There is evidence that the first tofu shops were located within Buddhist temples and monasteries and that the first master tofu makers were monks. In Japanese society tofu was first used exclusively by the upper class. Today, however, it is widely used among all people in China and Japan. Making tofu is still an art performed by "tofu masters," and their products are evaluated by connoisseurs in the same way that fine wines and cheeses are in the West.

Tofu is made by adding a salt to soymilk until the milk curdles. The curds are then pressed into cubes. Different varieties of tofu include firm, soft, and silken (a custardlike product). Tofu's versatility derives from its blandness and the porous quality that enables it to absorb the flavors of foods and spices it is cooked with. Tofu can thus be used in savory dishes as well as in desserts. Marinated cubes of tofu can be added to soups and stews. Soft tofu can be pureed and flavored to make cream-type soups, dips, or puddings.

Like soymilk, tofu is sold in aseptic packages that can be stored at room temperature for long periods. The tofu should be refrigerated once the package has been opened. Tofu may also be found in the store in water-filled tubs. This product must be refrigerated, and the water should be changed daily after the container has been opened. It is important to use refrigerated tofu within five days of opening the container. After that time, it may spoil.

Okara. Okara, the pulp left over when liquid is squeezed from soybeans to make soymilk or tofu, includes most of the fiber of the soybean. Fresh okara is rarely available in the West except to those who make their own soymilk or tofu. Okara can be cooked and used in main dishes in place of rice or other grains. Because it is very perishable, it should be refrigerated and used within a few days.

Yuba. The "skin" that forms on the surface of soymilk when it is heated is called yuba. It can be lifted off the soymilk in sheets, which are then dried. When rehydrated by being soaked in water, yuba makes a convenient wrapping for portions of rice or vegetables. It can also be deep-fried to make a snack chip.

Tempeh. Tempeh is an ancient Indonesian food made by combining cooked soybeans and grains with a mold culture and then incubating the mixture at a warm temperature for 18 to 24 hours. The resulting soybean cake has a strong, mushroomlike flavor and a tender but chewy texture. Tempeh can be marinated and cooked on the grill as a meat substitute; it also can be added to stews or soups or steamed, grated, and mixed with other ingredients to make sandwich spreads. Tempeh is usually sold in the frozen-food case in natural foods stores. It can be stored in the freezer for several months or for up to five days in the refrigerator. A visible coating of mold on tempeh is normal and harmless.

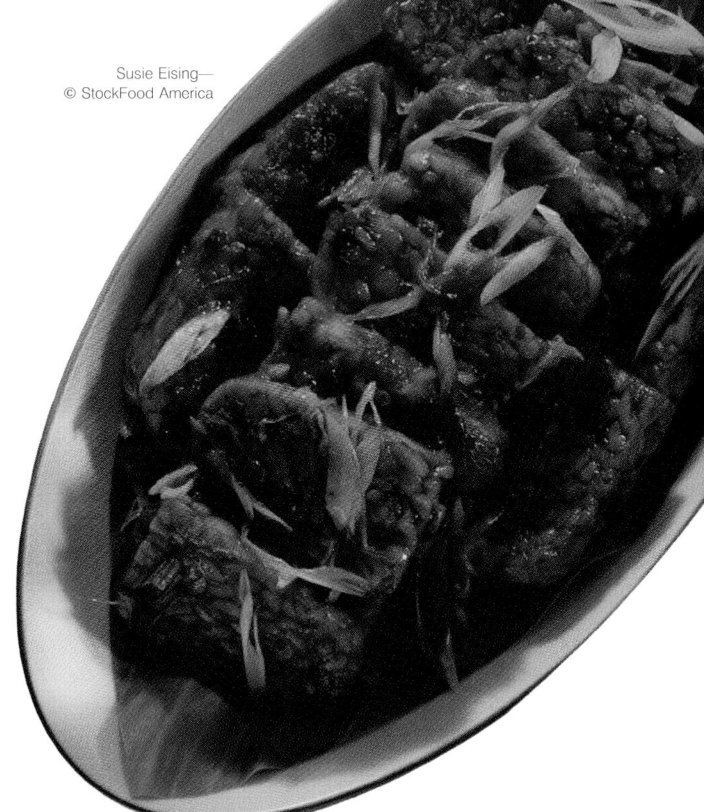

Tempeh (shown fried, with green onions), a soyfood that originated in Indonesia, has a mushroomlike flavor and chewy texture.

Miso. Miso, fermented soybean paste, is an essential condiment in every Chinese and Japanese kitchen. It is made by combining soybeans and a grain with salt and a mold culture. The resulting product is then stored in cedar vats to ferment for one to three years. Miso has a salty taste and can be used to make broths or added to sauces or stews. When refrigerated, miso can be kept for several months.

Soy sauce. True soy sauce, *shoyu,* is a fermented product that is aged for over a year and usually consists of a grain, such as wheat, combined with soybeans that have been processed to remove the fat. Most of the soy sauce sold in the U.S. is a synthetic product that is not aged. Tamari, which is similar to soy sauce in flavor, is the liquid left over when miso is made.

Modern soy products. Several nontraditional products made from soybeans are used as foods or food additives. The most important are textured soy protein and soy flour.

Textured soy protein, usually called textured vegetable protein, or TVP, is made from soy flour from which the fat has been removed. It is a dried, granular product that takes on the consistency of ground beef when rehydrated. TVP can be used in tomato-based dishes that call for ground beef, such as chili, tacos, sloppy joes, and spaghetti sauce. If stored in a tightly sealed container, TVP will keep at room temperature for several months. It is available in most natural foods stores and in the bulk-food section of some grocery stores.

Soy flour is often used along with other flours to boost the protein content of baked products. Because it has no gluten, it can be used in bread only in small amounts (otherwise, the bread will not rise). When added to cookies, muffins, or cakes, it promotes tenderness and delays the development of staleness. To keep it from becoming rancid, soy flour should be stored in the freezer.

Chris Johns—Tony Stone Images/PNI

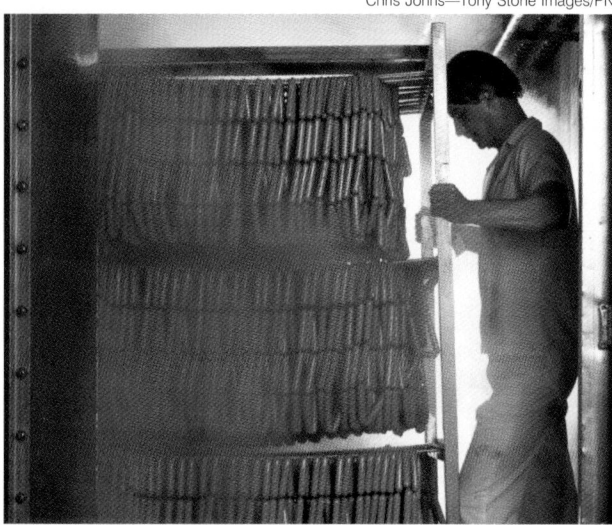

A variety of "second-generation" soyfoods have been created to satisfy the growing appetite for this low-fat source of protein. Today tofu is turning up everywhere—even in the form of hot dogs!

"Second-generation" soyfoods. A new class of soyfoods, many imitating meat and dairy products, has appeared in the U.S. over the past two decades as a response to the growing demand for low-fat vegetarian foods. These include vegetarian burgers, tofu hot dogs, imitation luncheon meats, and soy-based ice cream and cheeses.

One of nature's most nutritious foods

Not only are soyfoods rich in nutrients, but because they derive about 35% to 40% of their calories from protein, they are much higher in protein than most other vegetables. Moreover, the quality of the protein in soyfoods is equivalent to that in animal foods. Soybeans and many of the foods made from them are also a good source of B vitamins, especially vitamin B_6 and folic acid.

Depending on how they are processed, soyfoods can be an excellent source of calcium. Calcium salts are often used to make tofu, a process that produces a very calcium-rich product. Soymilk is sometimes fortified with calcium in order to increase its usefulness as a substitute for cow's milk. Soyfoods are also often high in iron, and although this iron usually is not absorbed well by the body, consuming a food rich in vitamin C (such as an orange) along with a soyfood can enhance iron absorption.

Soybeans are unique among legumes because compared with other beans, they are high in fat. Most of the fat in soybeans and the foods made from them is unsaturated, however, and like all plant foods, soybeans are free of cholesterol. Soyfoods are one of the few good plant sources of linolenic acid (an omega-3 fatty acid that is essential in the diet and abundant in fish and fish oils), a substance that may help to reduce risk for both cancer and heart disease. Although foods made from the soybean can derive as much as 50% of their calories from fat, reduced-fat versions are available (such as reduced-fat tofu, soymilk, and soy flour), and some soy products, like TVP, are virtually fat-free.

Health benefits: the evidence so far

Soybeans have long been popular in many parts of the world because of their nutritional value and versatility. The increasing interest in soyfoods in Western countries is due at least in part to growing evidence of their potential to help reduce the risk of certain chronic diseases, especially cancer, heart disease, and osteoporosis.

Cancer. Plant foods contain hundreds and perhaps thousands of biologically active components called phytochemicals. While these are not classified as nutrients, they exert physiological effects that may help to reduce the risk of chronic disease. Soybeans are an essentially unique source of one group of phytochemicals called isoflavones. Isoflavones are plant estrogens, or phytoestrogens. Like most phytoestrogens, they possess very weak estrogenic activity and are between 1/1,000 and 1/10,000 as potent as the estrogens produced by the body.

In women, high levels of estrogen in the bloodstream can increase the risk for breast cancer and other hormone-related cancers. It is believed that when estrogen enters a cell, it participates in a series of reactions that increase the likelihood of the normal cell's becoming a cancer cell. Isoflavones compete with estrogen for receptors on cells in breast tissue and, in theory, block estrogen from exerting its effects on the cells. Since isoflavones exert only weak estrogenic effects, they act essentially as antiestrogens.

There is some evidence that the estrogen-blocking effects of isoflavones may at least in part explain the lower rates of breast cancer seen in Asian countries, where the diet has traditionally been rich in soyfoods. One study involving female subjects in the U.K. and the U.S. found that women who added soyfoods to their diets experienced a marked increase (two to three days) in the length of the time between their menstrual periods. Longer menstrual cycles are associated with lower breast cancer risk, most likely because compared with women who have shorter cycles, women with longer cycles have a lower lifetime exposure to estrogen. Soy products from which the isoflavones are removed do not affect menstrual cycle length, which suggests that it is the isoflavones that are responsible for this effect.

Soy isoflavones appear to have anticancer effects independent of their antiestrogen activity, however. Hundreds of laboratory studies show that one isoflavone in particular, called genistein, inhibits the growth of most types of cancer cells, including lung, prostate, and colon cancer cells and leukemia cells, none of which is dependent on estrogen for growth. This growth-inhibiting property appears to be due to the effects of isoflavones on enzymes that regulate cell growth.

The relationship between soy and cancer is still speculative, but some data suggest that as little as one serving of soyfood per day may reduce the risk for a wide range of cancers. The soyfoods highest in isoflavones are whole soybeans, TVP, tempeh, tofu, and soymilk. Depending on how they are processed, meat substitutes may or may not contain isoflavones. Because no other commonly consumed foods contain isoflavones in appreciable amounts, eating soyfoods is the only known dietary means of ingesting these potentially beneficial substances.

Heart disease. Since 1967 nearly 40 clinical studies have demonstrated that soy protein can lower blood cholesterol levels. Soy protein consumption reduces cholesterol by about 10–15% more than traditional cholesterol-lowering diets, which simply limit intake of fat and cholesterol. Moreover, this effect is independent of the amount of fat in the diet. When soy protein replaces animal protein in the diet, cholesterol levels drop even if the fat in the two diets is similar in amount and type. Soy protein is effective in lowering cholesterol even when added to the diet with no other dietary changes.

Soy protein is most beneficial for people with high total blood cholesterol levels (above 240 mg per deciliter). Although as little as 25 g of soy protein per day is enough to lower cholesterol in some individuals, the more soy protein consumed, the greater the reduction. In some cases as much as 50 g may be needed to produce a response.

NEWS CAP

Beta-Carotene: A Dream Deferred

The dream that a simple vitamin pill might one day prevent cancer or heart disease remains, for the time being, just that. In fact, research published in 1995 and 1996 indicated that contrary to long-cherished expectations, some supplements may actually do more harm than good.

In January 1996 two large clinical trials evaluating the effects of vitamin supplements ended with disappointing results. In the Physicians' Health Study, a 12-year investigation of more than 22,000 male physicians, the men who took a beta-carotene supplement every other day had neither more nor less risk of disease or death than those who took a placebo. Beta-carotene, found naturally in dark green and yellow-orange fruits and vegetables—carrots, kale, spinach, sweet potatoes, cantaloupe, and mangoes, to name a few—is a vitamin A precursor (*i.e.,* it is converted into vitamin A in the body).

Even more disconcerting were the findings of the Beta Carotene and Retinol Efficacy Trial (CARET), which examined the effectiveness of a supplementation program in a group of people at risk for lung cancer and cardiovascular disease—smokers and former smokers and asbestos-exposed workers. When the researchers compared the subjects who received 30 mg per day of beta-carotene and 25,000 IU (international units) of vitamin A with those who received a placebo, they found that the supplement takers actually had a *greater* risk of both developing and dying from lung cancer and a higher death rate due to cardiovascular disease.

—Linda Tomchuck

In addition to the direct effects of soy protein on blood cholesterol levels, soy may affect heart disease risk in other ways. In the development of atherosclerosis (fatty deposits in the inner layer of the arteries), cholesterol must first interact with oxygen, a process called oxidation. Preventing the oxidation of cholesterol may be as important in reducing heart disease risk as decreasing blood cholesterol levels. Soy has the potential to directly inhibit cholesterol oxidation. In one study, when patients with cardiovascular disease consumed a soy product for six months, cholesterol oxidation was reduced by 50% compared with the control group. The isoflavone genistein may also reduce heart disease risk by inhibiting the formation of blood clots and the growth of cells that contribute to the artery-narrowing deposits.

Soy may therefore represent an effective and inexpensive nonpharmacological approach to lowering cholesterol and reducing heart disease risk for people with elevated cholesterol levels as well as for those with normal levels. In Italy the National Health Service provides soy protein free of charge to physicians for use in the treatment of high cholesterol.

Osteoporosis. Many factors affect bone health and risk for osteoporosis. Although adequate calcium intake is important for healthy bones, the amount of calcium retained by the body may be more important than the amount consumed. Calcium is normally lost through the urine, and factors that increase this loss can increase osteoporosis risk. Protein consumption increases the excretion of calcium in the urine; this observation may help to explain why, worldwide, populations with the highest intake of protein have the highest rates of osteoporosis. The high sulfur content of animal proteins (and also grains) appears to be responsible for the increase in urinary calcium excretion. Replacing animal foods in the diet with soyfoods (and with other legumes) inhibits this process and thereby helps to conserve calcium and protect bone health.

The isoflavones in soyfoods may also directly affect bone density. Bone is a dynamic substance, continuously being broken down, or resorbed, and rebuilt. When people age, resorption occurs more quickly than rebuilding, which can lead to a net loss of bone mass. In animal studies isoflavones have been shown to slow the speed of resorption. In fact, isoflavones are very similar in chemical structure to the drug ipriflavone, which is used in Europe and Asia to treat osteoporosis.

Soybeans and many of the foods made from them are also rich in well-absorbed calcium. For example, one cup of cooked soybeans provides about 175 mg of calcium, which is nearly one-fourth the recommended dietary allowance for adults. The calcium in soybeans is absorbed as well as that in dairy products.

Kidney disease. The kidneys filter the blood, sifting out unwanted chemicals and excreting them in the urine. In healthy people, diets high in protein have been shown to increase the rate at which the kidneys filter blood. Forcing the kidneys to work harder can increase the risk for renal disease in susceptible people. Replacing animal protein in the diet with soy protein has been shown to reduce the filtering rate and thus may help to protect the kidneys.

In patients with chronic kidney disease, on the other hand, high-protein diets actually slow kidney function. Protein-restricted diets are often advised for these people. Again, replacing animal protein with soy protein may improve kidney function in these patients. In addition, soy protein lowers blood cholesterol levels in patients with kidney disease, which can be especially important because the pathology of renal disease is believed to be similar to that of atherosclerosis.

Menopause. The decrease in estrogen production that signals menopause can cause a variety of symptoms, among them difficulty in regulating body temperature (manifested as night sweats and hot flashes). The severity of menopause symptoms varies throughout the world, however. For example, Asian women are typically one-third as likely as U.S. women to report symptoms. Soy consumption has been proposed as one explanation for this difference. Although soy isoflavones exhibit only very weak estrogenic activity, women who regularly eat soyfoods may have blood levels of isoflavones that are as much as 1,000 times higher than levels of natural estrogen. The estrogenic activity of soybean isoflavones may help to offset the effects of reduced estrogen production by the ovaries. Preliminary results of studies currently under way indicate that soyfoods are indeed effective in compensating for the decreased estrogen levels associated with menopause.

Tofu on your table

With mounting evidence of the many benefits of soyfoods, especially the reduced risk for some chronic diseases, it seems inevitable that Americans will be increasingly interested in incorporating soy into their diets. Because of the array of soy products available, it is becoming easier to include soy in "typical" American meals. One of the simplest ways to do this is to use TVP in spaghetti sauce, chili, and the many other dishes that call for ground beef. TVP is prepared by pouring ⅞ cup of boiling water over one cup of dry TVP and letting it stand for five minutes. Soymilk can also readily be used without making any radical dietary changes. In addition to being consumed by the glass and poured over cereal, it can be blended with frozen bananas, berries, or other fruit in milk shakes. Soymilk and soy flour can be added to pancake and muffin recipes.

Soft tofu can be pureed and flavored with dried soup mixes to make dips for chips or vegetables. It can also be blended with cooked pureed potatoes or spinach to create "cream" soups. Blended tofu, mixed with salt, parsley, and a small amount of olive oil, can be a substitute for ricotta cheese in lasagna or stuffed shells. Cubes of tofu, stir fried with almost any fresh vegetables, make a quick, delicious main dish.

Soy nuts (toasted, or roasted, soybeans) make a good snack alternative to peanuts or chips. Cooked soybeans can replace the beans in chili recipes and in barbecued or baked beans. Slices of tofu or tempeh can be marinated and grilled for an alternative to grilled meats; tofu that has been frozen, then defrosted, has a spongy but firm texture that absorbs sauces or marinades well and is easily grilled.

Last but not least, tofu can used (sweetened or not) in delectable desserts. "Cheeseless cheesecake" is one. Tofu, blended with melted chocolate and used as a "no-bake" pie filling, is another—one that no chocolate lover could resist!

—Virginia Kisch Messina, M.P.H., R.D., and Mark Messina, Ph.D.

Fundamentals of Fats

Public awareness of dietary fat is at an all-time high. In 1995 the International Food Information Council (IFIC), a food industry trade organization, commissioned a survey to find out how the U.S. news media had covered the subjects of diet and nutrition over a three-month period—in other words, what subjects were "hot" topics. The survey found that dietary fat was the number one story, receiving twice as much attention as any other single nutrition-related topic—more than vitamins, more than beta-carotene and other antioxidants, more even than calories, at one time the major American dietary preoccupation.

In part, this focus on fat reflects the scientific consensus that a high-fat diet increases the risk for many chronic diseases. At the same time, the intense interest in fat reflects this nutrient's remarkable biological diversity. Fat is composed of many individual compounds, called lipids, which are chemically quite different from one another. Lipids are defined as substances present in animal and plant cells that are generally insoluble in water and soluble in organic solvents. They are divided into three major classes: simple lipids, glycerophosphatides, and sphingolipids. The emphasis of the following will be on the simple lipids because these are the most abundant fats in food.

Not so simple after all

The simple lipids—also known as neutral lipids, neutral glycerides, or sometimes simply glycerides—are combinations of fatty acids and the organic substance glycerol. Fatty acids are molecules composed mostly of carbon and hydrogen atoms. The most abundant simple lipids are the triglycerides, which typically represent over 95% of the weight of most edible fats and oils. Triglycerides are compounds that contain one molecule of glycerol and three fatty acid molecules. (*See* Figure 1.) Most triglycerides are "mixed"—that is, they contain a combination of two or three different fatty acids rather than three identical ones. Other simple lipids are the monoglycerides (*i.e.,* one molecule of glycerol plus one fatty acid) and the diglycerides (one glycerol plus two fatty acids). Monoglycerides and diglycerides are seldom found in natural fats but can easily be made synthetically and are common ingredients in processed foods.

A fatty acid consists of a chain of an even number of carbon atoms with hydrogen atoms attached to the carbons along the length of the chain and a carboxyl group (COOH) at one end. Fatty acids are characterized according to chain length—*i.e.,* number of carbon atoms in the molecule. Common dietary fatty acids have between 12 and 22 carbon atoms and are classified as long-chain fatty acids; the American diet also contains small amounts of short-chain fatty acids (fewer than 8 carbon atoms) and medium-chain fatty acids (8–10 carbon atoms).

For nutritional purposes, fatty acids are usually categorized as either saturated or unsaturated, depending on the type of bonds that link the carbon atoms. Saturated fatty acids (SFAs; *e.g.,* palmitic acid, stearic acid) contain only single bonds between the carbon atoms. They have a relatively high melting

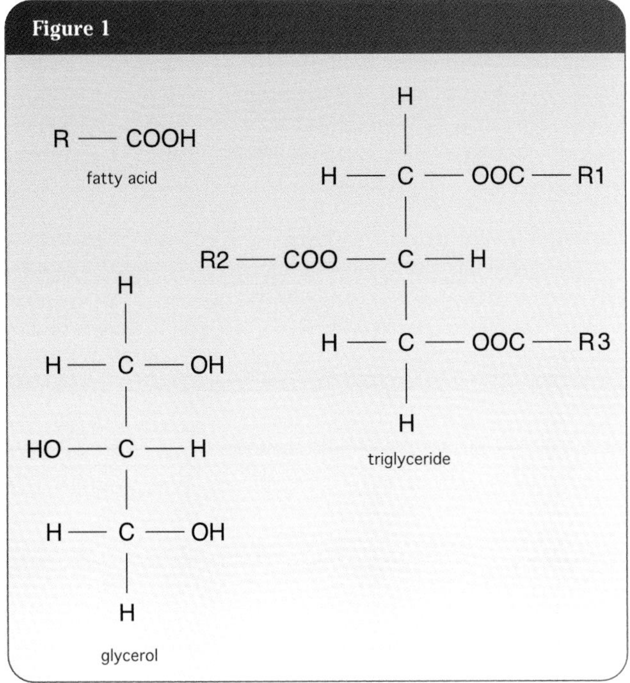

Figure 1

temperature and are usually solid at room temperature. Unsaturated fatty acids (*e.g.,* oleic acid, linoleic acid), in which one or more pairs of carbon atoms are joined by double bonds, tend to have low melting temperatures. The unsaturated fatty acids are further subdivided into monounsaturated fatty acids (MUFAs) and polyunsaturated fatty acids (PUFAs). MUFAs contain only one double bond; PUFAs contain more than one double bond.

The unsaturated fatty acids also are classified according to the position of the double bond (yielding the designations omega-9, omega-6, or omega-3) and the conformation of the double bond (yielding the designations *cis* or *trans*). In *cis* fatty acids the hydrogen atoms are located on the same side of the double bond, whereas in *trans* fatty acids the hydrogen atoms are located on opposite sides of the double bond. (*See* Figure 2.) Although there are small amounts of naturally occurring *trans* fatty acids in the diet (primarily in animal fats), most *trans* fatty acids are consumed in the form of vegetable oils that have been hydrogenated. Hydrogenation is the chemical process by which hydrogen molecules are added to unsaturated fatty acids at the position of the double bond. Hydrogenation has the effect of making liquid oils solid at room temperature.

Cholesterol, another substance that has been in the spotlight, is not a fat but rather a waxy compound that is classified as a lipid. Like fats, however, cholesterol is vital to life. It is a constituent of all animal cell membranes and is necessary for the synthesis of steroid hormones. Cholesterol is made in the liver and other organs and is transported in the blood in the form of particles called lipoproteins, which are combinations of lipids and proteins. In the condition known as atherosclerosis, cholesterol and other materials build up in localized deposits (plaques) inside the blood vessels, interfering with blood flow.

Cholesterol is present in the diet in essentially all animal products. After meat, egg yolks are the major source of cholesterol in the U.S. diet. One large yolk provides about 212 mg of cholesterol. A three-ounce portion of red meat or poultry contains considerably less, about 60–80 mg, but most Americans eat much more meat—especially ground beef—than eggs. Fish is also a source of dietary cholesterol, and some shellfish contain relatively large amounts; a three-ounce serving of cooked shrimp, for example, has 166 mg.

Many functions

Like protein and carbohydrate, fat is an essential nutrient that has many important biological attributes. Its primary role in the diet is to provide energy. Fat supplies more than twice as much energy (nine calories per gram) as carbohydrate or protein (four calories per gram). Moreover, fat is stored more efficiently than carbohydrate, which makes it the optimal nutrient for energy storage in the body. In persons who consume inadequate amounts of calories, fat, together with carbohydrate, acts to spare protein and thereby minimizes the breakdown of muscle for energy production and helps to preserve the body's lean tissues. During periods of growth, dietary fat can improve the growth rate because it conserves protein and so can be used to support weight gain.

Dietary fats provide essential fatty acids, substances needed by all mammals for normal growth and development. One of these, linoleic acid, must be obtained through food because it cannot be synthesized in the body. The dietary requirement for linoleic acid is approximately 3% of calories. When inadequate amounts are present in the diet, growth is impaired, and skin and hair are adversely affected.

Dietary fat is essential for the optimum absorption of fat-soluble vitamins such as vitamins A, D, and E. Thus, people who habitually consume inadequate levels of fat run the risk of suffering from vitamin deficiencies. Fat also contributes to satiety (the sensation of fullness) after consumption of food.

Fat has sensory as well as physiological functions. It contributes to the textural properties of food. For example, it is largely responsible for the "shortness" (*i.e.,* crumbliness) of biscuits, the melt-in-the-mouth properties of cheese, the different but characteristic textures of nuts and chocolate,

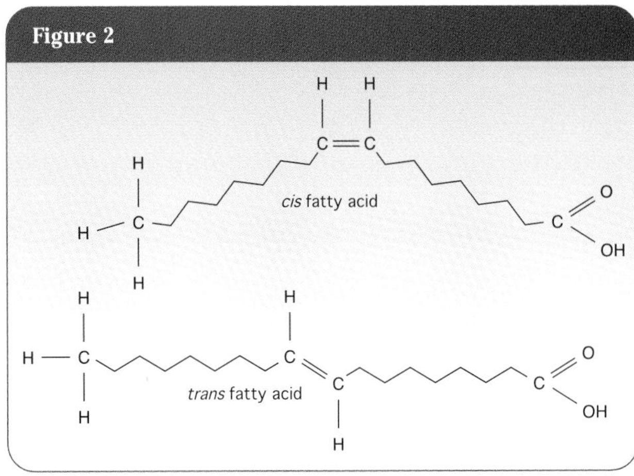

Figure 2

and the creamy smoothness of mayonnaise. Many fats have distinctive flavors and impart these to the foods in which they are present (*e.g.,* beef) or to which they are added (*e.g.,* olive-oil-based salad dressing). Bland-tasting fats modify the flavor of food by delaying the release of fat-soluble components of flavor compounds. The characteristic crunchy texture and appealing flavor of fried foods derive from the fact that fat can be heated to high temperatures without decomposing.

Taking dietary advice to heart

At the turn of the century, Americans were consuming approximately 32% of their calories as fat. Fat intake had increased to about 39% of calories by the late 1940s and rose to a little more than 40% in the 1970s.

During the 1960s and '70s, a series of pioneering epidemiological studies compared dietary patterns and heart disease rates in many different countries around the world. Their findings pointed to a single conclusion: the incidence of heart disease was high in populations that consumed a lot of saturated fats. Before long these data were translated into the dietary recommendations now so familiar to most Americans, advising them to reduce the amount of fat, and particularly saturated fat, in their diets.

This advice has clearly had an impact. Since the 1970s there has been a steady decrease in the percentage of fat calories in the U.S. diet; the most recent data (1990) indicate that Americans get about 34% of their calories from fat. Saturated fat intake also has declined, from 16% of calories in the late 1970s to 15% in the mid-1980s and 14% in 1990. Polyunsatu-

NEWS CAP

Good Reasons to Eat Liver and Legumes

Data continue to accumulate on the diverse health benefits of an adequate intake of the B vitamin folic acid (also called folate). Among the past year's findings:

- The role of folic acid in preventing birth defects was underscored by a study from the California Birth Defects Monitoring Program (reported in *The Lancet,* Aug. 12, 1995) that demonstrated that this nutrient—already known to reduce the risk of neural tube defects such as spina bifida and anencephaly—also helps to prevent cleft palate. In light of the accumulating evidence of the importance of folic acid in the diets of women of childbearing age, the FDA announced in February 1996 that as of Jan. 1, 1998, manufacturers of enriched grain products (bread, flour, corn meal, rice, pasta) will be required to add this nutrient to their products.
- Research linking adequate folic acid intake during pregnancy to the birth of healthy, normal infants has typically focused on maternal consumption of the nutrient from conception through the early weeks of fetal development. But according to a study in the April 1996 issue of the *American Journal of Clinical Nutrition,* maintaining an adequate level of folic acid *throughout* pregnancy can reduce a woman's chances of giving birth prematurely or having a low-birth-weight infant. Even though women may be eating fortified food products, the investigators said, they should still try to include in their diets foods that are naturally rich in folic acid (*e.g.,* liver, legumes, orange and grapefruit juices, and leafy green vegetables).
- An increased intake of folic acid by all U.S. adults—through diet, supplements, or both—could reduce the rate of heart disease. This conclusion was reached by epidemiologists at the University of Washington. Their meta-analysis of 38 studies, published in the *Journal of the American Medical Association* (Oct. 4, 1995), found that high blood levels of the substance called homocysteine are associated with an elevated risk of cardiovascular disease. They also found an inverse relationship between blood levels of folic acid and homocysteine. They concluded that if all U.S. adults received 400 μg (micrograms) of folic acid per day, the death rate from heart disease could be dramatically reduced.

  Until very recently homocysteine was virtually unheard of by most people. Now it appears that it may be as important as cholesterol. The relationship between homocysteine and heart disease is now the subject of intensive research.
- Is there a link between folic acid intake and cancer? Large-scale epidemiological investigations have indicated that people who eat foods rich in folic acid are at lower risk than others of developing colon cancer, and studies in animals have shown that folic acid depletion increases the risk of colorectal tumors. Several clinical trials are under way to see whether folic acid supplements (in amounts of 1,000–5,000 μg per day) might help to prevent recurrences of adenomatous polyps, the lesions that can develop into colon cancer.

—*Linda Tomchuck*

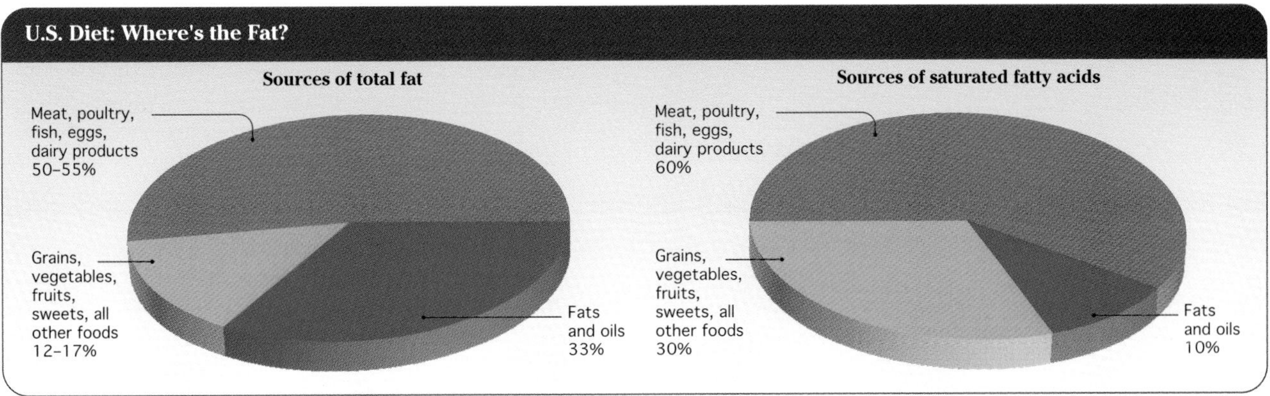

rated fats have increased from 4% of calories in 1940 to 7%, while monounsaturated fats have remained relatively stable at 16–17% of calories. Average cholesterol intake—410 mg per day—has declined markedly from the more than 500-mg-per-day figure of the late 1940s.

Meat (especially ground beef and beefsteak), poultry, fish, eggs, and dairy products are the major contributors of total fat and saturated fat to the U.S. diet, providing 50–55% of total fat and 60% of saturated fat. Fats and oils (*e.g.,* margarine, butter, vegetable oils) contribute 33% of total fat intake and 10% of saturated fat intake. Grains, vegetables, fruits, sweets, and all other foods account for 12–17% of total fat and 30% of saturated fat.

Are all fats equal?

Since the early studies that linked high-fat diets with heart disease, remarkable progress has been made in understanding the role of diet in health and illness. Some efforts have concentrated on elucidating how the amount and types of fat in the diet affect the risk for the chronic diseases that are the major causes of death in most industrialized countries. In the past few years, the research emphasis has narrowed even further, focusing on the effects of specific fatty acids on health. While there is still a great deal to learn, the available evidence indicates that the individual fatty acids have remarkably unique biological effects. A brief summary of this research follows.

SFAs: the chief culprits. The effects of SFAs on health have been investigated in both epidemiological and clinical studies. (Epidemiological studies look at the eating patterns and health status of entire populations, while clinical studies monitor the impact of specific dietary intakes on the health of individual subjects.) Data from both types of investigations have shown that certain SFAs raise blood cholesterol levels and, especially, levels of low-density lipoprotein (LDL) cholesterol, the so-called bad cholesterol, which is associated with increased risk of heart disease. In fact, SFA intake has more of an impact on blood cholesterol levels than any other dietary factor—including cholesterol. Controlled clinical trials have shown that for every 1% decrease in blood cholesterol levels, heart disease risk decreases 2–3%, and for every 1% increase in the SFA content of the diet, blood cholesterol will increase approximately two milligrams per deciliter (*i.e.,* about 1%). Thus, for every 1% decrease in dietary SFAs, a 2–3% decrease in heart disease risk can be expected.

In the past five years, it has become clear that the different types of SFAs have markedly different effects on cholesterol levels. Myristic acid (found in whole milk and butter, among other foods) is the most potent cholesterol-raising fatty acid, followed by palmitic acid (found in palm oils and meat) and then lauric acid (in tropical oils). In contrast, stearic acid (in meat and chocolate) is a unique SFA because it has essentially no effect on blood cholesterol.

Both epidemiological and clinical studies suggest that SFAs increase the risk of thrombosis (blood-clot formation), which plays a key role in the causation of both heart attack and stroke. Thus, while stearic acid does not increase cholesterol levels, some authorities believe it promotes clot formation. This remains to be proved, however.

Limited epidemiological evidence suggests an association between SFA intake and the development of colorectal, ovarian, and prostate cancers. In the prostate cancer studies, diets high in animal fats—and especially meat—were implicated. Evidence of an association is not proof of a cause-and-effect relationship, however. Further investigations are needed to corroborate these findings.

MUFAs: possibly protective. Epidemiological studies have reported a strong negative association between consumption of MUFAs and heart disease incidence. This finding is part of the basis for the enthusiasm surrounding the so-called Mediterranean diet. In Italy and Crete, where olive oil (which is 77% monounsaturated fat) is a staple of the diet, historically the rate of heart disease has been very low. Of course, people in Mediterranean regions also eat an abundance of fruits and vegetables, which are rich sources of fiber and antioxidants, also believed to have a preventive role in heart disease.

Numerous controlled clinical studies have reported that MUFAs have no independent effects on blood cholesterol levels. Compared with a low-fat diet (*e.g.,* less than 30% of calories from fat), however, a diet with as much as 40% fat derived largely from MUFAs increases levels of high-density lipoprotein (HDL) cholesterol—the "good" cholesterol that protects against heart disease. Some scientists believe that MUFAs also offer protection against heart disease by preventing the oxidation of LDL particles. (In the development of atherosclerosis, it is the oxidized LDL particle that contributes to the buildup of plaque in arteries.)

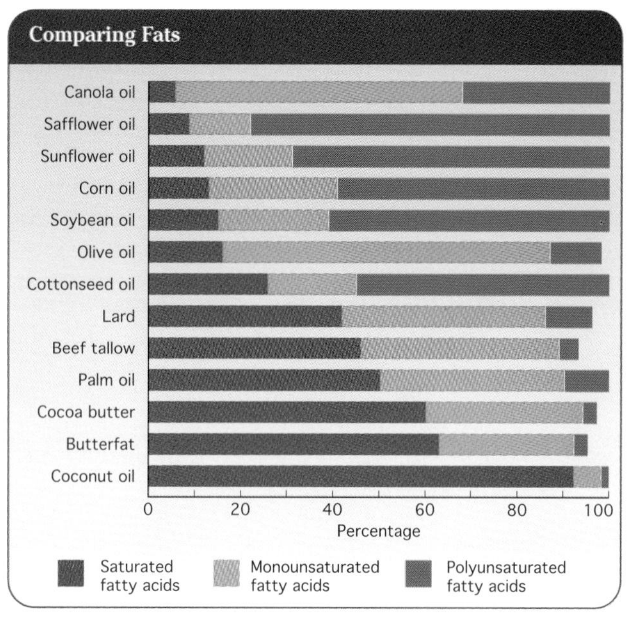

Traditional cholesterol-lowering diets are relatively high in carbohydrate and low in total fat. Recently, however, nutrition authorities have been impressed with the results of research showing the benefits of a diet low in SFAs but rich in MUFAs, especially for individuals with diabetes. Numerous studies have demonstrated that a diet high in MUFAs achieves the same reductions in total and LDL-cholesterol as a strict low-fat diet but does not decrease levels of cardioprotective HDL. Moreover, levels of plasma triglycerides (another risk factor for heart disease, especially in women) did not increase in those who ate a high-MUFA diet. In people with Type 2 (non-insulin-dependent) diabetes who adopt such a diet, blood glucose levels improve, as do insulin levels.

A recent study in Greece found that women whose diets were high in MUFAs (in the form of olive oil) were at lower risk than others of developing breast cancer. The women who consumed more olive oil, however, also ate more fruits and vegetables. The possible beneficial effects of these different foods are hard to separate scientifically, and in reality they may work together to promote health and/or protect against disease.

NEWS CAP

Eating Defensively

Researchers from many disciplines continue to investigate tantalizing links between diet and disease. Here are some major recent conclusions about the "You-are-what-you-eat" hypothesis:

- "So it may be true after all: eating **pasta** makes you fat," read the eye-catching headline in the *New York Times.* Nutrition scientists at Stanford, Harvard, and other respected institutions, however, begged to differ. What *does* make people fat, according to these experts, is eating too many calories—even if those calories are consumed in the form of low-fat foods that are rich in complex carbohydrates. While Americans have succeeded in reducing the proportion of fat in their diets, overall caloric intake has increased. This rise in calories, say the scientists, along with a failure to increase levels of physical activity, is the reason for the growing prevalence of obesity.
- Because breast cancer rates are comparatively low in countries where **low-fat diets** are the norm, epidemiologists have long speculated that a relationship must exist between dietary fat intake and breast cancer risk. This theory received a setback with the publication of an international study that analyzed the combined data from seven separate investigations and failed to find such a link. Altogether the pooled studies included more than 300,000 women in four countries. Data were obtained on their diets, and the subjects were then followed medically for up to seven years. The meta-analysis (published in *The New England Journal of Medicine,* Feb. 8, 1996) demonstrated that dietary fat intake in middle age and later life had no effect on breast cancer risk.
- Data from the Physicians' Health Study, a long-term investigation of the lifestyle, habits, and health of 22,000 male health professionals, revealed that **tomatoes,** whether eaten alone or in tomato-based foods such as spaghetti sauce, may reduce the risk of prostate cancer. Reporting in the *Journal of the National Cancer Institute* (Dec. 6, 1995), researchers from Harvard said that tomatoes and strawberries were the only foods among the many fruits and vegetables they studied that seemed to have a protective effect against prostate cancer. They also found that the benefits of eating tomatoes increased with the number of servings per week.

  The scientists speculated that the beneficial effect might be due to the high levels of the antioxidant lycopene in tomatoes. They were unable to account for the apparent benefits from strawberries and suggested that the finding was not reliable.
- Does eating **fish** a few times a week reduce a person's risk of develop-

PUFAs: mixed messages. The health effects of the PUFAs have been widely debated in recent years. The two subtypes of most interest are the omega-3s and the omega-6s.

Omega-6 PUFAs, found primarily in vegetable oils, are abundant in the U.S. diet. Studies of large populations have demonstrated an association between omega-6 PUFA intake and a low rate of heart disease. Controlled clinical studies consistently have shown omega-6s to have an independent cholesterol-lowering effect. For example, for every 1% increase in dietary omega-6 PUFA, blood cholesterol levels are expected to decrease by approximately 1%. Some laboratory evidence suggests, however, that omega-6 PUFAs may increase the oxidation of LDL, although it is not clear to what extent this occurs in the body, if at all.

Despite some evidence of a possible positive relationship between omega-6 PUFAs and cancer in experimental animals, there are no compelling and consistent data supporting an association between omega-6 PUFAs and human cancers. The presence of many confounding factors in the animal experiments makes it difficult to determine whether omega-6 PUFAs play any role at all in the development of cancer.

The omega-3 fatty acids are found primarily in fish and fish oils. A variety of benefits, from reduction of cholesterol and triglyceride levels to relief of inflammation in rheumatoid arthritis, have been claimed for omega-3s. With respect to the latter, however, the evidence has been contradictory. Studies like the much-publicized investigation conducted among the Greenland Eskimos in the 1970s have demonstrated low rates of heart disease among people who eat a diet rich in fatty fish (*e.g.,* salmon, mackerel), which are a major source of omega-3 PUFAs, but trials of fish-oil supplements have had mixed results. The subtle structural differences between the omega-6 PUFAs and the omega-3s have dramatic biological effects. In particular, while omega-3 fatty acids have little effect on blood cholesterol, they produce markedly lower triglyceride levels. Their most pronounced effect, however, is in hindering clot formation.

Truth about *trans*

Much has been written about the health effects of *trans* fatty acids, and the controversy has broadened into a debate about

ing heart disease? Yes—and no—according to two separate studies reported in 1995. A study at Harvard, published in April, found that consumption of fish had no effect on men's overall risk for heart disease. The following November, however, a team from the University of Washington reported that people who eat salmon and other fish rich in certain fatty acids may be protected against cardiac arrest (sudden heart stoppage due to disordered heart rhythm). The Washington scientists speculated that certain omega-3 oils found in these fish may help to regulate the movement of chemical compounds called electrolytes, necessary for maintaining normal heart rhythm.

- In an epidemiological study that examined risk factors for coronary heart disease (CHD) in more than 30,000 postmenopausal women (reported in *The New England Journal of Medicine,* May 2, 1996), investigators found that women who consumed the most **vitamin E-rich foods** (*e.g.,* vegetable oils, nuts, fortified grain products) had a 62% lower chance of dying of CHD than those whose diets had the lowest level of such foods. The use of vitamin E supplements was not associated with a reduced risk, however, nor was intake of vitamins A and C. Noting the inconsistent results of earlier investigations of the role of vitamin E in heart disease, an accompanying editorial concluded that the recent research on vitamin E—as well as that on beta-carotene and other antioxidant supplements—cannot be used as a basis for practical dietary recommendations.
- In the past several years, a possible link between **coffee** and CHD has been explored in numerous epidemiological studies—with quite different results. To those can be added the recent finding, based on 10 years' worth of data from the Nurses' Health Study, that there is no evidence of a positive association between coffee consumption and subsequent risk of CHD in women. This conclusion was published in the Feb. 14, 1996, issue of the *Journal of the American Medical Association.*
- Over a 10-year period, men who ate a diet high in **fiber** (from fruit, vegetable, and cereal sources) had a lower risk of CHD than others who consumed only low levels of fiber, according to a report in the *Journal of the American Medical Association* (Feb. 14, 1996). The subjects were participants in the Health Professionals Follow-up Study, a long-term investigation of some 50,000 physicians, dentists, pharmacists, and other health care workers aged 40 to 75. The results, said the authors of the report, suggest that dietary fiber—independent of the amount of fat in the diet—is an important component in the prevention of CHD.

—Linda Tomchuck

the use of the hydrogenated vegetable oils that contain these fatty acids.

To date, several epidemiological studies have examined the relationship between *trans* fatty acid intake and both lipids and lipoproteins in the blood. Although the evidence from some of the studies—but not all—does suggest a positive relationship between *trans* fatty acid intake and heart disease risk, it is important to appreciate the limitations of these studies. The Nurses' Health Study, a widely publicized long-term investigation of diet, lifestyle, and health in more than 100,000 female nurses, found that the risk of heart disease was increased by 50% in subjects at the highest levels of *trans* fatty acid intake as compared with those at the lowest level. There was no clear "dose-response relationship" at intermediate levels of intake, however. A similar positive relationship between *trans* fatty acid consumption and risk of myocardial infarction (heart attack) was reported in a study of men and women with heart disease, but again no proportional relationship was observed between levels of *trans* fatty acid intake and degree of disease risk. In both studies the lowest risk of heart disease was reported for subjects in the middle range of *trans* fatty acid intake.

Both of these investigations have inherent problems that cast doubt on the reliability of their findings. One difficulty is in the methods of dietary assessment. In large studies involving volunteers who live and eat at home (as opposed to being institutionalized or eating all of their meals in a controlled experimental setting), researchers must depend on the subjects' reports of their dietary intake, which may not be accurate. In addition, the *trans* fatty acid content of the food supply has not yet been thoroughly analyzed, so the exact amounts in certain foods are unknown.

A number of studies conducted 30 to 40 years ago to evaluate the effect of hydrogenated fats on blood lipid levels found that these substances increased cholesterol levels more than unhydrogenated liquid vegetable fats. When saturated fats such as butter, lard, and coconut oil were compared with both liquid and hydrogenated vegetable fats, however, blood cholesterol levels were elevated to the greatest extent with

Sources of Fatty Acids

Type	Dietary source
SATURATED FATTY ACIDS	
Lauric acid	Coconut oil, palm kernel oil
Myristic acid	Butterfat, milk fat, coconut oil
Palmitic acid	Palm oil, animal fat
Stearic acid	Cocoa butter, animal fat
UNSATURATED FATTY ACIDS	
Monounsaturated fatty acids	
Oleic acid	Olive oil, canola oil
Elaidic acid	Hydrogenated vegetable oil
Polyunsaturated fatty acids	
Omega-6 fatty acids	
Linoleic acid	Most vegetable oils (*e.g.,* soybean, corn, safflower)
Arachidonic acid	Lard, meat
Omega-3 fatty acids	
Linolenic acid	Soybean oil, canola oil
Eicosapentaenoic acid	Some fish oils
Docosahexaenoic acid	Some fish oils

NEWS CAP

Eat (Vegetables), Drink (Moderately), and Be Healthy

Vegetarianism and moderate consumption of alcoholic beverages can have a place in a healthy diet, according to the newest *Dietary Guidelines for Americans,* issued on Jan. 2, 1996. And these are not the only departures from the previous (1990) version.

Vegetarians can meet recommended dietary allowances, including the RDA for protein, as long as they eat a sufficient amount of food and have a varied diet. While the new guidelines acknowledge the scientific evidence that "moderate drinking is associated with a lower risk for coronary heart disease in some individuals," they also caution that alcohol has harmful effects when consumed in excess and that some people—including pregnant women—should not drink at all.

Dietary Guidelines for Americans is issued by a joint committee of the Department of Agriculture and the Department of Health and Human Services; the specific recommendations are revised every five years. What else is new or different in the latest version?

- Americans are strongly advised to control their weight. The previous directive to "maintain healthy weight" has been changed to: "Balance the food you eat with physical activity—maintain or improve your weight." The 1990 version stated that some weight gain in adulthood did not present a health risk; the revised guidelines warn that "most adults should not gain weight."
- "Eating is one of life's greatest pleasures." While this may not exactly be a revelation to most Americans, it is an idea that took time to be embraced by nutrition authorities.
- The *trans* fatty acids contained in partially hydrogenated vegetable oils (found in margarines, shortenings, and a variety of prepared foods) may raise blood cholesterol levels.
- Diets high in sugar do not cause hyperactivity in children, as some health professionals had previously speculated.

What has *not* changed? Americans are still being urged to:

- eat a varied diet
- choose foods low in fat
- include plenty of fruits, vegetables, and grains
- use sugar and salt only in moderation

—*Linda Tomchuck*

the saturated fats. In other words, replacing saturated fats (such as butter) with hydrogenated fats (such as margarine and shortening) lowered cholesterol levels, but replacing both with unhydrogenated liquid fats (liquid margarines and all types of cooking oils) lowered blood cholesterol the most.

It is only recently that studies have been designed specifically to examine the physiological effects of *trans* fatty acids. This research shows that *trans* fatty acids have an effect on total cholesterol and LDL levels that is intermediate to that of SFAs and unsaturated fatty acids—*i.e.,* compared with SFAs, *trans* fatty acids lower cholesterol levels, whereas compared with unsaturated fatty acids, they raise cholesterol levels. These findings are based on only a small number of studies, however; further work exploring the effects of *trans* fatty acids on both blood lipids and clotting factors is needed. Until then, recommendations to lower blood cholesterol levels continue to emphasize reductions in dietary SFAs. In this regard it is important to note that decreasing the consumption of both total and saturated fat will simultaneously reduce the intake of *trans* fatty acids. Substituting soft or liquid margarine for butter will help to decrease the amount of SFAs and *trans* fatty acids in the diet.

"Fake" fats

Food manufacturers have developed a number of novel technologies for producing reduced-fat and nonfat foods to help people reduce the amount of fat and calories in their diets. These new technologies cut the fat content of foods while maintaining many of the physical characteristics of fat that contribute to palatability.

Fat replacers can be divided into two categories: fat mimetics and fat substitutes. (The U.S. Food and Drug Administration [FDA] uses the term *fat substitutes* to describe both of these.) Fat mimetics are specially modified food products made with either starch or protein derived from food sources (*e.g.,* corn and potatoes in the case of starch and egg whites and milk in the case of protein), which is modified to provide fatlike properties. These fat replacers are called mimetics because they do not fully replace the functions of fats in foods—for example, they do not enhance or provide additional flavor as fat does, nor can they be cooked or used in frying. Fat mimetics are extremely useful, however, in holding moisture and providing a creamy, slippery "mouthfeel" similar to that of fat. Because these compounds are based on starch or proteins, they provide less than half the calories of fat. To compensate for the loss of flavor that comes with fat removal, foods made with fat mimetics are often high in sugar and salt.

"Now all we need is fake exercise."

Fat substitutes, in contrast, are synthetic substances that look and feel like fat and have physical and other properties similar to those of fat. In fact, these compounds are called substitutes because they theoretically can replace all of the fat in foods. Fat substitutes are synthesized by using fatty acids and thus provide characteristic properties such as flavor and creaminess and, in some cases, can be used for cooking and frying. Because some fat substitutes cannot be digested or absorbed and others may be only partially digested, they provide fewer or no calories compared with fat. A fairly large number of these products are under development. The most well known, and the only such synthetic substitute to be approved by the FDA, is sucrose polyester, or olestra, known by the brand name Olean. It is composed of six to eight fatty acids chemically linked to one sucrose (sugar) molecule. Because the olestra molecule is much larger and bulkier than a naturally occurring triglyceride, it is not digested by the body's intestinal enzymes and thus is not absorbed.

Fat replacers can be useful for people trying to modify their diets to meet current dietary recommendations, but the mass marketing of these products is not without controversy. Olestra, which has been the most widely studied, has been shown to inhibit the absorption of some fat-soluble vitamins and carotenoids, including beta-carotene (a precursor of vitamin A). To compensate for this effect, olestra is fortified with vitamins A, D, E, and K. Since the absorption of other carotenoids in food will also be affected, it is difficult to predict what the overall nutritional impact of olestra and similar substances will be. It is worth noting that similar nutrient interactions occur with other foods, and people seem to worry very little about them. For example, dietary fiber, particularly wheat bran, can reduce absorption of beta-carotene and zinc; likewise, milk, cheese, tea, and red wine can interfere with the absorption of a form of iron.

Short-term studies have suggested that people who eat fat-modified products as part of a strategy to decrease fat intake may make up for the calories they save by eating more. It has even been proposed that the body may compensate physiologically for the calorie deficit that results when fat-modified foods are substituted for others. On the other hand, some research indicates that use of fat-modified foods may decrease caloric intake. Clearly, much more work needs to be done before any firm conclusions can be drawn about the health impact of these products.

—Penny M. Kris-Etherton, Ph.D., R.D., Terry D. Etherton, Ph.D., and Vikkie A. Mustad, Ph.D.

Back to the Future

Americans are always looking for a shortcut to better health. And who can blame them? The U.S. spends more than any other country on health care—nearly $1 trillion in 1996—and one and a half times as much per capita as Switzerland, the next largest spender.

But money does not buy health. The average life span in the U.S. is less than that in Canada, Japan, and most Western European nations, and the U.S. infant mortality rate is higher. The major causes of death and disability are related to how much Americans eat (too much) and what they eat (too many animal products). Nearly every day—often while "on the run"—people in the U.S. consume the kinds of meals once reserved for holidays. Nonetheless, as the physician and humanist scholar Leon Kass of the University of Chicago observes, Americans are always hungry. The reason, Kass contends in his book *The Hungry Soul* (1994), is that they fail to appreciate the cultural and spiritual significance of the shared social meal—and, indeed, of food itself.

One group working to assuage this hunger is the Oldways Preservation & Exchange Trust. Oldways is a nonprofit educational organization based in Cambridge, Mass. Its primary objective is to preserve and promote healthful, environmentally sustainable food and agricultural traditions of diverse cultures—in other words, to preserve the "old ways." In addition, Oldways is committed to teaching the lessons—nutritional, culinary, and ecological—of these traditions to health professionals, farmers, chefs, restaurateurs, and the public at large. It hopes to have an impact on how American consumers shop, how families eat, how chefs cook, and how food growers and purveyors interact.

Pyramid power

Oldways was established in 1988 by K. Dun Gifford of Boston, a Harvard-educated lawyer and investment banker with a passion for food, wine, and the environment. What makes the group different from other organizations that promote sound nutrition or fine cuisine is its combination of scholarly grounding in science, strong social conscience, and commitment to culinary excellence. Oldways' international scientific advisory board includes some of the most respected names in nutrition, epidemiology, and medicine.

Oldways is probably best known to the public for its creation of "diet pyramids" based on traditional regional eating patterns, consisting, to date, of the Mediterranean and the Asian diet pyramids. (Latin-American and vegetarian diet pyramids are currently being prepared.) In order to "build" a pyramid, Oldways recruits top scientists, chefs, practicing physicians, and farmers from all over the world and asks them to evaluate and document the scientific and cultural bases of traditional diets—*i.e.,* those based on locally produced foods and consumed by many successive generations. While

USDA Food Guide Pyramid

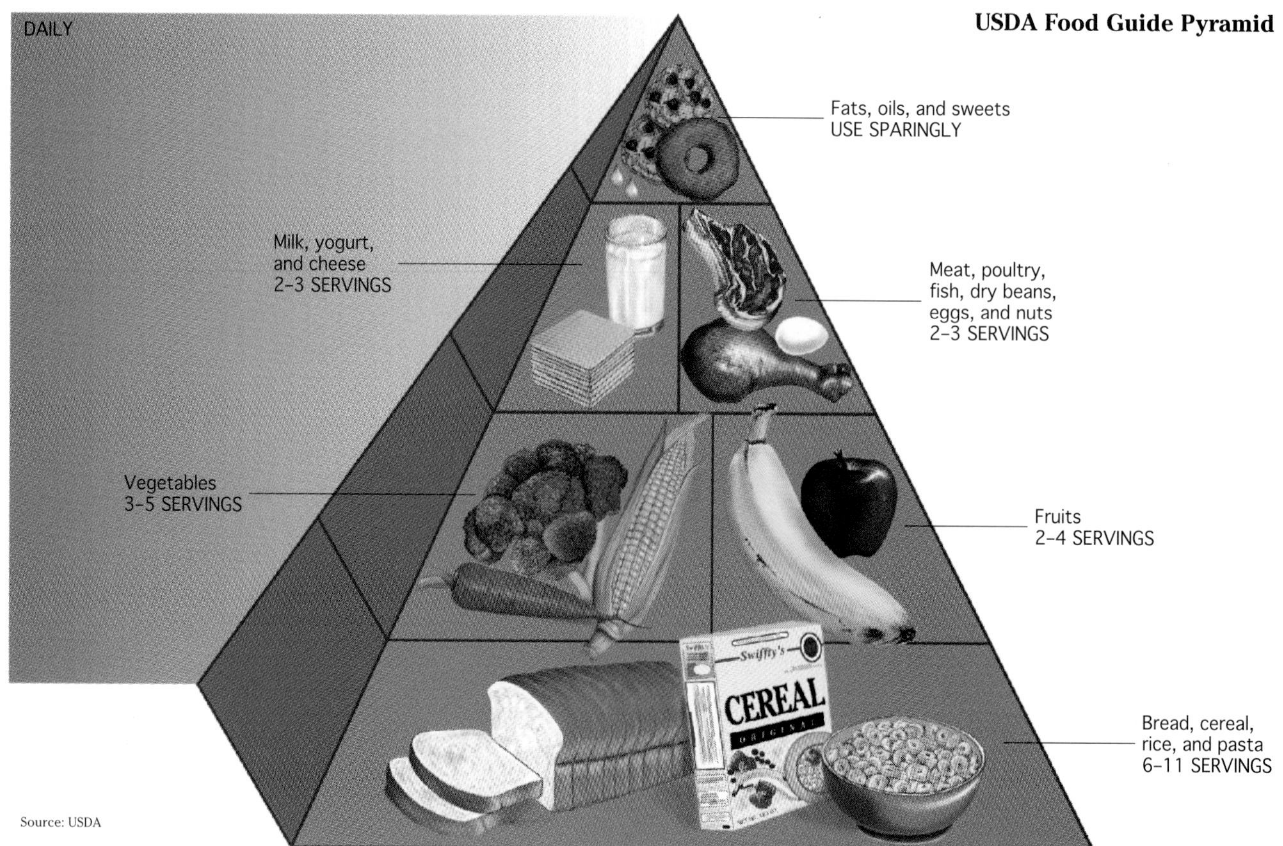

Source: USDA

Mediterranean Diet Pyramid

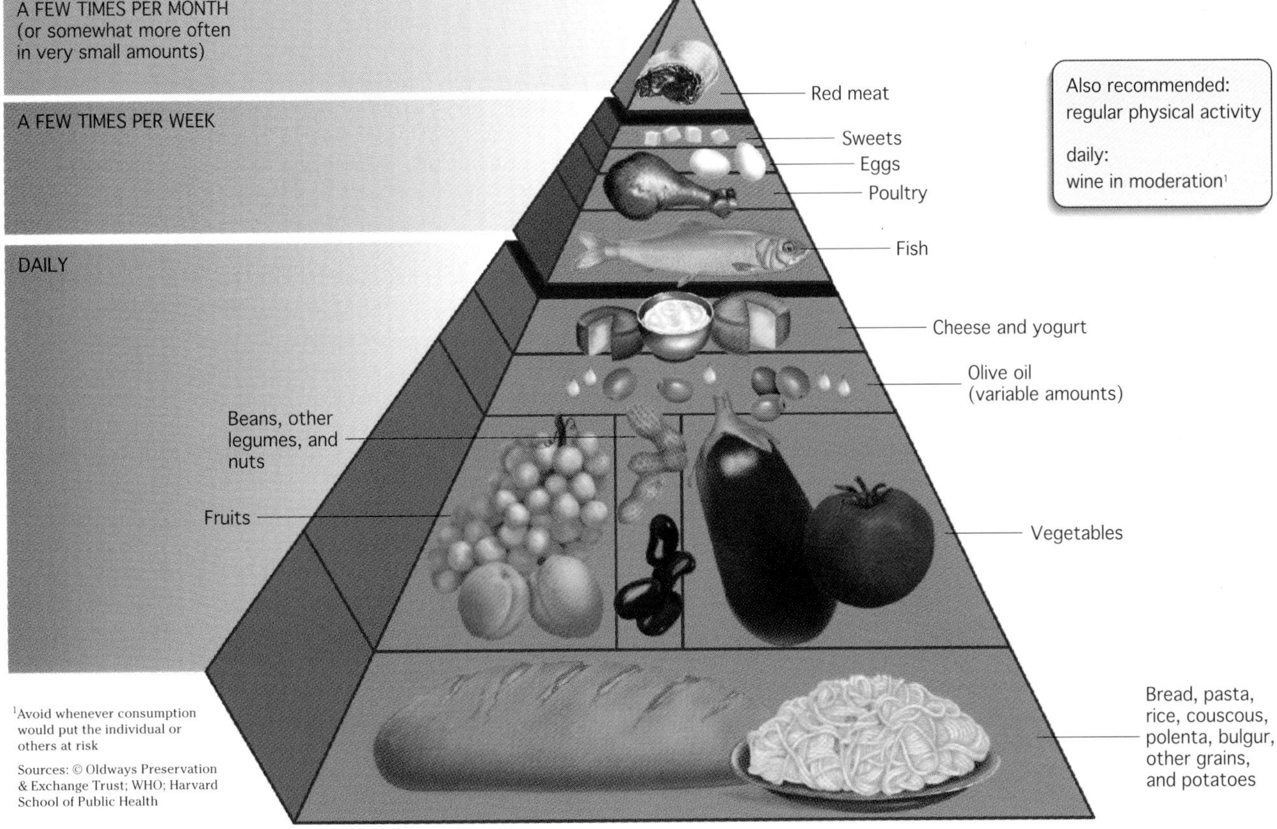

A FEW TIMES PER MONTH (or somewhat more often in very small amounts)

A FEW TIMES PER WEEK

DAILY

Red meat

Sweets

Eggs

Poultry

Fish

Cheese and yogurt

Olive oil (variable amounts)

Beans, other legumes, and nuts

Fruits

Vegetables

Bread, pasta, rice, couscous, polenta, bulgur, other grains, and potatoes

Also recommended: regular physical activity

daily: wine in moderation[1]

[1]Avoid whenever consumption would put the individual or others at risk

Sources: © Oldways Preservation & Exchange Trust; WHO; Harvard School of Public Health

Asian Diet Pyramid

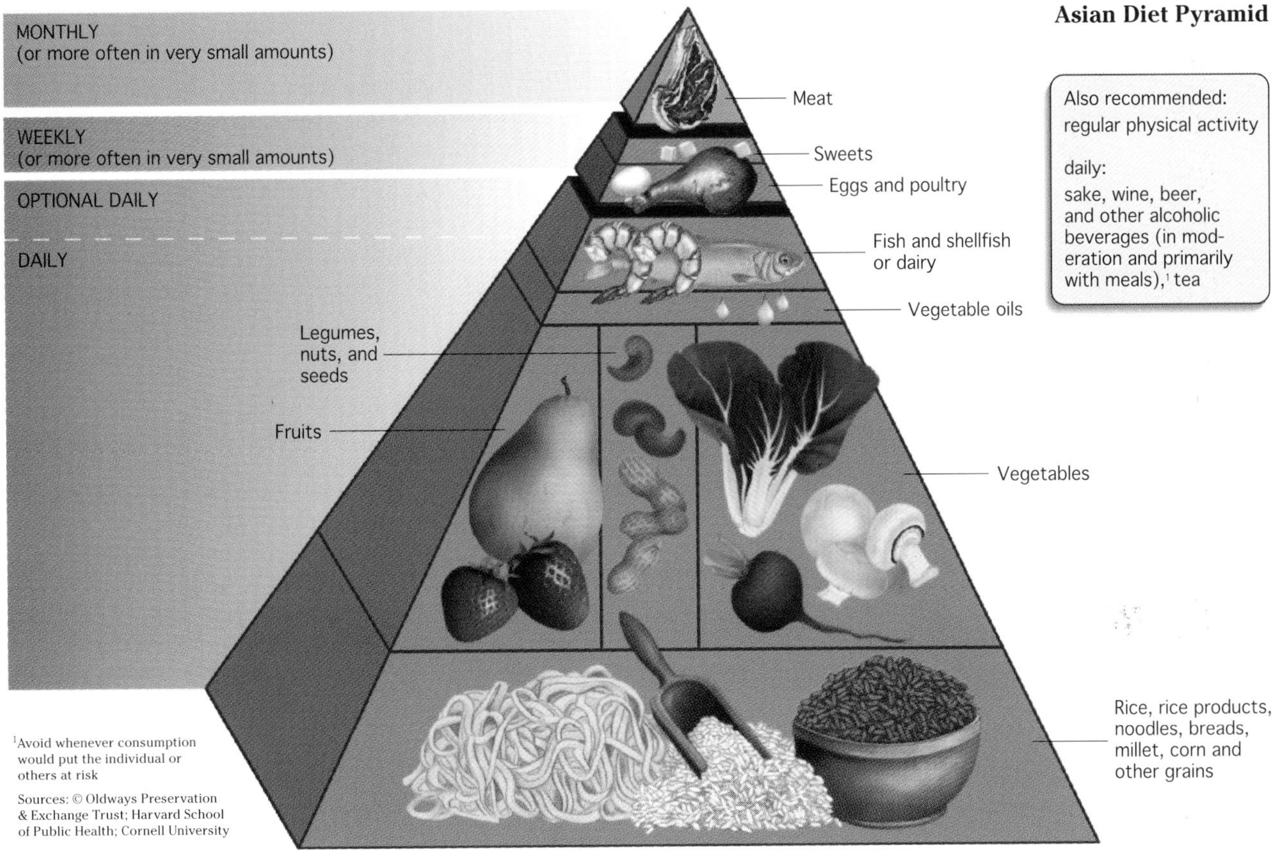

MONTHLY (or more often in very small amounts)

WEEKLY (or more often in very small amounts)

OPTIONAL DAILY

DAILY

Meat

Sweets

Eggs and poultry

Fish and shellfish or dairy

Vegetable oils

Legumes, nuts, and seeds

Fruits

Vegetables

Rice, rice products, noodles, breads, millet, corn and other grains

Also recommended: regular physical activity

daily: sake, wine, beer, and other alcoholic beverages (in moderation and primarily with meals),[1] tea

[1]Avoid whenever consumption would put the individual or others at risk

Sources: © Oldways Preservation & Exchange Trust; Harvard School of Public Health; Cornell University acknowledging that high-fat diets and sedentary lifestyles are major contributors to mortality in the U.S., Oldways does not promote a strict low-fat diet—or, indeed, any kind of prescribed eating pattern. Rather, it aims to identify populations that have naturally lower rates of heart disease and cancer than Americans have and find out what they eat and drink and how much they exercise.

Oldways recognizes the health and environmental benefits of a plant-centered diet, even though it is not a vegetarian organization. Its Mediterranean and Asian diet pyramids contrast markedly with the official Food Guide Pyramid issued in 1992 by the U.S. Department of Agriculture (shown on page 210). The USDA's pyramid, for example, includes nuts, beans, red meat, poultry, and fish in a single category ("eat every day") and thus makes no distinction in the frequency of consumption of animal and vegetable protein or saturated and unsaturated fat. In the Mediterranean and Asian pyramids, on the other hand, red meat is in the "eat a few times per month" category, and beans and other legumes join fruits and vegetables as foods that may be eaten daily. Oldways also takes a broader view of dietary health than the USDA, including "regular physical activity" and "wine in moderation" in its traditional Mediterranean diet. Many American experts, however, take issue with the Mediterranean diet's relatively high level of calories from fat (as much as 40%), even though the fats are largely unsaturated.

NEWS CAP

Finding "C" Level

How much vitamin C do people really need? A great deal more than the recommended dietary allowance (RDA) of 60 mg per day, according to a study sponsored by the National Institute of Diabetes and Digestive and Kidney Diseases and published in the *Proceedings of the National Academy of Sciences* (April 1996). Rather than identifying the level of vitamin C intake required for preventing dietary deficiency—which is how the RDA was determined—the investigators sought the "optimal" level necessary to promote good health. The number they arrived at: 200 mg.

The study, in which seven healthy young men consumed varying levels of vitamin C under strictly controlled conditions, refuted the benefits of megadoses of vitamin C advocated by the late chemist and Nobel laureate Linus Pauling. The researchers found instead that 200 mg per day is the level that results in full absorption of vitamin C by immune system cells and near saturation of the blood. They demonstrated that above the 400-mg-per-day level the body begins to excrete rather than absorb vitamin C and that levels above 1,000 mg—not uncommon among supplement takers—could prove hazardous to certain individuals. (Even 200 mg could be potentially harmful to some people—for example, those with a tendency to form kidney stones.)

Nutrition authorities point out that people who follow the current dietary recommendation to eat at least five servings of fruits and vegetables daily should easily be able to obtain 200 mg of vitamin C. Foods abundant in vitamin C include oranges, grapefruit, guava, strawberries, kiwifruit, broccoli, brussels sprouts, kohlrabi, and sweet peppers.

—Jeff Wallenfeldt

Eating and ethics

Buying food, according to the Oldways philosophy, is an activity with ethical—and even political—implications; it involves choices between good and bad, fresh and processed, locally grown and imported, and sustainable as opposed to solely commercial. When consumers buy tomatoes and bananas grown with chemicals, picked while green, shipped halfway around the world, and gassed with ethylene to turn them red or yellow at the point of sale, they are condoning a vast system of environmentally unsustainable practices. They are, in effect, voting with their forks.

The United Nations Conference on Environment and Development defines environmentally sustainable activities as those with "the capacity to meet the needs of the present without compromising the ability of future generations to meet their own needs." Likewise, sustainable resources are those that can renew themselves—from the fuel used to cook food to the agricultural and transportation technology needed to produce and deliver it and to the skills needed to prepare it.

Only in the short run, Oldways argues, do synthetic fertilizers, pesticides, and herbicides produce more affordable food. The long-term costs of pollution, erosion, and human exposure to harmful substances have yet to be counted. Also not yet counted is the cost to society of loss of diversity in the food supply. Who knows how many varieties of plants—the sources of many wonderful tastes, aromas, textures, and colors—have been abandoned by growers because they did not produce lucrative yields or because their products could not withstand five days of boxcar travel? While Oldways acknowledges that agribusiness—not the small family farm—is the source of the vast majority of Americans' food, it is highly critical of the way in which "factory farming" promotes the efficient production of only a small number—currently around 150—of the 80,000 plants available for cultivation.

The practice of growing only a few different kinds of, say, corn or potatoes not only limits the choices available to consumers but also can set the stage for famine, as happened in Ireland in 1845–46, when the potato crop, the main source of food for the Irish masses, was decimated by a fungal disease, and some 750,000 died as a result. Indeed, some agricultural authorities warn that another potato famine could occur at any time. Only a small number of potato varieties are grown today, and these particular varieties are extremely susceptible to some plant diseases.

(Top) Rafael Macia—Photo Researchers;
(bottom) Steve Smith—Westlight

Strategies for change

Oldways recognizes the enormous challenge it faces in trying to influence Americans' food preferences. To meet this challenge, the organization has adopted three strategies.

- The primary strategy is the compilation of the traditional diet pyramids. Experts from disciplines as varied as nutrition science, cultural anthropology, medicine, agriculture, and the culinary arts focus on one culture at a time. First, they study the traditional foodstuffs and dietary patterns; then they attempt to translate this knowledge into a practical eating plan that a contemporary American family could adopt.
- A second strategy is the sponsorship of the Chefs Collaborative 2000 project. The Collaborative is a group of chefs (now numbering over 1,000) who are committed to developing educational programs for consumers, teaching them how to shop for high-quality, fresh food. The group promotes awareness of sources such as farmers' markets and local organic farms. It also sponsors school-based programs designed to teach youngsters where food comes from, how different cultures grow and produce it, and how it gets from farm to market to table. So-called center-of-the-plate issues are a key focus of the youth education programs. For the Collaborative, *center of the plate* refers to meals in which plant-based foods are the main dishes and animal-based foods serve as side dishes or condiments. Although radically different from the typical Western diet, this simple, healthful approach reflects the way that most of the world still eats most of the time.

  Headed by Chicago chef and restaurateur Rick Bayless, the Collaborative seeks to unite the skills of professionals who love to cook with the knowledge of farmers dedicated to the principles of sustainable agriculture. Because the members of the Collaborative are keenly interested in flavor, their search for high-quality ingredients has made them an integral part of their own local "food communities." Such communities often start among the buyers and sellers at farmers' markets and extend to include growers and, in some cases, even ranchers and fishermen dedicated to supplying the most healthful meat, poultry, and seafood. By demanding quality, chefs have been able to exert influence over the way food is produced. Across the U.S. flourishing businesses that supply items like fresh herbs, salad greens, and free-range poultry have been established, thanks to the patronage of influential local chefs and restaurant owners. As Alice Waters, chef-owner of Chez Panisse in Berkeley, Calif., has written, the "search for good ingredients is pointless without a healthy agriculture and a healthy environment."
- The third strategy is called "Putting Pyramids into Practice." It involves teaching health professionals, especially practicing physicians, the basics of clinical nutrition. At a time when most Americans' health problems result from too much food rather than too little, the nutrition curriculum of many U.S. medical schools still consists chiefly of two first-year classroom lectures on vitamin and mineral deficiencies. To teach physicians, Oldways enlists both nutritionists, who know about food's nutritive value, and

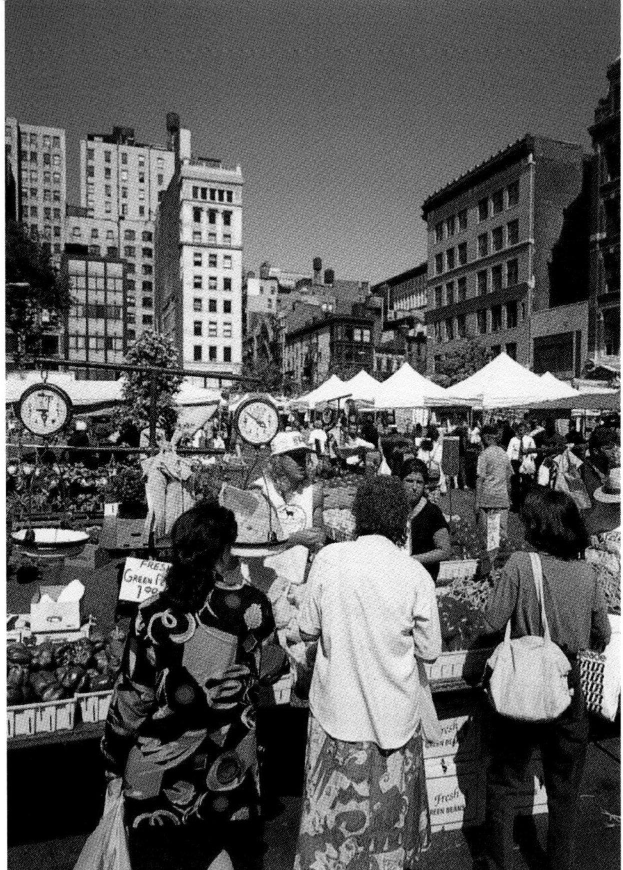

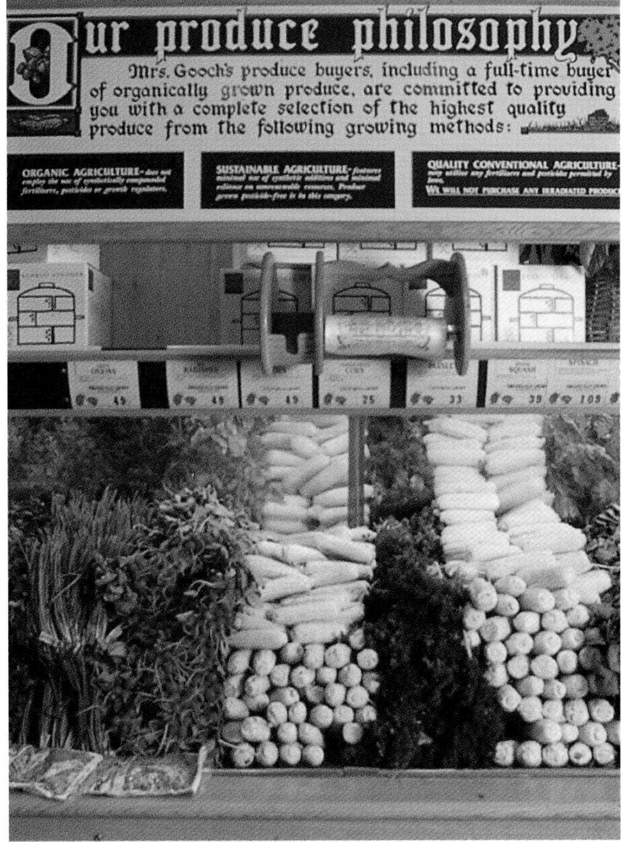

(Top) Shoppers at a farmers' market in New York City's Union Square take advantage of the opportunity to buy high-quality seasonal produce while at the same time supporting local growers. (Bottom) Consumers make an ethical, even a political, decision when they patronize stores that feature foods grown by environmentally sustainable methods.

In the kitchen of the Rialto restaurant in Cambridge, Mass., chef Jody Adams gives some youngsters a hands-on cooking lesson. Adams and other members of the Chefs Collaborative 2000 are committed to making Americans—adults and children alike—a "food literate" people.

chefs, who know about taste. Some pretty lively discussions occur when these professionals get together!

Rhythm of the seasons

Oldways believes that there is something wrong when there are more kinds of french fries being sold than varieties of potatoes being grown. By taking advantage of what other cultures have to offer, it hopes to right this imbalance.

In creating the Mediterranean and Asian diet pyramids, Oldways' experts have been struck by the way that traditional diets look to nature's seasonal variations for clues as to what people should eat and when. Regionally grown high-quality ingredients are the "secret" of nearly every good cook. What more could a Midwestern cook want in August than locally grown tomatoes picked at the peak of ripeness? Why would a baker in Maine make anything but blueberry pies and muffins in the summertime? Most shoppers know only too well how disappointing it is to bite into a mealy gas-ripened tomato in February or a hard, dry apple in May. Yet many growers choose commercial traits like long shelf life and packable shape over flavor, texture, and juiciness.

How can the average person put the Oldways philosophy into practice? Certainly one way is to go to farmers' markets and to buy locally grown foods. Another is to ask the supermarket manager where those March ears of corn and January zucchini were grown and whether their produce suppliers use synthetic chemicals on their crops. Still another is to devise healthful meals based on one of the traditional diet pyramids.

Ultimately, Oldways would like all Americans to regard food as a nourishing, delicious, colorful investment in their own and their family's health. And last but not least, Oldways urges people to teach their children how to cook!

—*John La Puma, M.D.*

NEWS CAP

Vitamin A Gets an F

A study of the pregnancy outcomes of more than 22,000 women found that excessive vitamin A supplementation—doses higher than 10,000 IU per day—may cause birth defects. (Some vitamin A capsules contain as much as 25,000 IU.) These findings were published in *The New England Journal of Medicine* (Nov. 23, 1995).

As a result of these findings, the U.S. Food and Drug Administration (FDA) issued new recommendations to women of childbearing age: limit the intake of foods and supplements containing preformed vitamin A (as distinct from its precursor beta-carotene) to 5,000 IU per day. Dietary sources of vitamin A include animal products, particularly liver, some vegetables, and fortified foods such as breakfast cereals.

—*Linda Tomchuck*

Accommodations in the Workplace: Smart Business

Do the right thing, the right way, and everyone benefits.
—Edward A. Brennan, former chairman and CEO of Sears, Roebuck and Co.

The Americans with Disabilities Act (ADA), signed into law by U.S. Pres. George Bush on July 26, 1990, continues to shape employment, governmental services, telecommunications, public accommodations, and, perhaps most important, public attitudes. Title I of the ADA, the most comprehensive federal law ever to address employment discrimination, took effect for U.S. businesses with 25 or more employees on July 26, 1992, and for businesses employing 15 or more on July 26, 1994. The implementation of the Title I provisions—those pertaining to the workplace—continues to spark intense public policy debate. Yet, on the whole, systematic study of Title I in operation has not been done.

Title I: an overview

Title I of the ADA prohibits businesses with 15 or more employees from discriminating against a qualified person with a disability in any aspect of employment: hiring, promotions, benefits, training, transfers, terminations, or any other facet of the employer-employee relationship. Under Title I, discrimination includes the failure to provide "reasonable accommodations" to a "qualified person with a disability" unless providing such an accommodation would create an "undue hardship for the employer." The concept of "reasonable accommodation" attempts to balance the bona fide needs of the employee against the costs and administrative burden to the employer. Persons covered by Title I encompass a wide range of individuals, including those with a physical or mental condition or impairment that substantially limits major life activities, those with a record of such a condition or impairment, and those regarded by others as having such a condition or impairment. Included are people with vision or hearing loss, HIV/AIDS, diabetes, mental illness, and mental retardation, to name a few, as well as people who have had cancer.

The concept of a *qualified* individual with a disability is central to Title I's goal of economic equality. An individual with a disability is qualified if he or she satisfies the prerequisites for the job—*e.g.,* has the educational background—and can perform essential job functions. In establishing qualifications and essential job functions, the employer must consider the applicant's experience and skills in conjunction with the possibility of making reasonable workplace accommodations.

As the agency charged with enforcing Title I, the Equal Employment Opportunity Commission (EEOC) emphasizes educational outreach—the dissemination of information, policy guidance, and technical assistance—to prevent discrimination from occurring. When a violation occurs, the EEOC encourages voluntary and informal resolution of disputes whenever possible. At the same time, the commission seeks to achieve firm, fair, and commonsense enforcement where noncompliance persists.

Does the ADA work?

The Annenberg Washington (D.C.) Program in Communications Policy Studies of Northwestern University (of Chicago) has carried out an intensive study of the pre- and post-ADA employment practices of one large U.S. employer, Sears, Roebuck and Co. The findings of that study were published in *Communicating the ADA* (1994), which has been used in corporate, educational, governmental, and media-based training and awareness programs. In 1996 a follow-up report was published. Both reports attempt to (1) stimulate discussion and debate of the issues that Sears (and other companies) face regarding the employment of persons with disabilities, (2) provide data, with a special focus on the costs and benefits of workplace accommodations and on the avoidance and resolution of disputes regarding employment practices, and (3) identify the broader implications of Sears's employment-related experiences so as to arrive at a philosophy for future policy making in U.S. business.

The long-term effectiveness of Title I depends upon continued study, education, and dialogue. On the basis of learning from models such as Sears, it has become clear that the following must be achieved:

- Myths must be dispelled about persons with disabilities.
- People must be informed of their rights and obligations under the act, and opportunities for workplace advancement must be equalized.
- Employers and employees must be enlightened so they can make informed decisions.
- Disputes must be diffused, avoided, and resolved whenever possible without formal litigation.

Sears: cataloging its successes

The impact of the ADA on U.S. business has been, and will continue to be, evolutionary, not revolutionary. In other words, change happens gradually and incrementally rather than suddenly and totally. Achievement of Title I's ultimate goals will remain a major challenge facing corporate America well into the 21st century. Although the experiences of any one corporate "laboratory" may be insufficient for drawing sweeping conclusions that apply throughout U.S. business, the in-depth study of Sears (with 300,000 employees, among whom an estimated 20,000 have disabilities) has been highly illuminating. Several achievements stand out.

Low costs and universal design. The Sears reports document, among other findings, that the costs of providing workplace accommodations for qualified employees with disabilities are low. Sears has shown that so-called universal design and access strategies fulfill the objective of including persons both with and without disabilities into productive workforce participation. The ADA encourages equality not only in employment opportunities but also in access to facilities and to information on the job. The benefits of universal design and accommodation strategies are generalizable to employees without disabilities (for instance, workplace safety in general is almost always enhanced when physical and environmental accommodations are made for people with physical disabilities).

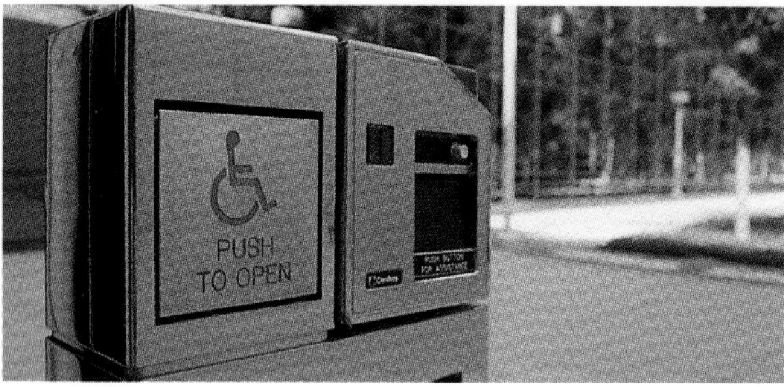

(Above) *At Sears, Roebuck and Co.'s corporate headquarters near Chicago, accommodations made in compliance with the Americans with Disabilities Act were neither costly nor complicated. More often than not, such accommodations enhance the working environment for* everyone.

Sears, Roebuck and Co.; photographs, Dan Sjostrom

Better business! Efforts to educate management and the workforce about the ADA and the capabilities of persons with disabilities are essential and, as already noted, must be based on facts, not myths. Sears has been resoundingly successful in educating and training employees at every level.

Sears is a company that has reached beyond mere compliance to transcendence—in ways that make strong economic sense. The ADA has played a catalytic role in fostering independence in the workplace among people with disabilities. Innovative corporate solutions for providing workplace access often have universal application and bottom-line economic benefits. Furthermore, the low costs of accommodations for employees with disabilities—at Sears and elsewhere—have themselves created unforeseen benefits for the companies—in terms of increased service to customers with and without disabilities, higher productivity levels, and greater effectiveness and efficiency in virtually all business dealings.

Dollars and cents. Figure 1 (*see* below) presents the cost of providing workplace accommodations to Sears employees with disabilities from 1993 to 1996 (the period immediately after the 1992 implementation date). The total cost of the 71 accommodations studied was $3,209, with the average cost being about $45. Sears found that 72% of accommodations entailed *no cost,* 17% cost less than $100, 10% cost less than $500, and only 1% cost more than $500; none cost more than $1,000. Examples of accommodations that require little or no cost include flexible scheduling, longer training periods, revised job descriptions, reasonable rest periods, enhanced lighting, adjusted workstations, and supported stools or chairs and back-belt supports.

Figure 1: Low Costs of Complying with the Americans with Disabilities Act

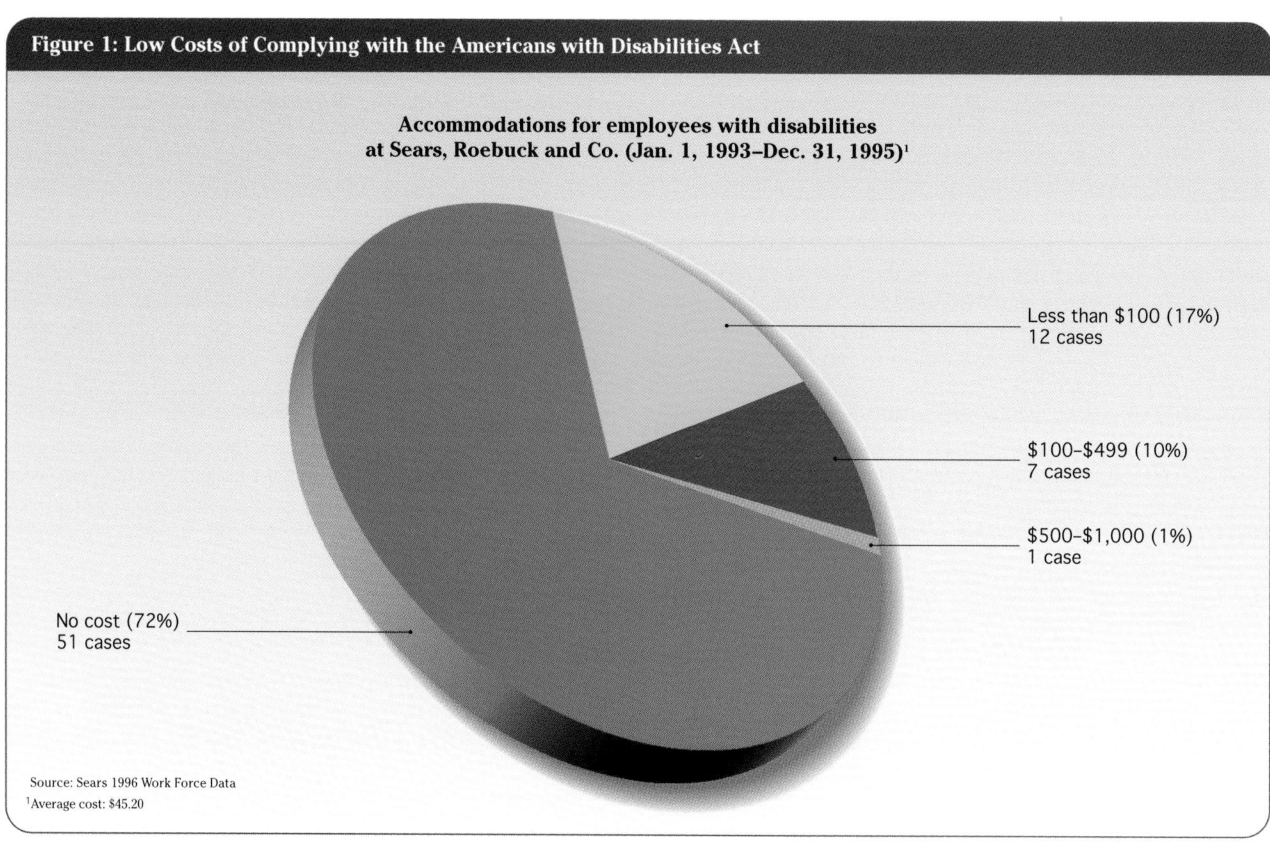

The cost of providing accommodations to Sears employees with disabilities during the years 1978 through 1992—prior to Title I's implementation—was also low. Almost all of the 436 accommodations studied during that period cost little or nothing, and only 3% cost more than $1,000; those 3%, involving state-of-the-art information technologies and communications systems, enabled groups of employees with and without disabilities to perform "information-intensive" jobs (*e.g.*, inputting large amounts of actuarial data for insurance purposes or processing credit card accounts) productively, cost-effectively, and safely.

The ADA has not been universally embraced by all businesses. One of the shortcomings that many U.S. companies have found in attempting to comply with Title I is the lack of standardized databases providing information on what accommodations are needed for whom. Sears, however, has assessed its large workforce by type of disability. Such an assessment was based on employees who actually requested and received workplace accommodations during the period Jan. 1, 1993, to Dec. 31, 1995 (Figure 2; *see* below). Almost half (47%) of the accommodations were for persons with orthopedic impairments, the average cost being about $43. Roughly one-third (31%) of the accommodations involved employees with sensory disabilities (primarily aural and visual impairments), at an average cost of about $75. Neurological impairments (*e.g.*, dyslexia, epilepsy, and others) accounted for 8% of the requested accommodations, at an average cost of $13. Behavioral impairments accounted for 7%, at an average cost of $0. Internal, skin, and "other" impairments totaled 4%, all with an average cost of $0.

Two general inferences may be drawn from these findings. First, from a business-planning perspective, the proportion of accommodations actually provided for employees with particular disabilities is quite consistent with the makeup of the workforce. Second, from an economic perspective, the direct costs associated with accommodations for any particular disability are low and do not deviate substantially from an overall average cost of $45.

Consider the case of Tony Norris, now a senior system specialist in Family Footwear at Sears's Merchandise Group's headquarters in Hoffman Estates, Ill., who started at the company in 1968 as a shoe salesman. In 1986 Norris had a spinal tumor removed and then had to undergo a dozen subsequent surgeries. He is now quadriplegic. Despite his impairments, Norris performs his job—handling about 4,000 "help-desk" inquiries a month—ably, largely because he has a voice-activated computer and breath-controlled telephone, and minor modifications were made to his workspace to accommodate his motorized wheelchair. "The computer has become part of me," Norris says, "and it's not all that expensive."

Six years after Norris' return to Sears, the inventory systems manager of the Sears Footwear Department said: "Though loyalty to a long-time employee was certainly an element of Sears's interest in bringing Tony back to the company, above all it was a good-sense business decision. Here was a trained, proven professional with a strong contribution to make. Logic dictated that an investment in accommodations would be 'paid back' many times in productivity and the ability to utilize his expertise."

Figure 2: Meeting Many Needs

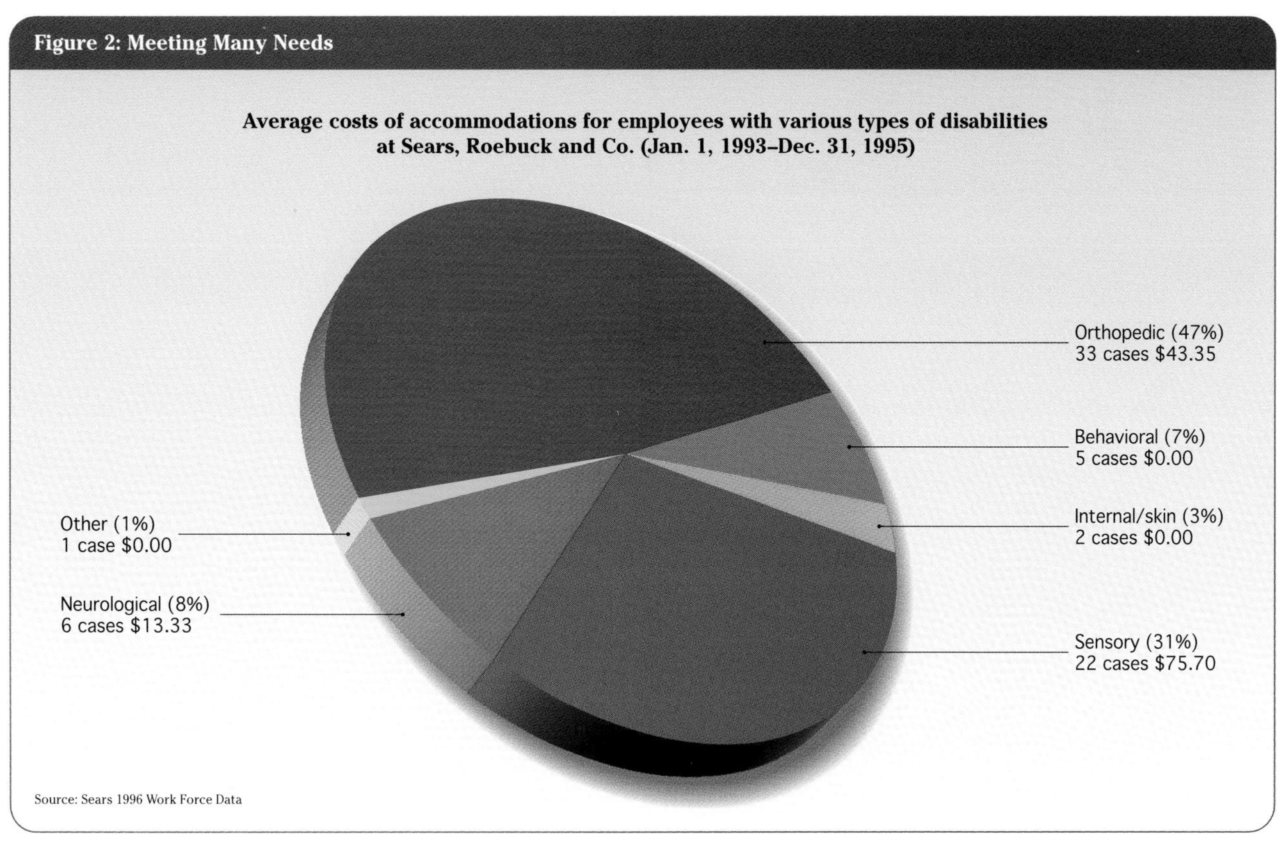

Source: Sears 1996 Work Force Data

The trend at Sears toward a reduction in overall cost of accommodations began well before the ADA and has been documented from 1978 to 1996. Such a trend is supported by other studies. A 1995 poll of more than 400 U.S. executives, conducted by the Harris Organization, showed that 80% of the respondents reported minimal or low increases in costs associated with accommodations in their workplaces; 75% reported that the average cost of employing a person with a disability was not greater than employing a person without a disability. The median cost for accommodations was $233 per employee, and from 1986 to 1995 the proportion making accommodations for employees with disabilities rose from 51% to 81% of the 400 companies represented by the survey.

Similar lowering of costs was associated with effective workplace accommodations that were tracked by the Job Accommodation Network (JAN); these included lowered job-training costs, increased worker productivity, lowered insurance requirements and fewer claims, and reduced rehabilitation costs after an injury on the job. A more recent JAN survey found that for every dollar invested in an effective accommodation, the companies concerned realized an average of $50 in benefits (*e.g.,* in the retention of qualified workers).

Staying out of court. Far from creating onerous legal burdens, the ADA has led to increasing numbers of companies adopting alternative dispute-resolution processes. Companies that comply with Title I on the whole experience relatively few disputes and are able to resolve most problems that arise at a low cost and by keeping qualified people at work.

Mary Ann Stephen has retinitis pigmentosa, an inherited progressive degeneration of both retinas. Stephen, an administrative assistant in Sears's legal department, is not legally blind and maintains much of the independence that fully sighted people enjoy. She is,

Tony Norris, who has been with Sears since 1968, is now a senior system specialist in Family Footwear. From his specially designed workstation, equipped with a voice-activated computer and a breath-controlled telephone, he fields about 4,000 "help-desk" inquiries a month.

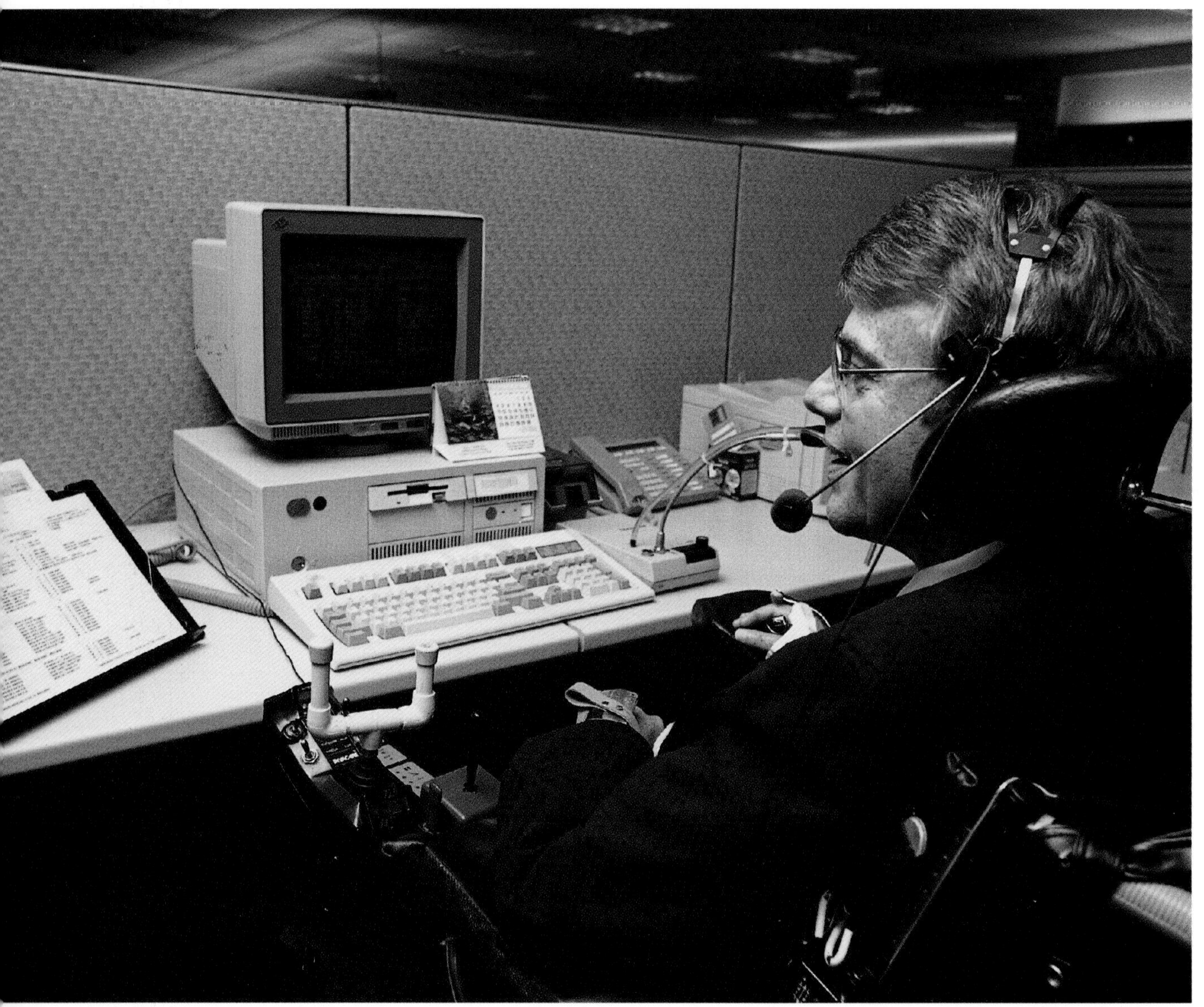

Sears, Roebuck and Co.

however, effectively blind at night and on hazy days and has a fair amount of difficulty reading. Stephen uses a text enlarger for reading printed material and a high-contrast computer monitor for reading computer files. "I asked for the monitor at my physician's recommendation. The boss said, 'Whatever you need, just order it.' They're happy to help me, and I appreciate it," Stephen says.

"I don't think of Mary Ann as having a disability," comments an attorney at Sears. "I think of her as a responsive, productive hard worker who performs equally with everyone else on the team. She has a good attitude, is willing to do any task we ask of her, and in short she doesn't let anything stop her, certainly not her vision problem that can be accommodated by special equipment."

What has enabled Sears to avoid litigation and foster cooperation (rather than confrontation) in managing disability-related issues? As a component of its Ethics and Business Policy Assist program, Sears established a toll-free telephone help line that is available to all employees for guidance on ADA-related questions. Inquiries are confidential, and advice and follow-up are provided. At each stage of the informal resolution process, responsibility is focused upon the affected employees and supervisors, encouraging problem solving at the local level. A study of 20 informally resolved ADA-related disputes at Sears from 1993 through 1995 revealed that roughly one-third (30%) of the total number of disputes involved individuals with orthopedic impairments and that more than three-quarters of the total cases (80%) were resolved successfully.

From Jan. 1, 1990, to Aug. 10, 1995, there were 141 formal Title I complaints filed with the EEOC against Sears, and these too were studied. Almost half of the charges filed against Sears (43%) involved orthopedic impairments. This relatively high proportion may reflect factors inherent in a large retail business, such as employees' standing on their feet all day or moving heavy appliances. On a national basis, only about 20% of ADA-related cases during the same period involved orthopedic impairments. The second largest category of charges filed against Sears with the EEOC involved behavioral impairments (15%); on a national basis, behavioral impairments (primarily mental illness) constituted 12% of the total.

Another finding from the Sears studies was that 41% of those employees who filed charges with the EEOC had evidence of a disability prior to their employment with Sears or prior to their current job at the company. More than one-quarter (29%) who filed charges were injured on the job; 18% were injured off the job. These findings do not support the assumption that Title I claims reflect issues that would otherwise be raised under traditional workers' compensation laws. Rather, the ADA fostered an antidiscriminatory climate; the EEOC gave those with discrimination complaints an outlet.

Of 138 charges that persons with disabilities filed with the EEOC against Sears during the period from 1990 to 1995 (prior to and after Title I implementation), 98% were resolved without trial litigation—with 12% settled, 9% withdrawn, and 33% dismissed. In 8% of the cases a "right to sue" letter was issued by the EEOC. In 34% of the cases, a decision by the EEOC was pending as of mid-1996, while trial court litigation was pending in only 2% of the cases. Thus, the overwhelming majority of formal Title I charges were resolved without resort to protracted litigation. Furthermore, as Sears has recognized, spending money on employees is a lot more cost-effective for the company than spending money on litigation fees.

While Sears has shown a commitment to resolving Title I disputes without resort to formal litigation, the same may not be true of many other companies. Nationally, as of December 1995, more than 54,000 Title I-related complaints had been filed with the EEOC.

Challenges ahead

The ADA has reflected a dramatic shift in American public policy toward the equal employment of persons with disabilities. Yet policy makers differ in their views of whether the ADA has played, or will play, a significant role in enhancing labor force participation of qualified persons with disabilities and in reducing dependence on government entitlement programs. Although unanswered questions remain, several points are clear:

- The ADA does not require employers to hire individuals with disabilities who are not qualified or to give preference to qualified individuals with disabilities over equally qualified individuals without disabilities.
- Title I does not require employers to make unduly costly accommodations for persons with disabilities.
- Better understanding is needed of individual disabilities and their relation to employment opportunity and career advancement.
- The study of disability policy should be interdisciplinary—*i.e.,* grounded in medicine, psychology, economics, law, ergonomics, and other fields.
- Every individual with a disability also has strengths and capabilities.
- Disability is a natural part of the human experience.

Assessing Title I compliance is a monumental task. No law, even one as far-reaching as the ADA, can be solely responsible for social change, nor can it specify a single way to ensure "civil rights." The implementation of the ADA will vary widely for employees with different disabilities and for businesses of different sizes and in different markets. There is a need for additional study of corporate policies and cultures that support equal employment opportunities for qualified persons with disabilities, particularly strategies that transcend "mere compliance" with the law.

When President Bush signed the ADA in a Rose Garden ceremony, he said that "every man, woman, and child with a disability [may] now pass through once-closed doors into a bright new era of equality, independence and freedom." Pres. Bill Clinton has expressed equally strong support for the act: "We must continue to voice our conviction that it is morally wrong to deny rights of citizenship to Americans with disabilities. We must remind others that our entire nation will share the economic and other benefits that will result from the full participation of all Americans." Sears is just one large corporate example of how the law functions at its best.

—Peter D. Blanck, Ph.D., J.D.

Al Eastman

Pedaling with a Passion: A Photo Essay

To say World Ride '95 is an ambitious undertaking is to say Michael Jordan is a decent basketball player.
—Scott Fowler, *Charlotte* (N.C.) *Observer*

Toleskaw ("Bolek") Zajiczek, whose hands were blown off by a grenade some 45 years ago, was one of hundreds of intrepid souls who participated in a round-the-world bicycle odyssey that began in Atlanta, Ga., on March 17, 1995, and concluded eight months later in Washington, D.C., having crossed more than a dozen countries. About half the riders had physical or mental disabilities.

Zajiczek, aged 65, cycled from Ireland to Moscow on a bike built with special armrests for his stumps. Exhilarated by his feat, he returned to his native Poland, where he helped organize a national bike ride for cyclists with disabilities. A little over three months later, thanks to the funds raised by boys and girls clubs of Poland, Zajiczek rejoined the World Riders in Los Angeles and pedaled his way to the U.S. capital. One who had the pleasure of knowing Bolek on the Old West stretch of the global ride was the novelist John Burnham Schwartz, who especially remembers Zajiczek's "perpetual expression of sunny stoicism." In his journal, Schwartz notes how dazzled he was by the way his Polish companion maneuvered "the smooth stumps of his forearms like wands—quick and warm and seemingly capable of anything."

Zajiczek was just one of many heroes on the unprecedented AXA World Ride '95, an event sponsored by the AXA insurance group of France and conceived and organized by World T.E.A.M. Sports, a not-for-profit organization based in Charlotte, N.C., and dedicated to promoting the participation of people with all types of disabilities in lifetime sports. (T.E.A.M. stands for "the exceptional athlete matters.") Greg LeMond, three-time winner of the Tour de France, served as honorary chairman, and more than two dozen corporate sponsors financed the $4 million venture. The ride would not have been possible without the visionary guidance and constant support of New York businessman James M. Benson, chairman of the board of directors of World T.E.A.M. Sports.

A core group of six cyclists, five with disabilities, completed the entire 20,963-km (13,026-mi) trek. About 250 individuals rode on one or more of the 14 stages (*see* map, page 222), and thousands of "day riders"—many with disabilities—joined the group as it made its way through communities in 16 countries: the United States, Ireland, the United Kingdom, France, Belgium, The Netherlands, Germany, the Czech Republic, Austria, Poland, Belarus, Russia, Mongolia, Kazakhstan, China, and Japan. The cycles were as diverse as the riders. Three of the core group rode on three-wheeled, hand-powered cycles across every conceivable type of terrain—cobblestones, superhighways, icy mountain passes, sandy steppes, and dung-covered pastures among them. A member of the core group, 41-year-old Steve Ackerman of Fort Collins, Colo., who is

"Core" riders Steve Ackerman (left) and Rory McCarthy (right) take the lead on hand-pedaled cycles as AXA World Ride '95 crosses Siberia.

(This page and opposite page) Photographs, Al Eastman

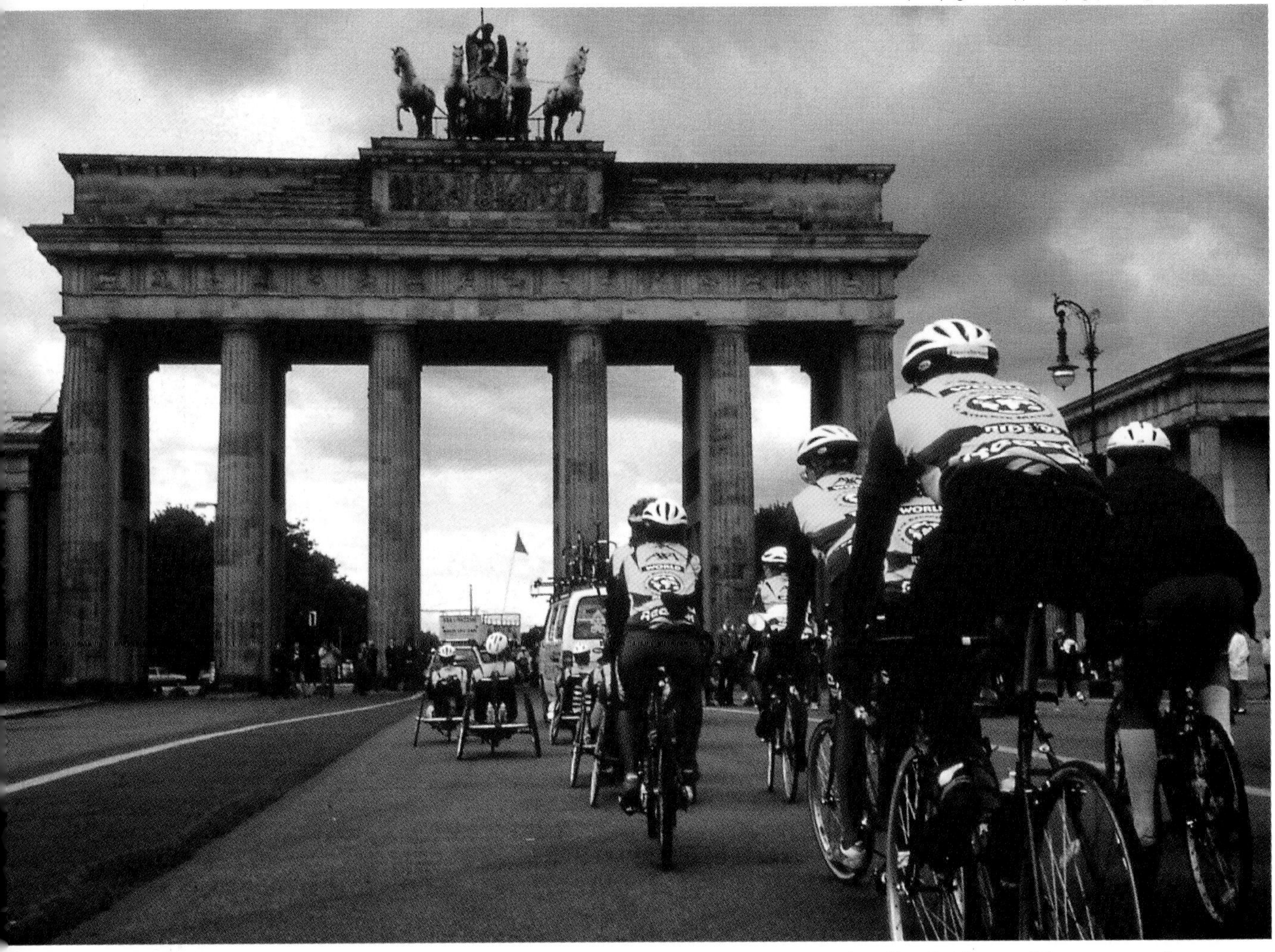

(Above) AXA World Ride '95 cyclists approach the Brandenburg Gate in Berlin on a fine spring day. Though riding conditions were not always so clement, one rider whose "sunny stoicism" never seemed to flag was 65-year-old Toleskaw Zajiczek of Poland (below right), who maneuvered bikes across Europe and the United States with the "smooth stumps of his forearms."

AXA WORLD RIDE '95

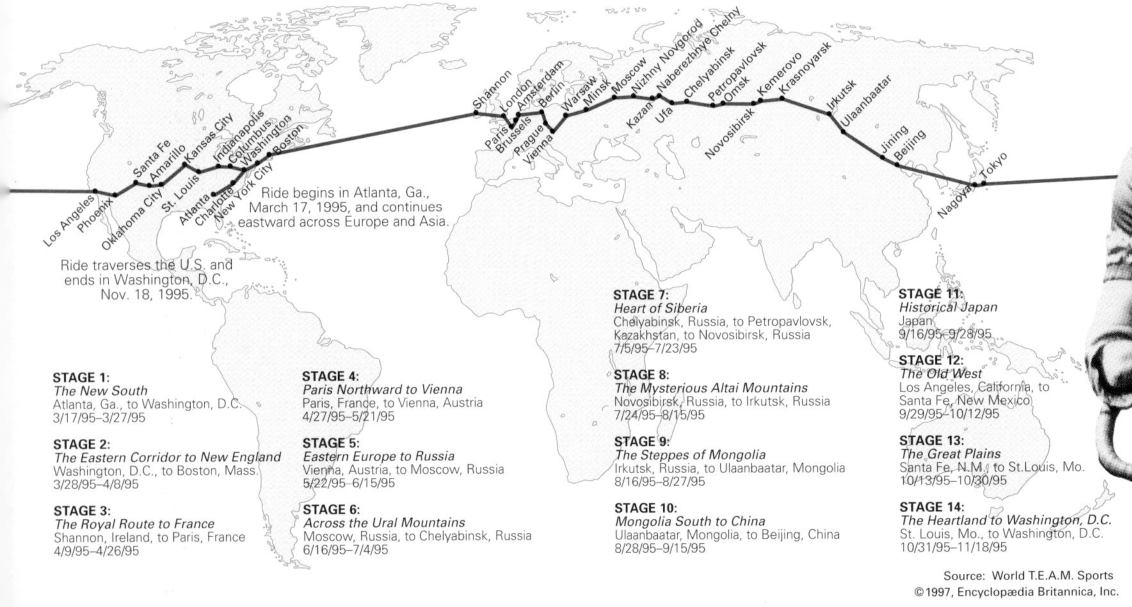
Los Angeles
Phoenix
Oklahoma City
Santa Fe
Amarillo
St. Louis
Kansas City
Indianapolis
Columbus
Atlanta
Charlotte
New York City
Washington
Boston
Ride begins in Atlanta, Ga., March 17, 1995, and continues eastward across Europe and Asia.
Ride traverses the U.S. and ends in Washington, D.C., Nov. 18, 1995.
Shannon
London
Paris
Brussels
Amsterdam
Berlin
Prague
Vienna
Warsaw
Minsk
Moscow
Nizhny Novgorod
Kazan
Naberezhnye Chelny
Ufa
Chelyabinsk
Petropavlovsk
Omsk
Novosibirsk
Kemerovo
Krasnoyarsk
Irkutsk
Ulaanbaatar
Jining
Beijing
Nagoya
Tokyo
STAGE 1:
The New South
Atlanta, Ga., to Washington, D.C.
3/17/95–3/27/95
STAGE 2:
The Eastern Corridor to New England
Washington, D.C., to Boston, Mass.
3/28/95–4/8/95
STAGE 3:
The Royal Route to France
Shannon, Ireland, to Paris, France
4/9/95–4/26/95
STAGE 4:
Paris Northward to Vienna
Paris, France, to Vienna, Austria
4/27/95–5/21/95
STAGE 5:
Eastern Europe to Russia
Vienna, Austria, to Moscow, Russia
5/22/95–6/15/95
STAGE 6:
Across the Ural Mountains
Moscow, Russia, to Chelyabinsk, Russia
6/16/95–7/4/95
STAGE 7:
Heart of Siberia
Chelyabinsk, Russia, to Petropavlovsk, Kazakhstan, to Novosibirsk, Russia
7/5/95–7/23/95
STAGE 8:
The Mysterious Altai Mountains
Novosibirsk, Russia, to Irkutsk, Russia
7/24/95–8/15/95
STAGE 9:
The Steppes of Mongolia
Irkutsk, Russia, to Ulaanbaatar, Mongolia
8/16/95–8/27/95
STAGE 10:
Mongolia South to China
Ulaanbaatar, Mongolia, to Beijing, China
8/28/95–9/15/95
STAGE 11:
Historical Japan
Japan
9/16/95–9/28/95
STAGE 12:
The Old West
Los Angeles, California, to Santa Fe, New Mexico
9/29/95–10/12/95
STAGE 13:
The Great Plains
Santa Fe, N.M., to St.Louis, Mo.
10/13/95–10/30/95
STAGE 14:
The Heartland to Washington, D.C.
St. Louis, Mo., to Washington, D.C.
10/31/95–11/18/95
Source: World T.E.A.M. Sports
©1997, Encyclopædia Britannica, Inc.

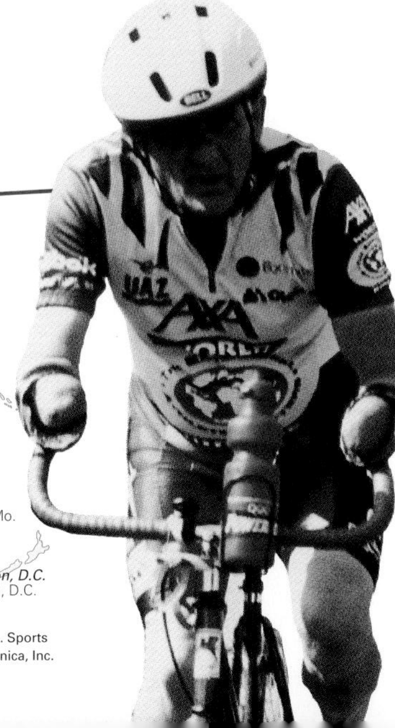

paralyzed from the waist down, remembers hand-pedaling his way across 1,000 roadless kilometers (600 mi) in Mongolia's Gobi Desert as "no picnic!" Cara Dunne, a 24-year-old law student who lost her sight to retinal cancer at age 5, rode about 1,600 km (1,000 mi) through Siberia on a tandem bike with the World T.E.A.M. Sports' executive director, Stephen Whisnant. Whisnant rode tandem with Tore Naerland, a blind Norwegian athlete, through Belarus.

The passionate participants in AXA World Ride '95 pedaled a lot more than unusual cycles; they "peddled" hope! As one rider put it, they showed the world that people with disabilities can do a lot more than "just survive"; they can "thrive." Along the way, an estimated 10,000 volunteers helped out in one fashion or another. In Siberia entire villages came out to cheer the riders on with the traditional greeting of flowers, bread, and salt. In West Virginia banners decorated the highways, and the cyclists were treated to big helpings of apple cobbler.

Obviously, such a journey required expert medical backup. The Hospital for Special Surgery of New York City was the principal medical sponsor and adviser. Cycling physicians and an exhaustively stocked medical supply van were part of the accompanying caravan. Fortunately, there were few medical mishaps. Of course, the riders experienced their fair share of routine injuries and illnesses—including lots of "road rash" and sore muscles, abrasions, upset stomachs, colds, sore throats, sprains, and strains. Probably the best remembered of all the afflictions were the monstrous mosquito bites that spared no one in Russia!

A van crash in the heart of Siberia was the most devastating event, but local teams responded quickly, and the ride's Russian interpreter, Sergey Berezny, who suffered a spinal injury, was treated in one of the best trauma centers in Russia. Ackerman developed a pressure sore, a serious skin wound that caused major tissue breakdown and threatened his health

(Below) The Savings Bank of the Russian Federation makes its sponsorship of 80 days of World Ride '95 a festive occasion. (Below center) Cara Dunne, a visually impaired tandem cyclist, receives flowers in Western Siberia. (Bottom left) Heavy rains in China make the going tough—even for support vans. (Bottom right) Blizzard conditions in the eastern United States fail to dampen the spirits of World Riders on the final stretch of their global odyssey.

(Top) The Washington Times; photograph, Christopher B. Corder; (bottom) Bruce Gellin

(Above) The triumphant finish of the unprecedented 20,000-km (13,000-mi) bicycle ride is celebrated in the U.S. capital on Saturday, Nov. 18, 1995, and "the possible dream" of some remarkably dedicated cyclists—with and without disabilities—is realized. (Left) At the end of the day, even the bicycles need something to lean on.

and life. Though his fellow riders and physicians urged him to quit, he was determined not to. At one point in Japan, he sought treatment from a faith healer. Amazingly, when his prospects seemed dimmest, his wound started to heal, and by the ride's triumphant finish, he was virtually out of danger.

On Thanksgiving Day 1995, the American public had a chance to witness scenes from the amazing 247-day ride when CBS Sports aired a 90-minute special, "World Ride: The Possible Dream," with Charles Kuralt as host and narrator. Kuralt introduced the program by saying, "The world is always saying to us, 'This thing you want to do is impossible; you can't do that.' Certain human beings always answer, 'Yes, I can.' " The show focused on the members of the core group—their struggles, hardships, fears, anger, courage, grit, resilience, and indomitable team spirit. Richard Sandomir of the *New York Times* wrote that "emotionally, no program in recent memory has exceeded CBS's 'World Ride: The Possible Dream.' "

Whisnant, who was a key planner of as well as a participant in the ride, says the goal was to bring communities of the world together, but he never imagined that the global enthusiasm for the event would be so great. Most important, he says, World Ride '95 "raised consciousness about disabled issues, especially in countries where support for and understanding of people with disabilities is minimal." Now plans are under way for a major World T.E.A.M. Sports-sponsored event in Vietnam at the end of 1997 and for another seven-to-eight-month transcontinental adventure in 1999.

—Ellen Bernstein

Global Warming: How Hazardous to Health?

Over the past 10 years, the profound impact of weather on human health has gained increasing recognition. Most people, of course, are aware that their moods are affected by the weather and that spring fever and cabin fever are real phenomena and not just inventions of the poets. Of greater interest to the medical and climatological research communities, however, is the impact of weather on a variety of medical conditions, some of them serious enough to result in death.

Most public health officials are all too aware of the toll exacted by the heat wave that hit Chicago in 1995. Outbreaks of many devastating infectious diseases, especially those transmitted by insects, are also closely related to meteorologic variations. With such events in mind, a number of federal and international agencies, including the U.S. National Institutes of Health and the World Health Organization (WHO), as well as professional organizations such as the American Public Health Association (APHA), have expressed concern that the global warming many atmospheric scientists expect over the next century will exacerbate the already important role of weather as an influence on human health.

Wake-up call

In November 1995 the United Nations convened a group of international experts to consider the possible social impacts of global warming; a detrimental effect on human health was considered to be among the most important of such impacts. In a report issued at the meeting, the UN Intergovernmental Panel on Climate Change (IPCC), which represents the expertise of more than 2,000 authorities worldwide, arrived at the following conclusions:

- The disturbance of physical systems (*e.g.,* weather patterns, sea level, water supplies) by climate change would pose risks to human health.
- The scale of such health consequences would be vast, affecting whole communities or populations.
- These health consequences would occur in various ways, via mechanisms of varying directness and complexity. Some would occur by relatively direct means (*e.g.,* deaths from heat waves and other extreme weather events); others would occur through indirect means (*e.g.,* changes in the geographic range of diseases carried by insects).
- Some of the consequences would be deferred or delayed.
- Most of the consequences would be adverse.

These troubling projections by the most respected scientists in the field should be a wake-up call to health professionals and the public alike. Even if these dire predictions are wrong, however, and the climate does not undergo dramatic change, the impact of weather on health will remain a significant one; moreover, this often underappreciated impact has broad public health implications.

Heat, health, and death

The extreme heat that affected cities in India, the U.S., and Western Europe in the summer of 1995 demonstrated something that has only recently become apparent: very high temperatures can kill many people very swiftly. Moreover, current research suggests that weather affects human death rates much more than might be expected. During extreme weather conditions like heat waves, deaths from all causes can rise 50% above typical levels. Although the total number of deaths in any locale is generally highest in winter, the most extreme weather-related increases in mortality are noted during the hottest weather.

Healthy people have efficient heat-regulatory mechanisms that enable their bodies to cope effectively with increases in temperature. For example, the body can increase heat loss through the skin by vasodilation (widening of the interior diameter of the blood vessels) and perspiration. Further, there is strong evidence that people can acclimatize to hot temperatures in a rather short period of time. Given heat waves of similar intensity early and late in the summer season, more people die during the earlier heat wave. No doubt some of this difference can be attributed to the death of the most vulnerable individuals during the first heat wave. Healthy people can easily adapt to continued heat, however; this capacity creates uncertainty for those attempting to predict the impact of global warming on heat-related deaths.

Deaths due to hot temperatures are largely a regional phenomenon. The most vulnerable cities appear to be those in the midlatitudes (*i.e.,* from about 30°–50° north or south of the Equator), where irregular but intense heat waves occur during most summers. A threshold temperature has been identified for many of these cities, indicating that there is a critical level of heat stress above which the body's physiological coping mechanisms become inadequate. In such cities increases in the death rate usually occur only during the 10–15% of summer days with temperatures above the threshold.

During the devastating July 1995 Chicago heat wave, the city morgue was so overwhelmed with corpses that refrigerated trucks were used to store bodies awaiting autopsy. The heat-related death toll was over 550.

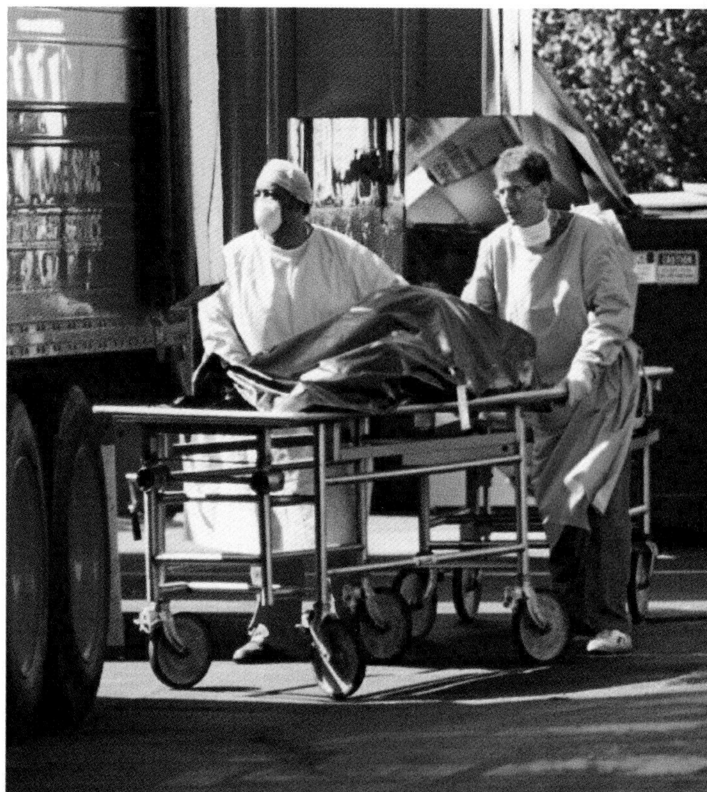

Charles Bennett—AP/Wide World

The actual threshold temperature in a given locale seems to depend upon the frequency of extreme heat. For example, the temperature exceeds 36° C (97° F) in St. Louis, Mo., with approximately the same frequency as it exceeds 32° C (90° F) in Detroit, Mich.; increases in mortality occur in both cities above these respective threshold temperatures. This differential again points to the ability of the body to acclimatize; people appear to respond to weather in a relative rather than an absolute fashion.

Surprisingly, cities in tropical regions seem to be less affected by heat-related deaths than those in the midlatitudes. Thresholds are more difficult to discern in tropical urban areas than in temperate cities, and it appears that the human response to the consistently high temperatures in tropical environments is another adaptive feature. Even in desert cities such as Phoenix, Ariz., heat-related mortality is less important than it is in New York, Chicago, or St. Louis. Another intriguing finding is the somewhat similar patterns in cities within the developed and less developed world. Contrary to expectations, heat-related mortality is not confined to the poorest cities. Although air-conditioning has mitigated the problem somewhat in the developed world, even the most modern large cities continue to have very pronounced increases in mortality during hot weather.

The impact of heat is not uniform across the population. The elderly and the very young are disproportionately affected, as their physiological capability to adapt to stressful conditions is less than that of young and middle-aged adults. Persons with preexisting cardiovascular disease are also less able to cope with extreme heat. In U.S. cities the poor are particularly vulnerable to hot weather because they often live in housing that is ill-designed for high temperatures, lack access to air-conditioning, and are exposed to the urban heat island effect. (Cities are, in effect, "heat islands" compared with the cooler rural areas that surround them.)

The increased frequency and intensity of heat waves expected with global warming may exacerbate the problem of heat-related mortality in summer, but there is uncertainty about the impact of such climate change on mortality rates in general. It is not clear whether declines in cold-related deaths will be equal to summertime increases. Research on this question has come to conflicting conclusions. In 1995 British scientists calculated that about 9,000 fewer winter-related deaths would occur annually by the year 2050 in England and Wales under typical climate-change scenarios that suggest temperature increases of 2°–2.5° C (3.6°–4.5° F). This decrease would more than offset any increase in heat-related deaths.

Various investigations conducted in the U.S., however, suggest that cold-related mortality will decline only slightly if global warming occurs, while heat-related deaths will increase sharply. Because a significant proportion of cold-related deaths are attributed to respiratory infections, which are most efficiently transmitted between people confined in poorly ventilated buildings, warmer winter weather could reduce infection risk if it encouraged outdoor activities. Still, it is questionable whether in most midlatitude cities the small increases expected in winter temperatures would lure people outdoors in great numbers. If the mean winter temperature in New York City increases from the present −1° C (30° F)

NEWS CAP

Agent Orange Update

Birth defects, prostate cancer, and a nerve disorder have been added to the list of health problems linked to Agent Orange, the herbicide that was used during the Vietnam War to defoliate the jungles of Southeast Asia. In April 1996 the Institute of Medicine (IOM) of the National Research Council published its second in a series of biennial reassessments of the health effects of Agent Orange exposure on Vietnam veterans.

In May, following a government review of the report, prostate cancer and the nerve condition peripheral neuropathy (a disorder affecting nerves outside the brain and spinal cord, which often causes numbness or tingling in the extremities) were added to the list of Agent Orange-associated illnesses for which the Department of Veterans Affairs provides medical benefits. The illnesses already recognized include cancer of the lung, larynx, and trachea and two cancers of the lymphoid tissues, Hodgkin's disease and non-Hodgkin's lymphoma.

The IOM report found what it called "limited or suggestive" evidence of an association between the birth defect spina bifida (the incomplete closure of the spine) and Agent Orange or its highly toxic contaminant, dioxin. This conclusion was based largely on a study of about 900 veterans who were directly involved in the handling of herbicides in Vietnam. Among 792 children born to these veterans, there were three cases of spina bifida, a rate of nearly four cases per 1,000, compared with only five per 10,000 in the general population.

With the exception of personnel known to have handled or sprayed herbicides, individual exposure levels of others who served in Vietnam are extremely difficult to determine. The government deems all 2.6 million Vietnam veterans to have been exposed and therefore eligible to qualify for medical benefits. Because children of veterans can receive such benefits only by an act of Congress, Pres. Bill Clinton requested legislation to extend coverage to persons with spina bifida who have a parent who served in Vietnam.

—Jeff Wallenfeldt

to 1° C (34° F) with global warming, how many more people will decide to venture outdoors for extended time periods?

Another uncertainty involves the trend in heat-related summer deaths, even if heat waves do become more severe. As mentioned above, death rates in tropical cities show little sensitivity to heat. If midlatitude cities become warmer, it is possible that their death rates might come to more closely resemble those of tropical cities. Some climate-change scenarios suggest that by the middle of the next century, New York City's summer weather may be very much like present-day summer in New Orleans, where there appears to be a minimal heat-mortality response. Is it possible, then, that heat-related mortality could actually decrease in midlatitude American cities? Most investigators contend that this will not be the case, but these questions point to the difficulties inherent in predicting the impacts of climate change on health.

Mosquitoes, flies, and ticks: on the move

The effect of global warming on the transmission of many infectious diseases may be of even greater concern than potential increases in temperature-related deaths. The Institute of Medicine of the U.S. National Research Council recently published a volume outlining a number of infectious diseases that are currently on the rise around the globe, including malaria, cholera, hantavirus infection, Lyme disease, and dengue fever. Most of these illnesses are transmitted by vectors, or carriers, such as mosquitoes, flies, ticks, and rodents, all of which are sensitive to a number of climatic factors. Although it is difficult to link specific increases in infectious disease to current variations in climate, it should be noted that most vectors thrive in warm, humid environments, and if such climates move poleward, it seems plausible that these diseases will begin to occur in regions where they do not now exist.

In tropical countries vectorborne diseases are often the major cause of illness and death. WHO estimates, for example, that up to half a billion people are currently infected with malaria, and almost 2.5 billion are at risk for the disease, as they live in environments conducive to successful reproduction of the vector mosquito. Currently, most vectorborne diseases are confined well within the climatic limits of their vectors. This pattern of distribution is due in part to biological factors that limit the survival of the infectious agent (often a virus or parasite) and in part to human efforts to control the vector's spread. Quarantines, vaccinations, pesticides, and drug treatment of infected individuals have successfully limited the geographic distribution of vectorborne diseases and should continue to do so even in the event of climate change.

The continued use of some of these control methods, however, raises uncertainties and even risks. Long-term pesticide use may favor the emergence of resistant strains of vectors or may kill natural predators that keep vector populations under control. In addition, climate-change-induced ecological alterations, such as the destruction of forests due to excessive heat, may upset natural vector-control mechanisms while simultaneously displacing human populations into areas (*e.g.,* rain forests cleared for agricultural use) where they are more likely to come in contact with the vector.

Crispin Hughes—Panos Pictures

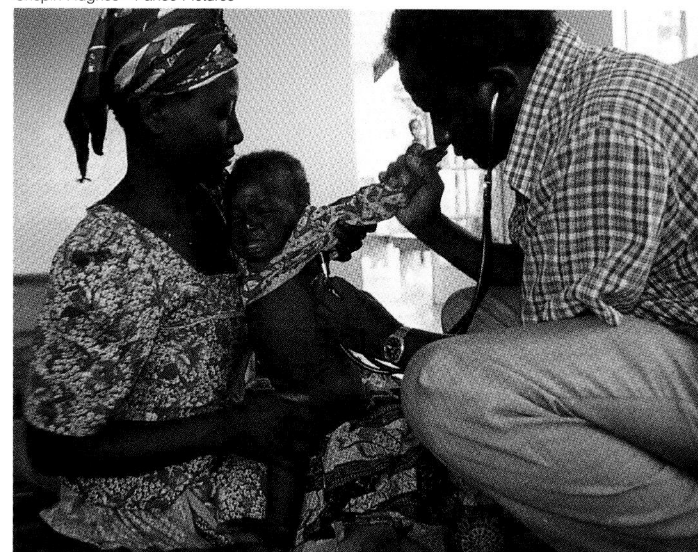

A Rwandan child is treated for malaria. In the late 1980s, following a period of unusually hot, wet weather, malaria rates in Rwanda soared; even areas that were previously malaria-free were affected.

Three that threaten

Although WHO and the IPCC are apprehensive that most vectorborne diseases will become more prevalent under global warming conditions, three particular afflictions—malaria, dengue fever, and onchocerciasis (river blindness)—are of special concern. All are transmitted by insects that survive best in warm, moist climatic conditions, and their health impacts are likely to be even more devastating in a warmer world than they are today.

Malaria. In less developed countries malaria kills one million to two million people annually and ranks at the top of all vectorborne diseases. Malaria is caused by a parasitic protozoan. The primary vectors of the parasite are mosquitoes of the genus *Anopheles.* The malarial parasite requires a temperature of at least 15° C (59° F) for completing its development within the mosquito, while the mosquito itself requires a temperature of at least 16° C (61° F) and prefers a relative humidity above 60%. The parasite develops even more quickly with elevated temperatures; at 30° C (86° F) its reproduction rate is more than twice that at 20° C (68° F).

Control of malaria has become increasingly difficult. The most virulent malarial parasite, *Plasmodium falciparum,* is resistant to most antimalarial drugs, and in many regions where the disease had been eliminated, it is now making a comeback, sometimes surpassing earlier recorded levels. Complicating the problem of malaria control is the resistance to insecticides that numerous mosquito species have developed.

Recent studies have documented the responsiveness of malaria incidence to local variations in climate. In Rwanda marked increases in the incidence and distribution of malaria were observed in 1987, when unusually hot, wet weather occurred. Increased prevalence of the disease was particularly striking in areas at higher altitudes, which formerly had been unaffected. On the basis of this and similar observations, it appears that a small rise in minimum temperature would facilitate the spread of malaria into large urban highland populations—like those of Nairobi, Kenya, and Harare, Zimbabwe—that are currently malaria-free. According to computer models of the spread of malaria given a warmer global climate, the likelihood of malaria epidemics would increase in both tropical and temperate regions. One such model predicts that as many as one million additional malaria deaths per year could be attributed to climate change by the middle of the next century.

Dengue. Dengue fever, also known as breakbone fever, is widespread in the Caribbean, tropical America, Oceania, Asia, and parts of Australia. The disease is characterized by the abrupt onset of fever, severe headache, muscle or joint pain, nausea, vomiting, and rash. A more severe manifestation, dengue hemorrhagic fever (DHF), is associated with leakage of plasma from the blood vessels, enlargement of the liver, and circulatory failure. Between 250,000 and 500,000 cases of DHF occur annually throughout the world. Without treatment, some 50% of patients will die. Over the past 15 years, epidemics of dengue have increased in both number and severity, especially in tropical urban centers. The proportion of DHF cases has also risen, especially in the latitudinal zone of the tropics between 30° N and 20° S.

The vector responsible for major epidemics of dengue is the mosquito *Aedes aegypti,* which reproduces most successfully in stored-water containers typically found near human habitation. Frosts or sustained cold temperatures kill adult mosquitoes and overwintering eggs and larvae and thus limit the occurrence of outbreaks in the U.S. Although there is as yet no clear evidence of regional climatic influence, annual epidemics of dengue have returned to Central and South America over the past decade. *A. aegypti* has reappeared in areas where it previously was eradicated, and in some South American and Mexican locations, the mosquito has been found at altitudes more than 610 m (2,000 ft) higher than previously reported. A recent outbreak in northern Mexico close to the Texas border put U.S. public health officials on alert. Dengue is a classic vectorborne disease that could be strongly affected by global warming. Not only would warmer weather shift the distribution of both vector and disease to higher latitudes or altitudes, but there is also evidence that *A. aegypti*'s biting rate increases as the temperature rises.

Onchocerciasis. Onchocerciasis, also called river blindness, is a particularly insidious vectorborne disease that affects 18 million people in Latin America and West Africa. The main vector is a blackfly that lives near rivers and in close proximity to humans who go to the riverbanks for their domestic water supply. The infectious agent is *Onchocerca volvulus,* a parasitic worm whose larva is transmitted to humans by the blackfly when it seeks a blood meal. The threadlike worm, or nematode, damages the skin, the lymphatic system, and sometimes the eye when it enters the body. The adult worm is viviparous (live-bearing) and produces millions of nematodes while in

In the wake of a recent outbreak of dengue in northern Mexico, the Texas Department of Health accelerated efforts to monitor potential breeding sites of the Aedes aegypti *mosquito, the vector of the disease-causing virus.*

Bruce Lee Smith—Gamma Liaison

the human body. The nematodes are mobile under the skin and migrate to various parts of the body, where they cause severe itching and, if they enter the eye, blindness. Climate plays an important role in the occurrence of onchocerciasis, since the blackfly requires fast-flowing water for successful reproduction, and the adult insect can be spread by wind.

A recent study of the impact of climate change on blackfly populations in West Africa showed that if temperature and precipitation were to change during the next century as predicted by climate models, blackfly populations might increase by as much as 25% at current breeding sites. Although onchocerciasis can be controlled somewhat by aerial application of pesticide to rivers and quite effectively by treatment of infected persons with the drug ivermectin, the anticipated increase in blackflies would lead to an expansion of the disease. Since the vectors, which are much smaller than a housefly, can travel hundreds of kilometers on wind currents, new habitats in areas previously unhospitable to the blackfly could be quickly colonized by the insect and the risk of onchocerciasis introduced into new locations.

Altered seas and skies

Over the past century, average sea surface temperature has increased by about 0.7° C (1.3° F). Marine growth of algae has been observed to increase in response to rising water temperature and increased availability of nitrogen in coastal waters, the latter a result of agricultural mismanagement and sewage release. The combination of increasing water temperatures and coastal land mismanagement has also contributed to the growth of populations of toxic phytoplankton (tiny water plants), which, in turn, has resulted in an increased incidence of shellfish poisoning in humans and the killing of large numbers of fish.

Scientists have recently found that the microorganism responsible for cholera, *Vibrio cholerae,* can persist in various algae and zooplankton (minute water animals) that thrive in the warm, nutrient-rich coastal waters. Diarrheal diseases like cholera affect people of all ages but are particularly burdensome to the young—in 1993 alone, for example, three million childhood deaths occurred in the less developed world as a result of dehydrating illnesses such as cholera. Large coastal accumulations of algae, called algal blooms, may have contributed to the recent cholera pandemic in Latin America, and the range of such blooms appears to be extending. Climatologists suspect that large-scale changes in marine ecosystems, such as advancing algal blooms, may already indicate sea surface temperature increases attributable to climate change.

A rise in sea level, caused by the thermal expansion of a warmer ocean and the melting of polar ice, may raise the level of the world's oceans by 0.5 m (about 1.6 ft), inundating large areas of low-lying land that is now densely populated or under cultivation. Less developed nations such as Bangladesh, where millions live at elevations near sea level, would be particularly hard hit. Even slight alterations in sea level could ruin nearly a fifth of the habitable land in Bangladesh through inundation and saltwater intrusion. Many health authorities fear that mass human migrations triggered by a rise in sea level could lead to urban overcrowding, overtaxed sanitation systems, and malnutrition—all precursors to infectious disease outbreaks.

Paul Harrison—Panos Pictures

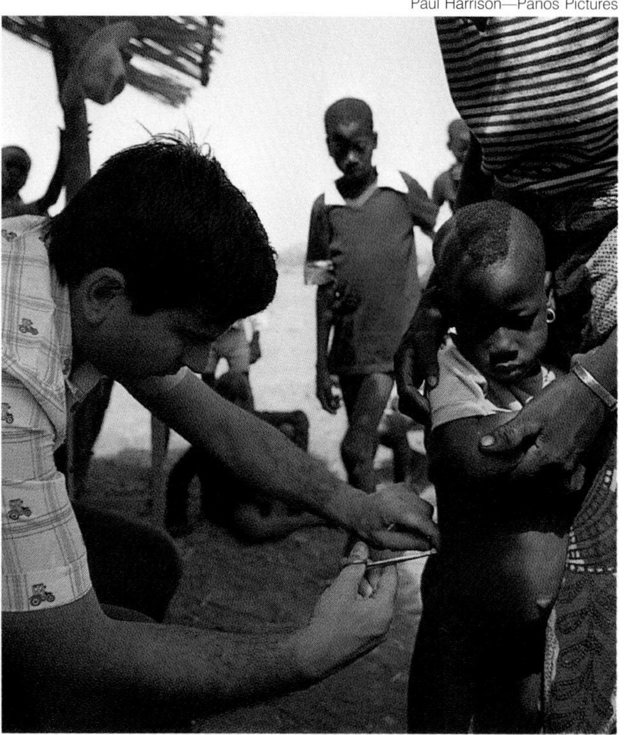

A "skin snip" test will reveal the extent of an African child's infection with the parasite that causes onchocerciasis, or river blindness, another disease whose spread could be influenced by climate change.

Stratospheric ozone depletion, accompanied by increases in biologically destructive ultraviolet-B (UVB) radiation, may exacerbate the impact of climate change on human health. UVB, the portion of sunlight that is responsible for most sunburn, wrinkles, and other skin problems, has a damaging effect on cellular proteins and genetic material. If the ozone layer continues to thin, UVB will penetrate to the Earth's surface in greater amounts. UVB exposure has been linked to skin cancer (especially the nonmelanoma skin cancers, basal cell and squamous cell carcinoma) and damage to the lens and retina of the eye.

Possibly the most harmful by-product of increasing exposure to UVB, however, is immunosuppression. Skin that has been exposed to excessive UVB radiation appears less capable than nonexposed skin of performing immune surveillance tasks. In UVB-damaged skin the Langerhans cells, which constitute the body's first line of defense against infections, are impaired or destroyed. UVB-damaged skin also possesses fewer T cells, which are vital to the proper functioning of the immune system. Excessive UVB exposure can affect the course of infectious diseases of the skin, such as onchocerciasis; it also appears to suppress the immune responses of the skin to herpes simplex type II virus and seems to trigger recurrence of skin lesions from preexisting herpes infection. In short, all available evidence points to the likelihood that by lowering human immune defenses, increased UVB exposure related to ozone depletion may augment the potential for new diseases to emerge—or for existing illnesses to resurge.

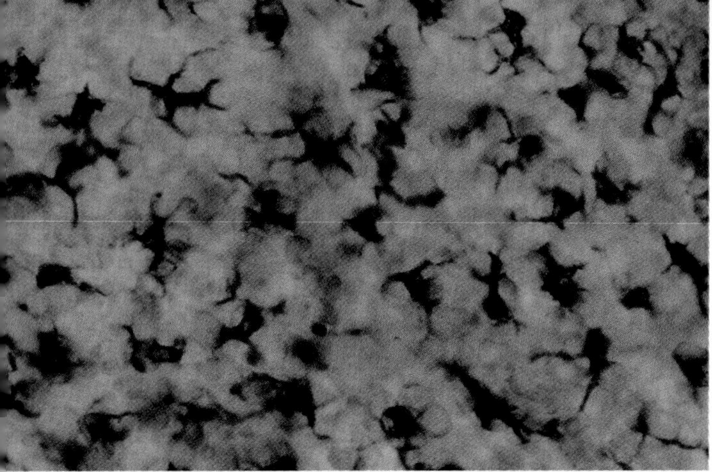

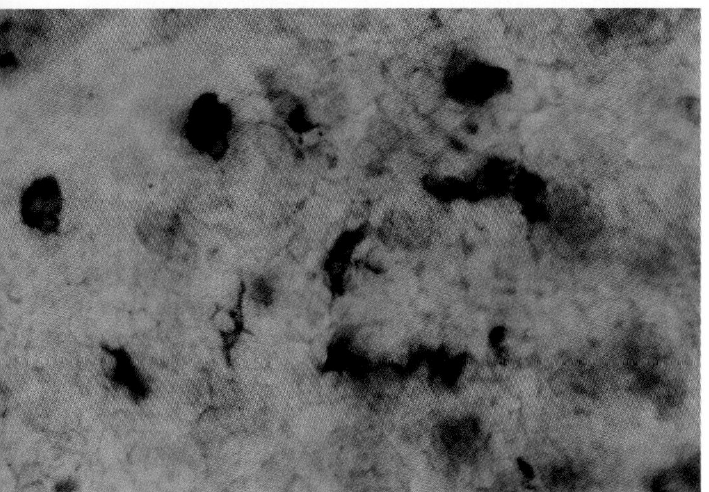

Amminikutty Jeevan, Margaret L. Kripke, University of Texas M.D. Anderson Cancer Center, Houston, Texas

Photomicrographs comparing normal human skin (top) with skin that has been exposed to ultraviolet-B (UVB) radiation (above); UBV damage is evidenced by depletion of the vital immune system cells known as Langerhans cells.

The next step

In September 1995, at the request of the White House, the National Academy of Sciences convened a conference on human health and global climate change. Addressing the meeting, Vice Pres. Al Gore emphasized the need for a coherent response to the health threats posed by global warming and warned of the dangers of delaying action.

That same year the APHA issued a statement citing global climate change as a major public health challenge. The statement strongly recommended improved monitoring of weather-related health problems through the use of state-of-the-art tools, such as remote sensing and geographic information systems. Remote sensing technology uses satellite imagery to provide data on changes in land-use patterns, habitat characteristics, and marine ecosystems. Geographic information systems are computer systems that can assemble, store, manipulate, and display data on such variables as disease distribution, climate variation, and demographic changes. In recent studies geographic information systems and satellite-generated vegetation maps were used to identify areas of the U.S. that would be receptive to dengue fever and Lyme disease.

The present system for monitoring weather-related health problems is generally inadequate, especially in less developed countries. One notable exception is WHO's Onchocerciasis Control Program, which monitors 300 locales in West Africa at least twice weekly to determine the numbers of blackflies and their movements over time. This surveillance program has led to improved efforts to control the disease, including eradication of the fly through pesticide use, provision of ivermectin to villagers in areas where the fly is prevalent, and collection of data on fly populations for use in computer modeling.

The IPCC has recommended that sophisticated watch/warning systems be developed to aid health authorities in predicting weather-related health problems. After the heat-related events of the summer of 1995, the National Oceanic and Atmospheric Administration (NOAA) endorsed implementation of new systems that would give public health officials in urban areas up to 48 hours to prepare for weather that could lead to significant increases in mortality. One such system was instituted in Philadelphia during that summer. The system forecasts the arrival of "oppressive" air masses, which represent weather situations historically associated with surges in death rates. A health watch is issued by the health commissioner if the air mass is forecast to arrive within 48 hours. A health warning is issued within 24 hours of arrival, and city agencies take steps to mitigate the potential impact of the stressful weather situation. One of these measures is to instruct the news media to advise the public that potentially dangerous weather is on the way and to offer suggestions on how to cope with the conditions. A telephone hot line is activated by the city to respond to specific questions, volunteers make personal visits to the homes of vulnerable individuals, and nursing homes are advised to prepare for impending conditions. Air-conditioned senior centers extend their hours of operation, and utility companies are urged not to shut off services during the heat warning. NOAA and the World Meteorological Organization are developing plans to broaden the scope of such systems and to offer all municipal health departments access to information on preparing for the arrival of oppressive weather.

While much remains to be done, major strides have been made in just the past few years toward developing a coordinated international program on the issue of climate and health. WHO, the World Meteorological Organization, and the UN Environment Programme have sponsored numerous meetings on this topic, and these have resulted in publications and plans for action. The need for better monitoring has been underscored, and various strategies have been suggested to reduce the impacts of weather and potential climate change on human health. Some of these strategies have already been implemented (*e.g.,* new watch/warning heat-advisory systems, improved surveillance of some vectorborne diseases), and professional organizations like the APHA are developing plans to educate health care workers and policy makers about efficient means to deal with climate-related health problems. These cooperative activities transcend the ongoing disagreement among atmospheric scientists about the scope, seriousness, and pace of climate change; those on all sides of the debate seem to agree that climate variability over the next century could have a serious health impact if strategies to avert such problems are not implemented.

—Laurence S. Kalkstein, Ph.D.

NEWS CAP

Do I Dare to Eat a Peach?

To eat or not to eat a peach, a strawberry, a green bean, or a brussels sprout? That is the question that the Environmental Working Group (EWG) set out to answer when it ranked 42 fruits and vegetables in order of their pesticide risk and recommended alternatives that would provide the same nutrients but contain only minimal pesticide residues. The group published its findings in *A Shopper's Guide to Pesticides in Produce* (1995).

The nonprofit research organization reviewed results of pesticide-residue tests that the Food and Drug Administration (FDA) performed on some 15,000 produce samples. Of all the foods tested, the most pesticide-laden were strawberries. As alternative sources of vitamin C, the EWG recommends blueberries, blackberries, oranges, grapefruit, kiwifruit, U.S.-grown cantaloupes, raspberries, and watermelons. The group estimates that by following its guidelines consumers could halve their pesticide-related health risks.

The rankings were based on both quantity and toxicity analyses. The quantity analysis measured the amount and number of pesticides found on a food sample or crop. The following questions were answered: (1) On what percentage of the crop was pesticide residue detected? (2) What percentage of the crop had two or more pesticides present? (3) What was the largest amount of pesticides found on a single sample? (4) How many pesticides were detected on the entire crop?

Once it had determined the contamination level of a food, the EWG established criteria by which the presence of pesticides could be understood relative to the health risks posed. Toxicity was determined by: (1) the potency of the average total residue of carcinogens, (2) the potency of the average total residue of neurotoxins (substances toxic to the nervous system), and (3) the average residue of endocrine and reproductive toxins (chemicals that disrupt hormonal function).

The 12 most contaminated fruits and vegetables in rank order were:

- strawberries
- bell peppers
- spinach
- U.S.-grown cherries
- peaches
- Mexican-grown cantaloupes
- celery
- apples
- apricots
- green beans
- Chilean-grown grapes
- cucumbers

The least contaminated types of produce were:

- avocados
- corn
- onions
- sweet potatoes
- cauliflower
- brussels sprouts
- U.S.-grown grapes
- bananas
- plums
- green onions
- watermelons
- broccoli

The EWG hoped its work would draw attention to a serious health issue, and indeed its efforts paid off. On Aug. 3, 1996, U.S. Pres. Bill Clinton signed into law the Food Quality Protection Act of 1996, a bill overhauling previous laws regulating pesticide residues in foods (some of which were considered too lenient, some too strict). Over a decade in the making, the new act had bipartisan support in both houses of Congress plus the endorsement of farmers, the food industry, environmentalists, and consumer groups. The legislation strengthens federal laws that govern chemical use and exposure and ends absolute prohibition of pesticides on produce when, for example, their use poses a one-in-a-million or less lifetime risk of cancer and when there is "reasonable certainty" that nobody will be harmed by their consumption. Most important, it mandates the most stringent limits for pesticide residues in foods consumed by infants and children. "I like to think of it as the 'peace of mind' act," said the president. "If a pesticide poses a danger to our children, then it won't be in our food." In addition, the legislation includes a "right to know" provision, requiring food stores to distribute information on pesticide residues and how consumers can minimize their risk from them.

The complete 45-page EWG report can be ordered from: Environmental Working Group, 1718 Connecticut Ave NW, Suite 600, Washington DC 20009; phone: 202-667-6982; fax: 202-232-2592; E-mail: info@ewg.org. It is also available on the World Wide Web at http://www.ewg.org.

Beyond shopping wisely, is there anything consumers can do to reduce their pesticide exposure? Authorities advise rinsing all fresh fruits and vegetables thoroughly in water. (Washing produce with detergents is *not* recommended.) Foods with edible peels should be scrubbed well, and the outer leaves of leafy vegetables like lettuce and cabbage should be discarded.

—*Katherine I. Gordon*

Ulcers Update

Approximately 10% of U.S. adults develop peptic ulcer disease sometime during their lifetime. An ulcer is a chronic sore located in the stomach or the first portion of the small intestine (the duodenum). In any one year about 4.5 million will experience ulcer symptoms, with 2.5 million of them seeking medical attention and about 500,000 being hospitalized. The annual cost attributed to peptic ulcer disease is $16 billion to $20 billion. The most common symptom of ulcer disease is pain in the upper abdomen that is relieved by eating or taking antacids. Until recently, peptic ulcer disease was thought to be related in some way to acid secretion, stress, or diet. In the last decade it has been proved that ulcer disease is one manifestation of an infection with a particular bacterium, *Helicobacter pylori*.

Legendary discovery

Today's insights into ulcers did not occur overnight. The story began long ago and includes research related to both peptic ulcer and gastric cancer. In 1930 gastric cancer was the most common cancer in American men. Since that time its incidence has fallen remarkably in the U.S., but it has remained high in many other countries. The last 100 years have witnessed a sharp increase followed by a decline in the frequency of peptic ulcer disease. Both gastric cancer and peptic ulcer disease are associated with chronic inflammation of the lining of the stomach, a condition called gastritis. Frequently, however, the term *gastritis* is used incorrectly by both patients and physicians to describe symptoms felt in the upper abdomen; in fact, most patients with gastritis do not have symptoms.

In 1985 Barry J. Marshall, then at Royal Perth Hospital in Australia, made himself sick in the name of science. He drank cultures of Helicobacter pylori *to demonstrate that the bacterium causes gastritis (in his case, a very painful inflammation of the stomach lining).*

Michael Bailey, University of Virginia

A rapid change in the frequency of a disease causes scientists to look for environmental factors that play a critical role in its development. For example, the rapid and dramatic increase in the incidence of lung cancer led scientists to evaluate and confirm the role of cigarette smoking as a causative factor. The observations that the incidence of gastric cancer and peptic ulcer varied greatly in different geographic regions and changed over time were strong evidence of the involvement of an environmental factor. One particularly intriguing fact was that individuals who migrated from regions with a high frequency of gastric cancer such as Japan, South Korea, or Peru to regions where gastric cancer was rare (*e.g.,* Canada, the U.S., or Germany) retained a high cancer risk. This observation suggested that exposure to an environmental factor or factors occurred at an early age. Attempts to find a single cause of gastritis were not fruitful until the mid-1970s, when pathologist Howard Steer in England noted that gastritis was associated with the presence of bacteria in the stomach. A similar observation was made independently by pathologist J. Robin Warren in Australia; in the early 1980s Barry J. Marshall, working with Warren and microbiologist Stewart Goodwin, succeeded in culturing the bacterium now known as *H. pylori. H. pylori* was proved to be the cause of gastritis when Marshall drank cultures of the bacteria and subsequently developed gastric inflammation. Cure of the infection, it had been shown, resulted in the healing of gastritis. These experiments proved that the bacterium did not simply colonize inflamed stomachs but actually caused the inflammation.

By the late 1980s it was generally accepted that infection with *H. pylori* causes gastritis, but proof was lacking that the infection is the cause of peptic ulcer disease. Proof was obtained in the early '90s when it was shown that elimination of the infection cures peptic ulcer disease and greatly reduces the likelihood of recurrence. Ulcer disease was transformed from a disease associated with stress to one caused either by infection with *H. pylori* or by the chronic use of nonsteroidal anti-inflammatory medications, such as aspirin, for treatment of arthritis. The stage was then set for development of effective therapies to cure the bacterial infection.

H. pylori are well adapted to living in the stomach, and the infected human stomach contains hundreds of millions of them. The bacteria do not invade the stomach wall but rather live in the mucous coating that lines the inside of the stomach cavity. The stomach is a very hostile place for bacterial survival, but *H. pylori* have adapted to living in an environment replete with acid and enzymes designed to digest dietary proteins. Some of the evolutionary adjustments that allow *H. pylori* to live under such conditions are their ability to avoid damage by acid, to swim rapidly with a darting motion through thick gastric mucus, and to attach to cells lining the stomach. Everyone with *H. pylori* infection has gastritis; however, no genetic features of the bacteria have been identified that reliably predict the fraction of infected individuals who will develop ulcer disease.

Becoming infected: who, when, where?

The primary reservoir for *H. pylori* infection is the human digestive tract. *H. pylori* has been cultured from human stools and has been detected in water contaminated with human wastes. The most common route of transmission is thought to be the fecal-oral route. The infection is usually acquired in childhood, and *H. pylori* infections cluster in families with children. While a single member of a family without children may be infected, the infection is commonly widespread in families with children. Such data suggest that infants and children not only are highly susceptible to infection but may have a role in spreading it as well. The two times in life when one is most likely to become infected are during childhood and as an adult living with young children in the family.

As with many other communicable diseases, the rate of acquisition of infection is higher under conditions of poor sanitation. Both the prevalence and the rate of acquisition of infection are high in people born in less developed countries. In the United States the frequency of *H. pylori* infection is low among those of high socioeconomic status. Because the infection is typically acquired in childhood, however, the critical factor affecting the likelihood of infection in adulthood is not an individual's current socioeconomic status but the status of his or her family during childhood. The features that promote transmission of the bacteria are those associated with poor hygiene, such as poverty and crowded living conditions.

Enlightened diagnosis

Most people who are infected with *H. pylori* do not know it, as they suffer no symptoms. Only about one in six infected persons will develop ulcer disease. The most common symptom of infection is recurring upper-abdominal pain that, as noted above, is relieved by food or antacid medication. When the infection is suspected, its presence can be confirmed by a variety of methods. The simplest approach is a blood test that detects antibodies against the bacterium.

Another method is a breath test that uses urea, the nitrogenous end-product of protein metabolism, to detect the presence of the enzyme urease. *H. pylori* contain large amounts of this enzyme, which splits urea into carbon dioxide and ammonia. This activity is thought to allow *H. pylori* to survive in the inhospitable acid environment of the stomach and to utilize the nitrogen from ammonia to help meet its metabolic requirements. The urea breath test is simple to administer. A small amount of urea is swallowed with water, and the presence of the bacterial enzyme in the stomach is identified by the rapid appearance in the breath of carbon dioxide produced from the urea. To identify that some of the exhaled carbon dioxide was generated from the urea, the test uses urea containing either the naturally occurring, nonradioactive isotope of carbon, carbon-13, or the radioactive isotope, carbon-14. The version of the test that uses radioactive carbon is not recommended for either children or pregnant women.

The original method of identifying the presence of *H. pylori* infection was endoscopy. Endoscopy is a procedure in which the patient swallows a flexible video camera, which allows a physician to view the stomach lining and obtain small biopsy samples. These scrapings are cultured in a laboratory dish or sectioned, stained, and examined under the microscope to see whether the bacteria are present. The availability of blood tests and the urea breath test has reduced the need to use the more difficult and invasive endoscopic procedure to diagnose *H. pylori* infection, but endoscopy is still required for obtaining a culture or excluding a malignancy. Such a culture, which determines the particular *H. pylori* strain, is especially important to help select the appropriate antibiotics for a patient who has failed to respond to standard antibiotic treatment. Because infection with *H. pylori* is difficult to cure, it is important after treatment to confirm that therapy has been successful. As the blood test remains positive for at least a year, even with clearing of infection, it cannot be used for this purpose. Either the urea breath test or endoscopy with biopsy is appropriate to prove that the bacteria have been eliminated.

Advances eliminate controversy

Although the understanding of the etiology of peptic ulcer disease has advanced by leaps and bounds, *H. pylori* infections have proved to be difficult to cure. A number of different treatment regimens have been devised; these will cure the infection in about 60% to 95% of patients. Current regimens require the taking of several antimicrobial drugs for one or more weeks. Unfortunately, like many other important bacterial pathogens today, *H. pylori* has readily become resistant to

Only in the past decade has it been proved that ulcers are an important manifestation of infection with H. pylori. *Hundreds of millions of the bacteria can live in the mucous layer lining the stomach. (The* H. pylori *shown below are magnified about 11,000 times.)*

P. Motta, Department of Anatomy, University "La Sapienza," Rome/Science Source/Photo Researchers

Infection-Free, Ulcer-Free[1]

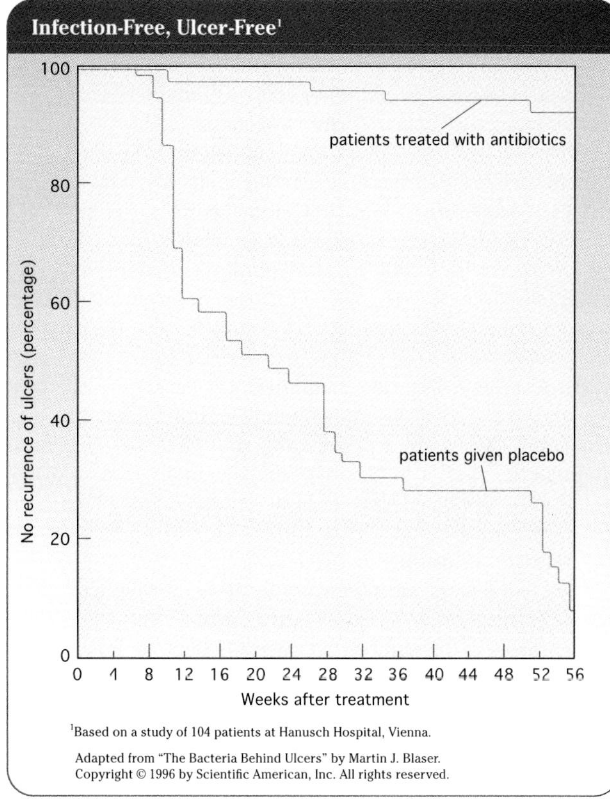

[1]Based on a study of 104 patients at Hanusch Hospital, Vienna.

Adapted from "The Bacteria Behind Ulcers" by Martin J. Blaser.

some of the most effective antimicrobials. The use of multiple drugs reduces the risk for development of resistance to a single antibiotic. One combination drug regimen—omeprazole and clarithromycin—was approved by the Food and Drug Administration (FDA) in April 1996. Another combination—ranitidine, bismuth subcitrate, and clarithromycin—was likely to be approved sometime after that. It is of interest that bismuth compounds (*e.g.,* Pepto-Bismol) were used for many years to treat ulcers, but only after the discovery of *H. pylori* was it recognized that the primary mode of action of bismuth was as an antibiotic. Worldwide, the most commonly used antibiotic combinations are tetracycline, metronidazole, and bismuth—often in conjunction with an antiulcer drug—and metronidazole, omeprazole, and clarithromycin. There are many unresolved questions regarding the optimal dosing schedules and durations of therapy.

Many myths and legends surround the "*Helicobacter pylori* story." One such myth is that it took a long time for antibacterial treatment to become widely used after Marshall's discovery. Actually, there was little delay. Previously available therapies for ulcer disease were effective in promoting healing of ulcers and providing relief from symptoms. Physicians wanted and needed proof that cure of the infection might cure ulcer disease and that the new approach to treatment was as effective as standard therapies. In addition, treatment of *H. pylori* infection could not be widely implemented until diagnostic tests and effective therapies had been developed and their uses and limitations established. By the time proof came that treatment of the infection actually cured ulcers (in the early 1990s), pharmaceutical companies had already begun trials to test new therapies. As noted, a new regimen has been approved and will be marketed in the U.S. in 1996. The urea breath test, which represents a rapid, noninvasive method of identifying the presence of the infection, is also brand new and is expected to become commercially available in 1996. In fact, the scientific knowledge of *H. pylori* organisms and the pathogenesis of infections has advanced rapidly, as many scientists turned their attention to this important problem as soon as it was identified. Most important, as data became available, there was general consensus among clinicians about how to diagnose and treat *H. pylori* infections.

The treatment dilemma

H. pylori infection is probably the most common chronic infection in humans. Because *H. pylori* infections are so widespread and the treatments are difficult, and not without risk, it is *not* currently recommended that *everyone* who is infected be treated. All patients with both *H. pylori* infection and peptic ulcer disease, however, should be treated, as it has been demonstrated conclusively that cure of the infection in such patients is of significant benefit. Unless *H. pylori* infection is cured, peptic ulcer disease requires chronic use of medication and is associated with a 15% to 20% lifetime risk of a major complication such as gastrointestinal hemorrhage. (The National Institutes of Health estimates that about 7,000 people die each year of ulcer-related complications.) Cure of the infection eliminates ulcer recurrences and thereby abolishes the symptoms associated with ulcer disease as well as any complications.

Currently, many patients with complaints that are suggestive of peptic ulcer disease are undergoing testing for *H. pylori* infection. Those who do have such an infection are receiving treatment on the premise that symptoms might be related to the infection. This is a controversial approach but not an unreasonable one.

Patients with primary gastric lymphoma, a malignant tumor of the lymphoid system, the system that produces cells and antibodies to regulate immunity, also should undergo treatment. With antibiotic therapy a majority of the tumors will go into remission and may even be cured.

Many of those patients with symptoms suggestive of an ulcer will not have ulcer disease but will have a condition called nonulcer dyspepsia. Most will not experience relief of symptoms with antibiotics because the symptoms were not caused by *H. pylori* infection. Though some noninfected patients will experience temporary improvement, such relief is not related to *H. pylori*. Abdominal symptoms, for example, can be caused by bacterial digestion of dietary sugars in the colon, and antibiotics may temporarily depress those bacteria and thus provide some transient relief. Patients with nonulcer dyspepsia represent a real dilemma if they obtain some benefit with the antibiotics. When the symptoms recur, they may want to be treated again because they are under the false impression that they have an infection that has not been cured. It will take a major effort to educate both physicians and patients about the reasonable expectations for therapy and the importance of confirming with the urea breath test that therapy has been successful.

What the future holds

Because infection with *H. pylori* is typically acquired in childhood, attempts are being made to identify behavioral modifications that could be instituted to prevent transmission. There are major research efforts under way to develop vaccines to prevent and possibly even to treat the infections. The results of vaccine experiments in animals so far have been encouraging, but moving from animal experiments to the development of an effective human vaccine against *H. pylori* will probably take a decade or more.

The progress in understanding, diagnosing, and treating *H. pylori*-related gastrointestinal disease has been remarkable and exciting. Medical scientists can realistically anticipate the day when peptic ulcer will be a historic disease. The recent approval by the FDA of the antibiotic combination therapy and the imminent approval of the urea breath test will provide the tools needed to identify and eliminate the infection from the groups of patients who are most likely to obtain some medical benefit. New and improved therapies are expected to be developed, and a vaccine has the potential to eliminate the infection and its associated diseases completely.

—*David Y. Graham, M.D.*

Hepatitis: From A to G

The word *hepatitis* is derived from the Greek words *hepar* ("liver") and *itis* ("inflammation"). It refers to any inflammation of the liver, regardless of the cause. Hepatitis may be either infectious—caused by an agent that produces infection—or noninfectious. Causes of noninfectious hepatitis include drugs and other substances that are toxic to the liver, the most common being alcohol.

At least six, and possibly seven, types of hepatitis-related viruses have been identified; these are the major infectious cause of the disease. Although other viruses also can produce inflammation of the liver, hepatitis is not their major clinical manifestation. Epstein-Barr virus, for example, causes infectious mononucleosis, a condition in which liver inflammation is a component. In addition, other types of infectious agents, including bacteria, fungi, and parasites, sometimes cause hepatitis.

Descriptions of hepatitis date to the 5th century BC. Beginning in the 8th century, periodic epidemics of the disease were documented. Many such epidemics occurred during wars, which thus inspired the term *campaign jaundice.* (Jaundice is the yellowish skin discoloration that is often a sign of hepatitis.) The term *infectious hepatitis* emerged in the late 19th and early 20th centuries. It was not until World War II, however, that it became clear that there were at least two distinct types of hepatitis. Since then, scientists have identified several more. Today the known hepatitis viruses are designated A, B, C, D, E, F, and G. Three of these—A, E, and F—are transmitted by contaminated food or water; B, C, D, and G are transmitted primarily by blood or bodily fluids. Over the past few decades, significant progress has been made in the understanding of these viruses, and advances in molecular biology have led to improved detection, treatment, and prevention.

Often misdiagnosed

The liver is the largest and heaviest solid organ in the body. It functions as both a factory, converting the nutrients in food into energy, and a waste-management plant, modifying various chemicals (including many drugs) and excreting them into the gastrointestinal tract through the bile ducts. When the liver is inflamed, these functions are impaired or stop altogether. In rare cases viral hepatitis leads to the massive destruction of liver cells, resulting in death.

The signs and symptoms of hepatitis are similar regardless of the cause; they include fatigue, loss of energy and appetite, fever, nausea, vomiting, abdominal pain, and, less commonly, rash and joint pains. These findings may be present in other disorders, and none is a specific indication of hepatitis. Consequently, the illness is often unsuspected or misdiagnosed. Some patients with hepatitis become jaundiced, developing, along with the typical yellow discoloration of the skin and the whites of the eyes, tea-colored urine and clay-colored bowel movements.

Even in patients who are symptom-free, evidence of either active or prior hepatitis infection can be detected by laboratory tests that assess liver function. The presence of liver damage, however, does not necessarily implicate a virus as the cause. Thus, specific diagnostic tests for the hepatitis viruses are necessary to identify the viral origin of liver inflammation.

Hepatitis A

Hepatitis A is the most common type of hepatitis worldwide. The illness does not lead to chronic liver disease, and most who are infected recover completely. The virus responsible is called the hepatitis A virus (HAV). According to the Centers for Disease Control and Prevention (CDC), about 143,000 cases of hepatitis A occur in the U.S. each year, with approximately 80 deaths. Worldwide the annual incidence exceeds 1.4 million cases. The disease occurs both sporadically (*i.e.,* as an occasional, single case) and in epidemic form. Illness develops in 15 to 50 days after infection, the average time being 28 days. HAV is generally transmitted by the fecal-oral route (*i.e.,* via ingestion of contaminated food or water) and may be spread by poor personal hygiene or inadequate sanitation. Among residents of developed countries, the spread of the virus occurs as a result of contact with infected individuals—particularly within households and in day-care centers—and travel in less developed countries.

In the past two years, hepatitis A outbreaks associated with the use of clotting factor have been reported among persons with hemophilia in Italy, Ireland, Germany, and Belgium. The first such cases in the U.S. were reported in late 1995; in response, the CDC suggested in February 1996 that physicians consider immunization against HAV for all susceptible patients receiving clotting factor.

There are three general strategies for prevention of hepatitis A. First, hygienic measures—sanitary disposal of human waste, maintenance of adequate water-quality standards—can reduce the risk of infection. Second, the disease may be prevented by an injection of immune serum globulin, a blood product made from immune system constituents of persons known to have been exposed to the virus. This form of prevention is called passive immunization. Unfortunately, if not administrated within two weeks following exposure, immune globulin (also called immunoglobulin) does not prevent hepatitis A, although it may decrease the severity of symptoms.

The third strategy for the prevention of hepatitis A is vaccination; the first vaccine approved for HAV in the U.S. became available in 1995; a second was licensed in 1996. The current vaccines are "killed," or inactivated, products, made by purifying HAV grown in the laboratory; the virus is then inactivated with chemicals. The inactivation method is essentially the same as that used for the inactivated poliovirus vaccine, better known as the Salk vaccine (after its discoverer, Jonas Salk). Inactivated HAV vaccines are very effective in producing an immune response and have been shown in two clinical studies to confer very high levels of protection against hepatitis A. Despite this record of success, a few questions remain about the future of inactivated HAV vaccines. For one, they are very expensive, which makes it unlikely that they will be widely used in less developed countries, where the disease is most prevalent. Second, the duration of the immune response to inactivated vaccines is still unknown, and it will take many more years of study before this information is available.

When viruses are grown for a long period of time in the laboratory, they often lose their ability to cause disease in humans. This reduction in virulence is called attenuation. Examples of live, attenuated vaccines include the Sabin vaccine for polio (named after Albert Sabin), the chicken pox vaccine, and the measles, mumps, and rubella vaccines. Such agents have several potential advantages over inactivated vaccines, including lower cost, the need for only a single dose, and, possibly, the induction of longer-lasting immunity.

An attenuated HAV vaccine was licensed in China in 1992, and several others have undergone limited clinical trials. In Chinese trials the vaccine produced an immune response in 96–99% of school-age recipients four weeks after immunization and prevented the development of hepatitis A. Although the attenuated HAV vaccine eventually may be widely used in less developed countries, concerns remain because it does not appear to stimulate immune responses as well as the inactivated vaccine, and it may even cause mild hepatitis in some cases.

Still another vaccine approach involves viruses that contain purposely altered genetic material. In the laboratory these so-called recombinant viruses have been shown to produce noninfectious HAV virus particles when they replicate, and in animal trials they have successfully generated antibodies against HAV. Thus, recombinant HAV vaccines appear to be feasible. Such agents could be produced more rapidly and less expensively than inactivated vaccines, but whether they offer a significant immunologic advantage remains to be determined.

Water-purification projects like this one in rural Rwanda are helping to reduce the risk of hepatitis A in less developed countries. Worldwide, this is the most common type of hepatitis, accounting for an estimated 1.4 million cases per year.

Betty Press—Panos Pictures

Hepatitis B

Because it was first observed to occur in patients after blood transfusions or exposure to used, nonsterile needles, hepatitis B was once commonly called serum hepatitis. After the isolation in 1967 of the viral protein dubbed Australia antigen (now known as hepatitis B surface antigen), the hepatitis B virus (HBV) itself was identified and characterized.

Unlike hepatitis A, hepatitis B causes both acute and chronic illness. The time between exposure to the virus and the onset of symptoms is from 40 days to 6 months, and the illness tends to be more severe and protracted than hepatitis A. Overall, some 5–10% of adult HBV infections become chronic, although some individuals with chronic infection do not develop active liver disease. Nevertheless, active liver disease leading to permanent scarring, or cirrhosis, of the liver can develop. The likelihood that hepatitis B will become chronic depends in part on the age of the individual at the time of infection and in part on the nature of the symptoms that develop during the acute infection. It appears that developing jaundice and having a more protracted illness are associated with a *decreased* risk of developing chronic infection. Some authorities postulate that the immune system is better able to eradicate the virus in these cases. Young children are at greater risk for chronic infection than are other age groups. The immune systems of newborns cannot effectively combat HBV infection; consequently, some 90% of children born to women with active hepatitis B become chronically infected.

Hepatitis B occurs worldwide, but infection rates are highest in Asia, Africa, and Oceania, where it is a significant cause of chronic liver disease. According to the World Health Organization, hepatitis B infection is the ninth major cause of death worldwide, and hundreds of millions of people are chronically infected. Carriers of the virus are about 100 times more likely to develop liver cancer (hepatocellular carcinoma) than are people who do not have HBV in their blood. HBV therefore is second only to tobacco as a known human carcinogen.

Fortunately, an effective vaccine is available to prevent HBV infection. As in the case of HAV, passive immunization with hepatitis B immunoglobulin can prevent infection or lessen symptoms if given within 48 hours after exposure. The immunoglobulin is prepared from the plasma of people with high levels of hepatitis B surface antibody. If hepatitis B immunoglobulin is given to an infant within 12 hours of birth, the baby's risk of developing persistent HBV infection is reduced by about 70%. Administering both hepatitis B immunoglobulin and the HBV vaccine to newborns at risk for the disease reduces the rate of transmission by more than 90%.

Because many countries, the U.S. included, did not recommend universal HBV immunization of children until around 1992, and most countries did not implement this policy until 1996, the duration of immunity remains a question. Only long-term observation of vaccinees will provide the answer. Booster doses could improve the duration of immunity, but it is not yet known if such a step will be necessary. Moreover, as more people are vaccinated, and the chance of exposure to HBV is reduced, the need for booster doses may also be reduced.

The first HBV vaccine was made in the late 1970s by purifying HBV particles from the blood of infected people and inactivating the virus by chemical treatment. Newer vaccines use the hepatitis B surface antigen to evoke an immune response. The antigen is produced by recombinant DNA technology, which thus decreases the cost and increases the safety of the vaccine. In Asia, where HBV infection is prevalent, mass immunization has been under way for many years. Pregnant women are routinely tested for HBV infection. The babies of those found to be infected usually receive HBV immunoglobulin within 12 hours of birth in addition to a full course of three doses of vaccine. Immunization rates are high in countries like Singapore, where mass immunization is conducted by the local government and health department.

The long-term success of mass immunization programs could be threatened by the emergence of mutated viruses against which the vaccine is useless. While such virus variants have been identified in individual patients, they do not seem to have been transmitted to others. Nevertheless, the spread of vaccine-resistant variants remains a possibility. If the number of potential variants is limited, it may be possible to alter the HBV vaccine to expand the effectiveness of immunization. In addition to vaccine-resistant mutations, scientists have also identified HBV variants that have other mutations. These virus variants, in which a specific region of the virus is altered, appear to cause more severe disease than the originally recognized types of HBV. Most cases of fulminant hepatitis (*i.e.,* extremely severe, rapidly progressing disease), which has a mortality rate of up to 50%, are associated with infection with these latter mutant viruses, although the connection between fulminant disease and infection with these mutants is still unclear.

Because of the severity of hepatitis B and the likelihood that the infection will become chronic, several different antiviral therapies have been tried. At present, alpha interferon appears to be the most effective; in selected patients it offers up to a 40% chance of long-term improvement. It is most effective in those with infection of relatively short duration and evidence of active liver inflammation. In patients with mild liver inflammation, however, the response to alpha interferon alone is poor.

Antiviral agents developed for treating other viruses also show promise against chronic hepatitis B. One that has been used in limited trials is 3TC, or lamivudine, a drug recently approved for treatment of HIV infection. A few antiviral drugs are being studied in combination with interferon, and it appears that some of these combinations may be more effective than either drug alone.

Hepatitis C

Once scientists had developed diagnostic tests for HBV, the U.S. and many other industrialized countries instituted universal screening of blood donors to prevent transmission of HBV via blood transfusion. Although this practice resulted in a significant reduction in the number of cases of post-transfusion hepatitis B, the overall incidence of transfusion-related hepatitis remained high. It became clear that most such cases were caused by neither HAV nor HBV; hence,

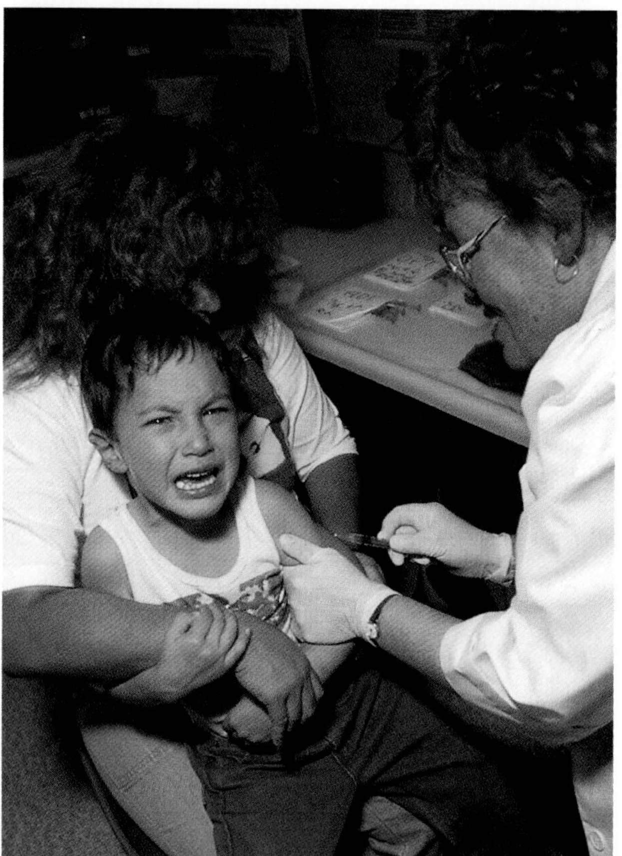

(Top) Hank Morgan—Rainbow/PNI; (bottom) David Manoug—Impact Visuals

(Left) Hepatitis B vaccine is purified during the manufacturing process. Today's vaccine, which uses a viral surface antigen to evoke an immune response, is less costly to produce than earlier versions, as well as being safer. (Bottom) A California youngster is immunized against hepatitis B. Current U.S. guidelines recommend that all children receive three doses of the vaccine during the first four years of life.

the term "non-A, non-B" (NANB) hepatitis was introduced. Many years of effort to find the responsible agent finally paid off in 1988 when researchers successfully identified the genetic material of the major posttransfusion NANB virus. They named the new agent the hepatitis C virus (HCV). Almost immediately, blood tests were developed to detect HCV antibodies, and testing of blood donors was begun. In the U.S., HCV is estimated to be responsible for about 170,000 infections a year.

Early diagnostic methods for HCV depended on the detection of antibodies to a viral protein. This test was reasonably sensitive, but because it was not specific for HCV, false-positive test results were common. In addition, some individuals in the early phase of HCV infection were missed. Subsequent tests offered increased sensitivity and specificity, but there remained some risk of false-positive tests. To further reduce this risk, more sophisticated assays were developed. These are used not for primary screening but to confirm the positive findings of the other screening tests. Unfortunately, some people with HCV infection lack the antibodies that are recognized by the confirming tests; thus, the current procedure still occasionally fails to detect a small percentage of HCV infections. Several methods now under development identify the virus itself rather than viral antibodies. Often such assays can detect HCV infection in people who test negative for HCV antibody.

Alpha interferon is the only treatment presently approved in the U.S. for hepatitis C virus infection. Only about half the patients respond to treatment, however, and about half of these will relapse when drug treatment is discontinued. Thus, at most, 25% of those who receive alpha interferon have a long-lasting response. In addition, the drug is very expensive, must be given by intramuscular injection, and has many side effects. Because of the many drawbacks of the only available therapy for HCV infection, and because two out of three who become infected develop chronic disease, HCV is currently the leading cause of chronic liver disease leading to liver transplantation.

It may be many years before a vaccine capable of preventing HCV infection becomes available. Passive immunization appears to delay the onset of infection but does not prevent it. At present, therefore, the only way to stop transmission of HCV is to prevent exposure to the virus. Screening of blood and organ donors is currently the best way to do this. Unfortunately, these measures do nothing to prevent the spread of HCV among one important risk group, injecting drug users. One British study found that the sexual partners of injecting drug users had risks of HCV infection that were two to four times normal; the drug injectors themselves had a more than 300-fold higher risk. The researchers suggested that needle sharing may, in fact, be the primary mode of HCV transmission.

Hepatitis D

Delta hepatitis, or hepatitis D virus (HDV) infection, was first detected in patients with hepatitis B and subsequently was found to occur only in conjunction with active HBV infection. HDV infection has been reported worldwide; the prevalence rate is particularly high in the Mediterranean Basin, South America, the Middle East, West Africa, and certain South Pacific islands. Transmission of HDV requires either simultaneous transmission of HBV or infection of HBV carriers with HDV. Like HBV, HDV is transmitted by sexual contact or by exposure to contaminated blood. HDV infection appears to be more severe, however, and up to 20% of people coinfected with hepatitis B and D die during the acute infection, compared with fewer than 1% of those who have hepatitis B alone. When chronic hepatitis B is complicated by HDV infection, a bout of acute hepatitis often occurs, followed in almost all cases by the development of chronic delta hepatitis. Up to 80% of persons with chronic delta hepatitis develop cirrhosis and complications of chronic liver disease. In contrast, only 15–30% of those with chronic hepatitis B experience complications of liver failure.

Those at risk for HDV infection include people with severe hepatitis B infection, patients with chronic hepatitis B who develop acute hepatitis, and those with rapidly progressive HBV-induced liver disease. Antibodies to HDV can be detected in the blood of individuals with chronic HBV and HDV infection. Chronic hepatitis D is treated with alpha interferon, administrated at high doses starting in the early phase of infection. Treatment should last for at least one year. Even if tests show that the patient's blood has been cleared of HDV, interferon should be continued until there is evidence that HBV too has been eliminated. Prevention of hepatitis B will automatically prevent hepatitis D; thus, hepatitis B vaccination and hepatitis B immunoglobulin are effective means of preventing coinfection with HDV.

Hepatitis E

In the early 1980s occasional cases and outbreaks of acute viral hepatitis were reported in Asia and India. These illnesses appeared to have been caused by an agent that was unrelated to either HAV or HBV. Transmission was primarily water- or foodborne; thus, the illness was originally called enterically transmitted non-A, non-B hepatitis (ET-NANB). The virus is now referred to as HEV.

One of the earliest reports of illness later attributed to this type of hepatitis came from New Delhi in 1955–56, when 30,000 cases of disease were identified following widespread fecal contamination of the city's drinking water. The virus was identified by electron microscopy in 1984, and in 1990 its genetic material was cloned. In recent years a great deal has been learned about HEV, and diagnostic tests have been developed.

The clinical manifestations of hepatitis E are similar to those of the other forms of viral hepatitis, except that severe infection and death are more common, occurring in more than 1% of cases. The death rate is particularly high among pregnant women—up to 50%. The diagnosis of acute hepatitis E is made by antibody testing and an epidemiological history that supports the probability of exposure to the virus. A recombinant DNA vaccine has proved successful in preventing HEV infection in experimental animals.

F and G: new guys on the block

Although HAV and HEV are responsible for almost all cases of enterically transmitted hepatitis, isolated cases have occurred that could not be attributed to either of these viruses or to HBV or HCV. These cases have been seen in England, northern Italy, France, the United States, and India. In 1994 a preliminary report by researchers in France suggested that a novel agent, which the authors called HFV (F for France), was responsible for these sporadic non-A, non-E hepatitis cases. HFV particles resemble HAV and HEV under the electron microscope, but the genetic material of HFV appears to be DNA rather than the RNA common to HAV and HEV. HFV may be responsible for up to 60% of enterically transmitted non-A, non-B hepatitis, but further work will be required before this virus can be firmly identified as a cause of human hepatitis.

Despite the fact that sensitive and specific tests to detect the hepatitis A, B, C, D, and E viruses have been available for a few years, a substantial portion of hepatitis cases could not be attributed to any of these organisms. The existence of these baffling cases strongly suggested that there were other, as-yet-unidentified hepatitis-causing agents. Indeed, in 1995 scientists found an entirely new group of three closely related hepatitis viruses, which they named the GB viruses (after the initials of the patient from whose blood they were first isolated).

Then, in January 1996, researchers announced that they had discovered still another hepatitis virus, which was designated HGV. Subsequent studies indicated that HGV and one of the GB viruses are virtually identical. HGV appears to be responsible for a substantial portion of cases of bloodborne and sexually transmitted hepatitis. It is capable of causing both acute and chronic disease.

While both HCV and HGV belong to the same genus in the flavivirus family (the family that includes the yellow fever and dengue fever viruses), they are only distantly related. Risk factors for HGV infection include blood transfusion, injecting drug use, and multiple sexual partners. Coinfection with HCV appears to be common—about 20% of those infected with HCV also show evidence of HGV infection. Approximately 15% of injecting drug users and 20% of multiple transfusion recipients have persistent HGV infection, and one recent study in the U.S. found that 1–2% of blood donors have a previously undetected HGV infection. Currently, there is no commercially available blood test to detect HGV; diagnosis depends on isolation of HGV RNA using a gene-amplification method. Little is known about the global distribution or clinical manifestations of the virus or the relationship, if any, with liver cancer. Nonetheless, the identification of HGV should rapidly lead to an increased understanding of this newly discovered source of infection.

—Jian-Qiu Han, M.D., and Jack Thomas Stapleton, M.D.

The Genetics of Violence: A Controversial Conference

If genes mold human physiology and physiology influences behavior, then behavior—including antisocial behavior such as violent crime—may have a genetic component. Crime, some scientists go on to argue, might therefore be understood and treated from a biological standpoint. And in a nation wracked by violence, many people consider the possibility that genetic research could one day help to prevent or control some forms of criminality to be too important to ignore.

Yet Americans have grim memories of "scientific" government programs for weeding out unwanted groups or behaviors. The eugenics movement, which led to the forced sterilization of thousands of supposedly feebleminded individuals starting in about 1900 and continuing into the 1970s, is the most haunting example. As a result, many sociologists, historians, minority advocates, and others doubt whether society can apply insights from genetic research cautiously or fairly.

How science can be used to combat criminal violence while averting a renewed campaign of state-sanctioned injustice was the troublesome question confronting participants at a conference on "The Meaning and Significance of Research on Genetics and Criminal Behavior," for which the University of Maryland served as host in September 1995. Researchers in behavioral genetics, neurobiology, animal behavior, and criminology mixed with historians, philosophers, and ethicists at the three-day conference, which surveyed the approaches researchers are taking today toward understanding the possible connections between genetics and crime, as well as some of the basic conceptual and ethical problems raised by these studies.

Can criminal tendencies be transmitted from parent to child in the same way as eye color or illnesses such as Huntington's disease—*i.e.,* through a special combination of genes? If so—and if it becomes possible to test whether an individual carries "criminal" genes—how should this knowledge be used? How can complex social traits such as criminality even be defined in biological terms?

Disagreement over such questions runs deep, as could be seen in the furor created by the conference itself. Supported by a grant from the U.S. National Institutes of Health (NIH), the conference was originally to have been held in 1992, but the agency withdrew its sponsorship after African-American leaders and others denounced the conference's subject as inherently racist and authoritarian. Conference organizer David Wasserman, a legal scholar and researcher at the University of Maryland's Institute for Philosophy and Public Policy, later

NEWS CAP

Mapping Human Genes: 3,600—and Counting

The Human Genome Project, the program to identify and analyze each of the estimated 50,000 to 100,000 human genes, marked the end of its first six years ahead of schedule and under budget. Genes currently are being discovered at the rate of several per month. The number of mapped genes grew from about 1,700 in 1990 to more than 3,600 in 1995.

The initial tasks of the project were to construct both a genetic linkage map and a physical map of the entire genome. A genetic linkage map identifies the relative position on each chromosome of genes and other distinctive DNA sequences—collectively called genetic markers—on the basis of how often certain markers are inherited together.

A physical map, on the other hand, provides the location of genetic markers on the chromosome in terms of the linear sequence of the bases (the structural units of DNA). A map with this level of detail is needed to achieve one of the chief goals of the project—determining the exact sequence of the three billion bases that constitute the human genome. The genomes of model organisms, including several bacteria, a yeast, a roundworm, and a mouse, also were to be mapped.

Considerable progress was made toward these goals in the past year. A major milestone was reached in April 1996 when an international team of scientists announced that they had completed work on the sequencing of the yeast genome. Comprehensive genetic maps of both human and mouse were published; this marked the completion of the genetic mapping phase of the project.

A partially completed physical map of the human genome, constructed by a research team at the Whitehead Institute for Biomedical Research, Cambridge, Mass., was published in the Dec. 22, 1995, issue of *Science.* The map consisted of sequence-tagged sites (STSs), short stretches of DNA that occur only once in the genome and whose location and sequence were already known. This version included about 15,000 STSs located about 200 kilobases (2,000 bases) apart. The team's targeted goal is to produce a map with 30,000 STSs at approximately 100-kilobase intervals. Although incomplete, the physical map affords enough information to allow researchers to begin the enormous task of sequencing the entire genome. Francis Collins, director of the National Center for Human Genome Research, Bethesda, Md., estimated that 99% of the sequence could be completed by the year 2002.

—*M.J. Friedrich*

won new NIH funding, allowing the conference to go forward with a revised agenda that focused more on the social and ethical difficulties raised by genetic studies of criminality than on the studies themselves. But the revisions did not mollify critics, some of whom appeared at the conference and angrily disrupted the proceedings.

Some protesters feared that even a discussion of genetic research on crime might presage action—notably action by law-enforcement agencies or the criminal justice system against groups that might be judged to be genetically predisposed to crime. The conference participants were also concerned about the potential abuses of the research, but they spent much of their time assessing the quality and significance of the research itself. Those conducting the work and those analyzing it from legal, ethical, or social perspectives all admitted at the conference's end that much remains to be learned about the connections between biology and criminal behavior—and whether these connections might be exploited wisely.

Discarded theories, unanswered questions

Research into the biological roots of violence and crime has a long and dubious pedigree. Many theories once thought to be compelling have since been discredited. In the early 1960s, for example, several researchers proposed that violent behavior by some men could be attributed to the presence of an extra Y chromosome in their cells. (The nucleus of virtually every human cell normally contains 46 chromosomes, including two sex chromosomes. Men carry one X and one Y chromosome, while women carry two X chromosomes. Occasionally, a human egg is fertilized by a defective sperm carrying two Y chromosomes, which creates an XYY male.) One study, published in the journal *Nature* in 1965, found that male prisoners confined to a mental hospital in Scotland carried extra Y chromosomes at a rate 20 times greater than that in the general population.

The media widely reported this and similar findings, and the idea that XYY men carry an extra dose of "maleness" and are therefore more aggressive became an item of popular lore. Subsequent studies exploded this idea, however, revealing that most XYY men in prisons had not committed violent crimes and that XYY men in the general population were not especially aggressive.

In fact, no ironclad proof has yet emerged linking criminal behavior to a person's genetic makeup. Many experts, including behavioral geneticists, neuropathologists, criminal justice experts, and others, believe that the time has come for a redoubled scientific effort to examine the question. One reason is that some recent statistical studies have suggested that criminal traits are heritable. (Geneticists say a trait is heritable if similarities in the trait among members of a group depend on how closely the group members are related by their genes.) Several studies of twins in North America, Japan, and Denmark, for example, indicate that if one twin has committed a crime, the likelihood that the other twin has also committed a

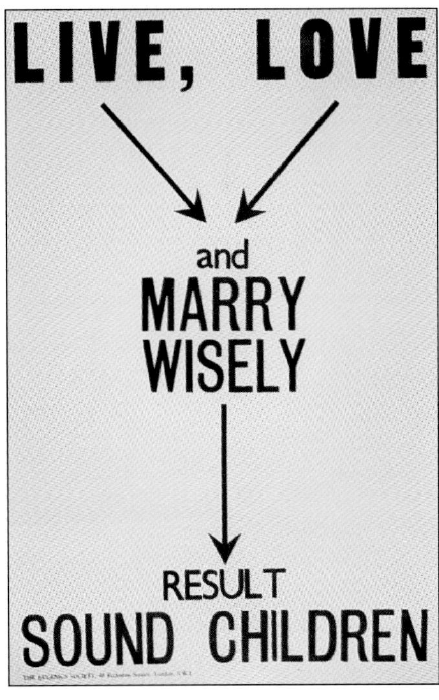

The posters at right are a grim reminder of an era when eugenic principles were used to justify oppression and even extermination of certain groups of people considered "undesirable" or "biologically inferior" by others.

Photographs, Wellcome Institute Library, London

crime is higher when the twins are monozygotic, or identical (descended from a single fertilized egg and therefore sharing exactly the same set of genes), than when they are dizygotic, or fraternal (descended from two eggs fertilized separately).

Another reason for the increased sense of urgency is the ongoing revolution in scientists' ability to decipher the genetic code of many organisms, including humans. The U.S. government-funded Human Genome Project, the envisioned 15-year effort to identify the chromosomal locations and nucleotide sequences of each of the estimated 50,000 to 100,000 human genes, is well on its way to completion. While it will take much longer to discover each gene's place in the body's complex biochemical pathways, the technological improvements spurred by the project will themselves make it feasible to screen a person's entire complement of DNA for "aberrant" genes—opening up the possibility of a systematic search for genetic markers of antisocial behavior.

Early controversy

Indeed, the NIH's National Center for Human Genome Research, which administers the Human Genome Project, was the initial sponsor of the planned Maryland conference. In 1992 the center's Ethical, Legal, and Social Implications Program approved a $78,000 grant for the conference, which was originally to be entitled "Genetic Factors in Crime: Findings, Uses, and Implications." According to a brochure written by Wasserman and borrowing language from the conference proposal, "genetic research holds out the prospect of identifying individuals who may be predisposed to certain kinds of criminal conduct, of isolating environmental features which trigger those predispositions, and of treating some predispositions with drugs and unintrusive therapies."

While thousands of academic conferences pass unnoticed by the general public each year, the Maryland conference was to be an exception. In a talk-show appearance on the Black Entertainment Television cable channel in July 1992, psychiatrist Peter Breggin, director of the Center for the Study of Psychiatry, Bethesda, Md., and an outspoken critic of the use of psychotropic medications, attacked the assumptions behind

Maryland psychiatrist Peter Breggin argues that studies of genetics and crime are scientifically baseless and inherently racist.

NEWS CAP

Cystic Fibrosis: Answers Raise Questions

Since the discovery in 1989 of the cystic fibrosis (CF) gene, significant strides have been made in managing this life-shortening disease. At the same time, those advances revealed unanticipated complexities that called into question long-held assumptions about CF. But in the past year or so, some scientifically important steps were taken toward better understanding of a complex condition.

CF is the most common genetic disorder of Caucasians; in the U.S. approximately one in every 2,500 children of European heritage is affected. The inheritance pattern is recessive—a child must inherit two copies of the defective gene, one from each parent, in order to develop the disease. Even when an individual inherits two defective copies of the gene, his or her illness does not follow a set course; age at onset, degree of severity, and clinical manifestations may vary widely.

The gene, called the *CFTR* (cystic fibrosis transmembrane conductance regulator) gene, normally encodes a protein that transports chloride across the cell membrane and thus enables cells to maintain a proper balance of salt and water. Mutations in the *CFTR* gene interfere with the proper functioning of the protein. The cells of epithelial tissues—mucus-secreting tissues that line many organs and ducts—are the body cells most affected by this dysfunction. In people with CF, epithelial tissues produce an excess of mucus. This excess is the most prominent underlying cause of CF symptoms. The mucus blocks the flow of vital secretions such as digestive enzymes. In the lungs, accumulation of mucus impairs breathing and traps infection-causing bacteria. Although treatment has increased survival, most CF patients do not live beyond age 30.

Tests that detect mutations in the gene can be used to diagnose CF prenatally and to screen prospective parents who may be carriers (*i.e.,* possess a single mutated copy of the *CFTR* gene). It had been hoped that once the gene was identified, the entire U.S. population could be screened. This the conference as scientifically baseless. Because a disproportionate number of Americans arrested for violent crimes are members of minority groups, Breggin argued, government funding of a conference on genetics and crime was tantamount to "the kind of racist behavior we saw on the part of Nazi Germany." After Breggin's appearance, calls protesting the conference flooded the NIH's Office of Minority Affairs.

Further undermining the originally planned conference were misperceptions that it was part of a federal multiagency "violence initiative" that was coordinated by Frederick Goodwin, then director of the Alcohol, Drug Abuse and Mental Health Administration. In describing the initiative before a federal mental health advisory committee earlier in 1992, Goodwin had provoked controversy with an ill-considered comparison between hyperaggressive monkeys in the wild and inner-city youths. "Maybe it isn't just the careless use of the word when people call certain areas of certain cities jungles," Goodwin had said. That remark drew strong criticism from members of the Congressional Black Caucus, and in his television appearance Breggin linked the Maryland conference to the violence initiative. (In fact, the decision to fund the conference was not connected to the initiative.)

In late July, reacting to mounting public criticism, then NIH director Bernadine Healy suspended the conference's grant. In September she informed the University of Maryland that before funds could be released, the conference would have to be redesigned to address critics' concerns. Wasserman and the university submitted a revised brochure and agenda to the NIH, but in April 1993 the NIH administration terminated the grant.

The university, protesting what it saw as a violation of academic freedom and of the NIH's contractual obligations, appealed the decision and prevailed. An administrative appeals board found the termination "arbitrary and capricious" and ordered the NIH administration to conditionally reinstate the grant, permitting Wasserman to put the conference back together. What resulted was an event with an increased budget and expanded agenda. The rescheduled conference included sessions devoted to findings, approaches, and possible uses of research on genetics and crime. It also scheduled individual sessions that would examine the quality of the research on crime and genetics, the legacy of previous attempts to link biology and crime, the public's perceptions of genetics research, and issues of race and discrimination.

Tantalizing leads

On Sept. 22, 1995, some 70 conference participants, including several reporters, finally gathered at Wye Woods, a secluded retreat on Maryland's eastern shore. Irving Gottesman, a behavioral geneticist from the University of Virginia, opened the meeting by presenting an overview of the results of current research on genetics and criminal behavior. While stressing that no behavioral trait can ever be attributed entirely to a person's genetic endowment, Gottesman also stated unapologetically that "genes are among the risk factors relevant to psychopathology." He summarized studies that found antisocial or criminal behavior to be highly correlated in monozygotic twins, whether they were reared together or apart. According to other studies, adopted children whose biological

idea proved impractical, however. For one thing, more than one altered version of the *CFTR* gene has been found, and most tests are not sensitive enough to detect every one. (The most common mutation accounts for about 70% of cases, but more than 400 other alterations have been identified.)

The results of a gene therapy trial reported in the autumn of 1995 were disappointing (*The New England Journal of Medicine,* Sept. 28, 1995). The researchers attempted to introduce healthy copies of the *CFTR* gene into the lungs of patients in order to reduce the buildup of mucus.

First, healthy copies of the gene were incorporated into the genetic material of adenoviruses, organisms that cause respiratory infections. The genetically altered adenoviruses were then applied to the patients' nasal passages. Although some nasal epithelial cells did take up the gene, insufficient amounts of the protein were produced. The investigators attributed the failure to the poor ability of the virus to enter the epithelial cells. They remained hopeful, however, that new techniques of gene delivery would produce better results.

An additional clue to the disease process may have been uncovered in 1996 by scientists at the University of Iowa College of Medicine, Iowa City. They reported (in *Cell,* April 19, 1996) that cells lining the inner surface of the lung produce a natural antibiotic-like substance capable of killing several microorganisms. This natural antibiotic is inactivated, however, in a high-salt environment such as that in the lungs of people with CF, a finding that could facilitate the search for more effective treatments.

In the meantime, investigators at the University of Alabama School of Medicine, Birmingham, reported (in *Nature Medicine,* April 1996) that one class of antibiotics commonly prescribed for treatment of infections in CF may actually combat the disease itself. Their findings suggested that the continued use of the antibiotics known as aminoglycosides (*e.g.,* gentamicin, streptomycin, neomycin) would be helpful for at least some patients. Though the CF challenge remains, these were small but hopeful steps in the right direction.

—*M.J. Friedrich*

parents have been arrested are two times more likely to have been convicted of a felony themselves than are adopted children whose adoptive parents have been arrested—evidence, Gottesman said, that while neither nature nor nurture rigidly determines a person's future, both are very important.

Abnormalities in the body's chemistry are one mechanism by which a person's genetic legacy makes itself felt, argued other researchers at the conference. Neurobiologist David Goldman of the National Institute on Alcohol Abuse and Alcoholism cited a 1993 study in which researchers tied repeated incidents of violence and arrest in members of a family in The Netherlands to an inherited defect in the gene that encodes (*i.e.,* directs the synthesis of) monoamine oxidase A, an enzyme that normally inactivates the neurotransmitter norepinephrine. A number of other single-gene changes have also been found to result in neuropsychiatric disorders, Goldman said, including a mutation in the gene encoding the thyroid hormone receptor molecule in some individuals with attention-deficit/hyperactivity disorder.

Psychologist Adrian Raine of the University of Southern California proposed that low arousal levels might be another heritable marker that predisposes an individual to criminal behavior. In one study in the United Kingdom, arousal-level indicators such as resting heart rate, skin electrical conductance, and electroencephalograph patterns were measured in 15-year-old schoolboys, and the subjects were followed for the next nine years. Heart rates were significantly lower among the boys who went on to be arrested. Perhaps low arousal is a sign of fearlessness, Raine speculated, or perhaps violent individuals seek special stimulation to compensate for their low arousal levels.

Animal behavior—which has the advantage of being easier to observe and manipulate than human behavior—was a third line of research discussed at the conference. Michael McGuire, an evolutionary psychologist at the University of California, Los Angeles, pointed out that a link between brain chemistry, social status, and aggression had emerged in extended studies of groups of vervet monkeys. Dominant monkeys tended to have high levels of the neurotransmitter serotonin, while submissive monkeys had low levels. (McGuire has found a similar pattern in human groups: leaders of college athletic teams, for example, tend to have higher serotonin levels than other teammates.) Yet monkeys with low serotonin were more likely than those with high serotonin to initiate violence against other monkeys. Moreover, if their status increased as a result, their serotonin levels increased accordingly.

"It would appear," McGuire said, "that monkeys are programmed to move along certain channels," with their brains' biochemistry preparing them to act out whatever behavior is most advantageous, given their social status. In McGuire's view, a low serotonin level is not a marker of predisposition to violence—at least not in the same way as a mutated monoamine oxidase gene—but it may equip individuals of low status in the community to take risks that could help raise their status. If the same mechanisms apply in human societies, such risk taking might often involve breaking the law.

Diana Fishbein, a criminologist then at the U.S. Department of Justice, said at the conference that she welcomed any progress biologists could make toward understanding what biological factors predispose some people to crime. While millions of Americans are exposed to environmental factors such as poverty, racism, and unemployment that place them at greater risk for violent or criminal behavior, she noted, most remain perfectly law-abiding. "Perhaps genetics can help tell us which people are most at risk," Fishbein said. If so, early interventions could be planned.

The specter of misuse

Many of the nonscientists participating in the conference, and even some of the scientists, leveled harsh criticism at theories linking genes and crime. Garland Allen, a biologist and historian at Washington University, St. Louis, Mo., and Andrew Futterman, a psychologist at the College of the Holy Cross, Worcester, Mass., noted in a jointly authored paper that definitions of human behaviors deemed "violent," "aggressive," "antisocial," and "criminal" are both social and legal in origin and can vary widely from one era to another and across cultures. Such traits are therefore impossible to measure in a standardized, quantified way and cannot be reliably correlated with genetic differences, they argued.

Even if there were accurate genetic tests for criminality, what should society do with this information? asked bioethicist Adrienne Asch of Wellesley (Mass.) College. She noted that it is acceptable to some to screen for and selectively abort fetuses with certain genetic disorders, such as Down syndrome. The advent of a similar genetic screen for predictors of antisocial personality, Asch postulated, would force the question of "whether we want a society that breeds some people out"—as the eugenics movement tried to accomplish—"rather than helping others to live comfortably with them."

During Machine Gun Week in Kentucky, a father teaches his son to shoot an M16 rifle, a weapon used by U.S. and South Vietnamese forces in the Vietnam War. Few would argue that environment and upbringing have as much to do with violent behavior as any genetic factors might.

Christopher Brown—Stock, Boston/PNI

© Wade Roush

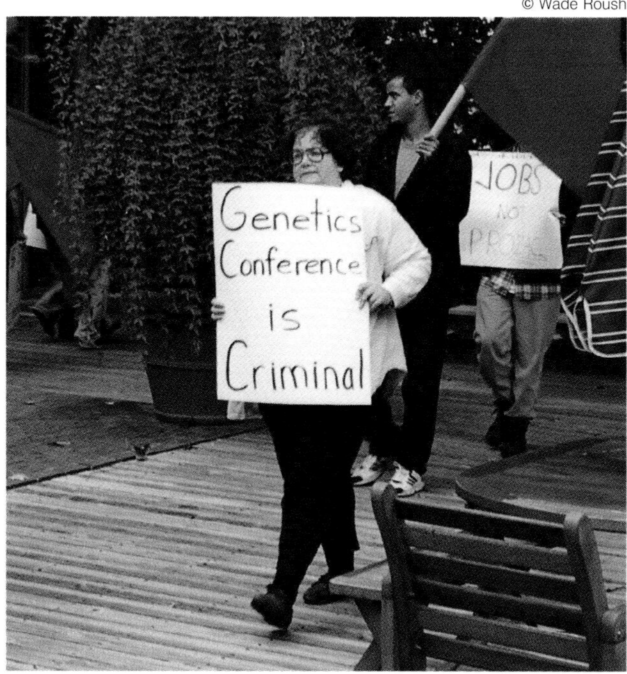

University of Maryland criminologist Katheryn Russell said she feared that genetic research would end by thrusting tests and therapies for genetic disorders disproportionately on the poor and on racial minorities, since these groups are often perceived to be the source of the U.S.'s crime problem. "The research can't be separated from the social and political climate," Russell said. "We cannot act as though we are conducting our academic research in a vacuum."

Violent emotions

Indeed, conference participants had a tangible reminder of the world outside when some 30 placard-toting demonstrators invaded the Wye Woods auditorium shouting, "Maryland conference, you can't hide—we know you're pushing genocide." A minor scuffle ensued, and though Wasserman tried to explain that the conference had been designed to take a critical look at genetic research, the protesters—including representatives of Support Coalition International, an alliance of

Protesters outside the conference on "The Meaning and Significance of Research on Genetics and Criminal Behavior" were a sharp reminder to the participants inside that their proceedings were not controversy-free.

NEWS CAP

Gene Therapy: Promise Unfulfilled

Gene therapy has been tested in more than 100 clinical trials involving some 600 patients since 1990. Although the promise of the technique is great, the field is still in its infancy, and results to date have been less than inspiring. This was the conclusion of a report released in December 1995 by an advisory panel appointed by Harold Varmus, director of the U.S. National Institutes of Health, to evaluate the success of gene therapy trials. Earlier in the year, several teams of researchers testing specific applications of gene therapy published their disappointing results.

Gene therapy is based on the idea that if a disorder is caused by a missing or defective gene, it can be treated by introducing a normal version of the gene into the patient's cells. Theoretically, the new gene should insert itself into the DNA of the cell, correcting the abnormality and ameliorating the disease. The approach was first used to treat a young girl with a fatal disorder of the immune system called severe combined immunodeficiency. The illness is caused by a defect in the gene that codes for the enzyme adenosine deaminase (ADA), which is necessary for the body to mount an effective immune response. Healthy copies of the ADA gene were introduced into the child's white blood cells. Five years later her blood cells contained functioning ADA genes and her immune system was working, but because she had also received injections of the enzyme, it was unclear whether gene therapy alone was responsible for her good health.

The results of gene therapy trials in patients with cystic fibrosis, Duchenne muscular dystrophy, and familial hypercholesterolemia (an inherited condition of extremely high blood cholesterol levels) were published during the second half of 1995. These data showed that the patients had derived no therapeutic benefits. In some cases genes were successfully transferred to the patient's cells but not in adequate numbers to correct the underlying defect.

On the heels of these publications came the report from the panel established by Varmus. Although the experts did not question the long-term potential of gene therapy, their report deemed the current state of the technology inadequate. In particular, the panel recommended that more efficient methods of gene delivery be developed. The document also emphasized that efforts to understand the entire disease process—not just the genetic aspects—of each disease in question must continue if successful therapies are to be devised. Criticism was also leveled at members of the research community and the media for raising unreasonable hopes for this still very new field.

—*M.J. Friedrich*

self-described "psychiatric survivors" endorsing Breggin's opposition to psychotropic medication—insisted on being heard out. Said one of the demonstrators, a student from Rutgers University, New Brunswick, N.J., "You might think that you have a right to do the research that you are doing, but the bottom line is that it will be used to subjugate people."

Meanwhile, outside the auditorium a group of six conference participants led by Allen staged their own protest event, issuing a press release denouncing "the presentation of circumstantial evidence and statistical manipulations as if they were rigorous scientific research that can inform decisions about public policy." The group said that research on genetics and crime "can play upon and feed into racist stereotypes and become justifications for racist oppression."

With Maryland state troopers looking on, the outside demonstrators eventually dispersed, and more restrained debate continued among researchers for another day. At the conference's close, some of the participants said that they had welcomed the disruptions. Many others, however, believed that the protesters and critics had mistaken the true tone of the meeting, which they contended was more cautious than assertive, as well as mindful of historical attempts to use biology to justify oppression. If, in the end, participants at the conference agreed on anything, it was that both the research and vigilance toward its uses must continue. "There are significant segments of the population who feel very strongly about the importance of this work, and about how the work is likely to affect their lives," said Paul Billings, a Stanford University physician. "Without a conference like this one we wouldn't have had a forum where this kind of data, and this kind of expression, can come out."

—Wade Roush, Ph.D.

NEWS CAP

Havoc in the Helix

The search for disease-causing genes continues to yield results. In the past year investigators have identified genes that, when mutated (*i.e.,* altered), are responsible for three rare inherited conditions: Werner's syndrome, a disease of premature aging that is also associated with an increased incidence of certain cancers; Friedreich's ataxia, a neurodegenerative ailment first manifested by loss of coordination; and progressive myoclonus epilepsy, a disorder characterized by seizures and mental deterioration.

A fourth recently discovered gene, called *FHIT* (for fragile histidine triad), has been linked to a variety of cancers, including stomach, esophageal, and colorectal. Researchers suspect that mutations in *FHIT* are involved in other malignancies as well.

Many of the genes in the human genome can cause disease if they are damaged or altered. The function of genes is to code for proteins—that is, to carry instructions that specify how a given protein is produced. Normal protein synthesis depends on the gene's basic structural units, called nucleotides, being arranged in a certain sequence, much as the letters of a word must be arranged in a given order for the word to be readable. When the sequence is altered, the directions for protein synthesis may become garbled, and the protein product can be abnormal—or even absent.

In the case of Werner's syndrome, for example, the gene, known as *WRN,* is thought to encode a kind of enzyme called a helicase. The enzyme's function is to unravel the two coiled strands of the helical (*i.e.,* spiral in shape) DNA molecule, a process vital to repair and replication of the genetic material. An abnormal helicase has the potential to disrupt proper functioning in every cell in the body. A defect in so basic a process could, in turn, accelerate aging—although exactly how this occurs is not yet understood. Because people with Werner's syndrome tend to develop an array of unusual cancers, scientists speculate that *WRN* is a cancer-promoting gene as well as an aging gene.

The gene responsible for Friedreich's ataxia encodes a protein called frataxin, about which little is known. The type of mutation involved, however, called a trinucleotide repeat (or triplet repeat), has been observed in other neurological disorders, including Huntington's disease. Researchers are now trying to determine how these repeated nucleotide sequences lead to deterioration of the brain.

The gene implicated in progressive myoclonus epilepsy encodes a protein called cystatin B, which normally blocks the degradation of other proteins within cells. The mechanism by which an aberrant form of the protein disrupts brain function is currently under investigation.

The *FHIT* gene codes for a tumor-suppressor protein—*i.e.,* one whose function is to inhibit uncontrolled cell growth. The gene is located at a so-called fragile site—a region of a chromosome that is prone to breakage—on chromosome 3. When this gene is mutated, its tumor-suppressing ability is lost, which predisposes the individual to various types of cancer. Scientists expect that these discoveries will lead to a deeper understanding of genetic disease and, perhaps, to new means of diagnosis, prevention, and treatment.

—M.J. Friedrich

U.S. Health Care Reform: Still on the Critical List

In order to carry on a coherent discussion of health care reform, it is necessary first to clarify the problem that a particular "reform" is intended to address and then to consider the desired outcomes of the reform. In regard to health care in the United States today, there is, for the most part, general agreement that the overall cost of health care is too high and has been growing at too great a rate and that there are too many uninsured and underinsured U.S. citizens who do not have access to comprehensive health care. The main health care reform policy questions then become: How can the growth in the cost of health care be reduced while, at the same time, all U.S. citizens are ensured access to comprehensive care? Can such reform be accomplished without diminishing the overall quality of health care?

It is highly unlikely that universal comprehensive coverage can be implemented without significantly increasing the overall level of health care spending. This reality appeared most evident in the summer of 1994, when it became clear that U.S. Pres. Bill Clinton's "American Health Security Act" was doomed, and by mid-fall of that year it was "dead."

While it is clear that there has been little if any health care *reform* in the U.S. over the past several years, there is no doubt that some revolutionary changes in the *provision* of health care have been occurring. In a nutshell: where once there were patients or consumers, there are now "covered lives." Where once there were physicians, there are now "providers." Where once people purchased health insurance to provide reimbursement for medical expenses, now insurers and their shareholders regard the medical expenses they pay out as a "loss" against potential profits. Where once health care was considered primarily a public service, today it is primarily a business.

While the goals of increasing access to care and reducing its costs are still major public policy concerns, the primary health care focus of the U.S. Congress for the past two years has been on cost containment (*i.e., financial* reform). There are those health policy analysts who hold that since access and quality are being virtually ignored, the cost-containment issue that Congress is addressing is only masquerading as health care reform.

Best in the world?

U.S. politicians and health care providers often boast that the U.S. has the finest health care system in the world. Is that really so? Can a system be the finest if a large proportion of the population does not receive or benefit from that care? A recent survey conducted by the London-based firm Market Line International ranked the health care systems of 30 countries. The following criteria were used:

- per capita health expenditures
- number of doctors per capita
- infant mortality
- life expectancy
- key causes of death
- level of accessibility of health care services

The highest-ranked country was Switzerland, followed by Sweden, Austria, and Japan. Canada was 6th; the U.S. ranked 12th, and the United Kingdom ranked 18th. The four top-rated countries were all found to have low infant-mortality rates, long life expectancies, high accessibility of care, and well-developed hospital systems. By contrast, the report stated that the U.S. system "provides poor value for money," leaving part of the population without access to care. Furthermore, despite its wealth, the U.S. has a notably high infant-mortality rate.

When thinking about means to reform the U.S. health care system, it is important to keep in mind that internationally the greatest cause of all ill health, suffering, and death (as listed in the *International Classification of Diseases*) is "extreme poverty," which is defined as "a level of income or expenditure below which people cannot afford a minimum nutritionally adequate diet and essential nonfood requirements," one of which, of course, is access to health care.

Shifting presidential priorities

In January 1994 President Clinton devoted about a third of his state of the union address to health care reform. He spoke about the country's health care crisis, the millions of Americans without health care coverage, and the skyrocketing cost of care. He called for a full guarantee of private health insurance that would provide comprehensive medical benefits for all Americans.

In his 1995 address, soon after the defeat of his health care reform proposal and the election of a Republican Congress, the president acknowledged that "we almost came to blows over health care, but we didn't do anything," adding that 1.5 million Americans had been added to the number of uninsured in the previous two years. He indicated that he still believed "our country has to move toward providing health security for every American family—but I know that last year

"Why come to me? I'm only a humble doctor. You should see a health-care provider."

we bit off more than we could chew." While Clinton did not call for universal coverage for either adults or children in 1995, as he had done the year before, he did ask the question: Can the U.S. "find a way to make sure that our children have health care"?

Instead of calling for a total overhaul of the health care system as he had in 1994, in 1995 Clinton called for a "step by step" approach to solving the problems and, at the very least, the passage of meaningful insurance reform so that no Americans would lose coverage when they changed jobs or lost a job or when a family member got sick.

In his most recent (1996) state of the union address, Clinton devoted only four paragraphs to health care. He again expressed concern about working families, who "must be able to buy health insurance policies they don't lose when they change jobs or when someone in their family gets sick." He acknowledged that over one million Americans in working families had lost their health insurance over the past two years; he then went on to suggest that Congress should "start by passing the bipartisan bill offered by Senators [Nancy] Kassebaum and [Edward] Kennedy to require insurance companies to stop dropping people when they switch jobs, or denying them coverage for preexisting conditions" (discussed in detail below). The president also called for the "preservation of the basic protections Medicare and Medicaid give, not just to the poor, but to people in working families, including children, people with disabilities, people with AIDS, and senior citizens in nursing homes."

Reform: morbid but not yet moribund

After the Republican takeover of Congress in 1994 (perceived in great part to be a reflection of voters' hostility toward "big government"), it appeared that most health care reform activities were on the back burner. In fact, the words *health care* appeared nowhere in the Republicans' "Contract with America." It soon became evident to the Republican members of Congress that in order to make good on several of the items that were mentioned in the contract—*e.g.,* tax cuts and balancing the budget—reductions in the amount of projected spending for both the Medicare and Medicaid programs would be essential. Thus, while health care was not on the initial Republican legislative agenda, it became part of it by necessity, and Congress was once again wrestling with health care "reform," albeit a highly stripped-down version. During most of 1995 and early 1996, it was primarily Medicare and Medicaid that were being debated, but as time passed it became evident that with the November 1996 elections approaching, there was little likelihood of reaching any agreement on either Medicare or Medicaid before 1997. Nonetheless, both Democrats and Republicans wanted to see some type of health care reform measure passed before the November elections.

On Aug. 21, 1996, U.S. Pres. Bill Clinton signs the Health Insurance Portability and Accountability Act of 1996 into law, with the bill's sponsors, Nancy Kassebaum and Edward M. Kennedy, looking on.

Richard Ellis—AFP

During the New Hampshire presidential primary in February 1996, candidate Pat Buchanan focused on the issue of economic insecurity and clearly struck a chord with the American public. As the issue of job insecurity came to the fore during the subsequent primaries, abetted by extensive media coverage of the downsizing of U.S. corporations, more and more Americans expressed anxiety about losing their health insurance. With such a significant number of voters concerned about the same issue, both the Democratic and Republican parties wanted to be associated with (and take credit for) passing legislation to alleviate the problem of the loss of health insurance.

The march toward managed care

A major change in the provision of health care in the United States over the past several years has been the significant increase in the number of people enrolled in managed-care plans and decrease in those enrolled in traditional indemnity (so-called fee-for-service) plans. A recent survey conducted by the consulting firm Foster Higgins found that in 1995, 71% of U.S. employees who were insured through their companies or employers were enrolled in managed-care plans, compared to 48% in 1992.

Managed-care plans attempt to limit costs by encouraging patients to utilize a network of health care providers (doctors and hospitals that have agreed to accept fixed fees). Such plans require patients to pay some or all of their bills if they go to health care providers outside the network or to accept capitated fees (preestablished fees for which providers agree to provide a given set of services).

A major criticism of paying for health care through a system of capitation is that if a provider or managed-care company receives a predetermined amount of money to provide a given set of services (irrespective of the number of services actually provided), there is an incentive to undertreat because the more services rendered, the less money the provider can keep as profit. The incentives of a capitation system contrast markedly with those of a fee-for-service payment system, under which reimbursement occurs only for services provided.

Given that both capitation and fee-for-service payment schemes have inherent undesirable incentives, which system is more (or less) deleterious to the public's health? There is no unequivocal answer to that question currently. A recent study published in *The New England Journal of Medicine* indicated that physicians paid on a capitated basis did as well as—and sometimes better than—HMOs in reducing the utilization of services. Thus, it appears that economic incentives have as strong an influence on physicians in controlling utilization of services as they do on HMOs. Recently there has been a spate of managed-care "horror stories" reported in the media. Most have had to do with the withholding of care by physicians and health plans because of the associated financial risk. Uwe Reinhardt, an economist at Princeton University, suggested that what is needed is legislation that requires the posting of a statement in "every doctor's office" detailing his or her financial arrangement with a managed-care plan.

Other health care delivery trends

An important but often not appreciated recent change has been the integration of health care providers—*e.g.,* managed-care plans, hospitals, clinics, and private physicians—into large umbrella corporations. In the state of Minnesota, which has been a leader in the development of managed care, there has been a significant increase in the number of formerly independent physicians who have sold their practices to become employees of big health care companies, thereby giving up their independence and linking their futures to those of companies that will control the flow of patients. In the major metropolitan area of Minneapolis and St. Paul, over half the physicians are no longer their own bosses. Currently four big corporations employ 40% of all primary care physicians, and 60% of the region's primary care doctors are employees or affiliates of 10 large managed-care organizations. Only 5% of primary care doctors are in solo or two-person practices (as compared with 42% in 1979). This major transformation has occurred with fairly little fanfare; a large majority of the public may not have even been aware of it. Sara Rosenbaum, director of the Washington, D.C.-based Center for Health Policy Research, characterized the change by saying, "It's been like the invasion of the body snatchers."

One of the concerns in regard to the consolidation of smaller health care organizations into bigger ones is that in the short run it will result in more cost shifting rather than in a genuine search for less-expensive ways to provide services; thus, public and private payers will continue to pressure insurers to cut premium costs while insurers pass the cost burden to providers through capitated payment systems. In the longer run, as managed care becomes even more pervasive, it will become necessary for successful providers to manage the risks of a population rather than shift risk up or down the health care delivery chain. A recent report by Health Trends Inc., "Restructuring the American Health-Market—Separating Myth from Reality," concluded that to survive, providers will have to change their focus from the management of illness to the prevention of its onset. Many consumers, as well as health policy analysts, seem to have forgotten that HMO stands for *health maintenance* organization.

The race to cut costs has put a squeeze on doctors' incomes and fostered a trend toward patients' having to pay a greater

Lara Jo Regan—Saba

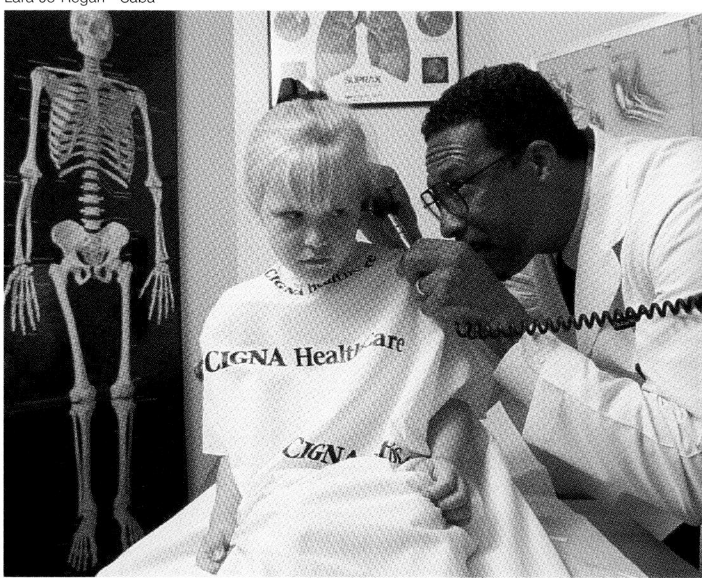

A pediatric patient is examined by a doctor with Cigna HealthCare of Arizona, a top-rated health maintenance organization with over 216,000 members statewide. One of the most dramatic recent trends in U.S. health care has been the march toward managed care.

share of their medical costs while having less say in choosing their doctors. It has also brought robust profits for many insurers. Stanford University economist Alain C. Enthoven, the "guru" of managed competition in health care, recently expressed concern that federal legislation could not keep up with—no less control—the pace of market-driven health system reforms. In response to this push toward competition and cost savings among managed-care plans, John F. Holahan, a health policy analyst with the Urban Institute in Washington, D.C., questioned whether the cost savings might well be "eroded through mergers and consolidations." Unfortunately, any improvements in efficiency resulting from managed competition would not help the 40 million-plus uninsured in the U.S. obtain insurance.

Still another little-appreciated trend has been the increasing acceptance of alternative forms of medicine as acceptable ways to treat chronic illnesses for which conventional medicine has not been effective. It has been estimated that Americans currently make more visits to alternative care providers than to primary care physicians, and they spend $14 billion a year on unconventional remedies. Even the federal government has given credence to the alternative care movement by establishing the Office of Alternative Medicine (OAM) at the National Institutes of Health. The OAM is funding research into such practices as acupuncture, hypnosis, and guided imagery. As many as 20 medical schools now offer courses in alternative, or "complementary," therapies, and some insurance companies are reimbursing patients for expenses incurred in alternative care treatment. Even some drug companies are starting to take notice. Pfizer Inc., for example, recently announced it would undertake a three-year study of traditional Chinese herbs. This trend is one that will have major implications for health care delivery and health care economics in future years.

Chris Maynard—Gamma Liaison

The proprietor of an herbal pharmacy in California prepares traditional Chinese remedies. The growing acceptance of alternative forms of medicine—by consumers, the medical establishment, the government, insurers, and drug companies—is sure to have an impact on future U.S. health care.

The politics of Medicare and Medicaid reform

One of the effects of the current political climate is that the debates over Medicare and Medicaid have consisted primarily of Democrats engaging in "mediscare" over the proposed Republican "cuts," while Republicans have challenged that unless the Democrats accept their proposed cuts, neither program will be "saved." As the *Washington* (D.C.) *Post* columnist E.J. Dionne, Jr., observed, "It's easier to convince voters that your opponent will hurt them than that you will somehow help them." The political rhetoric regarding Medicaid and Medicare has primarily been concerned with whether proposals to "reform" both programs would result in budgetary "cuts" or "increases." If by a cut it is meant that the actual budgeted dollar amount would be reduced, then neither Medicare nor Medicaid was to be cut. If, however, the budgeted amount would be increased but the amount of the increase would not be enough to either account for inflation or cover the costs of serving larger numbers of projected enrollees, then the increase could be considered a cut.

Medicare cuts: jeopardizing the health of older Americans. Given the politically highly charged issue of Medicare, it could be said that one of the braver undertakings of the Republicans in 1995 was to propose a plan to restrain the growth of Medicare. Medicare, along with Social Security, has been called the third rail of American politics because of the significant voting influence the elderly have demonstrated over the years. In fact, Speaker of the House Newt Gingrich ignored the advice of party leaders who had urged him to postpone discussion of Medicare until after the 1996 elections. Gingrich was acutely aware of the consequences of opening the Medicare Pandora's box, saying, "Medicare was the only thing we touched this year that could kill us. I've thought about it every day."

The importance to the Republicans of reducing federal expenditures on Medicare in order to balance the budget and reduce taxes was expressed by Rep. John Boehner, the fourth-ranking House Republican and chairman of the Medicare Conference Committee. He said, "If we're going to successfully balance the budget, we've got to deal with Medicare. Now nobody can disagree with that."

The Medicare proposal put forth by Gingrich depended on shifting millions of senior citizens into managed-care plans. The Republican proposal bore a strong resemblance to President Clinton's unsuccessful American Health Security Act. The speaker realized that such a proposal could well earn the enmity of hospitals, physicians, and organizations representing the elderly. While the Republicans were formulating their plan to reform Medicare, Gingrich, having learned several lessons from the American Health Security Act fiasco, was meeting with powerful interest groups representing the above constituencies.

In discussions with the American Medical Association, Gingrich was also able to persuade physicians to support his bill (after he agreed that the bill should be amended to protect doctors' fees). Even though doctors would get smaller increases in their fees, Gingrich assured them that they would be allowed to compete with insurance companies. When insurance companies made it clear that they did not want this competition, Gingrich placated insurers by promising that there would be new opportunities to sell new types of insurance packages in a more open Medicare market.

Months before the final details of the Republican bill were made clear, the American Hospital Association had begun to run ads that accused individual members of Congress of "conspiring to devastate Medicare." The association then found itself shut out of meetings and debates with members of Congress. "We knew exactly what we had to do," said Representative Boehner. "We had to smack 'em." Without much delay the ads stopped.

Throughout this time, the Republicans were able to keep to their party line on Medicare and develop a carefully formulated message—*i.e.,* Medicare was not going to be cut, although there would be a reduction in the rate of its growth. "We tested it and found out that if you talked about balancing the budget and Medicare in the same sentence you were asking for trouble, big trouble," commented Boehner, to which Gingrich added, "We learned that if you talked about 'preserving' and 'protecting' Medicare, it worked." Gingrich was also able to pacify the American Association of Retired Persons (AARP), the most influential group representing the elderly, by, among other things, promising to stave off a proposal to raise co-payments and deductibles for people who chose to remain in traditional fee-for-service plans. In addition, a recent attack on AARP's tax-exempt status dampened the association's enthusiasm for taking on the Republicans.

Eventually, when the White House staff realized how effective the Republicans had been in getting so many influential groups on their side, it, too, approached the lobbyists for the above groups, hoping to mount a late offensive against the Republican bill. In essence, the Democrats were told that it was too late.

By the 1995 congressional summer recess, the Republicans were thoroughly prepared to sell their plan to "save" Medicare. After the recess, however, the Democrats appeared to rise from the dead. They struck back, charging that the Republican Medicare proposal was in reality a way to give a tax break to the rich. Democrats accused Republicans of pulling a reverse Robin Hood—*i.e.,* robbing the old and poor to give more to the rich. Coincidentally or not, the amount of the $250 billion projected Medicare savings over a seven-year period was virtually the same as the $245 billion the Republicans proposed in tax cuts over the same period of time.

While the discussions of the "reform" of Medicare were quiescent during the presidential campaign, Medicare continued to play an important role in the campaign, with the

NEWS CAP

Covering the Costs of What Works

Therapies once relegated to the fringe or dismissed outright as "quackery" are gaining new legitimacy as more and more Americans turn to them (one in three, according to a Harvard Medical School study published a few years ago). Indeed, the term that many prefer for alternative therapies is *complementary medicine.* As the recently revised *Oxford Medical Companion* notes, the word *complementary* "expresses a welcome recognition that in matters as complex as the pursuit of health or the treatment of disease there is room for diverse approaches." Prominent among those approaches are diet and nutrition therapies, mind-body techniques (*e.g.,* biofeedback, meditation), manual healing methods (*e.g.,* massage, chiropractic, therapeutic touch), Chinese herbal medicines, acupuncture, Indian ayurvedic healing systems, and homeopathy.

Perhaps the most significant indication of the growing acceptance of these methods in the U.S. is the increasing number of insurance companies that have extended coverage to include them. Mutual of Omaha, for example, now covers a heart disease treatment program devised by cardiologist Dean Ornish at the University of California, San Francisco. The regimen includes yoga, stress management, meditation, exercise, and a low-fat vegetarian diet. Its cost (less than $4,000) is considerably lower than the average cost of more conventional treatment: $18,000 for angioplasty and $30,000–$40,000 for coronary artery bypass surgery. Other insurers (*e.g.,* American Western Life and Blue Cross of Washington and Alaska) have instituted plans that cover treatment by non-MDs such as naturopaths (who emphasize the use of natural agents such as sunlight and water in place of drugs and surgery).

It used to be that patients' claims for the success of alternative treatments were considered merely a reflection of the "placebo effect," in which a patient senses improvement simply because he or she wants to believe a purported cure is working. While many widely promoted unconventional methods are *not* sound, and some may be dangerous or even deadly, there is a growing body of evidence, supported by well-controlled scientific trials, showing that specific alternatives *do* work.

Herbert Benson, director of the Harvard Medical School Mind/Body Medical Institute, has been conducting studies on the benefits of spiritual, behavioral, and relaxation techniques for several decades. At a recent conference he noted that he now receives dozens of calls a month from health maintenance organizations (HMOs) wanting to know about alternative treatments. The calls come as no surprise to Benson; if such methods work, they are "just plain money in the bank for the HMOs," he commented.

—*Jeff Wallenfeldt*

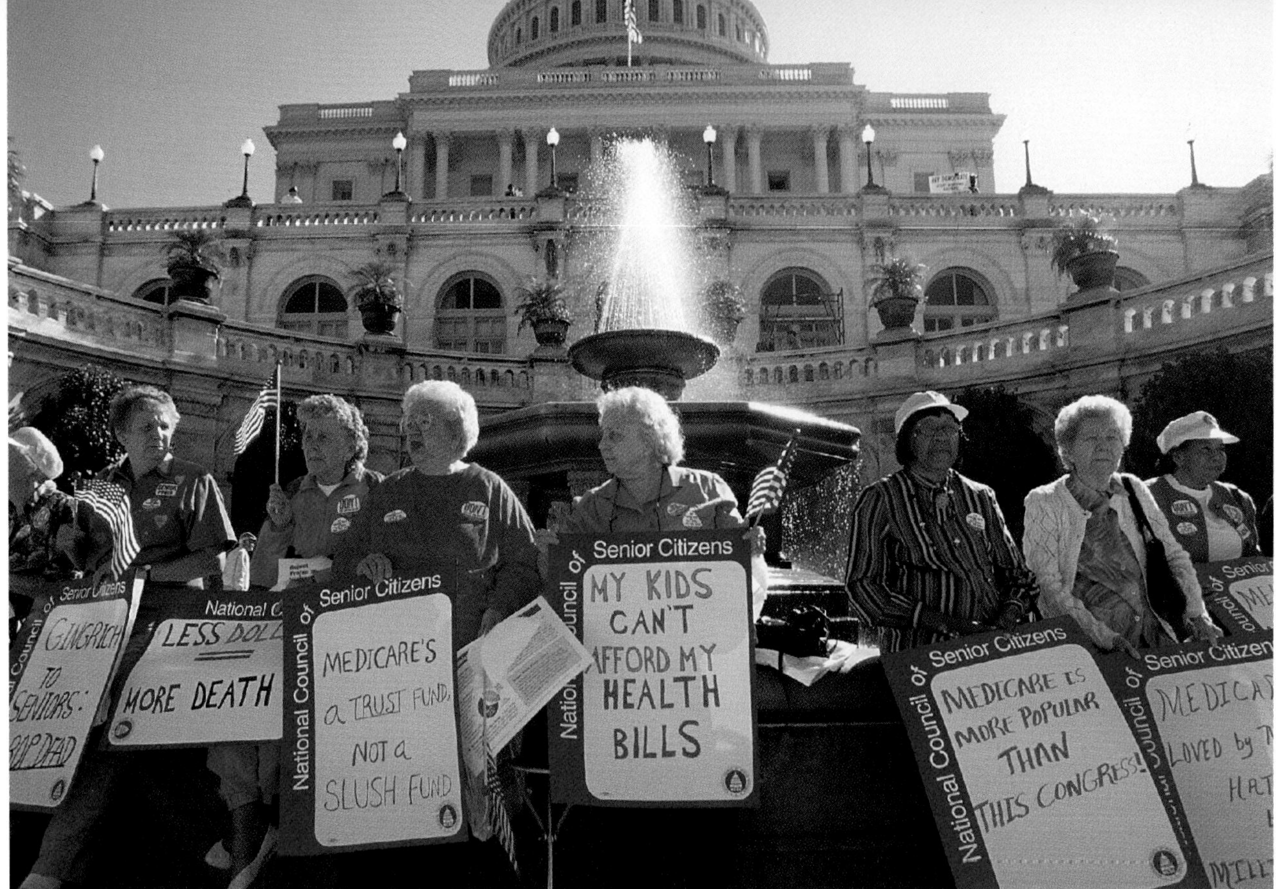

On Sept. 29, 1995, angry members of the National Council of Senior Citizens stage a rally on Capitol Hill, protesting proposed Republican plans to overhaul Medicare. Speaker of the House Newt Gingrich admitted, "Medicare was the only thing we touched this year that could kill us."

Democrats charging the Republicans with wanting to destroy it and the Republicans responding that they were only trying to save it from abuses.

Medicaid: even crueler cuts. While most of the media coverage of the 1995 and early 1996 health care debate concerned reforming Medicare, the less-reported-upon but more difficult and controversial issue was the reforming of Medicaid, the joint federal-state program established in 1965 to provide health coverage to the poor, the disabled, and the impoverished elderly. The Republican proposals to curb the growth of Medicare were and continue to be mild when compared with those for Medicaid. Currently the costs of Medicaid are split between the federal government (on average 57%) and the states (43%). The federal government sets minimum eligibility and coverage standards; thus, in the past whenever Congress expanded coverage, state spending was automatically raised. Between 1987 and 1994, Medicaid costs increased from 10% to 19% of state budgets.

While almost 70% of Medicaid's 36 billion beneficiaries are the nonelderly poor, pregnant women, and mothers and their children, almost 70% of Medicaid's budget ($156 billion in 1995) is spent for the other 30% of recipients: persons with disabilities and the impoverished elderly. About half of this 30% is spent for nursing home care. In addition, Medicaid does not cover all the poor. It misses many poor families who do not have health insurance and are not on welfare. In the past decade Congress has attempted to close some of these gaps by extending coverage to include greater numbers of pregnant women and poor children, which is one of the reasons the number of Medicaid beneficiaries has increased by 14 million since 1985.

The Republican proposal to reform Medicaid would convert it from an entitlement program (in which everyone who meets the eligibility requirements is covered irrespective of the resulting costs) to a block-grant program. Under a block-grant program, the automatic "entitlements" to benefits would end. States would instead receive a fixed amount of money for health services for the poor. Under the Republican proposal, states would be able to determine who was eligible, what services would be covered, and how much the federal and state shares of Medicaid would be. The Clinton administration, on the other hand, while wanting to lower the projected cost of Medicaid, also wanted to maintain more federal control and maintain the concept of entitlements.

"Reforming" health insurance

Recent data from a survey conducted by researchers from Harvard University indicated that the percentage of the United States population covered by insurance obtained through the workplace fell from 61% in 1992 to less than 57% in 1994; if the proposed reductions in Medicaid are implemented, the growing numbers of workers who lose job-based coverage in the future will increase the number of uninsured Americans to between 46 million and 66 million by the year 2002. Brookings Institution economist Henry Aaron recently predicted that any dramatic growth in the number of uninsured would lead to public discontent and "pressures for a revived and heightened role of government."

A study looking at the inadequacy of U.S. health insurance coverage, conducted by the Urban Institute, was released by the American College of Physicians in May 1996. Among the findings were that there were an unprecedented 42 million Americans without medical insurance, an increase of 3 million since 1993 (when the president launched his ill-fated effort for universal health care coverage). In addition, another 29 million (or 18.5% of those under the age of 65) were underinsured, which means that they could not afford out-of-pocket medical costs that exceeded 10% of family income. The study blamed the increase on the continuing decline in employer-provided coverage and on funding cuts for Medicaid. The study found as well that one-third of the uninsured lived in households with annual incomes of more than $30,000, which is twice the federally established poverty level for a family of four. Currently about 62% of Americans under age 65 get medical insurance through the workplace (as compared with 66% in 1983). Approximately 12.5 million, or about 9%, of the nonelderly population lost employer-sponsored coverage between 1988 and 1993 (the most recent year for which comparable data are available).

Confirming the findings of many previous studies, the Urban Institute concluded:

- Uninsured children who are injured are only 73% as likely as insured children to receive treatment.
- If it were not for the growth of Medicaid, which picked up many people who had lost their employer-based health insurance, the number of uninsured Americans would now be significantly higher.
- Lack of insurance can leave people without access to both preventive care and curative treatment, resulting in serious illness and huge unpaid bills.
- Lack of insurance is associated with a 25% higher risk of death than the risk for insured people of the same age and characteristics.

A recent study by the not-for-profit agency Employee Benefit Research Institute indicated that those with lower incomes have a far greater chance of being uninsured, and, for the most part, they lack insurance because they cannot afford to purchase it. For people with low or modest incomes, paying $2,500–$5,000 a year in insurance premiums takes a huge bite out of their take-home pay.

Unfortunately, current attempts to reform insurance cannot change the basic nature and principles of insurance. If insurance companies are forced to provide health care coverage to people who are all at predictably high risk of needing care, without being able to charge a sufficiently high premium, they will not be able to remain in business. It is unlikely that an attempt to "reform" health insurance without reforming the rest of the health care delivery system can solve the current U.S. health care dilemma.

Since it is the insurance industry that has been denying health insurance to employees who have lost their jobs and to those who are at higher risk for illness, it seems that an appealing solution would be to place the onus on the industry and thereby prohibit insurers from denying coverage to anyone who seeks it. Realistically, though, if insurers are forced to accept "bad risks," *somebody* will have to pay. Either those who are considered "high risk" will pay, or everyone who has insurance will.

In the proposed 1996 House and Senate legislation, there were no caps on premiums. If the premiums for the very people for whom the legislation was targeted were to get too high, those people would not be able to afford to purchase insurance. If the response to this unintended consequence is to cap the premiums, the costs of health insurance for everyone would go up as the companies attempted to recoup their losses. Higher overall insurance costs would make it harder for considerably more Americans to afford coverage, and this would have the effect of swelling the ranks of the uninsured.

Bipartisan bill signed into law

Ironically, two years after President Clinton warned that an incremental health care reform plan that addressed only health insurance reform would likely do more harm than good, he signed such a bill. House and Senate versions of the legislation, now known as the Health Insurance Portability and Accountability Act of 1996 (or the Kassebaum-Kennedy Act), were passed in the spring of 1996. On July 31 House and Senate negotiators resolved lingering differences over their respective bills in a conference committee, creating a single bill that passed in both houses of Congress and was signed into law by the president on August 21.

While both the House and Senate versions would have guaranteed that most people would be eligible for health insurance after changing or losing their jobs and would not be denied coverage because of preexisting medical conditions, there were two major differences between the bills. The Senate bill contained a provision that would have required insurers to cover treatment for mental illness in the same manner they cover physical illness. The House bill had no such provision. The second, more contentious difference between bills had to do with medical savings accounts (MSAs), which are discussed in more detail below. The House bill included a provision permitting the creation of MSAs, which are tax-deductible savings accounts to be used solely for medical expenses by people who have policies with high deductibles or so-called catastrophic health insurance. The Senate bill contained no such provision. While a compromise on MSAs was reached by the House and Senate, a compromise was not reached on mental health coverage. The latter, therefore, is not addressed in the law.

Under the new law, insurance companies can no longer "cherry pick"—seek only healthy people and exclude "bad risks"—*i.e.,* people who have a history of illness or a record of making large claims. The law also makes it illegal to discriminate against persons with a genetic predisposition to a particular disease or to deny or limit coverage to victims of domestic abuse. Some major features of the bill are:

- *Group insurance portability.* A misconception in regard to the concept of portability is that people will be able to take their own insurance policies with them when they change jobs—in other words, that the *policy* is portable. It is not. Rather, portability means that people can move to a new job and obtain new insurance, or they can leave a job and be able to get new insurance on their own. In either case, the new insurance may not have the same level of benefits as the previous plan, and it may well cost more.
- *Individual insurance availability.* Insurers who offer individual coverage will be required to offer an individual policy

to anyone who (1) has had coverage for at least 18 months, (2) is not eligible for coverage under any group plan, and (3) has exhausted so-called COBRA coverage. (COBRA is a federal law that allows eligible people to keep their insurance for a short time after leaving their jobs.) The law does not set price limits for individual policies.

- *Small business insurance availability.* The act requires guaranteed issue of policies to small businesses (with between 2 and 50 employees) that can afford to purchase insurance. Insurers are required not only to offer policies to small businesses but to renew them. Businesses can be dropped only for nonpayment of premiums and/or fraud.
- *Exclusions based on health status.* Insurers are prohibited from refusing coverage or renewal of coverage to an individual because of that person's health status. Insurers are prohibited from using health status (or preexisting illness) as grounds to deny coverage to any individual who is a member of a company's group insurance plan. Moreover, while the law does not include the mental illness parity clause contained in the original Senate bill, it does make it illegal for insurers to deny policies to those who have mental illnesses.
- *Guaranteed renewability.* Insurers are required to renew most policies. An insurer could terminate coverage for group plans or individual policies by giving at least 180 days' notice, but any insurer that did so would be barred from selling policies in that state for five years.
- *Health insurance deductibility.* The law will increase the tax deductibility of health insurance premiums for self-employed people and their dependents from 30% to 80% by the year 2006.
- *Long-term care.* The law treats long-term care premiums like standard tax-deductible premiums. Up to $63,875 per year in benefits received under a long-term insurance policy—for example, for home care—would be exempt from taxes.
- *MSAs.* A four-year MSA "experiment" will be implemented on Jan. 1, 1997. The trial will be limited to an initial population of about 750,000 individuals with high-deductible or catastrophic health insurance plans who work at companies with 50 or fewer employees or are self-employed or uninsured. To prevent the MSAs from being used as tax shelters, the law limits annual contributions by individuals to 65% of the deductible and by those with family policies to 75% of the deductible.

While the new law will be of help to those who otherwise would not have been able to obtain insurance after they lost or left their jobs, it is unlikely to solve the problems of the large majority of the uninsured who cannot afford insurance. As Gail Wilensky, former administrator of the Medicare and Medicaid programs, said prior to passage of the law, "The main reason people lack insurance is lack of money." Similarly, Robert D. Reischauer, the former Congressional Budget Office director, said, "Kassebaum-Kennedy is not going to do much for most of the 40 million uninsured whose lack of insurance stems from lack of money."

How many of those 40 million will be affected by the new law is difficult to predict. Certainly those employed in small businesses that can afford to purchase insurance but have been denied coverage owing to preexisting conditions among their employees will benefit. Others who will benefit are the four million people who are reported to be in "job lock"—*i.e.,* stuck in jobs they do not want solely for the sake of keeping their insurance.

In signing the act the president said:

> *Health care reform is measured by how many lives it improves. With this bill we take a long step toward the kind of health care reform our nation needs. It seals the cracks that swallow as many as 25 million Americans who can't get insurance or who fear they'll lose it. Now they're going to be protected. Never has such a measure been more needed for our people. . . . But now we need to build on what we have achieved. . . . The game is not over. . . . I'm suited up and ready to play.*

Hubbub over MSAs

While the details of MSAs can vary, their overall concept is as follows: Instead of providing employees with a comprehensive health insurance policy that covers expenses above a low deductible (the amount the insured person pays before the policy kicks in), employers would buy a less expensive plan that would cover only medical expenses above a much higher deductible. After the purchase of that policy, the employer would deposit the money it saves on premiums into an MSA. Conceptually, the idea behind an MSA is similar to that behind individual retirement accounts (IRAs), which were instituted in the United States in 1974. Just as IRAs are intended to supplement a person's pension income, MSAs are intended to help defray the costs of health care. Both IRAs and MSAs rely on tax breaks.

With some restrictions, individuals are now allowed to make tax-deferred contributions to IRAs. However, under current law, while an employer can deduct the cost of conventional health insurance provided to employees (a cost that is not treated as taxable income for workers), money that employers now place in an employee MSA is considered as taxable income.

To cover medical expenses individuals could draw money from their accounts without a tax penalty. Withdrawals made for other purposes would be taxable and subject to a withdrawal penalty of 10% for those aged 59½ and younger. If money in the MSA was left over at the year's end, it could be rolled over to create a bigger account for the following year, or the employee could treat it as taxable income and spend it for some other purpose.

Like any "reform" proposal, MSAs are quite controversial. Those who support them claim that they:

- encourage patients to make health care choices and to take responsibility for staying well and avoiding unnecessary health care costs
- encourage careful "shopping" whenever medical services are needed
- foster an increase in the use of preventive care owing to the inherent incentives to stay healthy
- give individuals the incentive to question the costs of the care they receive

Those opposed to MSAs argue that they:

- are really a scheme to transfer money from sick people to healthy people and from those in lower tax brackets to those in higher tax brackets
- would undermine the country's entire health care system by making health insurance too expensive for those who are likely to be sick
- would increase the number of uninsured by forcing more people out of the insurance net
- would discourage people from seeking preventive care since under an MSA an individual would be spending money from his or her own account (the less affluent might well decide to use their money for something else or save it until they became really sick)

In signing the Health Insurance Portability and Accountability Act, the president said that he had "opposed an open-ended, unconstrained expansion of MSAs because of [his] concern that MSAs may create incentives for healthier people to select catastrophic health coverage." Even though at least 15 states had enacted some form of MSA by late summer 1996, there were too few reliable data to determine how effective MSAs would be if implemented on a national scale or whether they would help control costs by making people more aware of the cost of their care. An interesting study of MSAs, recently completed by the Urban Institute, suggested that people may see the money going into MSAs as a "bonus" and use it, for example, to pay for services that currently are not covered, such as cosmetic surgery and vision-correction devices. If this were to occur, it could well be that overall health care spending would actually rise once the deductible had been met, as there would be little disincentive to use high-cost care. This could mean that the overall impact of MSAs would be not to reduce costs but rather to increase provider earnings. It is likely, the institute projected, that MSAs would cost the federal government an additional $2 billion or more per year, which is not quite what the proponents of MSAs would wish for.

A recent study by the RAND Corporation, however, suggested that tax-sheltered MSAs would have little effect on either total outlays for those under age 65 or on accessibility of insurance for the very rich. The study concluded that the incentive of a $3,000 deductible would reduce total health care spending by individuals by at most $250. On June 13, 1996, *New York Times* economics writer Peter Passell suggested that the battle over MSAs is an "exercise in ideology—much like the battle over raising the minimum wage from a pittance to a near pittance."

John Burry, Jr., chairman and chief executive officer of Blue Cross & Blue Shield of Ohio, suggested that the "come-on" for MSAs is that everyone wins. Though the concept is very seductive, he said, "it won't work," adding that MSAs are a "social distraction, a gimmick."

State Sen. Dennis Kucinich of Ohio, a state that planned to create MSAs in 1996, warned that only two groups would benefit from them: "people who have never been sick and the people who own insurance companies." Kucinich dubbed MSAs "medical scam accounts" and said that the "concept flies in the face of shared-risk insurance, and we're going from all for one and one for all to every man and woman for himself and herself."

NEWS CAP

No Appointment Necessary

The Internet, home video, and CD-ROMs are fast becoming health information's most promising venues. The newest kid on the block is America's Health Network (AHN), a round-the-clock cable channel launched in March 1996. AHN's format consists of two-hour segments called "Ask the Doctor," which are supported by the Mayo Clinic and feature specialists from across the country. During each segment an expert in a particular field (*e.g.*, pediatrics, sports medicine, or nutrition) answers questions from a studio audience and call-in viewers. Approximately every 23 minutes a 7½-minute "Health Mall" is aired, marketing products that are relevant to the particular "Ask the Doctor" discussion. For example, viewers can call a number to buy developmental toys during "Ask the Pediatrician."

Sixteen hours of every day's programming are live, and 8 are repeats. Future programming will include medical research segments presented by *The New England Journal of Medicine* and Reuters Health Information Services.

AHN's president and chief operating officer, Joseph A. Maddox, Jr., predicts financial success for the new cable TV enterprise because of the public's great appetite for health news and advertisers' attraction to AHN's target audience. "The cable universe itself is affluent, and people with an interest in health care are even more affluent," said Maddox, who anticipated that AHN would reach nine million viewers by the end of 1996.

—Joseph Turow, Ph.D.

Calling Sherlock Holmes

The American people and their government representatives are presently challenged with reforming the current pluralistic health care system in such a way that all U.S. citizens would receive comprehensive high-quality health care at a reasonable cost. This will not be easy in a society that is as ambivalent about the issue of individual rights versus the welfare of the community as it is about the right of all citizens to have their basic needs (including that of health care) guaranteed by their government. As one of the most vivid characters in English fiction, the mastermind detective Sherlock Holmes, once observed: diagnosing a problem is one thing; resolving it, however, is quite another!

—Lester E. Block, D.D.S., M.P.H.

Patient Privacy in a Computerized World

The practice of medicine is in a period of upheaval in most of the industrialized countries. Contributing to the upheaval are the application of information technology to medical practice, advances in molecular biology and genetics, and the introduction of measures to control the mounting costs of medical care. Each of these elements impinges on the others.

Computerization of medical records is proceeding rapidly in many settings—physicians' offices, hospitals, pharmacies, and managed-care networks—as well as in settings that handle medical billing and other administrative functions. Computerized records are favored because they provide rapid access to patient information, permit simultaneous viewings by many parties in different locations, and, with the assistance of various software programs, facilitate sophisticated analyses of test results and other patient data. Each of these capabilities may improve the quality of care that a patient receives, and some believe that computerization can also reduce costs and aid research.

From paper to computer

The replacement of paper records by computer records is being actively promoted by the computer and telecommunications industries and by some parties in government and medicine. At the same time, patients' rights, civil liberties, and consumer-protection groups have raised questions about the impact of computerization on the practice of medicine and on the patient's ability to obtain confidential medical care. Official "privacy commissions" in Canada and several European countries have objected to some medical computerization schemes because of their potential negative impact on the maintenance of medical record confidentiality.

Traditionally, medical records have been viewed as a resource to aid in patient care and to use in legal proceedings, should the need arise. When use has been restricted to these contexts, the number of parties who have viewed medical records has been relatively small. The confidentiality of medical records has been further protected by law, regulation, and long-standing custom.

Increasingly, however, medical records that identify individuals are being used in the pursuit of new objectives. Computerization facilitates this expansion by making possible the aggregation and rapid transfer of information. Among the important developments that are fostering the expansion of access to personal medical records are:

- the growing proportion of medical care that is delivered under the auspices of health care networks or large managed-care facilities
- increased demands by corporate and governmental entities for access to patient information in order to manage and administer the delivery of medical care and to control costs
- the proliferation of commercial schemes that involve patient data

Computerized patient records that are easily accessed and readily transferred to other parties with the click of a button may facilitate the work of large managed-care organizations—and may even help to keep the costs of health care down—but the uses of such records, containing highly sensitive personal information, infringe upon patients' privacy in troubling ways.

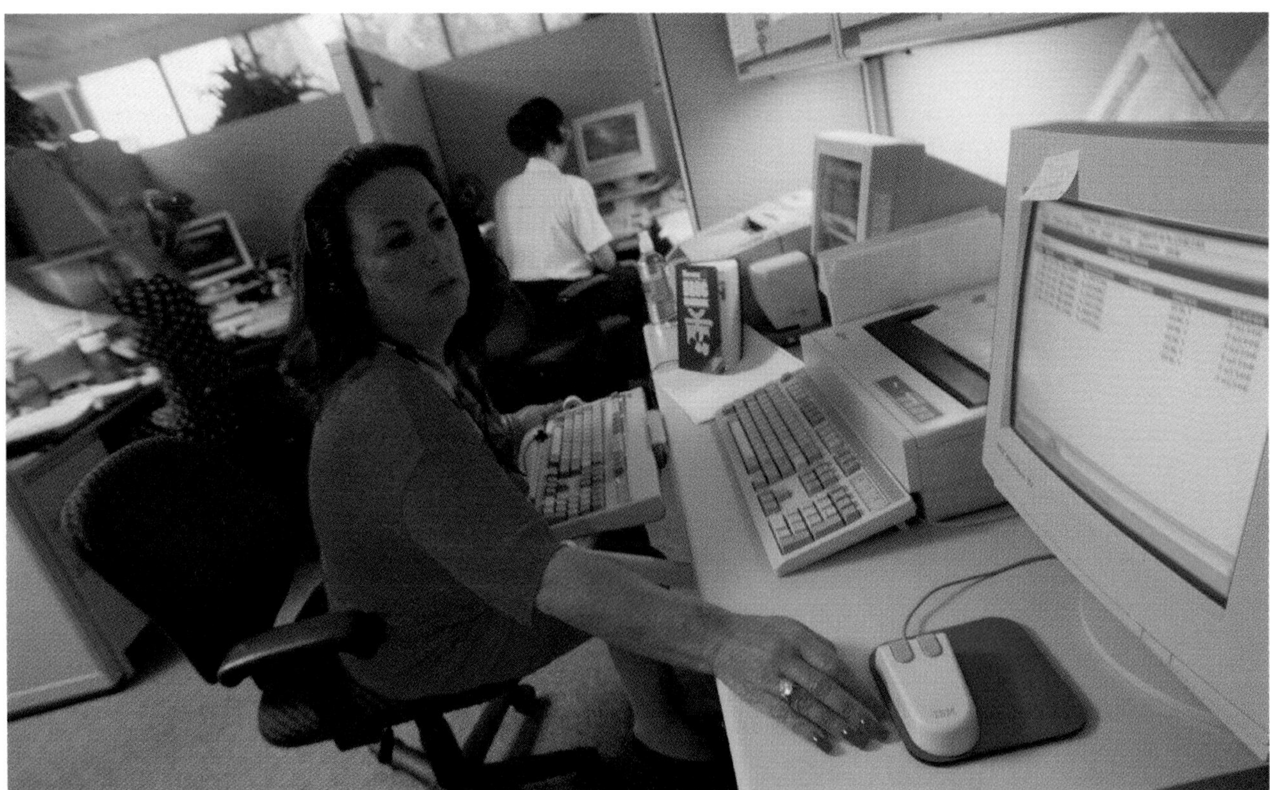

Lara Jo Regan—Saba

- the increase in statistical research projects that require access to the records of large populations, sometimes total populations, such as all the residents of a state
- the blurring of the distinction between actions to promote personal health and programs to promote public health

Redefining privacy

Although technical means are available to restrict and control dissemination of information within computer networks, they tend not to be utilized, particularly if they are perceived as too costly or as interfering with other goals. Current developments tend to promote information dissemination rather than restriction. At present only the patient who pays out of pocket for care received in the offices of physicians with independent practices can realistically expect privacy. Even this patient may need to use a pseudonym in order not to leave a computer record trail.

Given the difficulties of restoring privacy in its traditional sense, many information experts and lawmakers have directed their attention to redefining privacy. Paul M. Schwartz, an authority on privacy issues, has argued that the notion of privacy as "informational seclusion" is of limited utility under present circumstances and that there should be a shift in thinking to the notion of "privacy as participation." The advantage of this "model," according to Schwartz, is that it "recognizes that in many instances the processing of personal information will take place," whether people wish it or not.

In the privacy-as-participation model, confidentiality goals are achieved if there is regulation of the flow of information rather than prevention of information transfers. The primary objective of privacy legislation in this context is not to prevent facts about a patient's health from being known but to give the individual access to—and a chance to amend—records pertaining to him or her and to forestall certain harmful consequences that may occur as a result of the disclosure of personal information—consequences such as a job applicant's facing restricted employment opportunities. Measures of these sorts are known as "fair information practices."

Recent conflicts over medical privacy legislation illustrate the different points of view of the adherents of "privacy" and the adherents of "privacy redefined." The former seek legislation that recognizes privacy as desirable in itself and that tightly restricts all disclosures of personal medical information. They resist legislation based on notions of fair information practices because they are skeptical about the ability of legislation of this kind to achieve its stated goals and because such legislation fails to recognize privacy as an intrinsic good. Adherents of privacy redefined argue that privacy as traditionally understood is no longer possible and is an impediment to medical and social progress. They emphasize the benefits that may arise from the availability of information and argue that the potential harmful effects can at least be mitigated by well-designed legislation.

Toward patient-protective legislation

In the U.S. these two points of view have been manifest in the debates that have occurred in Congress with respect to the Medical Records Confidentiality Act of 1995 (later renamed the Medical Records Confidentiality Act of 1996), a bill cosponsored by Senators Robert Bennett and Patrick Leahy. The proponents of this bill have claimed that it sets the highest feasible standard in a computerized environment and that its provisions will prevent the improper use of medical information that identifies the individual. They argue that the provisions of the bill that grant permission to disclose a patient's records without that patient's consent are necessary on the basis of the legitimate "need to know" of various parties—such as public health officials, medical researchers, law-enforcement officials, and governmental and professional oversight bodies.

The critics of the bill, however, are far from satisfied. They argue that it fails to adhere to the fundamental principle of medical privacy, namely, that in the absence of informed consent, "an individual's right of privacy with respect to personal medical information shall not be eliminated or limited except in circumstances where there is an overwhelming and compelling public interest." They claim that the bill fails both to regulate insider access (disclosures within provider networks) in an effective way and to set strict standards for external disclosures. The Medical Privacy Coalition, an alliance of patients' rights, civil liberties, and consumer-protection advocates, headed by Denise Nagel, a psychiatrist from Lexington, Mass., has drafted an alternative bill and is supporting the introduction of more stringent legislation.

Massachusetts psychiatrist Denise Nagel heads the Medical Privacy Coalition, a group that opposes the Medical Records Confidentiality Act of 1996 because it does not go far enough to ensure strict standards for the disclosure of information on patients.

Rick Friedman—Black Star

Medical Records and Patient Privacy: The Public's Opinion[1]

	To the best of your knowledge, have you ever had medical information about yourself disclosed, without your permission, to someone else?	Do you think laws should be passed that prohibit health care organizations from giving out medical information without first obtaining the patient's permission?
Yes	8%	87%
No	88%	8%
Not sure	4%	5%

[1] Questions asked in a *TIME*/CNN telephone poll of 406 U.S. adults conducted by Yankelovich Partners on Feb. 22, 1996.

Reprinted with permission of *TIME*/CNN and Yankelovich Partners.

The inclusion of a section on administrative simplification in the Health Insurance Portability and Accountability Act of 1996, which passed Congress in August, intensified this debate. The administrative simplification provisions establish the framework for a national electronic data-collection and data-transfer system for personal medical data and require that the secretary of health and human services adopt a system of unique health identifiers for every patient, health care provider, and health plan. The proponents of the Medical Records Confidentiality Act of 1996 argue that this bill is a necessary and adequate response to the threats to confidentiality entailed by the administrative simplification section, while the bill's opponents argue that it is much too weak to be effective in this regard.

Patient privacy in England

These debates are similar to those that have occurred recently in England, where the National Health Service is setting up a national computer network to handle information about all medical care in the U.K. The British Medical Association (BMA) has instructed its members not to participate in this network unless patients are given control over who has access to their records and strong security provisions are put in place, such as the encryption of records (*i.e.,* conversion of information into codes so that the information can be read only by individuals with a key for decoding it).

The BMA rejects the need-to-know criterion—a position that it outlined in its 1996 report *Security in Clinical Information Systems:*

> *The BMA does not accept that "need-to-know" is an acceptable basis for access control decisions. The concept of "need-to-know" implies and encourages the surreptitious erosion of the patient's privilege for the sake of administrative convenience.*

The document also states: "Needs do not confer rights."

Whose "need to know"?

A major difficulty with the need-to-know criterion is that it is infinitely expandable. In 1991 the National Academy Press published a major study by the Institute of Medicine entitled *The Computer-Based Patient Record: An Essential Technology for Health Care*. The authors of this study, which advocated the adoption of the computer-based record, stated that the number of parties with a potential need to know was so large that they could not even attempt to provide a complete list. Nevertheless, they went on to cite many parties—including journalists, researchers, and government policy makers—none of whom was directly involved in patient care.

To most people confidentiality in medical care implies that only persons directly involved in their care will have access to their medical records and that those persons will be bound by strict ethical and legal standards that prohibit further disclosure. Even if access is regulated and limited to medical professionals, *e.g.,* all the physicians and nurses in a provider network, the patient is unlikely to accept that his or her records are "confidential" if large numbers of people have access to them.

The patient's uneasiness may well be justified. As the number of authorized record viewers increases, it becomes more and more difficult to control the flow of information. It is well recognized by security experts that the larger the number of persons with authorized access to restricted records, the greater the probability that there will be improper conduct in the use of those records. Moreover, the likelihood of improper conduct is heightened when the contents of records are considered valuable.

Medical information is potentially valuable to many commercial enterprises (including health maintenance organizations [HMOs] and health care networks, insurers, pharmaceutical and medical equipment companies, and research firms), as well as to employers, detectives, information brokers, political campaign managers, and others. These parties with a "desire to know" the contents of medical records may use various strategies, some of them illegal or of borderline legality, to obtain information from those who have been granted authorized access to records based on the need-to-know criterion. The 1995 indictment of 25 people in Maryland in connection with a scheme in which clerks sold information about identified individual patients, obtained from the state's Medicaid database, to four HMOs is a case in point.

Lingering questions

The promise of computerized medicine is that it will make needed information quickly available and put new resources at the disposal of health care providers. Telemedicine may improve medical care in rural areas by making expertise available via computer from urban medical centers. The consolidation of an individual's medical records may help physicians spot problems that would otherwise go undetected. Computer analyses may provide clues, if not definitive information, about the effectiveness of different treatments.

Each of these achievements, however, may be purchased at the price of a loss of patient privacy and of confidentiality of records, so the critical question is, Who will decide? Who will decide when the patient's medical records or physical being (as seen with the naked eye or with the aid of medical instruments) will be put on view? Is this the beginning of an era of "bodies on tap," in which large numbers of health care providers and others in the health care industry will have routine access to words, pictures, and sounds that convey the details of an individual's bodily functioning? Will the computer be primarily a tool of patient management, or can it be used to support patient autonomy?

Real-world threats

Information can be used in many ways—including as a means for the management and control of individuals. As noted above, medical information in the hands of corporations, schools, and governmental agencies can be used to determine employment and educational opportunities and access to insurance and to medical care. Employers can use medical information as a means of manipulating insurance coverage, managing employee behavior, and reducing corporate medical costs. Indeed, these practices are already occurring.

Public health surveillance can assume a new character when public health agencies have access to everyone's medical history. Public health authorities may link medical information to other information and use it to influence educational, environmental, and social policies in ways that limit the citizen's right to liberty and freedom of association, as well as the right "to be let alone" (the traditional definition of privacy). Public health authorities may take on responsibility for individual health and attempt to regulate individual behavior.

The explosion of genetic information poses grave ethical dilemmas. A worst-case scenario is the use of such information for eugenic control. Eugenics legislation is not unknown in the U.S. Ruth Hubbard and Elijah Wald point out in *Exploding the Gene Myth* (1993): "By 1931, some thirty states had compulsory sterilization laws on the books, aimed mostly at the 'insane' and the 'feebleminded.' These categories were loosely defined to include many recent immigrants and others who were functionally illiterate or who knew little English." Such laws remain on the books in some states.

Is patient privacy a thing of the past?

Over a century ago the U.S. Supreme Court set a high standard with respect to privacy and individual autonomy in *Union Pacific Railway* v. *Botsford* (1891). The court held that "no right is more sacred, or is more carefully guarded by the common law, than the right of every individual to the possession and control of his own person." Medical practice has long been torn between respect for this standard, which is expressed in the requirement that patient consent be obtained for treatment and for disclosure of information about a patient, and the desire to manage patients in pursuit of their well-being.

The introduction of the computer into medicine heightens the conflict between these two approaches. The computer is not a neutral tool, as it lends itself easily to abrogations of patient autonomy. A basic principle of policies supporting individual autonomy should be that a patient's consent must be obtained before his or her records are disclosed on a computer network. While a patient's refusal of computerized disclosure may in some cases lessen the quality of care that the patient can receive (*e.g.,* if the patient refuses a telemedicine consultation concerning his or her case), the U.S. legal system supports the right of the patient to make such a choice.

The American Medical Association has already expressed concern over the link between the consent requirement and the computerization of patient information. In the 1994 edition of its *Code of Medical Ethics,* the AMA's Council on Ethical and Judicial Affairs stated:

> *The patient . . . should be advised about the existence of computerized data bases in which medical information concerning the patient is stored. . . . All individuals and organizations with some form of access to the computerized data bases, and the level of access permitted, should be specifically identified in advance. Full disclosure of this information to the patient is necessary in obtaining informed consent to treatment.*

But what if the patient does not consent? Should treatment then be denied? The BMA has answered that it should not:

> *Finally, there is the issue of the patient's consent to have his record kept on a computer system at all. It is unethical to discriminate against a patient who demands that his records be kept on paper instead; his fears may well be justified if he is a celebrity.*

In the view of the American Civil Liberties Union, it is not only celebrities who may have reason to worry. The ACLU advocates the passage of legislation that will give every patient control over which personal medical information goes into a computer network and which information does not.

—Beverly Woodward, Ph.D.

Death in the 1990s

> *The Russian writer Count Leo Tolstoy, dying on the platform of a country railway station in 1910, murmured, "And the mujiks [Russian peasants], how do the mujiks die?"*

Death is the last taboo. Most people are uncomfortable talking about it (their own death, that is)—except perhaps those with fatal illnesses. "Well, it's morbid. Just thinking about it gives me the creeps," they protest. While people who live in industrialized Western nations may have banished death from their comfortable lives, death continues to stalk the planet, reaping its annual harvest in human lives. Each year some 50 million people die.

In North America and much of Western Europe, attitudes toward death are being re-examined because many now face a "technological death." Advances in medical technology have given many Westerners a genuine choice between life and death. (This is not a "choice" available to people in less developed countries.) Nearly half of all Americans now die in hospital intensive care units (ICUs) surrounded by the paraphernalia of medical technology. Many elderly people are released from intensive care only to be readmitted to the hospital a short time later to die in pain and distress.

In the first edition of his book *Medical Nemesis* (1975) the Austrian philosopher and social critic Ivan Illich complained about the "medicalization" of death since the end of World War II, which led people to see themselves as "two-legged bundles of diagnoses." Illich concluded that heroic medical strategies had inspired unrealistic expectations in patients. Writing in the *British Medical Journal* (*BMJ*), Dec. 23/30, 1995, Illich identified a further movement away from the traditional art of dying in Western culture. His concern today is with the "systematization" of medicine. New technologies and management systems have changed people's perception of medical treatment, including terminal care, in such a way that the latter is seen to be the final phase in a lifelong managed postponement of the breakdown of a biological system. Illich now sees an "amortal society," in which there are no dead. Rather, people are just parts of vast interlocking systems.

"Angels of Compassion," © Michael Tice, 1993

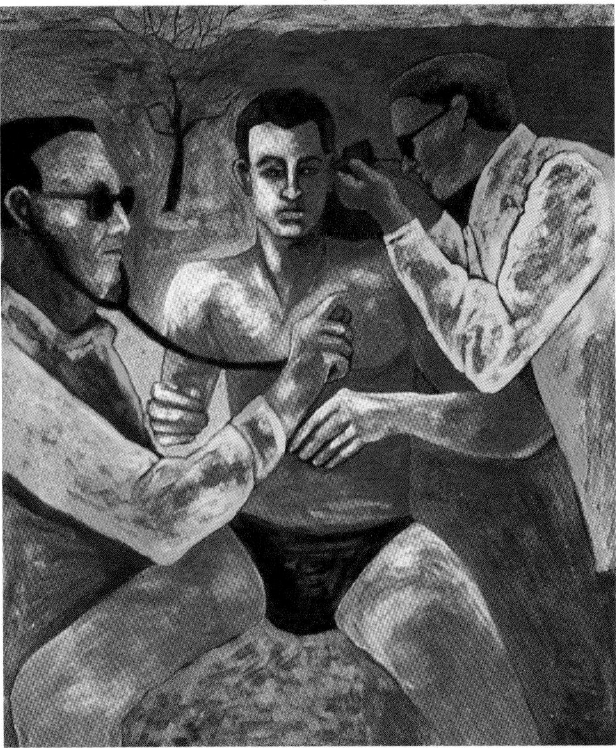

The Austrian social critic Ivan Illich has criticized the "heroic" strategies of doctors that leave patients feeling like "two-legged bundles of diagnoses." Psychiatrist Elisabeth Kübler-Ross has questioned whether medicine has become a "depersonalized science in the service of prolonging life rather than diminishing human suffering."

By addressing these bioethical dilemmas, internationally respected medical publications such as the *BMJ* and the *Journal of the American Medical Association* (*JAMA*) have begun to break the last taboo. Within the past year, the journals have published major reports and editorials about the reluctance of physicians to talk to patients about death and to heed patients' wishes concerning resuscitation and pain relief.

Death in the past: simple and elaborate

Things were very different in earlier centuries, when people were encouraged to prepare for imminent death. In the tradition of the Greek physician Galen, who lived in the 2nd century AD, doctors learned the signs of approaching death and would withdraw. Nature broke the healing contract at that point, and the doctor was expected to acknowledge his or her limitations.

In the centuries before the technological age, dying was generally a simple affair. One was usually forewarned by a natural sign, frequently by a premonition. Death could not be cheated. A set ritual was begun as soon as an intimation of the end was perceived. Sometimes death rituals were elaborate. The Egyptians, Tibetans, Mayans, and Aztecs all provided funereal texts of spells, hymns, and prayers to guide people into the next world. The oldest of these is the Egyptian Book of the Dead, which is a collection of texts dating from about 2350 BC.

In the Middle Ages in Europe, treatises called *ars moriendi* helped people achieve "a good death." *De praeparatione ad mortem* ("Preparation for Death") by Desiderius Erasmus in the 15th century gave instruction on preparation for the afterlife. The plagues that swept Asia and Europe in the 14th and 15th centuries (such as the Black Death of 1347), meting out indiscriminate death, could have engendered the notion of the dance macabre, in which pope, king, ploughman, and maid were all cut down in the same way by death's scythe.

Remnants of ritual

In the technological vastness of the postindustrial age, medical science has virtually obliterated the role played by ritual in older societies to meet the needs of the fatally ill. There are still some cultures, however, that have maintained their traditions. The Inuit people place their dying elderly on ice floes, there to pass from this world. This practice may seem barbaric to many, but it is the vestige of an older attitude toward death, an unsentimental view. Is it possible that the Inuit, resting peacefully on a bed of ice, has a more benevolent end than the many Americans and Western Europeans who die in an ICU?

In Mexico each year on the Day of the Dead, pre-Christian beliefs are still celebrated. Death is seen as a part of everyday life, and it is treated with humor and even affection. The deceased on this day "come back" to visit friends and relatives on Earth and partake of the pleasures of the living.

The Mayans of the Yucatán still bury their dead with provisions for a journey. Christianity also perceives death as a journey, the destination being either heaven or hell. Most religions, in fact, adhere to strict rites to help people in their final hours of life.

To Muslims the time of death is etched in fate and cannot be changed. There is the need, therefore, always to be prepared, and since everything belongs to God, the deceased person's body must be given back to God. Strict instructions are laid down in the Qur'an about correct disposal of the body. The body is returned home, washed, wrapped in a clean white cloth, and, after being taken to the mosque for a short prayer, buried as soon as possible. Men are expected to show restraint at the funeral, and women are not allowed to go (because they might display emotional weakness). Three days are allowed for grieving and mourning.

Deathbed scene from the Book of Hours of Catherine of Cleves, c. *1435—a time when death was viewed as a natural part of the life cycle; families attended their dying loved ones at home, offering whatever comforts and solace they could.*

Joe Viesti—Viesti Associates, Inc.

Considerable ritual still surrounds the Mexican Day of the Dead (November 2), a festive—never morbid—celebration of the continuity of life. In Michoacan state (above) it is common for families to have sumptuous early-morning picnics on elaborately decorated grave sites of their deceased.

Islamic medicine does not reject all technology. Resuscitation techniques, for example, are allowed for those who can afford them. In 1993 Imran, a 23-year-old medical student in Karachi, Pak., was diagnosed with systemic lupus erythematosus, an autoimmune rheumatic disorder that is sometimes fatal. After treatment with anti-inflammatory immunosuppressive drugs, he experienced a remission and returned to his studies and diligently prepared for his finals. In 1996, however, his health declined, and he endured a long battle in intensive care. When it was clear that his death was imminent, he showed no bitterness, maintaining that one should not doubt that God had his own reasons. In his last days he had a premonition of the end and told his mother he had "passed." The will of God had prevailed; he could do no more in this life and hoped to go to a better place.

The "good death" gone?

Is it possible to return to the old idea of a good death? Could the old maxim that a wise person needs to cultivate an *amicus mortis,* one who tells the bitter truth and stays to the end, be revived? Elisabeth Kübler-Ross, the Swiss-born psychiatrist and leader in the field of thanatology (a discipline concerned with the idea of death and the psychological mechanisms of coping with dying), views today's society as one bent on ignoring or avoiding death. She neatly sums up the dilemma facing physicians: "We have to ask ourselves whether medicine is to remain a humanitarian and respected profession or a new but depersonalized science in the service of prolonging life rather than diminishing human suffering." In spite of the death-and-dying movement of the last 20 or so years, no consensus exists yet, outside of a few clear-cut cases, about medical priorities at the end of life.

Studies reported in late 1995 in *JAMA* examined the attitudes of doctors toward terminally ill patients and the attitudes of patients in nursing homes toward ICU treatments, as well as the cost-effectiveness of medical technology applied to end-of-life crises. The Study to Understand Prognoses and Preferences for Outcomes and Risks of Treatments (better known as SUPPORT) was carried out in five teaching hospitals across the U.S. Its objective was to improve end-of-life decision making and reduce the frequency of a mechanically supported, painful, and prolonged process of dying. Phase I of SUPPORT (an observational study of more than 4,000 patients) documented shortcomings in communication, the frequency of aggressive treatment, and the common characteristics of hospital deaths. Phase II (a controlled clinical trial) encouraged attentive treatment of pain by health care professionals and meaningful physician-patient communication; during the study specially trained nurses had close contact with doctors, family, and the patient to elicit preferences and improve understanding of outcomes.

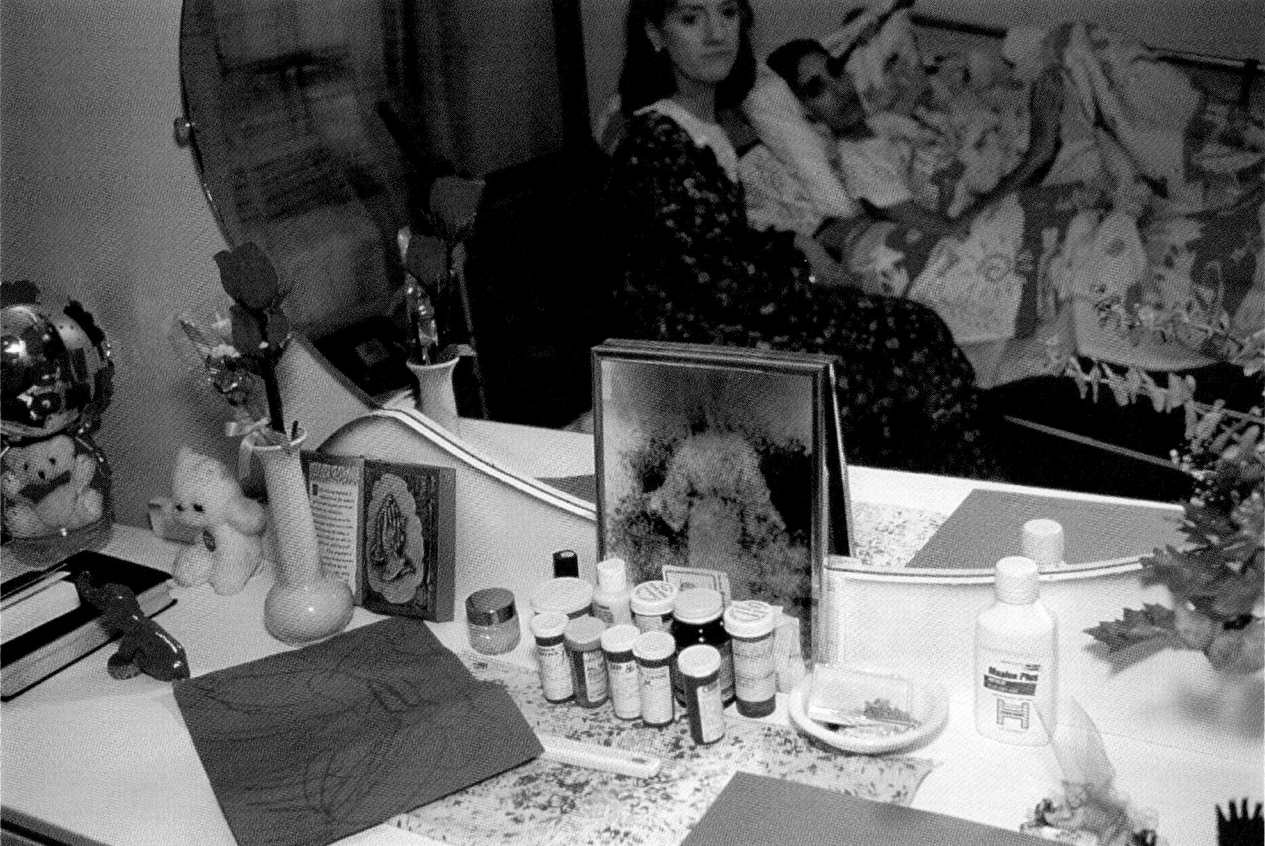

Photograph of "Amalia's Dresser, NYC, 1994." A terminally ill patient receives hospice care at home, which allows her to have a gentle and dignified death. By contrast, most Americans die in hospitals, where inappropriate medical heroics only increase the pain and isolation of death.

Numerous serious problems with terminal care were revealed by the two phases of SUPPORT. Broadly, doctors were reluctant to talk openly to patients. Of the 60% of patients who opted for cardiopulmonary resuscitation (CPR), 14% changed their mind when they were told in detail what the technique involved—for instance, the use of defibrillation and mechanical ventilation. The authors of the report commented, "Why this information did not have more of an impact on treatment preferences remains unclear." Perhaps doctors do not talk to patients about treatment because treatment can be extremely unpleasant.

Among the many conclusions of reports published in the Nov. 15, Nov. 22/29, and Dec. 13, 1995, issues of *JAMA* were:

- No one knows when to discontinue treatment.
- "Do not resuscitate" (DNR) orders are frequently ignored.
- Doctors do not listen to patients' wishes and are not candid when conveying bad news.
- Pain is managed poorly.
- Interventions by SUPPORT team nurses on behalf of patients had no effect on outcomes.
- Doctors' decisions leave many families nearly broke.
- Despite having preferences regarding life-sustaining treatments, relatively few nursing home residents have discussed these with care providers or family.
- Nursing home residents and terminally ill patients are typically excluded from discussions about their care.

While acknowledging the fears of doctors that patients could choose ineffective and expensive options if given the opportunity, the SUPPORT investigators were critical of the medical profession's attitude toward end-of-life treatment. Doctors failed to communicate with patients on such important issues as the use of interventional therapies like CPR and enteral feeding (nourishment given via a tube that passes through the stomach into the intestines) or noninterventional measures such as DNR orders. Moreover, they were unlikely to consider that treatment might be futile.

In an editorial in *JAMA* (Nov. 22/29, 1995), physician and medical ethicist Bernard Lo at the University of California, San Francisco, who served as a consultant to SUPPORT, was highly critical of the fact that prognoses were obtained by physicians in only 59% of SUPPORT cases, that physicians had little appreciation of patients' preferences on CPR, and that physicians did not appreciate or adequately treat patients' pain. Lo concluded:

> *The SUPPORT data present a challenge to physicians. It would be simple if computers and nurses alone could improve the care of seriously ill patients. Instead, physicians will need to change hospital culture and practices and our own behavior. These are daunting tasks, particularly at a time when many physicians complain that managed care is undermining professional autonomy and reducing*

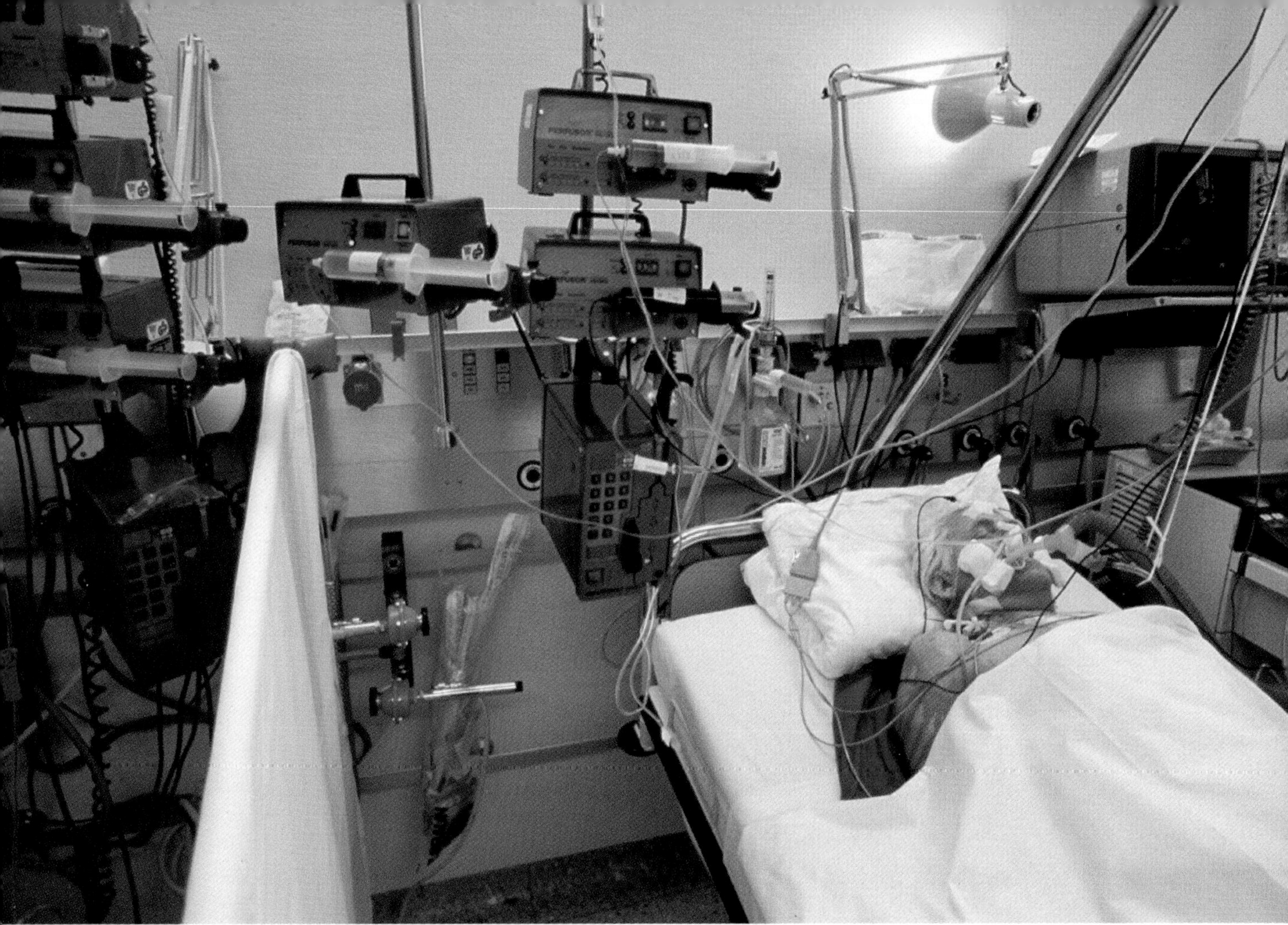

The aggressive measures routinely taken in intensive care units have raised questions about the manner in which physicians handle end-of-life crises. Studies show that doctors frequently disregard the wishes of patients and that their decisions to prolong life leave many families financially devastated.

us to pawns in impersonal organizations. Although our resources may be restricted, nonetheless, we need to reaffirm our traditional responsibility for relieving pain, responding to patients' concerns, helping them make difficult decisions, and respecting their informed choices.

The costs of medical care will become an ever-heavier burden on the state and taxpayer. One of the *JAMA* reports (Nov. 15, 1995) focused on the *limits* of care and the potential *ineffectiveness* of care. The conclusion was that aggressive treatment of patients in the "potentially ineffective care" category consumed vast resources. Families were often faced with massive medical bills that quickly gobbled up any funds in the estate of the deceased. That care, however, did little good for the patients.

Living longer, choosing death

Advances in medical science and improved diets and living conditions have increased life expectancy and almost eliminated child mortality in the wealthy industrialized countries of the West. In *The Fireside Book of Death* (1990) psychiatrist Robert Wilkins speculated that few Westerners living today will have seen a dead body before they are 40. At a conference held in Las Vegas, Nev., in December 1995, Ronald Klatz, president of the American Academy of Anti-Aging Medicine, said that Western society was about to enter "a truly golden age of youthful vibrancy limited only by [the individual's] decision to live or die." Though few experts would go as far as Michael Rose, professor of evolutionary biology at the University of California, Irvine, who believes it eventually will be possible for people to live for 200 years or more, there is a growing consensus that most North Americans and Western Europeans will be living longer and longer.

Many experts, such as Caleb Finch, professor of gerontology at the University of Southern California, will give no figure for a maximum human life span. He and others are pursuing novel antiaging strategies in the quest for "eternal youth." Added to this are the advances in freezing human organs for transplantation and the recent extension (in the U.K.) from 5 to 10 years for storing frozen embryos. New cryonic techniques will no doubt encourage more people to think of immortality. In fact, cryopreservation (frozen storage) has been proposed as a means to store corpses and diseased human tissue that would later be amenable to any new treatments that science devises.

The growing number of elderly, the current lack of a cure for AIDS, and many other issues are now forcing more and more people to confront and talk about death as a reality. Advocates of assisted suicide and groups like the Hemlock Society and Exit have been trying for some time to break the last taboo. Between June 1990 and September 1996 retired Michigan pathologist Jack Kevorkian had participated in or provided the means for 40 suicides. On May 14, 1996, Kevorkian was acquitted of criminal charges for his role in helping two chronically ill women die in 1991. This was his fifth acquittal at his third criminal trial. Kevorkian was triumphant. Jurors, who had deliberated for 13 hours, said that they were especially moved by the videotapes of the two women and by testimony from their families and Kevorkian. In a commentary in the *New York Times* (May 19, 1996), Jeff Stryker, a health policy analyst, noted that "Dr. Kevorkian's efforts not only show how difficult physician-assisted suicide may be to regulate in practice but also how rapidly attitudes are changing from the courtroom to the bedside."

Writing in the *Chicago Tribune* (May 21, 1996), David Orentlicher, former director of the American Medical Association's (AMA's) Division of Medical Ethics, said:

> *It is the intolerable suffering of dying patients that has kept Kevorkian in business. . . . But dying patients should not have to turn to Dr. Kevorkian, his canisters of carbon monoxide and his rusted minivan for help. . . . It is time now to consider what kinds of regulation ought to be implemented to ensure that patients who should have access to assisted suicide can have that access through their own physician and in a setting that is dignified. . . .*
>
> *In his six years of assisting suicides, Dr. Kevorkian has provided us important insights into the needs of patients and the shortcomings of medical practice. It is time now to implement the lessons we have learned.*

During the AMA's annual meeting of its governing body, the House of Delegates, in late June 1996, the subject of doctor-assisted suicide was brought to the floor for debate. Delegates overwhelmingly rejected a proposal to end the association's opposition to assisted suicide. The Board of Trustees of the AMA released a report categorically stating that "The physician's role is to affirm life, not hasten its demise." At the same time, the report recommended that members of the medical profession embark on an educational campaign to promote the use of pain-reducing treatments for critically ill and terminal patients.

In early 1996 a court case in the U.S. broke new ground in the debate over assisted suicide. Gerald Klooster, a retired obstetrician-gynecologist of Castro Valley, Calif., had been diagnosed with Alzheimer's disease at age 63. After his diagnosis he began to speak about committing suicide in order to spare his family the necessity of having to cope with his decline and loss of dignity. When Klooster contacted Kevorkian, his son Chip became alarmed and demanded custody of his dad. Klooster's wife, Ruth, contended that they had an appointment with Kevorkian but only to explore their options. Shortly thereafter a protracted family feud broke out. In April a court settlement was reached, ruling out assisted suicide for Klooster, designating that he would live with his 37-year-old daughter, and eliminating Chip from the family will. The disinherited son defended his dramatic action of taking his father from the family, saying, "We would all be visiting my father's grave site today if I hadn't rescued him. My father would have been Dr. Kevorkian's 27th victim." In June a California judge ordered that Klooster be returned home to live with his wife. Under the new arrangement the daughter would provide respite care on weekends and whenever it was needed. Chip remained estranged. While there have been suits in which relatives have attempted to prevent "pulling the plug" on treatment of the terminally ill, the Klooster case was thought to be the first in which someone had gone to court to prevent a relative's assisted suicide.

A recent survey conducted by David A. Asch, a specialist in internal medicine and a medical ethicist at the University of Pennsylvania School of Medicine, found that one in five nurses in ICUs reported that they had helped patients die. Assistance took several forms, the most common being the administration of an opiate narcotic that would relieve pain but also might hasten death. While many ethicists were critical of the survey, published in *The New England Journal of Medicine* (May 23, 1996), and felt it exaggerated the participation of nurses in the deaths of patients, Asch's findings suggested that codes of ethics in ICUs may, in fact, be overlooked when critically or terminally ill patients are in pain.

Lori Grinker—Contact Press Images/PNI

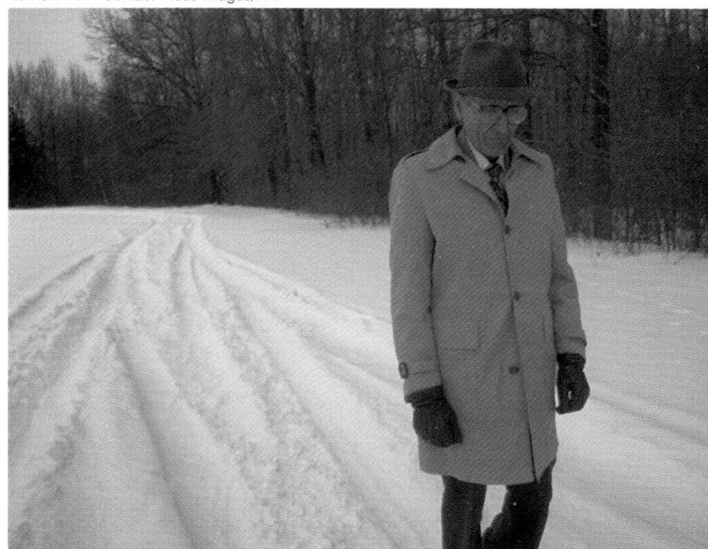

It seems nothing will stop the 68-year-old retired pathologist and assisted-suicide proponent Jack Kevorkian from aiding those who seek his services. As one medical ethicist has noted, "It is the intolerable suffering of dying patients that has kept Kevorkian in business."

It is evident from the number of reported cases of assisted suicide that attitudes toward death are changing fast. It has been alleged that Pres. François Mitterrand of France decided to call a halt to the chemotherapy for prostate cancer that was keeping him alive. He died within three days after stopping all drugs but painkillers.

As the millennial year 2000 approaches and people achieve greater prosperity and live longer lives, they will have more choices to make. Before the next millennium is up, it may be that everyone will have to decide the time and place of his or her own death.

—*Jerry Mason*

Latin America: The New "Hot Zone"

Practically every day, it seems, a news story appears warning of a dread disease, never before known, that is now dramatically making its presence felt in some far-off place—or, even more frighteningly, somewhere near home. Equally common are stories about the reappearance of ancient scourges like tuberculosis and cholera, reminders that infectious diseases of the past are still very much a threat to human health.

Latin America, like all parts of the world, has had its share of new and resurgent diseases, and this region's experiences, especially with viral infections, point to both the perils of these illnesses and the discouraging prospects for their control in a world where any pathogen is only an airplane flight away. Infections caused by viruses are of particular interest because their emergence and transmission reflect many quintessential 20th-century developments: the rise of megacities, massive rural-to-urban population movements, deforestation, burgeoning international travel, and widespread fiscal crises. The following enumerates the more important viral diseases that have surfaced in Latin America in the past few years. A concluding section explores the conditions underlying the emergence of these disorders and the beginning of a global strategy for prevention and control.

Dengue: an Asian import

The year 1995 witnessed the largest outbreak of dengue fever—also known simply as dengue—in the Americas in more than a decade; well over 200,000 cases were reported, including thousands of cases of the deadly variant called dengue hemorrhagic fever, which ended in scores of deaths. For public health officials the epidemic was a clear signal that this viral disease had arrived in the Americas in full force. The affected areas included much of the Caribbean and Central and South America, with thousands of cases reported in Mexico and local transmission documented in southern Texas. Some international travelers undoubtedly returned home to North America, Europe, Asia, and Africa with dengue among their souvenirs.

A youngster is treated for dengue at a medical center in Achuapa, Nicaragua, in October 1995, during the largest outbreak of dengue to affect the Americas in more than a decade.

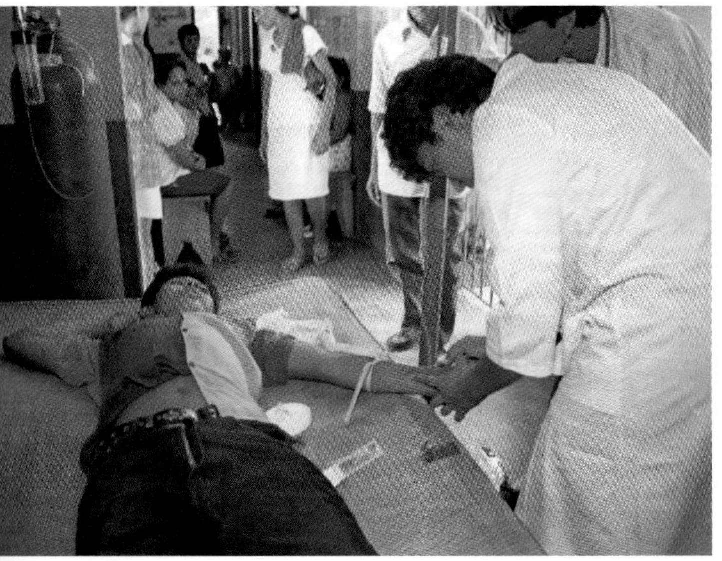

AFP

To understand the complexity of the disease and the challenges of dengue control, it is instructive to examine the recent history of dengue viruses, both in the Americas and globally. The dengue virus is transmitted by the mosquito *Aedes aegypti*. Four distinct viruses can cause classic dengue fever, an illness characterized by high fever, blinding headache and pain in the eyes, and, most notably, severe pain in the bones—indeed, it is often called "breakbone fever." Most patients are bedridden for a week or so but generally recover without any residual affects. Unfortunately, those who have suffered a single bout of dengue are protected only against reinfection by that particular type of dengue virus, so they remain susceptible to the other three viral types. Subsequent dengue infections may again lead to classic dengue fever, but they also carry the risk of dengue hemorrhagic fever, which may result in leakage of plasma (the liquid portion of the blood) into the tissues, shock, and, if not properly treated, death. The type 3 dengue virus was introduced into the Americas in 1995; types 1, 2, and 4 had arrived earlier.

The real culprit is not the dengue virus, however, but rather the mosquito that serves as its vector, or carrier, without which the virus would have no way of spreading (dengue is not transmitted from person to person). *A. aegypti* is a master at coexisting with humans, and as human populations have grown and dispersed, so has this mosquito. Originally from Africa, *A. aegypti* circled the globe with early trading ships, breeding in stored-water containers, taking its blood meals from unsuspecting crew and passengers, and disembarking at each warm port city to seek a new home, just as the human travelers did. Today *A. aegypti* is present in most cities in warm climates, where it breeds in any kind of container capable of retaining water for the week or so required for the mosquito larva's aquatic development. Discarded tires, empty beer and soda cans, and plastic bottles collect rainwater and serve as welcome sites for breeding, as do buckets, flowerpots, clogged drain spouts, and hundreds of other products of modern society. Controlling *A. aegypti* is thus a very real challenge, as it is human habits and lifestyle that are the source of both the problem and the solution. Moreover, *A. aegypti* is also an important vector of the yellow fever virus.

Although dengue was mentioned in early medical writings, it has been only since the end of World War II that dengue and dengue hemorrhagic fever have had a significant impact on human health, starting in Southeast Asia with the rebuilding of war-damaged cities and the expansion of urban centers. As populations grew, dengue fever outbreaks became more common. Initially only a single type was responsible for the outbreaks; then multiple types began to circulate, one after another, and finally, more or less simultaneous transmission of all four occurred. With the circulation of multiple types of dengue, the more serious dengue hemorrhagic fever appeared, sporadically at first and then more regularly. As dengue viruses became increasingly common, the disease began to affect progressively younger individuals, who constitute the only remaining susceptible group. Today in Asia dengue and dengue hemorrhagic fever are most common among school-age children, and rather than emerging in periodic epidemics, both of these diseases are now present in Asia virtually all the time. This pattern is now being replayed in Latin America, and the future is clear; unless *A. aegypti* is controlled, dengue incidence will rise, hospitalizations due to dengue hemorrhagic fever will increase, and more deaths will occur. Increasingly, the victims will be children.

Return of yellow fever

Like the dengue virus, the yellow fever virus is transmitted by mosquitoes. Unlike dengue, however, which results in relatively few deaths, yellow fever is often fatal. Onset is sudden, and symptoms last for a week or more. Severely ill patients progress from fever to liver failure, internal bleeding (leading to the classic "black vomit"), and, in up to half or more of those hospitalized, death. There is no effective treatment or cure, but an excellent vaccine is available that offers probable lifelong immunity. Whereas with dengue, humans appear to be the only significant vertebrate host in the mosquito-human-mosquito transmission cycle, yellow fever has a "silent" jungle cycle that involves forest-dwelling mosquitoes and monkeys. Thus, the yellow fever virus continually circulates in nature in the jungles of Africa and the Amazon Basin. Humans become infected when they enter the jungle for work or recreation and are fed upon by infected jungle mosquitoes. If the infected individual returns home to a rural village, mosquitoes there, including *A. aegypti,* may feed upon the person while the virus is present in the bloodstream. Village-dwelling insects then become infected and subsequently transmit the virus to other human villagers. Because most people who live in endemic areas have been immunized, too few susceptible individuals are present to sustain continued transmission. If, however, an

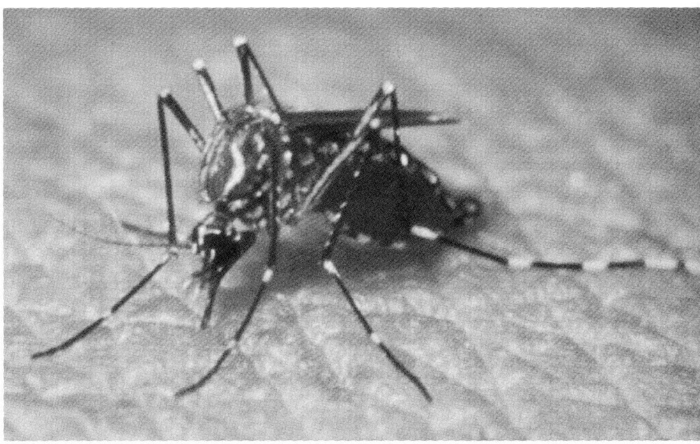

(Right) A female Aedes aegypti *mosquito prepares to ingest a meal of human blood. This species is an important vector of infectious diseases, including dengue and yellow fever. (Below) Any container in which water is allowed to stand for a week or more is a potential site for the development of* A. aegypti *larvae.*

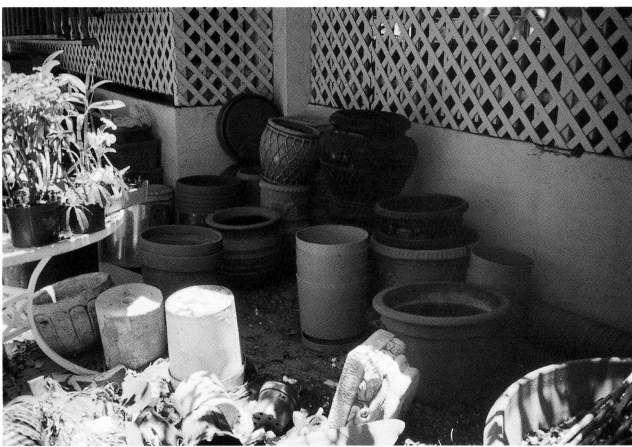

Centers for Disease Control and Prevention, San Juan, Puerto Rico; (top) Marco Suárez

Centers for Disease Control and Prevention, Fort Collins, Colo.

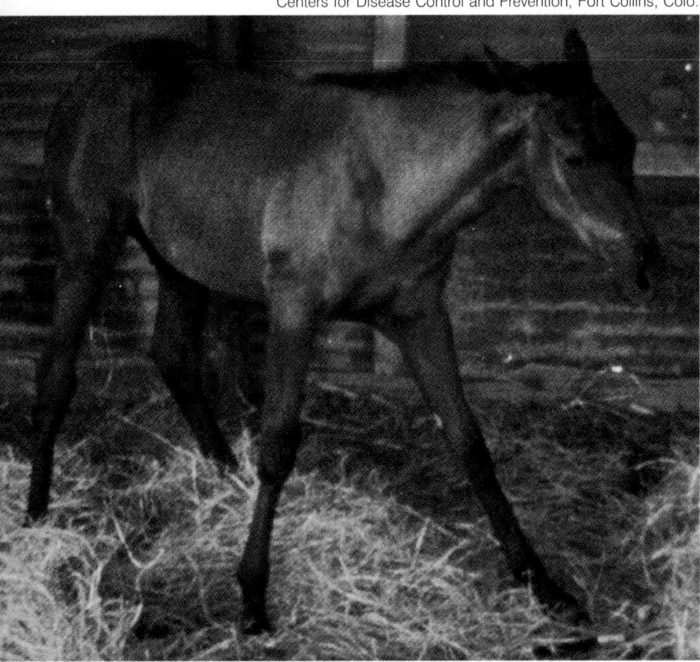

A horse with the characteristic signs of Venezuelan equine encephalitis. In 1995, after an absence of more than 20 years, this illness reappeared in Latin America in the form of a major epidemic.

infected person returns to an urban center where *A. aegypti* population densities are high and vaccination coverage low, then conditions are prime for a major urban outbreak of yellow fever. Unfortunately, this is precisely the set of conditions that now exists in many Latin-American cities, and as a consequence, urban transmission of yellow fever virus is perhaps the region's greatest health hazard. Ironically, despite dramatic advances in public health and medicine in the past 100 years, one of the same diseases that threatened human health at the start of the century remains a menace at century's end.

The threat of yellow fever is most acute on the fringes of the Amazon Basin, where human vaccination coverage is likely to be low, vector mosquito populations are high, and the virus is known to be present among the jungle primates and mosquitoes. A Peruvian epidemic in 1995, perhaps the largest jungle yellow fever outbreak ever recorded, serves to exemplify the growing threat of this disease. During the early 1990s rising coffee prices led to the expansion of coffee plantations into newly cleared forest areas. Many of the workers brought in to help clear the fields and plant the crop had not been vaccinated for yellow fever. Consequently, between January and July 1995, 440 workers, family members, and others were infected with yellow fever, and 169 died. Fortunately, the dispersion of infected people did not seed other outbreaks, but many experts believe that it is only a matter of time before a migrant worker infected with the yellow fever virus returns to Rio de Janeiro or São Paulo, Brazil, or another major tropical city infested with *A. aegypti,* triggering an epidemic of devastating proportions.

In its 1992 report on emerging infectious diseases, the Institute of Medicine (IOM), a branch of the U.S. National Research Council, created a sort of worst-case scenario for an outbreak of yellow fever in New Orleans, La., where the disease was once endemic. With a human population today of about one-half million, an abundant population of mosquitoes, including both *A. aegypti* and the recently introduced Asian tiger mosquito, *A. albopictus,* and a low rate of vaccination coverage, New Orleans possesses conditions that could be considered ideal for an epidemic. The IOM estimated that given the difficulty of obtaining a sufficient supply of yellow fever vaccine (the vaccine is no longer manufactured in the U.S. and would have to be imported) and the logistic problems of effective mosquito control, an estimated 100,000 of the city's residents could become ill with yellow fever, and 10,000 would likely die within a 90-day period. If one were to consider the same scenario in one of the Latin-American megacities, with a population 10 times or more that of New Orleans, it quickly becomes clear why public health officials in Latin America are gravely concerned about the possibility of urban yellow fever transmission.

Sick horses and humans in Venezuela

In the 1960s and early 1970s, Latin America experienced a serious outbreak of Venezuelan equine encephalitis (VEE). The epidemic originated in northern South America, spread through Central America and Mexico, and in 1971 entered southern Texas. Thousands of horses, donkeys, and mules were infected, and many died. Likewise, hundreds of people became ill, and several fatal cases were documented. Because enormously high levels of virus circulate in the blood of horses infected with VEE, many mosquito species normally considered to be only pests rather than disease vectors became infected and were able to transmit the virus. The abundance of mosquitoes capable of spreading the virus and the relocation of horses—some of which were incubating the disease when transported—served to amplify the epidemic and introduce it into new areas.

The outbreak finally ended in the United States following administration of 2,250,000 doses of VEE vaccine to horses and application of insecticide over more than 3.2 million ha (8 million ac) in Texas and Louisiana. In Latin America, where such costly interventions were not feasible, the epidemic ultimately burnt itself out after all the susceptible animals had become infected. The economic impact was difficult to estimate, since many rural villagers lost equines that were critical to their livelihoods.

Over the ensuing 20-plus years, the equine population has decreased in numbers, and the animals that survived the epidemic—and were therefore immune to reinfection—have been replaced by a new population of susceptible animals. Consequently, many authorities were concerned that the stage was set for another VEE epidemic. Indeed, their fears were well founded, for in October and November 1995, a major outbreak of VEE occurred, this time in Venezuela and Colombia. By the end of October 1995, over 45,000 people had been infected and hundreds of horses had died. It remained to be seen if this outbreak heralded the beginning of yet another major epizootic (*i.e.,* a disease affecting a large population of one animal species).

Hemorrhagic fevers: unhealthy harvest

One group of highly pathogenic South American viruses is maintained and transmitted by field mice. These viruses belong to the arenavirus family, Arenaviridae. The name comes from the Latin *arenosus,* which means "sandy"—under the electron microscope the surface of each virus particle appears to be covered with grains of sand. Each of the viruses is named for the location where it was first discovered: Machupo virus (the cause of Bolivian hemorrhagic fever), Junin virus (Argentine hemorrhagic fever), Guanarito virus (Venezuelan hemorrhagic fever), and Sabia virus (Brazilian hemorrhagic fever). Little is known about the latter, as it was only recently discovered. The others are spread not by common house mice or rats but rather by species that live in the bush, especially in agricultural areas, where they forage for food along the perimeter of the fields. As expected, humans who become infected with these viruses are predominantly farmers and their families, exposed through contact with the rodents or their infectious urine or droppings. Transmission has also been documented in hospital and laboratory settings, on occasion with fatal outcomes.

The clinical disease caused by all of these viruses is basically the same and is characterized by fever, weakness, headache, and eye pain. Patients are generally bedridden, and those who suffer severe disease may progress to bleeding, shock, and ultimately, in 15% to 30% of those hospitalized, death, depending upon the treatment they receive. Studies of Lassa fever, an infection caused by a related arenavirus (Lassa virus) found in Africa, have demonstrated the effectiveness of the antiviral drug ribavirin, and laboratory and animal tests suggest that this agent will work against the Latin-American arenaviruses as well.

Argentine hemorrhagic fever. Because it is endemic in the rich, fertile pampas of northern Argentina, Argentine hemorrhagic fever has considerable economic importance to the region in addition to its medical significance. The first recognized epidemic was in 1951–52; since then, outbreaks have occurred annually and have involved approximately 300–800 people per year. If provided only with supportive care, about 30–40% of hospitalized patients will die. Doctors in Argentina, however, have developed a process of collecting plasma (the fluid portion of the blood, which contains immune system components) from survivors and administering it to those who are acutely ill, and by so doing they have reduced the death rate to less than 1% when the treatment is given early in the course of disease.

Junin virus, the causative organism, is carried by the mouse *Calomys musculinus* and perhaps other species. Over the years, the distribution of the virus has grown and changed until today it involves large segments of several provinces west of the capital city of Buenos Aires. The reason for this expansion is not well understood; perhaps the creation of new agricultural areas or changes in farming practices are to blame, but at present nobody knows for sure. After more than a decade of work, collaborating scientists from Argentina and the U.S. succeeded in developing a vaccine for Junin virus. Between 1985 and 1988, this vaccine was tested in extensive safety trials among more than 300 human volunteers in the U.S.

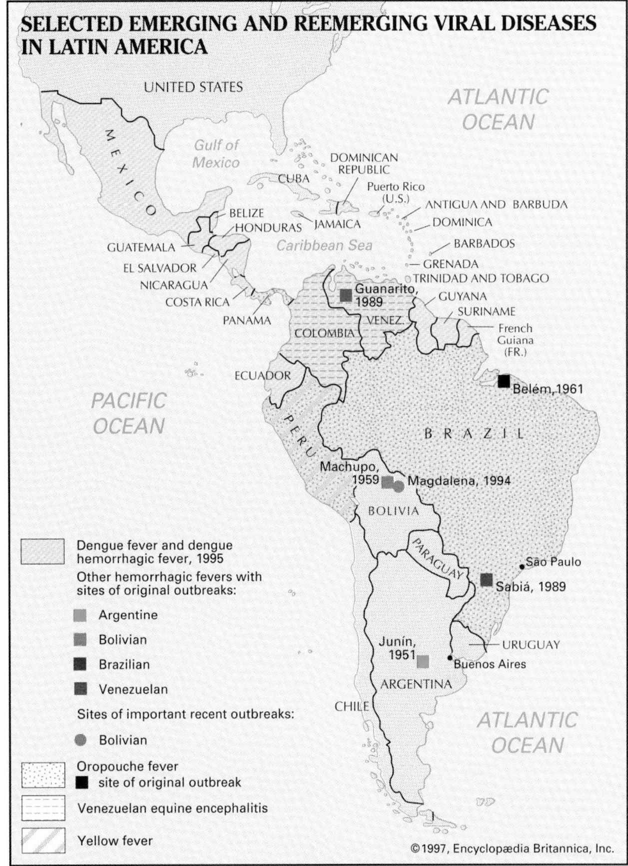

and later Argentina; then from 1988 to 1990, it was tested for both safety and efficacy in more than 6,500 persons at risk for the disease. The vaccine clearly proved efficacious and is now being offered to those at risk in the endemic area. This collaboration represents successful international cooperation in the fight against emerging diseases at its best.

Bolivian hemorrhagic fever. Like its cousin Junin virus, Machupo virus, the cause of Bolivian hemorrhagic fever, is also maintained by a rodent of the genus *Calomys,* in this case *C. callosus,* a species that lives along the borders between tropical grassland and forest on the eastern plains of Bolivia and adjacent areas in Brazil and Paraguay. The disease was first recognized in 1959, and by 1962 Bolivian health officials had reported 470 cases. Thirty percent of those who became ill died. In 1963–64 a large outbreak occurred in the town of San Joaquin after a population explosion among *C. callosus* led to an invasion of the town by hundreds of these mice. Following this outbreak only isolated and sporadic cases were seen, and scientists began to wonder if the virus had disappeared.

They got their answer in July 1994 when a cluster of new cases was identified among a family residing in Magdalena, a small town of about 5,000 inhabitants in the north-central district of Beni near the border with Brazil. Seven family members aged 10 months to 50 years were ill, and all but the first person to become infected died. Other isolated cases of Bolivian hemorrhagic fever were identified but, fortunately, no major outbreak occurred.

(Opposite page, top) © Claus Meyer—Black Star/PNI; (bottom) © Bruno Barbey—Magnum/PNI

During the 1994 outbreak a laboratory worker was exposed to the virus when a test tube containing blood from one of the patients broke. She was treated with ribavirin immediately. She developed a febrile disease but recovered completely; it could not be established if she was actually infected with Machupo virus or just coincidentally developed a bad cold.

Venezuelan hemorrhagic fever. An outbreak of severe hemorrhagic fever began in the city of Guanarito in the central Venezuelan state of Portuguesa in September 1989. At first doctors suspected dengue hemorrhagic fever or perhaps yellow fever, but laboratory tests ruled out these more common infectious disorders, and it soon became clear that a new disease had struck. Subsequent studies identified the cause as a new arenavirus, which was later named Guanarito after the site of the first outbreak. Studies have now confirmed the basic similarities between Guanarito virus and other Latin-American arenaviruses—the clinical course is quite similar, with the very real potential for fatal outcome, and as in the case of Junin and Machupo viruses, a rodent appears to be the reservoir for human infections. A different species of field mouse, the cane mouse, *Zygodontomys brevicauda,* appears to be involved, however. As with other Latin-American arenaviruses, the people most likely to become infected are those living in rural environments associated with agriculture; most cases occur in persons over the age of 16 or so, although both sexes are affected almost equally, a pattern that is somewhat unique to Guanarito virus. By early 1996 about 120 cases had been recognized; over half of these occurred between December and March, the dry season in Portuguesa state, when there is considerable agricultural activity.

Like other Latin-American arenaviruses, Guanarito virus persists in infected rodents, making itself increasingly known as humans enter the rodents' forest habitat in growing numbers. Authorities now familiar with this pattern cannot help but wonder how many other infectious organisms are awaiting discovery as the forests of the region continue to be invaded. Indeed, scientists studying Guanarito virus have recently identified another arenavirus, designated Pirital virus and found in another rodent species (*Sigmodon alstoni,* the cotton rat), but it is still unclear if this agent can cause human disease. Clearly these are not "new" viruses; they undoubtedly have been in existence for hundreds or even thousands of years, but they are only now becoming known.

Sabia virus: a cautionary tale

One of the most tragic episodes in the annals of emerging disease is the story of Sabia virus—not because of the magnitude of the outbreak but because of the personal story of the first reported victim. A previously healthy Brazilian woman, in her mid-20s and engaged to be married, began to feel ill in December 1989. She was repeatedly seen by doctors; then on Jan. 12, 1990, she was finally hospitalized. Over the next four days, her condition deteriorated. Fever, headache, muscle pains, vomiting, and weakness progressed to bleeding disorders, convulsions, and shock before she eventually died. The attending physicians were at a loss as to how to treat her, nor could they identify the cause of her illness. Initially they suspected everything from a systemic bacterial infection to leptospirosis, malaria, hepatitis, or yellow fever, but all of these diagnoses proved to be wrong. A blood sample drawn while the woman was hospitalized was tested at the Adolfo Lutz Institute in São Paulo after her death. A virus was indeed present in the sample, but because a major dengue outbreak was in progress, and the laboratory was already overwhelmed, the organism, which proved not to be dengue, was stored for later study.

Subsequently, the virus was examined by electron microscopy, and the characteristic sandlike surface projections typical of arenaviruses were seen, which prompted the scientists in São Paulo to request help from colleagues at the Evandro Chagas Institute in Belém, Brazil, who had more experience with arenaviruses and possessed the appropriate reagents needed to identify the virus. There a laboratory technician given the task of characterizing the virus became infected and suffered a severe disease similar to that of the first victim. He was hospitalized but survived and recovered fully. Work was halted in Belém, and the virus was next sent to the world-famous Yale Arbovirus Research Unit at Yale University School of Medicine. By then it was clear that this was a new, highly pathogenic arenavirus. It was designated Sabia virus, after the community where the first patient had been staying when she became ill.

As investigators at Yale attempted to further characterize the organism, a test tube broke in a centrifuge, and while cleaning up the accident, a scientist was apparently infected by aerosolized viral particles. Initially the researcher did not realize the seriousness of the accident, and when he came down with a fever several days later, a recurrence of malaria was suspected. It was only later when an astute clinician ruled out malaria, noted that blood tests were suggestive of a viral infection, and asked about recent work in the laboratory that the likelihood of another Sabia infection was discovered. The scientist was quickly hospitalized under isolation conditions and started on ribavirin. Fortunately, the infection was aborted, and the patient recovered fully. For now, the story ends here: three victims, one death. When and where Sabia—or another new arenavirus—will strike is not known, but it is certain that the saga of the Latin-American arenaviruses is not yet finished.

Oropouche fever: deforestation's legacy

Unlike the other viral diseases described above, Oropouche fever is not fatal; those infected suffer a fever, headache, muscle and joint pains, and sometimes nausea and vomiting, usually lasting up to a week and followed by complete recovery. The disease is of note, however, because it is an excellent example of how changes in land use and human behavior have created the conditions that allowed a rare, insignificant virus to become a major public health problem. Whereas urban sprawl and waste have created ideal breeding grounds for the mosquitoes that transmit dengue, the increased incidence of Oropouche fever appears to be a direct result of deforestation of the Amazon Basin and the agriculture practices that followed.

Oropouche virus was first discovered in Trinidad when it was isolated from the blood of an ailing forest worker.

(Top) The clearing of rain-forest land for agricultural use is thought to be responsible for increased incidence of Oropouche fever, a viral illness transmitted by gnats that breed in vegetation discarded by banana and cacao growers. (Above) The advent of megacities, the burgeoning of populations of urban poor, and dramatic increases in travel and trade all have played a part in the recent resurgence of infectious diseases in Latin America.

Later, studies in Belém found isolated examples of infected mosquitoes and sloths. Little was known about the natural history of the virus or its epidemic potential until 1961, however, the year of the first recognized Oropouche outbreak in Belém, in which an estimated 11,000 persons were infected. Since then about 30 epidemics have occurred across the Amazon Basin, into Peru and even in Panama. The total number of cases has been difficult to estimate, since in recent years Oropouche outbreaks have coincided with the transmission of dengue fever, and the two are clinically quite similar. Nonetheless, each of two of the better-documented large Oropouche outbreaks led to an estimated 100,000 cases; a total of nearly a million people have probably been stricken, and the numbers are likely to grow as agricultural development continues.

The mode of transmission of the Oropouche virus has always been perplexing, but scientists now think that tiny biting gnats (sometimes dubbed "no-see-ums") are the vector. These insects are small enough to fly right through normal window screening, and they readily feed on humans. The prime suspect vector of Oropouche virus is *Culicoides paraensis,* a species that breeds in decomposing organic matter, especially rotting banana tree stalks and the discarded husks of cacao. These wastes have become extremely common throughout the tropics as land cultivation has spread, and this has led to very high population densities of *Culicoides,* often followed by epidemic waves of Oropouche fever. As development of the region continues, increasing outbreaks of Oropouche are likely, both in areas where it has not been seen previously and recurring in cities already affected.

Nature's balance disrupted

The diseases cited above have one thing in common; they are becoming increasingly prevalent or, in the case of yellow fever, threatening to become so. The reasons for their growing prevalence are as different as the viruses themselves. Nonetheless, a few common themes appear. Aside from dengue, all of these viruses are really zoonoses—that is, organisms that affect animals primarily and humans only incidentally—and all are transmitted by an animal vector, either insect or rodent. As humans encroach into the areas where these viruses coexist with their zoonotic hosts, the balance of nature is disrupted and human disease follows.

The obvious question, then, is why do humans force themselves into these areas? Clearly, many of the basic forces influencing the world today contribute; these include population growth and poverty, leading to deforestation and invasion by humans into new areas, and urban growth and its attendant squalor, with the shear number of people outpacing the abilities of municipalities to provide clean water and sanitation. Another factor that plays a part in the emergence of new diseases is the dramatic increase in travel, both nationally and internationally, enabling an individual to be infected in one corner of the world but become ill in a distant place, at the same time introducing a new virus into that place.

Still another factor is the expansion of international trade, which has served as an alternative vehicle for disease or disease vectors. The Asian tiger mosquito, for example, was introduced into both North and South America with shipments of used truck tires from Asia. The tires were stored outside prior to shipment, rainwater collected in them, and *A. albopictus* eggs were deposited around the waterline. Even though the tires may have been dried prior to shipment, the drought-resistant eggs survived and were ready to hatch when the tires again were flooded with rainwater after reaching their destination on the other side of the Pacific Ocean. The result: a new, competent vector species, which also happens to be an aggressive pest, was introduced into the Americas. A decade after its introduction, the species is well entrenched as a solid part of the local fauna in much of North and South America.

A global strategy

The single most important step in addressing the problem of new and resurging infectious diseases, not only in Latin America but indeed globally, has been acknowledgment of the problem. In the United States this came about initially in 1988 when concerned scientists organized a meeting in Washington, D.C., to discuss emerging viral illnesses. The conference was followed in 1992 by the IOM report *Emerging Infections: Microbial Threats to Health in the United States,* which highlighted many of the shortcomings, both national and international, in disease surveillance, training of fieldworkers, and other key aspects of public health. This publication, in turn, stimulated the U.S. Centers for Disease Control and Prevention to develop a carefully crafted plan to address emerging diseases. In recognition of the fact that infectious illnesses quite obviously do not respect national borders, a significant part of that plan focuses on international health.

The World Health Organization (WHO) also has taken notice of emerging diseases; in 1995, during the World Health Assembly, where the annual agenda for international health is set, a resolution was endorsed establishing a global strategy to address the problem. That strategy has four basic objectives: (1) to improve recognition of new, emerging, and resurgent diseases through better surveillance; (2) to build or, in many cases, rebuild the public health infrastructure of many nations because these critical assets have deteriorated over years of economic cuts and neglect; (3) to encourage applied research activities—for example, application of recent advances in biotechnology to diagnostic testing and tools for epidemiological research; and, finally, (4) to use the fruits of these efforts to enhance the prevention and control of infectious diseases.

These fundamental objectives have formed the basis for implementation plans now under way in each of the six WHO regions. The Pan American Health Organization was the first WHO regional office to serve as host to an organizational meeting, develop a specific regional plan, and gain approval for it by its regional advisory board. Implementation of that plan is now in full swing, with initial efforts focusing on improved communication, better national disease surveillance and reporting, and improved diagnostic laboratory capabilities. Most Latin-American nations are strongly behind these efforts, and the overall outlook is one of optimism. While

(continued on page 274)

NEWS CAP

Malaria Update: Don't Forget the Bednet

Just 30 years ago, malaria was on the slate for eradication. Today the optimism of the post-World War II era appears surprisingly naive as the disease reemerges with a vengeance. Scientists at the World Health Organization fear that over the coming decade malaria parasites resistant to all known drugs could easily emerge from Southeast Asia and spread into parts of Africa, where the transmission of infection is especially intense. That, say the scientists, would be a disastrous turning point in the history of a dreadful disease.

Every year, between 300 million and 500 million people become infected with malaria, and one million to two million die of the disease, the vast majority of them being children in Africa. In terms of disease burden—measured in years of healthy life lost, or "disability-adjusted life years"—only six other illnesses claim a heavier toll in the world's less developed countries.

The ease of international travel has made people in industrialized nations, too, increasingly vulnerable to malaria. About one in every 200 business travelers to Kenya returns home with the parasite; the United States now reports about 1,000 cases a year. And as human populations migrate at an increasingly rapid rate, even supposedly safe regions are now seeing occasional cases of locally transmitted malaria. In 1994 researchers reported two cases in suburban New Jersey, in individuals who had had no connection with endemic countries.

In humans malaria is caused by four protozoan parasites belonging to the genus *Plasmodium;* the most virulent species is *P. falciparum* and the most widespread, *P. vivax.* Alarmingly, resistant strains of the parasite are emerging much faster than new drugs. By the mid-1990s all malaria-endemic regions except Central America had reported some degree of resistance to the mainstay of antimalarial drugs, chloroquine. In addition, resistance to another first-line treatment, sulfadoxine/pyrimethamine, has developed in Southeast Asia, South America, and some African countries. In parts of Thailand more than half of all *Plasmodium* strains are resistant to the newer drug mefloquine; even quinine, reserved for severe malaria, seems to be losing its power there. Drug resistance has emerged more slowly in Africa, but that situation is now changing.

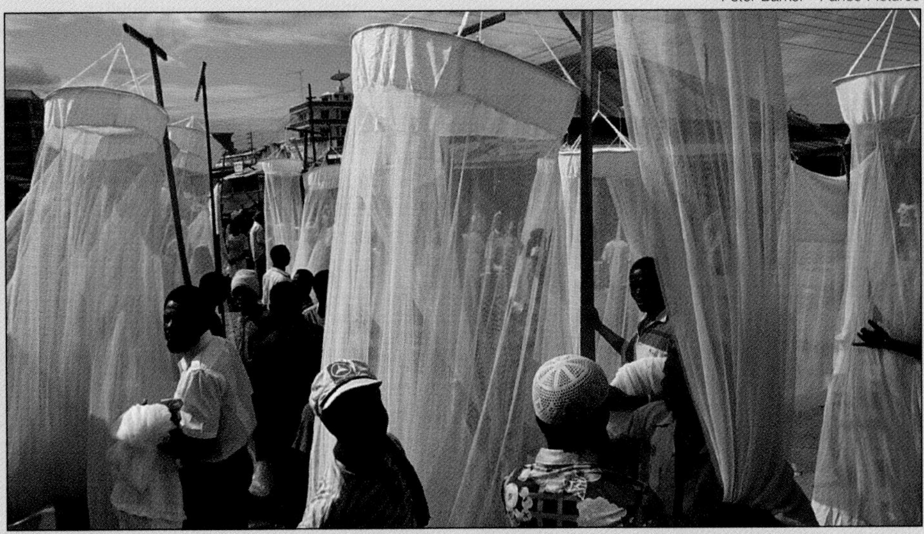
Peter Barker—Panos Pictures

Currently there are no licensed vaccines for malaria. However, hopes ran high in the early '90s when a synthetic vaccine devised by Colombian biochemist Manuel Patarroyo produced encouraging results in Latin America and Tanzania (promoting Patarroyo to hero status). But those hopes were dashed in 1995 when, in trials in West Africa, the vaccine failed to protect young children from getting the disease. Meanwhile, other potential vaccines are being developed, including an "altruistic" vaccine that does not stop its human recipient from becoming infected but prevents the parasites from being spread to other persons. Such a vaccine works by interfering with the parasite's ability to reproduce in the gut of the mosquito that carries it and transmits it to humans. Safety trials of an altruistic vaccine called pfs-25 began in late 1995.

While the world waits for a vaccine, humbler preventive solutions will have to do. The simple bednet treated with insecticide has proved highly effective, even in the most endemic areas. For the foreseeable future, at least, no traveler heading for a malarious region should leave home without one.

—*Phyllida Brown*

(continued from page 272)
the problem is far from solved, most public health authorities agree that a meaningful plan is in place, and concrete steps are being taken to implement it.

Elsewhere, many years of basic research are finally starting to pay off. An excellent example is the Junin vaccine already mentioned. Likewise, a vaccine capable of protecting against all four dengue virus types is now in pilot production, with safety tests due to begin in 1996 or early 1997. Advances in molecular virology have enabled scientists to quickly characterize new viruses that are closely related antigenically and genetically. And field studies of the drug ribavirin in Africa have provided the technical basis for exploration of its value in treating emerging infections in Latin America.

Progress is being made on the social front as well. With the recognition of the growing importance of dengue and dengue hemorrhagic fever and the threat of urban outbreaks of yellow fever, public health officials in Brazil are now seriously considering investing substantial sums to eradicate the vector, *A. aegypti.* Community action campaigns have already been developed in many Latin-American countries in an attempt to control *A. aegypti,* and some city governments are tackling the difficult task of improving living conditions in the slums, providing electricity and clean water.

On the right track

It should be apparent that there will be no "quick fixes" for the problem of emerging diseases. The root causes go to the most basic of human needs: a place to live and food to eat. Moreover, these needs are being shared by ever-increasing numbers of people. These pressures will continue to force people into previously uninhabited areas where "new" viruses will be encountered; cities will continue to grow, and well-adapted vectors such as *A. aegypti* will thrive. Countering these trends will require all segments of society to work together, both nationally and internationally. A plan has been developed and is now being implemented, but it will be costly—it has been estimated that the U.S. program alone will cost as much as $125 million when fully implemented—and it will take time, dedication, and persistence. Fortunately, the effort under way appears to be on the right track and has a good chance of succeeding.

—James W. LeDuc, Ph.D.

Immunization Update

The year 1996 marks the bicentennial of the world's first vaccine, Edward Jenner's homegrown inoculation against smallpox. Jenner, an English country physician, derived his preparation from cowpox pustules on the arms of a dairymaid; an eight-year-old boy, James Phipps, was the first recipient. Jenner called his experimental procedure "vaccination" (from the Latin word *vacca,* "cow"). Subsequently, the manufacturing process was refined, and smallpox vaccine became the weapon that by 1977 had eradicated a merciless disease from the planet. The celebration of this 200th anniversary of the first vaccine is a perfect time to reflect on the monumental impact that vaccines have had—in terms of lives and money saved and suffering eliminated—and to consider the promise that these uniquely efficient tools hold for the health and well-being of humankind in the future.

Success stories

Following Jenner's discovery, it took nearly two centuries to control and eradicate smallpox. Over the years, however, the time between the development, production, and delivery of subsequent vaccines (also known as immunizations)—and the virtual control and elimination of the diseases they are meant to protect against—diminished substantially. For example, the push to develop an effective vaccine against paralytic poliomyelitis (polio) began in the late 1930s, when an experimental model of the disease was established and the poliovirus was first isolated. In 1949 the advent of tissue culture technology meant that the virus could be reliably grown in a laboratory. Only five years later, Jonas Salk's inactivated polio vaccine (IPV) was developed, tested, and licensed, and just a few years later (1960), another approach to polio vaccination, Albert Sabin's oral polio vaccine (OPV), was first used. (The former is delivered by injection; the latter, now given as drops but probably best known for its sugar-cube mode of delivery.) The broad use of these vaccines brought about a rapid decline in polio incidence. In the United States this decline in disease led to the closing of large hospital wards (with their rows upon rows of iron lungs) and the relegation of immunization campaign paraphernalia—*e.g.,* March of Dimes posters featuring childhood polio victims—to historical archives. In the U.S. the last case of naturally occurring (also known as "wild-type") polio was in 1979. Today national immunization campaigns around the world are making major headway. In Latin America, for example, the last case of wild-type poliomyelitis occurred in Peru in 1991. Following in the footsteps of smallpox eradication, an international campaign to eradicate polio by the year 2000 is being waged. This effort, organized by the World Health Organization, seems likely to succeed.

More recently, the development and initial licensing of safe and effective vaccines against *Haemophilus influenzae* type b (Hib) disease resulted in a dramatic reduction of this disease in the United States. Prior to the initial introduction of an Hib vaccine in 1985, approximately one in 200 children in the U.S. suffered from severe infections—primarily meningitis and pneumonia—caused by this bacterium, and nearly 20,000 children under five years of age were hospitalized each year. The widespread use of Hib vaccine in infants reduced the incidence of infection to such a remarkable extent that in 1995 only 270 cases were reported to the Centers for Disease Control and Prevention (CDC) in Atlanta, Ga.

Refined and designed

These monumental successes represent victories from an era when vaccine development was a purely empirical science (based on trial and error). Scientific and technical leaps in the fields of immunology, molecular biology, and genetics in the 1970s and '80s substantially broadened the horizons for vaccine development. New generations of highly refined and

Simon Fraser—Science Source/Photo Researchers

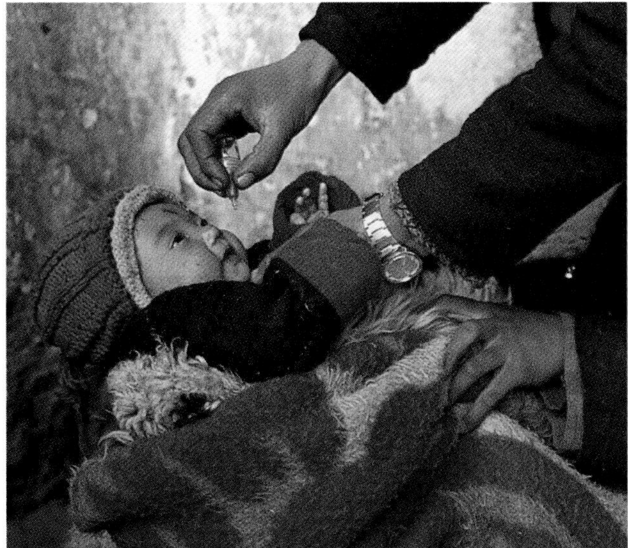

A child in India receives oral polio vaccine. In 1994 polio was declared conquered in the Western Hemisphere. A campaign to eradicate the disease from the rest of the world by the year 2000 is well under way.

genetically engineered (*i.e.,* designed) vaccines will, in the near future, protect against a long list of infectious diseases. In addition, now that several chronic diseases such as cervical cancer and stomach ulcers have been traced to chronic infections, vaccines under development may prevent these conditions as well, in the same way that hepatitis B vaccine will prevent liver cancers caused by hepatitis B.

The timetable for the development of any single vaccine is lengthy, and success is uncertain until the product is licensed and used. Licensure of the classical vaccines, such as those against rubella and polio, took place decades after identification of the respective pathogens. New technologies such as recombinant DNA approaches (discussed below) may truly accelerate the development process, but there are also significant obstacles. Physical, biochemical, engineering, and logistic challenges are inevitably encountered in the process of scaling up manufacturing processes from laboratory experiments to mass production. Vaccine manufacturers must ensure that mass-marketed vaccine products are the same as those that were demonstrated to be safe and immunogenic (able to produce an immune response) in clinical trials, which evaluated vaccines that were produced in smaller pilot lots.

Vaccine pipeline. There are a large number of candidate vaccines in the research and development pipeline—many of which are likely to be discarded as they proceed along the evaluation pathway when they come to dead ends. For example, if a candidate vaccine has too many side effects, it will not proceed from limited (Phase 1) trials in a small number of healthy adults to trials involving large numbers of adults and sometimes children (Phase 2). If the protective effect (immune response) does not seem promising during Phase 2 trials, few manufacturers will be willing to invest the necessary resources for an efficacy (Phase 3) trial. Only vaccines reaching this level of evaluation will be tested for efficacy in Phase 3 trials (involving 10,000–100,000 volunteers). In addition to these clinical trials, before a vaccine will be licensed, the manufacturer must perform additional laboratory studies that are needed to ensure safety, purity, and potency of the vaccine and consistency in the manufacturing process.

Logistic considerations. The steps that follow the decision to develop a new vaccine—from concept through licensing—are, in theory, straightforward. In reality, however, many questions must be answered and logistic considerations addressed—a process that involves numerous players: research scientists, biotechnology and vaccine companies, public-sector manufacturers, users (*e.g.,* health care providers, insurance companies, immunization program managers), and, ultimately, recipients. Consequently, even in this age of recombinant DNA technology, the process of developing a new vaccine is unlikely to take less than a decade or, conservatively, to cost less than $200 million.

In 1985 the Institute of Medicine (IOM) of the National Research Council was commissioned by the National Institutes of Health (NIH) to review the growing field of "vaccinology" and define priorities for vaccine research and development. The IOM committee considered, among other things, the technical feasibility of developing new vaccines, the epidemiology of the diseases that the vaccines would protect against, target populations, the relative efficacy of each new vaccine (*i.e.,* the extent to which illness and death would be reduced), and the relative cost-effectiveness of this prevention strategy. This evaluation approach enabled the IOM to establish priorities. Identified as the highest priorities were vaccines against Hib, varicella (chicken pox), hepatitis B, and typhoid. In the decade following the IOM report, all of these immunizations were developed and tested, and they are now licensed in the U.S. Currently, hepatitis B and Hib vaccines are being incorporated into global immunization programs.

Because vaccinology has advanced so dramatically in the past decade, the IOM has again been requested to review priorities for vaccine development. The evaluation in progress, which is expected to be completed by the end of 1996, is examining not only traditional vaccines against infectious diseases but potential vaccines to protect against allergies, autoimmune diseases, and cancer.

Emerging technologies

While there are ever-increasing numbers of conceptual approaches to vaccine development, two stand out as particularly promising: DNA vaccines—a revolutionary step forward in vaccine methodology—and genetically manipulated plants that may be the vaccine "factories" of the future.

DNA vaccines. In experiments in mice, when plasmids (extrachromosomal genetic particles) containing DNA from a microbial pathogen are injected into muscle, they instruct the cells to produce antigens (substances that are recognized by the body as foreign) that mimic those of the pathogen and create a strong response to the antigen. That observation has already begun to revolutionize human vaccine design. This technology allows for the design of specific gene sequences. Thus, a desired antigen (the molecule that will stimulate the immune system and results in protective immunity) can be created. As a potential vaccine, the plasmid may then be

Merck & Co., Inc.; photograph, Maureen Murphy

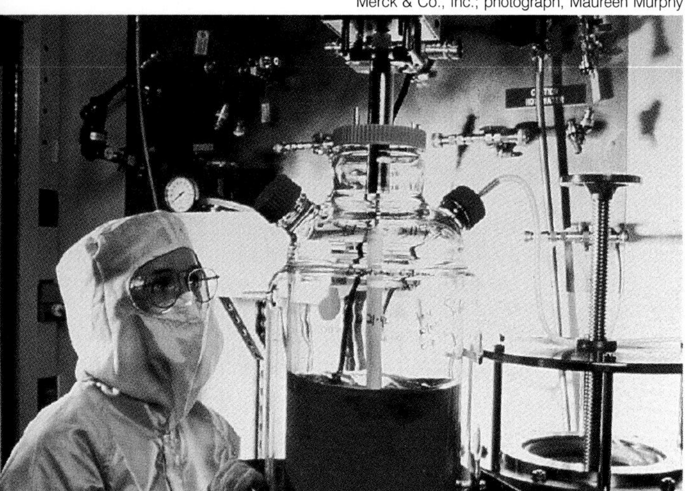

Manufacture of hepatitis A vaccine. Scientists spent several decades developing two recently licensed vaccine products that protect against the highly infectious, liver-damaging hepatitis A virus.

administered either by injection, by nasal spray, or orally. This scientifically elegant approach may be the technological leap scientists have been waiting for—one that will allow a whole new generation of vaccines to be developed. It is now theoretically possible to construct vaccines that will protect against several infectious diseases at once and thereby reduce the number of doses needed to generate an effective immune response. Despite what may appear to be complex products, these vaccines may prove to be relatively inexpensive to produce. Animal studies have proceeded at an accelerated pace, and this has allowed the first human trials of DNA vaccines against influenza and HIV infection to begin in 1996.

Banana-based vaccines? An unlikely offshoot of the "Green Revolution" is the ability to manipulate the genes of certain plants in such a way as to produce desirable traits (such as disease resistance). How does this apply to vaccine development? Desirable genes that are incorporated into such transgenic plants express proteins that, when used as a vaccine, are recognized by the recipient's immune system. Such recognition results in an immune response that stands ready to protect the immunized individual against infection by specific pathogens. Among the plants that are being explored as vehicles for vaccines are bananas and potatoes. Indeed, this technology may eventually create "edible" vaccines that would have several theoretical advantages over existing vaccines. Production of such products would be relatively inexpensive and could occur in less developed countries, where cost-effective, easily delivered vaccines are needed most.

Newly licensed vaccines

Today's technologies have already enabled several new and improved vaccines to be developed and, in the past year or so, marketed. These newly licensed products protect against pertussis (whooping cough), hepatitis A, varicella, and typhoid.

Acellular pertussis. Pertussis, a respiratory disease that produces prolonged cough, generally with a characteristic "whoop," can lead to choking, seizures, and even death. It is a disease that affects more than 50 million people around the world annually, causing about 500,000 deaths. In the U.S. whole-cell pertussis vaccines have been responsible for reducing infection from a peak of more than 260,000 cases in 1934 to about 4,300 cases in 1995. Although whole-cell pertussis vaccines were used effectively for decades, they were associated with occasional adverse reactions (*e.g.,* fever, seizures, encephalopathy [brain tissue alterations]). Parents' fears of adverse effects caused immunization rates to plunge. The whole-cell vaccine is made from killed, inactivated preparations of the whole cell of the pertussis toxin, which includes dozens of cellular components that are thought to be associated with the reactogenicity (side effects) ranging from fever and redness and pain at the injection site to seizures and acute encephalopathy. For the past 15 years, the U.S. has focused on developing safer pertussis vaccines. This research effort bore fruit in 1995 with the conclusion of several large Phase 3 clinical trials of highly purified acellular pertussis (aP) vaccines. The new vaccines are made up of one or more inactivated, purified, or recombinant antigens. The trials (conducted in Sweden, Italy, Germany, and Senegal) all used slightly different study designs, vaccine schedules, and case definitions for pertussis, which made direct comparisons difficult. But several conclusions could be drawn. The new acellular vaccines as a group are much less reactogenic than whole-cell products, with low rates of fever and local reactions and few, if any, episodes of seizures and other acute idiosyncratic events. Also, most of the acellular pertussis vaccines were found to be as effective as or more effective than several whole-cell vaccines.

Although acellular pertussis vaccines for use in infants have been licensed and available in other countries, one of the many acellular pertussis vaccines recently evaluated (Tripedia) was first licensed in the U.S. in 1996. In these new products, acellular pertussis vaccine is combined with vaccines against diphtheria and tetanus (DTaP) but not yet with other childhood vaccines (such as Hib, hepatitis B, or polio). Therefore, as noted above, the new pertussis vaccines initially will increase the total number of injections that are required for a child to be fully immunized. The development of safer pertussis vaccines marks the culmination of an unprecedented collaboration between industry, parents, physicians, researchers, and government and serves as a model for the development of new and improved vaccines.

Hepatitis A. Hepatitis A is principally an infection of children, in whom the illness is usually mild and often not detected. In other words, children are the main reservoir of the virus. In contrast, infected adults may be severely ill for several weeks. Two new vaccines that protect against hepatitis A (Havrix and VAQTA) are likely to replace the use of serum-derived immune globulin (gamma globulin, or immunoglobulin) in many situations. Although the latter has been used for decades, it offers limited protection for three to six months.

The new vaccines are recommended for adults at heightened risk for exposure to hepatitis A—military personnel and other persons traveling to or working in countries in which hepatitis A is endemic, homosexual men, injecting drug users, persons with an occupational risk for infection (mainly lab

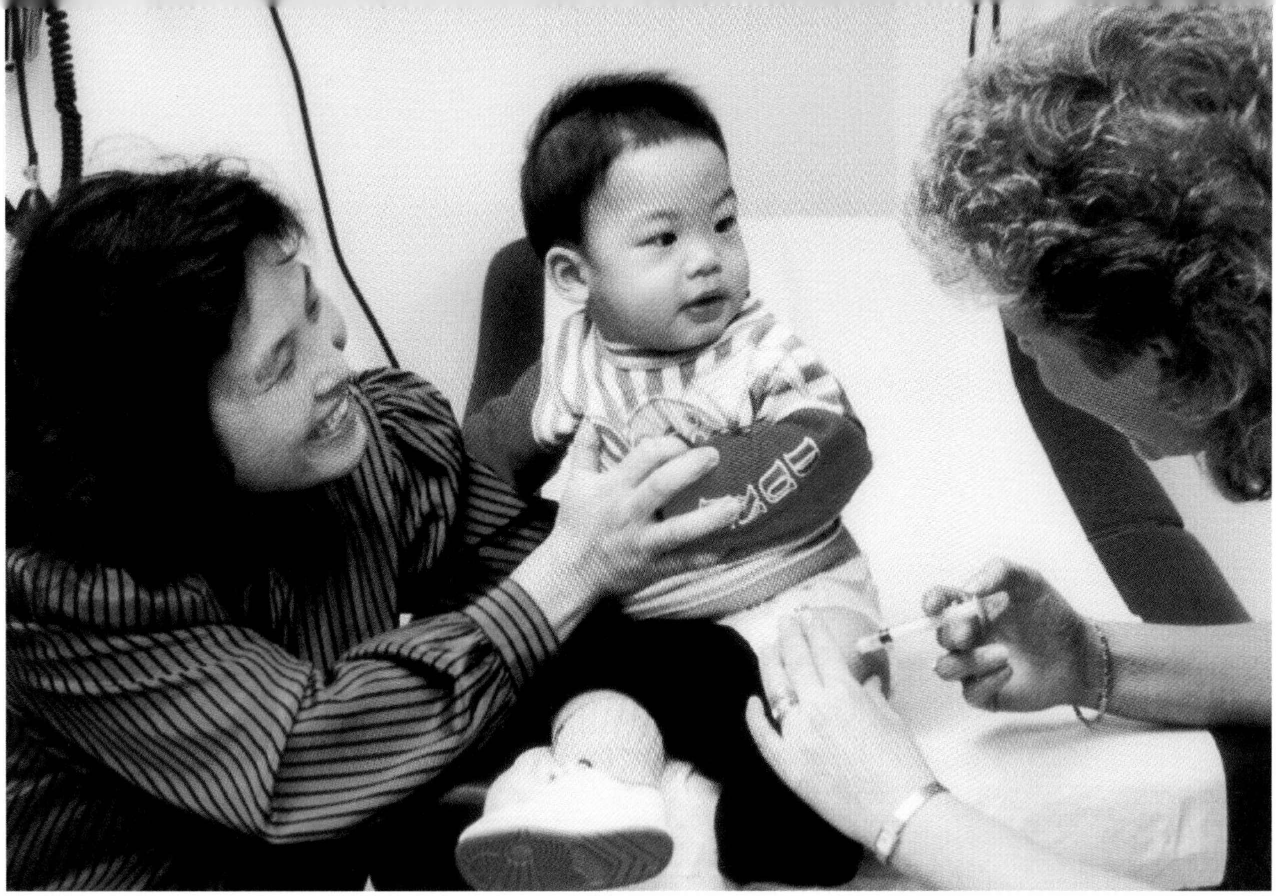

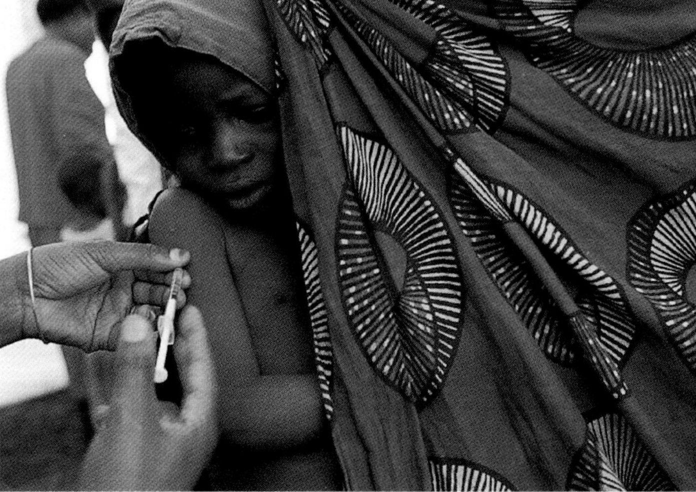

(Top) Timothy Vang seems to know that having measles, mumps, or rubella (German measles) would hurt a lot more than the single shot it takes to prevent them. (Above left) Batman and Robin take a tough stance on vaccines. (Above right) A Rwandan child in a refugee camp is immunized against measles—a shot that could be lifesaving. Crowding and poor sanitation tend to promote the spread of virulent infections.

workers who handle live hepatitis A virus), and persons in whom hepatitis is likely to be unusually severe (such as persons with preexisting liver disease).

Currently it is not universally recommended that day-care workers, food handlers, or others be immunized. In adults the new vaccines require two doses administered at least six months apart; therefore, they may not be especially practical for the international traveler who requires such protection on short notice. For short-term and/or occasional travelers who are unlikely to require long-lasting immunity against the hepatitis A virus, immunoglobulin may still be the preferred protection.

Varicella. Chicken pox is mainly a disease of children. It is usually self-limited and usually weathered without substantial complications or sequelae. In mild cases varicella may cause fever and can predispose to superimposed bacterial skin infections and lead to scarring. In severe cases, especially in immunocompromised children and adults, varicella infection can be fatal. Changing demographic factors, however, such as the increasing numbers of children in day care, increased the demand for a chicken pox vaccine; most day-care centers and schools will not allow children with chicken pox to attend until they have fully recovered. The first varicella vaccine (Varivax) was licensed in 1995.

(Top and bottom left) Immunization Action Coalition; (bottom right) Steve Lehman—RÉA/Saba

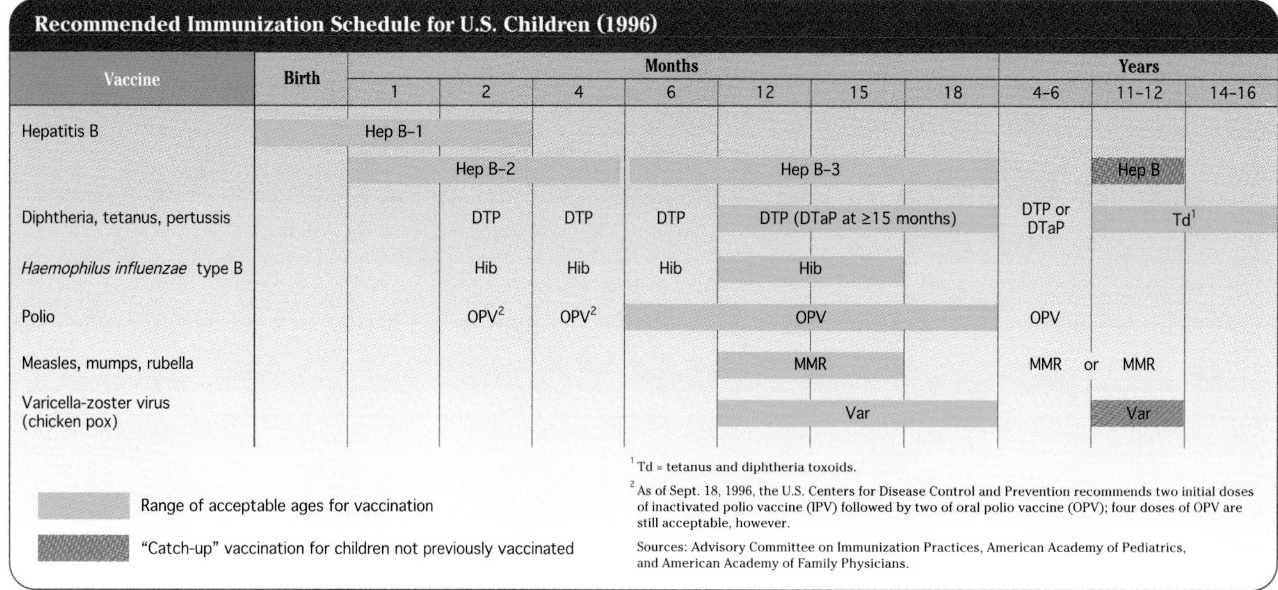

Recommended Immunization Schedule for U.S. Children (1996)

Vaccine	Birth	Months 1	2	4	6	12	15	18	Years 4-6	11-12	14-16
Hepatitis B		Hep B-1									
			Hep B-2			Hep B-3				Hep B	
Diphtheria, tetanus, pertussis			DTP	DTP	DTP	DTP (DTaP at ≥15 months)			DTP or DTaP	Td[1]	
Haemophilus influenzae type B			Hib	Hib	Hib	Hib					
Polio			OPV[2]	OPV[2]		OPV			OPV		
Measles, mumps, rubella						MMR			MMR or	MMR	
Varicella-zoster virus (chicken pox)						Var				Var	

Range of acceptable ages for vaccination

"Catch-up" vaccination for children not previously vaccinated

[1] Td = tetanus and diphtheria toxoids.

[2] As of Sept. 18, 1996, the U.S. Centers for Disease Control and Prevention recommends two initial doses of inactivated polio vaccine (IPV) followed by two of oral polio vaccine (OPV); four doses of OPV are still acceptable, however.

Sources: Advisory Committee on Immunization Practices, American Academy of Pediatrics, and American Academy of Family Physicians.

Currently, it is recommended that all children in the U.S. receive the vaccine. The vaccine is also recommended for certain susceptible adolescents and adults: health care workers, household contacts of immunocompromised persons, and persons living or working in an environment with a high risk for varicella virus transmission (*e.g.,* day-care attendants).

Shingles (zoster) is a recrudescence of latent varicella infection; the virus remains quiescent in the nervous system for decades. Common in the elderly, this painful condition can be relentless and debilitating. Preliminary evidence suggests that chicken pox vaccine recipients may have a lower incidence of zoster in later life, and those who are affected may have a milder infection. It is not yet clear, however, which adults should receive Varivax. Those adults who have had chicken pox in the past are assumed to be immune already. It is currently estimated that only about 10% of the adult population is likely to be susceptible to varicella and thus may need the vaccine. At present, the most cost-effective approach is to carry out serological testing (analysis of the watery serum portion of the blood) to determine susceptibility prior to immunization of adults without an obvious history of varicella.

Typhoid. Typhoid, also called typhoid fever, is an acute infectious disease of humans caused by the bacterium *Salmonella typhi.* The bacterium usually enters the body through the mouth by the ingestion of contaminated food or water, penetrates the intestinal wall, and enters the bloodstream within 24 to 72 hours, causing septicemia (blood poisoning) and systemic infection.

Typhoid vaccines have been available since the beginning of the 20th century, but these have not been entirely effective, safe, or beneficial. Immunization against typhoid is not required for travel to or from countries in which typhoid is endemic, such as Peru, India, Pakistan, and Chile. However, the availability of new efficacious typhoid vaccines with greatly improved safety profiles now makes vaccination of international travelers possible and probably beneficial. An oral vaccine (requiring four doses over seven days) became available in 1994, and a new single-dose injected typhoid vaccine (Vi CPS) was licensed in 1995. Individuals who should avoid the live-attenuated oral vaccine are those who are immunocompromised, pregnant, or receiving antibiotics or mefloquine (for malaria).

AIDS vaccines: not yet

Despite early optimism that an AIDS vaccine would rapidly follow the discovery of HIV, the virus that causes AIDS, the development of such a vaccine continues to be impeded by both scientific and financial obstacles. While over 20 candidate vaccines to prevent AIDS have been given to uninfected human volunteers since 1988, to date no large-scale trials have been undertaken because no candidate vaccine has been found to be promising enough. Researchers and public health officials in Thailand, where approximately one million of the country's 60 million citizens may be HIV-positive, are now considering a large efficacy trial to assess a first-generation vaccine. Though the vaccine is likely to be only partially effective, this is seen as a worthwhile interim goal.

In February 1996 a conference on "Advances in AIDS Vaccine Development" was dominated by the unveiling of a new strategic plan by the National Institute of Allergy and Infectious Diseases (NIAID). The plan reinforced the need for continuing both basic research and empirical research in the development of vaccines against HIV. It acknowledged that many companies involved in HIV vaccine research and development had either terminated their programs or reduced their investments over the past two to three years. Most important, the plan emphasized the need for "more and better-defined partnerships between NIAID and industry sponsors of vaccine development."

Though AIDS is a global disease, the HIV subtypes that cause it are not the same all over the world. International health specialists have expressed concern that costly vaccine-development efforts are not being targeted at strains of the virus that are prevalent in the less developed world and that a number of potential vaccine approaches have been underexplored. Recognizing this, the Rockefeller Foundation in New York City, in conjunction with the United Nations AIDS Program, the Merieux Foundation of France, and the U.S.-based "Until There's a Cure" program, launched the International AIDS Vaccine Initiative (IAVI). This effort is focusing on developing vaccines that are suitable for use in the areas of the world where HIV infection is spreading most rapidly.

Immunization strategies and controversies

In his first month in office, U.S. Pres. Bill Clinton introduced a new entitlement program designed to improve childhood immunization rates. As conceived, the Vaccines for Children (VFC) program would provide free vaccines to children for whom vaccine costs were seen as an obstacle to getting immunized. The program commenced in October 1994 despite lingering controversy about whether price alone was the ma-

NEWS CAP

Smallpox Virus: On Death Row

Exactly 200 years after Edward Jenner discovered a vaccine for smallpox, and nearly 20 years after the last case of this once-dreaded disease was detected (in Somalia), the governing board of the World Health Organization (WHO) voted to destroy the last stocks of the smallpox (variola) virus on the planet. The fate of the existing stocks had been deliberated for more than a decade, during which time several "execution dates" had been set and several stays granted. Finally, in May 1996 the board signed the death warrant for the samples that are presently being held in two maximum security laboratories—at the Russian Federation's Russian State Research Center of Virology and Biotechnology in Koltsovo and at the Centers for Disease Control and Prevention in Atlanta, Ga.

The date set for the virus's demise was June 30, 1999. The board recommended that in the interim scientists take advantage of recently acquired genetic information to answer any remaining scientific questions about the virus. (The complete genomes of two representative smallpox strains have now been sequenced.)

Shortly after WHO officially declared smallpox eradicated from the globe in 1980, it was proposed that all virus stocks held in research facilities be obliterated. Some scientists, however, considered the call for destruction rash and premature, stressing that there was still much to be learned about variola and that careful study of the virus might offer valuable clues to a number of other viral diseases, including AIDS. The scientists argued, moreover, that just as gene sequencing was unknown only a few years ago, new techniques could be developed in the near future that would provide further insights into the smallpox agent. To do away with the virus completely would mean that some potentially important information would be irrevocably lost. Still another consideration was that the extinction of the virus would be the first intentional elimination of a biological species.

London School of Hygiene & Tropical Medicine/Science Source/Photo Researchers

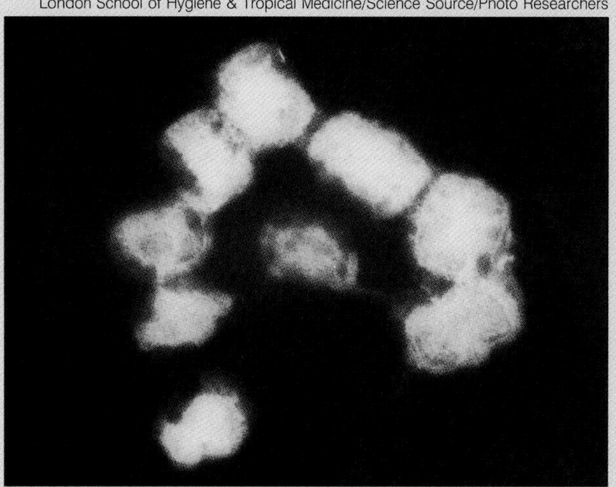

In making the final decision, the international scientific community acknowledged that viable sources of smallpox virus *may* exist in cadavers in the permafrost (a permanent frozen layer below the Earth's surface) and possibly in some other laboratories. In the end, though, the potential threat that the virus would pose to an unimmunized population, were it to escape from a lab, was judged to outweigh any theoretical benefits of preserving it.

It took nearly two centuries to move from Jenner's vaccine to the global eradication of a scourge. It was only about 30 years ago that smallpox was still endemic in 31 countries. At that time some 10 million–15 million people were infected each year, of whom nearly 2 million died, and millions of survivors were left disfigured or blinded for life. The smallpox-eradication effort lasted a little over 10 years and cost $313 million—an investment that has already been recouped many times over in savings on vaccines and medical care and in the suspension of vigorous international surveillance activities. Money well spent!

—Bruce G. Gellin, M.D., M.P.H.

jor barrier. Most authorities agree that cost is only one factor. Others include parental negligence, complacency about the need for immunizations, public health clinics' being in inconvenient locations or having inconvenient hours of operation, and poor record keeping on the part of immunization facilities. Compounding the latter obstacle is the increasingly complicated children's immunization schedule. To be fully compliant, a child must have 16 individual immunizations given in five or more separate clinic visits in the first two years of life. Yet in 1996 rates of immunization coverage and the federal expenditure on immunizations ($938 million) were at an all-time high, while rates of vaccine-preventable diseases in children were at an all-time low.

Currently, vaccines can prevent 10 childhood diseases: polio, diphtheria, tetanus, pertussis, measles, mumps, rubella (German measles), hepatitis B, varicella, and Hib. Because most must be administered by injection, "combination" vaccines that protect against several diseases with a single injection are being sought to help simplify the schedule. Unfortunately, until combination vaccines become available, new and improved vaccines that will initially be licensed as single products will further complicate childhood immunization schedules. For example, the development of a safer vaccine against pertussis and the recently recommended change from OPV to IPV (*see* below) will have the interim effect of increasing the number of injections and medical visits required for a child to be fully compliant with the recommended immunization schedule (*see* page 278).

From Salk to Sabin to Salk again. A growing debate over what constitutes the safest and most effective polio vaccine recently led to a subtle shift in the U.S. polio immunization policy. Ever since the licensing of two different polio vaccines in the early 1960s, the U.S. and most of the rest of the world have relied on Sabin's OPV. OPV's advantages include its ease of administration (oral), its lower production costs, and the fact that this approach mimics the wild-type virus's natural route of transmission and stimulates the mucosal immune system. In the latter instance, however, it is possible that the vaccine will cause poliomyelitis (known as vaccine-associated paralytic polio) in the recipient or in persons in close contact with a vaccinated child. Such events are extremely rare (occurring less than once in every two million doses given). Nonetheless, concerns about the safety of the vaccine, especially in light of the limited risk of acquiring a natural polio infection in the U.S., have caused immunization officials to reconsider the risks and benefits of OPV.

In June 1996 the CDC's Advisory Committee on Immunization Practices revised its recommendations and suggested that the country shift toward increasing use of IPV for the initial two doses, when the risk of neurological virulence from OPV appears to be greatest. That recommendation became official Sept. 18, 1996. For now, the substitution of IPV for OPV will add more injections to the childhood immunization schedule, which causes practitioners and public health officials to worry that this shift will create yet another barrier to full compliance with the recommended childhood vaccines. These matters are being addressed.

—Bruce G. Gellin, M.D., M.P.H., and Regina Rabinovich, M.D., M.P.H.

Tracking Trouble: Disease Surveillance via the Internet

The 20th century has witnessed monumental achievements in the control of infectious diseases. Smallpox, one of the great historic scourges, was eradicated from the world in 1977, and in 1994, in the first step toward global polio eradication, wild poliovirus was declared officially eliminated from the Western Hemisphere. Many deadly bacterial diseases have been controlled by immunization and antibiotic therapy, and improved nutrition and living conditions have dramatically reduced the incidence of infectious disease in industrialized countries. While these successes have been accumulating, however, paradoxically, the world has also been witnessing outbreaks of "new" infections.

Perhaps the greatest shock has been the AIDS pandemic. Unknown two decades ago, AIDS is now a prominent global health concern. AIDS, like many of the plagues of the past, falls into the category of seemingly new diseases that appear suddenly. Other recent examples include hantavirus pulmonary syndrome in the southwestern United States, which killed at least 16 persons in May and June 1993; Lyme disease; hemolytic uremic syndrome (a foodborne infection caused by certain strains of the common bacterium *Escherichia coli* in meat); bovine spongiform encephalopathy, or "mad cow disease" in British cattle; and Ebola hemorrhagic fever in Africa (a 1995 outbreak in Kikwit, Zaire, made international headlines; a subsequent outbreak in 1996 had less of a news impact). In addition, antibiotic-resistant bacteria are an increasingly common clinical problem, provoking fears that medicine may soon be without effective treatments for many severe or fatal bacterial infections.

Emerging infections: global vulnerability

Emerging infections can be defined as those that either have newly appeared in the population or are rapidly increasing in incidence or expanding in geographic range. Although emerging infections may seem random and unpredictable, they are not. Specific factors precipitating disease emergence can be identified in virtually all cases. Many emerging infections of humans, including the most novel, are existing infections of other species. An opportunity to infect humans usually comes as a result of changing ecological or environmental conditions that increase contact between humans and the environmental source of the infection. Other infections are already present in a human population somewhere in the world but reach new populations as a result of mass migrations or movement of people from rural areas to cities. The conditions of modern life make these factors increasingly prevalent; thus, it is reasonable to expect emerging diseases to increase in number and virulence. Past scourges can also recur. Reemerging, or resurgent, diseases, often well understood and well recognized as public health threats, suddenly increase or reappear because previously active public health measures have lapsed or sanitary infrastructures have deteriorated.

The history of HIV is illuminating. HIV may have originated as a cross-species transfer of an existing virus (perhaps from monkeys) in places where people were in contact with the natural host. After its probable first move from a rural area in Africa into an initial city, HIV-1 (the primary AIDS virus) spread along highways to other cities and later by long-distance modes (notably air travel) to increasingly distant places. Social factors (*e.g.,* people moving to cities, expansion of the commercial sex trade, intravenous drug use and exposure to contaminated hypodermic apparatuses) were essential to the spread of HIV in humans. Other diseases are likely to emerge or undergo a resurgence in the future as a result of similar opportunities. In industrialized countries high-density settings such as day-care centers, prisons, and shelters for the homeless often allow common and new diseases to spread rapidly once they have gained a foothold. Tuberculosis, now increasingly seen in drug-resistant forms, is a recent example.

No country is invulnerable. A "new" infection may first come to light in a human population anywhere in the world. Hantavirus pulmonary syndrome (1993) and Legionnaires' disease (1976) were both identified first in the U.S. but now occur in other parts of the world as well. Under suitable circumstances, a new infection appearing first in one "hot spot" could then span entire continents within days or weeks. New strains of influenza often originate in China but then spread quickly around the world. HIV has taken much longer, but it, too, appears well on its way to covering the globe.

Thinking globally, acting locally

The sudden appearance of these "new" diseases emphasizes humanity's continuing vulnerability to infectious diseases, both familiar and unfamiliar. This situation is not likely to change in the foreseeable future. Consequently, the only prudent action is to be prepared for these inevitable events. The simple first step, supported by every expert analysis, is global epidemiological monitoring, or surveillance—a worldwide "early-warning system" to recognize new diseases and spot increases in known diseases—backed up by a system to ensure an appropriate response.

A formal system for comprehensive surveillance would involve a network of facilities with special capabilities, including sophisticated laboratories and epidemiological expertise. Facilities would be on the lookout for diseases of concern or unusual signs or symptoms in patients. Blood or tissue samples from these patients would be collected and tested in the laboratory to identify the likely cause of disease, while epidemiologists would investigate details of transmission and determine whether there were additional cases.

Developing such a system will require improving national capabilities and effectively coordinating all of these activities on an international basis, which will take considerable time and resources. Effective communications will be essential to tie the network together. Ideally, reporting should be as rapid as possible, preferably almost instantaneous—in "real time." If the goal is to recognize an infection as early as possible, and, as history demonstrates, potentially serious infections can originate anywhere in the world, an effective system will depend especially on monitoring at the local level. Such widespread monitoring has generally been considered too difficult to be practicable because of the enormous number of locations that would have to be included.

Romeo Gacad—AFP

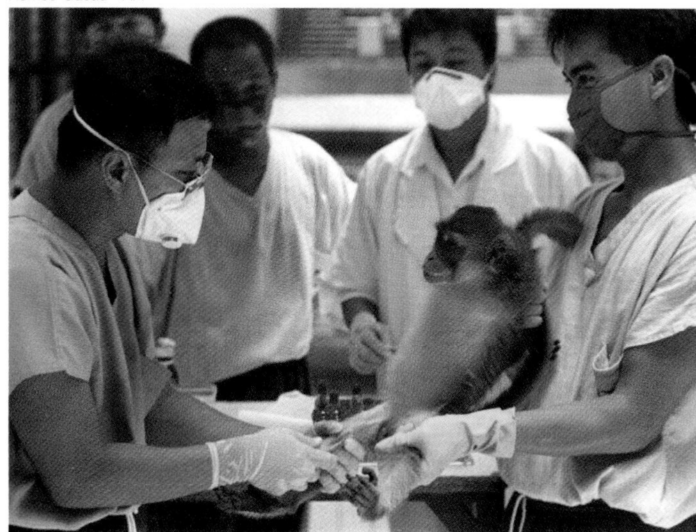

In May 1996 scientists collect blood from a monkey at a primate breeding facility in the Philippines after two macaques shipped from the same supplier to a research laboratory in Texas were found to be carrying a strain of the Ebola virus—one that is not known to infect humans.

The ProMED prototype

Believing that the increasing availability of the Internet had finally made it possible to improve communications and tackle this problem, a group of scientists established an electronic network in August 1994 as an experimental prototype for an informal monitoring system. ProMED (the Program for Monitoring Emerging Diseases) was begun as part of an international initiative launched in September 1993 under the auspices of the Federation of American Scientists to bring together international experts and concerned parties to plan and promote a global early-warning-and-response system. Under the leadership of viral epidemiologist Jack Woodall, formerly with the World Health Organization (WHO), a ProMED working group, in partnership with SatelLife, a nonprofit organization that has been working for several years to provide Internet links and access to medical databases to less developed countries, established an electronic network (now called ProMED-mail) on the Internet. In order to ensure that less developed countries would have full access to the system, the ProMED group opted for the most basic format possible, an E-mail list server. That means that information for ProMED-mail is submitted to a central computer, or file server (at SatelLife in Boston), in the form of a simple E-mail text message. The system redistributes the message by E-mail to every "subscriber" on the list. To allay concerns over irrelevant or erroneous information, each message submitted to the network is routinely read and reformatted by an editor, or "moderator," before being distributed. Woodall has ably served as director and chief moderator of the ProMED E-mail network since its inception.

Anyone can subscribe, and at last count (in early July 1996) the list had grown to over 5,000 subscribers in over 100 countries. Although most are people with a professional interest in disease tracking, such as public health and infection-control specialists, subscribers run the gamut from high-school students to top government health officials. Among the outbreaks ProMED-mail has tracked have been:

- a newly identified virus causing fatal respiratory illness in 14 racehorses and their trainer in Australia in 1994
- reappearance of the same virus in Australia in 1996
- Japanese encephalitis, a serious mosquitoborne disease, in Australia in April 1995
- avian influenza in Mexico
- a plant disease that caused severe crop losses in Costa Rica
- the outbreak of Ebola virus responsible for several hundred deaths in Zaire in May 1995
- epidemics in the Western Hemisphere of two important mosquitoborne diseases, Venezuelan equine encephalitis and dengue, in 1995
- cases of cholera in various parts of Asia and Africa
- various parasites, including *Cryptosporidium,* in urban water supplies

In addition to real-time reporting and relatively low overhead costs, an electronic network has other distinct advantages. The collective wisdom of a large group of experts can be brought to bear on a single problem. In several instances perplexing cases reported on the ProMED-mail network have elicited expert advice from other subscribers. Another advantage is that isolated case reports appearing on the network may be noticed by other subscribers who are aware of similar problems; thus, a pattern might be established when it otherwise might have escaped notice. The information is also electronically archived and can later be searched to identify disease clusters or associations. For example, it was possible to note increases in bacterial meningitis in several parts of the world in 1995. Such outbreaks are believed to be part of a still poorly understood cyclic phenomenon.

Tracking outbreaks: new sites and systems

ProMED-mail was set up as an experimental prototype for instant reporting of disease outbreaks and interactive discussion of related infection-control problems. ProMED-mail, however, is not the only such system; the Internet boasts other valuable resources whose purpose is to provide general information on infectious diseases. The intense press coverage of the 1995 Ebola virus outbreak in Zaire generated a tremendous public demand for information. In response to this need, independent software developer David Ornstein created the Ebola Page on the World Wide Web, which rapidly became one of the most heavily accessed sites on the Internet. After the epidemic ended, Ornstein and his colleagues expanded the content of the site, renamed Outbreak, to include information on other infectious diseases. The federal Centers for Disease Control and Prevention (CDC) in Atlanta, Ga., and WHO in Geneva are among the official agencies that have developed Web sites providing excellent current information.

What began in 1995 as the Ebola Page on the World Wide Web was later expanded by its creator and renamed Outbreak. This is one of several Internet sites devoted to tracking emerging and resurgent diseases.

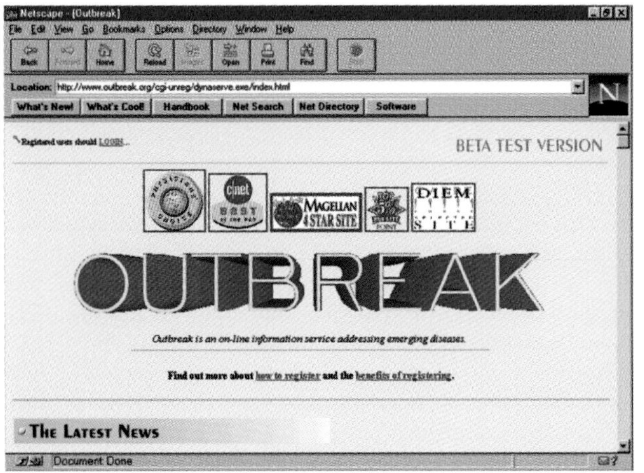

Courtesy of David Ornstein

Of course, the Internet does not solve all the problems of communicating information about infectious disease threats worldwide, but once the infrastructure is in place, costs of using the system are relatively low. Other benefits are obvious: communications are rapid and can include many parties simultaneously. Although there are still large geographic areas not yet connected, especially in less developed countries, the Internet, with assistance from governments and the private sector, is rapidly expanding its global base.

How imminent is a full-capacity fully functioning global network? During the September 1993 meeting at which ProMED was launched, 60 experts from around the world assessed the situation and discussed ways to plan and implement a global-monitoring program. The participants unanimously agreed that existing capabilities for surveillance of infectious diseases, both at the national level and internationally, were greatly fragmented and in critical need of strengthening. At that time there were insufficient coordination and communication between those existing facilities. Nevertheless, the participants agreed that with appropriate investment the needed networks could readily be established by building on systems that were already functioning effectively and by filling in notable gaps. Although much remains to be done, there have been encouraging signs of progress. New initiatives have recently been announced by WHO and by several governments, including those of the U.S. and the other members of the G-7 group of industrialized nations.

Connecting

To subscribe to **ProMED-mail,** interested parties can send an E-mail message to: majordomo@usa.healthnet.org. Either of the following two addresses offers access to the ProMED-mail archives, as well as links to other relevant sites:

- http://www.fas.org/promed (Federation of American Scientists ProMED home page)
- http://www.healthnet.org/promed.html (SatelLife Healthnet ProMED home page)

The other Internet sites providing up-to-date disease-surveillance information mentioned above are:

- **Outbreak** http://www.outbreak.org
- **Centers for Disease Control and Prevention** http://www.cdc.gov
- **World Health Organization** http://www.who.ch

—*Stephen S. Morse, Ph.D.*

Chronic Obstructive Pulmonary Disease: Insights and Advances

Great strides have been made in recent years in understanding the causes and mechanisms of chronic obstructive pulmonary disease, or COPD, a clinical term for a range of afflictions that includes asthma, chronic bronchitis, and emphysema. Though the condition is a growing problem in the industrialized nations of the world, it can be prevented or, in cases when it becomes established, effectively managed. The latter, however, requires that both the public and health care providers become aware of the insidious nature of COPD.

It has now been shown—through the Chronic Obstructive Pulmonary Disease Early Intervention Trial, or Lung Health Study, sponsored by the National Institutes of Health—that middle-aged smokers averaging 31 cigarettes per day and having mild degrees of airflow obstruction suffer greater losses in lung function over a period of five years if they continue to smoke. By contrast, if these patients quit smoking, their lung function may actually show improvement at first, followed by a plateau and then a very modest decline. In fact, over a five-year observation period, patients who were successful in stopping smoking essentially lost no lung function. The most common cause of death in this study was lung cancer; heart attack or stroke was the second most common cause. During the course of this study, which involved nearly 6,000 patients, no deaths from COPD occurred because the degree of functional impairment was mild. What this means is that early airflow abnormalities are surrogate markers of the risk of dying from other causes, namely, lung cancer, heart attack, and stroke. Nonetheless, COPD is the fourth leading cause of death in the U.S.; in 1997 there will be some 100,000 or more deaths from COPD, and the death rate continues to rise.

Lung maladies: closely interrelated

Chronic obstructive pulmonary disease is an inclusive term that describes a lung malady that has components of chronic and asthmatic bronchitis and emphysema. The lungs are made up of branching airways that provide the pathway for air entry and exit. The major airway, or windpipe (trachea), divides into two main bronchi (the term *bronchitis* refers to an inflammation of these main airways and their subsequent branches). Each bronchial tube in turn divides into smaller and smaller orders of air passages, with each airway generation dividing into two, until some 22 divisions result in 100,000 small air passages that feed the surface membrane of the lung. This surface membrane comprises some 300 million alveoli (saclike structures), which are lined by myriad tiny blood vessels (capillaries). Gas exchange takes place at this air-blood interface, which is 1/50 the thickness of tissue paper.

Emphysema is a dilatation and finally destruction of these fine gas-exchange structures. Since the alveoli contain elastic fiber, loss of elasticity is characteristic of emphysema. Chronic bronchitis and asthmatic bronchitis are closely related, and both play a part in COPD. "Asthmatic" refers to inflammatory and spastic episodic narrowing of the air passages, which, if unchecked, becomes chronic and results in fixed, narrowed airways. When airways are compromised and the lungs' elasticity is reduced, abnormal airflow results.

COPD refers to the overlapping processes just described. All of these states (*i.e.,* asthmatic bronchitis, chronic bronchitis, and emphysema) are characterized by cough, shortness of breath, and sometimes wheeze—in varying degrees of severity. In the early stages of COPD, symptoms may be absent or only subtle and not appreciated by either the patient or his or her physician.

The surface membrane of the lung—the air-blood interface (below left)—comprises some 300 million alveoli (air sacs) lined by tiny blood vessels; it is here that gas exchange takes place. Emphysema results in the dilatation and eventual destruction of these fine gas-exchange structures (right).

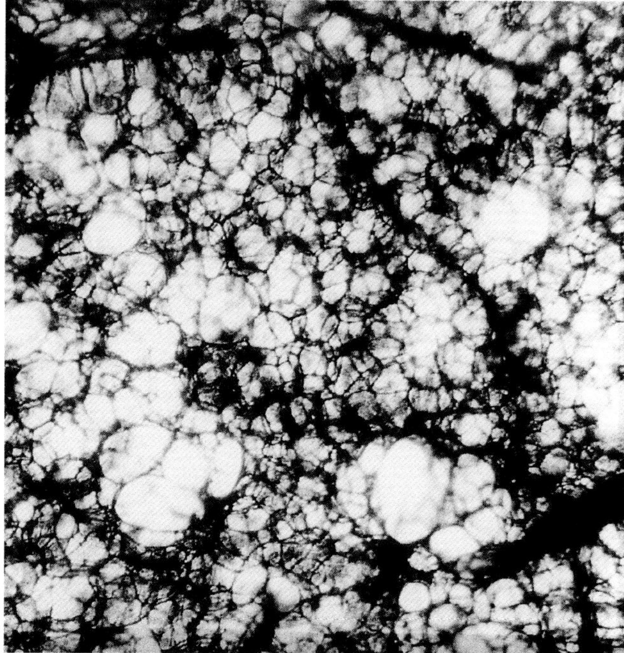

University of Colorado Health Sciences Center

A smokers' disease—and more

COPD can be considered a smokers' disease. It clusters in families and worsens with age. Although this broad statement is a true one, it fails to provide insight into many of the intricate processes that result in the development of this lung condition. As already indicated, COPD is a complex disease state that involves numerous overlapping processes. By far, the greatest risk factor is smoking, which is responsible for some 80–90% of COPD. This fact is extremely important because cigarette avoidance is the major target for both prevention and treatment.

The other clearly established risk factor is known as the alpha-1-antitrypsin (AAT) deficiency state. This scientific term refers to a material produced in the liver, which reaches the lungs when they are in a state of inflammation, usually associated with a viral or bacterial infection. Infectious agents are killed by white blood cells that release oxidants and enzymes called elastases, the major defense that human bodies have against infectious invaders. Sometimes, however, oxidants and elastases are produced in excessive amounts that can damage the airways and alveoli themselves. It is also important to note the connection of AAT to smoking; the by-products of cigarette smoke may inactivate normal AAT function.

The purpose of AAT is to modulate, or reduce the impact of, these inflammatory processes so that the lung is not damaged while it rids itself of harmful invaders. Insufficient AAT allows lung damage to occur. The AAT-deficiency state is definitely of a hereditary nature, but the genetics are complicated owing to the fact that different genes produce the protective AAT material in varying quantities and of various quality. Although only a small minority of patients with COPD (3–5%) have a deficiency in AAT, this disease state is important conceptually because it focuses upon the basic biological nature of COPD. Furthermore, there are preliminary approaches to AAT-replacement treatment under way. In the future this form of therapy may be given to COPD patients in much the same way that insulin is given for the control of diabetes.

Other causes of COPD are occupational (grain workers and mine workers, for example, may be exposed to excessive dust on the job). Repeated childhood infections and probably an allergic factor, which in its full-blown form is associated with hay fever, hives, and even acute episodic asthma, also contribute to COPD. By contrast, allergic asthma is not included in the COPD spectrum (because different mechanisms are involved in its development and because it is a reversible condition).

A recent survey of lifelong nonsmokers suggested a significant prevalence of COPD. That conclusion, however, is based on self-reporting and thus may not be accurate. No proof of airflow obstruction was present in this survey, which again raises questions about the validity of the conclusion that COPD is relatively common in nonsmokers.

Insidious course

The natural course, or total duration, of COPD is usually 20–40 years. At the onset no symptoms are present; physical examinations are normal, and common tests for lung abnormalities such as chest X-rays are also normal. Nonetheless, significant lung damage may be present. That damage may be overlooked by patients and their families, as well as by the individual's personal physician. The symptom-free period is probably 10–15 years.

This is usually followed by a period of relatively mild symptoms, where cough is prominent and exercise capacity is gradually reduced. Patients may feel that they are simply "out of shape" or slowing down, since this phase of disease begins most commonly in the late 40s or early 50s. The presence of mild to moderate symptoms usually does not alert either the patient or the physician that something is seriously wrong and that a detailed assessment and organized treatment should be pursued.

More disabling symptoms occur in the mid- to late 50s or early 60s. By this time lung function is usually reduced by 50–70%, and serious complications of COPD are already beginning to occur. With treatment, however, patients can live well into their 70s and 80s.

The typical course suggests that the prevalence of severe COPD will rise dramatically in the near future. As the world prepares to meet the needs of its rapidly aging population, it must consider COPD and its potential to cause debilitation and death. This is all the more reason to heighten the awareness of COPD now: the public needs to be educated. The health care delivery system needs to be prepared to diagnose and treat COPD effectively. And the government needs to launch public health campaigns to prevent smoking-related lung disease and to fund research on COPD cures.

The peak flow meter (below), widely used to monitor asthma, measures the greatest flow of air a patient can generate when blowing out from fully inflated lungs. Far more accurate assessments of COPD are made with the spirometer (opposite page); the patient blows into a transducer that is connected to a monitor that produces readings of airflow (forced expiratory volume in one second) and air volume (forced vital capacity).

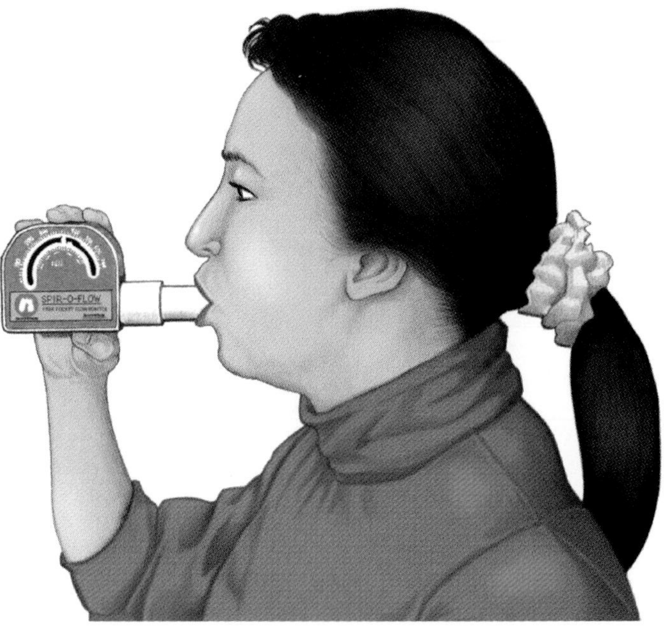

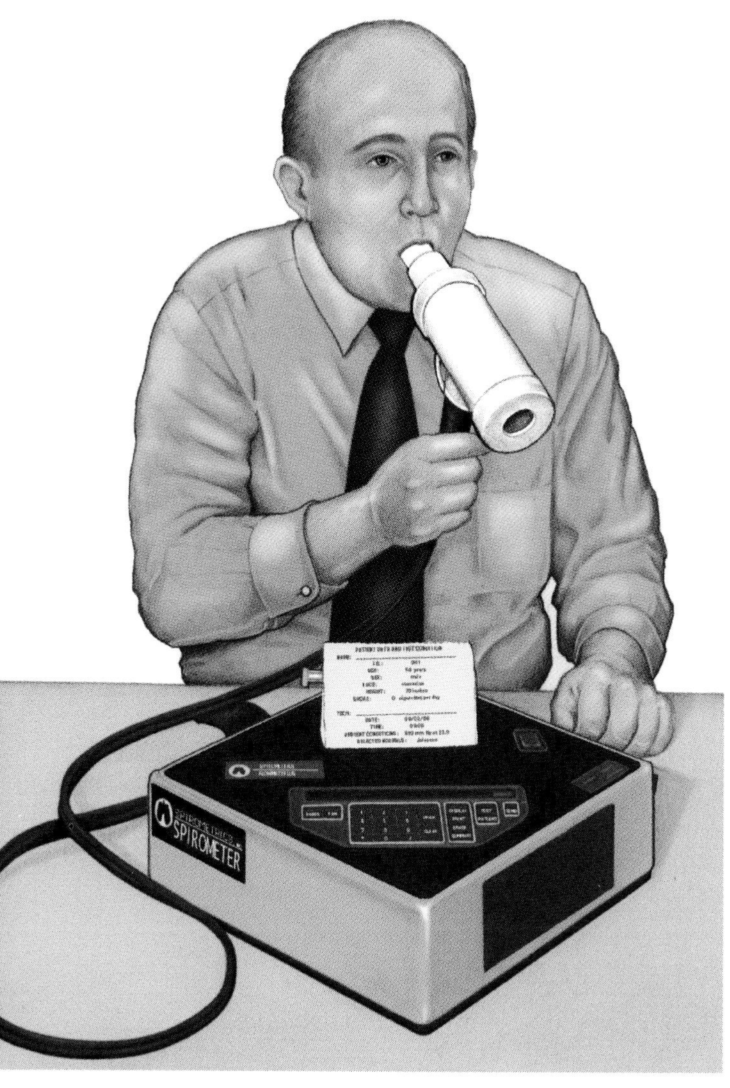

Diagnostic process

Perhaps the most important part of diagnosing COPD is to ascertain the patient's smoking history, including the age of starting and the intensity of smoking. Smoking histories are commonly expressed as "pack-years," so a person who smokes one pack per day for a year has had a one-pack-year exposure; 2 packs per day for 10 years is 20 pack-years; and 3 packs per day for 20 years amounts to 60 pack-years. The threshold for the development of clinically significant COPD appears to be somewhere around 10 pack-years, depending upon the age of starting and the intensity of smoking. Sometimes the patient will report a smokers' cough or a feeling of breathlessness under exercise conditions. Other important factors in the patient's history are COPD in relatives, *i.e.,* a positive family history, and occupational and environmental exposures to dust or smoke (including secondhand tobacco smoke).

A physical examination is part of the assessment, though it usually is not very revealing. Careful studies have shown that even experienced physicians have difficulty in diagnosing COPD of moderate severity. The only way to diagnose COPD accurately is with measurements of airflow and air volume, tests done by devices that are quite simple.

The simplest device is the so-called peak flow meter. Peak flow is a "snapshot" of the greatest flow of air a patient can generate when blowing out from fully inflated lungs. Peak flow measurements are much more useful in asthma, however, than in COPD. The most important device for assessing COPD is a spirometer. Unfortunately, however, only about 30% of primary care physicians have spirometers in their offices.

The way the spirometer works is that the patient blows into a flow indicator (transducer), which is connected to a machine that creates a recording of airflow and volume on a strip of paper—much like an electrocardiograph machine. The flow test is called the forced expiratory volume in one second (FEV_1). This refers to the *amount* of air that one can blow out in one second and is expressed in liters (roughly equivalent to quarts). The *volume* of air is the total amount of air that can be blown out of fully inflated lungs and is called the forced vital capacity (FVC). The term *vital capacity* alone refers to the capacity to live; not surprisingly, FVC is a fundamental measurement not only in COPD but in other disease states as well. Indeed, reductions in FVC are predictive of premature mortality from *all* causes, including heart attack, stroke, and lung cancer.

Spirometry is much simpler than electrocardiography, yet despite years of campaigning by this author and many of his colleagues in the pulmonary disease field, the majority of primary care providers—*i.e.,* general internists, family practitioners, physician assistants, and nurse practitioners—still have not availed themselves of this fundamental device. There simply is no other way to assess COPD accurately. All patients, especially smokers, should have spirometric measurements periodically; they should know their spirometric "numbers," just as they know their systolic and diastolic blood pressure numbers. Thanks to a successful campaign by the National Heart, Lung, and Blood Institute—the National Cholesterol Education Program, launched in 1985—most Americans have had their cholesterol measured, and many know their lipoprotein values. As a result, they have reduced their risk of coronary heart disease. A similar public health effort might be successful in reducing the incidence of advanced, life-threatening COPD.

The best treatment

Extensive studies have resulted in a fairly systematic approach to the management of COPD—an approach that can reduce symptoms and greatly improve the quality of life. In fact, it can extend survival for a considerable number of years. Briefly considered, the main elements of treatment are as follows:

- *Smoking cessation.* By far the most important element of treatment for any stage of COPD is giving up smoking. Ideally, the patient quits *before* he or she develops symptoms and before lung function has been reduced too far. Smoking cessation requires the patient's own motivation and efforts to quit; behavior modification therapy and group support may also be helpful, and for those who suffer intolerable withdrawal symptoms, nicotine replacement in the form of gum or patches may be an additional aid. The majority of smokers who stop, however, do so on their own, using the "cold turkey" method—*i.e.,* setting a quitting date and then ceasing the habit.

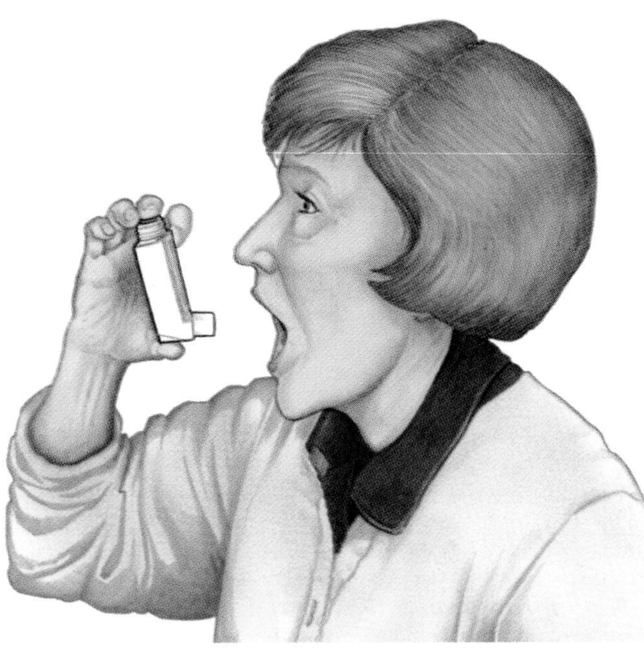

Metered-dose inhalers are held just in front of the open mouth; the patient presses the canister to release a precise amount of bronchodilating medication while simultaneously inhaling.

- *Vaccines.* Vaccines are helpful for preventing infectious complications of COPD. Influenza (flu) virus vaccine should be given each fall. It is about 80% effective in reducing serious infection in the airways and alveoli. Influenza pneumonia can be fatal, and, in fact, flu kills about 80,000 people each year in the United States alone. Vaccination against pneumococcal pneumonia is also available; though probably not as effective as flu vaccination, it is still useful in reducing the incidence and severity of this common and often life-threatening form of pneumonia, to which COPD patients are highly vulnerable.
- *Bronchodilators.* Even patients with severe airway inflammation may improve airflow by using a variety of inhaled bronchodilators. Most commonly, these drugs are provided by so-called metered-dose devices. Such devices also can deliver anti-inflammatory drugs directly into the lungs.
- *Antibiotics and corticosteroids.* Antibiotics are helpful for infectious exacerbations of COPD. Potent oral anti-inflammatory drugs, known as corticosteroids (*e.g.,* prednisone), can abort inflammatory exacerbations. The strategic use of antibiotics and corticosteroids should be under the direction of a physician; however, many patients are instructed to initiate such therapy at the first sign that their disease is worsening.
- *Oxygen.* Oxygen has been proved to extend the length of life of patients with advanced COPD for three to five years or, in many, even longer. Oxygen systems that are truly portable are now available; these have improved exercise tolerance and reduced heart strain, which can be complications associated with COPD. Oxygen is administered most commonly via small plastic tubes in the nostrils; some patients receive it by the transtracheal route, through a plastic catheter placed directly into the trachea. Today about 800,000 patients benefit from regular oxygen therapy, which reduces hospitalizations and improves not only the quality but the length of life.
- *Pulmonary rehabilitation.* Motivated patients can benefit greatly from improved exercise tolerance. Pulmonary rehabilitation includes patient education, special breathing exercises, and strength training for upper and lower extremities. Normal walking is probably the best exercise for COPD. More formalized exercise prescriptions are usually reserved for patients with special degrees of impairment. Exercise can help reduce the sensation of shortness of breath in COPD and is *not,* as many patients fear, dangerous.
- *Pursed-lip breathing* helps COPD patients move more air in and out of their airways and breathe more efficiently and can help exercisers, such as walkers, exercise for longer periods.

An antidisease diet?

Patients with early stages of disease may have significant shortness of breath on stressful exercise, which causes them to curtail anything that makes them feel uncomfortable. These patients are generally unfit from a cardiovascular point of view. In addition, a high level of depression and anxiety often occurs in all stages of COPD. This is probably why COPD patients are typically so dependent on tobacco; they use this drug to deal with the depression and anxiety. Although the reasons are unclear, smokers with COPD tend to eat a diet that is low in antioxidants, high in fat, and low in fiber. This is the worst possible diet for anyone who is on the disastrous pathway to COPD. Although evidence is incomplete, it is generally believed that eating foods high in antioxidants (*i.e.,* beta-carotene, vitamin C, vitamin E, and certain minerals, such as selenium, copper, and manganese, that are contained in multivitamin preparations) has the potential to reduce oxidative damage to the lung. In any case, it seems reasonable for those at risk for COPD to follow such a diet.

Looking to the future

A new initiative of the National Heart, Lung, and Blood Institute is the National Lung Health Education Program (NLHEP). The NLHEP is patterned after the highly successful National Hypertension Education Program, the aforementioned National Cholesterol Education Program, and the National Asthma Education Program. The new campaign is focusing on early identification of and intervention in COPD and is directed toward primary care physicians. A major public health education program will also be launched in 1996. It is hoped that the NLHEP will result in wide use of spirometry in doctors' offices and in patients knowing their "lung health numbers."

Thinking of COPD as primarily a smokers' disease with some familial predisposition, a high degree of nicotine addiction, and a poor diet for combating the damaging effects of cigarette smoke offers a new global concept. Once the public and the medical profession have become enlightened and realize that COPD is a major constitutional health problem, it will be possible to reduce its impact. Early identification and intervention are the keys.

—Thomas L. Petty, M.D.

Courtesy of the National Alliance for the Mentally Ill

NAMI
"As for me,
you must know I shouldn't precisely
have chosen madness
if there had been any choice
What consoles me is that
I am beginning to consider madness
as an illness like any other,
and that I accept it as such."
VINCENT VAN GOGH, 1889
IN A LETTER TO HIS BROTHER THEO

Depression Update

In the last 30 years, depression has gone from being one of the least understood to one of the best understood of the many emotional disorders mental health professionals are asked to treat. Fortunately, depression is highly responsive to good treatment, and good treatment is widely available from a variety of sources.

What is depression?

The mental health profession officially categorizes depression as a mood disorder but also recognizes that it can take many different forms. Prevalent as it is, depression elicits symptoms that vary widely from individual to individual.

It is best to think of depression as a complex disorder that affects many aspects of the sufferer's life. It can affect the *body*—producing sleep and appetite disturbances, diminished sex drive, fatigue, and anxiety. It can affect the *mind*—interfering with ability to think clearly, be attentive, remember details, or make decisions. It may also lead to errors in judgment. It can affect *behavior*—triggering crying spells, leading to suicide attempts, or causing drug or alcohol abuse. (In fact, substance abusers often use drugs or alcohol as "self-medication" in an attempt to cope with their depressive symptoms.) Depression can affect *emotions*—causing one to feel sad, desperate, guilty, worthless, or hopeless. Finally, it can affect *interpersonal relationships*—making it hard to relate to others and leading to destructive relationship choices or to social withdrawal and isolation.

The two main forms of depression are major depressive disorder (also known as "unipolar depression" because it generates depression only) and bipolar disorder (also known as manic-depressive disorder because it generates mania—emotional highs marked by euphoria—as well as depression). Major depression is by far the more common form and is the focus here.

It can happen to anyone

Depression is currently the most common psychological disorder in the United States. It affects both sexes, as well as people of all ages, racial and ethnic groups, and socioeconomic levels. Some groups, however, have higher rates than others. Women, for example, are diagnosed as depressed two to three times more often than men. The highest rates are for persons aged 25–44, while adolescents represent the group in which rates are increasing fastest. The group that is probably the most underdiagnosed is the elderly. Several recent studies have shown that people over the age of 60 are at least as likely to suffer from depression as any other group. According to the National Institute of Mental Health, 3% of elderly Americans are clinically (severely) depressed; 7–12% have milder forms but could benefit from therapy. Unfortunately, owing to the prevalence of other medical disorders

Educational campaigns are spreading the word that depression is not the dark and enigmatic malady it once was and that treatment is widely available.

in older people, their psychological state may be overlooked by medical personnel. Thus, many who could be receiving effective treatment for depression are not.

Depression can be a completely normal response to painful circumstances, such as the death of a loved one, the loss of a valued job, an ongoing painful stressor (like a debilitating illness), or a serious threat to one's sense of security or self-esteem. In such cases, depression is usually a short-term experience and is a quite reasonable response to whatever has happened. If depression persists for at least two weeks and adversely affects one's ability to function, however, it may be evidence of something more serious. Talking with a mental health professional will allow for an objective assessment of the problem.

High costs

Depression is extremely costly on many levels. The emotional costs of grief, pain, and despair are the most obvious ones. The physical costs are paid out in frequent illnesses, persistent physical discomfort, frequent trips to see doctors, and even an unwillingness to maintain one's own health. The social costs are evident in family conflicts, high divorce rates, poor parenting, and sometimes profound antisocial behavior (such as drunk driving).

Finally, the financial costs are substantial. A recent U.S. study estimated that depression costs the country $53 billion a year. This includes occupational costs: lost workdays (due to absences), poor performance (including injuries on the job and tasks needing to be redone), and lost potential earnings (as a result of inability to work or suicide).

Understanding the causes

Psychotherapists generally agree that biological, psychological, and sociological factors can combine to cause depression. Hence, a biopsychosocial model of depression is the most widely accepted view of the disorder. Recognizing that depression has many causes can help sufferers come to terms with their problem. It is important that they understand they are not suffering from a disorder of personal weakness, nor is depression a disorder arising from character flaws or from just feeling sorry for oneself. These are all-too-common—but unenlightened—explanations that only exacerbate the stigma of mental problems. In the great majority of cases, depression is a *real* disorder that is both diagnosable and treatable.

Biologically, there is some evidence to suggest that depression can be transmitted genetically from parent to offspring, but this genetic-transmission factor appears to account for only a minority of cases of major (unipolar) depression. On the other hand, a genetic factor is often the major culprit in bipolar disorder, which is one reason that the latter is best treated as a physical illness, with appropriate medication.

One of the great neuroscientific breakthroughs of recent times is the understanding that specific neurotransmitters (the brain's chemical messengers) are related to mood and can be influenced by antidepressant medications. Antidepressant medications are presumed to affect what are commonly described as chemical imbalances in the brain in which certain neurotransmitters, such as serotonin, are believed to be present in abnormally low concentrations.

Depression can also be caused by other physical factors, such as certain medications (including some hypertension drugs like reserpine, some beta-blockers like propranalol, and many other drugs as well) and physical conditions (*e.g.,* hypothyroidism, chronic fatigue syndrome). Likewise, other physical and mental disorders can coexist with and sometimes disguise the presence of depression. These are called "co-morbid" conditions; in fact, the majority of depression sufferers have a co-morbid condition. The most common co-morbid conditions are anxiety disorders, of which obsessive-compulsive disorder is a specific one, substance-use disorders, and personality disorders. If one has depression-like symptoms, it is wise to have a thorough physical examination in

NEWS CAP

Panic in the ER

People experiencing a panic attack for the first time may believe they are having a heart attack and be admitted to a hospital. Even medical experts can be fooled. Panic disorder is a mental illness characterized by the sudden appearance of intense anxiety. It may be accompanied by conditions that are symptomatic of cardiac seizure: chest pain, tingling sensations, numbness, palpitations, shortness of breath, trembling, nausea, chills, hot flashes, dizziness, and fear of dying, among them. Psychologists from the Montreal Heart Institute monitored 441 patients who went to an emergency room complaining of chest pain and found that 108 (about 25%) met the diagnostic criteria for panic disorder. The attending cardiologists, however, identified mental illness in only two patients, releasing 81 with a noncardiac pain diagnosis. The psychologists reported these findings at an American Heart Association meeting in January 1996.

Of course, not all first-time panic attacks are necessarily signs of panic disorder; often they are a direct physiological consequence of a medical condition, a side effect of a drug, or an adverse reaction to a chemical substance. It is the unanticipated recurrence of the attacks that makes them diagnosable as a mental disorder.

First classified as a disease about two decades ago, panic disorder afflicts an estimated one in 75 people worldwide. Although difficult to diagnose because of its symptomatic similarities to other illnesses, panic disorder is highly treatable with behavior therapy and sometimes with antidepressants or tranquilizers.

—Tom Michael

Table 1: Psychotherapies—Strong Medicine

Type	Focus of treatment	Goals for patient	Methods
Interpersonal therapy	identifying and correcting deficits in social skills	to define and resolve issues in main areas—*e.g.*, abnormal grief following significant loss, interpersonal disputes, role transitions, and interpersonal deficits	exploratory techniques, encouragement of the expression of feelings, clarification of communication style, and use of the therapeutic relationship
Cognitive therapy	identifying and correcting errors in thinking (cognitive distortions)	to learn self-identification and self-correction strategies when interpreting events or making choices that otherwise may be depressingly inaccurate	use of behavioral "experiments," homework assignments, and Socratic questioning, as well as exploration of thought content and style
Behavioral therapy	diminishing hurtful or unsuccessful behaviors while teaching and encouraging the use of rewarding behaviors	to identify and develop the skills necessary to manage interactions and tasks skillfully and with maximum emotional reward	relaxation training, assertiveness training, role playing, learning from someone who demonstrates the desired behavior, graduated task assignments, and time management

order to determine whether there may be a specific physical reason for the depression. In addition, a psychological evaluation should assess the possibility of a co-morbid condition so that the complexity of the patient's *whole* problem is not underestimated.

Psychologically, depression can be caused by a variety of factors. As noted previously, traumatic and painful life events may be a cause. Often, however, depression is a product of how one *interprets* life events rather than the events themselves. This is especially true if one lacks the personal resources to cope with stressful events. One may have poor problem-solving capabilities or erroneous, self-limiting beliefs. Thus, almost any stressful or hurtful experience has the potential to be depressing if it is misinterpreted or if one responds to the event inappropriately.

Depression is strongly affected by social and cultural influences. The rates of depression in the United States and other countries have risen dramatically in recent decades, and many authorities interpret this rise as a response to rapidly changing social conditions (for example, a societal de-emphasis on the traditional nuclear family and increased social isolation resulting from reliance on technology).

It is interesting to note that people's cultural backgrounds affect the way their symptoms are expressed and communicated. In some cultures, for example, depression may be experienced mostly in physical terms; in others, mostly in emotional terms. The American Psychiatric Association's *Diagnostic and Statistical Manual of Mental Disorders*, fourth edition, points out that complaints of "nerves" and headaches are more common manifestations of depression in Latino and Mediterranean cultures; weakness, fatigue, and "imbalance" are more common in Asian cultures; and "heartbroken" is the expression used among Hopi Indians for depression. Social and cultural expectations may also affect how certain people view others' symptoms. Some people may be more concerned or worried about someone who is irritable and eats poorly than about one who is sad and withdrawn.

Overcoming depression: what works best?

Cure is generally not an appropriate term for describing the result of the treatment of depression. A better word is *management*. Depression can go away, mood can lift, and the sufferer can feel like his or her old self again. Because depression is a part of life experience, and unfortunate things can and do happen to everybody, everyone is likely to suffer at one time or another to one degree or another. The primary goals of psychotherapeutic treatments for depression are to learn to recognize what events trigger depressive episodes and to apply preventive strategies whenever possible, to limit the destructive influence of depression when an episode occurs, and to generate a remission of symptoms as quickly and thoroughly as possible.

Psychotherapy and antidepressant medications are the two most commonly used treatments today. Individual patients' responses vary, and either approach (alone or in combination) holds promise for providing relief.

Recently, the Agency for Health Care Policy and Research (AHCPR), a branch of the U.S. Public Health Service, established "clinical-practice guidelines" for health care providers who treat depression. It also issued a comprehensive guide for patients. (*See* "Resources for Consumers," page 291.) In order to develop guidelines characterizing "effective treatment," a panel of experts reviewed over 100,000 recent research publications comparing different treatments. Such a comprehensive review by top mental health professionals is testimony to the fact that depression is a subject that has received a huge amount of attention from researchers and clinicians. It also indicates that there is a great deal known, objectively, about what does and does not work and that some treatments are demonstrably better than others. This should be especially reassuring for patients.

The AHCPR panel concluded that psychotherapy is a highly effective form of treatment for depression, the three most effective psychotherapies being interpersonal, cognitive,

Table 2: Selected Drugs from Today's Antidepressant Armamentarium

Antidepressant class/drug	General indications/contraindications	Side effects (vary from patient to patient)
Tricyclics desipramine (Norpramin) nortriptyline (Pamelor) imipramine (Tofranil) amitriptyline (Elavil) protriptyline (Vivactil) doxepin (Sinequan)	owing to their sedating effects, tricyclics are useful for patients with insomnia; they may pose a risk for individuals with cardiovascular disease, such as arrhythmias	*most common:* dry mouth and constipation *others:* weight gain, dizziness caused by a drop in blood pressure on sitting or standing up (orthostatic hypotension), changes in sexual desire, difficulty urinating, increased sweating, and sedation; in overdose can be lethal
Selective serotonin reuptake inhibitors (SSRIs) fluoxetine (Prozac) sertraline (Zoloft) paroxetine (Paxil) fluvoxamine (Luvox)	SSRIs are generally the first-line choice because they have fewer side effects than other antidepressants, do not require blood monitoring, and are safe in overdose	insomnia, agitation, sexual dysfunction, occasional nausea or heartburn, headache, occasional drowsiness, dizziness, tremor, diarrhea/constipation, and dry mouth
Monoamine oxidase inhibitors (MAOIs) isocarboxazid (Marplan)[1] tranylcypromine (Parnate) phenelzine (Nardil)	can cause severe and sudden rise in blood pressure if ingested with certain drugs (*e.g.,* over-the-counter cold preparations, diet pills, and amphetamines) or foods containing tyramine (*e.g.,* red wines, aged cheeses); interact with epinephrine, an ingredient in some topical anesthetics; not advised if patient is taking other antidepressants	weight gain, agitation, insomnia, sexual dysfunction, disturbed appetite, and faintness (similar to orthostatic hypotension)
bupropion (Wellbutrin)	does not interact significantly with other drugs; at high doses can cause seizures in some people, most commonly those who have seizure disorders, anorexia, or bulimia; used experimentally to counteract sexual side effects of SSRIs	agitation, insomnia, sedation, blurred vision, dizziness, headache/migraine, dry mouth, tremor, appetite loss, weight loss, excessive sweating, rapid heart beats, constipation, and rashes
trazodone (Desyrel)	often used with another antidepressant to alleviate insomnia induced by the initial drug	drowsiness, faintness, nausea, and vomiting
maprotiline (Ludiomil)	to treat agitation and anxiety associated with depression; not advised for people with seizure disorders; somewhat risky for patients with cardiovascular disease	similar to side effects of tricyclics

[1] Discontinued December 1993.

Adapted from the December 1995 issue of the *Harvard Women's Health Watch,* © 1995, President and Fellows of Harvard College.

and behavioral. Table 1 summarizes these treatment models. Some common denominators of the three types are:

- an emphasis on therapy as an *active process* of experimenting with new behaviors and perceptions
- a duration of treatment that is *time-limited—i.e.,* treatment does not go on indefinitely
- a focus on solving *current problems* rather than rehashing old issues from childhood
- a concentration on *symptom relief* rather than on more abstract personality issues
- an emphasis on achieving *present goals* without dwelling on past failures
- an emphasis on building *coping skills* that can be applied in the future

The key characteristics of a good psychotherapist are warmth, empathy, acceptance, openness, knowledgeability, and a willingness to be both an ally and a guide. The research on therapy's effectiveness makes it clear that it is less the person's academic degree or title (psychologist, counselor, behaviorist, psychiatrist, social worker, or family therapist) and more the person's personal characteristics and clinical skills. There are many ways to find a reputable and qualified therapist. Some useful resources are listed on page 291.

What about medications? As noted earlier, depression has obvious biological components and consequences. On that basis alone, the appropriate use of antidepressant medication is wholly justified. It is unfortunate that many people fear and avoid medication because they assume only "sick people" need medication. On the other hand, some patients readily seek drugs because they believe that pills offer a quick and easy solution. (They do not.) Each person's depression varies, as do his or her treatment responses, but on the whole the evidence is clear that receiving good psychotherapy in addition to taking appropriate medication is far more effective than taking medication alone.

The AHCPR guidelines suggest that medication be considered when the following conditions exist:

- the individual's depression is severe
- the individual has suffered at least two prior depression episodes

- there is a family history of depression
- the individual specifically wants medication as the sole intervention

If one is considering antidepressant medication, here are some useful pointers: (1) In most states only a physician (M.D.) can prescribe medications. Ideally, one should consult a psychiatrist or psychopharmacologist (an M.D. with advanced training in the use of medications in treatment) for a complete evaluation and an individually tailored prescription. (2) There are several classes of antidepressant medications; Table 2 (page 290) lists the most commonly prescribed drugs according to their class. Two of the classes, tricyclic antidepressants and monoamine oxidase inhibitors (MAOIs), have been widely used for decades and are effective for about 70% of depressed patients. Their use, unfortunately, is complicated by the need for careful dose adjustments and also by the wide range of adverse effects that reflect the influence of these drugs on a variety of biological systems. The availability of the newer class of antidepressant drugs, the selective serotonin reuptake inhibitors (SSRIs), has been an important recent development for treatment of depression. The first approved and marketed SSRI in the U.S. was fluoxetine (Prozac). Because it does not require careful dose adjustments and has far fewer side effects than the other antidepressants, Prozac quickly became the most widely prescribed antidepressant. (3) No single antidepressant is clearly more effective than another. It is unknown how any individual will respond to a specific medication in terms of side effects or symptom remission. Therefore, one must be willing to experiment a little under the supervision of a competent M.D. (4) The AHCPR panel recommended staying on effective medication from four to nine months following remission. More recent studies suggest staying on antidepressant medications up to 18 months. In any case, antidepressant treatment is usually a time-limited treatment plan.

High ratings for psychotherapy. In June 1995 an article by psychologist David Antonuccio, "Psychotherapy for Depression: No Stronger Medicine," was published in *American Psychologist*. More recently, Antonuccio and his colleagues, at the University of Nevada School of Medicine and the Reno Veterans Affairs Medical Center, published the results of their comprehensive analysis of the treatment literature showing statistically that psychotherapy is at least as effective as medications and in some ways is superior. When symptoms are largely of a physical nature (sleep or appetite disturbance, for example), medications can work especially well. When one's life skills are deficient or one needs emotional support, an empathic psychotherapist can make all the difference.

A study of a quite different type was published in the November 1995 issue of *Consumer Reports*. Readers of the periodical responded to questions about their own experience with therapy. In other words, *Consumer Reports* examined what happens in the "real world," where therapists exercise clinical judgment and switch or modify approaches as necessity dictates. Likewise, in the real world clients shop for therapists and stay in treatment as long as they need or want to (or as long as their insurance allows). This differs from standard "controlled" treatment studies, in which subjects are assigned to a therapist for a specific period of time.

Under these real-world conditions, the benefits of therapy were overwhelmingly affirmed: 87% of *Consumer Reports* respondents reported improvement with whatever treatment they received. Most relevant, perhaps, was that consumers rated psychotherapy alone as highly as psychotherapy in combination with medication. Moreover, most respondents who took drugs reported some unwanted side effects.

Depression is no longer the dark mystery it once was. The mental health profession has learned a great deal about who gets depressed and why and, most important, what to do about it. In the great majority of cases, depression sufferers can be helped. They can learn specific skills in thinking, behaving, and relating to others and thereby rediscover the joys of life.

—Michael D. Yapko, Ph.D.

Resources for Consumers

- When seeking help for depression, many people consult their family physicians first.

- Anyone can obtain his or her own copy of *Depression Is a Treatable Illness: A Patient's Guide* from the **U.S. Department of Health and Human Services** by phoning 800-358-9295 or writing to the **Agency for Health Care Policy and Research:**
  AHCPR Publications Clearinghouse
  PO Box 8547
  Silver Spring MD 20907
  An Internet version of the *Guide* is available at
  http://www.medaccess.com/guides/cpgs/CPG_01.htm
  or *http://www.mentalhealth.com/bookah/p44-dp.html*

- General information about depression and mental illness can be obtained from the following:[1]

American Association for Marriage and Family Therapy
1133 15th St NW Suite 300
Washington DC 20005
http://www.aamft.org/
American Psychiatric Association 202-682-6000
American Psychiatric Nurses Association 202-857-1133
American Psychological Association 202-336-5800
Depression/Awareness, Recognition, and Treatment 800-421-4211
National Alliance for the Mentally Ill 703-524-7600 or 800-950-6264
National Foundation for Depressive Illness, Inc. 800-248-4344
National Institute of Mental Health 301-443-4513
5600 Fishers Ln Room 7C 02
Rockville MD 20857
National Mental Health Association 800-969-6642

- For a free pamphlet on depression or other mental disorders (which an also be ordered in bulk), phone the Public Affairs department of the **American Psychiatric Association** 202-682-6220.

[1] Some organizations will provide names of qualified, reputable psychotherapists.

Diabetes Update

Two types of diabetes mellitus—insulin-dependent and non-insulin-dependent—and two related metabolic syndromes are responsible for increasing rates of illness and death in the United States and many other developed nations. A limited ability of the human body to utilize carbohydrates, leading to blood glucose levels (also known as blood sugar levels) that are higher than normal but not as high as those associated with diabetes, particularly after meals, is called impaired glucose tolerance. In addition, some individuals are resistant to the action of insulin, the hormone that regulates glucose, and have the syndrome that is known as insulin resistance, even though their blood sugar levels are normal.

Insulin-dependent diabetes mellitus

Usually diagnosed early in life, insulin-dependent diabetes mellitus (IDDM, or Type 1 diabetes) is an autoimmune disease. The term *autoimmune* in this case means the body makes substances called antibodies, which destroy the cells responsible for insulin production, the beta cells (β cells) of the islets of Langerhans in the pancreas. Although IDDM has a hereditary component and has been associated with certain changes in the immunogenic genes, the precise factors responsible for beginning the β-cell-destruction process are unknown.

In general, the onset of IDDM is acute, with patients experiencing increased thirst, increased urination, weight loss, and sometimes even diabetic coma—symptoms caused by elevated blood sugars. In the absence of insulin, the body cannot use glucose. For that reason, fat becomes the primary energy source; the breakdown products of fat (ketones) accumulate in the blood, which results in ketoacidosis—an increased acidity of the body fluids and tissues—producing severe symptoms and, if untreated, death.

Since IDDM results from the lack of insulin production, the only available treatment is insulin injection. Though there have been reports recently suggesting that a deficiency of the trace minerals selenium, chromium, or zinc could cause IDDM, these hypotheses have not been supported by scientific research.

Prevention of IDDM? There are two types of research investigating the possibility of preventing IDDM. Both involve identifying patients early in the course of their disease. In the current Diabetes Prevention Trial–Type 1 (DPT-1), patients with the potential for developing IDDM—children or siblings of patients with IDDM who are identified by screening for anti-islet antibodies—are treated with small amounts of insulin to determine whether "resting" the pancreas will prevent the progression to actual IDDM.

A second series of studies has used agents that suppress the immune process. The most important agent that has been tested is the immunosuppressant cyclosporine. Since the early 1980s this drug has been widely used to suppress rejection of transplanted organs. Whereas some research has suggested that cyclosporine slows the progression or halts the destruction of the islets in IDDM, most studies have shown that once cyclosporine is stopped, the immune process resumes its course and clinical IDDM follows. Furthermore, cyclosporine is associated with kidney damage and has the potential risk of accelerating the renal disease that is one of the serious complications of IDDM.

New treatments. In addition to the trials attempting to prevent insulin-dependent diabetes, a number of new agents are being studied that may improve the treatment of diabetes and/or prevent its complications. One of these is a synthetic insulin of recombinant DNA origin called insulin lispro (Humalog). Humalog, developed by Eli Lilly and Co., was approved by the U.S. Food Drug Administration (FDA) and became available in 1996. This new type of insulin has the advantage of acting very rapidly within the body; thus, it can be self-injected at mealtime to control the increased blood sugar that occurs after eating. It has the potential both for improving diabetes control and for making insulin injections more convenient, since preinjection of insulin 30–45 minutes prior to meals is not necessary.

In 1983 the National Institute for Diabetes and Digestive and Kidney Diseases began the landmark Diabetes Control and Complications Trial, which lasted for a decade. The trial showed conclusively that intensive treatment of IDDM, so-called tight glucose control, will delay the onset and slow the progression of major diabetes complications. Although tight glucose control has been shown to impede the eye, kidney, and neurological complications of diabetes, attaining near-normal blood sugar is difficult, very costly, and associated with an increased risk of hypoglycemia (abnormal decrease in blood sugar levels). Therefore, an intensive search is presently under way for agents that will prevent a large majority of IDDM complications. Two types of agents have been studied: aldose reductase inhibitors and aminoguanidine. Trials of aldose reductase inhibitors are based on the theory that the complications of diabetes are due to the accumulation of the toxic substance sorbitol in the cells. Although aldose reductase inhibitors do prevent the buildup of sorbitol, the trials thus far have been disappointing. There is some suggestion that symptomatic neurological complications may be improved, but as yet there is no definitive evidence that the eye and kidney complications can be prevented by these agents.

Aminoguanidine prevents the formulation of toxic substances called advanced glycation end products, which result from the high blood sugar levels in patients with diabetes. In experimental animals, aminoguanidine has proved quite effective in preventing kidney complications. The clinical trials are only in their early stages, however, and thus far no data on humans have been reported.

Non-insulin-dependent diabetes mellitus

Non-insulin-dependent diabetes mellitus (NIDDM), which is also known as Type 2 diabetes, is by far the more common form of the disease. Of the approximately 16 million people in the U.S. who are affected by diabetes mellitus, over 90% have NIDDM. NIDDM afflicts certain ethnic groups more than others. African-Americans, Latinos, and American Indians, for example, all have high rates. (In contrast, Caucasians have nearly twice the incidence of insulin-dependent diabetes as African-Americans or Latinos.)

NIDDM is much more subtle than IDDM, and probably as many as half of the existing cases are presently undiagnosed. (NIDDM typically goes undiagnosed for an average of six years because the symptoms are very nonspecific and the high blood sugars are usually less severe than in IDDM.) The vast majority of scientific evidence suggests that the specific diabetes complications of NIDDM (of the eye, kidney, and nerves) can be prevented by improved glucose control. The means of achieving a state of glucose control in NIDDM differ from those in IDDM; patients with the former can be treated with a prudent diet and exercise, sometimes in combination with oral hypoglycemic agents.

It has been known for decades that the hyperglycemia (excess of sugar in the blood) seen in NIDDM is improved with diet. About 50–90% of patients with newly diagnosed NIDDM will have normalization of their blood sugars when they are placed on a diet of 1,200–1,500 calories per day; normalization usually occurs in less than two weeks. The decrease in calories and subsequent associated weight loss are responsible for the improvement in blood sugar control. An increase in insulin sensitivity is seen with a weight loss of 4.5–11 kg (10–25 lb). Unfortunately, dietary therapy generally fails in patients with NIDDM because weight loss in most patients tends not to be steady or consistent and is rarely maintained.

There is some controversy about the appropriate proportions of fat, protein, and carbohydrates in the NIDDM diet. The current American Diabetes Association (ADA) recommendations leave wide leeway for individual choice—specifying only that carbohydrate consumption should account for between 40% and 60% of total calories, protein for 15–20%, and fat for no more than 30%. Most people find it hard to maintain a diet that has less than 30% fat. Rather than focusing on specific nutrients, it is better for patients with NIDDM to maintain a caloric intake that will result in gradual weight loss over time.

More recently, there have been a number of studies suggesting that exercise is a powerful sensitizer to insulin and that the insulin resistance syndrome seen in both NIDDM and impaired glucose tolerance can be improved by relatively moderate exercise. Twenty minutes of exercise three times a week is associated with an improvement in insulin sensitivity, a reduction in hyperglycemia, a lowering of blood pressure, and an increase in high-density lipoprotein cholesterol ("good" cholesterol). These positive changes occur even in the absence of weight loss. Over time, the proportion of body fat also decreases with moderate exercise. Owing to these benefits, exercise is a critical component in the nonpharmacological treatment of impaired glucose tolerance and NIDDM. (Longer physical activity periods of about 40 minutes three times a week are needed for weight loss.)

Nonetheless, as NIDDM progresses, the pancreas becomes increasingly unable to produce adequate amounts of insulin to overcome the insulin resistance that underlies the condition (*see* below). Patients then may require insulin either alone or in combination with oral agents to control their blood sugar.

New treatments. In the United States only one class of oral agents has been available over the last several decades, the sulfonylureas. These oral antidiabetic drugs stimulate the pancreas to produce insulin but are effective only if some of the insulin-secreting cells remain active. Some common sulfonylurea drugs are acetohexamide, chloropropamide, glipizide, glyburide, tolazamide, tolbutamide, and glimepiride (released to the U.S. market in 1996).

Recently, however, two new agents have been approved for U.S. marketing. The first agent was metformin (Glucophage), which has been used in other countries for about 30 years. Its basic pharmacological effect is to reduce resistance to insulin, which thus reduces the amount of glucose produced by the liver and increases the amount of glucose taken up by muscle. (Some patients experience gastrointestinal side effects such as nausea or diarrhea.) Metformin is approximately equal in potency to the most commonly used sulfonylureas. In patients who have both NIDDM and obesity (a very common occurrence), metformin may be particularly useful because it is associated with weight loss in many patients. Metformin and the sulfonylureas also can be used in combination in patients who do not respond adequately to either agent alone. Metformin is not advised for use in patients who have kidney or liver dysfunction or severe cardiac disease.

The second new oral antidiabetic agent, acarbose (Precose), has been in use in Europe for several years. Acarbose is a drug that prevents the breakdown of sugars in the stomach and duodenum. This reduces the rate of absorption of these sugars and lowers the rise in blood sugar that occurs after meals. Although less potent than the other oral agents, acarbose may be of benefit to patients who have high blood sugar after meals. The main side effects are gastrointestinal.

Bayer Corporation

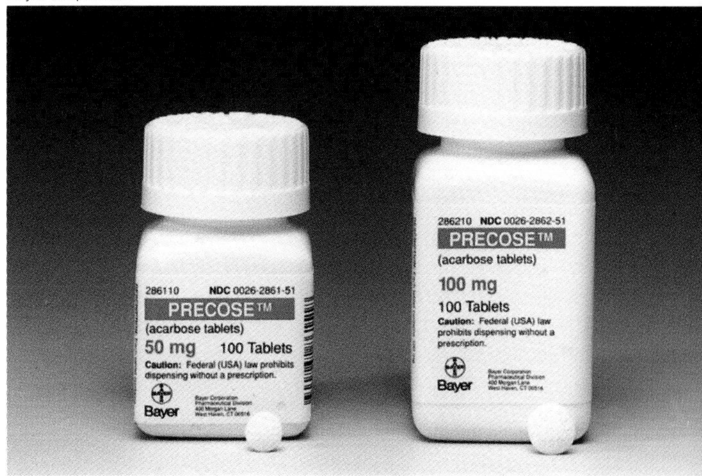

One of two new antidiabetic agents, acarbose (Precose) works by slowing carbohydrate breakdown and glucose absorption in the small intestine.

In NIDDM the most common cause of death is cardiovascular disease (heart attacks, strokes, occlusion of the peripheral vessels). Although diabetes is associated with an increased incidence of cardiovascular disease, there have not been controlled clinical trials demonstrating that the improved management of blood sugars per se lowers the incidence of cardiovascular disease. There are a number of reasons why such trials have not been undertaken. A major one is that concomitant risk factors for cardiovascular disease occur in many patients with NIDDM. These include hypertension, an

Eric Kamp—Phototake

Because optimal management of diabetes depends on frequent blood glucose monitoring, aggressive efforts are being made to devise accurate self-monitoring methods that do not require a finger prick.

elevated level of low-density lipoprotein (the "bad" cholesterol), a low level of "good" high-density lipoprotein, and obesity. Findings from the Nurses' Health Study (published in *Annals of Internal Medicine,* April 1, 1995) indicated that modest weight gains (of 7–11 kg [15–25 lb]) were associated with a doubling of future risk for NIDDM. A reduction in the rate of cardiovascular disease in NIDDM is likely when *all* of the above conditions are treated. Thus, the optimal therapy is an integrated one that treats obesity, hyperglycemia, hypertension, and abnormal lipids. This therapeutic regimen usually begins with lifestyle changes (dietary modifications, weight loss, exercise, smoking cessation), with the addition of appropriate pharmacological agents as needed.

Toward painless blood sugar monitoring

In all types of diabetes, it is necessary to have a measure of average blood sugar control, since the complications of diabetes are highly correlated with the duration of diabetes and its metabolic control. In all large clinical trials, glycated hemoglobin (hemoglobin A_{1c}) has been used as the "gold standard" for measurement of metabolic control. The reason is that this substance is a measure of the average blood sugar in the preceding one to two months. Thus, it can distinguish between patients with excellent, fair, or poor metabolic control. The recommendation of the ADA is that patients should maintain their diabetic control within 1% of the upper limit of the normal value. (The normal value varies, depending on the technique that is used to measure the glycated hemoglobin; all patients should know both their glycated hemoglobin value and the upper limit of normal.) Further, the ADA recommends that any patient who has a glycated hemoglobin above 2% of the upper limit of normal change his or her therapeutic regimen. These figures are derived from a number of studies that suggest that for every 10% lowering of the glycated hemoglobin, there is an approximate 40% decrease in the development of future complications.

Although glycated hemoglobin is an excellent integrated measure of blood sugar control, it cannot be used to determine optimal day-to-day therapy. For this, the patient must institute self-monitoring of blood glucose. The frequency of self-monitoring depends upon a variety of clinical factors, including the type of diabetes, the prescribed therapy, and the inherent instability of diabetes. In general, patients with IDDM require more frequent monitoring than those with NIDDM. The ADA currently recommends that all patients taking insulin monitor their blood sugar; the frequency of monitoring should be sufficient to enable adjustments to their insulin regimen if need be. Monitoring frequency should be increased during times of adjustment of the therapeutic regimen or during acute illnesses.

Because of the inconvenience and physical pain associated with monitoring, a number of techniques for the noninvasive monitoring of blood sugar have been under study. These generally fall into two classes of devices. The first class uses near-infrared spectroscopy to detect glucose levels through the skin. Although this technique has been shown to be promising, it has not been reliable enough thus far to be approved for clinical use. The devices tend to be bulky and expensive. They also may require a considerable amount of maintenance in order to ensure that they are measuring blood sugar levels accurately.

A second type of noninvasive device involves the movement of glucose through tissues by a variety of mechanisms. The most recent innovation has been the use of reverse iontophoresis—the passing of a small electric current over the skin, causing ions and glucose to come to the surface of the skin to be measured. Recent reports suggest that this method is feasible. Again, however, no clinical devices have thus far been approved for general use.

Related syndromes: recent insights

As many as 11% of the adults in the United States have impaired glucose tolerance. These patients have fasting and/or postmeal blood sugars that are above the normal range (less than 115 mg/dl [milligrams per deciliter] before meals and less than 140 mg/dl after meals) but not diagnostic of diabetes (fasting blood sugars of 140 mg/dl or more or postmeal blood sugars of 200 mg/dl or more). About one-third of these patients will subsequently develop non-insulin-dependent diabetes mellitus. Individuals with impaired glucose tolerance have been clearly shown to have an increased incidence of cardiovascular disease. Because of both the cardiovascular disease associated with impaired glucose tolerance and the subsequent development of NIDDM, a number of studies have been proposed to try to prevent the conversion of patients with impaired glucose tolerance to those with diabetes. The largest of such trials, the Diabetes Prevention Program (DPP), was initiated in the U.S. in mid-1996. This study eventually will enroll approximately 4,000 patients with impaired glucose tolerance into treatment groups that include diet and exercise and the use of metformin or a new, as-yet-unapproved therapeutic agent, troglitazone, which reduces insulin resistance. Should any of the regimens prove successful in either reducing cardiovascular disease or preventing the conversion to NIDDM, future morbidity and mortality associated with diabetes could be reduced considerably.

The insulin resistance syndrome was first described by Gerald Reaven, of Stanford University Medical School, in 1988. Reaven dubbed the constellation of conditions "syndrome X"; it is also sometimes called the "deadly quartet." Many people, particularly those with a family history of NIDDM, have increased insulin concentrations even though their glucose levels are normal. These people are usually obese and are likely to have so-called visceral obesity—a waist-hip ratio greater than 0.9 in men and 0.8 in women. (Waist-hip ratio is calculated by measuring the waist at the level of the navel, measuring the hips and buttocks at their largest point, and then dividing the waist measurement by the hip-buttocks measurement. The American Heart Association recommends that a woman's waist-hip ratio be no larger than 0.8 and a man's no greater than 1.0.) In addition, insulin-resistant individuals have a high incidence of hypertension and abnormal blood lipids, and a number of studies have shown that they have an increased incidence of cardiovascular disease.

The insulin resistance syndrome precedes the development of impaired glucose tolerance and subsequent NIDDM and may affect as much as 25% of the U.S. population. Given the increasing incidence of obesity in the United States and Western Europe, this syndrome is likely to become one of the most important health problems in the developed world in the 21st century. The treatment of insulin resistance syndrome, consisting of a weight-loss diet, exercise, smoking cessation, and appropriate treatment of hypertension and abnormal blood lipids when they are present, is thus of critical importance.

—*Charles M. Clark, Jr., M.D., and Ana Priscu, M.D.*

NEWS CAP

Obesity: The Plot Thickens

Significant progress has been made in the past year in understanding how the body's weight-regulating mechanism can go awry and cause obesity. The new findings have helped to clarify earlier reports that pointed to a genetic cause for some cases of obesity.

In December 1994 scientists at Rockefeller University, New York City, announced that they had identified a gene in mice—the *ob* gene—that instructs fat cells to produce the hormone leptin. The hormone travels through the bloodstream, arriving at the brain with a message instructing the body to stop eating. Mice that either carried defective copies of the *ob* gene or were missing the gene altogether did not produce this chemical messenger and consequently grew to three to five times their normal weight. When injected with leptin, however, the obese mice ate less and slimmed down, which raised hopes that a similar treatment could be used in humans.

Subsequent studies suggested that defective leptin production might not be the most important factor in the development of human obesity. Leptin levels in many obese individuals were measured and found to be quite high. In fact, elevated leptin levels correlated positively with a high percentage of body fat. This finding indicated that the gene that coded for leptin was in working order. Obesity in these individuals seemed to stem from a fault in the brain's response to the signal instead of a problem in the signal itself.

Investigations conducted in the past year on rats and mice support this theory. In the part of the brain called the hypothalamus, an area known to regulate feeding behavior, researchers identified a receptor for leptin, believed to be an integral component of the signaling pathway that controls eating. (Signaling involves a chemical message being sent to a cell's nucleus—the area where DNA is found—to turn production of a gene on or off.) When leptin binds to the receptor, production of neuropeptide Y, a strong appetite stimulant, is decreased. The bound receptor may also increase production of the appetite suppressant glucagonlike peptide-1, recently shown to be active in the hypothalamus.

Remi Benali—Gamma Liaison

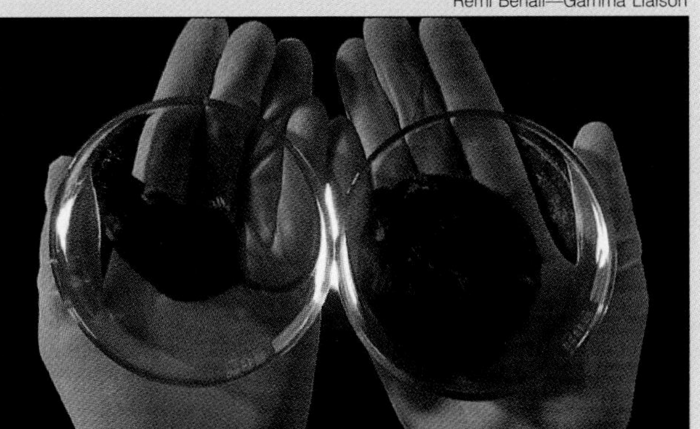

The chubby mouse on the right has a defective obesity gene; so does its counterpart, but after receiving leptin injections over several weeks, the mouse on the left lost more than 30% of its fat.

A defect in the receptor or in one of these appetite-regulating peptides could undermine the chemical balancing act the body performs to maintain a stable weight. Thus, obesity may be caused by a variety of underlying biochemical mechanisms. Moreover, by mid-1996 scientists had identified five different obesity-related genes in mice, some of which were known to have human counterparts. As metabolic researchers—and frustrated dieters—have long suspected, obesity is a far-from-simple problem.

—*M.J. Friedrich*

Parkinson's Disease Update

Parkinson's disease is a neurological disorder marked by gradual deterioration of the ability to move normally. The term *parkinsonism* refers to a syndrome characterized by tremor, muscular rigidity, and slowness of movement (bradykinesia). When these problems are the result of a degenerative disorder of unknown cause, the illness is called Parkinson's disease (PD), named after the British surgeon James Parkinson, who first described it in 1817. When the motor (*i.e.,* movement) disturbances are a result of other definable diseases or identifiable causes (such as environmental exposures), the ailment is called secondary, or symptomatic, parkinsonism. PD, therefore, is distinguished from some conditions that resemble it by the fact that it is an idiopathic disorder (one whose cause is unknown).

The annual incidence (the number of new cases that occur each year) is about 20 per 100,000 persons; the prevalence (the total number of cases existing at one time) is between 100 and 170 per 100,000. While it can occur at any age, PD is primarily an illness associated with aging. The incidence rate peaks at around age 70. About 1–2% of the over-80 population are affected. Men and women are equally likely to develop the disease.

The incidence and prevalence of secondary parkinsonism vary widely depending on the underlying causes. Parkinsonism that develops as a side effect of drugs—for example, antipsychotic medications like haloperidol—is quite common. Arteriosclerotic parkinsonism, which is caused by small strokes deep within the brain, also occurs relatively frequently. There are, in addition, many other extremely rare neurodegenerative conditions that have parkinsonian features.

Disease signs

The major clinical features of PD, like those of parkinsonism, are tremor, rigidity, and bradykinesia. The disease is often mildly asymmetrical at first, but it generally involves both sides of the body. The tremor is usually most noticeable in the arms and hands and, more specifically, the fingers. It is most apparent when the hands are not occupied with any activity. In fact, unlike many other tremors, the characteristic involuntary movements of PD decrease when the patient makes a purposeful movement—for example, reaching for an object. (Some patients also experience other types of tremors during voluntary muscle action.) Although over half of all people with PD notice the tremor before other symptoms, the other typical features of the disease are usually present at the time of diagnosis.

Rigidity—increased muscle tone evident as increased resistance to passive stretching of muscles—can readily be felt by the physician in a physical exam. The characteristic rigidity of PD has a unique quality known as "cogwheeling"; if the examiner bends the patient's forearm or wrist, he or she feels not a smooth resistance but a series of ratchetlike engagements, as of cogs on a wheel. Rigidity is also apparent in the posture of patients and the typical flexed, or bent, position of the neck, trunk, elbows, wrists, hips, and knees. Despite the rigidity, there is no actual loss of muscle strength.

Bradykinesia literally means "slowness of movement." It is probably the most disabling feature of the disease because it can affect all volitional actions as well as many that are largely involuntary, such as blinking and swallowing. People with PD also have difficulty initiating movements, such as rising from a chair or starting to walk. It is the bradykinesia that gives rise to the characteristic masklike, expressionless face of the Parkinson's patient. Drooling (from less-frequent-than-normal swallowing), soft, mumbled speech, and small, illegible handwriting are also common manifestations of bradykinesia.

Abnormal gait and balance occur frequently in PD. The patient walks with a forward-stooped posture and tends to gather speed as he or she moves. The steps are short and shuffling, and the normal swing of the arms is decreased. When turning, the patient does not pivot but takes several small steps and turns en bloc. Balance is especially unsteady when the individual is turning. Loss of balance can be severe enough to interfere with standing and even with unsupported sitting. Difficulty in walking and a tendency to fall may be the first sign of problems resulting from PD.

The disease also may affect the autonomic nervous system, which regulates many basic body functions. Patients may experience increased sweating, low blood pressure when standing, sexual impotence, constipation, and incontinence. Sleep disturbances—inability to fall asleep, inability to remain asleep, reversal of normal sleep pattern (*i.e.,* sleeping during the day, wakefulness at night)—are common complications of PD.

At least 90% of patients have subtle but measurable intellectual changes, and more than 40% experience a dementia syndrome. The cognitive impairment of PD includes difficulty with memory, slowing of thinking, and problems with so-called executive tasks governed by the frontal lobe of the brain (for example, the ability to organize and plan). Speech can be soft and mumbled, but the disease spares other language functions. The dementia syndrome of PD has multiple causes. Some patients probably have Alzheimer's disease in addition to PD. Even in the absence of Alzheimer's disease, however, PD itself appears to cause intellectual as well as motor system abnormalities. Depression is also very common, affecting 40–60% of patients at some time during the illness. The depression appears to have a biological basis and is not directly related to the severity of the disease or the degree of disability.

All the symptoms of PD gradually and inevitably worsen. With progressive immobility, patients become increasingly susceptible to infection and malnutrition. Without treatment, they usually die within 8–10 years of diagnosis. Survival can be prolonged with treatment, but life expectancy is still reduced.

Difficulties in diagnosis

PD and secondary parkinsonism may be difficult to distinguish. The resting tremor is less prominent in drug-induced parkinsonism than in PD, and the presence of small strokes in arteriosclerotic parkinsonism may be indicated by other symptoms suggestive of blood vessel disease. Parkinsonism due to drugs or environmental toxins usually cannot be definitively diagnosed, however, unless the harmful exposure can be identified. The other degenerative conditions that may resemble

PD are marked by combinations of additional neurological signs such as abnormalities of eye movement, ataxia (loss of coordination), and abnormal reflexes.

Establishing a precise diagnosis of PD can be quite difficult. In fact, in only about 75% of those diagnosed with PD is the diagnosis subsequently confirmed by the autopsy findings. A diagnostic evaluation of patients with newly discovered parkinsonism, including blood tests and brain imaging, may help to distinguish those with true PD from those with other problems.

The disease process

PD is characterized by two anatomic changes in the brain: loss of pigmented nerve cells and the presence of abnormal structures called Lewy bodies in some regions of the brain. The principal part of the brain affected is the area known as the substantia nigra, two thin layers of pigmented nerve cells, or neurons, located in the midbrain.

The pigmented neurons are the source of the chemical neurotransmitter dopamine, which acts on neurons of the striatum, a collection of brain structures named for their streaked appearance. Both the substantia nigra and the striatum are components of the basal ganglia (from the Greek *ganglion,* "knot"), knotlike masses of tissue located deep within the brain. Dopamine deficiency in the basal ganglia is the major factor in the disease process in both PD and secondary parkinsonism. Because normal dopamine levels must be reduced by about 80% before symptoms become obvious, the illness is usually quite advanced by the time of diagnosis. Another feature of PD is loss of neurons in a group of cells in the brain stem called the locus ceruleus, which produce the neurotransmitter norepinephrine.

The basal ganglia and the brain region called the thalamus are part of a complex system of feedback loops that connect with other components of the motor system to control movement. Dopamine deficiency in the basal ganglia, along with the resulting overactivity of other neurotransmitters such as acetylcholine, disrupts function in some of these feedback loops. As a consequence, neurons that normally inhibit nerve impulses from the thalamus to the motor cortex become overactive. Motor system activity diminishes, which results in the typical symptoms of parkinsonism. Insight into these underlying mechanisms has suggested several possible treatment options: replacement of dopamine, stimulation of dopamine receptors, retardation or prevention of the loss of pigmented neurons, and selective destruction of the overactive pathways in the motor system.

Unraveling the cause

When explaining what is responsible for the dopamine deficiency in parkinsonism, neurologists generally distinguish two categories of illness. In one are the cases due to known, specific causes, including viral infections, medications, toxic exposures, and damage to the basal ganglia from trauma or reduced blood flow to the brain. In the second category is idiopathic PD, in which, as the term implies, deterioration of the dopamine-producing cells is due to unknown factors—although scientists have several theories about the underlying mechanisms in this process.

Despite the fact that PD appears to be a sporadic illness (*i.e.,* one that occurs in single or occasional instances) rather than a familial disease, families with many affected members are known. The existence of such families suggests that a genetic factor may play a part in susceptibility to the disorder. Several teams of researchers have studied identical and fraternal twins in an attempt to determine the extent to which genetic factors might explain the occurrence of PD. In twin studies scientists look at the proportion of twin pairs in which

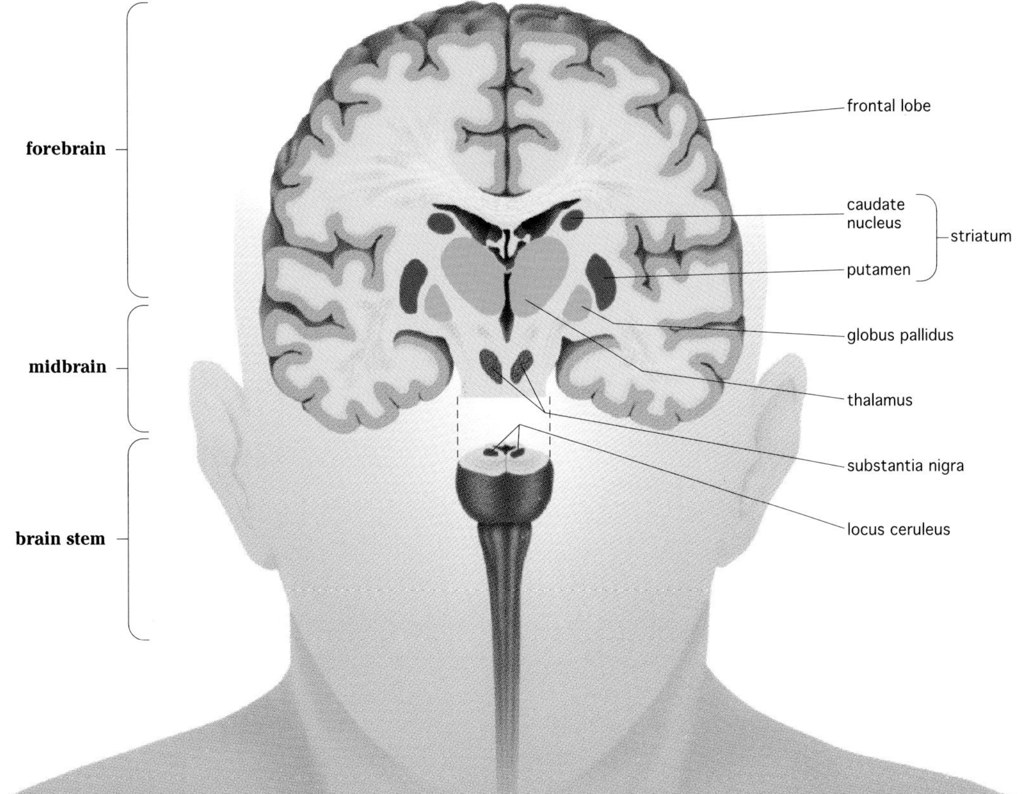

both are affected by the disease in question. This proportion is called the concordance rate. If concordance is higher in identical twins, who share all their genes, than in fraternal twins, who are no more closely related than other siblings, it would be presumed that the illness or trait under study has a genetic component.

Early twin studies of PD showed no greater concordance in identical than in fraternal twins. These studies were flawed, however, in that they often did not use sensitive criteria for diagnosing PD and did not follow subjects long enough to detect the later onset of illness in some individuals. Recent family studies have shown that relatives of persons diagnosed with PD have a higher-than-normal risk of developing the disease, which suggests that there *is* a major role for inheritance in PD. The genetic influence is not the only factor, however. Thus, some people who inherit the illness may not develop symptoms; conversely, many persons with PD have no relatives with the disorder. These findings suggest that PD may be the result of interactions between several genes or between genetic and environmental influences.

Infectious agents and environmental factors have been proposed as possible causes of PD. The best evidence that infection may play a part is the development of so-called postencephalitic parkinsonism in the survivors of a global epidemic of encephalitis (inflammation of the brain) that occurred between 1917 and 1929. (The 1973 book *Awakenings*

NEWS CAP

Mad Cow Chronology

Ten years ago agriculture authorities in Great Britain diagnosed the first cases of a lethal neurological disorder called bovine spongiform encephalopathy (BSE) in beef and dairy cattle. The disease quickly grew to epidemic proportions; by 1993, 1,000 cases per week were being reported.

In March 1996 a scientific committee in the U.K. reported 10 unusual cases of an extremely rare, always fatal human equivalent of BSE known as Creutzfeldt-Jakob disease (CJD). CJD is usually seen only in middle-aged or older people, but the British patients were younger—a few even in their teens—and their illness had other clinical and pathological features not typical of CJD. These differences led scientists to theorize that the recently reported cases represented a new variant of CJD. There was immediate speculation that the ingestion of beef from BSE-infected cattle was responsible for these unusual cases of CJD. Fears of a new and deadly foodborne disease made headlines worldwide.

Without delay, most countries in Europe and many other parts of the world imposed a ban on the importation of British beef and beef products. In Britain many farmers faced the loss of their herds—and their livelihoods—and British consumers the loss of confidence in the safety of their food supply. The controversy over the government's handling of the matter even threatened the political future of Prime Minister John Major.

BSE, sometimes called mad cow disease, is one of several spongiform brain diseases (or spongiform encephalopathies) that affect animals. (Destruction of nerve cells leaves the brains of affected animals riddled with holes, much like the holes in a sponge—hence, the term *spongiform.*) Mink, deer, and various species of cats have also been known to develop such illnesses. The most common spongiform brain disease of animals is scrapie, a condition of sheep and goats that has been recognized in Europe for more than 200 years. The symptoms of BSE and scrapie are similar; they include behavioral changes (agitation, nervousness), loss of coordination, and muscle tremors and twitches. Both are inevitably fatal.

CJD strikes only one person in a million per year; the incidence is vir-

A British farmer ponders the future of his herd after the government's announcement that millions of cattle would be destroyed to prevent the spread of so-called mad cow disease.

Murdo Macleod—FSP/Gamma Liaison

by the British-born neurologist Oliver Sacks and the motion picture based on the book explored the lives of some of those affected by postencephalitic parkinsonism.) In rare cases the condition occurs in the aftermath of other viral infections, although no other such epidemics are known.

Other factors have been postulated to increase a person's chances of developing PD, including a previous history of head trauma. Epidemiologists have observed that the disorder occurs more frequently in northern latitudes and among those who live in rural as compared with urban environments. Among the most curious lifestyle associations has been the persistent observation that smokers are at lower risk for PD than nonsmokers. Some researchers speculate that this apparent protective effect may be the result of the death of many smokers before they reach the age of peak risk for PD. Others suggest that people may stop smoking when they develop the disease. Another, more plausible possibility is that the nicotine in tobacco may stimulate the dopamine system of the brain.

Exposure to certain neurotoxins—for example, manganese, carbon disulfide, carbon monoxide, or mercury—can cause parkinsonism. Another toxic chemical linked to the disorder was identified in the early 1980s after a cluster of young drug addicts near San Francisco experienced the rapid onset of parkinsonism. Through careful medical sleuthing, neuroscientists discovered that these addicts had injected a chem-

tually the same worldwide. The disease is marked by progressive decline in intellectual function and loss of the ability to control movement. A majority of those affected die within 3 to 12 months after diagnosis. Although a small percentage of CJD cases are familial, the majority are sporadic (occurring occasionally or singly). Transmission of CJD via organ and tissue transplants has been documented. In a handful of cases, spread of the disease was traced to injections of growth hormone made from human pituitary extract. As a rule, however, the cause is unknown.

What BSE and CJD have in common is that both are believed to be caused by a novel infectious agent known as a prion (short for proteinaceous infectious particle). Prions are misshapen versions of proteins normally found in the body. Unlike all other known pathogens—viruses, bacteria, fungi—prions have no genetic material, no DNA or RNA. They apparently cause disease by inducing their normal counterparts in the body to change shape. Before prions were discovered, slow-acting viruses had been assumed to be responsible for the spongiform brain diseases. All of these disorders, human and animal, have long incubation periods—that is, many years elapse between exposure to the infectious agent and onset of symptoms.

Where did BSE come from, and why was it first identified in 1986? Most authorities believe that the scrapie prion was transmitted to cattle via livestock feed. Until 1988 British farmers fed their cattle a protein supplement that was made originally from sheep offal (viscera and other leftover parts of butchered animals) and later included cattle parts. The use of solvents in the processing of livestock carcasses was phased out in the late 1970s and early '80s, and authorities now speculate that these solvents may have rendered prions in the meat harmless. Although the practice of using animal parts in livestock feed was banned in Britain in July 1988—because of suspicions that it was responsible for the BSE outbreak—cases of the disease continued to be reported, reaching a peak in 1992–93. Although BSE incidence has declined steadily since then, recent research has confirmed that the illness can sometimes be transmitted from cow to calf, which would explain why British cattle continued to develop BSE even after the ban.

In the wake of the disclosure of the unusual CJD cases in Britain, beef sales in Europe and elsewhere plummeted. Under pressure from the European Union, Britain agreed to slaughter and destroy the carcasses of all cattle over 30 months old—more than four million animals. Although herds in the United States reportedly were free of BSE, and the importation of British beef ceased in 1985, many Americans, too, had second thoughts about

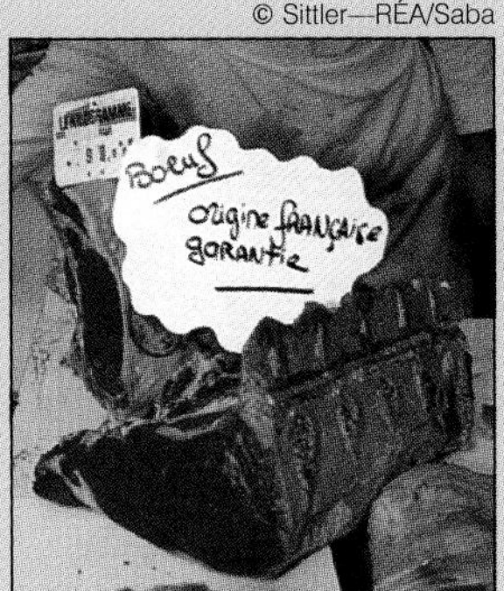

Sign in a Parisian market assures customers that its beef is from cattle raised in France.

their beef-eating habits. (Live cattle have not been imported from Britain—or any other country known to have reported BSE—since 1989.)

Can humans contract BSE by eating beef from infected cows? While this question has not been answered definitively, French scientists have demonstrated that monkeys injected with brain tissue from BSE-infected cows can develop a disease similar to the new CJD variant. The French finding presents the strongest case yet for the hypothesis linking the recent CJD cases to the consumption of contaminated beef.

—Linda Tomchuck

ical known as 1-methyl-4-phenyl-1,2,3,6-tetrahydropyridine (MPTP), a substance created inadvertently in the manufacture of an illicit drug. In the body MPTP is converted into a chemical that impairs the functioning of the mitochondria—tiny, subcellular energy-producing structures—in neurons. Only about 100 cases of parkinsonism were attributed to MPTP exposure, but the discovery of this substance enabled scientists to create animal models of PD that have increased the understanding of the illness tremendously and allow for potential new therapies to be tested in animals before being tried in humans.

Some patients who have no history of exposure to MPTP appear to have enzyme abnormalities that affect the mitochondria in much the same way as the chemical does. Other processes that have been implicated in PD—the accumulation of iron molecules in the substantia nigra, the formation of free radicals (unstable molecules that cause cellular damage)—also impair the functioning of the mitochondria. Therefore, abnormalities in the energy-producing processes of the mitochondria may be a common link in many possible causes of PD. Even the genetic influence may operate through this mechanism. Scientists know, for example, that one specific gene mutation affects the capacity of the mitochondria to metabolize a compound called debrisoquine; this same genetic alteration is associated with a higher rate of PD.

Some herbicides are chemically related to MPTP, and these or other environmental toxins theoretically could have neurotoxic effects similar to those of MPTP. The increased incidence of PD in rural as compared with urban areas may be due to exposure to herbicides, pesticides, and other toxic substances in the rural air and water.

Drug therapy

Medication becomes necessary in PD when the tremor and bradykinesia begin to interfere with the patient's ability to work and socialize. In the past, patients relied on anticholinergic drugs (substances that block the action of acetylcholine) to help restore the balance between dopamine and acetylcholine within the basal ganglia. These drugs were more effective for the tremor than for rigidity or bradykinesia. Anticholinergic medications and the antiviral drug amantadine (which was serendipitously found to stimulate dopamine release) are still used in young patients with mild symptoms. Because of the high incidence of side effects, however, these agents must be used with caution, if at all, in elderly persons.

Neurotransmitter replacement. The discovery of dopamine deficiency in PD was the first breakthrough in the understanding of the disease process and led to the strategy of neurotransmitter replacement therapy. Since the late 1960s dopamine replacement has been the mainstay of treatment. While dopamine does not get into the brain easily, its precursor levodopa, also called L-dopa, does. Once in the brain, levodopa is converted to dopamine. Levodopa is dramatically effective for all the symptoms of PD but is especially so for the bradykinesia and rigidity.

Because levodopa is converted to dopamine in other parts of the body besides the brain (*e.g.,* the stomach, intestines, and blood vessels), not all of the levodopa administered to patients will reach the brain and have an effect on the symptoms. The amount of dopamine reaching the brain can be maximized, however, by combining levodopa with a substance that blocks the conversion of levodopa to dopamine elsewhere in the body. One such substance is carbidopa.

Many dosage forms of levodopa-carbidopa are available; by using different ratios of the two, physicians are able to tailor the dosage to the individual patient's needs. Sustained-release formulations, which have a longer duration of action, are also available. Common side effects of levodopa are nausea, dizziness, confusion, and hallucinations. These problems can be reduced by careful adjustment of the dose.

After several years of therapy, the efficacy of levodopa decreases and new side effects emerge. These complications include involuntary movements associated with peak blood levels of the medication and a "wearing-off" effect as the drug level dwindles. Another complication consists of unpredictable fluctuations in motor system activity, known as the "on-off" phenomenon and characterized by alternating periods of uncontrolled movements and "freezing." The use of the lowest dose that controls symptoms early in the disease may forestall the development of these disabling and difficult-to-manage problems.

When symptoms are unresponsive to a moderate dose of levodopa, a second line of drugs, the dopamine agonists (drugs that mimic the effects of dopamine), is added to the regimen. Bromocriptine, pergolide, and other dopamine agonists act directly on the dopamine receptors in the brain. These drugs are not as effective as levodopa, but given along with levodopa, they may improve efficacy and smooth out the fluctuations in response to levodopa. The dopamine agonists have the same side effects as levodopa.

Levodopa gets into the brain by means of a transport system that also carries amino acids, the building blocks of protein, from the bloodstream into the brain. After a protein-containing meal, these amino acids compete with levodopa to get into the brain. For some patients a diet consisting of complex carbohydrates (fruits, vegetables, and grains) during the day and a low-protein evening meal increases the effectiveness of levodopa. This is not necessary or helpful for all patients, however.

Muhammad Ali carries the Olympic torch at the 1996 Summer Games. The former world heavyweight champion is not the first boxer to have developed parkinsonism as a result of brain damage incurred in the ring.

Doug Mills—AP/Wide World

Neuroprotective therapy. The discovery that MPTP becomes toxic in the body led to a new use for an old drug. Deprenyl, now called selegiline, was found to protect animals exposed to MPTP from developing parkinsonism. Neuroscientists theorized that a similar mechanism could protect human neurons from the toxic effects of free radicals. A large multicenter study concluded that selegiline does slow the progression of PD and delays the time until symptomatic therapy is necessary. It may be, however, that selegiline does not have a protective effect but rather improves symptoms by enhancing the action of dopamine in the brain. Whether selegiline merely provides mild relief of symptoms or has a neuroprotective effect, it is often the first drug used in newly diagnosed PD patients, and some patients do not require additional medications for some time. Except for reducing the wearing-off effect, selegiline is not beneficial in those who have advanced disease.

Because of the hypothesis that excess oxidation damages neurons in PD, antioxidants have been studied for their possible neuroprotective effect. The antioxidant vitamin E (tocopherol) was evaluated in the same large trial that examined selegiline, but that study found no benefit from vitamin E. Other antioxidants, known as lazaroids, confer protection against MPTP toxicity in animals but have not yet been tested in humans.

Neuroscientists have speculated about a variety of other neuroprotective mechanisms that might prevent progression of PD. One such strategy would use dopamine-transport blockers or dopamine agonists to reduce a possible toxic overactivity of dopamine early in the course of the illness. Other potential neuroprotective strategies might include the use of agents called iron chelators, which remove iron from the body and thus would decrease iron accumulation in the substantia nigra; drugs that would block toxic effects of excessive calcium on neurons; and nerve growth factors that would stimulate cells of the substantia nigra. None of these possibilities has been studied in humans yet. Neuroprotective therapy may not be feasible until scientists discover methods to diagnose presymptomatic PD, since, as mentioned above, 80% of the nigral neurons have been lost by the time the disease becomes clinically evident.

Surgical treatment

In the 1950s surgical procedures that destroyed parts of the basal ganglia or thalamus were performed to reduce or eliminate some Parkinson's symptoms. Surgical approaches were largely abandoned after levodopa was introduced, but interest revived in the 1990s. Currently, two approaches to surgical treatment are being tried—tissue transplantation and stereotactic surgery.

In the initial experiments with tissue transplantation, surgeons took dopamine-producing cells from the patients' own adrenal glands and inserted them into the striatum. This surgery was not very successful and was plagued by complications. More recent transplantation surgery has used fetal brain tissue as the source of dopamine-generating cells. The use of fetal tissue—which is taken from aborted fetuses—has been controversial in the U.S., and research has, until fairly recently, been limited. (A moratorium on fetal tissue research was rescinded by Pres. Bill Clinton in January 1993.) A great deal more work in this field has been done in Sweden.

The evidence to date shows that transplanted fetal tissue can survive in the brain of Parkinson's patients and does produce dopamine. Using positron emission tomography scanning, which allows visualization of metabolic activity in the brain, scientists have confirmed increased dopaminergic activity following transplantation. Some transplant recipients have experienced dramatic improvement in their symptoms. More often, however, improvement is modest, and patients still require medication. Many questions regarding the best technique, the most likely candidates, and the clinical efficacy of the procedure—and the ethics of fetal tissue transplantation per se—must be answered before it can be considered to be a therapy suitable for large numbers of PD patients. Moreover, even newer approaches, such as genetically engineered implantable dopamine-producing cells, are on the horizon.

Advances in medical imaging of the brain have led to refinements in the procedure known as stereotactic lesion surgery. The term *stereotactic* refers to a technique for orienting the tip of an instrument (such as a needle or an electrode) in three planes in order to target a precise spot in the brain. Using magnetic resonance imaging to guide their instruments, surgeons can destroy small areas within the basal ganglia. This surgery is called ventral pallidotomy, or simply pallidotomy, after the brain structure—the globus pallidus—involved. The procedure works by purposely damaging that part of the motor system pathway where there is excess inhibitory activity. Before destroying any brain tissue, the neurosurgeon electrically stimulates the target area in the brain of the conscious but locally anesthetized patient, who will experience involuntary movements or visual symptoms (*e.g.,* partial loss of vision) if the probe is affecting the optical tract or other vital structures adjacent to the target. After locating the safest, most effective spot, the surgeon then makes a permanent lesion several millimeters in length. Many patients have significant improvement in tremor, rigidity, bradykinesia, and overall function, as well as experiencing a reduction in medication-related complications. Most patients need to continue to take dopamine-replacement medications, however. Because of the testing for the exact site during surgery, complications from misplaced lesions—slurred speech, weakness, partial loss of vision—are rare.

Stereotactic surgery is not a treatment of first choice, however. It is reserved for patients with poor response to or severe complications from medications. Because the lesion is created only on one side of the brain, the improvement is most noticeable on the opposite side of the body. If the procedure is successful in reducing symptoms on one side, a second surgery may be planned. Stereotactic thalamotomy (destruction of part of the thalamus of the brain) is a variant that may be more effective for the tremor in PD, but it has more complications. Implantation of an electrical stimulation device into the thalamus is another innovative surgical approach that reduces tremor. It has the advantage of being a reversible procedure with few side effects.

—Michael E. Mahler, M.D.,
and David B. Reuben, M.D.

New Responsibility and Respect for Nurses

When an ambulance rushed this author's husband to the hospital last year with strokelike symptoms, he was immediately examined, tests were ordered, a tentative diagnosis was made, emergency treatment was instituted, and he was admitted for further observation—all by a nurse practitioner. Care was prompt, appropriate, and personal. The patient and his wife were consulted and informed even during the urgent proceedings. Two days later he was released from the hospital with no lasting effects of the cerebrovascular incident. It is not unusual that a nurse should play such a key role on the contemporary health care scene.

Catherine Smith—Impact Visuals

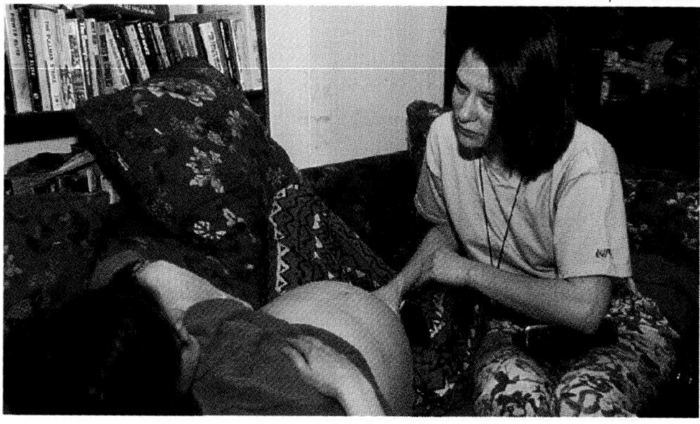

A nurse-midwife makes a house call, checking to see that all is well with a mother-to-be in her ninth month of pregnancy.

Nurses in the '90s

Today patients in the United States who require anesthesia for surgery may well find themselves in the capable hands of certified nurse anesthetists, who are involved in 65% of all anesthesia administration. Worldwide, nurses are authorized to administer anesthesia in more than 107 countries; they do so in 70–80% of surgical cases or, in some less developed nations, in virtually all instances.

In the past two decades, the proportion of childbirths attended by nurse-midwives in hospitals and other settings in the U.S. has increased from less than 1% to close to 5%. This occurred at a time when medicine became increasingly "high-tech" and the number of cesarean sections skyrocketed. In many countries, where childbirth is more commonly a "low-tech" event—and recognized as a natural phenomenon—midwives handle essentially all maternity care at lower costs and with fewer surgical interventions than in the industrialized world and with healthy outcomes for mother and child.

In a remote village in southern Africa, Latin America, or southwestern Asia, the community mobilizer for health, sanitation, and housing services may well be a nurse. In the rural or inner-city U.S. or in South Korea, clinics serving the entire community may well be run entirely by nurses.

Consider the following situations:

- Clients in a giant managed health care system may discover that the case manager for their highly complex plan of care is a nurse—sometimes visible, sometimes behind the scenes.
- A family that belongs to a health maintenance organization, or HMO, may be assigned a nurse practitioner as its primary care provider and "gatekeeper" to today's mazelike medical care system.
- The nurse making minute-by-minute decisions at the bedside of a patient in intensive care, whose condition is highly unstable, may be a clinical nurse specialist with a master's degree. He or she is not only highly qualified but board-certified to care for those with particular diseases or symptoms and to administer specialized treatments.
- The chief executive officer of a hospital or health care system may be a nurse (with additional training in economics or business administration). She or he may also serve on the board of the Federal Reserve Bank and/or several large corporations.
- The university professor and principal investigator of a research team studying major problems in pain management, wound healing, the care of premature infants, or the cost savings associated with various treatments (so-called outcomes research) may be an R.N.-Ph.D.
- The expert called upon to teach good health and safety practices in community centers, industrial settings, or public schools may be a specially trained public health, occupational health, or school nurse.
- The owner and operator of the neighborhood rehabilitation center, nursing home, hospice, or home health care agency may be a nurse entrepreneur who has invested his or her career (and personal savings) in providing care when and where it is needed most.
- Among the shingles hanging outside many a local medical arts building may be those of independent nurse practitioners, offering a wide array of primary care services to the public—services that are reimbursable by the government or a private insurer.
- The executive officer of a large philanthropic foundation that dispenses hundreds of millions of dollars to support innovative and experimental projects shaping the future of health care locally or abroad may be a nurse.
- The attorney representing a client in high-stakes health care litigation may be a nurse with training in the law.
- The provost or president of a large public research university or a small liberal arts college may be a nurse and professor who has ascended to the top of the academic ladder through teaching, research, and administrative excellence.
- The executive director of a local or national Red Cross agency, organizing and directing thousands of volunteers in times of disaster, may be a nurse.
- The head of a national family-planning program may be a nurse.
- A member of a country's parliament, the minister of health, the representative to the United Nations, or a chief delegate to the World Health Assembly may be a nurse.
- A lieutenant governor of a state or province, the chief of staff for the majority leader of the U.S. Senate, the head of the U.S. Health Care Financing Administration responsible for the Medicaid and Medicare programs, the "czar" of the federal AIDS program, or the director of the Social Security Administration may be a nurse.

In fact, all of the above positions are presently or have been held by nurses. Adapting to current social, economic, and health care trends, nurses today are stepping up to higher levels of education and research and accordingly are reaching out with greater knowledge, skill, confidence, and independence into expanded roles and settings.

Meeting challenges

Worldwide the nursing profession is responding to myriad health care needs and challenges, including:

- the global commitment of the World Health Organization (WHO) to health promotion and disease prevention and community-focused health services
- consumer demands and expectations that are higher than ever before and are overwhelming the health care budgets in many industrialized nations
- efforts to control escalating health care costs, resulting in fewer and more intensive hospitalizations for patients, including the mentally ill
- the remarkable advances in technology in hospitals and, more recently, in home-based care of the chronically and terminally ill
- the fragmentation of care resulting from a high degree of specialization and from the rapid movement of patients from setting to setting and from health care provider to provider
- the needlessly high infant and maternal mortality in many nations, both industrialized and less developed
- the rampant spread of infectious diseases such as AIDS, malaria, cholera, and tuberculosis, all of which are preventable and some of which formerly were curable but now are resistant to treatment
- the increase in the number of elderly persons in the world and the corresponding increase in aging-associated health problems
- patients' increasing dependence on community support systems such as home care services, meals-on-wheels, etc.
- the ever-growing need for health care expertise in ethical dilemmas and in key public policy issues, where patients' lives may hang in the balance or the health care of large populations is influenced

Around the world, public health nurses are meeting vital needs of young and old, sick and well, rich and poor. (Left bottom) In Seattle, Wash., a visiting nurse checks blood pressures in a senior citizens center. (Below) A nurse in Cambodia distributes information about malaria prevention to schoolchildren.

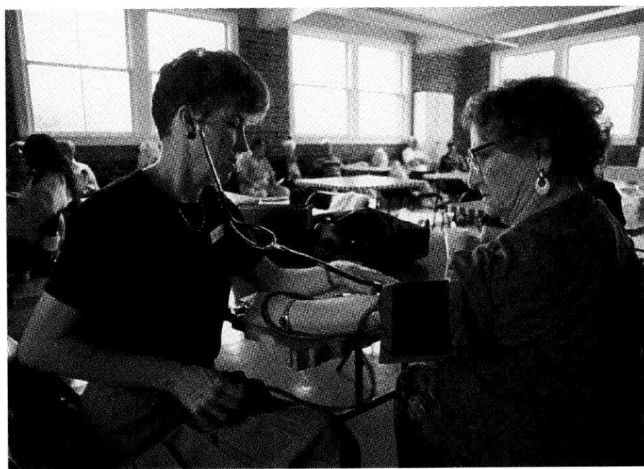

(Left) Matthew McVay—Stock, Boston; (right) P. Merchez—WHO

Andy Levin—Photo Researchers

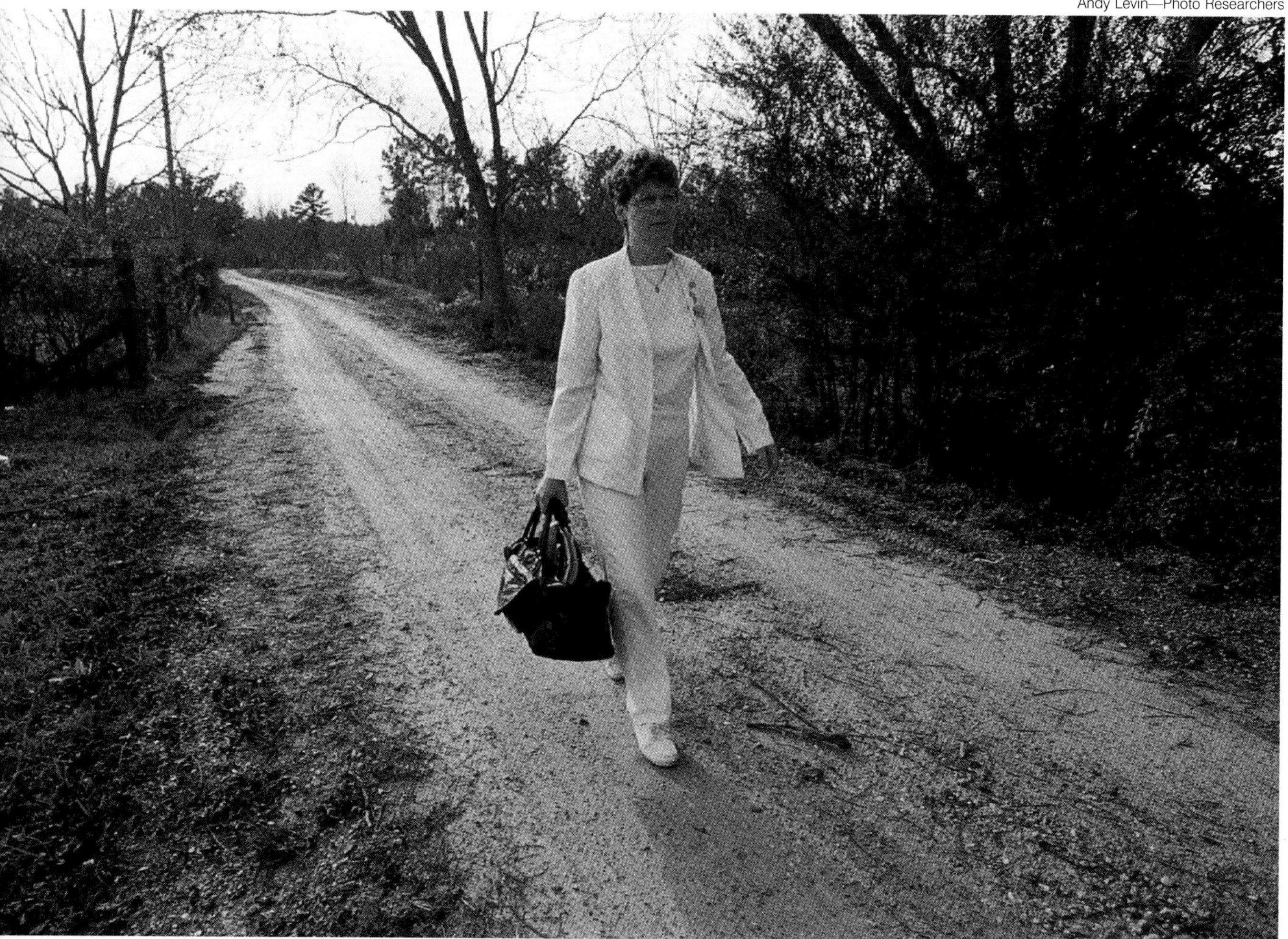

A nurse practitioner heads down a country road in Mississippi to see patients who depend on her. Internationally, more nurses than any other health care providers reach out to the underserved and practice in rural, remote, and poor areas.

Why nurses?

Nurses have been called upon to meet these diverse challenges for quite a number of reasons. First and foremost, nurses constitute the largest group of health care providers in most countries and throughout the world. It is difficult to arrive at exact figures because nursing and nurses are defined variably around the globe but, as just one example of their significant numbers, there are more than 2.2 million registered nurses in the United States alone. Also, nurses are geographically more evenly distributed than other health care providers. More nurses practice in rural, remote, and poor areas than any other health care providers. In fact, nurses have searched out the vulnerable, underserved populations—the homeless, refugees, substance abusers, the elderly, and persons with HIV/AIDS.

The World Bank has estimated that a global ratio of 2:1 to 4:1 qualified nurses to physicians (with approximately one or two doctors per 10,000 population overall) is adequate to provide the minimum package of health care services in the most cost-effective manner. In addition to being ubiquitous and cost-effective, nurses possess a number of attributes that equip them well for meeting the many challenges in the current health care environment. For example, the nursing profession has historically placed a great deal of emphasis on health promotion (*i.e.,* preventing illness by educating the public). At the other extreme of the health care continuum, in the high-tech hospital setting, nurses have provided 24-hour continuity of care. Traditionally nurses have also been team players, contributing good "people" skills and versatility to the complicated processes of health care delivery. "Care, cure, coordination, and collaboration" have been nursing's stock-in-trade for decades. Furthermore, public trust is another asset nurses bring to the contemporary health care scene. Numerous consumer surveys indicate that nurses are viewed as competent, pragmatic, truthful, and ethical.

When these qualities are matched to the needs and challenges of the modern-day health care marketplace, the increasing value of nurses in a changing world becomes quite evident. All these factors also help explain why shortages of nurses are chronic and endemic, despite the growing supply. The demand rises with the heightened awareness that a fully qualified, well-supported nurse "working smart" is the best investment in health care.

(Top and bottom) Photographs, Alain McLaughlin—Impact Visuals

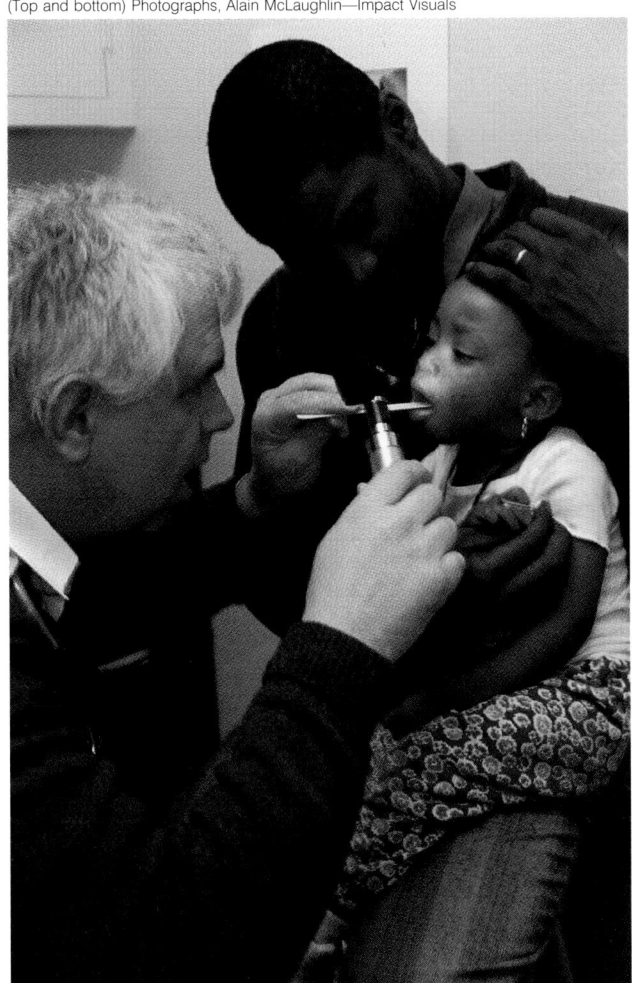

Looking forward

To enable today's nurses to meet current challenges and tomorrow's nurses to meet future challenges, a number of changes have had to occur in the profession, in the health care industry, and in health policy and law. Six critical factors that are having a major impact on the expansion of nurses' roles are addressed below.

1. Organized advocacy. The support of nursing and health care organizations has been a fundamental factor in nursing's advancement. Changes at the grassroots of nursing have been stimulated and assisted by a number of governmental and nongovernmental organizations (NGOs) on all levels. Moving up the tiers of the governmental system are the local, state, and federal departments or ministries of health and, internationally, WHO, with its six geographic regions. The International Labour Organisation (ILO), a UN agency, specifically addresses economic and general welfare issues for workers in all occupations, including nursing. Principal among the NGOs advocating for nursing are the 114 national nurses associations constituting the International Council of Nurses (ICN). Conveniently, the ICN, WHO, and the ILO are all headquartered in Geneva, where their close proximity permits intensive communication and cooperation. Through a variety of projects, addressed jointly and singly by these organizations, the profession has been strengthened and empowered to meet the challenges of the late 20th century and the early 21st century.

(Left) A pediatric nurse at a family health clinic in San Francisco examines a patient with a sore throat. (Below) At a state hospital in California, nurses meet for a change-of-shift report. Nurses have a well-earned reputation as team players; without their work as carers, curers, coordinators, and collaborators, hospitals would hardly function.

Ansell Horn—Impact Visuals

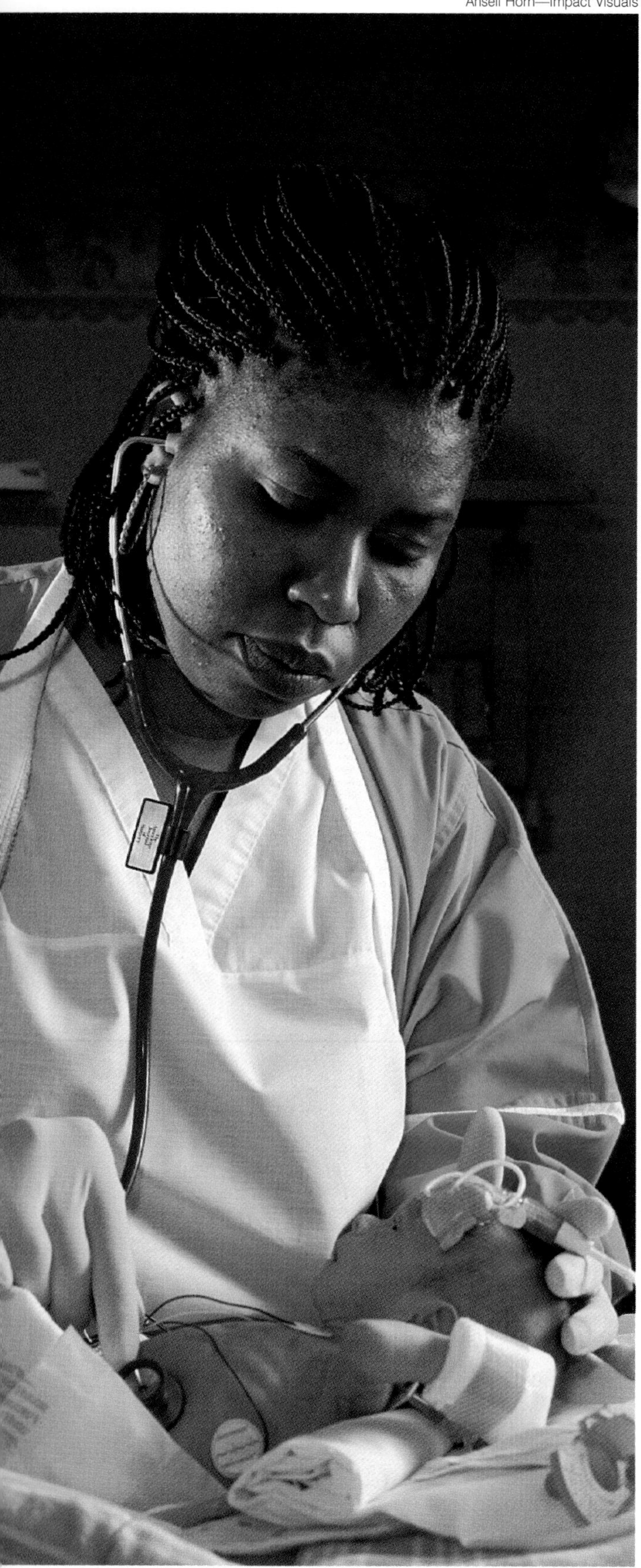

2. Education, research, and practice. Nursing education has had to change dramatically to enable the profession's expanded role in health care. Traditional hospital-based programs do not provide community nursing experience or the liberal arts curricula of universities and thus have not been adequate in scope or breadth. Moreover, they have isolated nursing students from the mainstream of higher education. To remedy this situation, the preparation of nurses is now occurring increasingly in academic settings. In fact, in some countries nursing education has moved exclusively into the universities. Despite the extension and reform of nursing education, the cost of educating a nurse is only a fraction of the cost required for educating a physician. This opens the field to more persons; it also helps keep the costs of health care down—costs that are eventually borne by the public. Improvements in education have also led to improvements in research and practice. There is good evidence that advanced practice nurses improve patient care.

3. Nursing practice laws. A third factor enabling—or inhibiting—the expanded role of nurses is legal authorization. In most countries the limits of nursing practice are set at the federal level. In the U.S. and some other decentralized countries, however, the authority resides with state or provincial governments.

As nurses have become better and better educated and their roles have been enlarged, the legal scope of their practice has had to be extended accordingly. In recent years, largely through the combined efforts of the ICN and WHO, there has been an accelerated movement to extend the practice boundaries of the profession. In some countries nurses are now authorized to diagnose, prescribe medication, and even admit patients to hospitals under their care. Some jurisdictions have delegated to the nursing regulatory body (a nursing council or nursing board) the authority to set and revise the limits of practice in accordance with health care trends and the enhanced capabilities of nurses. The goal of such regulation is public safety.

4. Third-party reimbursement. The government or private health insurers, known as the "third party," pay for some or all of health care in most countries. When nurses provide "expanded" services, the health care system must provide for their reimbursement, just as it does for physician-rendered services. In nations with centralized, single-payer health systems, such adjustments have been easily accommodated. In the United States, ongoing negotiations with the federal government, state agencies, and private insurance companies have inched forward to gain authorization for reimbursement of advanced nursing services. A major tool in the negotiations for third-party reimbursement has been the widely documented efficacy and cost-effectiveness of care rendered by highly qualified nurses.

5. Compensation and recognition. Incentives are another enabling factor in the advanced-practice movement. Nurses are encouraged to seek additional education and to assume roles of greater scope and responsibility when health care consumers recognize their expertise and seek out their care

A nurse practitioner examines a healthy newborn baby in the maternity unit of a New York City hospital.

and when they are appropriately compensated by employers. The profession long suffered from the "a-nurse-is-a-nurse" complex, and little motivation was provided for nurses to better themselves. Progress has been made in establishing career ladders and salary structures distinguishing nurses with higher qualifications and greater responsibilities. Nevertheless, inequities in salaries and practice privileges persist, and these could have the effect of preventing the profession from realizing its true potential.

Nursing, a largely female profession, has long been a natural standard-bearer for the economic and social rights of women. Battles continue to be waged on many fronts and at many levels, with nurses and nursing organizations often leading the fray. As just one example, many nurses were at the negotiating tables of the UN Fourth World Conference on Women in Beijing in September 1995, where they spoke persuasively for the educational, economic, and health rights of women around the world.

6. Public awareness and acceptance. Public response is a sixth key factor influencing nursing's progressive development. In order to benefit from all that nurses of the 1990s have to offer, society must appreciate the high level of education that stands behind those services. The public must also comprehend the relative costs of expert nursing care within an increasingly expensive and troubled health care system.

The public must not only be willing to accept and seek out those services but also be discriminating in doing so. In assuming more responsibility for their own health, people should be aware of the many distinctions within the nursing profession. As a practical measure, to indicate these distinctions most nurses wear pins on their uniforms or lab coats indicating R.N. (registered nurse), M.S. (a nurse with a master of science degree), C.C.N.S. (certified clinical nurse specialist), C.A.P.N. (certified advanced practice nurse), nurse anesthetist, nurse-midwife, and, increasingly, Ph.D. If such information is not readily apparent, consumers should not hesitate to inquire; generic labels such as "nursing staff" or "patient care attendant" tell nothing about the qualifications of the care provider.

Nursing's dynamism

The impact of new roles and new responsibilities for nurses has already been dramatic. Studies show that the expanded services provided by well-qualified nurses are different in nature from those provided by physicians. For example, nurses spend more time with patients; the treatments they provide are often more conservative and less intrusive. Most telling, outcomes are as good or better in terms of health status and cost savings. Consumers react positively to such care and ask for more. As sweeping changes occur in health care technology and in the structure and priorities of health care systems, nurses will continue to be at the patient's side, assuring quality care, providing expertise, and offering comfort when and where they are needed.

—Margretta Madden Styles, R.N., Ed.D.

NEWS CAP

Valor in Oklahoma City

On May 6, 1996, at a formal ceremony in Washington, D.C., the American Red Cross and the American Nurses Association (ANA) honored 10 outstanding professionals with the first-ever "Nurse Hero" awards. The awards celebrate individuals whose extraordinary commitment to nursing is marked by acts that exceed professional expectations in life-threatening situations.

The event closely followed the one-year anniversary of the worst act of terrorism in U.S. history: the bombing of the Alfred P. Murrah Federal Building in Oklahoma City, Okla., on April 19, 1995. A huge car bomb, planted in a rented truck, exploded, destroying the federal building, damaging 70 nearby buildings, cruelly ending the lives of 169 people, and injuring more than 600. It was on that tragic day that two of the Nurse Hero award recipients demonstrated their bravery.

Photographs, ANA

Rebecca Needham Anderson

Capt. Marion L. Duncan

As soon as Rebecca Needham Anderson heard the first 911 call after the bombing, she proceeded to the shattered federal building and began administering aid to the wounded. She had been on the scene only a short while when a loosened piece of concrete struck her on the head; five days later she died. Her eyes, heart, liver, and kidneys were all removed to become donor organs.

Capt. Marion L. Duncan accompanied a surgeon into the collapsing building later that day to rescue the last known survivor. He succeeded in saving the life of a young woman trapped inside and delivered himself to safety as well.

Eight other Nurse Hero awards were presented. All went to individuals who risked their own lives to save others.

—Katherine I. Gordon

Focus on Low Vision

With her wet arms glistening like knives and her feet beating the water into a soufflé of white foam, Trischa Zorn churns up the lanes of an Olympic-size pool just like any other internationally competitive swimmer. But when Zorn—who has won no fewer that 40 gold medals and was a finalist for *Sports Illustrated*'s sportsperson of the year (1988)—looks at a road sign, she pulls out a smaller-than-palm-size telescope; the powerful, optically ground lenses bring distant, otherwise unintelligible letters into focus.

Like an estimated three million Americans, Zorn has functional eyesight that is categorized by eye care professionals as "low vision." Though not totally blind, she has sharply limited useful vision. Generally the eyesight of persons with low vision is not improved by medicine, surgery, or ordinary corrective lenses, although that does not mean they cannot be helped. Low vision is usually defined as 20/70 visual acuity or less in the better eye. Zorn's sight is considerably worse than that; born 32 years ago without irises (a condition known as aniridia), she has an estimated 20/900 visual acuity in her better eye, the left. In fact, in most U.S. states Zorn would far exceed the criteria for legal blindness, which is defined as a visual acuity of 20/200 or less, or a visual field restriction of 20° diameter or less, in the better eye (corrected with eyeglasses). But in her rather extraordinary case, very minimal vision combined with her own considerable grit has allowed her to avoid books in Braille, a Seeing Eye dog, and even a white cane.

Illuminating findings

A recent survey conducted by Louis Harris and Associates, Inc., for the Lighthouse Inc., the world's leading resource on vision impairment, found that a large majority of middle-aged and older Americans fear vision loss more than any other physical impairment: 71% of those surveyed feared becoming blind more than becoming deaf; 76% feared blindness more than being wheelchair-bound; 70% feared sight loss more than loss of a limb. The only "impairment" feared more than blindness was mental or emotional illness.

The survey also showed that while vision impairment cuts across socioeconomic strata, certain groups are at higher risk than others. Broadly speaking, vision impairment is more prevalent among those with the lowest social and economic resources. Similarly, the survey found that gender, economic status, marital status, living arrangements, ethnicity, education, and general health status distinguish those with the most severe forms of vision impairment from those with more moderate degrees of impairment.

The anatomy of low vision

In normal vision, light enters the eye through its clear window, the cornea; then passes through the lens, which allows the eye to vary its focus from infinity to close objects; and finally forms an image on the central part of the retina, the macula lutea (or macula). Within the macula, vision is sharpest at the small pit called the fovea. The photoreceptors (rods and cones) in the retina transform these light images into tiny electric impulses that are sent by way of the optic nerve to the visual region of the brain, where vision actually takes place. The "field of vision" includes central vision—what one sees when looking straight ahead—and peripheral (side) vision.

Anything that interrupts, disturbs, or degrades the normal pathway of light to the retina or the impulses that move along the optic nerve to the brain can cause vision to deteriorate. People with low vision may see color, light, movement, dimension, size, and shape, but objects may be highly blurred, faded, or distorted, or they may jump around, be "not all there," or simply not be visible at all. Typically, the person with low vision has difficulty reading a newspaper or going shopping in a supermarket. This is still a higher level of acuity than that of the legally blind person with maximal vision. The latter would barely be able to perceive a large boldface newspaper headline.

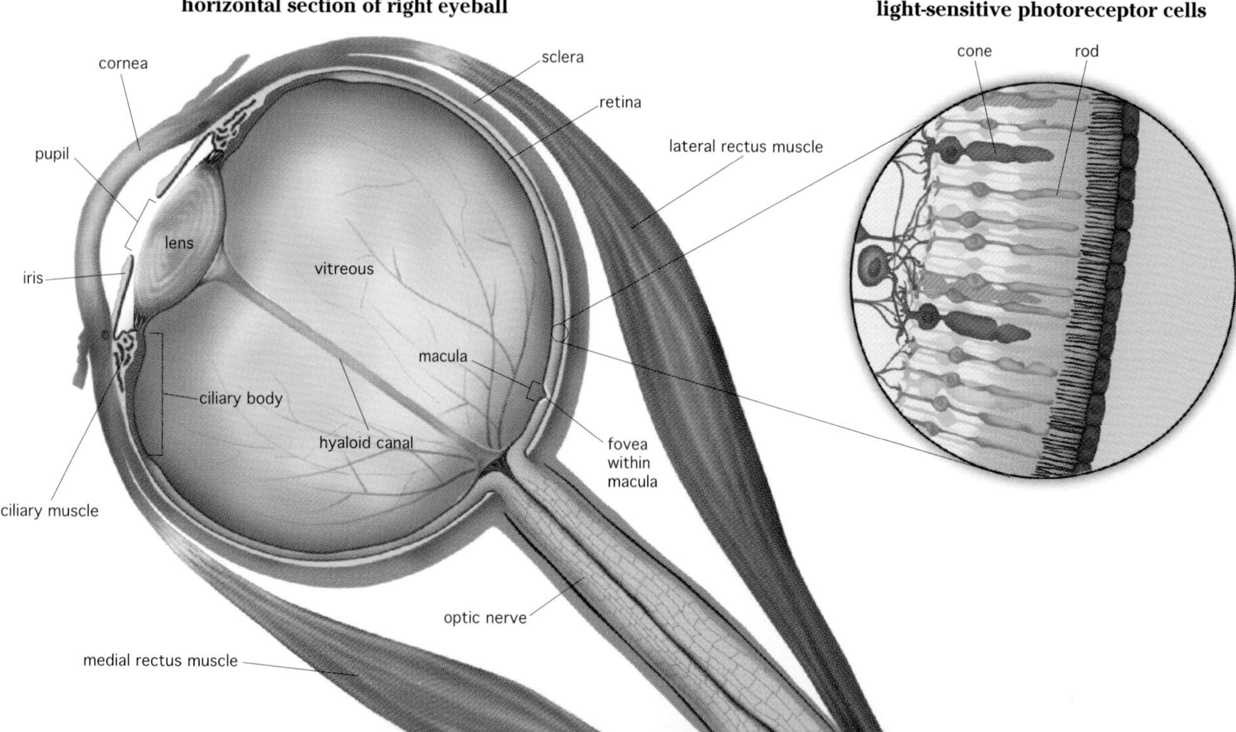

Leading causes of impaired sight

While impaired vision can occur at any age, individuals aged 65 and older are more likely than younger people to suffer from low vision. Not only is the affliction more common in seniors, but the impact on their lives is more severe; 40% of low-vision patients over 65 report significant limitations in their everyday activities. By contrast, Zorn was a leading contender in many events at the 1996 Paralympic Games in Atlanta, Ga., and works as a teacher-administrator with mildly mentally handicapped youngsters. While her athletic prowess is unusual, studies have shown that fewer than 20% of those aged 45 and younger with low vision are severely limited in their capability to function and work.

The four leading causes of vision loss in the U.S. and most industrialized nations are described below and are all primarily age-related: macular degeneration, cataracts, glaucoma, and diabetic retinopathy. Other common eye diseases that can diminish sight and occur at any age are corneal dystrophies, retinal detachments, and optic nerve diseases. Still other contributors to sight loss are strokes, tumors, and ocular trauma.

Macular degeneration. Ten million elderly Americans experience visual impairments associated with age-related macular degeneration (AMD), which makes it the leading cause of vision impairment in the U.S. The National Advisory Eye Council estimates that each year more than 165,000 Americans develop AMD. Development of the disorder is usually a slow process, occurring over a period of years. Less often, macular degeneration is acute in onset, caused by a leakage of fluid into the macular area. Those who are affected may have problems reading and recognizing faces but have adequate peripheral vision, allowing them to get around. While there is no cure for macular degeneration, some patients can benefit from laser surgery (but time is of the essence). Most patients, however, can benefit from high-magnification vision aids. Additionally, because ultraviolet (UV) light is one of the causative or exacerbating factors in AMD, affected individuals should protect their eyes by wearing UV-blocking sunglasses.

Cataracts. Cataracts are opacities that cause the crystalline lens in the eye to lose its transparency. In advanced stages cataracts may limit vision to a point where eyeglasses and magnifiers offer no improvement. Although cataracts usually progress very slowly over many years, they may be surgically removed at any stage of development. In fact, cataract surgery is the most common operation performed on Americans aged 65 years and over (with an estimated 1,350,000 cataract-removal procedures being performed yearly at a cost of approximately $3.4 billion). Even though the success rate for cataract removal is about 95%, not everyone who could benefit undergoes the surgery; thus, cataracts remain an important cause of visual loss in the United States.

Glaucoma. Abnormally high pressure within the eye is the usual cause of glaucoma. In most cases the increased pressure does not cause discomfort or any noticeable vision change for years. Rather, it gradually "sneaks up" and robs the individual of, first, peripheral vision and, then, central vision. It usually can be treated by medications, but more severe cases may require surgery or laser treatments to lower the internal eye pressures. Some groups of people are at higher risk than others; African-Americans, for example, are up to five times more likely to develop glaucoma than whites, especially when the eye disease is associated with diabetes, blood vessel disease, or a family history of glaucoma.

John Nienhuis—Sports Illustrated

Trischa Zorn has extremely low vision, but that has not stopped her from being a champion swimmer or from having a fulfilling out-of-pool career.

Diabetic retinopathy. Damage to the retina (occurring centrally and/or peripherally) is one of the most common complications of diabetes mellitus. At least half of the 16 million Americans with diabetes have some form of diabetic eye disease, resulting from faulty or inadequate insulin production. As many as 24,000 people go blind annually from diabetic retinopathy, and it is the leading cause of blindness among working-age Americans. If detected early, these complications can be treated with medications, lasers, or other forms of surgery. Long-standing diabetes, by contrast, can damage the blood vessels of the retina and precipitate the development of cataracts or glaucoma and eventually blindness. The severity of vision loss depends on several factors—the type of diabetes (insulin-dependent or non-insulin-dependent, also called Types 1 and 2, respectively), the age of onset of diabetes, and control of blood sugar levels. Examinations at regular intervals are recommended for a proper assessment of diabetic eye disease in all persons at risk.

Superior services underutilized

In the U.S. support services for the sight-impaired abound. Unfortunately, however, many people, including doctors, still are not fully informed about the help that is available to those with low vision. This results in wide underutilization of the services offered. According to the national survey commissioned by the Lighthouse Inc., 40% of older Americans did not know that there were public agencies providing vision rehabilitation services and that these were available in their own communities; those individuals who suffered from low vision were even less aware. Although cost and transportation to the facilities that offer such services are certainly factors that contribute to underutilization, the lack of public awareness remains a chronic problem. Consequently, in 1996 the National Eye Institute of the U.S. National Institutes of Health, Bethesda, Md., initiated a major campaign to inform the public about the disabilities that are associated with low vision and what can be done about them.

Low-vision services are provided by ophthalmologists, optometrists, and other professionals who have been specially trained and have the necessary equipment to assess a patient's visual functioning and prescribe appropriate low-vision aids. Other team members may include rehabilitation counselors, special education teachers, and orientation and mobility instructors, as well as occupational and physical therapists, psychologists, medical social workers, audiologists, and family physicians.

At the outset a comprehensive examination by a qualified ophthalmologist or optometrist should be performed to determine the nature and extent of vision loss and how to make the most of whatever eyesight remains. The examination should include a detailed medical history that determines overall ocular health and assesses the patient's attitude and expectations. A subjective evaluation of the eyes' focusing system is done to ascertain the best-possible prescription for high-magnification eyeglasses or other suitable optical devices. Subjective tests are also done to assess fields of vision, macular function (using the Amsler grid test), and contrast sensitivity of each eye. Objective tests evaluate the patient's ocular health status and measure intraocular pressures. Additional tests determine how well the two eyes fixate together, adapt to dark conditions, and perceive colors.

Visual acuity is determined by use of the Snellen chart (named for the 19th-century Dutch ophthalmologist Hermann Snellen). The chart consists of series of letters of varying sizes representing what the normal eye should see clearly at 20 ft, 30 ft, up to 200 ft. Each eye is tested separately. Thus, if an eye can read a row of letters that the "normal" eye reads at 20 ft, then visual acuity in that eye is 20/20. If the first row of letters that can be read on the chart is what the normal eye should see at 200 ft, then visual acuity is 20/200.

The Snellen chart, with the big E on top, relies on the individual's ability to read black letters of graduated sizes against a white background. This traditional means of testing acuity, however, is not always suitable for low-vision patients. It makes the task of seeing letters especially difficult for glaucoma patients with tunnel vision (loss of peripheral vision) and AMD patients with a blind spot in their central vision. Recently, though, charts have been developed specifically for the evaluation of low-vision patients. Bailey-Lovie charts, named for their developers at the University of California, Berkeley, School of Optometry, are more standardized than Snellen charts, having the same number of letters in each row, which affords more uniform reading down the chart. This allows for more sensitive scoring and provides better detection of subtle acuity changes in the low-vision patient. The newer charts can also evaluate the ability of the eyes to perceive different levels of contrast.

Low-tech aids: easy and affordable

Low-vision rehabilitation services aim to make the most of whatever residual sight an individual has. Sometimes this is simply a matter of making minor environmental modifications—such as moving a television set away from a window that causes glare or using an adjustable "goosenecked" lamp that aims bright light directly onto the reading material or work area. Many low-vision patients benefit from the use of nonoptical adaptive devices such as large-print publications, enlarged telephone buttons, high-contrast watch faces, and "talking" machines (alarm clocks, computers, timers, scales, etc.).

Long before prescription eyeglasses were common, simple handheld magnifying lenses were used to enhance vision. Today there are many optically improved aids that help low-vision patients. These include special high-prescription eyeglasses, handheld or stand magnifiers, prisms, mirrored optical systems, spectacle-mounted telescopes, and loupes. Like the pocket-size monocular favored by Zorn, most such aids are easy to use and reasonable in cost.

Most optical aids employ some type of magnification system. The purpose of such aids is to enlarge the image to be viewed over a wider area of retina and thereby increase the number of messages sent from the rods and cones to the brain. No single low-vision aid has been designed to enhance all the functions of the sight-impaired eye. For this reason a person may need a combination of aids for different viewing purposes.

UV light has been shown to be at least partially responsible for the photochemical ocular damage that occurs in some cases of cataract and macular degeneration. Newly developed glare-control lenses called Corning Performance Filter (CPF) lenses help protect the eyes from excessive exposure to harmful UV light. Patients with low vision tend to be hypersensitive to glare and bright light, whether from the sun or an artificial light source; CPF lenses minimize the discomfort that brightness and glare can cause. CPF lenses are photochromic—*i.e.,* they alter according to the light source, from a lemon yellow indoors to dark brown outdoors. Today they are increasingly being recommended for cataract patients before and after surgery and for those with macular degeneration, diabetic retinopathy, retinitis pigmentosa (a hereditary degenerative eye disease marked by night blindness, constriction of the visual field, and pigment changes in the retina), and other conditions that cause severe light sensitivity. All prospective CPF users need to try different series of lenses to find the filter level that is most appropriate for them individually.

High-tech help

Only recently has the research community turned its efforts to the low-vision field in general and to enhancing the reading ability of low-vision patients in particular. This emphasis has accelerated the development of a wide variety of electronic magnification aids such as personal computers with special low-vision software, closed-circuit television systems, optical scanning devices with voice (also called optical character reading devices), portable video magnifiers, head-mounted video display systems, and flat-screen display systems. The current pace of the technological revolution virtually ensures that many practical, improved new vision aids will emerge in the next few years.

Besides improving the tools for examination, diagnosis, and treatment of patients, high-tech innovations have expanded the horizons of those with low vision in some quite amazing ways. Audio technology, for example, has played a major role in increasing the level and scope of competition of low-vision and even blind athletes. Open-water endurance swimmers, such as those swimming the English Channel, wear caps fitted with tiny one-way FM radios that allow them to hear directional instructions from their coaches. Some pools used for competition are now equipped with motion-detector alarms that beep when swimmers approach the wall.

Personal computers. Several major computer companies, such as Apple and IBM, have adapted current computer technology for individuals with disabilities so that they can fully participate in special education programs. Many standard computers can magnify print size on the screen a specified number of times and also allow the selection of large-size fonts. In some cases large monitors enlarge print size enough so that people with low vision can continue using a standard computer. There are also contrast-enhancement and glare-reducing filters that attach to the monitor. Other computer enhancements scan printed material into the computer and convert it into a machine-readable format that can be read, enlarged, edited, and stored on the computer; such material can also be reproduced in either speech or Braille. The latter, optical character readers (OCRs), are especially useful to individuals who are severely visually impaired or blind. Special OCRs are used in conjunction with character-recognition software.

Computer users also benefit from a growing number of resources on the Internet aimed at persons with visual impairments. Internet bulletin boards, for example, offer information on the latest vision-enhancing technologies, post job openings for those with low vision, and enable computer users who are visually impaired or blind to exchange information and ideas and share concerns and resources.

Video views. Closed-circuit television (CCTV) systems can electronically enhance a video image in a variety of ways—*e.g.,* by enlarging, moving, or freezing it. Because images can be magnified up to 60 times, such systems are useful for, say, reading a letter or writing a check and especially for prolonged reading and writing tasks. The CCTV's components are a mounted camera, a self-contained light source, a lens that magnifies standard print to various sizes, and a monitor. Some models have special digital contrast-enhancement features that improve text reading. Others allow the user to view images in either positive or reverse video mode, in green, amber, or other user-selected colors.

Recently developed portable handheld electronic magnifiers connect in minutes to any television set to provide enhanced viewing or reading for those with low vision. Similar units are available on a portable flat-screen display system.

The Aladdin personal reader is a moderately priced aid that makes it possible for most people with low vision, even some who are legally blind, to manage everyday tasks—like writing a check or reading a recipe—easily and without giving up their independence.

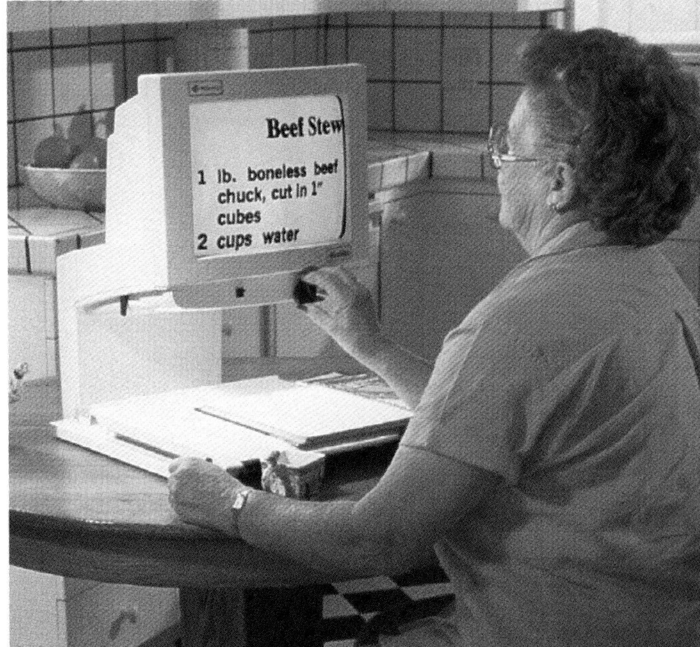

Photographs courtesy of Telesensory

Space-age innovation. One of the newest devices for low vision is the product of collaborative research by the National Aeronautics and Space Administration, the Wilmer Eye Institute of Johns Hopkins University, Baltimore, Md., and the U.S. Department of Veterans Affairs. The Low Vision Enhancement System, or LVES (pronounced "Elvis"), has distinct advantages over the other high-tech vision aids. For one thing, the system is portable, battery-operated, and head-mounted. The head mount looks like a virtual reality goggle, has a black-and-white video display unit equipped with three video cameras, and provides a range of magnification from 1.7 to 7.5 power (and up to 10.5 power for reading). The wearer's field of view inside the headset is 50° wide × 40° high, similar to the view on a large-screen projection television at a 1.2-m (4-ft) distance.

Unlike CCTVs, which are limited to certain tasks such as reading, writing, and viewing pictures, LVES can be used for a variety of tasks, since it leaves both of the user's hands free. LVES works as a magnifier, telescope, contrast enhancer, and CCTV all in one system, and it focuses both near and far automatically. Another LVES feature is a zoom lens that can vary the distance-viewing magnification and focuses automatically. This remarkable invention is meant mainly for stationary tasks and situations in which the user is either sitting or standing still. Nonetheless, with proper training a visually impaired person can use it while walking, as an aid for orientation and mobility. It is not meant for use during activities such as driving, boating, flying an airplane, or bicycling. At present these units are quite costly (about $5,800, plus training costs).

The amazing Low Vision Enhancement System is worn on the head, goes anywhere, and leaves hands free to work or play. Best of all, this portable space-age electronic vision system allows the person with minimal sight to view the world with a remarkable degree of clarity.

Courtesy of Visionics

Aids plus attitude

One of the pioneering low-vision rehabilitation facilities in the U.S., the Low Vision Service of the Eye Center of the University of Illinois at Chicago, emphasizes that:

> *Good low vision care includes instruction and encouragement in the use of recommended devices and techniques. Follow-up care also is important. The rehabilitation program may need to be revised if persons with low vision have further changes in vision or in what they need to do.*
>
> *Loss of vision affects each person in unique and profound ways. No one low vision aid can solve all the problems that a visual impairment causes. However, the combination of low vision devices, techniques, services and resources has the potential to greatly help a visually impaired person.*

Trischa Zorn is convinced that individual attitude and family support are probably more important than the most sophisticated technological aids in determining how the person with low vision ultimately copes—or does not cope—with his or her impaired vision. In speaking of her own situation, Zorn says, "The doctors told my parents I'd be institutionalized or dependent on them for the rest of my life, but my folks were convinced otherwise. They never sheltered me and they let me try to accomplish anything I thought I could."

Low-vision specialists have made great strides in developing new aids for patients. Designed to help people function at their highest potential, the devices and services available through public and private agencies enable those with progressive and/or irreversible impairments to lead productive and independent lives.

—*Weylin G. Eng, O.D.,*
and Robert C. Yeager, M.J.

LOW-VISION RESOURCES

- The Lighthouse Information and Resource Service
  telephone 800-334-5497

- The American Academy of Ophthalmology offers *Resources for Individuals with Visual Impairment,* a listing of services, organizations, and general information sources:
  655 Beach St
  PO Box 7424
  San Francisco CA 94120-7424
  telephone 415-561-8500; fax 415-561-8567

Osteoporosis Update

Osteoporosis is the condition of skeletal fragility responsible for most bone fractures in the elderly. The largest toll is taken by hip fractures and compression, or crush, fractures of the vertebral bodies. (The latter are responsible for the spine deformity known as the "dowager's hump.") Together these injuries cost the U.S. on the order of $10 billion each year, a figure that is expected to increase dramatically as the proportion of elderly people in the population rises. While not confined to females or the aged, the disorder is nevertheless most common in older women.

The bone fragility that characterizes osteoporosis is due to a combination of bone loss and microarchitectural damage (*i.e.,* microscopic structural deterioration). Bone loss occurs during remodeling—the cyclical process of bone formation and resorption—when the amount of bone removed exceeds the amount replaced. Microarchitectural damage accumulates over time as a consequence of both usage and errors in remodeling.

Until fairly recently, osteoporosis often was not diagnosed until fractures occurred. Today, however, reduced bone mass can easily be measured by a variety of techniques collectively termed bone densitometry. Thus, one of the major contributors to skeletal weakening now can be detected in advance of fracture, which offers the promise of better prevention and control of osteoporosis.

Treatment news

In 1995, for the first time in over 10 years, the U.S. Food and Drug Administration (FDA) approved a new treatment for osteoporosis. It also approved a new dosage form of an already available hormonal treatment and gave serious consideration to yet a third agent. All three therapies are already on the market in various other countries around the world and, in some cases, have been available for many years.

Bisphosphonates. The new drug approved in 1995, alendronate (Fosamax), belongs to a family of compounds called bisphosphonates. Another less-potent bisphosphonate, etidronate (Didronel), used to treat other bone disorders, has been widely prescribed in the U.S. for the past 5–10 years as a treatment for osteoporosis even though the FDA has not approved it for this use. Several pharmaceutical firms are developing their own versions of the basic bisphosphonate structure; hence, several more drugs in this class are likely to be approved by the FDA in years to come.

The bisphosphonates act by suppressing bone remodeling, mainly by interfering with the function of osteoclasts, the bone-destroying cells that resorb damaged or weakened bone tissue. Resorption is the first step in the remodeling process; it removes damaged bone and makes room for fresh, new bone. Thus, suppression of remodeling slows or stops the bone loss that constitutes part of the basis for osteoporosis. The beneficial effect does not stop there, however. Because the body depends upon the dissolving action of osteoclasts to make calcium available during periods of fasting, bisphosphonate therapy tends to decrease the ready availability of the calcium stored in the body's "bone bank." The therapy thereby

Larry Mulvehill—Science Source/Photo Researchers

Compression, or crush, fractures of the vertebral bodies are responsible for the spinal deformity known as the "dowager's hump."

evokes increased production of calcium-conserving hormones (*e.g.,* parathyroid hormone); this both partially counteracts the bisphosphonate's effect on the osteoclasts and improves intestinal absorption and retention of calcium from food. The net result, at least in the case of alendronate, is a slow bone gain—about 1% per year in the spine at optimal doses. A greater rate of gain probably is not possible with any bisphosphonate, since notable increase in bone mass requires active remodeling and all of these agents suppress remodeling. Nevertheless, simply stopping bone loss is beneficial, and even a small gain is better than none at all.

Alendronate is taken by mouth once a day on an empty stomach. The duration of treatment is indefinite. Like all bisphosphonates, it must be taken with calcium and can be taken along with estrogen, although the effects of the combination have not been well studied. Alendronate has negligible side effects when taken as directed. Any person with vertebral compression fractures and a diagnosis of osteoporosis, or anyone with severely reduced bone mass who is considered to be at risk for spine fractures, is a candidate for bisphosphonate treatment.

Fluoride. Fluoride, in one formulation or another, has been available for over 30 years and is approved for treatment of osteoporosis in several Western European countries. In November 1995 a medical advisory panel to the FDA recommended that the agency approve a slow-release formulation of the agent for treatment of osteoporosis.

Unlike the bisphosphonates, which suppress remodeling, fluoride directly stimulates the osteoblasts, or bone-forming cells, particularly in the spine. The result is that vertebral bone mass, for example, increases at a rate of 4–5% per year. Quantitatively normal bone mass can be restored in many individuals with a few years' treatment. The slow-release form of the compound may also reduce the risk of further fractures.

As mentioned above, the bone weakness of osteoporosis is due not just to thinning and loss of bone but also to microscopic architectural damage, specifically loss of the connections between structural elements in the bone. Bony tissue in the vertebrae and at the ends of the long bones is

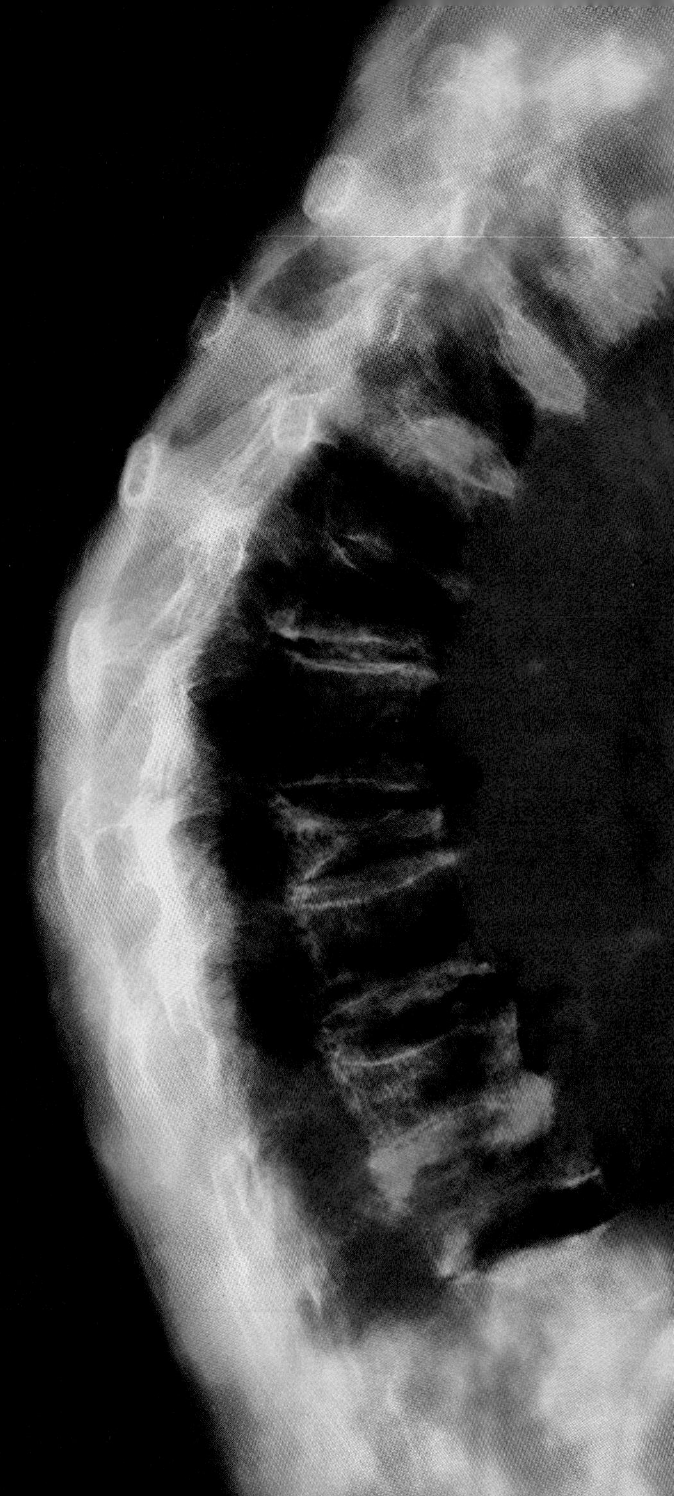

Mehau Kulyk—Science Source/Photo Researchers

A color-enhanced X-ray of the curved spine of a woman with osteoporosis, a condition with enormous social and financial costs that are likely to increase as the population ages. Much of the current research focuses on identifying risk factors for bone thinning.

not solid but instead consists of a three-dimensional lattice of bony plates and spicules, collectively called trabeculae, or trabecular elements. Vertically oriented trabeculae ordinarily carry most of the weight of the body, and horizontally oriented trabeculae brace the vertical structures and keep them from buckling under the load. Loss of connections between these lattice elements greatly weakens the structure out of all proportion to the actual loss of bone tissue.

Both fluoride and the bisphosphonates, by thickening existing structures, improve one of the components of bone weakness in osteoporosis, but they do not repair the severed connections in the bony lattice. Thus, even a potent bone-forming agent like fluoride cannot be expected to fully restore normal bone strength. Furthermore, there is no known medical treatment that can restore compressed vertebrae to their original shape once they have fractured. Drug treatments, therefore, cannot straighten the characteristic spine deformity of osteoporosis. When osteoporosis is diagnosed after fractures have developed, some degree of damage and the resulting fragility inevitably persist.

For both bisphosphonates and fluoride, correct dosage is important. In the case of bisphosphonates, too little will fail to stop the bone loss, and too much, while halting loss, will suppress remodeling to the extent that further gain is precluded. Determining the right dosage is not easy. Bisphosphonates are very poorly absorbed when taken by mouth (roughly only 1% of the ingested dose is absorbed), and absorption efficiency varies substantially from person to person. In the setting of the doctor's office, there is no good way to assess absorption of these agents. Hence, with standardized dosage regimens it is possible that some patients will get too much and others too little, even if overall the average is about right. The same concern exists for fluoride—too little fails to stimulate the osteoblasts, while too much has toxic effects on them. Fluoride absorption is more consistent than that of the bisphosphonates, however, and fluoride blood levels can be readily measured. Thus, it is easier to find the right dosage of fluoride for each patient.

Calcitonin. A nasal-spray form of calcitonin (Miacalcin), a hormonal preparation that slows osteoclastic bone resorption, was approved in 1995 for the treatment of osteoporosis. Previously calcitonin had to be administered by injection, generally every day or every other day. The nasal spray should prove more convenient for patients who can benefit from this agent. The spray is used daily, in alternate nostrils, at a recommended dosage of 200 IU (international units).

Aids to diagnosis

When the protein matrix of bone is laid down during the formative phase of remodeling, or when the matrix is demolished during the resorptive phase, various protein by-products or fragments are released into the bloodstream and excreted in the urine. Some of these substances are also produced in small quantities in the remodeling of other tissues, such as tendons and skin, but others are quite specific for bone. As a group, these substances are called bone biochemical markers, or simply bone biomarkers. Scientists' ability to measure such markers in blood and urine has advanced greatly in recent years.

The various bone biomarkers reflect the level of bone remodeling in a general way, but not all of them respond equivalently to changes in remodeling induced by drugs, diet, and other factors. The reasons for these differences remain unclear. Nevertheless, companies producing kits for the measurement of bone biomarkers have promoted them aggressively, and the potential profitability of these kits has been touted in the financial press. Despite the advertising claims, the kits do not provide definitive diagnosis of osteoporosis, and it is still too early to say how useful they will be as an adjunct to other diagnostic procedures.

Because biomarker levels do reflect bone remodeling, it is likely that biomarker tests may help in choosing a therapy, particularly as more treatment options become available. Thus, a high remodeling rate is believed to predict a good response to a remodeling suppressor such as a bisphosphonate; a low remodeling rate, a poor response. By contrast, fluoride, because it stimulates bone, may be the treatment of choice when remodeling is sluggish.

It also seems likely that the biomarkers will be useful in monitoring the progress of treatment. Physicians need to know how well a given treatment is working: is remodeling suppressed in a patient receiving estrogen or a bisphosphonate and, if so, by how much? Similarly, is formation augmented in a patient taking fluoride? Measuring one or more biomarkers a few weeks after starting treatment should help answer such questions.

Bone densitometry is generally not very helpful as a monitoring technique. The reason is that successful treatment adds new bone to that already present at a relatively slow rate; in most patients the differences produced by treatment usually are not large enough to be detected reliably for at least two years. By contrast, biomarkers change substantially within weeks or months of starting treatment and thus seem likely to prove more sensitive indicators of a specific therapy's impact on the remodeling process.

Calcium and vitamin D: how much is enough?

The current recommended dietary allowances (RDAs) for calcium and vitamin D in adults are 800 mg and 200 IU per day, respectively, but recent studies suggest that both figures are much too low and that many osteoporotic fractures could be prevented if intakes of both nutrients were higher.

Nutrient requirements are revised periodically, but the basic system used in the U.S. was worked out many years ago, using 1920s technology. The classic approach was to see how much of a given nutrient had to be ingested to prevent a specific disease. In the case of vitamin D, the disease was rickets, a childhood bone disorder now rarely seen in the U.S. but still common in some parts of the world. More recently, however, scientists have assessed nutrient needs by looking at the body systems in which a particular nutrient works and determining how much is required for the system to function optimally. This newer approach recognizes that "disease" is often only the last stage in a downhill process and that "health" is more than the absence of disease.

Adopting such an approach, a 1994 National Institutes of Health consensus conference recommended a calcium intake of at least 1,000 mg per day for young to middle-aged adults and 1,500 mg per day for everyone over age 65. Similarly, agreement is emerging among bone biologists that the vitamin D requirement for adults is probably 600 IU per day and rises with age to about 800 IU. These values are two to four times the current RDAs. While this is a big change, it is supported by persuasive data. The evidence is of two sorts. Studies in which older adults received calcium and/or vitamin D supplements that elevated their total intakes to these higher levels showed impressive reductions in fracture risk. This finding would be compelling in its own right, but it has also been demonstrated that these higher intakes are precisely the amounts needed for fully healthy physiological functioning. Thus, the two approaches converge on the same higher levels. Three brief examples, drawn from recent research, illustrate this physiological approach to determining nutrient requirements.

Bone serves as the body's calcium reservoir. When a person's dietary calcium intake is not adequate to offset daily losses (through skin, urine, and digestive juices), the body makes up the deficit by breaking down bone to release its calcium. Over the short term, this is an appropriate way for a reserve to function. Over the long term, however, if calcium withdrawals exceed deposits, bone strength suffers. A recent study in France showed that women in their 80s eating their habitual diets were ingesting about 500 mg of calcium per day and were losing bone at a rate of about 3% per year. When they were given 1,200 mg of calcium and 800 IU of vitamin D (in addition to their usual dietary intake of both nutrients), bone loss was completely arrested, and fractures were reduced dramatically.

Parathyroid hormone is the chemical messenger the body uses to cause bone to release calcium. Unlike other hormones, the levels of which tend to fall with aging, levels of parathyroid hormone in the blood rise with age. The reason was unclear until recently. Studies published in 1996 show that with sufficient calcium consumption, the elevated levels typical of the elderly return to the normal values seen in younger years. One reason for the high parathyroid hormone levels in older people is that intestinal calcium absorption efficiency declines with age, which renders existing calcium intakes—already inadequate—even more so. Another reason is that older people get less vitamin D from sunlight exposure than do young people. Thus, with advancing age the shortfall of both nutrients gets worse. In response, the body produces more and more parathyroid hormone to help it withdraw calcium from the bone bank.

A third example involves the annual cycle of bone loss (and partial repair) in persons living in northern latitudes. In wintertime they get relatively little solar vitamin D, in part because they tend to bundle up against the cold and in part because the Sun is too low in the sky to allow penetration of the atmosphere by ultraviolet wavelengths that convert precursor compounds in the skin to vitamin D. As a result, people who do not take supplemental vitamin D sometimes end up with severely depleted vitamin D stores by late March. This shortage is manifested by a detectable decrease in bone mass, particularly at the spine and hip. (Since vitamin D augments calcium absorption, vitamin D depletion produces much the same kind of effect on bone as primary calcium deficiency.) It turns out, however, that this annual bone loss, reaching its low point in late winter, occurs only in people getting the equivalent of the current RDA for vitamin D or less. Those who get 600 IU per day or more show no winter bone loss at all.

For all of these reasons, nutrition experts now believe that the current RDAs for both calcium and vitamin D are too low. The best advice for adults is to get 600–800 IU of vitamin D per day and 1,500–2,000 mg of calcium, preferably from foods rich in these nutrients. It is important to stress, however, that these levels should not be exceeded. More will do no good and could be harmful. Since vitamin D is naturally present in only a very few foods (fish-liver oils, egg yolks, fish, organ meats) and is added as an enrichment only to milk, people trying to consume extra vitamin D must either drink more milk, take a vitamin D supplement, or do both.

Factors Contributing to Increased Fracture Risk

- Low bone density
- Family history of hip fracture
- Propensity for falling
- Thinness, weight loss in adulthood
- Inactivity and frailty
- Use of long-acting tranquilizers
- Advanced age
- Tall stature and susceptible bone geometry
- Low vitamin D levels
- Low calcium intake
- Poor balance and slow reflex responses

Body Mass Index: Relevant to Fracture Risk

Height (meters; feet and inches in parentheses)	Weight range (kilograms; pounds in parentheses) for BMI of 22–26
1.52 m (5' 0")	50.8-60.3 (112-133)
1.55 m (5' 1")	52.6-62.1 (116-137)
1.57 m (5' 2")	54.4-64.4 (120-142)
1.60 m (5' 3")	56.2-66.2 (124-146)
1.63 m (5' 4")	58.1-68.5 (128-151)
1.65 m (5' 5")	59.9-70.8 (132-156)
1.68 m (5' 6")	61.7-73.0 (136-161)
1.70 m (5' 7")	63.5-75.3 (140-166)
1.73 m (5' 8")	65.3-77.6 (144-171)
1.75 m (5' 9")	67.6-79.8 (149-176)
1.78 m (5' 10")	69.4-82.1 (153-181)
1.80 m (5' 11")	71.2-84.5 (157-186)
1.83 m (6' 0")	73.5-86.6 (162-191)

Reevaluating risk factors

The significance of osteoporosis as a health problem lies in the fact that it increases the individual's risk of sustaining bone fractures. Fractures, in turn, are debilitating and, especially in the elderly, can have complications that lead to death. A great deal of recent research has focused on the relative contributions of the different factors that influence an individual's risk of fractures. Low bone density, which the experts once thought was everything in osteoporosis, is now recognized as only one of many factors—and not always the most important one.

Some of the factors known to increase the risk of fracture are listed in the upper table at left. They are largely independent of one another in the sense that each adds a further degree of risk. Thus, a person with five or more of the factors is at much greater risk than someone with only two. While some of the factors listed—for example, advanced age—are self-explanatory, the part played by others is not so obvious. Weight loss and thinness are particularly worthy of discussion because of the high value placed on thinness by women in the U.S. Bone density is directly related to body weight: the heavier the person, the stronger the skeleton. The fracture protection conferred by weight can be attributed only partly to the greater bone mass of the heavy individual. The other advantage of a higher body weight is the presence of increased padding over the bony prominences, which helps cushion the force of a fall. Thus, a woman who weighs 54.4 kg (120 lb) at age 25 and gains 11 kg (24 lb) over the ensuing 50 years has a 40% lower fracture risk at age 75 than a woman who maintains her young-adult weight. A gain of another 11 kg decreases the risk by yet another 40%.

A recent report that linked lean adult weights to lower death rates would seem to contradict the notion that weight gain in adulthood might have any health benefits. The association between increased life expectancy and added weight operates only at a body mass index (BMI) of 26 or greater, however, whereas optimal weight for a woman translates into a BMI in the range of 22–26 kg/m^2. (*See* lower table at left. BMI, a method of adjusting weight for height, is calculated by dividing weight in kilograms by the square of height in meters. A woman who is 1.7 m [5 ft 7 in] tall and weighs 68 kg [150 lb] has a BMI of 23.5.)

Tallness is another factor that merits explanation. Simply put, when a tall woman falls, she has farther to go than a short woman before hitting the ground. "Bone geometry" refers to the configuration of the bones and specifically, with regard to the development of osteoporosis, to the shape of the hipbone and the size of the vertebral bodies. Relative to their height, Caucasians have longer femoral necks (the angled segment of the upper femur, or thighbone) than do Asians. Engineering analysis shows that a long femoral neck is structurally weaker than a short one. This fact explains why, at the same bone density, Asians have about half the hip-fracture rate of Caucasians. Similarly, vertebrae that are small for body size are weaker than vertebrae that are large for body size, even though both contain the same amount of bony material.

—Robert P. Heaney, M.D.

New Tools for ENT

The practice of otolaryngology (also known as *otorhinolaryngology; head and neck surgery;* and *ear, nose, and throat,* or ENT) has been changing rapidly in the 1990s owing to advances in technology. New technology has made it possible to do less-invasive procedures with better results, which both reduces hospital stays and allows for shorter recovery times. This not only cuts down on medical costs but saves money for businesses by decreasing medical leave time. The most effective treatments for disorders of the ear, nose, and throat would not be possible without two key tools: the endoscope, primitive versions of which came into use in the 19th century, and several different types of lasers (used in surgery since the 1960s but in otolaryngology only quite recently).

History of the endoscope

Historically, the endoscope—a small, narrow telescope—has been used by the otolaryngologist in attempts to view the depths of the human head and neck anatomy and thereby understand how disease affects the body. This probing capability has the potential to significantly enhance the diagnosis and treatment of disease. Very recently, improvements in the device have made it a truly invaluable tool. Only in the last 20 years have reductions in scope size allowed physicians to have a precise view of the inside of the nose.

Early scopes were difficult to set up and did not give the otolaryngologist a clear picture of the paranasal sinus system (cavities within the face that are lined with mucous membranes) or diseases affecting it. The optics of the endoscope were greatly improved in the 1950s, when researchers at the Karl Storz Co. in Germany developed the Hopkins rod lens.

A laryngoscope, developed in 1857 by Ludwig Türck and Jan Czermak of Vienna, allowed the otolaryngologist to inspect the internal passages and structures of the nose and throat in a way that previously had not been possible. The device, however, relied upon a mirror and thus afforded only an indirect view. Truly revolutionary tools were still to come.

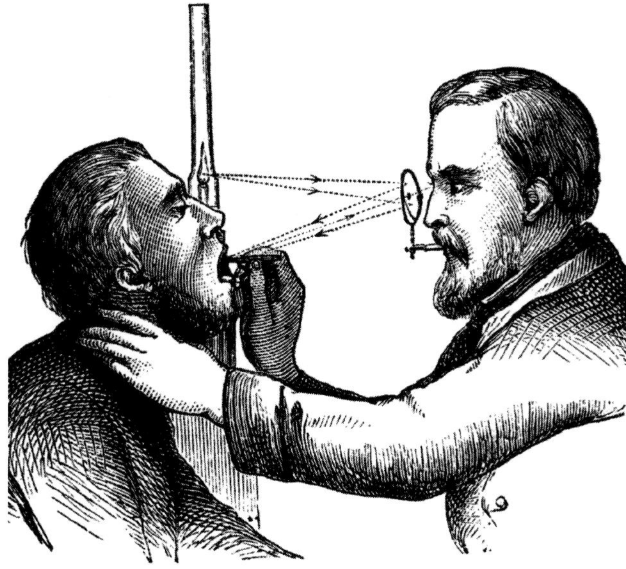

Ann Ronan at Image Select

This new lens allowed for an increased field of vision and a smaller scope diameter, both of which made the handling of the instrument much easier. During the 1970s, with the aid of newer versions of the endoscope that offered much better views and even smaller scopes (eventually as small as 2.7 mm [0.11 in] in diameter), Walter Messerklinger, chairman of the university otolaryngology clinic in Graz, Austria, was the first physician to do a detailed study of the mode of secretion transport through the nasal mucosa and sinuses. This study led to a clearer understanding of the pathophysiology of sinus disease and its diagnosis. By the early 1990s, innovations in endoscope technology had been reflected in an improved comprehension of sinus disease.

Anatomy and disease of the sinuses

To appreciate the significance of Messerklinger's study, one needs to understand the function of the sinuses and how they are affected by disease. Four pairs of sinus cavities in the head produce approximately one liter (one quart) of thin, watery mucus a day; tiny brushlike cilia easily sweep this mucus through openings in the paranasal sinuses, into the nose, and onto the back of the throat. (The mucus is then swallowed or expelled.) The frontal (one pair), ethmoid (two pairs), and maxillary (one pair) sinuses all drain into the nose through a small area—technically termed the ostiomeatal complex—that acts as an outlet for all the sinus structures. Using the nasal endoscope to study this area, Messerklinger not only came to appreciate the complex drainage system in the head but adapted that knowledge to the treatment of disease. He realized that continual drainage through the sinuses and nose helped to keep the nose free of dust and bacteria, which are swept to the back of the throat and swallowed.

Most causes of sinus inflammation (otherwise known as sinusitis) originate in the nose and begin with a blockage in the natural pathway of mucus drainage. Allergy, illness, or abnormalities in the nasal anatomy are by far the most common causes of blockage. A cold or flu often triggers swelling in the nasal lining that blocks the sinus openings and thereby causes a retention of secretions, which sets the stage for sinus infection. This stagnant mucus becomes a perfect milieu for the rapid bacterial growth that characterizes sinusitis. Inhaled allergens often can cause the nasal lining to swell and prevent the cilia from sweeping away the mucus, which creates an environment conducive to rapid bacterial growth. Environmental insults (*e.g.,* smoke, air pollution) will do the same thing. Anatomic problems may also be the cause of an obstruction of the sinus structures (*e.g.,* a deviated septum impinging on the sinus outflow or a polyp growing in the nose). By using the endoscope to examine the mucus pathway, the otolaryngologist can see if infection is present and what is causing the infection if it does exist. Medical management can then take place in the doctor's office (without the use of X-rays).

Sinusitis: today's treatments

The initial medical treatment of sinus disease is to attack the cause of the blockage. Inflammation is usually reduced with

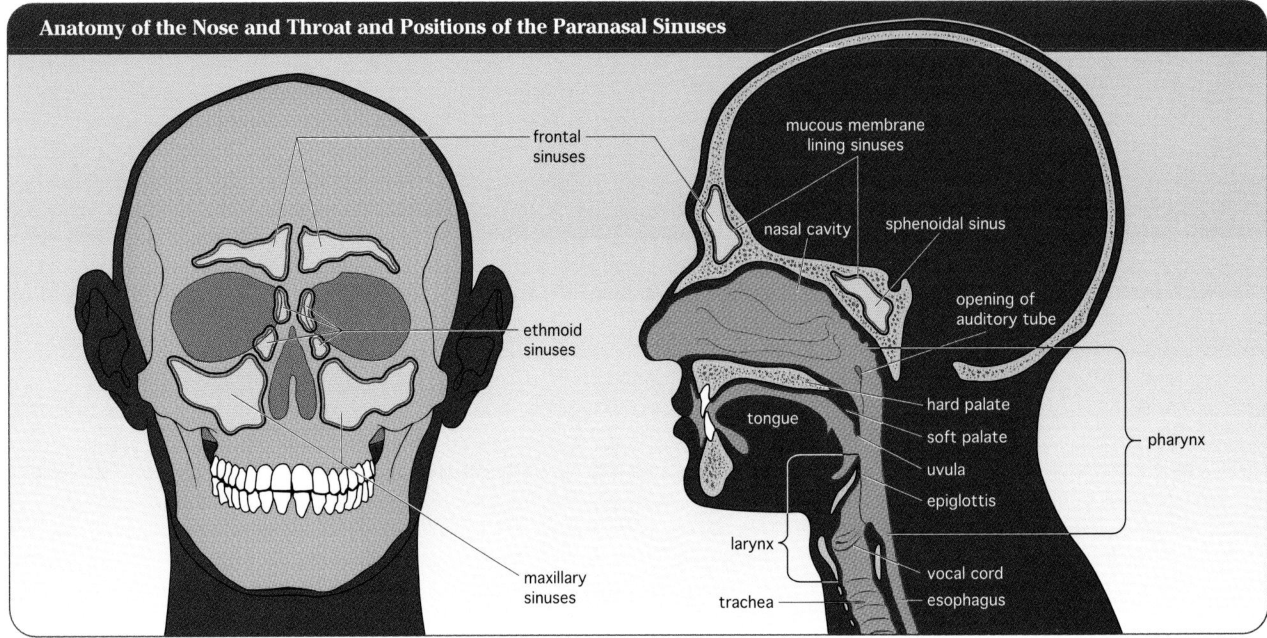

antibiotics; swelling is reduced with decongestants; mucus is thinned with expectorants. (Because of their drying effect, antihistamines are rarely used to treat sinus disease.) An old "home remedy" that has become an established treatment in recent years is saline lavage. To perform a lavage, the physician adds one teaspoon of salt to a pint of warm water and administers the mixture with a bulb syringe. The nose is aggressively irrigated by forcing the saline into the sinus system. This procedure cleans the nasal lining of thickened secretions and polluting allergens. It also restores the function of the cilia.

Surgical intervention is considered only when initial medical management has failed. A computed tomography (CT) scan will be ordered if surgery is contemplated. CT produces detailed cross-sections of the head that give the surgeon a clear picture of the anatomy of the nose and sinuses and the extent of disease affecting them. Such a picture is important because of the proximity of the eyes and brain to the sinuses. Surgical complications involving those delicate organs can thus be avoided.

In recent years the endoscope and other microinstruments have allowed the otolaryngologist to address the problem of blockage directly by removing only the diseased tissue. Before the endoscope was invented, it was necessary for the surgeon to do a more radical operation in order to gain access to the sinuses. Owing to the visualization that is possible with the endoscope, the surgeon can get directly to the sinus blockage. Endoscopic surgery involves no external incisions, less blood loss, and a shorter hospital stay for the patient. Postoperatively, the endoscope allows the surgeon to carefully monitor the healing process during office visits.

The flexible endoscope: a modern miracle

The improvements in the endoscope have made it a remarkably adaptable tool. The flexible scope, with its small diameter, makes it possible to perform procedures that go beyond the sinus structures. While the rigid scope is most effective for rhinogenic disease (that which originates in the nose), the flexible scope readily allows the physician to pass the scope through the nose and down the back of the throat to examine deeper organs—the lower pharynx, the larynx, and the entrance to the esophagus. Because the procedure requires only a small amount of local anesthesia, it can be done easily in the doctor's office.

Treating children. Many of the most exciting advances in otolaryngology have come from the treatment of airway disease in children. Traditionally, a large metal scope with a light attached was used to evaluate the tiny airway. The passage of the scope required a general anesthetic, was achieved with difficulty, and did not allow for an adequate evaluation of the dynamics of respiration in the child—a key component in the effective treatment of airway disease. Now, as a result of the development of a flexible scope, the exam can be done under local anesthesia, which allows the physician to study the larynx and better assess the young person's respiration. Owing to the simplicity of the procedure, the need for an operation or more elaborate therapy is circumvented.

Teaching tool. With the advent of highly advanced endoscopes, training for a specialty in otolaryngology has been greatly enhanced. Since a number of ENT procedures are performed on anatomic structures that are difficult to gain access to, for years surgery could not be demonstrated to ENT residents easily, if at all. With the use of a camera attached to the flexible scope, surgery now can be viewed by many students simultaneously—and better understood. Experienced surgeons can now videotape their operations to be used as teaching material or to help develop more refined procedures. These enhanced teaching methods pay off in three distinct ways: (1) they result in more highly trained surgeons, (2) they allow for further advancements in the field of otolaryngology, and (3) they improve care for the patient.

(Top) Stryker Endoscopy; (bottom) Mitsubishi Cable America, Inc.

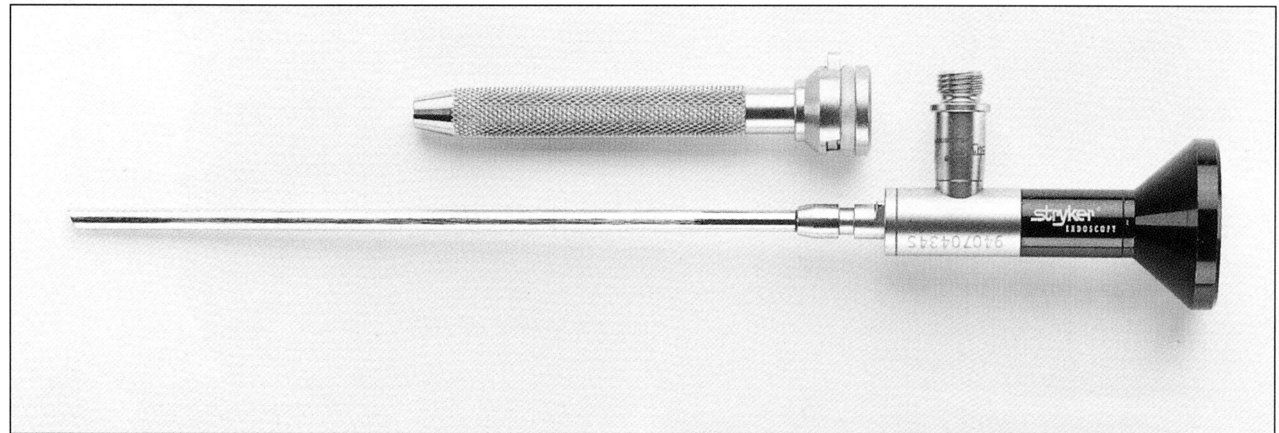

State-of-the-art ENT tools. (Above) The rigid endoscope, shown with its handle (top) detached, is most often used by ENT specialists to treat disease originating in the nose (rhinogenic disease). (Right) This endoscope—the ultrathin flexible nasopharyngoscope—makes it possible for procedures to be performed on parts of the anatomy that are otherwise virtually impossible to reach, including the pharynx, the larynx, and the entrance to the esophagus.

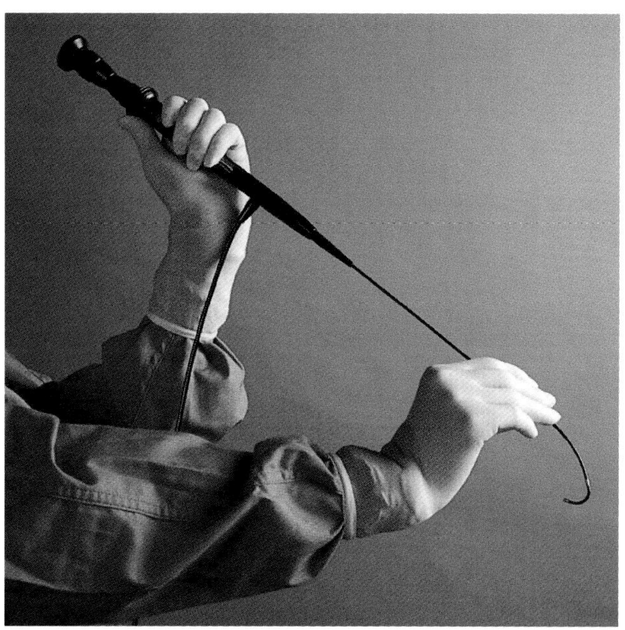

Lasers in ENT

The laser was introduced as a surgical tool in the 1960s but has gained popularity in ENT only in the last two decades. The advantages and disadvantages of the laser are still being determined as various models are developed and tested. Lasers are specifically designed surgical tools and, like all surgical instruments, are most effective for particular procedures. Similar to a scalpel, the laser is used primarily to remove tissue. Lasers can be utilized at different wavelengths to achieve different results. To its advantage, the laser's intense beam of light can literally vaporize tissue cells and "spot-weld" bleeding vessels, causing them to coagulate effectively. On the other hand, lasers are expensive and tedious to use; moreover, their use requires careful protection of the patient and surgical personnel. Eyeglasses must be worn, since looking directly into a laser can burn the retina. Because the laser causes certain materials to combust, surgical gear for laser procedures must be carefully chosen. Presently, a number of lasers are available, each with its own special features.

The first laser treatment. The first laser used in the ear, nose, or throat (initially for surgery in the larynx) was the carbon dioxide (CO_2) laser. Because the CO_2 laser (10.6 μm [micrometers] wavelength) is well absorbed by water, human tissues that are high in water content conduct its energy well. During a procedure the laser's energy is concentrated at the point of impact, and the resulting intense local heating effectively vaporizes target tissue cells. Vaporization is accomplished with relatively minimal spread of energy through the surrounding tissue. This type of laser continues to work well in laryngeal surgery because of its ability to modify tissue precisely with minimal thermal damage to surrounding areas. The CO_2 laser is also used to treat small growths in the larynx, obstructions in the airway, and benign growths (such as polyps, nodules, and cysts) on the vocal cords. Coupling the CO_2 laser with an operating microscope (for a better field of vision) provides unparalleled surgical precision. Its particular disadvantages, however, are that the delivery system is bulky and has limited maneuverability and that the laser has suboptimal hemostatic ability; that is, it may not completely stop bleeding. A new flexible CO_2 laser is currently being developed, which should greatly improve delivery.

Newer lasers, new possibilities. In the 1980s newer lasers with different wavelengths were introduced. Among these were the KTP/532 (a potassium titanyl phosphate laser used at a 532-nm [nanometer] wavelength) and argon lasers, which are more effective at inhibiting bleeding than the CO_2 laser. These newer lasers can be used in more flexible, smaller-diameter microscopes that are incorporated into delicate handpieces to enable greater precision during surgery. For use in the nose, the KTP/532 is the primary laser of choice. In order to best treat vascular tissue, vascular tumors, and swelling (in the hope of improving breathing), the KTP/532 is equipped with a suction attachment. This specially designed component allows for simultaneous delivery of the laser en-

Stryker Endoscopy, the originator of the patented "Hummer" used for microendoscopy

ergy with a continuous suctioning of the wispy smoke from the vaporized tissue, allowing for better visualization of the area.

In the treatment of nasal polyps, the KTP laser is often used for an initial "debulking" of diseased tissue. Once the polyp has been whittled to a manageable size, the laser is no longer a practical tool, however. Eliminating the polyp with a laser would be both time-consuming and tedious. Nasal polyps are better handled with a recently developed instrument called the microdebrider, or "hummer." Originally used by orthopedists for joint surgery, the microdebrider makes a pleasant humming sound as it operates, hence its nickname. Similar in size to the endoscope, the microdebrider consists of a motor and a central suction channel with a handpiece attached to a long narrow tube. Inside the hollow tube is a disposable rotating blade. The tube has an open mouth at one end through which the blade can gain access to the polyp. The hummer sucks the polyp into its side-facing mouth, and the small portion of tissue is immediately cut by the rotating blade. This suck-and-slice motion is repeated with every rotation of the blade, and the device literally gobbles up the

An illustration depicts laser-assisted uvula-palatoplasty (LAUP), in which a strip of the soft palate is removed to cure snoring; this is one of the most popular applications of ENT laser technology.

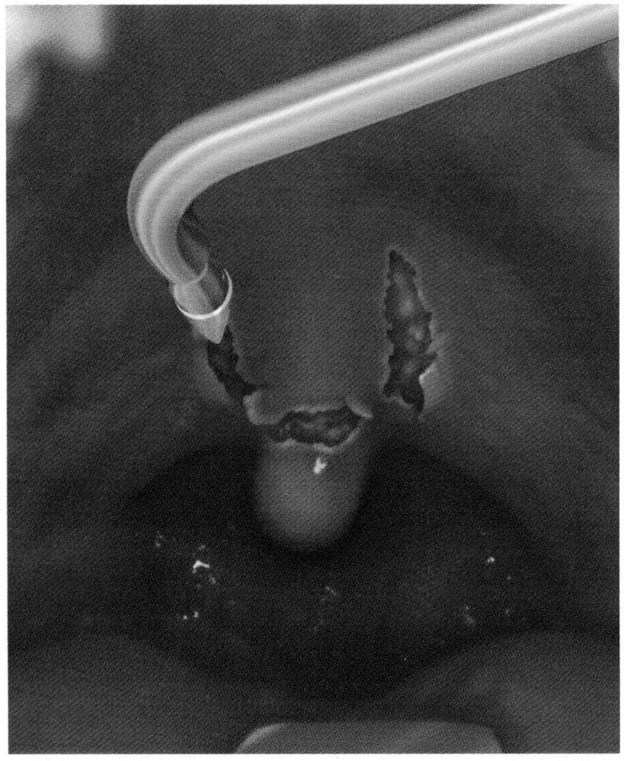

Courtesy of Surgical Laser Technologies

The microdebrider, originally developed by orthopedists for joint surgery, is used in ENT to remove nasal polyps. The instrument is also known as the "hummer" because of the sound it makes as it operates.

polyp. Any blood that might obscure the operative field is removed by the continuous suction.

For treating disease in the ear, both the CO_2 and KTP/532 lasers are frequently used. Because the middle ear contains many small, delicate bones, surgery in this area requires great care and a high level of precision in order to avoid complications. The laser's precision allows for effective removal of both adhesions and granulation tissue (a fleshy mass of scar-forming tissue that temporarily replaces cells lost through trauma). Lasers also work well in the removal of sections of bone to be replaced by prosthetic material. Though the CO_2 laser was long the standard instrument for many procedures in the ear, the KTP model has recently become more popular in most types of ear surgery. Because the latter has a wavelength visible to the naked eye, it has an advantage over the older, less advanced CO_2 beam, which is invisible. When the beam is invisible, a "carrier beam" must be attached so that the surgeon can guide the instrument; in the tight confines of the middle ear, this poses a danger, as the laser beam and carrier beam may become disconnected from one another. In such a situation there is a potential for the surgeon to inadvertently misdirect the laser. Use of the visible KTP laser eliminates this problem.

The argon laser is used primarily to treat vascular lesions of the skin because of its rapid absorption by melanin and hemoglobin. The Nd:YAG laser (1.06 μm wavelength) is used most often to remove obstructing lesions of the trachea and bronchial tubes. The most serious drawback to using the Nd:YAG laser is that hemorrhage is a frequent and dangerous complication associated with surgery of these structures. The laser can achieve the necessary deep penetration into the tissue but sometimes at the expense of the patient's safety.

Snoring cure. Perhaps the most popular use of the laser in otolaryngology is in a cure for snoring that involves a procedure known as laser-assisted uvula-palatoplasty, or LAUP. In a large majority of patients, snoring is thought to be caused by fluttering of the soft palate. The LAUP laser is used to remove a central strip of the palate (including the uvula). Scarring then occurs at the site of the laser application, which stiffens the palate. The procedure can be done in a doctor's office under local anesthesia, and 70% of patients are said to benefit. However, long-term results of LAUP are unknown; furthermore, some physicians are of the opinion that the same results can be achieved with electrocautery (removal of tissue using electricity) at considerably less expense.

—Michael A. Allan, M.D.

Toddlers at the Table

Parents tend to be scrupulous about feeding their newborn infants, following the pediatrician's advice to a T so that whether an infant is breast-fed or formula-fed, he or she receives optimal nourishment during the first year of life. Too often, however, this is not the case when the infant becomes a toddler. In fact, many parents make mistakes when it comes to feeding their one-to-three-year-olds—mistakes that can have serious health consequences as the child grows up. Here are some circumstances that contribute to the problem:

- By the time an infant reaches one year of age, parents are usually told by their baby's doctor to start offering table foods. This translates into a toddler's eating a diet that is much higher in salt and sugar than was the case during the first year of life. The reason for this is that the commercially available infant foods the child had been eating—assuming he or she has been weaned from the breast—have no salt added and usually have no added sugar, whereas adult table foods usually contain large amounts of salt and sugar (added for the sake of taste).
- After one year of age, the toddler has fewer regularly scheduled "well-baby" checkups. Parents thus have fewer opportunities to discuss proper nutrition with the child's pediatrician.
- Since a toddler's rate of weight gain is much slower than an infant's, it is normal for the appetite to decrease starting at around one year of age. Many parents are not aware of this and do not realize that their toddler simply needs less food than previously. This situation often leads to forced feeding and unpleasant, tension-filled mealtimes. Fighting with a toddler about food not only is unsuccessful but may cause harm in the long run by interfering with the establishment of healthy eating habits. A 1994 study of slightly older children (aged three to five) found that overcontrol of children's eating by parents led to fat children.
- In the majority of cases, both breast-feeding and the use of an iron-fortified formula end by age one. The one-year-old usually is started on regular cow's milk, which does not contain any appreciable amount of iron.
- As infancy ends and toddlerhood begins, parents usually discontinue infant cereals, which are iron-fortified by law with at least 60% of a one-to-three-year-old's recommended dietary allowance (RDA) for iron; in their place the toddler is fed "adult" cereals, which are not iron-fortified or contain considerably smaller amounts of iron.
- As the toddler starts understanding more and more and begins actively using language, parents tend to use food as a bribe or reward, and the foods used are almost always nonnutritious and high in sugar and fat.
- Toddlers typically spend hours a day watching television. Slipped into cartoons and other young children's programming during the Saturday 7–10:30 AM "prime-time" period is a constant stream of commercials for sugar-coated ce-

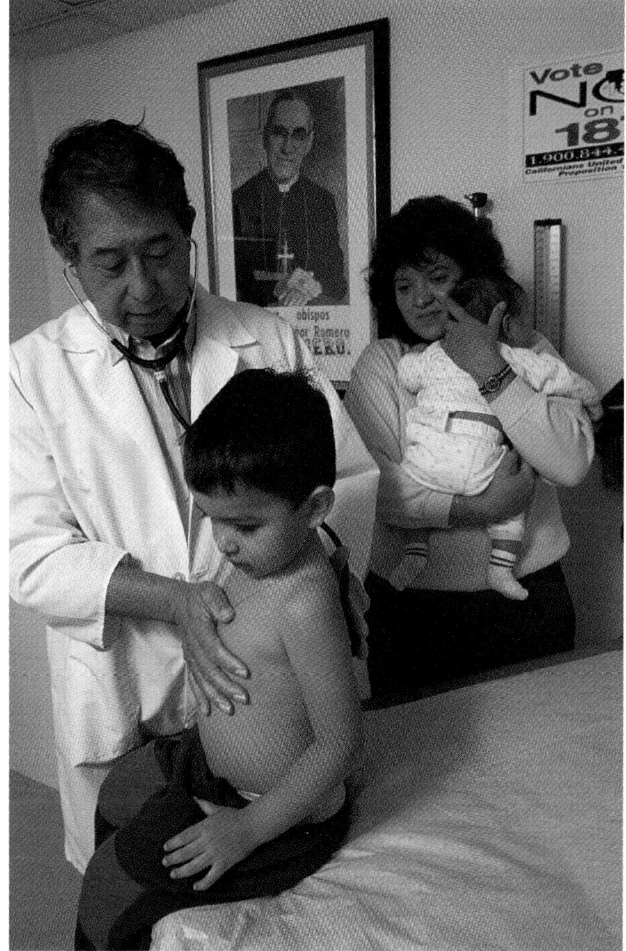

Parents tend to get plenty of advice about feeding infants but little when it comes to feeding one-to-three-year-olds. Daily battles over food may ensue, and as many a parent will testify, getting toddlers to eat—no less eat properly—can be no picnic!

(Top) A. Ramey—Stock, Boston; (bottom) Cathy Melloan—Tony Stone Images reals, candy, soft drinks, fatty fast foods, and other items of very limited nutritional value. According to researchers from the University of Minnesota, who collectively viewed more than 50 hours of Saturday-morning programs (on the ABC, CBS, NBC, Fox, and Nickelodeon networks), not even one advertisement promoted the eating of fruits and/or vegetables. About one-half of the commercials were for foods such as cookies, chips, cakes, pastries, and soft drinks—all products that are loaded with fat, sugar, or both.

Overfed and undernourished

What is the result of all this? Too many toddlers eat diets that are low in iron, high in sugar and salt, high in saturated fat, and, more often than not, very poorly balanced and non-nutritious. There are three major nutrition-related problems affecting today's toddlers; fortunately, all are preventable if some fairly simple steps are taken.

Iron-clad iron needs. A toddler should have 10 mg of iron per day. Iron is an essential element that cannot be manufactured by the body and therefore must be supplied by foods or a supplement. A recent U.S. government-sponsored study demonstrated that the iron intake of toddlers is lower than the RDA specified for the one-to-three age group. A recent clinical investigation evaluating the iron status of a large group of children between one and three years of age concluded that about one-third of the toddlers had some degree of iron deficiency. Such iron deficiency can be associated with loss of appetite, failure to thrive, increased irritability, pica (a craving for nonfood substances), breath holding, fatigue, and poor school performance. Iron deficiency, especially between one and three years of age, may have very significant ramifications in terms of the brain. Since almost all brain growth occurs during the first two years of life, it is crucial that sufficient iron be supplied for optimal brain development during this period.

A number of studies have proved that iron-deficiency anemia during the first year of life may result in irreversible brain damage—that is, even after the anemia has been corrected. No such studies have as yet been carried out for the one-to-two-year-old age group, but it makes intuitive sense that an anemic state during this period of rapid brain growth would cause harm.

This common problem, with its serious consequences, can be prevented by offering the toddler iron-rich foods such as poultry, fish, lean red meats, iron-fortified cereals, iron-fortified grain products, green leafy vegetables, and dried fruits. Serving citrus fruits and juices at the same meal will enhance the iron absorption. Since the toddler's appetite tends to be small to start with, giving too much milk (more than 480–720 ml [16–24 fl oz, or 2–3 cups] a day) or more than 240–480 ml (1–2 cups) of juice per day may further decrease the appetite for iron-rich foods. An iron supplement or an iron-fortified nutritional drink may be indicated for those toddlers who simply refuse to eat enough iron-containing foods. This should be discussed with the child's doctor.

Tubby kids are no joke. As compared with 20 years ago, the incidence of obesity in U.S. children has risen dramatically. Considered by many physicians to be the most important nutritional problem affecting children of all ages, obesity often begins during the toddler years. Because there is a well-established genetic factor for obesity, youngsters most at risk are those with obese parents. Genetics, however, is only one part of the problem. A much more significant factor is environment.

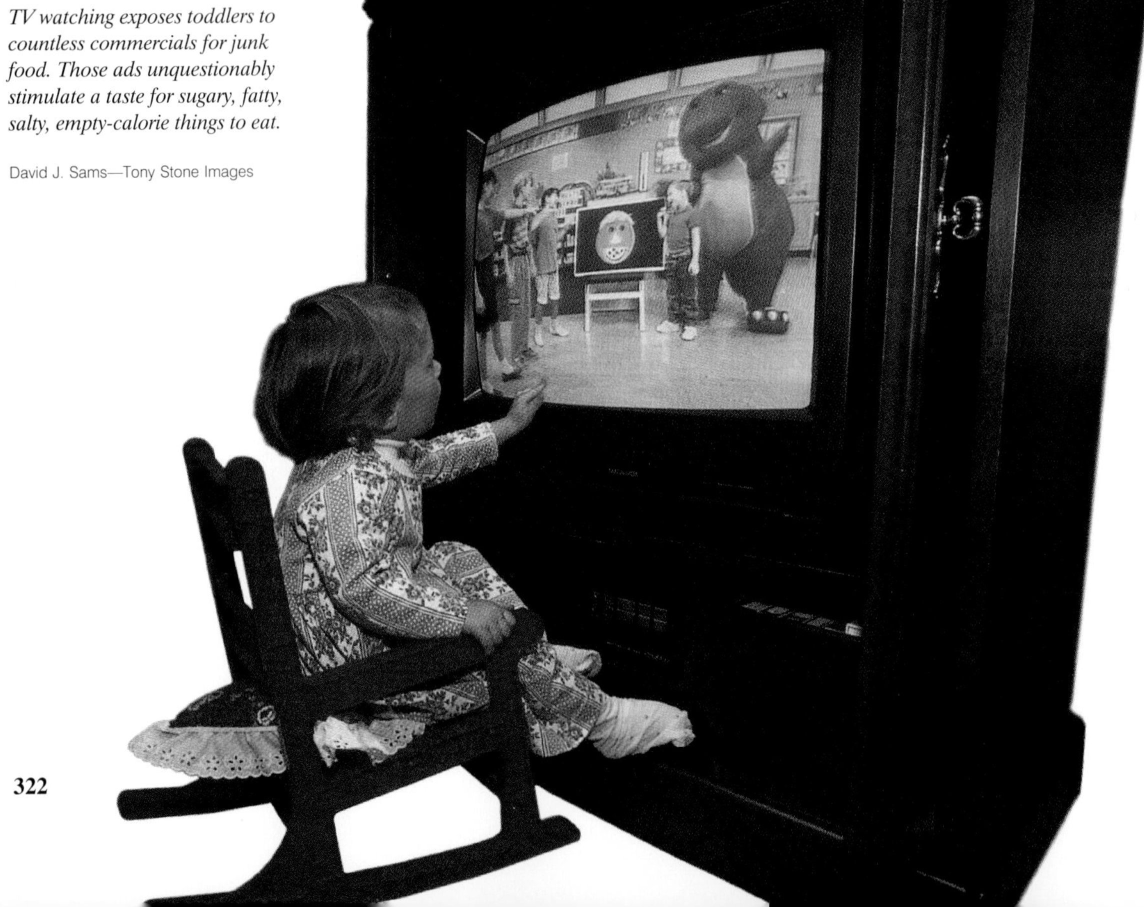

TV watching exposes toddlers to countless commercials for junk food. Those ads unquestionably stimulate a taste for sugary, fatty, salty, empty-calorie things to eat.

David J. Sams—Tony Stone Images

(Top) Martha Cooper—Peter Arnold, Inc.; (bottom) Gabor Demien—Stock, Boston

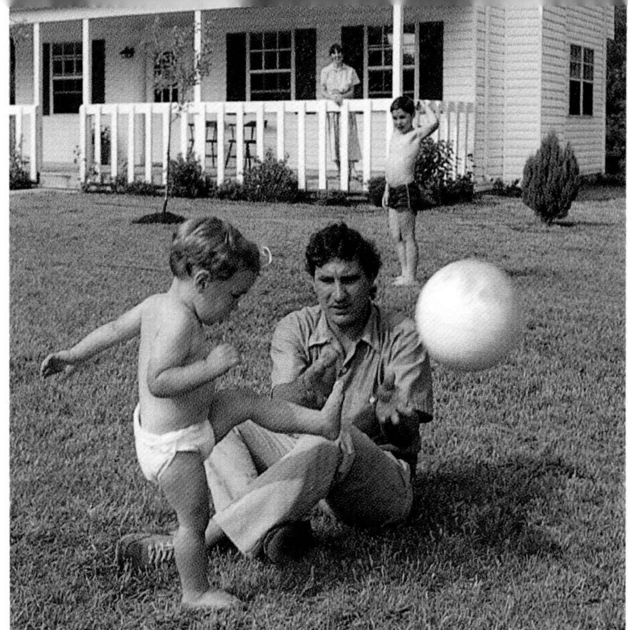

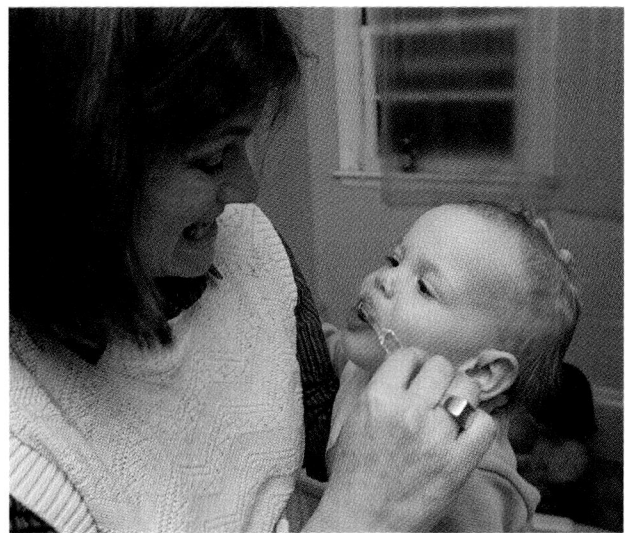

Obesity and dental caries are all too common in U.S. kids. Both are preventable. Parents should encourage physical activity among all their children—toddlers included—and brush and floss toddlers' teeth daily.

A toddler's physician will be able to determine if a youngster is overweight on the basis of the child's age, height, sex, and body build. If a weight problem exists, the doctor may make specific dietary suggestions. Parents can do a great deal to prevent obesity in their toddlers. The following are steps they can take:

- A variety of nutritious foods from all the food groups should be offered, but foods that are high in fat and sugar should be strictly limited. A practice to be discouraged is the serving of unmeasured portions ("family-style" eating).
- Families should "fat proof" their homes. This means not buying, or eliminating, *all* nonnutritious high-sugar, high-fat, high-calorie junk foods. Such a step might meet stiff resistance from the children in the household because they are continuously being "brainwashed" by television advertising. In 1995 the *Archives of Pediatrics & Adolescent Medicine* published the results of a study on children's television programs, which found that 91% of food advertisements were for foods high in fat, salt, or sugar. The study also found that although new regulations had led to shorter advertisements, ads were more numerous.
- Last but not at all least, parents must encourage physical activities for the whole family—including the toddler. Not only can family exercise be fun, but it will discourage what this author refers to as the "S.O.B. [Sitting On Behind] syndrome" among all members of the household.

Too much tooth decay. Dental caries, or cavities, develop when sugar and bacteria combine in the mouth and act to eat away at the surface of the teeth. The results of the first national study to assess the dental health of U.S. children who still had their baby teeth was published in the March 1996 issue of the *Journal of the American Dental Association.* Remarkably, 40% of children had cavities in their primary teeth. So-called baby-bottle tooth decay—the result of the practice of letting a baby sleep with a bottle propped in his or her mouth, which creates a perfect environment for bacteria—was a major reason for caries in teeth. Children of low-income families had the worst problems; recent cutbacks in Medicaid funds meant that many toddlers had received little or no dental health care. Toddlers should not be offered sugary snacks and should never be put to bed with a bottle of milk or juice. At least once a day, the toddler's teeth should be brushed with a fluoride-containing toothpaste and flossed. A fluoride supplement is recommended when the local water supply does not have added fluoride. These simple preventive measures have been proved to be very effective in reducing dental cavities. All children also should have dental checkups regularly (once a year or more often).

Prudence endorsed

The Committee on Nutrition of the American Academy of Pediatrics (AAP) recommends that children eat a variety of foods to support growth and to reach or maintain a desirable body weight. The committee recommends that children over two years of age receive 30% of their daily calories from fat and less than 10% of their daily calories from saturated fat (the so-called 30/10 diet). They should have no more than 300 mg of cholesterol per day. These numbers are approximates; actual amounts can be averaged over a period of days. In other words, toddlers aged two years old should follow the so-called prudent diet—a diet that is much lower in saturated fat and cholesterol and higher in fruits, vegetables, and whole grains than the typical "American diet." This translates into the use of low-fat milk, few portions of fatty red meats, and no more than three or four eggs per week. The rationale for this recommendation is that such a diet will reduce the risk of atherosclerosis (buildup of fatty deposits in the arteries) in later life.

Since eating habits are established early in life, teaching two- and three-year-old children to eat and enjoy the 30/10 diet will make it much more likely that they will continue to eat the same type of diet as they grow up. (One-year-old toddlers need not begin this prudent diet yet.)

There has been some voluble controversy as to whether this prudent diet is appropriate for toddlers. Will it inhibit proper growth and development? Will reducing the amount of fat in a child's diet do more harm than good? The consensus among pediatricians and nutritionists is that the diet recommended by the AAP will not in any way interfere with normal growth and development, nor will it lead to failure-to-thrive problems after age two. This is a healthy, well-balanced diet, and all children over two should be on it.

The milk question

Milk is the main source of calcium in the toddler's diet. Whole milk is recommended until age two because a certain amount of fat is needed for optimal brain growth during this period. This is followed by a gradual change to low-fat milk after age two. There has been some recent controversy as to whether toddlers, after weaning from breast milk or infant formula, should drink any milk at all. There are physicians who believe that cow's milk may be unhealthy and that sufficient intake of calcium can be achieved with a totally nondairy diet. Some who hold that children should not drink milk cite studies in rats and mice that have shown a relationship between the development of diabetes mellitus and milk intake. Others believe that there is a high incidence of childhood allergy to the protein in cow's milk, which is another reason to discourage milk consumption. This, however, is not the consensus among most experts in the field, who believe that milk and

Lawrence Migdale—Stock, Boston

Milk is an important source of calcium; low-fat milk, limited to two to three cups a day, is recommended for toddlers once they reach age two.

NEWS CAP

Score Two for Prevention

Although preventive medicine rarely yields the kind of dramatic results achieved by miracle drugs or daring surgery, it is unquestionably capable of producing remarkable triumphs. Such has been the case with two fairly recently instituted interventions, both intended to save the lives of infants and children: (1) the packaging of medications in containers that children cannot open, and (2) putting infants to sleep on their backs.

Two and a half decades ago, the U.S. Congress passed the Poison Prevention Packaging Act, which mandated that all toxic substances used in or around the home—including prescription drugs—be packaged in child-resistant containers. A comprehensive study reported in the *Journal of the American Medical Association* (June 5, 1996) concluded that in the period from 1974 through 1992, there was a 45% drop in the annual death rate of children under age five who had accidentally swallowed prescription medications. The drop in mortality would have been even steeper, the report suggested, had it not been for the fact that the law allows people to request that their prescriptions have "nonchildproof" caps. Indeed, many adults, especially those with arthritis or other conditions that impair dexterity or strength—as well as those who do not like the inconvenience of the harder-to-open containers—take advantage of this option. For this reason, the Consumer Product Safety Commission is currently revising its protocol for testing child-resistant packages to promote designs that thwart children but do not frustrate adults.

"Back to Sleep," a two-year-old national public education campaign alerting U.S. parents and child-care professionals to put infants to sleep on their backs rather than on their stomachs, has had a decided impact on deaths from sudden infant death syndrome (SIDS). SIDS, also known as "crib death" or "cot death," is the leading killer of U.S. infants in the first year of life. In the late 1980s and early '90s, epidemiological studies carried out around the world suggested that the prone (*i.e.,* face down) sleeping position significantly increases the risk of SIDS. Since 1994, when "Back to Sleep" was launched, SIDS deaths have declined by 30%. Telephone surveys found that in 1995, 71% of mothers of newborns said they put their babies to sleep on their backs (compared with only 30% in 1994). Duane Alexander, director of the National Institute of Child Health and Human Development, estimated in July 1996 that 1,500 young lives had been saved in the U.S. and that even more had been saved in other countries where similar campaigns had been under way longer and where SIDS rates were higher.

—Linda Tomchuck

milk products are safe and necessary to ensure an adequate calcium intake. On the diabetes-milk question pediatrician Ronald Kleinman, a past chairman of the AAP's Committee on Nutrition, has stated: "The relationship between the ingestion of dairy products and diabetes in humans is still at the very preliminary stage. Dairy products are a rich and valuable source of minerals, protein, and energy for growing children. There is no reason to eliminate cow's milk and dairy products from the diet of infants and children."

Milk should be limited to 480–720 ml per day so that toddlers have an appetite left for solid foods. Cheese and yogurt also provide excellent sources of calcium. Nondairy foods that are rich in calcium include green leafy vegetables, salmon and sardines with the bones, some soy products, and calcium-supplemented juices. As noted before, however, it is also a good idea to limit juice intake to 240–480 ml per day; many toddlers spoil their appetites by drinking huge quantities of juice—especially apple juice. Water rather than juice may be offered to satisfy the toddler's thirst. The use of *sweetened* juices, fruit drinks, or soft drinks should be discouraged, since they provide only "empty calories."

The salt question

Although certain studies show no relationship between the development of hypertension (high blood pressure) and salt (sodium) intake, there is an established link between the two in at least some individuals. Consequently, it is probably best that toddlers not acquire a taste for highly salted foods. Experts recommend that toddlers' daily sodium intake be limited to no more than 225 mg per day for one-to-two-year-olds and 300 mg per day for two-to-three-year-olds. Little or no salt should be used in cooking (other seasonings are fine), and salt shakers should be kept off the table. It is good practice to steer toddlers away from highly salted foods such as potato chips and any products that are high in sodium; this includes ketchup, pickles, TV dinners, and other kids' favorites. Parents should check the labels on all processed foods for their sodium content.

The supplement question

Vitamin and mineral supplements may be recommended for individual toddlers by their physicians if their diets are not nutritious and well-balanced. If a toddler eats well, he or she may not require any form of supplementation, but it is best to consult the youngster's doctor in most cases.

Finicky eaters

Despite the fact that many toddlers are very finicky eaters, it is important for parents to offer them a variety of foods from each of the major food groups: (1) breads, cereals, and other grains, (2) fruits and vegetables, (3) meat, poultry, fish, eggs, and legumes (chickpeas, lentils, kidney beans, and black beans), and (4) milk, cheese, and yogurt. There is no reason to be concerned if a toddler does not have a serving from each of these food groups every day. If parents regularly offer their toddlers a variety of well-balanced foods in a pleasant environment and allow the child to regulate his or her own caloric intake, even the pickiest eater will gradually develop healthy eating habits.

The following are some suggestions that the family can follow to make mealtimes for and with toddlers happy and healthy:

- Make portions of food small, about one-third of an adult portion; offer a second helping later if the toddler is still hungry.
- Allow toddlers to feed themselves. Offer them appropriate eating utensils, but do not worry if they choose to use fingers instead. Mealtime is an ideal time for children to explore their independence.
- Try to set an example. Toddlers imitate their parents and older siblings when choosing foods; they learn to eat what those around them eat.
- Mealtimes should be pleasant, peaceful family gatherings. Attempt to minimize distractions from eating, such as television and family arguments.
- Within reason, try to respect a toddler's likes and dislikes about food choices.
- Introduce new foods in small portions with gentle encouragement but without forcing.
- Never make an issue of finishing any particular food or about joining the "clean-plate" club.
- Parents should decide when, where, and what foods toddlers eat, but the toddler should decide how much to eat.
- Avoid serving foods that may cause a one-to-three-year-old to choke (*e.g.,* raw carrots, popcorn, hard candy, and nuts). It is a good practice to peel the skin off grapes and hot dogs and to cut foods into small, easily chewed, easily swallowed pieces.

There is nothing wrong with snacks. In fact, well-selected between-meal foods can meet the nutritional needs of almost any toddler.

Robert E. Daemmrich—Tony Stone Images

Smart snacking

Snacks can be an excellent source of good nutrition. They should be offered between meals, not right after meals, and should not be used as a reward or bribe. The following are some nutritious snack foods from the four major food groups:

- crackers with cheese or peanut butter
- fresh fruit, cut up
- pretzels that are not overly salty
- breadsticks
- yogurt
- hard-boiled eggs on occasion
- leftover "finger foods" such as chicken pieces or meatloaf, cut up
- frozen juice "pops"
- cut-up raw vegetables
- custard or pudding
- cereal with milk and fruit
- graham crackers

Some last words

Because children between one year and three years of age grow more slowly than infants, it is perfectly normal for them not to have big appetites. Parents should rest assured that no toddler will starve if he or she skips a meal or two. Needless to say, there are tremendous pressures nowadays for people to live life "in the fast lane." In the process, parents may not take the time to eat properly and may pay little attention to getting sound nutrition—for themselves or their young ones. Indeed, more and more meals are eaten on the run, outside the home, and in fast-food restaurants, while traditional family meals are fewer and farther between. Meanwhile, there is an omnipresent advertising industry pushing the wrong foods. Getting a toddler to eat well may not be easy, but if parents take the time and are successful, they will be doing their children a very important favor in terms of their future health and well-being.

—Alvin N. Eden, M.D.

NEWS CAP

Iraq's Children: Paying the Price of Politics

Since the end of the Persian Gulf War in 1991 and the institution of economic sanctions following the war, malnutrition and mortality have increased among Iraqi children. This finding came from a study conducted under the auspices of the United Nations Food and Agriculture Organization, which was published as a letter to the editor in *The Lancet* (Dec. 2, 1995). Among the findings were that in the capital city of Baghdad the mortality rate for infants (children under one year of age) had doubled between August 1991 and August 1995, and it had increased fivefold for children under five years old. Malnutrition also saw a dramatic rise over the same time span. Stunting (a measure of height-for-age) had doubled, while underweight (weight-for-age) and wasting (weight-for-height) had quadrupled.

These data are consistent with the harsh economic and social conditions in Iraq today; clean water and affordable food are scarce, and medical care and the public health infrastructure are deteriorating rapidly. The economic sanctions imposed upon Iraq by the UN and the Iraqi government's refusal to use its limited resources to improve health conditions had led to the deaths of an estimated 567,000 children by late 1995. Mary C. Smith Fawzi and Sarah Zaidi, the authors of the UN report, noted that this estimate was probably low, as it extrapolated the mortality rates in Baghdad to the remainder of Iraq; in more remote areas, conditions are known to be much worse.

On May 20, 1996, Iraq agreed to accept an oil-for-food deal that first was proposed under a UN Security Council resolution in 1995. Baghdad initially had rejected the "humiliating terms" of the resolution and claimed it would rather let its people go hungry. Under the accord, Iraq would be allowed to sell $2 billion worth of oil on the international market over six months. Those profits would enable it to buy food, medicines, and other humanitarian supplies for its people. The resolution would not take effect for at least several months; Iraq's president, Saddam Hussein, had first to submit an acceptable plan for the equitable distribution of the goods. The UN Department of Humanitarian Affairs would oversee the distribution and make sure that all relief supplies reached those for whom they were intended, particularly suffering Iraqi children.

—James Hennelly

Antonio Ribeiro—Gamma Liaison

New Drugs Approved by the Food and Drug Administration, January 1995–July 1996

PRIORITY APPROVALS[1]

Generic name (brand name)	Manufacturer	Use	Selected side effects
albendazole (Albenza)	SmithKline Beecham	cystic disease caused by pork tapeworm larvae and dog tapeworm larvae	changes in liver enzymes; abdominal pain; nausea; vomiting; headache
alendronate sodium (Fosamax)	Merck	osteoporosis and Paget's disease of bone	abdominal pain; constipation; diarrhea; flatulence; esophageal ulcer; difficulty swallowing; muscular and skeletal pain; headache
amifostine (Ethyol)	U.S. Bioscience	reduction of kidney toxicity associated with cisplatin therapy for advanced ovarian cancer	low blood pressure; nausea; vomiting; flushing; chills; dizziness; drowsiness; hiccups; sneezing
cidofovir (Vistide)	Gilead Sciences Inc.	cytomegalovirus infection of the retina	kidney toxicity; low white blood cell count; fever; infection; shortness of breath
corticorelin ovine triflutate (Acthrel)	Ferring	diagnostic aid for determining cause of Cushing's syndrome	flushing of face, neck, and upper chest; rapid heartbeat; low blood pressure; difficulty breathing; chest tightness
dexrazoxane (Zinecard)	Pharmacia & Upjohn	reduction of cardiac toxicity associated with doxorubicin therapy for breast cancer	injection-site pain
docetaxel (Taxotere)	Rhône-Poulenc Rorer	breast cancer in patients who have not responded to standard therapies	low white blood cell count; anemia; low platelet count; fluid retention; rash; hair loss; nausea; vomiting; diarrhea; low blood pressure; inflammation of the mouth; changes in liver enzymes
epoprostenol (Flolan)	Glaxo Wellcome	primary pulmonary hypertension (increased resistance to blood flow in the arteries that supply the lungs)	injection-site pain and/or infection
gemcitabine (Gemzar)	Lilly	pancreatic cancer	low white blood cell count; nausea; vomiting; fever; edema (accumulation of fluid in the tissues); rash; flulike symptoms; hair loss
indinavir (Crixivan)	Merck	HIV infection	kidney stones; elevated levels of the pigment bilirubin (a sign of impaired liver function); abdominal pain; weakness; nausea; diarrhea; vomiting; headache; taste disturbance
irinotecan (Camptosar)	Pharmacia & Upjohn	colorectal cancer in patients whose disease has relapsed or progressed on 5-fluorouracil therapy	diarrhea; low white blood cell count; nausea; vomiting; abdominal cramping
lamivudine (Epivir)	Glaxo Wellcome	HIV infection (in combination with other drugs)	headache; nausea; malaise and fatigue; diarrhea; nerve damage; low white blood cell count; anemia; inflammation of the pancreas
latanoprost (Xalatan)	Pharmacia & Upjohn	relief of intraocular pressure in open-angle glaucoma	increased brown coloring of the iris of the eye; blurred vision; ocular stinging and/or itching
mycophenolate mofetil (Cellcept)	Roche Bioscience	prevention of organ rejection in kidney transplantation	diarrhea; low white blood cell count; vomiting; localized or disseminated infection; increased risk of lymphoma
nevirapine (Viramune)	Boehringer Ingelheim; Roxane	HIV infection (in combination with other drugs)	severe rash; changes in liver enzymes
porfimer sodium (Photofrin)	QLT Phototherapeutics	obstructive throat cancer in patients who cannot be treated by laser therapy	light-sensitivity reaction; localized redness; back pain; chest pain; fever; constipation; nausea; vomiting; atrial fibrillation (a rapid, irregular heartbeat); inability to sleep; anemia; difficulty breathing; fluid accumulation in chest cavity
riluzole (Rilutek)	Rhône-Poulenc Rorer	amyotrophic lateral sclerosis (ALS; Lou Gehrig's disease)	weakness; nausea; dizziness; decreased lung function; diarrhea; abdominal pain; pneumonia; vomiting; vertigo; weight loss; drowsiness

New Drugs Approved by the Food and Drug Administration, January 1995–July 1996

Generic name (brand name)	Manufacturer	Use	Selected side effects
PRIORITY APPROVALS (continued)			
ritonavir (Norvir)	Abbott	HIV infection	nausea; diarrhea; vomiting
saquinavir (Invirase)	Roche Bioscience	HIV infection (in combination with other drugs)	diarrhea; abdominal discomfort; nausea
topotecan (Hycamtin)	SmithKline Beecham	ovarian cancer	low white blood cell count; nausea; vomiting; diarrhea; constipation; abdominal pain; hair loss; fatigue; fever
sodium phenylbutyrate (Buphenyl)	Ucyclyd	urea cycle disorders (a group of congenital metabolic diseases)	absence of menstrual periods; body odor; taste aversion; decreased appetite
STANDARD APPROVALS[2]			
acarbose (Precose)	Bayer	management of high blood sugar in non-insulin-dependent diabetes	flatulence; diarrhea; abdominal pain; changes in liver enzymes
adapalene (Differin)	Galderma	acne	skin redness and/or scaling, dryness, itching, burning, stinging, tingling
anastrazole (Arimidex)	Zeneca	advanced breast cancer in postmenopausal women with progression following tamoxifen therapy	weakness; nausea; headache; hot flashes; pain; back pain; difficulty breathing; vomiting; cough; diarrhea
arcitumomab (CEA-scan)	Immunomedics	diagnostic imaging in colorectal cancer	fever; upset stomach; bursitis; headache; rash
azelaic acid (Azelex)	Allergan	acne	skin itching and/or burning, stinging, tingling, redness, dryness; rash
bicalutamide (Casodex)	Zeneca	advanced prostate cancer (in combination with hormone treatment)	hot flashes; diarrhea; breast enlargement and/or tenderness; constipation; back pain; weakness; pelvic pain; nausea; infection
carvedilol (Coreg)	SmithKline Beecham	high blood pressure	drop in blood pressure when changing position; dizziness; diarrhea; low platelet count; elevation of triglycerides; swelling; urinary tract infection
cefipime (Maxipime)	Bristol-Myers Squibb	urinary tract infections, skin infections, pneumonia	rash; vein inflammation; pain
ceftibuten dihydrate (Cedax)	Schering-Plough	bronchitis, otitis media (middle ear infection), pharyngitis, tonsillitis	nausea; headache; diarrhea; upset stomach; dizziness; abdominal pain; vomiting
cetirizine (Zyrtec)	Pfizer	relief of nasal allergy symptoms and chronic rash	drowsiness; fatigue; dry mouth; sore throat; dizziness; headache; nausea
dirithromycin (Dynabac)	Lilly	bronchitis, pneumonia, pharyngitis, tonsillitis	abdominal pain; headache; nausea; diarrhea; vomiting; upset stomach
fexofenadine (Allegra)	Hoechst Marion Roussel	seasonal allergy symptoms (e.g., nasal inflammation, itchy eyes)	[none]
fosphenytoin (Cerebyx)	Warner-Lambert	prevention and treatment of seizures	rapid eye movements; dizziness; itching; headache; drowsiness; muscle incoordination
glimepiride (Amaryl)	Hoechst Marion Roussel	management of high blood sugar in non-insulin-dependent diabetes mellitus	low blood sugar; dizziness; weakness; nausea
ibutilide fumarate (Corvert)	Pharmacia & Upjohn	atrial fibrillation or flutter (conditions of rapid, irregular heartbeat)	rapid heart rate; low blood pressure
insulin lispro (Humalog)	Lilly	rapid-acting insulin analog for diabetes (new form of insulin)	low blood sugar; itching
iopromide (Ultravist)	Berlex	diagnostic imaging of blood vessels	risk of heart attack and/or stroke; back pain; headache; nausea; urinary urgency
iodixanol (Visipaque)	Nycomed	diagnostic imaging of blood vessels	chest pain; nausea; headache and/or migraine; vertigo; rash; taste disturbance

New Drugs Approved by the Food and Drug Administration, January 1995–July 1996

Generic name (brand name)	Manufacturer	Use	Selected side effects
STANDARD APPROVALS (continued)			
ioxilan (Oxilan)	Cook Imaging	diagnostic imaging of blood vessels	headache; fever; chest pain; nausea
lansoprazole (Prevacid)	TAP Pharmaceuticals	duodenal ulcer, erosive esophagitis, persistent oversecretion of stomach acid	abdominal pain; diarrhea; nausea; headache
losartan potassium (Cozaar)	Merck	high blood pressure	dizziness; leg pain; respiratory infection
mirtazapine (Remeron)	Organon	depression	low white blood cell count; drowsiness; nausea; weight gain
moexipril (Univasc)	Schwarz Pharma	high blood pressure	cough; dizziness
nalmefene (Revex)	Ohmeda	opioid drug overdose	nausea; vomiting; rapid heart rate; high blood pressure; fever; dizziness
nisoldipine (Sular)	Bayer; Zeneca	high blood pressure	swelling; headache; dizziness; palpitations; sore throat; blood vessel dilation
remifentanil (Ultiva)	Glaxo Wellcome	general anesthesia	depression of respiration; slow heartbeat; low blood pressure; muscle rigidity
sevoflurane (Ultane)	Abbott	general surgical anesthesia	nausea; vomiting; cough; slow heart rate; low blood pressure; rapid heartbeat; agitation; throat spasm; dizziness; drowsiness
technetium Tc 99m tetrofosmin (Myoview)	Medi-Physics	diagnostic imaging of heart muscle	high blood pressure; torsades de pointes (a type of irregular heart rhythm); vomiting; abdominal discomfort; skin allergy; low blood pressure; dizziness; rise in white blood cell count
tramadol (Ultram)	McNeil	analgesic for moderate to moderately severe pain	dizziness; vertigo; nausea; constipation; headache; drowsiness
trandolapril (Mavik)	Knoll	high blood pressure	cough; dizziness; diarrhea
BIOLOGICS OR VACCINES[3]			
hepatitis A vaccine (Havrix)	SmithKline Beecham	prevention of hepatitis A infection	headache; fatigue; fever; nausea; malaise
hepatitis A vaccine (Vaqta)	Merck	prevention of hepatitis A infection	fever; sore throat; abdominal pain
interferon-beta-1a (Avonex)	Biogen	relapsing forms of multiple sclerosis	fever; chills; muscle aches; fatigue; weakness
respiratory syncytial virus immune globulin (RespiGam)	MedImmune; Wyeth-Ayerst	prevention of respiratory syncytial virus infection	fever
varicella-zoster virus vaccine (Varivax)	Merck	prevention of chicken pox	injection-site pain; mild chicken pox-like rash; fever; upper respiratory illness; cough; irritability; diarrhea; joint pain
NEW INDICATIONS, FORMULATIONS, OR COMBINATIONS			
alprostadil injection (Caverject)	Pharmacia & Upjohn	erectile dysfunction (previously approved for opening of arteries in newborns with congenital heart defects)	penile pain; prolonged erection; development of fibrous penile tissue; high blood pressure; headache; upper respiratory infection; sinus inflammation; flulike symptoms
alteplase (t-PA; Activase)	Genentech	acute ischemic stroke (previously approved for heart attack)	intracranial bleeding
amiodarone (Cordarone I.V.)	Wyeth-Ayerst	recurring ventricular fibrillation and unstable tachycardia (disturbances of heart rhythm; injectable formulation)	low blood pressure; changes in liver enzymes; nausea; slow heartbeat
amlodipine and benazepril (Lotrel)	Ciba-Geigy	high blood pressure (formerly available as separate drugs)	cough, edema (accumulation of fluid in the tissues)

New Drugs Approved by the Food and Drug Administration, January 1995–July 1996

NEW INDICATIONS, FORMULATIONS, OR COMBINATIONS (continued)

Generic name (brand name)	Manufacturer	Use	Selected side effects
amphotericin B lipid complex (Abelcet)	The Liposome Co.	aspergillosis (a fungal infection) in patients who do not respond to or cannot tolerate regular amphotericin B (liposomal formulation)	chills; fever; increased serum creatinine levels (a sign of kidney dysfunction); gastrointestinal bleeding; respiratory failure; multiple organ failure; sepsis
azithromycin (Zithromax)	Pfizer	AIDS-related *Mycobacterium avium* complex infection (a bacterial infection; previously approved for respiratory, skin, urethral, and cervical infections)	diarrhea; nausea; abdominal pain
bleomycin (Blenoxane)	Bristol-Myers Squibb	malignant pleural effusions (exudation of fluid into the pleural membranes as a complication of lung cancer; previously approved for squamous cell carcinoma, lymphoma, and testicular carcinoma)	local pain; lung inflammation; development of fibrous tissue in the lungs; low blood pressure; skin redness; rash; hair loss
butoconazole nitrate (Femstat 3)	Roche	over-the-counter treatment for vaginal yeast infection (formerly prescription-only)	vaginal burning and/or itching, discharge, soreness, swelling; generalized itching
calcitonin-salmon nasal spray (Miacalcin)	Sandoz	osteoporosis (nasal-spray formulation)	nasal inflammation; back pain; flushing; nausea; allergic reaction
cimetidine (Tagamet HB)	SmithKline Beecham	over-the-counter heartburn and acid indigestion treatment and prevention (formerly prescription-only ulcer treatment)	interaction with other drugs, including theophylline, warfarin, and phenytoin
clarithromycin (Biaxin)	Abbott	*Helicobacter pylori*-associated duodenal ulcers (in combination with omeprazole); prevention of AIDS-related *Mycobacterium avium* complex infection (a bacterial infection; previously approved for treatment of *M. avium* complex and other infections)	diarrhea; nausea; distortion of taste perception; upset stomach; abdominal pain; headache
conjugated estrogens and medroxyprogesterone acetate (Prempro, Premphase)	Wyeth-Ayerst	single estrogen/progestin pill for hormone replacement therapy and treatment of osteoporosis (formerly available only as separate pills)	breakthrough bleeding; breast tenderness; nausea; skin discoloration; weight gain or loss; changes in libido
daunorubicin liposomal formulation (DaunoXome)	NeXstar	AIDS-related Kaposi's sarcoma (liposomal formulation; formerly available in nonliposomal formulation for treatment of leukemia)	blood cell suppression; back pain; flushing; chest tightness; cardiac symptoms
dexfenfluramine (Redux)	Interneuron; Wyeth-Ayerst	obesity (new formulation of the drug fenfluramine)	diarrhea; dry mouth; drowsiness; risk of primary pulmonary hypertension (increased resistance to blood flow in the arteries that supply the lungs)
dinoprostone (Cervidil)	Controlled Therapeutics	promotion of cervical dilation prior to childbirth (vaginal-insert formulation)	fetal heart rate abnormality; uterine contractile abnormality; drug interaction with oxytocin
diphtheria/tetanus/ acellular pertussis vaccine (Tripedia)	Connaught	infant whooping cough vaccination, first three doses (previously approved for fourth and fifth booster doses)	local skin redness, swelling, and pain; weight loss; vomiting; drowsiness; persistent crying
divalproex (Depakote)	Abbott	prevention of chronic migraine headache; treatment of manic phase of bipolar disorder (previously approved for epilepsy)	nausea; upset stomach; diarrhea; vomiting; weakness; fatigue; drowsiness; dizziness; risk of liver failure
doxazosin (Cardura)	Pfizer	benign enlargement of prostate gland (previously approved for high blood pressure)	dizziness; weight gain; drowsiness; fatigue
doxorubicin liposomal formulation (Doxil)	Sequus	AIDS-related Kaposi's sarcoma in patients whose disease has progressed on chemotherapy (liposomal formulation)	skin eruptions of hands and feet; low white blood cell count; anemia; nausea; weakness; fever; chest pain; hair loss; vomiting
estradiol transdermal patch (Vivelle)	Ciba-Geigy	low-dose estrogen replacement therapy (transdermal formulation)	headache; breast tenderness; skin irritation; fluid retention
estradiol vaginal ring (Estring)	Pharmacia & Upjohn	local treatment for vaginal and urogenital postmenopausal atrophy (vaginal-insert formulation)	vaginal secretions; abdominal pain; genital itching; nausea; breast tenderness; fluid retention

New Drugs Approved by the Food and Drug Administration, January 1995–July 1996

NEW INDICATIONS, FORMULATIONS, OR COMBINATIONS (continued)

Generic name (brand name)	Manufacturer	Use	Selected side effects
etoposide phosphate (Etopophos)	Bristol-Myers Squibb	small-cell lung cancer, testicular tumors (new formulation of etoposide)	low blood cell counts; nausea; vomiting; chills; fever; rapid heart rate; shortness of breath; low blood pressure
famciclovir (Famvir)	SmithKline Beecham	recurrent genital herpes (previously approved for shingles)	headache; nausea
famotidine (Pepcid AC)	Merck	over-the-counter heartburn and acid indigestion treatment and prevention (formerly prescription-only for treatment of ulcers)	headache; dizziness; constipation; diarrhea
fluticasone propionate (Flovent)	Glaxo Wellcome	asthma (oral-inhalation form, formerly available as nasal spray for nasal inflammation)	sore throat; nasal congestion; respiratory infection; flu; headache; oral candidiasis (fungal infection of mouth); hoarseness
ganciclovir intraocular implant (Vitrasert)	Chiron; Roche	AIDS-related cytomegalovirus infection of the retina (implantable formulation)	temporary decrease in visual acuity; eye infection; retinal detachment; cataracts
ganciclovir oral formulation (Cytovene)	Roche	AIDS-related cytomegalovirus infection of the retina (oral formulation)	fever; abdominal pain; diarrhea; nausea; low white blood cell count
goserelin acetate (Zoladex)	Zeneca	advanced breast cancer palliative treatment (previously approved for prostate cancer and endometriosis)	vaginal swelling and itching; headache; emotional lability; decreased libido; sweating
interferon alpha (Intron A)	Schering-Plough	malignant melanoma (previously approved for hairy cell leukemia, genital warts, and chronic hepatitis B and C)	fatigue; low white blood cell count; muscle pain; appetite loss; nausea; changes in liver enzymes
interferon alpha (Roferon-A)	Roche	chronic myelogenous leukemia (previously approved for hairy cell leukemia and Kaposi's sarcoma)	anemia; low white blood cell count; low platelet count; fever; chills; muscle pain; appetite loss; nausea; headache
ipratropium bromide (Atrovent)	Boehringer Ingelheim	nasal inflammation and allergies (nasal-spray form; formerly available in oral-inhalation form for chronic obstructive lung disease)	mouth and throat dryness; cough; headache; nausea; dizziness; blurred vision
itraconazole (Sporanox)	Janssen	onychomycosis (fungal infection of toe- and fingernails; previously approved for other fungal infections)	changes in liver enzymes; gastrointestinal disorders; rash; high blood pressure; low blood pressure; headache; muscle pain; vertigo
ketoprofen (Actron)	Bayer	over-the-counter pain remedy (formerly prescription-only)	upset stomach; nausea; abdominal pain; diarrhea; constipation; flatulence; weight loss; headache; dizziness
ketoprofen (Orudis KT)	Whitehall-Robins	over-the-counter pain remedy (formerly prescription-only)	upset stomach; nausea; abdominal pain; diarrhea; constipation; flatulence; weight loss; headache; dizziness
lansoprazole (Prevacid)	TAP Holdings	maintenance of healing in erosive esophagitis (previously approved for duodenal ulcer, erosive esophagitis, and hypersecretion of stomach acid)	abdominal pain; diarrhea; nausea
lisinopril (Zestril, Prinivil)	Zeneca; Merck	improved survival after acute heart attack (previously approved for high blood pressure and heart failure)	low blood pressure; kidney dysfunction; cough; chest pain; skin rash; swelling
lovastatin (Mevacor)	Merck	slowing of progression of coronary atherosclerosis in patients with coronary heart disease (previously approved for cholesterol lowering)	headache; diarrhea; rash; abdominal pain; flatulence; nausea; constipation
miconazole (Monistat 3)	Ortho Advanced Care Products	over-the-counter treatment for vaginal yeast infection (formerly prescription-only)	vaginal itching and burning; abdominal cramping; headache; rash
minoxidil (Rogaine)	Pharmacia & Upjohn	over-the-counter hair-growth treatment for male and female hair loss (formerly prescription-only)	skin irritation; eczema
nicotine gum (Nicorette)	SmithKline Beecham	over-the-counter smoking-cessation therapy (formerly prescription-only)	oral tingling; bleeding of gums; diarrhea; upset stomach; nausea; hiccups; tooth disorders

New Drugs Approved by the Food and Drug Administration, January 1995–July 1996

Generic name (brand name)	Manufacturer	Use	Selected side effects
NEW INDICATIONS, FORMULATIONS, OR COMBINATIONS (continued)			
nicotine nasal spray (Nicotrol NS)	McNeil; Pharmacia & Upjohn	smoking-cessation therapy (nasal-spray formulation)	[none]
nicotine patch (NicoDerm)	SmithKline Beecham; Hoechst Marion Roussel	over-the-counter smoking-cessation aid (formerly prescription-only)	skin redness and/or itching, burning
nicotine patch (Nicotrol)	McNeil	over-the-counter smoking-cessation aid (formerly prescription-only)	skin redness and/or itching, burning
nizatidine (Axid AR)	Lilly	over-the-counter heartburn treatment (formerly prescription-only)	anemia; rash
ofloxacin ophthalmic solution (Ocuflox)	Allergan	corneal ulcers (previously approved for bacterial conjunctivitis)	ocular burning and/or stinging, redness, dryness, light sensitivity; blurred vision
omeprazole (Prilosec)	Astra; Merck	*Helicobacter pylori* -induced duodenal ulcers (in combination with clarithromycin), gastric ulcers (previously approved for duodenal ulcers, erosive esophagitis, and gastrointestinal reflux disease)	dizziness; rash; constipation; cough; back pain
paroxetine (Paxil)	SmithKline Beecham	obsessive compulsive disorder, panic disorder (previously approved for depression)	weakness; sweating; nausea; decreased appetite; drowsiness; dizziness; inability to sleep; tremor; nervousness; ejaculatory disturbance
pravastatin (Pravachol)	Bristol-Myers Squibb	reduction of heart attack risk and slowing of progression of coronary atherosclerosis (previously approved for cholesterol lowering)	rash; heartburn; fatigue; headache; dizziness
ranitidine (Zantac 75)	Glaxo Wellcome	over-the-counter heartburn treatment (formerly prescription-only)	constipation; diarrhea; nausea; abdominal pain
sumatriptan succinate tablets (Imitrex)	Cerenex (division of Glaxo Wellcome)	migraine headache (oral formulation)	tingling; weakness; warm/hot sensation; feeling of heaviness or tightness
terbinafine tablets (Lamisil)	Sandoz	onychomycosis (fungal infection of toe- and fingernails; formerly available in cream form for athlete's foot, jock itch, and ringworm)	diarrhea; rash; upset stomach; changes in liver enzymes; itching; taste disturbance; nausea; abdominal pain
testosterone patch (Androderm)	Theratech; SmithKline Beecham	testosterone deficiency in men (transdermal formulation)	skin redness and/or itching
tretinoin (Renova)	Ortho	sun-damaged skin (previously approved for acne)	skin peeling and/or burning, stinging, redness, itching
tretinoin (Vesanoid)	Roche	acute promyelocytic leukemia that has relapsed after anthracycline chemotherapy (oral formulation)	respiratory symptoms
valacyclovir (Valtrex)	Glaxo Wellcome	herpes zoster (shingles), recurrent genital herpes (new formulation of acyclovir)	nausea; headache; diarrhea; dizziness
DUPLICATE OF AVAILABLE PRODUCT			
somatropin (Bio-Tropin)	Bio-Technology General	human growth hormone treatment for children with growth failure	headache; injection-site pain
somatropin (Genotropin)	Pharmacia & Upjohn	human growth hormone treatment for children with growth failure	injection-site pain; rash; swelling; headache; blood in urine; thyroid deficiency
somatropin (Norditropin)	Novo Nordisk	human growth hormone treatment for children with growth failure	nausea; headache; muscle pain and/or weakness; mild increases in blood sugar and urinary sugar

[1] New compounds (*i.e.,* new molecular entities) to treat serious illnesses for which no adequate alternative therapy exists.
[2] New compounds that provide some, little, or no therapeutic gain over products already available.
[3] Products such as serums, toxins, blood components, etc., used to prevent, treat, or cure disease.

—prepared by Danielle Foullon

Aspirin: Ageless Remedy

In 1997 aspirin will celebrate its 100th birthday. Laboratory records of the German chemical and pharmaceutical firm Friedrich Bayer & Co. for Oct. 10, 1897, describe the chemical transformation of salicylic acid into acetylsalicylic acid—aspirin—by a young industrial chemist, Felix Hoffmann. Despite its unpleasant taste and troublesome side effects, salicylic acid was widely used in the 19th century as a remedy for the pain and inflammation of rheumatism. Hoffmann hoped to create a compound that would be easier for his father, a rheumatism sufferer, to tolerate.

Because of its long history and easy availability, aspirin is no longer thought of as a wonder drug. However, recent findings about its potential to prevent life-threatening disease have reawakened appreciation for this remarkably safe and effective drug.

A long history

Salicylic acid goes back many thousands of years. It is a constituent of several plants long used as medicaments. The Ebers papyrus, an Egyptian compilation of medical texts that dates from about 1550 BC, recommended that a decoction of the dried leaves of myrtle be applied to a woman's abdomen and back to expel rheumatic pains from the womb. A thousand years later Hippocrates championed the juices of the poplar tree for treating eye diseases and those of willow bark for alleviating pain in childbirth. All of these remedies contained salicylates (derivatives of salicylic acid).

In AD 30 the Roman encyclopedist Celsus described the four classic signs of inflammation—rubor (redness), calor (heat), dolor (pain), and tumor (swelling)—and used extracts of willow leaves to relieve them. Over the course of the 1st and 2nd centuries AD in the Roman world, the medicinal use of salicylate-containing plants was further developed. Additional uses—*e.g.,* as plasters for wounds and treatments for menstrual discomfort and dysentery—were found during the Middle Ages. In Asia, too, these botanical substances were being applied therapeutically.

On June 2, 1763, the Rev. Edward Stone of Chipping Norton in Oxfordshire, England, read a paper to the Royal Society on the use of willow bark in fever. Stone had tasted the bark and was surprised by its extraordinary bitterness, which reminded him of the taste of cinchona bark (the source of quinine), then being used to treat malaria. He believed in the "doctrine of signatures," which held that the cure for a disease is often found in the same location where the malady occurs. Since, in Stone's words, the "willow delights in a moist and wet soil, where agues [fevers, often with chills or sweating] chiefly abound," he gathered a pound of willow bark, dried it in a baker's oven, and pulverized it. The powdered bark was taken mixed with a liquid. Stone's greatest success was with doses of one dram (1.8 g, or 1⁄16 oz), which he reported using in about 50 patients safely and with good results. He concluded his paper: "I have no other motives for

The bark and leaves of the weeping willow, Salix alba, *were one of the chief sources of salicylates until the mid-19th century, when chemists in Germany discovered how to synthesize salicylic acid in the laboratory.*

Andy Purcell—Bruce Coleman Limited

(This page and opposite page) Photographs, Bayer AG

As a young chemist at the German pharmaceutical firm of Friedrich Bayer & Co., Felix Hoffmann (top) sought to develop a compound that would have the pain-relieving and anti-inflammatory properties of salicylic acid without its side effects. In 1897 he succeeded in creating acetylsalicylic acid—better known as aspirin. (Above) The new remedy was tested in Bayer's pharmacology laboratory; in 1899 the company's research director, Heinrich Dreser (second from right), launched aspirin as a commercial product.

publishing this valuable specific, than that it may have a fair and full trial in all its variety of circumstances and situations, and that the world may reap the benefits accruing from it."

Stone's wishes have certainly been realized; world production of aspirin has been estimated at 36,000 tons a year and average consumption in developed countries at about 70 tablets per person per year. Without the discovery in recent years of a great many aspirin substitutes, consumption would surely be many times higher.

Salicylic acid was synthesized in Germany in 1860. Its ready supply and lower cost compared with that of the natural substance, which was extracted from plants, led to even wider usage—as an external antiseptic, as an antipyretic (*i.e.,* fever reducer), and in the treatment of rheumatism. As Hoffmann had hoped, his father found aspirin much more palatable than salicylic acid, and Bayer's research director, Heinrich Dreser, recognized that he had an important new drug on his hands. In 1899 he launched aspirin on the market, at the same time writing a paper suggesting that aspirin was a convenient way of supplying the body with the active substance salicylate. This point is still debated, but most of the evidence now shows that aspirin works in its own right.

Inner workings

Aspirin has dozens of modern imitators such as ibuprofen, indomethacin, piroxicam, and sulindac. Despite the diversity of their chemical structures, they all share certain therapeutic properties. In varying doses they alleviate the swelling, redness, and pain of inflammation, reduce a fever, and relieve a headache. They also share to a greater or lesser extent a number of the same type of side effects. Depending on dose, they may cause gastric upset and may even ulcerate the stomach lining. In high doses they can delay the birth process and, in overdose, damage the kidneys. An intriguing—and therapeutically relevant—side effect of some of these aspirin-like drugs is that they also interfere with the process by which the tiny blood cells called platelets clump together in order to stem the flow of blood from a cut.

When a chemically diverse group of drugs all share some of the same qualities (which, in themselves, have little connection with each other), it is a fairly safe assumption that the drugs' actions are based on a single biochemical intervention. For many years pharmacologists searched without success for such a common mode of action. Then, in 1971, one of these authors (John Vane) and his colleagues, working at the Royal College of Surgeons in London, discovered that aspirin and drugs like it inhibit an enzyme that generates a family of potent substances known as prostaglandins.

Prostaglandins were first identified in 1935 by the Swedish physiologist Ulf Svante von Euler (later to become a Nobel laureate). Von Euler observed that semen caused uterine muscle to contract and relax. Thinking that this property of semen came from the prostate gland, he called the active substance prostaglandin. Through von Euler's later work and that of other scientists, it is now known that there are many different prostaglandins and that they can be made and released by almost every cell in the body. Some of them, when injected into humans or animals, produce the signs of

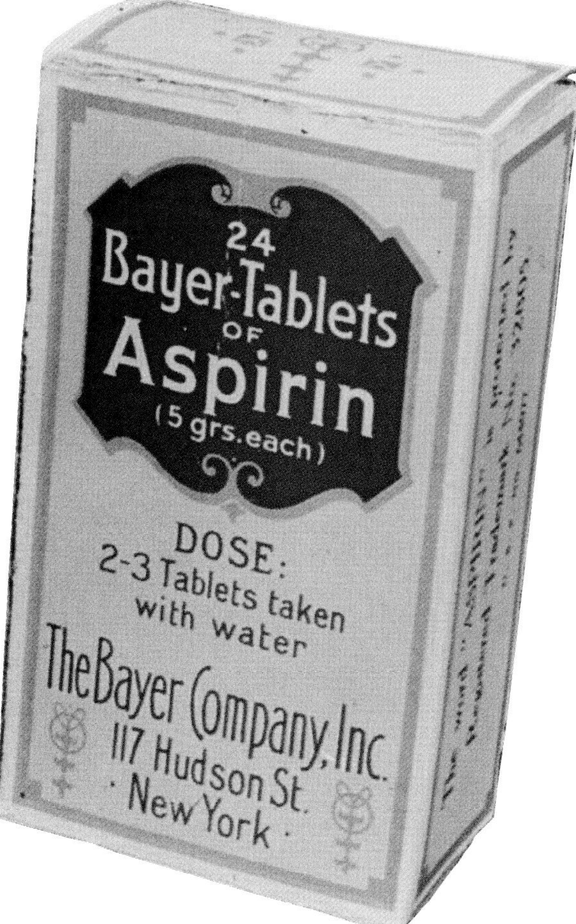

When first marketed, aspirin was sold in the form of a powder (left). The now-familiar aspirin tablet became available a short time later; the package (bottom left) dates from around 1914. Today, nearly a century after aspirin's introduction, medical researchers continue to seek and find new uses for this remarkable remedy.

inflammation and cause fever and headache. An examination of the fluid from a rheumatic knee joint or from the brain of an animal with fever reveals the presence of an excess of prostaglandins. The idea that aspirin-like drugs produce their effects by preventing the generation of prostaglandins received reinforcement from the finding that prostaglandins are released in inflammation and produce swelling, redness, fever, and pain. Thus, scientists concluded, local trauma disturbs the tissues, causing them to release many mediators of inflammation, including prostaglandins, which, in turn, cause inflammation. By removing the prostaglandins, aspirin has a therapeutic effect.

At the same time, the integrity of the stomach lining and continued blood flow to the kidneys are to some extent dependent on the constant physiological generation of a protective prostaglandin; when this substance is removed by aspirin, the drug's typical side effects occur. The most common of these is an upset stomach, caused by aspirin's removal of protective prostaglandins as well as by its local irritant action on the stomach lining (a property not shared to the same degree by other aspirin-like compounds). Some drug manufacturers overcome this irritant effect by placing a special coating on the aspirin tablet, designed to carry it through the stomach before the aspirin is released. In preventing the tablet from dissolving in the stomach, however, these so-called enteric coatings also delay absorption. Moreover, even after it enters the bloodstream, aspirin continues to inhibit production of the protective prostaglandins in the stomach lining.

In 1990 scientists working at the Monsanto Co. proposed that the prostaglandins formed in the stomach and kidneys and those formed in inflamed tissues are made by different enzymes. Molecular biologists at Brigham Young University, Provo, Utah, and other academic institutions then identified an enzyme that appeared only when inflammation was present. It seemed possible, given these findings, that scientists would be able to design aspirin-like drugs to attack selectively the enzyme that makes pro-inflammatory prostaglandins. Several pharmaceutical companies now have such drugs in different stages of development.

An aspirin a day . . . ?

Even though aspirin had its origins in ancient times, scientists learn something new about it virtually every day. Recent investigations have focused on the potential of aspirin to prevent such diverse ailments as heart attack and colon cancer. The following is a brief summary of some of this research.

Cardiovascular disorders. Considerable interest has focused on the antiplatelet effects of aspirin—that is, its ability to counter clumping, or aggregation, of platelets. In the event of an injury, the platelets stick to the sides of a cut or wound and to each other until a "dam," or thrombus, has formed, which thus halts blood loss.

In the last step in aspirin manufacture, the tablets are coated with an ultrafine protective film of acrylic resin. Worldwide, many thousands of tons of acetylsalicylic acid are processed into aspirin every year.

A member of the prostaglandin family called thromboxane is released by the platelets when they are called into action, and it is this substance that makes them stick together. Aspirin, by preventing thromboxane formation, reduces platelet clumping and will prolong the time that a cut will bleed. Scientists also know that platelet thrombi sometimes form within the circulation, and when such a thrombus blocks an artery to the heart or brain, a heart attack or stroke ensues.

Once the antithromboxane activity of aspirin was understood, it was proposed that a daily dose of aspirin might prevent a heart attack or stroke. Large-scale clinical trials were started, at first using fairly high doses of aspirin comparable to those used in treating arthritis—up to six tablets per day. (In the U.S. a single tablet is 325 mg, but the dosage varies slightly from country to country; a tablet in the U.K. is 300 mg.) In 1976, however, Vane (then at the Wellcome Research Laboratories in England) and his colleagues discovered yet another prostaglandin, which they named prostacyclin. This prostaglandin is made by blood vessels and helps to protect them from thrombi by preventing platelets from sticking together. Obviously, stopping the generation of prostacyclin may be harmful, so the search was on to try to find a dose of aspirin that would affect platelet aggregation but not the ability of the blood vessel to make prostacyclin.

Careful work showed that a daily dose of aspirin as low as 75 mg—about a quarter of a tablet—was enough to neutralize thromboxane formation by platelets but was too low to have a substantial effect on prostacyclin production by the blood vessel wall. This selective effect was fascinating in itself. It turned out that aspirin affects the platelets immediately after it is absorbed into the blood draining the stomach. It is then carried by the bloodstream through the liver, where enzymes turn some of it into salicylate; when the blood reaches the arteries of the systemic circulation, it contains very little aspirin but a lot of salicylate, which has little or no action on prostacyclin formation.

Interestingly, aspirin attacks both of the enzymes that form prostaglandins—cyclooxygenase-1, the housekeeping, or constitutive, enzyme in the stomach, blood vessels, and kidneys, and cyclooxygenase-2, which is induced by inflammation. Indeed, the drug is more powerful against cyclooxygenase-1 than against cyclooxygenase-2, a fact that nicely explains the propensity of aspirin to damage the stomach. This fact also accounts for the antiplatelet action of aspirin, as platelets contain only cyclooxygenase-1.

The benefits of a regular low dose of aspirin in preventing a recurrence of heart attack or stroke were first demonstrated in male cardiovascular patients. Subsequent studies confirmed that women who had a history of these conditions could also benefit from prophylactic use of aspirin. Clinical studies performed over many years and recently subjected to sophisticated statistical analyses have shown that regular aspirin use can reduce the recurrence of heart attack or stroke by up to 50%.

Aspirin's usefulness in the primary prevention of heart attack or stroke (*i.e.,* to avert a first occurrence) remains a matter of question. Large-scale U.S. and British studies that sought to resolve the matter were inconclusive. At the present time, therefore, most cardiologists advise the use of daily low-dose aspirin for primary prevention only in people with established risk factors for cardiovascular disease (*e.g.,* family history of cardiovascular disease, elevated cholesterol levels, obesity, smoking).

Aspirin's antiplatelet effects have also been shown to reduce the likelihood of death from blood clots in the lungs and large veins in both men and women. Regular administration of low doses of aspirin increases the success rate of grafted arteries and veins and improves the healing of leg ulcers. The important action of aspirin in both these conditions is clearly to prevent the obstruction of blood vessels by platelet clumps and thus to improve the circulation.

Pregnancy-induced high blood pressure. More than 10% of women pregnant for the first time develop high blood pressure (preeclampsia), which can result in fetal growth retardation and in some cases maternal death. (Preeclampsia may also occur in subsequent pregnancies.) Infants affected by fetal growth retardation are smaller than normal because they do not receive an adequate blood supply in the womb. In addition, many such fetuses fail to develop normally and are born prematurely because the placental blood vessels have become obstructed by platelet thrombi.

Giving regular low doses of aspirin throughout pregnancy to women with a history of high blood pressure or fetal growth retardation in a previous pregnancy has resulted in delivery of healthy infants. The drug reduces the amount of thromboxane released by the platelets and thus decreases their tendency to form thrombi in the placental blood vessels. It also alters the balance between thromboxane and prostacyclin in the maternal blood vessels. A predominance of prostacyclin, the protective prostaglandin, improves both the maternal circulation and blood flow through the placenta.

Colorectal cancer. Cancers of the colon and rectum are the second most common cause of cancer death in the U.S., taking approximately 60,000 lives each year. In the 1970s researchers in Scandinavia observed that there were fewer intestinal cancers among patients receiving aspirin-like drugs for rheumatoid arthritis or taking antithrombotic doses of aspirin than among the general population. Subsequent epidemiological studies in large numbers of adults for more than 10 years concluded that prolonged use of aspirin and other aspirin-like drugs halved the risk of fatal cancer of the esophagus, stomach, colon, and rectum. Other types of cancer were not affected, and acetaminophen (Tylenol, Datril, etc.) did not protect against cancers of the intestine. Several aspirin-like drugs were also shown to reduce the incidence of polyps, the growths that often develop into colonic and rectal tumors. Experimentally induced tumors of the colon in rats and mice similarly regressed after treatment with aspirin, indomethacin, piroxicam, or sulindac.

Is the beneficial action of aspirin in colon cancer due to reduced prostaglandin formation? This may be the case, since most tumor cells, including bowel cancer cells, make greater amounts of prostaglandins than normal cells, and excessive amounts of prostaglandins are found in the blood and urine of patients with bowel cancer. Some prostaglandins promote the growth of cancer cells and inhibit the activity of cells of the immune system that normally fight the cancer. Removal of prostaglandins may lead to an increase in the rate of tumor cell death. The difference in prostaglandin production between cancerous and normal cells is a difference in the level of the inflammatory form of cyclooxygenase. Therefore, the selective inhibitors of this enzyme now under development may also have a potential as anticancer drugs.

Unwanted effects

Although it is an extremely safe drug, aspirin has many mild side effects and some potentially serious ones. As mentioned above, prolonged use of aspirin can damage the stomach lining and cause ulcers throughout the digestive tract. There is no evidence that even high doses of aspirin taken for long periods of time cause kidney damage. Treatment with some of the other, more potent antirheumatic drugs, however, produces toxic effects on the kidney. Again, this problem should not occur with the aspirin-like drugs currently under development, which prevent the generation of inflammatory but not protective prostaglandins. These new medications may become available (after extensive clinical trials) early in the 21st century.

Reye's syndrome. In the 1980s several studies suggested an association between aspirin use and a rare disease of children and young teenagers called Reye's syndrome. The illness is characterized by inflammation of the brain, sometimes leading to delirium and coma, and severe liver damage. Symptoms include irritability, personality changes, lethargy, and vomiting. Although it occurs in fewer than 10 children per million aged under 16, Reye's syndrome is serious—about one-quarter of affected youngsters die. Those who survive may have permanent brain damage.

Reye's syndrome usually occurs after chicken pox or influenza and is believed to arise from an interaction between a virus and the patient's immune system, possibly modified by an outside agent. When children have chicken pox or flu, they often receive antipyretic drugs, including aspirin, and several studies have pointed to aspirin as the external agent in the pathogenesis of Reye's syndrome. Many of the children who developed Reye's syndrome also had preexisting inherited metabolic disorders that rendered them vulnerable to aspirin-mediated alterations in liver metabolism. The evidence of aspirin's role is not entirely conclusive, although it certainly is bolstered by the fact that since 1985, when the U.S. government warned against the use of aspirin in children with chicken pox or flu, the incidence of Reye's syndrome has dropped to the lowest rate in 12 years.

Since 1986 all aspirin sold in the U.S. has been required to carry a warning label cautioning against the use of the drug in children and teenagers with symptoms of chicken pox or flu. Likewise, after discussions between the Committee on Safety of Medicines and the makers of aspirin in the U.K., it was agreed to withdraw children's aspirin from the market there and to warn against aspirin use in children under 12 with chicken pox or flu.

Aspirin-induced asthma. In about 10% of adults who suffer from asthma, swallowing aspirin precipitates an asthma attack. As well as experiencing narrowing of the airways, these individuals may develop allergic rhinitis (sneezing, runny nose) and gastrointestinal or skin reactions. Since other drugs that prevent the formation of prostaglandins also cause these symptoms, some authorities suggested that the crucial factor in aspirin-sensitive asthma might be inhibition of the enzyme that makes prostaglandins.

Prostaglandins are made from the fatty acid arachidonic acid. As mentioned above, the process also involves one of two very similar cyclooxygenase enzymes. Arachidonic acid can also be transformed by another group of enzymes—the lipoxygenases—into leukotrienes, chemical substances related to but different from the prostaglandins. Leukotrienes are particularly effective in causing narrowing of air passages (bronchoconstriction) and, thus, wheezing in asthmatics. Research has shown that compared with asthma patients who are not aspirin-sensitive, those with aspirin sensitivity have higher levels of leukotrienes in their lungs and urine after they take a dose of aspirin. Therefore, asthma attacks in aspirin-sensitive individuals could well be due to overformation of bronchoconstrictor leukotrienes from excess arachidonic acid whose conversion into prostaglandins has been blocked by aspirin. This hypothesis was reinforced when it was discovered that a drug that inactivates the lipoxygenase enzyme also prevents aspirin-induced asthma. Interestingly, unlike aspirin, acetaminophen and salicylate itself do not precipitate asthmatic episodes.

To take or not to take

Because alcohol is a mild irritant to the stomach lining, the use of aspirin and alcohol together may cause more gastric damage than either taken alone. Some research indicates that moderate amounts of alcohol enhance the antiplatelet effect of aspirin taken to prevent heart attacks.

"Sounds like a heart attack. Tell him to take two aspirin and call my office in the morning."

Aspirin exacerbates the danger of blood loss in patients with bleeding disorders. Similarly, while moderate doses of aspirin during pregnancy will not harm the fetus, the drug should be avoided if possible just prior to and during childbirth. If taken during these times, aspirin is likely to increase maternal bleeding, delay the progress of labor, and cause premature closure of fetal blood vessels that should remain open until birth. All of these effects are related to aspirin's ability to block prostaglandin formation. For example, prostaglandin secretion during labor stimulates uterine contractions and thus helps to expel the fetus. Aspirin, because it reduces the production of prostaglandins, slows contractions and thus delays birth. Aspirin and other anti-inflammatory drugs may also reduce the effectiveness of intrauterine contraceptive devices, because such devices depend on the local production of prostaglandins to exert their contraceptive effect—*i.e.,* to prevent the implantation of the ovum in the uterus.

How much is too much?

Large doses of aspirin (30 or more tablets) are toxic to the brain. In an average person, a single dose of 30 or more tablets causes ringing in the ears, nausea, and vomiting. Ingestion of around 80 tablets produces more extreme toxicity, which is evidenced by severe vomiting, overbreathing (hyperventilation), rise in body temperature, mental confusion, coma, and convulsions. A fatal overdose leads to death from kidney failure. Continuous overdosing with more than 15 tablets per day also produces ringing in the ears, overbreathing, acid urine, coma, and convulsions. Salicylate poisoning is treated by washing out the stomach to rid it of any undigested aspirin and by making the urine alkaline to hasten removal from the body of aspirin that already has been absorbed into the bloodstream.

The future

Clearly, aspirin has had a long and useful life. Even should its popularity be eroded by the creation of newer and more specific inhibitors of the enzyme involved in inflammation, it will continue to be important as a prophylactic to reduce heart attacks and strokes.

Recent reports have suggested that aspirin and some other nonsteroidal anti-inflammatory drugs may slow the progress of Alzheimer's disease, dementia, cystic fibrosis, and AIDS. Most aspirin-like drugs do not easily penetrate the physiological barrier known as the blood-brain barrier (which prevents many substances circulating in the blood from entering the brain tissue), but a few such drugs are able to get through. A small clinical study of one of these, indomethacin, suggested that Alzheimer's disease does not progress as rapidly in patients taking the medication as in those not taking it. Eventually, aspirin may also prove to be a cheap and effective agent for helping reduce the incidence of cancer of the colon and possibly other forms of cancer. Other new applications undoubtedly will emerge as scientists learn more about the actions of this fascinating drug.

—Sir John Vane, D.Sc., F.R.S., and Regina Botting, Ph.D.

Take the Plunge: Swimming for Health

The year 1896 was a good one for swimming. The first modern Olympic Games, held in Athens, included swimming events in the Bay of Zea, off the Greek mainland. During the same year in San Francisco, the Sutro Baths, a spectacular recreational facility, was opened for the public. Swimmers had a choice of seven pools of varying sizes and temperatures. Adolph Sutro, an engineering genius (and San Francisco's mayor from 1895 to 1897), designed and built his pleasure palace for the enjoyment of entire families. Sutro always held swimming to be "the very best exercise." As an engineer, he understood the nature of water and how to utilize its dynamics for the body's benefit.

Water's wonders

When the body is cradled by the water, its range of motion, flexibility, energy expenditure, and coordination are all enhanced. The wonder of water is its buoyancy. In neck-deep water the body's apparent weight is one-tenth of its true weight on land. This hydrostatic support of water allows movement to take place without stress on joints, muscles, and organs. Swimming works against the resistance of the water, displacing it in all directions. It strengthens all the major muscle groups simultaneously and improves heart and lung efficiency. Immersion in water produces an "air-conditioning" effect on the body; swimming feels good because it is done in a refreshing "no-sweat" environment.

Adolph Sutro, master engineer and mayor of San Francisco from 1895 to 1897, built his most lavish construction, the Sutro Baths, in 1896. The sumptuous facility included 7 pools, 500 dressing rooms, promenades, 3 restaurants, and more—all under a spectacular glass dome.

Collection of Marilyn Blaisdell

Swimming is an aerobic fitness activity utilizing the cardiovascular system. Furthermore, swimming laps results in the release of natural mood-elevating hormones, endorphins, into the body, which produces an "exerciser's high." An obvious advantage of swimming is the psychological benefit of retreating to the pool and removing one's self from the stress and clamor of the day to the solitude of being cloaked by the water. Fitness swimmers often speak of this meditative and restorative effect on the psyche. For example, Lori Santamorena, a Canadian bank official, says, "Swimming laps helps me focus and put things into perspective, both for work and personal matters. Water is my friend. It's like going back to the womb."

A class of four-year-olds stays afloat with the aid of kickboards. They are among an estimated 4.5 million U.S. children who take swimming lessons each year—lessons they will benefit from all their lives.

Robert E. Daemmrich—Tony Stone Images

Statistics

Swimming is democratic. There are no age limits, ethnic barriers, or necessary skill levels. It provides a lifetime fitness activity. Over 60 million Americans say that they participate in aquatic activities—at summer camps, public and private schools, country clubs, community and municipal recreation centers, YMCAs and YWCAs, health clubs, spas, and resorts.

The National Spa and Pool Institute reports that there are approximately 6.6 million swimming pools in the United States. In 1995 the American Red Cross alone trained 175,000 lifeguards. The National Recreation and Park Association estimates that 4.5 million children take "learn-to-swim" lessons per year. According to the National Interscholastic Swimming Coaches Association of America, there are 5,500 high-school swimming pools and nearly 200,000 students participating in swimming, diving, and water polo.

The American Swimming Coaches Association tabulates approximately 500 colleges that offer men's and/or women's swimming and diving programs nationwide. And there are over 30,000 men and women who are registered with U.S. Masters Swimming, Inc., many of whom are fitness swimmers. These are adults from 19 to 102 years old, grouped according to age, who compete in a full complement of swimming events.

The Fédération Internationale de Natation Amateur (FINA), based in Switzerland, is the governing body for all competitive aquatic activities worldwide. Since 1986 FINA has served as host of World Masters Championships in Japan, Australia, Brazil, the U.S., Canada, and, in 1996, Sheffield, England, where more than 4,500 Masters swimmers from some 1,280 clubs representing 46 nations competed.

Swim strokes

All swim strokes begin from a streamlined body position. Each arm motion consists of a catch, pull, and recovery. The breathing pattern and leg kick combine with the arm stroke and coordinate for forward propulsion.

The crawl: getting it right. The *crawl* (or *freestyle,* as it is called in competition), is the most popular swimming stroke and is usually the first swimming stroke learned in North America. "I can swim but I can't breathe." This is the most frequently heard comment by reluctant "crawlers." This stroke begins from a prone streamlined position with the face submerged to the hairline. The skill that needs to be learned for the crawl stroke is rhythmic breathing and the coordination of breathing with the arm motion. As one turns the head to one side, one inhales, with the opposite arm extended forward. The breath is taken through nose and mouth, with the head pivoting downward into the water while exhaling through both nose and mouth, forming bubbles continuously. The most important advice is *never hold the breath!*

The crawl stroke utilizes the alternating flutter kick. The body should maintain a streamlined position while arms provide more forward propulsion than the legs. For greater upper-body and stroke efficiency, one can use the "S-shaped" pull—tracing a question mark with the right arm and a reverse question mark with the left. This way one moves "still"

Thomas Zimmermann—Tony Stone Images

Triathlon enthusiasts plunge into the first segment of what will be a grueling long-distance competition by any standards—one that includes a 1.5-km open-water swim, a 40-km bicycle race, and, last but not least, a 10-km run.

water instead of water already in motion. A "body roll" adds greater power and efficiency to the crawl stroke by using the strong back and shoulder muscles during the arm pull.

Backstroke: shoulder power. The backstroke is begun from a streamlined back-float position that allows for regular breathing because the face is out of the water. Arms move in an alternating backward "windmill" motion. A continuous flutter kick is employed. To swim most efficiently, one should use the bent-arm "S-shaped" pull. This allows the body to roll alternately in the direction of each pull, engaging the large muscles of the back and shoulders for extra power.

The backstroke made simple. In the elementary backstroke, both arms and legs are entirely under water, moving simultaneously and symmetrically from a streamlined back-float position. The arms begin at one's sides; then the fingertips slide up along the body to the underarms for the recovery, in which the arms extend outward from the shoulders. Finally the arms sweep straight downward to the outer thighs for the pull. This glide position is held momentarily before one begins the cycle again. The elementary backstroke usually employs either the frog or the whip kick. The conventional frog kick is executed by bending the knees wider than hip width before the legs extend and snap together. The competitive whip kick is done with the knees bending at a point narrower than hip width before the lower legs snap together for the propulsion phase. Despite its simplicity, the elementary backstroke offers a good muscular and aerobic workout for the arms and legs.

Breaststroke: European elegance. In Europe the breaststroke is usually the first stroke taught. It begins from a streamlined prone-float position with the face in the water; one raises the head to inhale while pulling forward symmetrically under water with a "heart-shaped" arm motion. One submerges the face and exhales through both nose and mouth as the arms extend forward and glide. The kick is done symmetrically under water; it helps strengthen and tone inner and outer thighs. Two kicks are popular: the frog kick and the whip kick. With either, the stroke is smooth and elegant.

Winging it: the butterfly. The butterfly is often considered the most challenging, energetic stroke. Begun from a prone position, the stroke involves the arms pulling simultaneously in a symmetrical "keyhole" stroke. The head and shoulders rise out of the water so one can inhale while simultaneously pulling backward. The arms then recover out of the water, and one exhales. The dolphin kick is done with the legs moving in an undulating motion, which promotes flexibility of the back, but the butterfly is generally not advised for those with lower-back problems.

Choosing sides. One begins the sidestroke in a streamlined position, on either side. Because one's face remains above the waterline, one can breathe freely. Inhaling is done while pulling and kicking; exhaling is coordinated with extending the body and getting a good glide. The sidestroke arm motion is either an overarm motion, in which the hand and arm come out of the water, or a sweeping motion through the water. The sidestroke kick can be either a scissors kick (top leg forward) or an inverted scissors kick (top leg back). The body tucks as legs and arms come together. The arms and legs share equal power in this relaxing, two-phased stroke.

First things first

Most swimmers who seek to get fit find it most convenient to swim in a pool—indoors or out. But while working out in a pool is the norm, one can also swim for fitness in an open body of water such as a lake, bay, quarry, stream, or ocean. Open-water swim adherents say they enjoy the heightened experience of sustaining the momentum of their stroke—with no walls and no turns or flips necessary. Also, open bodies of water often are salt water or brackish (a mix of salt and fresh water), which has the advantage of providing extra buoyancy. Many experienced swimmers enjoy competing in open-water events. In triathlon competitions, open-water distance swimming is one of the three sports (distance bicycling and running are the other two).

NEWS CAP

Playing Fair: Drug Testing at the Olympics

Performance-enhancing drugs can make the difference between winning and losing the gold. Just ask Canadian sprinter Ben Johnson, winner and loser at the 1988 Olympic Summer Games in Seoul, South Korea.

Anticipation. Anticipating substance abuse at the 1996 Olympic Summer Games in Atlanta, Ga., the U.S. Olympic Committee sought to ensure that no one came out of the blocks with an unfair advantage; the committee had budgeted $1.5 million for drug testing and education. More than ever before, U.S. athletes were randomly called upon to produce urine samples that were then subjected to highly sensitive tests that could detect even tiny amounts of banned substances. Testing was mandatory for all medal winners.

Yet, as testing procedures became more refined, illegal doping techniques employed by cheating athletes became increasingly sophisticated. As officials focused on testing for anabolic steroids (synthetic steroid hormones that temporarily increase muscle size and power), some athletes began using endogenous hormones (synthesized by the body). Their belief was that endogenous, or "natural," hormones could not be detected as easily. Testosterone was the "drug of choice" among the determined competitors. Officials, however, countered with tests that measured the levels of testosterone and the related hormone epitestosterone (the former may vary over time, but the latter changes only after doping).

The tests are not foolproof, however, and some Olympic hopefuls responded by carefully manipulating their hormone levels to produce false results. Others going for the gold turned to substances that have shorter half-lives and thus are eliminated from the body in a relatively short time, which reduces the chances of detection.

Regrettably, a few of the losers in this game of hide-and-seek had not even intended to play; some athletes tested positive for the use of drugs they did not know were illegal. There are very fine distinctions; for example, phenylephrine HCL and pheniramine maleate (Dristan Nasal Mist) are illegal, but oxymetazoline HCL (Dristan Long Lasting Nasal Spray) is not; terfenadine (Seldane) is okay, but terfenadine with the common decongestant pseudoephedrine (Seldane-D) is not. So that athletes would know the rules, the Olympic Committee provided a confidential hot line. Another up-to-date source is the *Athletic Drug Reference,* published by Clean Data, Inc. (for the drug company Glaxo, Inc.).

Jeff Rouse, captain of the U.S. men's Olympic swim team, who won a silver medal in the 100-m backstroke in 1992 (and then a gold medal for the same event in '96), spent much of the time between Olympics launching a campaign that called for random testing of athletes outside competition, harsher penalties for all offenders, and a lifetime ban from Olympic competition for any swimmer who tests positive. His militant stance won him both friends and foes (and even some personal threats of sabotage). Nonetheless, Rouse maintained that getting strict sooner rather than later was the only way.

Winners and losers. Accusations of steroid use surfaced in Atlanta when a previously unheralded 26-year-old Irish swimmer, Michelle Smith, made big waves by winning three

The crème de la crème of open-water distance swims is the English Channel, the narrow seaway between Calais, France, and Dover, England—a swim of approximately 38 km (24 mi). There are many other challenging open-water competitive events around the world.

Then, too, there are those who find it invigorating to take midwinter dips. "Polar Bear" club members annually appear on the beach at Coney Island in Brooklyn, N.Y., where they splash into the frigid waters of the Atlantic Ocean on New Year's Day. Similar events occur in many other cold-climate locales. In the U.S, Midwestern "polar bears" brave the Great Lakes every January 1. A similar activity that attracts some hearty Russians is called "walrusing"; the enthusiasts cut a hole in the surface of a frozen lake and then courageously plunge into the icy but stimulating waters below.

Fitness swimming tips for everyone

The latest official U.S. fitness guidelines say that one should get a medical checkup before beginning an exercise program if one has a very sedentary lifestyle, if one has two or more known cardiovascular risk factors or other health problems, and if one is a man over age 40 or a woman over 50 with risk factors. Younger, healthy people need not consult a physician but should always start their exercise program slowly and build up gradually. Some other tips and protocols for swimmers are as follows:

- Always swim with supervision. Never swim alone!
- A swim workout should include the key elements of any workout: a five-minute warm-up, the main set, and a five-minute cooldown. An ideal recommended total workout

gold medals and one bronze. Smith, who had failed to win a medal in two previous Olympics, knocked an astounding 19 seconds off her personal best time in taking the gold in the 400-m freestyle. She also won gold medals in the 200-m and 400-m individual medley and a bronze in the 200-m butterfly. In the full glare of the media, Smith, who had passed four drug tests since May 1996, denied all accusations. Those accusations were prompted not only by the brilliance of her out-of-nowhere performance but also because her husband and trainer, former Dutch discus thrower Erik de Bruin, had been suspended from competition after testing positive for steroid use in 1993. Controversy may have tarnished Smith's performance in Atlanta, but back in Ireland she was celebrated as a national hero.

Richard Mackson—Sports Illustrated

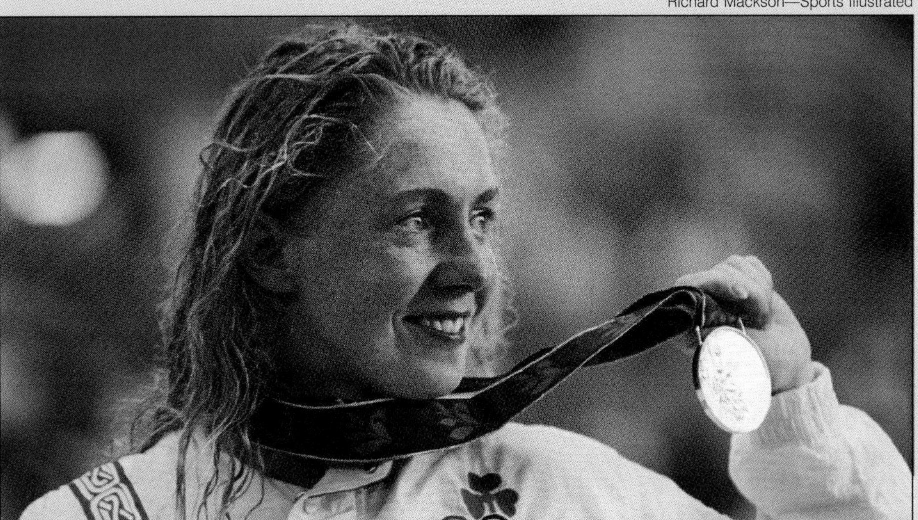

Irish swimming phenomenon Michelle Smith, 26, went home from the 1996 Summer Olympics with three gold medals and one bronze, under heavy suspicion that she had used performance-enhancing drugs.

There was no ambiguity, however, in the tests that revealed that two track-and-field competitors, Bulgarian triple jumper Iva Prandzheva and Russian hurdler Natalya Shekodanova, had used performance-enhancing drugs. The day after the completion of the Games, the International Olympic Committee (IOC) announced that Prandzheva, who finished fourth in her event, had tested positive for the anabolic steroid metadienone, while Shekodanova, the seventh-place finisher in the 100-m hurdles, tested positive for stanozolol, the drug responsible for Johnson's downfall. The results were detected by standard testing equipment rather than new high-resolution mass spectrometers, which are reportedly three times more effective in identifying steroids. Five other athletes were exonerated when the IOC announced that there was insufficient evidence to indicate that the implicated drug bromantan was a stimulant.

The real losers, though, were neither those who were "caught" inadvertently nor those who were caught for true deception but rather those who used banned substances and paid with their lives. Reportedly, six European cyclists died before the 1996 Olympics after using a dangerous synthetic version of erythropoietin, which increases the oxygen-carrying capacity of blood.

—*Jeff Wallenfeldt*

time is 30–45 minutes, swimming three to four days a week on alternate days.

- One should be considerate of other swimmers—*e.g.,* circling counterclockwise when more than two swimmers are in one lane. To pass a slower swimmer, one should tap the person on the foot and pass at the wall just before turning. (Swimming, however, is not to be a contact sport!)
- One should drink plenty of water both before and after swimming. Having a water bottle to drink from during a long swim is recommended.
- One should pace all workouts and rest when necessary. "Start slowly" and "listen to the body" are the rules for any safe exercise program.
- If pain, shortness of breath, dizziness, or disorientation occurs during exercise, one should stop swimming and rest out of the water.

When one chooses to swim in open water, there are certain considerations that will ensure safety.

- One should always apply waterproof sunscreen.
- One should research the open body of water before swimming in it—*i.e.,* know about its tides, currents, marine life, boats and other vessels, possible pollutants, etc. One should not take unnecessary chances, particularly in storms.
- It is important to acclimatize oneself to the colder water before becoming immersed. Hypothermia (cooling of the body's core temperature below normal range) is a real risk and therefore must be a concern for the open-water swimmer.
- Open-water swimmers often wear wet suits, which help keep the body warm as well as add to the water's buoyancy.
- In open water one should swim parallel to the shore. One should swim with a buddy and/or be followed by someone in a small craft.

It is easy to overestimate one's ability, but, more important, it is dangerous!

(continued on page 346)

Author Jane Katz has competed in every World Masters Championship, sponsored by the Switzerland-based Fédération Internationale de Natation Amateur—taking home gold medals from each.

© Douglas Kirkland

NEWS CAP

Mop That Floor, Tread That Mill

Everyone has heard it before: to be physically fit, one must engage in an activity that gets the pulse revved up to a "target" zone (based on one's age and maximum heart rate) for 20 minutes. Right? Wrong.

According to a consensus development panel convened by the National Institutes of Health in December 1995, it is not necessary to swim the Hellespont to reap significant cardiovascular benefits from exercise. Citing recent studies indicating that more than 50% of Americans get little or no exercise and mindful of the fact that heart disease remains the single greatest cause of death in the U.S., the panel of experts on physical activity and cardiovascular disease stated that 30 minutes of moderate exercise per day can lower mortality and reduce heart disease for those who are inactive but otherwise healthy. Swimming, cycling, brisk walking, and even yard work and house cleaning qualify as moderate exercise. Moreover, three 10-minute stints a day are perfectly acceptable.

The panel also refuted the notion that anyone about to undertake a physical fitness program should first consult a physician. While it is recommended that men over 40 and women over 50 with two or more cardiovascular risk factors (*i.e.,* sedentary lifestyle, diabetes, high blood pressure, elevated cholesterol levels, cigarette smoking, obesity) check with their doctors first, the panel gave the go-ahead for most people to start exercising right away.

The get-up-and-exercise message was reaffirmed in a big way on the eve of the opening of the Centennial Olympic Games with the release of *Physical Activity and Health: A Report of the Surgeon General.* Two years in the making, the first surgeon general's report on fitness was issued on July 11, 1996, at a White House ceremony. The six-chapter document recommends *any* activity that burns 150 calories per day or 1,000 calories per week—*e.g.,* washing and waxing a car for 45 minutes or pushing a stroller 2.4 km (1.5 mi) in 30 minutes. The report was called "a passport to good health for all Americans" by Donna E. Shalala, secretary of health and human services, and "more than a summary of the science . . . a national call to action" by acting surgeon general Audrey F. Manley. Vice Pres. Al Gore, present at the ceremony, said, "To put it as politely as possible: Americans, take a walk!"

Across the Atlantic, England's Health Education Authority launched the £9 million "Active for Life" campaign in 1996 to get its population off their duffs. A recent survey showed that 60% of men and 70% of women were insufficiently active, even though they knew exercise would be good for them. Realistic activities like walking part of the way to work or school, dancing, and taking stairs instead of an elevator are the types of exercise that the British are recommending.

No matter which side of the Atlantic they are on, those who choose to expend their energy indoors on a machine may be interested in the findings of researchers from the Medical College of Wisconsin and Veterans Affairs Medical Center, Milwaukee, published in the *Journal of the American Medical Association* (May 8, 1996). The investigators compared the workouts provided by six types of machines: a stationary bicycle, a cycle ergometer that works the arms and legs, a cross-country ski machine, a rowing ergometer, a stair-stepper, and a treadmill. Exercising at a perceived level of exertion that was "somewhat hard" on a treadmill burned the most calories (about 700 per hour) and provided the best overall aerobic exercise. The energy expenditure was lowest (498 calories per hour) for subjects who rode the stationary cycle.

—Jeff Wallenfeldt

Many Ways to Burn 150 Calories

More vigorous, less time

Climbing stairs for 15 minutes

Shoveling snow for 15 minutes

Running 1 1/2 miles in 15 minutes

Jumping rope for 15 minutes

Bicycling 4 miles in 15 minutes

Playing a game of basketball for 15–20 minutes

Playing wheelchair basketball for 20 minutes

Swimming laps for 20 minutes

Performing water aerobics for 30 minutes

Walking 2 miles in 30 minutes

Raking leaves for 30 minutes

Pushing a stroller 1 1/2 miles in 30 minutes

Dancing fast for 30 minutes

Bicycling 5 miles in 30 minutes

Shooting baskets for 30 minutes

Walking 1 3/4 miles in 35 minutes

Wheeling oneself in a wheelchair for 30–40 minutes

Gardening for 30–45 minutes

Playing touch football for 30–45 minutes

Playing volleyball for 45 minutes

Washing windows or floors for 45–60 minutes

Washing and waxing a car for 45–60 minutes

Less vigorous, more time

C Goll

Source: *Physical Activity and Health: A Report of the Surgeon General*, 1996.

These senior citizens enjoying a water aerobics class know that one does not need to be a master swimmer to derive benefits—and pleasure—from the water. The water's buoyancy enables a wide range of motion and considerable energy expenditure without straining joints or muscles.

(continued from page 344)

Gearing up

What does one need besides water and the motivation to take the plunge? The following are useful:

- A comfortable *swimsuit* is basic.
- *Goggles* help protect eyes and improve underwater vision.
- A *swim cap* helps keep hair dry and protected from chlorine; wearing a cap also streamlines the body.
- Various *aquatic equipment* can add variety to a swim workout. For example, *hand paddles* can be used to help strengthen upper-body muscles. *Kickboards* aid in supporting the upper body, enabling the swimmer to exercise the legs alone. *Pull-buoys* add buoyancy and support for the lower body. *Fins* are useful for providing added resistance for large leg muscles and helping to develop flexibility of feet and ankles.
- A *pace-clock* or a *waterproof wristwatch* can be used for timing oneself.
- A *log* can be used for recording one's distance, timing, and progress.

Rx: swim!

Physical Activity and Health: A Report of the Surgeon General, *released in July 1996, has determined that a lack of physical activity is detrimental to your health.*

Today swimming is medicine, which, when properly prescribed, can help prevent or alleviate many disabling conditions such as heart disease, stroke, hypertension, and diabetes, as well as obesity, arthritis, and depression, among others. Many people who are limited in their ability to exercise on land can benefit greatly from the buoyancy, freedom of movement, and safety of being in water. Those who choose to swim for fitness or do in-water exercise can gain the physical and psychological benefits of either type of program.

Obesity. Overweight people often use fitness swimming as part of an initial conditioning program and to help them lose weight at a safe rate. The buoyancy of the water cushions the body, reducing the strain on the heart and lungs, easing discomfort, and minimizing the risk of an orthopedic injury—all of which can occur while exercising on land.

Arthritis. The warmth of the water, its buoyancy, and the resistance it provides make swimming and in-water exercise especially effective in decreasing the pain and stiffness of arthritis. Many arthritis sufferers enjoy greater joint flexibility, comfort, and mobility as a result of their water workouts.

Osteoporosis. The loss of bone density that is common in postmenopausal women can be reduced by weight-bearing exercise such as water aerobics performed in shallow water. In particular, those at risk for osteoporosis benefit from the frequent turns and push-offs in a fitness-swimming workout. Here swimming in small pools, such as those found in some health clubs, hotels, and backyards, is a plus. Swimming, of course, is only one part of osteoporosis prevention. Hormone replacement therapy, calcium, vitamin D, fluoride, and various new drugs may also be prescribed.

Asthma. Because the air near the surface of water is generally freer of dust and pollutants than most outdoor air, a swimming pool can be the ideal exercise environment and swimming the ideal form of physical activity for the person with asthma. A number of Olympic swimmers have histories of asthma—1996 gold medalists Tom Dolan and Amy Van Dyken among them.

Some people suffer from "exercise-induced asthma"—airway narrowing that occurs minutes after one begins a vigorous activity; for them, energetic exercise may be the only condition that provokes an attack. This does not mean that they should not exercise, however. The exerciser can usually avoid exertion-induced symptoms with appropriate management of the asthma. Usually inhaled anti-inflammatory medications used 5–60 minutes before swimming will prevent symptoms for as long as several hours. To be safest, the swimmer with asthma should always take appropriate medication (usually an inhaler) to the pool and should inform the lifeguard of his or her medical condition.

The physically challenged. The water provides a positive environment for persons with physical disabilities. Passage of the Americans with Disabilities Act in 1990 stipulated that persons with disabilities must have access to all public accommodations and commercial facilities, which include health clubs, gymnasiums, and swimming pools. There are aquatic programs that enable persons with physical disabilities to participate along with able-bodied persons in recreational swimming programs. There are also adapted swimming competitions such as the Paralympics and the Special Olympics.

Mental health. Therapists have been gratified by the positive response that people with a wide range of psychological problems have shown to water activities. From their participation in aquatic exercise, those suffering from depression, anxiety, and other psychological or emotional disorders derive the benefits of relaxation, increased vigor, and increased self-esteem at the mastery of new skills.

Aquatic advice

Swimming burns calories at a higher rate than many other physical activities. Swimmers can burn up as many as 600 calories per hour. (Variables including exertion level, swimming ability, body weight, and water temperature can affect this number.) Swimming thus is good for weight loss. Those who are attempting to maintain their weight should replace the calories burned with nutritious foods.

Chlorine is a basic water sanitizer used to kill bacteria in pools. The amount of chlorine used in properly maintained swimming pools is not harmful to human health. Chlorine can, however, affect the skin's natural oils; one can prevent dry skin by showering after swimming and applying a moisturizing lotion. Dyed, permed, or chemically processed hair is prone to damage in chlorinated water, but swimmers can easily keep hair protected and dry by wearing a well-fitting latex or silicone swim cap. Wearing a Lycra cap under a silicone cap provides added comfort and dryness. New ionization technology for pool water has been developed, which provides an alternative for pool sanitation.

Athlete's foot (tinea pedis) can easily occur in the pool area and in locker rooms and showers if feet are not dried properly. There are many over-the-counter antifungal preparations to help treat the condition.

To help protect against "swimmer's ear" (otitis externa; an inflammation of the outer ear), one can use swimmers' earplugs to protect the ear canal. An alternative is to use a small amount of lamb's wool coated with petroleum jelly

Photographs, Tony Stone Images;
(opposite page) Zigy Kalunzy; (below) Robert E. Daemmrich

At the 1992 Paralympic Games in Barcelona, Spain, male amputees compete in one of many swimming events. Swimming is a sport in which physically challenged athletes from around the world continue to excel.

Courtesy of Jane Katz

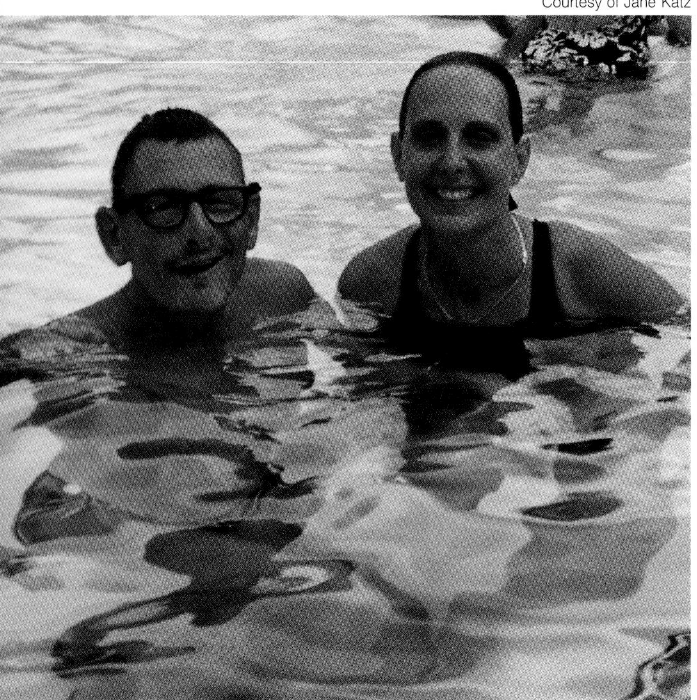

John Williams of San Diego, Calif. (left), is an aquatic instructor who works with people with disabilities and special exercise needs. Williams, who is affected by cerebral palsy, is an inspiration to all who know him—including the author (right)—in or out of the pool.

to seal the ear canal. Goggles are highly recommended if one normally wears contact lenses. Glasses wearers can order special prescription goggles or now can buy over-the-counter Speedo goggles that are available in diopter increments from −1.5 to −8.0.

Swimming during menstruation is possible and can even be helpful—as long as a tampon is used. During menstruation, women who swim report less severe cramps and lower back pain. Some women find that premenstrual distress is lessened. This may be because water and salt are removed from the body during swimming; being in the water is a natural diuretic. Women can swim safely during pregnancy if they use a few commonsense precautions, such as avoiding crowded pools, extreme water temperatures, and overexertion.

Swimmers with a fever, a bad cold, or upper-respiratory discomfort should remain out of the water until they have recovered. Vaginitis and cystitis are inflammations and may be uncomfortable but do not preclude swimming. If a woman has a yeast infection requiring treatment, she should consult a physician and follow his or her advice about swimming. According to the Centers for Disease Control and Prevention, HIV infection and AIDS are not spread in swimming pools. With most common skin disorders, people can continue swimming. Anyone who has an open sore or more serious skin condition should check with his or her doctor first.

Sensible safety precautions should be followed in the locker room. Water shoes, for example, are recommended for sure footing on wet floors, and toiletries should be kept in small plastic, rather than glass, containers. Thorough drying of hair, skin, ears, and feet helps the swimmer stay healthy.

See you poolside!

The Centennial Olympic Games in Atlanta, Ga., left the legacy of another state-of-the-art natatorium that is now part of the stock of great aquatic facilities around the world. Thousands of fitness swimmers and aquatic exercisers will enjoy the use of these pools well into the 21st century.

The decades of the '70s and '80s spawned a new industry of health pursuits. The baby-boomer generation spearheaded this fitness revolution. It is this same demographic group that, having experienced shin splints and other mementos of high-impact aerobics, is now finding its way into swimming pools, often at the recommendation of sports medicine specialists. The 1968 Olympic decathlon gold medalist, Bill Toomey, for example, has recently taken up swimming and exercising in water as therapy following back surgery.

Swimming is for everyone, a lifetime fitness activity whose appeal is increasing globally. All signs suggest that swimming will remain a preferred fitness activity in the 21st century.

—Jane Katz, Ed.D.

FITNESS SWIMMING RESOURCES

Publications

- Katz, Jane, Ed.D. *The All-American Aquatic Handbook: Your Passport to Lifetime Fitness.* Boston: Allyn and Bacon, 1996; telephone 1-800-278-3525.
- Katz, Jane, Ed.D. *The New W.E.T. Workout®: Water Exercise Techniques for Strengthening, Toning, and Lifetime Fitness.* New York: Facts on File, 1996; telephone 1-800-322-8755.
- *Aquatics International* magazine
6151 Powers Ferry Rd NW
Atlanta GA 30339
(770) 955-2500

Organizations

- Fédération Internationale de Natation Amateur (FINA)
avenue de Beaumont 9
Rez-de-chaussée
1012 Lausanne, Switzerland
(41-21) 312-66-02
- International Swimming Hall of Fame
1 Hall of Fame Dr
Fort Lauderdale FL 33316
(305) 462-6536
- National Spa and Pool Institute
2111 Eisenhower Ave
Alexandria VA 22314
(703) 838-0083
- Special Olympics International
1325 G Street NW, Suite 500
Washington DC 20005
(202) 628-3630
- U.S. Masters Swimming, Inc.
2 Peter Ave
Rutland MA 01543
(508) 886-6631

Update on Birth Control Pills

Women have sought for centuries to control their reproductive destiny. Oral contraceptives (OCs) offer them an extremely effective method of birth control. Over the past decade 25% to 30% of women of childbearing age in the United States have used OCs, or about 18.7 million women a year. Some three-quarters of all U.S. women—more than 40 million—have used them at some point in their lives for an average of five years. So well established are OCs as the contraceptive choice of American women that women occasionally will say, "I'm on birth control"—meaning, "I'm on birth control pills"—just as *the Pill* is a common shorthand for all birth control pills.

The formulations known as combined oral contraceptives contain two hormones, an estrogen and a progestin, that are quite similar to those made by the female body during the reproductive years. Over 95% of women who take birth control pills use a combined OC. The combined pills work primarily by stopping ovulation, but they also affect the lining of the uterus and the mucus of the cervix in ways that prevent fertilization and implantation. Three OCs marketed in the United States contain a progestin alone. These progestin-only pills may be appropriate for some women who, for various health reasons, cannot take estrogen.

Since 1960 close to 60 brands of OCs have been marketed in the U.S. alone. One could argue that there have actually been far too many pills for women—or even their doctors—to fully understand the differences. Adding to the confusion, in several instances pills with exactly the same kind of estrogen and progestin in exactly the same dosage have been marketed under different brand names. (Worldwide more than 100 brands of combined OCs are being sold, but all are variations of six or seven basic formulations. Occasionally similar names are used in different countries for quite different formulations.)

The nearly 40 years of experience in oral contraceptive prescribing and use have enabled medical scientists to reach several firm conclusions:

- A dramatic decline in the dose of both the estrogen and progestin components makes today's OCs much safer than their predecessors.
- A vast literature on prescribing OCs provides insight into who should and should not use this form of contraception.
- Medical scientists have made important discoveries about the noncontraceptive benefits of OCs, and women are often given birth control pills to produce desirable effects other than prevention of unwanted pregnancies.
- Controversy and negative publicity have never been far from the Pill. The debate over the risk for deep vein thrombosis in women taking so-called third-generation pills is only the most recent example.

The following explores each of these points in detail.

Safer pills

To a great extent, the increased safety of combined birth control pills is due to a decrease in hormone dosage. Today's combined oral contraceptives contain far less estrogen, progestin, or both than the pills used a generation ago. Most OCs today contain estrogen in the form of ethinyl estradiol. In fact, all of the so-called low-dose pills (those with less than 50 µg [micrograms] of estrogen) use ethinyl estradiol as the estrogen component of the formulation. The amount of ethinyl estradiol has declined from 100 µg in 1960 to as little as 20 µg in some current pills.

Even more dramatic has been the decrease in the amount of one commonly used progestin, norethindrone. One of the earliest combined pills provided 10 mg of norethindrone. Today most combined pills contain 0.5 mg, and one has only 0.4 mg—96% less than that first-generation pill. The decreased dosage, and thus the increased safety of birth control pills, has led to a movement in the U.S. to make them available over the counter (that is, without a prescription).

Better guidelines

The question of who can and cannot use OCs has been on the minds of American women and their clinicians since 1960, when the Pill first went on the market in the U.S. Initially, birth control pills were prescribed to almost any woman who wanted them. A decade later concern about OC users' increased risks for cardiovascular disorders (strokes, blood clots in the veins and lungs) caused the pendulum to swing in the opposite direction. This trend toward restriction may have gone too far, though, and made it unnecessarily difficult for some women who were good candidates for OCs to obtain them.

Preventing Unwanted Pregnancies

Contraceptive use by U.S. women aged 15–44

Method	Married women using method (percentage)	Unmarried women using method (percentage)	Total
Pill	28	52	39
Sterilization	27	10	19
Condom	19	33	25
Withdrawal	6	11	8
Rhythm	5	4	4
Diaphragm	4	4	4
Sponge	3	3	3
Suppository	1	3	3
Douche	<0.5	4	3
IUD	1	1	1
Foam	1	1	1
Cream/jelly	1	1	1
Implant	<0.5	1	1
Cervical cap	<0.5	<0.5	<0.5
All methods, total	97	92	94
None	3	8	6

Note: Individuals may use more than one method.

Adapted from Jacqueline Darroch Forrest and Richard R. Fordyce, "Women's Contraceptive Attitudes and Use in 1992," *Family Planning Perspectives,* vol. 25, no. 4 (July/August 1993)

Robert Burke—Gamma Liaison

Birth control pills are the contraceptive of choice among U.S. women, taken by 25–30% of women of childbearing age over the past decade—or about 18.7 million women a year.

In the mid-1990s the World Health Organization (WHO) convened clinicians from throughout the world to devise a system for determining the appropriateness of oral contraceptive use. That system established rankings from one to four for medical conditions that should be taken into consideration by a physician in deciding whether to prescribe birth control pills for a particular patient. A given health status or disease may be graded as a condition for which (1) there is no restriction on the use of combined OCs, (2) the advantages of using combined pills generally outweigh the theoretical or proven risks, (3) the theoretical or proven risks usually outweigh the advantages, or (4) the use of combined pills presents an unacceptable health risk. Under the new system some women with conditions that formerly would have excluded them as candidates for OCs—for example, being over age 40 (even if a healthy nonsmoker) or having had surgery for gallbladder disease—are now eligible (in grade 2) to take combined pills. On the other hand, being a smoker over age 35 or having current symptomatic gallbladder disease (both grade-3 conditions) probably rules out OC use. Conditions in grade 4—for example, active viral hepatitis, liver tumors—definitely preclude the use of birth control pills.

Broader uses

Contraception is not the sole reason women take birth control pills. OC use may have a number of beneficial effects on a woman's menstrual cycles, helping to regulate irregular cycles and, most important, diminishing menstrual cramps, pain, and blood loss. Studies have shown that OCs reduce the risk for ovarian cancer and cancer of the endometrium (the lining of the uterus), benign breast masses, and ovarian cysts.

Birth control pills have also been used to reduce premenstrual symptoms, to treat endometriosis (abnormal growth of endometrial tissue) and acne, and to prevent ectopic pregnancy. It should be noted, however, that a woman using the Pill is not certain to receive all these benefits. In fact, some women may actually find that one or more of these problems become worse when they take OCs.

Unintended pregnancies: not an exception

In spite of the wide range of contraceptive options available to U.S. women, most pregnancies are unintended (*i.e.,* mistimed or altogether unwanted). During the 1970s and early 1980s, the proportion of births that were unintended at conception decreased. Between 1982 and 1988, however, this trend was reversed, and the reversal appears to be continuing into the 1990s. In 1990 about 44% of all births were the result of unintended pregnancy. Among teens, 95% of pregnancies were unintended.

There are several basic reasons why couples experience unplanned pregnancies:

- They do not use any contraceptive.
- They use a contraceptive but do not use it correctly.
- They use a contraceptive but do not use it every time they have intercourse.
- They use a contraceptive consistently and correctly but still become pregnant—*i.e.,* the contraceptive fails.

Just how successful *is* contraception? In 1988 the 60.3% of U.S. women who used contraceptives had 47% of the unintended pregnancies, while the 6.7% of women who used no contraception (but were not trying to conceive) had 53% of the unintended pregnancies. Expressed another way, 1.5 million of the 34.9 million contraceptive users became pregnant, but 1.7 million—or nearly half—of the 3.9 million women using no contraception had unintended pregnancies.

Unplanned pregnancies have many adverse repercussions—for the woman, her family, and society at large. About half of all unintended pregnancies are terminated by abortion, for example, and, as noted above, an enormous percentage involve teenagers, who are ill-equipped to be parents. Unplanned additions to families exert economic and emotional pressures on each family member. Further, women who do not plan to become pregnant are less likely than others to get appropriate prenatal care. They are also more likely to smoke and drink during pregnancy, practices that have been linked to birth defects. Low birth weight and infant mortality are increased in unintended pregnancies.

There is no question that contraception reduces the rate of unintended pregnancies. A serious effort must be made to use contraceptives correctly and consistently, however, and it is important to choose a method with the lowest possible failure rate. Couples using methods other than condoms should strongly consider condoms as a backup, especially if there is any risk of infection. After having one or two children, women might want to consider the intrauterine device (IUD) called the copper T 380A, a contraceptive that has an extremely low failure rate and can be left in place for a prolonged period (at least 10 years) but that may slightly increase the risk for pelvic infection. Once an individual's family is complete, permanent sterilization—vasectomy for men or tubal ligation for women—may be considered an option. Anyone who chooses permanent sterilization should, of course, understand that these procedures are very difficult to reverse.

(continued on page 352)

NEWS CAP

Better Paps

Cancer of the uterine cervix is a gynecologic cancer that is highly preventable; still, it strikes about 500,000 women in the world yearly. In the U.S. alone, an estimated 65,000 new cases were diagnosed in 1995, and some 5,000 American women were killed by the disease. This has troubled health care professionals, who attribute the unnecessarily high mortality rate to two factors: women's failure to be tested and errors in the testing process.

George Papanicolaou's cancer-screening technique, known as the Pap smear, was introduced around 1940, and its implementation decreased the death rate from cervical cancer by more than 70%. The Pap smear is simple, affordable, and widely available—but not foolproof. Technicians who analyze Pap smears are responsible for screening up to 24 million cells per day—100,000–300,000 per slide—so an abnormality can easily be missed. Despite quality-control standards, a false-negative result is reported as often as 30% of the time.

The medical community hopes to see a decrease in false-negative reports, as well as fatalities, with the introduction of two computer-aided quality-control products: Papnet and AutoPap. Both were approved by the U.S. Food and Drug Administration in 1995.

Papnet, developed by Neuromedical Systems Inc., Suffern, N.Y., is an interactive computer-assisted screening process. Once slides have been reviewed by a laboratory technician, those smears that are judged to be negative are submitted for visual enhancement and review by Papnet. The computer technology, which originally was created to detect missiles for the "Star Wars" defense system, uses neural network technology to select the 128 most suspicious cells from a Pap smear and magnify them 1,000 times. Papnet thus provides a more precise rescreening (double-check testing). Papnet does not attempt to diagnose by itself or to replace the diagnostician; rather it facilitates recognition of suspicious cells by a trained technician. Those smears determined to be suspicious are returned to the originating laboratory in the form of magnified images for further review by technicians.

AutoPap is a fully automated system designed to detect cell abnormalities. Produced by Neopath Inc., Redmond, Wash., AutoPap is designed to be utilized by laboratories on-site. Pap smears that have been determined by technicians to contain no abnormalities are retested by AutoPap's algorithm technology, which distinguishes normal cells from abnormal ones. Those smears determined by AutoPap to contain abnormalities are further reviewed by a laboratory technician.

It has been predicted that computerized screening devices could detect up to 50% of abnormalities that would otherwise have been overlooked in the 50 million Pap smears performed each year in the U.S. In addition, regular testing of women in high-risk groups—for example, those who are sexually active at a young age, have multiple sexual partners, have a history of sexually transmitted disease, or were exposed to the drug diethylstilbestrol, or DES, in utero—could further diminish the incidence of cervical cancer.

—*Katherine I. Gordon*

Papnet's neural network computing technology searches Pap smears for suspicious-looking cells that may have been missed by conventional screening methods. Abnormal cells are then magnified on a high-resolution video screen for interpretation by a skilled technician.

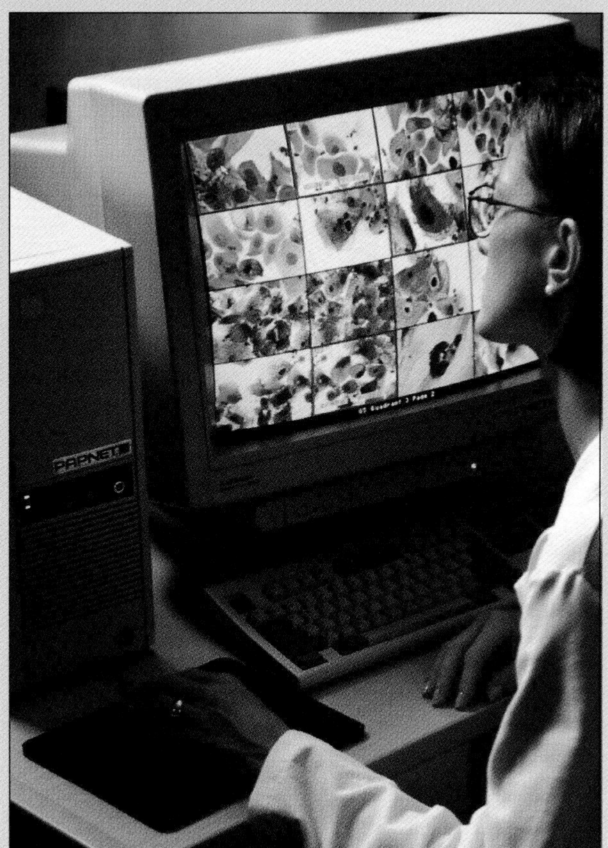

Neuromedical Systems, Inc.

(continued from page 350)

Emergency contraception: the secret is out

Even after unprotected intercourse has occurred, a woman in the U.S. has a choice of three methods to prevent pregnancy. Two rely on available OCs, and the third involves the use of the copper T 380A IUD.

A number of combined birth control pills may be effective as postcoital contraceptives if taken within 72 hours of unprotected intercourse. A high dosage is used (approximately 200 micrograms of ethinyl estradiol and 2 mg of progestin) and is administered twice over a period of 12 hours. Because nausea may result from the higher-than-normal dosage of hormones, many women also take an antinausea medication. Less frequently progestin-only pills are used for postcoital contraception. They cause little or no nausea or vomiting, but an extremely large dose (about 40 pills) is needed to produce the desired effect.

The copper T 380A has two main advantages over postcoital pills: the window of time it may be used is longer—it can be inserted as late as five to seven days after unprotected intercourse—and it is definitely more effective. Moreover, if the woman chooses not to remove the device after the possibility of pregnancy has passed, she has the benefit of a reliable long-term form of contraception.

Emergency postcoital contraceptives remain a well-kept secret, in spite of the fact that they have been available for some 25 years. The challenge facing concerned health care professionals is to inform both women and their clinicians that there are ways to prevent pregnancy after unprotected intercourse. Women need to know in advance that they can reassure themselves in the case of rape—or any time they think their contraceptive might not have worked.

Women can also call a toll-free telephone number—1-800-584-9911—to learn the phone numbers of three providers of emergency contraceptives in their local areas. This same service will explain the three options for emergency contraception, tell a woman where she can get written information, and inform clinicians what to do if they would like their names to be given to hot-line callers. The list of referrals now includes 1,500 physicians from every state in the U.S.

The latest alarm

Concerns about the health risks of OCs seem to arise periodically. In the late 1960s reports surfaced of an increased incidence of blood clots and strokes linked to the use of birth control pills. As mentioned above, those first-generation pills contained relatively high doses of estrogen. Pill-related cardiovascular complications declined when manufacturers decreased the estrogen content of their products. These low-dose pills represented the second generation of OCs.

The most recent alarm involves reports of an increased risk for venous thrombosis (*i.e.,* blood clot in a vein) among users of so-called third-generation pills. The third-generation OCs, which became available in the U.S. only in the 1990s, differ from earlier formulations in that they contain newer progestins, which were developed for the purpose of further reducing the risk for cardiovascular problems. These progestins are desogestrel, gestodene, and norgestimate. Of the three, desogestrel is by far the most commonly used. Gestodene, widely used in Great Britain and elsewhere in Europe, has not been approved by the Food and Drug Administration and so is not a component of any OC sold in the U.S. Norgestimate (present in two of the third-generation pills marketed in the U.S.) was not implicated in recent reports linking third-generation pills and blood clots.

The recent scare was touched off in October 1995 when women and their physicians in Britain and throughout Europe were warned that an increased rate of venous blood clots was being reported among users of certain brands of oral contraceptives. An advisory sent to all British doctors and pharmacists on Oct. 18, 1995, triggered a massive increase in visits to physicians and caused what has been called Britain's biggest pill scare in 20 years. The warning, which involved several brands of OCs being taken by some 1.5 million British women alone, was based on the findings of three studies that had not yet been published and were not released for another two months.

In the meantime, a newsletter from the Margaret Pyke Family Planning Centre in London attempted to allay some of the concerns by putting the risks for thrombosis into context. Apparently, many women were not sufficiently reassured. The number of abortions in Britain rose in the period from December 1995 to February 1996 and, despite advice to women to discuss with their doctors whether to change contraceptives, some OC users stopped using the pills immediately after news of the advisory became public.

The studies in question were finally published in the Dec. 16, 1995, issue of *The Lancet.* The findings were summed up in an accompanying commentary by the University of Washington epidemiologist Noel Weiss. Weiss wrote:

> *The latest results provide reasonably strong evidence that users of third-generation OCs have a higher risk of venous thromboembolic disease than do users of other OCs, and further suggest that the newer OCs are in fact responsible. Each study was large, and each came to the same conclusion: that there was approximately a two-fold difference in risk between current users of third-generation OCs and other OCs.*

Why was there relatively little alarm over these findings in the U.S.? One reason may be that the increased risk found in these studies was quite small. This fact was emphasized in a statement issued by the Association of Reproductive Health Professionals, which concluded, "A small risk doubled is still a small risk. In fact, the risk of deep vein thrombosis from pregnancy is much greater than the risk associated with birth control pills."

A second reason for the more moderate U.S. reaction is that most pills used by American women do not contain either of the two hormones cited in the studies as potentially harmful. Because the third progestin, norgestimate, was not implicated, women and their clinicians who want to continue its use can probably feel comfortable in this decision.

(continued on page 354)

NEWS CAP

Teens Have a Future with Foster

Henry W. Foster, Jr., who did not get the job of surgeon general after M. Joycelyn Elders' departure from that office in December 1994, did get another high government appointment, one that suits him to a T. At a White House ceremony on Jan. 29, 1996, U.S. Pres. Bill Clinton announced that he was appointing Foster to be his senior adviser on a national problem of epidemic proportions: teenage pregnancy.

About one million teenage girls in the U.S. become pregnant each year, and as many as 95% of these pregnancies are unintended. Although these rates had been declining for about 15 years, they increased from 1986 to 1991 and are still higher than they were 20 years ago. The U.S. has the highest rate of teen pregnancy in the developed world—more than double that of England, Iceland, Canada, Norway, and Sweden; almost as high as that of Jordan, the Philippines, and Thailand; and almost 10 times higher than the teen pregnancy rate in Japan.

Why is teen pregnancy considered a high-priority problem? Largely because it is linked to so many other societal ills: poverty, illiteracy, and unemployment, to name a few. Recent statistics show that teenage mothers are more likely than older mothers to rely on public assistance, are less likely to finish high school or go to college, and have only half the earning potential of women who do not give birth until they have reached the age of 25. The findings of the most comprehensive study to date on the costs of teen pregnancy in the U.S. estimated that $7 billion would be spent in 1996 on the social problems resulting from births to women under age 18.

Also contributing to teen pregnancy's high-priority status are major health concerns. Pregnant adolescents are less likely than older mothers to receive adequate prenatal care and are more likely to have low-birth-weight babies. Teenage mothers have a high incidence of pregnancy complications, including hypertension, anemia, and cephalopelvic disproportion (a condition in which the maternal pelvis is small in relation to the fetal head). They are also less likely to have the parenting skills necessary to raise a healthy child.

These are all matters that Foster has tackled with unquestioned success. In 1987 he started the "I Have a Future" program at Meharry Medical College (Nashville, Tenn.), aimed at teenage residents of Nashville's public housing projects. Teens in the program, which is still active, attend after-school meetings during which older role models show them what they have to look forward to if they *delay* parenthood. Participants discover the many new vistas that can be open to them. For example, they visit college campuses, take field trips to historic sites, or simply go to an airport for the first time.

Greg Gibson—AP/Wide World

Pres. Bill Clinton with his adviser on teenage pregnancy, Henry Foster.

What has the program achieved? Teen pregnancy rates for Nashville have declined, and "I Have a Future" participants are staying in school longer. Foster has long believed that "I Have a Future" should be initiated on a national scale, and now it will be. His goals are to: (1) educate young people about health, sexuality, conflict resolution, and drug and alcohol abuse; (2) encourage abstinence but provide contraception for those who are sexually active; and (3) expand the opportunities of teens (by improving their job skills, helping them become self-reliant, and encouraging them to establish their own value systems).

Foster earned a bachelor of science degree from Morehouse College, Atlanta, Ga. (1954), and his M.D. from the University of Arkansas (1958). He has since practiced gynecology and obstetrics, been a professor and acting president at Meharry, and worked as a consultant to the U.S. Department of Health and Human Services.

Foster chooses not to see his rejection as surgeon general as a defeat. In his words, "When one door closes, another one opens."

—*Katherine I. Gordon*

(continued from page 352)

Women who continue to use or are considering using either of the desogestrel-containing products on the market in the U.S. (Desogen and Ortho-Cept) need to be aware of the new data. Some clinicians believe current users of desogestrel pills can safely continue taking them if the women are experiencing no problems—particularly if they have had difficulties with other OCs—but are recommending that no new users be started on pills containing desogestrel.

There was a silver lining to the news that emerged from Europe in late 1995—namely, evidence that women using older progestins were at *less* of an increased risk for blood-clotting complications than had previously been documented. Data from the FDA showed that 10–15 cases of nonfatal venous thrombosis occurred annually among women taking older, low-dose pills. The risk to those using desogestrel- or gestodene-containing products was 20 to 30 per 100,000 women. By comparison, for healthy nonpregnant women who were not taking hormones, the rate of venous thrombosis was 4 per 100,000. To put these figures into perspective, this complication occurs among pregnant women at a rate of 60 per 100,000.

Further, not all women taking the newer progestins are at equal risk of developing blood clots. Another report in the December 16 issue of *The Lancet* identified a genetic marker called the factor V Leiden mutation, which seems to account for the majority of cases of idiopathic venous thrombosis (*i.e.,* those for which there is no clear underlying cause). Women who carry the mutation have resistence to a blood protein that prevents clotting. The factor V Leiden mutation is not uncommon, occurring in some 3% to 10% of people, and a screening test may eventually be available to identify women with the mutation in advance of prescribing OCs. If a woman has both risk factors for venous thrombosis—that is, she is using a desogestrel-containing pill and is a carrier of the factor V Leiden mutation—her risk for blood-clotting complications is 50 times greater than that of a woman who has neither risk factor.

A crucial question that remains is whether OC users should reevaluate the Pill in light of these studies. While women should always be aware of new findings arising as a result of increased experience with birth control pills, they should understand that the new data do not contradict several long-standing and accepted facts:

- OCs are one of the best-studied medications ever taken by large numbers of people.
- They are extremely safe.
- They have a number of benefits over and above their remarkable effectiveness as a contraceptive.

The question of the risk of desogestrel and gestodene pills became even more complex with the publication in January 1996 of an international study of the incidence of heart attack in women taking third-generation pills. The investigators concluded that the risk for heart attack was appreciably lower among women using the third-generation pills—comparable to that among women who did not use oral contraception and two to three times lower than that among women using second-generation OCs. It is possible, therefore, that the increased risk for venous thrombosis associated with third-generation oral contraceptives may be offset by a reduced incidence of acute heart attack.

Is this the final word? Unfortunately, it probably is not. As the above clearly demonstrates, having more data does not necessarily clarify a situation. Sometimes it simply adds to the complexity and confusion. The best course of action for women and their doctors is to follow developments closely and make maximum use of all available sources of information.

—*Robert A. Hatcher, M.D., M.P.H.*

Tobacco and Health: Continuing Saga

On June 6, 1996, the United States Council of State and Territorial Epidemiologists voted unanimously to add cigarette smoking to the list of conditions that are regularly reported to the federal Centers for Disease Control and Prevention (CDC). Smoking was the first *behavior* to be designated a nationally notifiable condition; all other notifiable conditions are diseases or illnesses. The significance of this move was noted in the CDC's *Morbidity and Mortality Weekly Report* (June 28, 1996):

> *Most importantly, this action underscores the role of tobacco use as the leading preventable cause of death in the United States and the need to conduct national public health surveillance for both conventional disease outcomes and for underlying causes (e.g., smoking and other risky behaviors) amenable to public health intervention.*

In 1995–96 antismoking advocates triumphantly proclaimed that the days of *healthy* profits reaped by an industry that promotes an *unhealthy* habit were numbered. The powerful tobacco industry was faced with several major legal actions against it. In addition, three widely publicized books added to the negative image of the cigarette manufacturers: *Smokescreen: The Truth Behind the Tobacco Industry Cover-Up* by Philip J. Hilts, *The Cigarette Papers* by Stanton A. Glantz, and *Ashes to Ashes: America's Hundred-Year Cigarette War, the Public Health, and the Unabashed Triumph of Philip Morris* by Richard Kluger.

Undoubtedly, the most sweeping action against the tobacco giants was that taken by the U.S. Food and Drug Administration (FDA) when it proposed to regulate the sale and promotion of tobacco products to all minors. In response to the FDA proposal, which was supported by Pres. Bill Clinton, the Philip Morris company put forth its own set of measures to keep tobacco products out of the hands and mouths of youth.

Smokers lose

The medical dangers of smoking continue to mount. In the past year studies either found or confirmed that:

- Women smokers are at increased risk for reproductive problems (*e.g.,* miscarriage, low-birth-weight babies, ectopic pregnancy, and reduced fertility).
- The proportion of smokers dying from lung cancer is at an all-time high.

(Top) Cathy Melloan—Tony Stone Images; (bottom) Evan Johnson—Impact Visuals/PNI

- Secondhand, or passive, smoke is even more harmful than was previously recognized. One group of researchers, at Bowman Gray School of Medicine in Winston-Salem, N.C., found that nonsmokers exposed to secondhand smoke were at greater risk for atherosclerosis than unexposed nonsmokers. The investigators found that the arteries of subjects exposed to passive smoke thickened 10% faster than did the arteries of unexposed subjects.
- Smokers are more likely than nonsmokers to develop diabetes, have a heart attack or stroke, or suffer from insomnia, snoring, and other sleep-related problems.
- Smokers are more likely than nonsmokers to have premature facial wrinkling and a number of other skin conditions. Dermatologist Jeffrey B. Smith at the University of South Florida published a report in the journal *Dermatology* in 1996 tabulating the adverse manifestations of smoking on the skin. For example, smoking thickens and fragments the elastic fibers of skin, depletes the skin's oxygen supply, and prevents collagen formation, all of which lead to disintegration of skin tissues and profound, early wrinkling. Smoking increases the risk of skin cancers as well as cancers of the mouth, lip, penis, anus, and vulva. Smoking also delays wound healing, appears to increase the risk of psoriasis, and is related to blood vessel disease in the lower legs that results in poor circulation, tingling, burning, and ulcer formation.

In addition to these and other adverse effects of smoking are recent neurochemical findings. Research has shown that when nicotine is introduced into the human nervous system, it stimulates the release of dopamine, a brain chemical associated with the experience of pleasure. A study conducted at the Brookhaven National Laboratory, Upton, Long Island, N.Y., and reported in the journal *Nature* (Feb. 22, 1996) found that an unknown substance in tobacco smoke reduces the levels of an enzyme (monoamine oxidase B) that breaks down dopamine. Dopamine levels in the brain are thereby increased, which accentuates the pleasure-enhancing effects of smoking. On the basis of these findings, addiction researchers believe that cigarettes should be considered a "gateway drug"—in other words, one that can lead to the use of dangerous illicit substances. Meanwhile, in the past year or so it has come to light that cigarette manufacturers deliberately manipulate the nicotine content of cigarettes. In so doing, they virtually guarantee addiction and continued use of tobacco products.

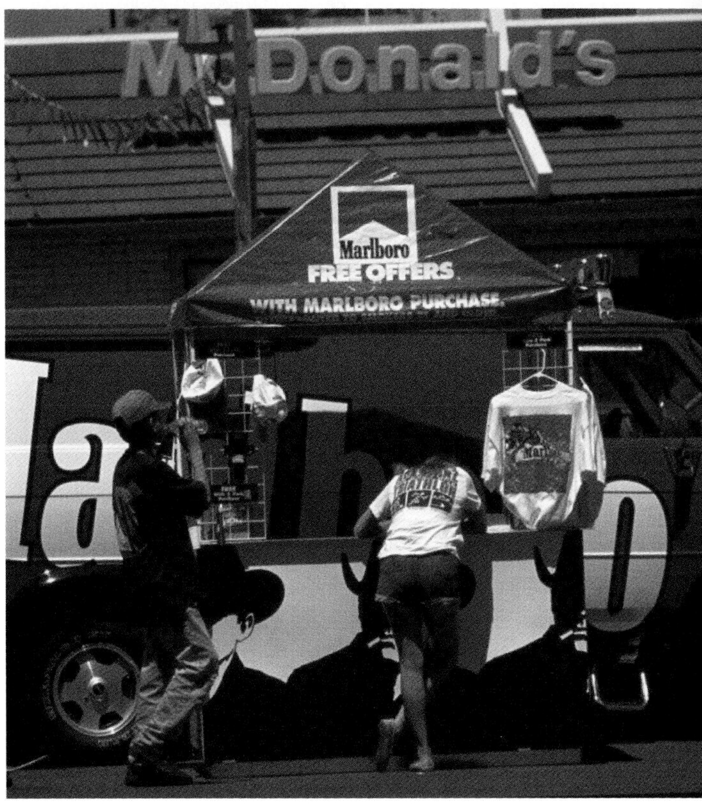

Quitters win

For anyone who smokes and has any doubts about whether quitting pays off, the American Cancer Society (ACS) points out that:

- Within 20 minutes of smoking the last cigarette, blood pressure drops to its normal level.

Tough new federal regulations that have the health and well-being of the U.S.'s young people in mind will, among other things, banish Joe Camel from all signs or billboards that are within 300 m (1,000 ft) of schoolyards or playgrounds. The advertising crackdown will also make giveaways of cigarettes or products—hats, T-shirts, etc.—that bear the names or logos of cigarette manufacturers a thing of the past.

National Center for Tobacco-Free Kids

With ads that target the young and impressionable, tobacco companies are addicting a whole new generation of customers—a practice that the Campaign for Tobacco-Free Kids is determined to snuff out.

- After eight hours the amount of carbon monoxide in the blood returns to normal.
- Within two days the ability to taste and smell improves.
- In one to nine months coughing, sinus congestion, fatigue, and shortness of breath decrease; cilia—hairlike structures in the air passages that rid the lungs of foreign materials—regain normal function.
- In five years the risk of dying from lung cancer decreases by 50%.
- After 15 years the risk of cardiovascular disease is almost that of a nonsmoker, as is the risk of dying from lung cancer.

No more Joe Camel

In light of growing evidence of the harm caused by tobacco use, the FDA is fighting for full jurisdictional control over the tobacco industry. The FDA argues that by definition nicotine is a drug: a product "intended to affect the structure or any function of the body." If the FDA wins such control, it could decide to ban tobacco use altogether. A more likely step, however, would be to limit young people's access to tobacco products and thereby reduce the number of future smokers. The agency set the following goals for tobacco control: (1) to diminish advertising's appeal to minors by (a) restricting the types of ads used (*e.g.,* no more Joe Camel), (b) banning the production of promotional items such as free hats and T-shirts, and (c) prohibiting the marketing of tobacco products in places where children are likely to be exposed to it (*e.g.,* on billboards near schools or in large-circulation magazines with a predominantly youthful target audience); (2) to limit cigarette availability to minors; and (3) to further educate the public about the dangers of smoking.

Ultimately, the FDA hopes to protect children and adolescents from being enticed by sophisticated promotional efforts, because the overwhelming majority of adult tobacco users get hooked before age 18. The reason the FDA took this major step when it did was that it had solid evidence that cigarette manufacturers intentionally manipulate the level and form of nicotine in their products. A new study, published in the American Marketing Association's *Journal of Marketing* (April 1996), clearly supported the steps taken by the FDA by demonstrating that young people are three times more sensitive to advertising of tobacco products than adults, even if the ads are directed toward adults. John Banzhaf, executive director of Action on Smoking and Health (ASH), Washington, D.C., commented that the recent marketing study was the first "to directly demonstrate the very strong relationship between the intensity of cigarette advertising and the resulting brand market shares among adults versus young people."

In early 1996 the National Center for Tobacco-Free Kids was established in Washington, D.C., with a $20 million grant from the Robert Wood Johnson Foundation, $10 million from the ACS, and additional support from many other groups, such as the National PTA, the National Association of Secondary School Principals, the American Medical Association, and the American Heart Association. One of the center's main undertakings is the Campaign for Tobacco-Free Kids, a nationwide advertising and information sweep to deter youths from commencing the decidedly harmful habit. The hard-hitting messages of the campaign are directed not only at vulnerable youngsters but at physicians as well. Recent public service advertisements of the campaign appearing in the *Journal of the American Medical Association (JAMA)* have directly attacked tobacco lobbyists: "After decades of lying about addiction and disease, tobacco companies have launched a last-ditch scheme to continue marketing to kids: flood Congress with cash." The same *JAMA* ad appealed to doctors to write their members of Congress and "tell them America's children aren't for sale."

Tobacco giants tremble

These and other efforts, combined with the most serious legal challenges the tobacco giants have ever faced, have had the $45 billion industry gasping for breath. Thus threatened, tobacco companies have proposed their own crusade to reduce smoking among youths. Philip Morris USA, for example, appealed to the public in full-page newspaper ads, asking that "everyone—including our critics—join together in pursuing [the] common goal [of ending underage tobacco use]." Philip Morris' agenda includes (1) banning the imprint of tobacco-product names and logos on nontobacco items (*e.g.,* T-shirts, caps, jackets), (2) banning vending machine cigarette sales, and (3) earmarking $250 million over the next five years to enforce restrictions on teenage smoking.

Although the Philip Morris proposals appeared to mirror those of the FDA, public health professionals failed to see them in that light. They alleged, for example, that the "common ground solution" proposed by Philip Morris fell far short of the government's health-oriented objectives. ASH saw the tobacco giant's offer to self-regulate as having "many loopholes, limitations, and even contradictions." Ultimately, antismoking advocates predicted that after a lot of sound and fury, there would be little change in the status quo; despite its apparent stance against underage smoking, the powerful tobacco industry would likely continue to play by its own profit-oriented rules.

—Katherine I. Gordon

NEWS CAP

Glaucoma: Lasers Take the Pressure Off

Laser surgery is as effective as or better than drugs in treating glaucoma, the leading cause of blindness in the U.S. A study reported in the *American Journal of Ophthalmology* (December 1995) pointed to laser treatment as a practical alternative to the conventional medical therapies for glaucoma, eyedrops or oral medications, which can cause such troublesome side effects as elevated blood pressure, headaches, and respiratory problems.

Chronic, or open-angle, glaucoma, the most common form of the disease, results when pressure builds up in the eye because the fluid that normally passes through the pupil and into the front of the eye fails to drain properly through sievelike permeable tissue. Untreated, this elevated intraocular pressure can lead to nerve damage and loss of vision. Argon laser therapy as the initial treatment relieves the pressure by stimulating a reaction that increases the permeability of the meshwork tissue.

The study, which was conducted at several U.S. medical centers, tracked 203 glaucoma patients for an average of seven years. Each of the subjects received laser treatment for one eye and drug therapy for the other. Not only did the eyes treated with the laser respond as well as those treated medically; they also showed a greater reduction in intraocular pressure and a reduced need for additional drug therapy. In addition, vision loss was reduced in the laser-treated eyes. Perhaps most important, there were no serious side effects from the laser surgery. The study's director cautioned, however, that none of the existing treatments is a final answer for long-term control of glaucoma.

—*Jeff Wallenfeldt*

NEWS CAP

Remembering TV's Toughest Surgeon

Actor Vince Edwards, best remembered for his starring role in the 1960s television series "Ben Casey," died of pancreatic cancer in Los Angeles on March 11, 1996, at the age of 67. Often compared to motion picture star Burt Lancaster because of his rugged, handsome features and gruff speech, Edwards as neurosurgeon Ben Casey was the quintessential TV doctor. The show's creator, James Moser, envisioned Casey as a James Deansian rebel in surgical scrubs.

The program debuted in the autumn of 1961 and remained in prime time until 1966. By then, the show and its star had made such a lasting impression on both the viewing public and industry executives that it became the model for TV "doctor shows" for years to come.

During the show's five-year run, life began to imitate art in hospitals across America. Any doctor who was tough or brooding, exhibited a quick temper, or showed unrestrained idealism risked being accused by colleagues of "pulling a Ben Casey." Edwards, who went on to star in other television programs and motion pictures, never forgot his most acclaimed role, saying that he would always be committed to perpetuating the image of the "godlike kind of a man" he felt Ben Casey represented.

—*Joseph Turow, Ph.D.*

Globe Photos

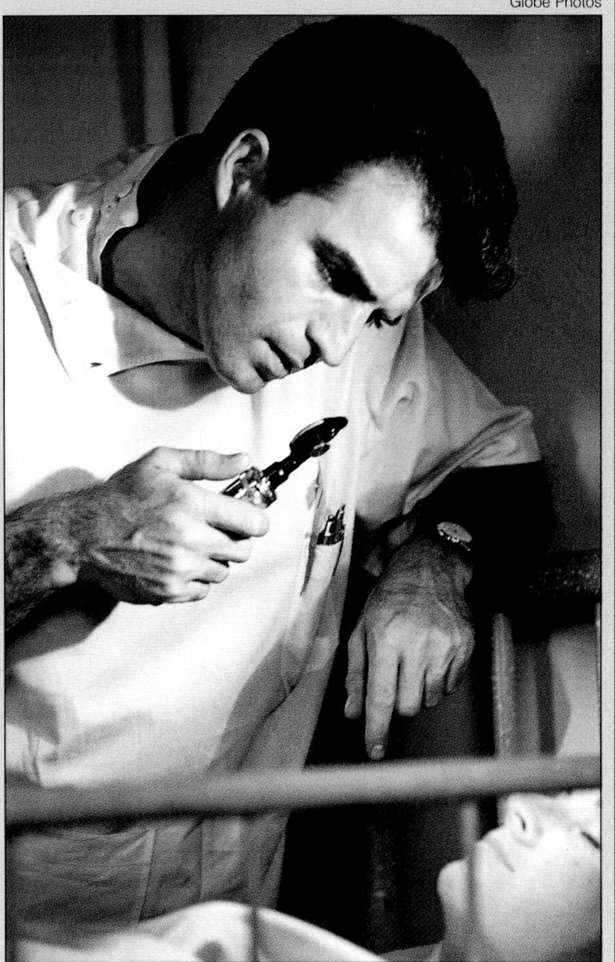

Xenotransplantation Considered

End-stage organ failure—the irreversible deterioration of, most commonly, the heart, liver, or kidneys—is one of the most significant public health issues facing the U.S. today. Heart disease, for example, kills 10 times as many Americans as HIV infection and breast cancer combined. It is a disease with an increasing incidence and a cost of between $5 billion and $25 billion per year. Preventive therapies have had little impact on end-stage organ failure and are unlikely to do so in the near future. The single most effective therapy is transplantation.

The demand for organs far outstrips the supply: only 15% of all Americans waiting for transplants will receive them. It has been estimated that in the U.S. alone about 40,000 people under the age of 65 could benefit from heart transplantation each year, yet only about 2,000 human hearts are available annually. Mandatory seat belt laws have reduced the number of deaths from automobile crashes—a major source of donor organs—and public education about organ donation has not significantly increased donation rates. Between 20% and 30% of Americans on waiting lists for heart or liver transplants die before an organ becomes available. (The percentage of those who die while awaiting kidney transplants is significantly smaller, in part because of the availability of dialysis.) Among heart transplant candidates the likelihood of dying while waiting for a donor organ is even greater than the risk of death in the first year after transplantation surgery.

Although still an experimental procedure, cross-species transplantation, or xenotransplantation (from the Greek *xenos,* meaning "strange" or "foreign"), offers a promising alternative to the use of human organs. Given the shortage of donor organs and the constantly increasing demand, alternatives to allografts (same-species transplants) require serious investigation if clinical transplantation is to meet the current need and to continue the exponential growth pattern established over the past quarter century.

A brief history

Clinical cross-species transplantation dates to the early 20th century, when unsuccessful attempts were made to replace failing human kidneys with organs from rabbits, pigs, goats, lambs, and nonhuman primates. Following these early failures, the practice was abandoned for over 40 years. In 1963 xenotransplantation pioneer Keith Reemtsma and his colleagues at Tulane University, New Orleans, La., transplanted chimpanzee kidneys into six human patients; the grafted organs not only survived but functioned for as long as nine months. The Tulane team used a regimen of immunosuppressive drugs that would be considered antiquated by today's standards.

Later that year the pioneering transplant surgeon Thomas E. Starzl, then at the University of Colorado, reported six baboon-to-human kidney transplants surviving between 10 and 60 days (mean survival, 36 days), using azathioprine and steroid drugs to suppress the immune function of the organ recipients. Surprisingly, this relatively long survival was achieved despite the fact that half of the recipients received organs from animals whose blood types were incompatible with their own—a practice that carries a significant risk of rejection.

Since 1964, when James Hardy and colleagues at the University of Mississippi performed the world's first heart xenotransplant, using a chimpanzee as a donor, there have been eight documented attempts at clinical heart xenotransplantation. Five of the donors were nonhuman primates (two baboons, three chimpanzees), and three were domesticated farm animals (one sheep, two pigs). The longest survivor was the newborn infant known as Baby Fae, whose baboon heart functioned for 20 days despite an initially unrecognized mismatch in blood type. In 1968 Denton Cooley (Texas Heart Institute) and Donald Ross (National Heart Hospital, London) transplanted a sheep and a pig heart, respectively, into dying patients. Both grafts immediately failed upon reperfusion (restarting of the blood circulation), presumably owing to an immediate, severe rejection reaction (hyperacute rejection). More recently, surgeons at the Silesian Academy of Medicine, Zabrze, Poland, tried circulating a patient's blood through a pig donor heart prior to transplantation to remove from the blood human antibodies that would attack the pig tissues. In this case, although the graft recipient died about 24 hours after the surgery, there was no evidence of hyperacute rejection.

Since 1992 surgeons at the University of Pittsburgh, Pa., have performed two baboon-to-human liver transplants; one patient survived for 70 days and the other for 26. An important lesson learned by these investigators was that their overwhelming concern for preventing rejection prompted them to employ a particularly harsh regimen of immunosuppressive drugs, which rendered the transplant recipients highly susceptible to infection. As these cases show, the prevention of rejection in xenotransplantation is currently achieved at the price of augmented immunosuppression and, consequently, an increased risk of infection.

A temporary measure?

With increasing worldwide clinical experience in transplantation, it has been demonstrated that both rejection and infection can be managed successfully in most patients who receive human organs. The use of the immunosuppressive agent cyclosporine, introduced in the late 1970s, has resulted in excellent survival rates in allograft recipients and has reduced the incidence of infection- and rejection-associated illnesses in these patients.

The immunologic barrier that must be overcome in xenotransplantation is unquestionably greater than that in allotransplantation. While considerable advances have been made in the field of heart and kidney xenotransplantation since the first clinical applications in the 1960s, it remains uncertain whether even xenotransplantation from species closely related to humans—nonhuman primates like the chimpanzee and baboon—can become an accepted therapy.

Although these "closely related" xenografts have not consistently achieved long-term survival in humans, it is clear that heart, kidney, and liver xenografts from baboons and chimpanzees have been able to support human life for periods ranging from weeks to months. It is precisely this fact

Organs Donated Versus Patients Waiting

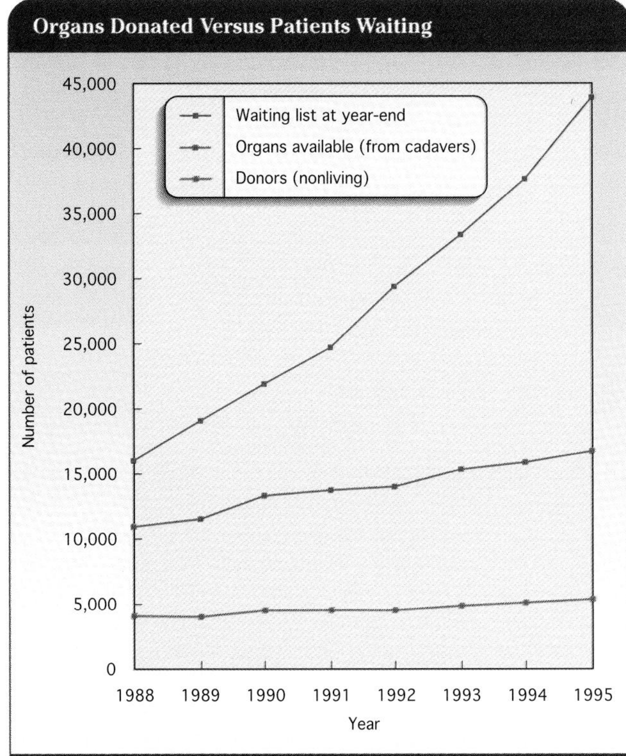

On the Waiting List

Age group (years)	Number of patients[1]								
	Kidney	Liver	Pancreas	Kidney-pancreas	Intestine	Heart	Heart-lung	Lung	TOTALS
0–5	83	322	3	9	37	93	5	10	562
6–10	132	151	2	0	14	27	8	15	349
11–17	374	180	5	0	7	75	21	87	749
18–49	19,310	3,120	265	1,275	14	1,300	164	1,140	26,588
50–64	10,441	2,411	18	92	3	1,945	23	795	15,728
65+	2,329	391	1	1	0	182	0	27	2,931
TOTALS	32,669	6,575	294	1,377	75	3,622	221	2,074	46,907

[1]As of June 30, 1996.
Note: Some patients are listed with more than one transplant center; therefore, the number of registrations may be greater than the actual number of patients.

Adapted from information obtained from United Network for Organ Sharing.

that certain investigators hope to exploit in so-called clinical bridging studies, in which an animal organ would provide temporary heart, kidney, or liver support for a dying patient waiting to receive a suitable human donor organ—as has already been done in some cases with mechanical heart-assist devices. Bridging strategies cannot alleviate the shortage of human donor organs, however, and are therefore epidemiologically inconsequential. Some authorities view bridge-to-transplantation xenografts as a test of feasibility, with the potential to eventually establish xenotransplantation as an acceptable alternative to allotransplantation. Success in this more ambitious latter goal would clearly help to alleviate the human donor organ shortage.

Understanding rejection

Historically, rejection in xenotransplantation has been divided into two categories according to the mechanism involved. In one category are rejection reactions in which preformed natural antibodies against donor tissues are present in the patient's blood; such is the case in xenografts between distantly related species. The other category consists of rejection responses in which preformed antibodies are absent; such is the case in xenografts between closely related species. Thus, while rejection involving distantly related species—hyperacute rejection—commonly takes place rapidly (within a few minutes to a few hours), that between closely related species—acute or chronic rejection—may take substantially longer.

The chief function of the immune system is to distinguish substances that are "self" from all those that are foreign, or "nonself" (*e.g.,* viruses, bacteria, foreign tissues), and to effectively destroy the latter. The human immune system has two branches, cellular immunity and humoral immunity. Cellular immunity involves many types of cells, including lymphocytes (white blood cells) and macrophages, which recognize and attack the tissues of transplanted organs. Humoral immunity involves antibodies and the proteins known collectively as complement; these immune system constituents act even more rapidly and violently to destroy organ transplants.

Although distantly related xenotransplantation has come to be associated primarily with antibody-mediated immune responses and closely related xenotransplantation primarily with cell-mediated responses, both the antibody-mediated and cell-mediated arms of the immune system are potentially active in every rejection event. Indeed, the only difference between the categories of rejection is the immune mechanism that predominates in the given rejection episode (*e.g.,* antibody-mediated mechanisms predominate in hyperacute rejection, and cell-mediated mechanisms predominate in acute rejection). In general, this predominance is also time-related. Thus, to a great extent the clinician can judge which arm of the immune response is exerting the most influence on the rejection episode simply by observing the time interval between transplantation and rejection.

Donor organs from nonhuman primates have been favored by those seeking to minimize the genetic disparity between animal donors and human recipients. Chimpanzees are the most compatible with respect to such criteria as size and blood types, but because they are an endangered species, they are not an acceptable source of organs for clinical xenotransplantation. An alternative is the baboon, which is not endangered and is anatomically and physiologically quite similar to humans. Adult baboons reach a maximum weight of only about 30 kg (70 lb), however, which would limit the clinical application of baboon-to-human transplants to pediatric patients and small adults. The infrequency of blood group O among baboons (a blood type compatible with all others in the ABO blood group) is a further drawback to the use of baboons as sources of donor organs.

Still another obstacle is the limited number of colony-bred baboons. Because of the potential for the spread of infectious agents, animals captured in the wild are not ideal sources of donor organs. Most experts agree that colony-bred baboons

Courtesy of Imutran

In an attempt to overcome some of the immunologic barriers to the use of pigs as sources of transplantable organs, scientists have developed so-called transgenic pigs, animals whose tissues contain genes for human proteins that inhibit the rejection response.

would make more suitable donors, but because such animals number only in the hundreds, they are likely to provide only enough organs to serve the needs of the pediatric population with end-stage organ failure.

Despite the fact that nonhuman primates represent the best immunologic alternative to human allografts, ethical concerns and the problems of small size and limited populations have created a renewed enthusiasm for the use of other animals as organ donors. The pig, in fact, fulfills all the criteria for an organ donor: it is available in large numbers (approximately 90 million are slaughtered yearly for the food needs of the U.S. alone); it can be bred in a controlled environment so as to minimize the risks of potentially transmissible disease; and it has strikingly similar cardiac anatomy and physiology when compared with humans. Further, the use of pigs as organ donors is not likely to evoke the kind of opposition that the use of organs from nonhuman primates has.

The immunologic barriers between the species remain a major problem, however. A number of strategies are currently under investigation to overcome these obstacles, mostly involving treatments that rid the recipient's blood of immune factors that would attack the pig tissues. Another approach is to breed genetically altered pigs whose tissues contain genes for human complement inhibitors (proteins that normally protect human cells from damage by the body's own complement). Three of these inhibitors have been produced in transgenic pigs or mice, and they appear promising in protecting against complement-mediated hyperacute rejection of the animal organ.

Still another alternative is to genetically modify pig endothelial cells (the cells that line the blood vessels and hollow organs) so that a molecule called alpha-gal, which stimulates the human immune response, is either absent from the endothelial cells of the donor organ or is present in significantly reduced numbers. This has been accomplished in mice by breeding animals that lack the gene that codes for a particular enzyme, which, in turn, is necessary for the manufacture of alpha-gal. The technology necessary to similarly manipulate the genes of higher mammals is not yet available. Genetic modification of potential xenograft donors is an area of very active and exciting research and probably will be the source of the major advancements required for xenotransplantation to become a clinical reality.

Infectious disease risk: how real?

On the basis of the current knowledge of infections transmitted via allogenic transplantation and the evolving knowledge of zoonoses (diseases communicable to humans from other animals), the organisms of greatest concern in xenotransplantation are herpesviruses and retroviruses. The potential for xenozoonoses—*i.e.,* animal diseases transmitted to humans via donor organs—appears to be greatest with the baboon; therefore, infections that could spread from baboons to humans are the focus of this discussion. In addition to herpesviruses and retroviruses, other infectious agents with potential for transmission via baboon-to-human organ transplants include the organisms that cause toxoplasmosis, tuberculosis, and an inflammatory brain condition. Less likely to be found in animals raised in captivity in the U.S. are filoviruses (*e.g.,* the Marburg and Ebola viruses), monkeypox, and simian hemorrhagic fever virus. Several other pathogens are highly unlikely to be transmitted with an organ transplant, but donor animals should probably be screened for them in order to ensure the safety of recipients.

The three viruses most prevalent in the baboon belong to the herpesvirus family: cytomegalovirus (CMV); a baboon equivalent of Epstein-Barr virus (EBV); and simian agent 8 (SA8). The latter, which is similar to herpes simplex virus types 1 and 2 of humans, is endemic in baboons. Its ability to cause disease in humans remains unknown. There have been no documented cases of human disease with SA8, but baboons with evidence of active infection probably should be excluded as donors. While potentially subject to transmission via transplantation, the other two baboon herpesviruses, which are similar to their human counterparts, have not been shown to cause infection in humans.

The risk of transmission of an animal disease in xenotransplantation is probably restricted to the xenograft recipient. Nevertheless, the potential exists for such illnesses to be transmitted to others, which creates a possible public health concern. The risk of transmitting recognized zoonotic pathogens can be reduced, if not eliminated, by strictly regulating the vendors of donor animals, screening individual donor animals for the major transmissible agents, and following strict sterile procedures during organ harvesting. While the threat of unrecognized pathogens cannot be eliminated, the majority of experts feel that this risk is small.

Second only to xenograft recipients with respect to risk of zoonotic infection are health care personnel who come in contact with recipients. All such workers should be fully informed of potential health hazards, and any individual who wishes to be exempt from caring for xenograft patients should be permitted to do so. A registry must be kept of all health care workers who come in physical contact with xenograft recipients, and such workers must be carefully monitored for unexpected or unexplained symptoms or illnesses. Because of the difficulty of monitoring for the unknown, the surveillance process should include notifying the office of the principal investigator (head of the research team) in the experimental xenotransplantation program of any unexplained illness in exposed health care workers.

Ethical and moral considerations

As cardiac xenotransplantation has advanced, inevitably ethical debates have arisen over the appropriateness of this endeavor. Indeed, many have raised the question of whether it is ethically warranted for humans to use animals in this manner. As Thomasine Kushner (University of California, Berkeley) and Raymond Belliotti (State University of New York) noted in their 1985 article "Baby Fae: A Beastly Business" (published in the *Journal of Medical Ethics*), in order for unequal treatment of two groups of beings to be moral, it must be justified. That is, the unequal treatment of being X and being Y must be justified by a morally relevant difference between them. In this context, for example, children may be relieved of many of the social responsibilities held by adults.

Clearly, in order for xenotransplantation research to be justifiable, a morally relevant distinction between humans and animals must be made. It is not enough to state that animals can be used for any purpose humans deem fit simply because they are members of a different species. Indeed, as many authorities have pointed out, some humans who have diminished mental capacities will never approach the cognitive and emotional level exhibited by some primates. Is there a vital difference between humans and other animals that can serve as a rationale for the use of animals for experimentation? If not, the procedures discussed above could not be justified, because the act of doing good for the human patient would not outweigh the absence of regard for the animal.

Kushner and Belliotti pointed to the human ability to carry out complex cognitions as the morally significant difference between humans and other species. The medical ethics authority Arthur Caplan at the University of Pennsylvania's Center for Bioethics has cited as the key distinction the capacity for complex emotional relationships between human beings. But even if one accepts these distinctions as morally valid, the question of human beings with diminished mental capacities remains. Are they less human than their unimpaired counterparts? Should they be used as research subjects or as organ donors? Those who approve of animal research but oppose the harvesting of donor organs from anencephalic infants or brain-dead individuals focus on the impact that such a practice would have on other human beings, namely, the families of the donors. As Caplan has said with regard to anencephalic infants, "It is in the relationships with others, both family and strangers, that the moral worth and standing of these children are grounded."

If one accepts that the morally reasonable distinction between humans and animals is rooted in the complex emotional relationships that humans share and nonhumans do not, then Caplan's argument appears valid. Even if one does accept that there is a valid moral distinction between humans and animals, however, the next logical question becomes, Is it necessary to use primates in this manner? Ethical justification does not make an action a moral imperative. Disputes regarding animal experimentation notwithstanding, the ethical issues raised regarding the advancement of xenotransplantation from the experimental to the clinical arena are strikingly similar to those put forth 30 years ago in reference to the then new field of allotransplantation. As was the case in 1967, when the South African surgeon Christiaan N. Barnard performed the first successful heart transplant, it is necessary today to evaluate whether a sufficient level of success has been attained experimentally to warrant the clinical application of xenotransplantation.

The medical sociologists Renee Fox (University of Pennsylvania) and Judith Swazey (Boston University) have suggested that the assessment of any experimental therapy should address three critical questions. First, in the laboratory, what defines "success" of a level sufficient to warrant advancement to the clinical arena? Second, under what clinical conditions should this advancement proceed? And third, in the clinical arena, what defines "success" of a sufficient level to warrant further evaluations?

A comparison of the current status of experimental accomplishments in xenotransplantation with that of early allotransplantation yields the following answers. First, graft survival in animal models of xenotransplantation (*e.g.,* monkey-to-baboon transplants) has been comparable to that achieved in experimental allotransplantation prior to 1967. Second, with the current knowledge of allotransplantation has also come a greater awareness of its limitations. Thus, the clinical conditions under which xenotransplantation might proceed could be fulfilled by the presence of a candidate for allotransplantation with end-stage organ failure for whom a human donor could not be found in time. And finally, as was the case for allotransplantation, the measure of clinical "success" of xenotransplantation might be considered *any* duration of graft survival and the goal to strive for extended survival.

Fairness and scarcity

The fair and equitable distribution of organs is an issue that has troubled society ever since transplantation became an accepted therapy. In the U.S. organs are allocated by federal law through an agency called the United Network for Organ Sharing (UNOS). It is responsible for maintaining a national registry of patients classified by blood type, weight, organ needed, date of admission to the waiting list, and severity of illness. Preference is given to transplant centers in proximity to the hospital performing the harvest; if these centers have no candidates for the organ in question, it is released to institutions in a wider geographic area. The selection of recipients is based upon the waiting time accrued (first come, first served), the severity of illness (sicker patients take precedence), the patient's blood type, and the patient's weight (infant-sized

Ezio Petersen—UPI

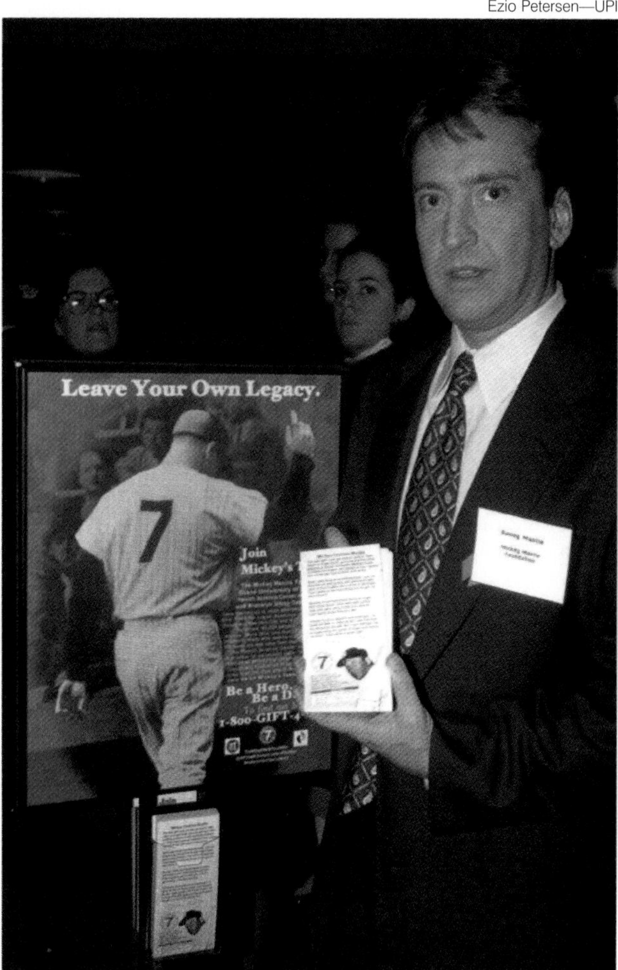

Danny Mantle, son of baseball legend Mickey Mantle, distributes organ donor cards made available by the Mickey Mantle Foundation, a charitable organization founded by his late father. Given a few extra weeks of life by a stranger's selfless gift of a liver, the senior Mantle, who died in 1995, vowed to work to eliminate deaths due to organ shortages.

organs could not be used for adults and vice versa). Despite the attention given to celebrity organ recipients like Mickey Mantle and television star Larry Hagman, the system works to the benefit of gravely ill patients—which both of them were—and is designed to save lives. Organs cannot be bought and sold, and the distribution system has many levels of checks and balances. No transplant center wishes to lose organs for its own patients because another center has manipulated the system or secured financial favors.

The distribution of xenografts will necessarily require some modification of this system, depending upon the availability of organs and the success of the implants. In the immediate future, xenotransplantation will most likely first undergo clinical trials as a bridge-to-transplantation procedure before being applied as "destination" therapy. Some authorities question the wisdom of all bridging strategies, whether biological or mechanical. They argue that the use of bridge transplants not only increases complications in recipients—thereby diminishing the overall success of the transplantation effort—but also fails to directly address the shortage of human organ donors. But as the experience with mechanical hearts has already demonstrated, patients who use such devices as bridges to a human organ experience improvements in liver, kidney, and other organ function during the period of device support. Thus, many investigators feel that bridge xenotransplants—like their mechanical counterparts—will allow patients to await transplantation in a more stable clinical state, which would render them better candidates for survival after allotransplantation. Indeed, for the pediatric population, it is also reasonable to suggest that because of the current disparity between the size of the most commonly available donors and that of the recipients most in need, the use of xenografts as bridges may actually increase the efficiency of donor organ usage. Further, while the initial clinical experiences with xenografts will not have a direct impact on the human donor organ shortage, they represent a necessary step that must be taken if xenotransplantation is ever to reach its full potential.

The future

The future of clinical xenotransplantation rests largely on the ability of medical scientists to develop more sophisticated immunosuppressive therapy. If, for example, physicians could employ therapies specific to the particular arm of the immune system predominating in the rejection process, they could combat it more efficiently and effectively. A better understanding of the actual mechanism of rejection also would allow for more accurately targeted treatment. These kinds of therapies could replace the profound and generalized immunosuppression currently in use.

Over the past quarter century, substantial strides have been made in the understanding of xenograft rejection. It seems reasonable to assume that the day will come when xenotransplantation will no longer be viewed as experimental. The ultimate goal of its advancement, however, must be to alleviate the shortage of human donor organs.

But what of the initial human xenograft recipients, those willing—but desperate—subjects of experimentation? Are the risks they will face justified by the fact that this unproven treatment may be their only alternative? In answer to these questions, it is useful to consider the observation made in the 1950s by the pioneering lung cancer epidemiologist Michael B. Shimkin: "To do nothing, or to prevent others from doing anything, is itself a type of experiment."

That xenotransplantation has the potential to alleviate human suffering—and that this goal justifies continued research—was emphasized in the report *Xenotransplantation: Science, Ethics, and Public Policy,* issued by the Institute of Medicine (IOM) in July 1996. The report noted that xenotransplantation is still an experimental procedure and one that poses unique risks. Overall, however, the IOM document supported continued research into xenotransplantation and took a less tentative position than a similar report issued simultaneously by a bioethics commission in the U.K. The experts in both countries agreed, however, that medical innovation requires a balancing of risks and benefits and that xenotransplantation research should proceed under careful scrutiny and with appropriate safeguards.

—Robert E. Michler, M.D.

World Health Data

The information presented here reflects the most recent published statistical figures that were available to the editors of *Medical and Health Annual* in mid-1996. Sources include principal intergovernmental organizations—*e.g.,* the World Health Organization (WHO; Geneva), the United Nations (New York City), and their regional offices and affiliated organizations; national statistical offices worldwide; principal U.S. authorities—the National Center for Health Statistics, the Centers for Disease Control and Prevention; and on-line resources of the Internet.

Certain terms used in this section have specific meaning in a public health context:

incidence New cases of a disease or condition diagnosed during a specified period of time; may be reported as the "total number of cases," or as a "rate per [1,000, 10,000, or 100,000]," when referred to a specified population.

prevalence Total cases, including new and all existing cases; may be reported as a total or as a rate.

safe water Treated surface and untreated but uncontaminated ground waters that are accessible within 200 meters (urban) or that can be obtained without excessive expenditure of time (rural).

attended birth Birth attended by a physician, nurse, midwife, trained primary health care worker, or traditional birth attendant.

The application of other terms may differ according to their national contexts—availability of "health services within one hour's travel" means availability of *appropriate* services (different for the U.S. and, say, India) in one hour's travel (travel services differing as much as health services).

Most of the figures provided are "best estimates" and may conceal a considerable range of variation—geographic, economic, or demographic—within any single national value. Because the scope and priorities of national data-collection systems differ greatly, coverage of some subjects may be incomplete.

Symbols and abbreviations:

...	not available
<,>	less than/greater than
≤	equal to or less than
≥	equal to or greater than
AIDS	acquired immune deficiency syndrome
FAO	Food and Agriculture Organization
HIV	human immunodeficiency virus
UNDP	United Nations Development Programme

World/Regional Summary

Persons per Doctor
(World average: 720)

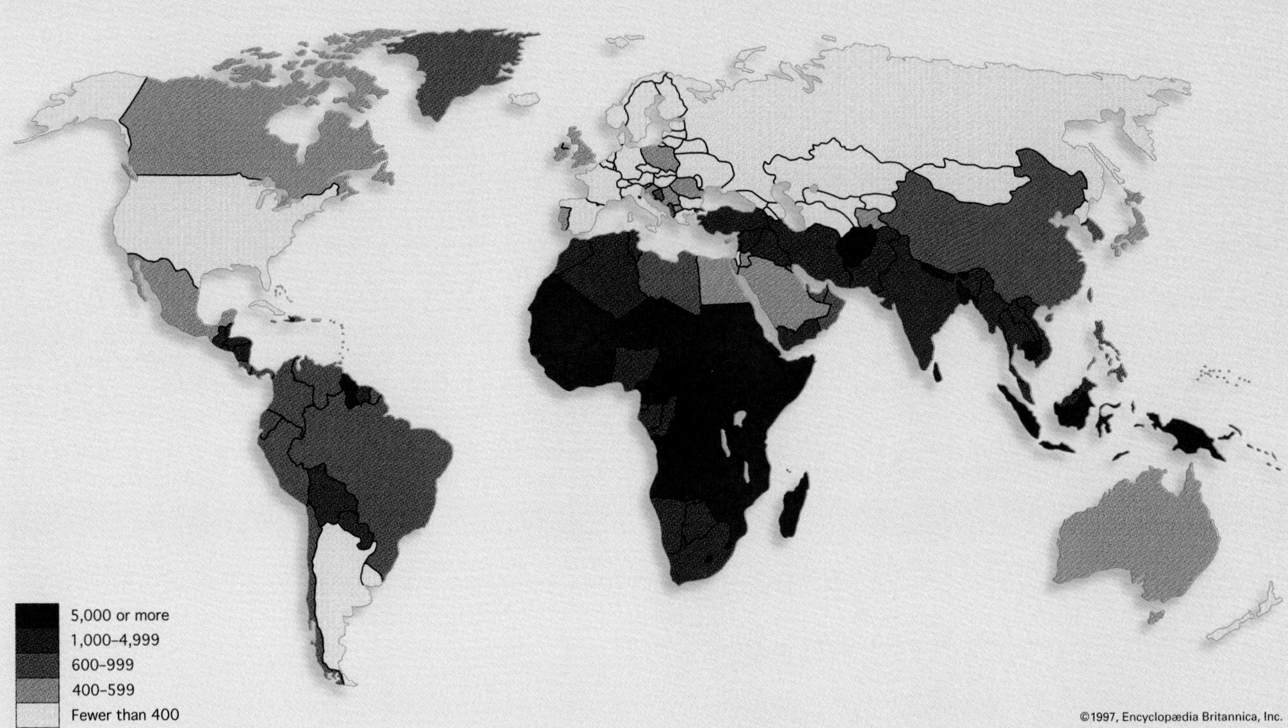

Health Indicators
(World and Component Regions)

Continent/region/bloc/country	Life expectancy		Other			
	Male (years)	Female (years)	Persons per doctor	Infant mortality per 1,000 births	Pop. having safe water (%)	Food (% FAO recommended minimum), 1992
WORLD	64.2	68.4	720	63.1	76	115
AFRICA	53.4	56.5	2,820	92.8	50	97
Central Africa	49.7	53.0	12,770	97.0	42	89
East Africa	47.4	50.4	12,700	108.9	40	81
North Africa	63.4	66.4	980	64.0	73	123
Southern Africa	61.6	67.3	1,680	50.2	56	109
West Africa	51.3	54.2	6,820	96.1	46	94
AMERICAS	68.3	74.5	520	33.5	88	126
Anglo-America[1]	72.4	79.2	390	8.3	100	139
Canada	74.7	81.7	460	6.3	100	116
United States	72.1	78.9	390	8.5	100	141
Latin America	65.7	71.6	660	43.1	80	116
Caribbean	63.7	68.2	480	58.0	75	106
Central America	64.3	69.5	1,190	45.1	64	107
Mexico	66.5	73.1	580	27.1	84	135
South America	65.9	71.7	690	47.6	81	113
Andean Group[2]	68.0	72.5	870	38.8	78	103
Brazil	63.8	70.4	720	60.0	87	118
Other South America	67.8	74.3	410	30.7	67	120
ASIA	64.6	67.5	980	63.7	73	113
Eastern Asia	69.7	73.6	630	24.2	73	117
China	69.1	72.4	630	26.0	69	116
Japan	76.6	83.0	570	4.5	97	124
South Korea	68.0	76.0	860	15.0	93	140
Other Eastern Asia	70.1	75.8	520	17.8	99	121
South Asia	60.0	60.9	2,350	90.6	77	104
India	60.4	61.2	2,140	88.0	79	108
Pakistan	62.0	64.0	2,110	83.0	68	100
Other South Asia	56.4	56.8	5,740	108.9	70	87
Southeast Asia	61.0	65.2	2,690	66.5	54	116
ASEAN[3]	61.8	66.1	2,550	63.2	57	116
Non-ASEAN	55.2	59.0	4,160	86.2	33	114
Southwest Asia	64.9	69.6	590	50.2	86	120
Central Asia	64.2	71.8	290	32.9	100	...
Gulf Cooperation Council[4]	69.6	72.7	570	22.9	95	115
Iran	65.0	67.0	1,600	60.0	89	119
Other Southwest Asia	64.1	69.3	690	56.5	78	122
EUROPE	68.5	76.7	290	11.5	99	133
Eastern Europe	62.8	73.2	280	16.8	99	123
Russia	57.7	71.1	240	18.6	100	...
Ukraine	65.3	74.7	230	14.0	100	...
Other Eastern Europe	67.1	74.8	370	16.4	97	123
Western Europe	73.5	79.9	300	6.8	100	135
European Union (EU)	73.4	79.9	300	6.9	100	136
France	73.1	81.3	370	7.3	100	144
Germany	72.5	79.0	310	5.8	100	126
Italy	73.6	80.2	190	8.3	100	141
Spain	74.6	80.5	250	7.4	100	151
United Kingdom	74.4	79.7	450	6.6	100	132
Other EU[5]	73.1	79.3	340	6.6	100	133
Non-EU	74.5	80.9	310	5.7	100	124
OCEANIA	70.5	76.2	520	24.7	88	122
Australia	74.5	80.8	450	5.8	100	120
Pacific Ocean islands	63.8	68.0	740	42.6	67	126

[1]Anglo-America includes Canada, the United States, Greenland, Bermuda, and St. Pierre and Miquelon.
[2]Bolivia, Colombia, Ecuador, Peru, Venezuela.
[3]Association of Southeast Asian Nations (Brunei, Indonesia, Malaysia, the Philippines, Singapore, Thailand, Vietnam).
[4]Bahrain, Kuwait, Oman, Qatar, Saudi Arabia, the United Arab Emirates.
[5]Finland, Greece, Ireland, Luxembourg, The Netherlands, Portugal, Sweden.

Household and Community Health Indicators
(Selected Countries)

	% persons in communities having:			% households having:	
	Health services (one hour's travel)	Safe water	Sanitary waste disposal	Inside toilet/ water closet	Refrigerator
AFRICA					
Algeria	98	79	77	68.9	...
Egypt	99	80	50	...	...
Ethiopia	46	25	19	55.2	...
Kenya	77	53	77	53.3	...
Morocco	70	55	41	50.2	...
Nigeria	66	40	35	7.0	...
South Africa	...	70	...	50.3	...
Sudan, The	70	60	22	...	...
Tanzania	80	50	64	...	...
Zaire	26	27	23	...	...
NORTH AMERICA					
Canada	100	100	99	99.4	99.6
Mexico	78	83	50	45.0	23.0
United States	100	98	85	98.9	99.5
SOUTH AMERICA					
Argentina	71	71	68	95.1	...
Brazil	...	87	83	...	71.1
Colombia	60	87	63	77.9	...
Peru	75	71	59	78.0	70.3[1]
Venezuela	...	79	94	84.4	74.2
ASIA					
Bangladesh	45	97	34	12.5	...
China	92	93[2]	97	25.2	25.0
India	85	81	29	23.7	...
Indonesia	80	62	51	26.6	...
Iran	80	84	67	43.6	...
Iraq	93	44	70	...	...
Japan	100	95	100	74.7	98.9
Korea, North	80	...	74	...	...
Korea, South	100	93	100	51.3	93.1
Malaysia	88	78	94	...	...
Myanmar (Burma)	60	38	36	...	...
Nepal	...	46	21	6.1	...
Pakistan	55	79	33	25.1	...
Philippines	76	85	69	35.0	20.7
Saudi Arabia	97	95	86	...	...
Taiwan	...	86	69	94.2	99.1
Thailand	90	86	74	40.9	25.7
Turkey	100	100	83	70.6	83.1
Uzbekistan	...	...	18	...	...
Vietnam	90	36	22	...	...
EUROPE					
France	...	100	100	93.5	97.9
Germany	...	...	...	98.3	77.8
Italy	100	99	99	98.5	91.0
Poland	100	100	100	68.9	97.7[3]
Romania	100	100	49	...	...
Russia[4]	100	94	93	...	95.0
Spain	97	100	100	97.1	97.9
Sweden	100	100	100	98.0	...
Ukraine	100	100[2]	49	...	...
United Kingdom	100	100	96	99.8	99.1
OCEANIA					
Australia	100	...	73	92.2	99.6
New Zealand	100	97	100[2]	97.1	76.5[5]

[1]Metropolitan Lima.
[2]Urban households.
[3]Households of employed persons.
[4]Data refer to the former U.S.S.R.
[5]Combined refrigerator-freezers only.

Sources: UNDP, *Human Development Report* (1996); WHO, *Progress Towards Health for All* (1994); national statistical offices.

Maternal Health
(Selected Countries)

	Percentage of deliveries				Deaths per 100,000 live births
	Prenatal care	Attended by trained personnel	Tetanus toxoid vaccine (pregnant women, 2 or more doses)	Babies of low birth weight (less than 2,500 g[1])	Maternal mortality
AFRICA					
Algeria	<40	15	36	9	160
Egypt	40–59	41	52	10	170
Ethiopia	40–59	14	22	16	1,400
Kenya	60–79	54	72	16	650
Morocco	<40	31	64	9	610
Nigeria	60–79	37	27	16	1,000
South Africa	≥90	90	26	12	230
Sudan, The	...	69	65	15	660
Tanzania	≥90	53	31	14	770
Zaire	...	33	20	15	870
NORTH AMERICA					
Canada	≥90	99	...	6	6
Mexico	60–79	77	42	12	110
United States	≥90	99	...	7	12
SOUTH AMERICA					
Argentina	40–59	87	...	6	100
Brazil	60–79	95	62	11	220
Colombia	60–79	81	14	10	100
Peru	60–79	52	21	11	280
Venezuela	60–79	69	...	9	120
ASIA					
Bangladesh	<40	10	94	50	850
China	80–89	94	11	9	95
India	40–59	33	81	33	570
Indonesia	60–79	36	64	14	650
Iran	40–59	70	82	9	120
Iraq	40–59	50	72	15	310
Japan	≥90	100	...	6	18
Korea, North	≥90	100	95	...	70
Korea, South	80–89	89	...	9	130
Malaysia	60–79	87	79	10	80
Myanmar (Burma)	80–89	57	61	16	580
Nepal	<40	6	19	...	1,500
Pakistan	<40	35	39	25	340
Philippines	60–79	53	48	15	280
Saudi Arabia	80–89	90	62	7	130
Taiwan	...	...	...	...	8
Thailand	60–79	71	86	13	200
Turkey	40–59	76	38	8	180
Uzbekistan	...	...	...	...	55
Vietnam	≥90	95	82	17	160
EUROPE					
France	≥90	94	...	5	15
Germany	≥90	99	...	6	22
Italy	≥90	100	...	5	12
Poland	≥90	100	...	8	19
Romania	≥90	100	...	7	130
Russia	...		...	...	75
Spain	≥90	96	...	4	7
Sweden	≥90	100	...	5	7
Ukraine	...	...	...	...	50
United Kingdom	≥90	100	...	7	9
OCEANIA					
Australia	≥90	99	...	6	9
New Zealand	≥90	99	...	6	26

[1]Approximately 5½ lb.

Sources: WHO, *The World Health Report 1995, 1996;*
UNDP, *Human Development Report* (1996);
UNICEF, *The State of the World's Children* (1996).

Infant/Child Health
(Selected Countries)

	Deaths per 1,000 live births		Percentage of children immunized (age 12 months and under)			
	Infant mortality rate (deaths in first 12 months)	Child mortality rate (deaths in first 5 years)	Bacillus Calmette-Guérin (TB) vaccine	Diphtheria/ pertussis/ tetanus vaccine (3rd dose)	Oral polio vaccine (3rd dose)	Measles vaccine
AFRICA						
Algeria	49	56	93	75	75	69
Egypt	73	61	85	82	83	82
Ethiopia	113	174	65	57	57	54
Kenya	68	107	92	84	84	73
Morocco	80	62	99	93	93	92
Nigeria	81	149	55	44	45	50
South Africa	50	76	95	73	72	76
Sudan, The	115	75	88	76	77	74
Tanzania	83	128	86	79	78	75
Zaire	89	133	51	35	36	41
NORTH AMERICA						
Canada	7	8	...	93	89	98
Mexico	34	41	98	92	92	90
United States	8	10	...	94	84	89
SOUTH AMERICA						
Argentina	26	23	96	66	70	76
Brazil	70	56	90	69	95	78
Colombia	41	36	99	91	92	77
Peru	73	61	95	94	92	97
Venezuela	25	22	95	63	73	94
ASIA						
Bangladesh	148	102	100	91	92	96
China	44	41	94	93	94	89
India	124	77	97	92	92	84
Indonesia	65	52	95	91	91	89
Iran	62	32	99	97	97	95
Iraq	62	52	99	91	91	95
Japan	6	4	91	85	91	68
Korea, North	27	23	99	96	99	98
Korea, South	13	10	93	93	93	92
Malaysia	23	12	100	90	90	81
Myanmar (Burma)	99	78	74	69	69	66
Nepal	126	93	85	77	78	78
Pakistan	107	82	65	55	55	53
Philippines	48	39	91	85	86	86
Saudi Arabia	31	26	93	97	97	94
Taiwan	5	6	...	...	...	...
Thailand	43	35	98	93	93	86
Turkey	68	58	90	86	86	75
Uzbekistan	48	39	93	65	79	71
Vietnam	59	40	96	93	94	95
EUROPE						
France	9	7	78	89	92	76
Germany	7	6	...	80	80	75
Italy	9	7	...	50	98	50
Poland	18	13	94	95	96	96
Romania	29	22	100	98	94	93
Russia	26	20	96	72	88	91
Spain	8	7	...	88	88	90
Sweden	6	5	...	99[1]	99	96
Ukraine	20	16	92	94	95	96
United Kingdom	8	7	...	92	94	92
OCEANIA						
Australia	8	6	...	95	72	86
New Zealand	10	9	20	84	84	87

[1]Diphtheria only.

Resources for Health Care (Selected Countries)

	Persons per doctor	Persons per dentist	Persons per nurse	Persons per pharmacist	Persons per midwife
AFRICA					
Algeria	1,010	3,380	...	9,920	...
Egypt	550	3,690	1,240	1,610	...
Ethiopia	30,200	...	14,290	123,080	...
Kenya	7,020	40,120	980	44,030	...
Morocco	3,360	22,850	1,940	11,680	279,240
Nigeria	4,690	77,430	1,640	15,840	1,610
South Africa	1,530	9,850	250	4,220	...
Sudan, The	10,000	...	...	...	...
Tanzania	19,780	...	...	...	...
Zaire	15,580	913,070	1,360	634,510	...
NORTH AMERICA					
Canada	460	1,920	110	1,270	...
Mexico	580	18,250	600	...	...
United States	390	1,380	130	1,420	86,040
SOUTH AMERICA					
Argentina	370	1,510	1,780	44,490	...
Brazil	720	1,260	3,450	2,620	...
Colombia	910	2,420	720	...	...
Peru	940	2,830	1,490	3,700	6,250
Venezuela	630	2,570	390	3,510	...
ASIA					
Bangladesh	5,180	160,620	10,630	14,450	12,040
China	630	...	1,120	2,850	21,430
India	2,140	78,230	2,550	...	4,410
Indonesia	7,400	45,020	2,860[1]	96,820	...[1]
Iran	1,600	11,940	1,140[1]	...	...[1]
Iraq	1,920	11,580	1,380	11,770	...
Japan	570	1,610	160	770	5,480
Korea, North	370	...	...	...	...
Korea, South	860	3,620	410	1,080	5,410
Malaysia	2,480	13,150	480	15,630	...
Myanmar (Burma)	3,720	42,900	5,030	...	5,290
Nepal	12,620	...	6,790	39,030	7,610
Pakistan	2,110	55,310	6,560	34,220	7,120
Philippines	850	41,270	4,490	81,100	5,400
Saudi Arabia	520	8,330	340	9,050	...
Taiwan	770	2,970	390	1,120	20,980
Thailand	4,250	21,310	650	12,340	2,910
Turkey	1,110	5,340	1,250	3,550	1,840
Uzbekistan	290	...	90[1]	...	...[1]
Vietnam	2,490	...	1,330	10,970	5,940
EUROPE					
France	370	1,490	180	1,110	5,120
Germany	310	1,400	110[1]	1,890	...[1]
Italy	190	5,250	330	1,050	...
Poland	440	2,230	190	2,010	1,590
Romania	530	3,550	...	3,540	...
Russia	240	3,140	150	20,240	1,260
Spain	250	3,190	230	990	6,290
Sweden	390	1,780	90[1]	1,560	...[1]
Ukraine	230	...	80[1]	...	...[1]
United Kingdom	450	3,230	200	1,520	2,310
OCEANIA					
Australia	450	2,580	90[1]	1,510	...[1]
New Zealand	310	1,840	80[1]	1,010	...[1]

[1]Nurses includes midwives.

Sources: International Monetary Fund, *Government Finance Statistics Yearbook* (1995); UNICEF, *State of the World's Children* (1996); national statistical offices.

Institutional Resources

	% of central government expenditure on health	Hospitals			Access of population to essential drugs (%)
		Total number	Beds per 10,000 population	Occupancy rate	
AFRICA					
Algeria	...	284[1]	22	...	81-95
Egypt	2.4	6,416	20	...	81-95
Ethiopia	3.2	86	3	...	50-80
Kenya	5.0	877	14	...	50-80
Morocco	3.0	203[2]	11[2]	52.9[2]	50-80
Nigeria	1.0	11,588	12	...	<50
South Africa	...	834[3]	39[3]	...	50-80
Sudan, The	...	...	8	...	<50
Tanzania	6.0	...	11	...	50-80
Zaire	0.7	400	21	...	<50
NORTH AMERICA					
Canada	5.6	1,079	50	...	>95
Mexico	2.0	1,539	10	64.7[1]	50-80
United States	18.3	6,580	46	64.6[4]	>95
SOUTH AMERICA					
Argentina	2.8	...	44	51.9[1]	81-95
Brazil	5.2	35,701	37	...	50-80
Colombia	5.4	947	14	57.2	50-80
Peru	5.0	427	17	...	50-80
Venezuela	10.0	610	26	69.7[1]	50-80
ASIA					
Bangladesh	5.0	891	3	...	50-80
China	0.4	60,784	24	71.1	50-80
India	1.8	15,067	8	...	50-80
Indonesia	2.7	971	6	...	50-80
Iran	8.9	609	15	...	81-95
Iraq	...	177	18	42.4	50-80
Japan	1.6	9,963	136	...	>95
Korea, North	...	...	135	...	50-80
Korea, South	0.7	...	29[5]	75.1[5]	>95
Malaysia	5.6	264	22	...	81-95
Myanmar (Burma)	4.7	717	6	...	<50
Nepal	4.7	114	3	...	<50
Pakistan	1.0	10,905	6	...	50-80
Philippines	3.0	1,723	11	62.1	50-80
Saudi Arabia	6.0	229	21	...	>95
Taiwan	...	810	48	...	50-80
Thailand	8.2	1,097	17	...	50-80
Turkey	4.0	857	24	...	>95
Uzbekistan	...	1,388	85	...	50-80
Vietnam	...	12,500	27	...	50-80
EUROPE					
France	16.0	3,834	120	83.0	>95
Germany	18.0	2,381	80	83.9	>95
Italy	10.0	1,926	68	69.8	>95
Poland	...	752	63	72.5	81-95
Romania	8.1	...	95	...	81-95
Russia	1.4	12,265	119	83.2	50-80
Spain	6.2	813	42	76.7	>95
Sweden	0.2	...	52	78.0	>95
Ukraine	...	3,900	130	...	81-95
United Kingdom	14.0	2,423	54	80.6	>95
OCEANIA					
Australia	13.1	1,071[6]	50	...	>95
New Zealand	15.6	330	77	93.3[1]	>95

[1]Government hospitals only.

[2]Public sector only.

[3]Data exclude the former African independent states of Bophuthatswana, Ciskei, Transkei, and Venda.

[4]5,261 community hospitals only.

[5]General and specialized hospitals only.

[6]General hospitals only.

Sources: International Monetary Fund, *Government Finance Statistics Yearbook* (1995); UNICEF, *State of the World's Children* (1996); national statistical offices.

Adult HIV-Infection Prevalence, Early 1995

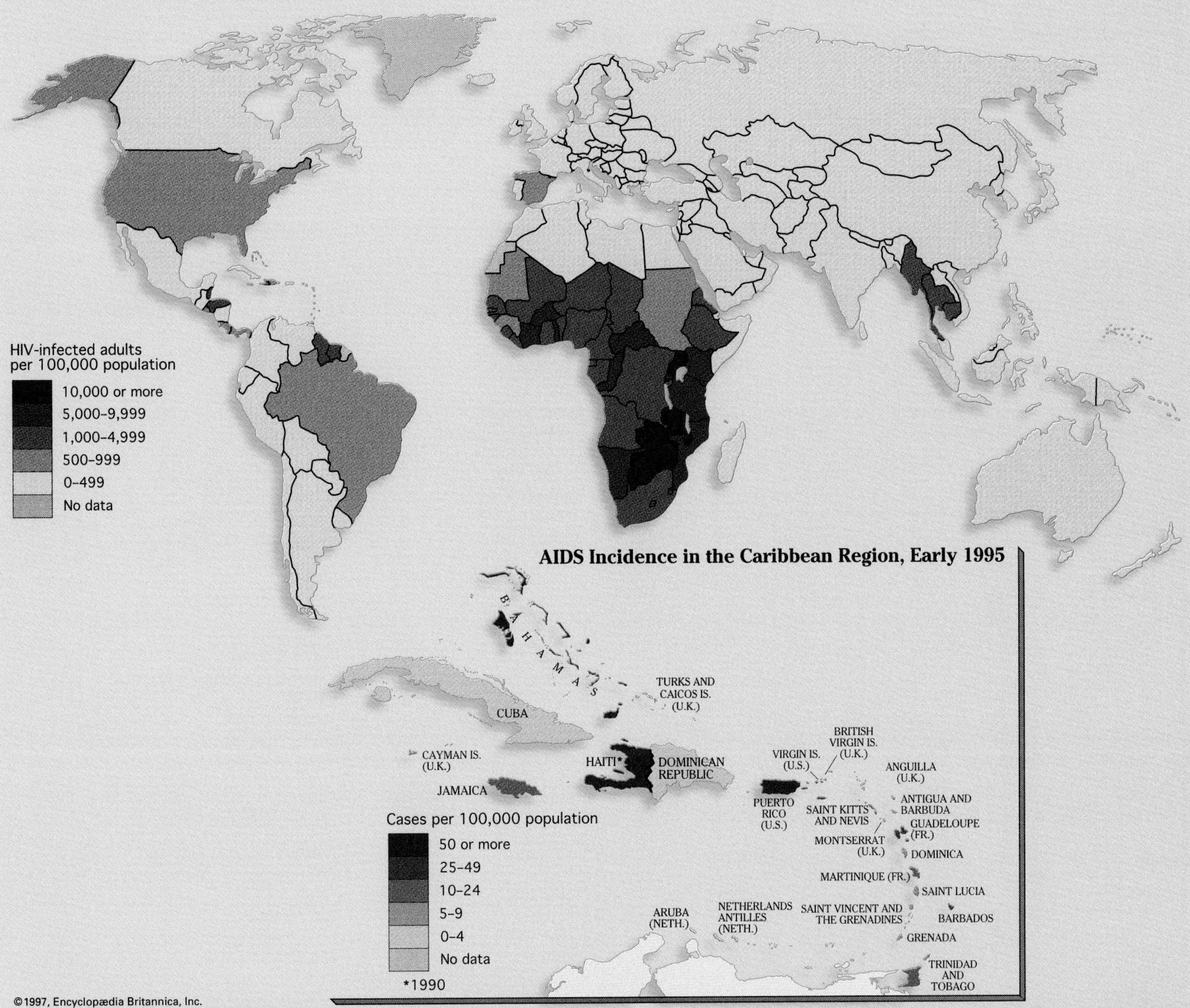

AIDS Cases Reported to WHO by Continent per Year Based on Reports Received Through Dec. 15, 1995

	New Cases						Cumulative Cases					
Year	Africa	Americas	Asia	Europe	Oceania	TOTALS	Africa	Americas	Asia	Europe	Oceania	TOTALS
1979	0	2	0	0	0	2	0	2	0	0	0	2
1980	0	185	1	17	0	203	0	187	1	17	0	205
1981	0	322	1	20	0	343	0	509	2	37	0	548
1982	2	1,156	1	80	91	1,330	2	1,665	3	117	91	1,878
1983	17	3,352	8	295	6	3,678	19	5,017	11	412	97	5,556
1984	187	6,680	8	570	76	7,521	206	11,697	19	982	173	13,077
1985	521	12,682	27	1,475	142	14,847	727	24,379	46	2,457	315	27,924
1986	5,438	21,322	86	2,395	252	29,493	6,165	45,701	132	4,852	567	57,417
1987	16,854	34,562	150	9,640	324	61,530	23,019	80,263	282	14,492	891	118,947
1988	28,212	47,697	176	10,811	598	87,494	51,231	127,960	458	25,303	1,489	206,441
1989	41,295	56,202	288	14,355	699	112,839	92,526	184,162	746	39,658	2,188	319,280
1990	54,528	65,041	478	17,311	770	138,128	147,054	249,203	1,224	56,969	2,958	457,408
1991	72,756	78,579	838	18,937	897	172,007	219,810	327,782	2,062	75,906	3,855	629,415
1992	73,631	99,881	2,039	20,697	866	197,114	293,441	427,663	4,101	96,603	4,721	826,529
1993	67,124	100,731	7,368	22,053	879	198,155	360,565	528,394	11,469	118,656	5,600	1,024,684
1994	65,684	83,475	11,707	23,541	906	185,313	426,249	611,869	23,176	142,197	6,506	1,209,997
1995[1]	16,486	47,793	5,454	11,906	174	81,813	442,735	659,662	28,630	154,103	6,680	1,291,810
TOTALS	442,735	659,662	28,630	154,103	6,680	1,291,810	442,735	659,662	28,630	154,103	6,680	1,291,810

[1]Partial data.

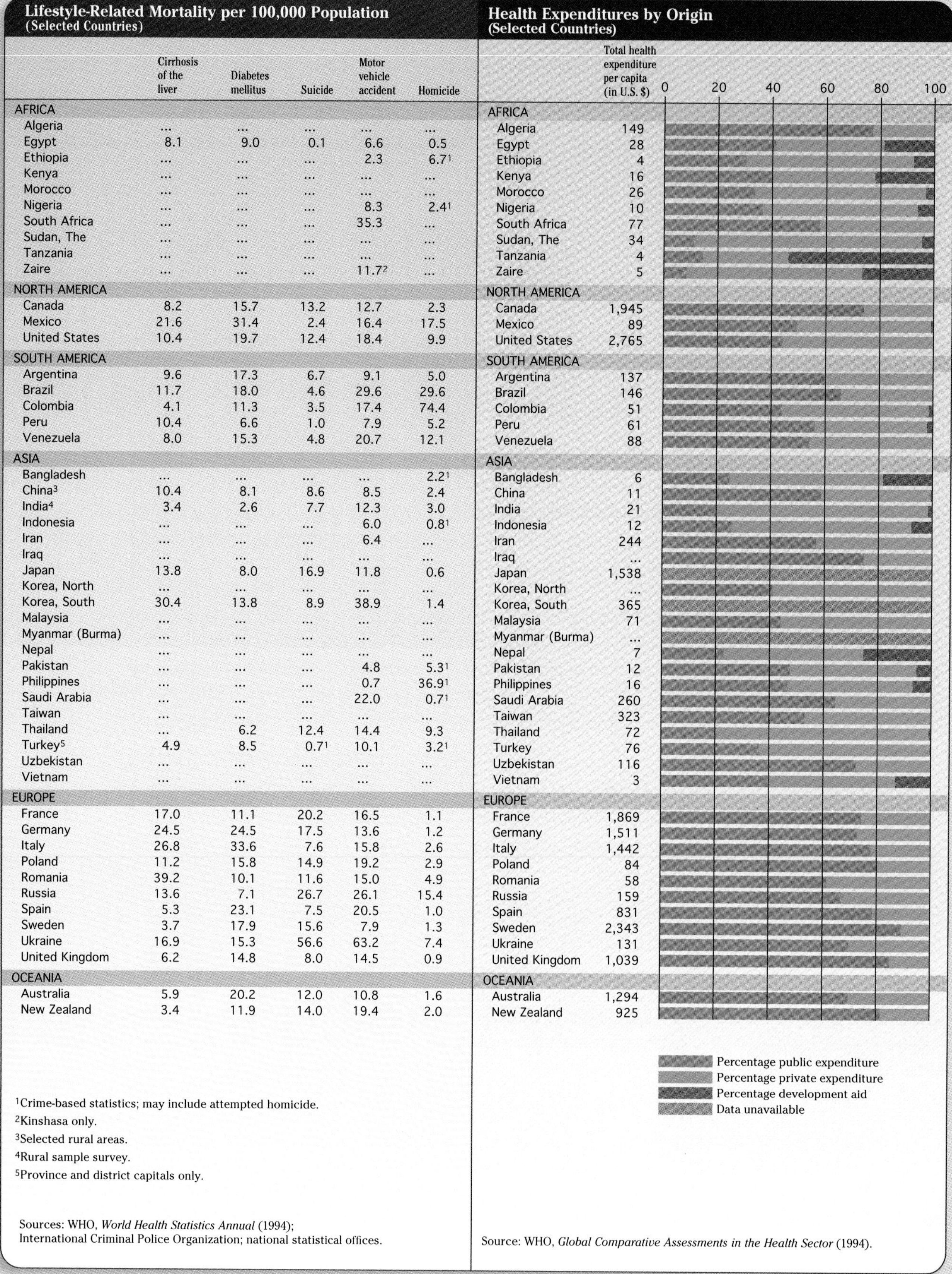

Lifestyle-Related Mortality per 100,000 Population (Selected Countries)

	Cirrhosis of the liver	Diabetes mellitus	Suicide	Motor vehicle accident	Homicide
AFRICA					
Algeria	...	...	...	...	...
Egypt	8.1	9.0	0.1	6.6	0.5
Ethiopia	...	...	...	2.3	6.7[1]
Kenya	...	...	...	...	...
Morocco	...	...	...	...	...
Nigeria	...	...	...	8.3	2.4[1]
South Africa	...	...	...	35.3	...
Sudan, The	...	...	...	...	...
Tanzania	...	...	...	...	...
Zaire	...	...	...	11.7[2]	...
NORTH AMERICA					
Canada	8.2	15.7	13.2	12.7	2.3
Mexico	21.6	31.4	2.4	16.4	17.5
United States	10.4	19.7	12.4	18.4	9.9
SOUTH AMERICA					
Argentina	9.6	17.3	6.7	9.1	5.0
Brazil	11.7	18.0	4.6	29.6	29.6
Colombia	4.1	11.3	3.5	17.4	74.4
Peru	10.4	6.6	1.0	7.9	5.2
Venezuela	8.0	15.3	4.8	20.7	12.1
ASIA					
Bangladesh	...	...	...	...	2.2[1]
China[3]	10.4	8.1	8.6	8.5	2.4
India[4]	3.4	2.6	7.7	12.3	3.0
Indonesia	...	...	...	6.0	0.8[1]
Iran	...	...	...	6.4	...
Iraq	...	...	...	...	...
Japan	13.8	8.0	16.9	11.8	0.6
Korea, North	...	...	...	...	...
Korea, South	30.4	13.8	8.9	38.9	1.4
Malaysia	...	...	...	...	...
Myanmar (Burma)	...	...	...	...	...
Nepal	...	...	...	...	...
Pakistan	...	...	...	4.8	5.3[1]
Philippines	...	...	...	0.7	36.9[1]
Saudi Arabia	...	...	...	22.0	0.7[1]
Taiwan	...	...	...	...	...
Thailand	...	6.2	12.4	14.4	9.3
Turkey[5]	4.9	8.5	0.7[1]	10.1	3.2[1]
Uzbekistan	...	...	...	...	...
Vietnam	...	...	...	...	...
EUROPE					
France	17.0	11.1	20.2	16.5	1.1
Germany	24.5	24.5	17.5	13.6	1.2
Italy	26.8	33.6	7.6	15.8	2.6
Poland	11.2	15.8	14.9	19.2	2.9
Romania	39.2	10.1	11.6	15.0	4.9
Russia	13.6	7.1	26.7	26.1	15.4
Spain	5.3	23.1	7.5	20.5	1.0
Sweden	3.7	17.9	15.6	7.9	1.3
Ukraine	16.9	15.3	56.6	63.2	7.4
United Kingdom	6.2	14.8	8.0	14.5	0.9
OCEANIA					
Australia	5.9	20.2	12.0	10.8	1.6
New Zealand	3.4	11.9	14.0	19.4	2.0

[1]Crime-based statistics; may include attempted homicide.
[2]Kinshasa only.
[3]Selected rural areas.
[4]Rural sample survey.
[5]Province and district capitals only.

Sources: WHO, *World Health Statistics Annual* (1994); International Criminal Police Organization; national statistical offices.

Health Expenditures by Origin (Selected Countries)

	Total health expenditure per capita (in U.S. $)
AFRICA	
Algeria	149
Egypt	28
Ethiopia	4
Kenya	16
Morocco	26
Nigeria	10
South Africa	77
Sudan, The	34
Tanzania	4
Zaire	5
NORTH AMERICA	
Canada	1,945
Mexico	89
United States	2,765
SOUTH AMERICA	
Argentina	137
Brazil	146
Colombia	51
Peru	61
Venezuela	88
ASIA	
Bangladesh	6
China	11
India	21
Indonesia	12
Iran	244
Iraq	...
Japan	1,538
Korea, North	...
Korea, South	365
Malaysia	71
Myanmar (Burma)	...
Nepal	7
Pakistan	12
Philippines	16
Saudi Arabia	260
Taiwan	323
Thailand	72
Turkey	76
Uzbekistan	116
Vietnam	3
EUROPE	
France	1,869
Germany	1,511
Italy	1,442
Poland	84
Romania	58
Russia	159
Spain	831
Sweden	2,343
Ukraine	131
United Kingdom	1,039
OCEANIA	
Australia	1,294
New Zealand	925

Source: WHO, *Global Comparative Assessments in the Health Sector* (1994).

Environmental Pollution

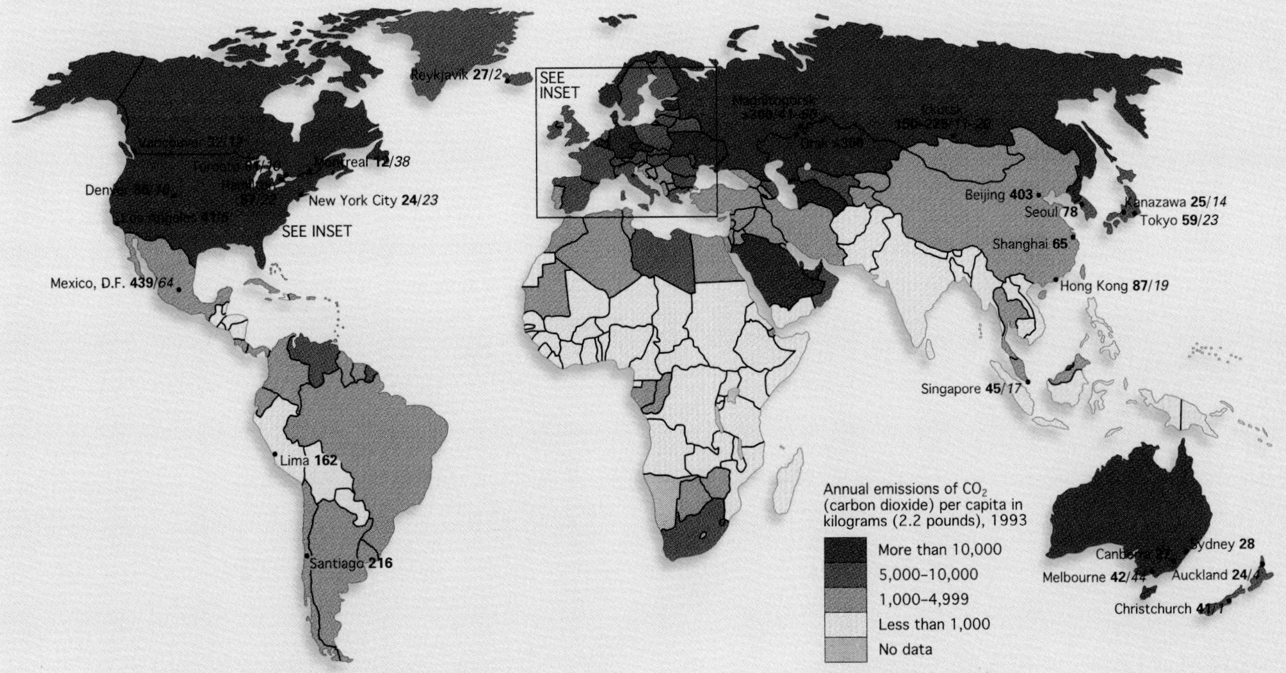

Reykjavík 27/2 · Montreal 12/38 · New York City 24/23 · Mexico, D.F. 439/64 · Lima 162 · Santiago 216 · Beijing 403 · Seoul 78 · Kanazawa 25/14 · Tokyo 59/23 · Shanghai 65 · Hong Kong 87/19 · Singapore 45/17 · Sydney 28 · Melbourne 42/4 · Auckland 24/4 · Christchurch 41/1

Annual emissions of CO_2 (carbon dioxide) per capita in kilograms (2.2 pounds), 1993

- More than 10,000
- 5,000–10,000
- 1,000–4,999
- Less than 1,000
- No data

Total suspended particulates shown in **bold**.
SO_2 (sulfur dioxide) level shown in *italic*.
Annual mean concentrations given for selected cities in micrograms per cubic meter of air.

The 30 United States metropolitan statistical areas with the highest average levels of suspended particulates (particles measured fall in the range of 2.5–10 microns). Values shown are given in micrograms per cubic meter of air and represent average levels from 1990 to 1994. SO_2 levels were converted from a parts per million ratio into micrograms per cubic meter of air (at 25°C [77°F]) and represent 1993 annual averages.

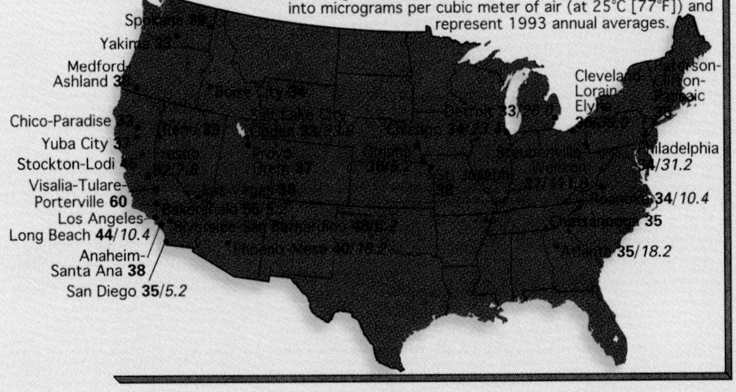

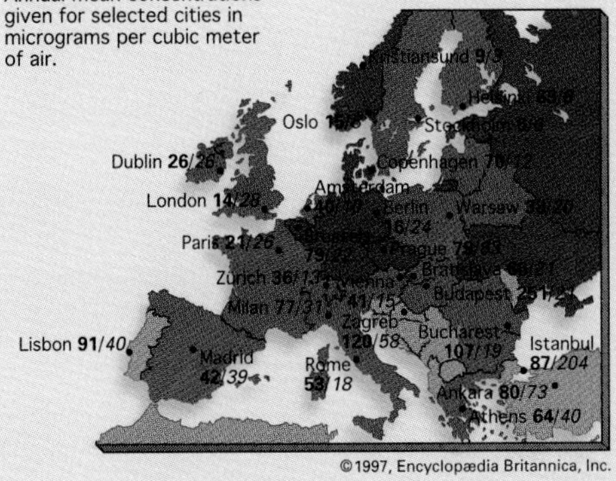

Medford-Ashland · Chico-Paradise · Yuba City · Stockton-Lodi · Visalia-Tulare-Porterville 60 · Los Angeles-Long Beach 44/10.4 · Anaheim-Santa Ana 38 · San Diego 35/5.2 · Philadelphia 31.2 · 34/10.4 · Chattanooga 35 · Atlanta 35/18.2

Lisbon 91/40 · Dublin 26/26 · London 14/26 · Paris 21/26 · Zürich 36/13 · Milan 77/31 · Madrid 42/39 · Rome 53/18 · Zagreb 120/58 · Bucharest 107/19 · Istanbul 87/204 · Ankara 80/73 · Athens 64/40 · Oslo · Copenhagen 70/12 · Amsterdam · Berlin 18/24 · Warsaw · Prague · Budapest

Outbreaks: Emerging and Reemerging Infectious Diseases, 1995–96

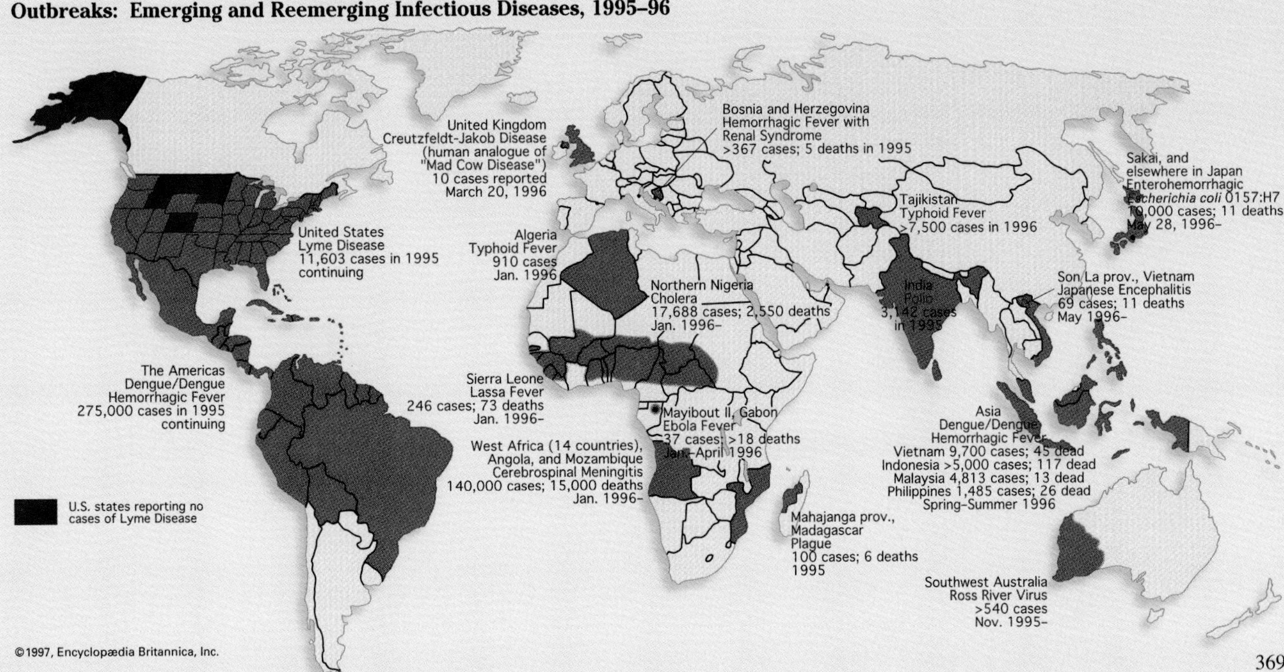

United States, Deaths due to Injury, 1993

Selected causes by type of accident or manner of injury	
TOTAL DEATHS DUE TO INJURIES	151,061
UNINTENTIONAL INJURIES/ACCIDENTS	90,523
Transport accidents	44,409
Railway	670
Highway	42,076
Water	763
Air and space	859
Poisoning and medical mishap	11,261
Drugs (licit and illicit), medications, and biologics	7,382
Gases and vapors	660
Complications of medical and surgical care	2,724
Falls	13,141
Fire	3,900
Lightning	57
Other accidents	15,049
Drowning	3,807
Inhalation and ingestion of food or other object	3,160
Firearm	1,521
Handgun	260
Other	1,261
Explosive material	178
Hot substance or object, corrosive material, and steam	130
Electric current	548
Adverse effects of drugs in therapeutic use	201
SUICIDE	31,102
HOMICIDE	25,653
Assault by firearm	18,271
Assault by cutting and piercing instrument	3,204

Source: National Center for Health Statistics.

United States, National Health Care Expenditures by Kind, 1994

Personal 87.6%
Government 3.0%
Other 9.4%
Dentist services 4.4%
Nursing home care 7.6%
Other professional services 5.2%
Drugs and other medical nondurables 8.3%
Vision products and other medical durables 1.4%
Other personal health care 2.3%
Program administration 6.2%
Government public health activities 3.0%
Noncommercial research 1.7%
Construction 1.5%
Hospital services 35.7%
Home health care 2.8%
Physician services 19.9%

Source: U.S. Department of Health and Human Services, Health Care Financing Administration, *Health Care Financing Review,* vol. 17, no. 3, HCFA Pub. no. 03383 (1996).

United States,[1] Physicians by Specialty,[2] 1994

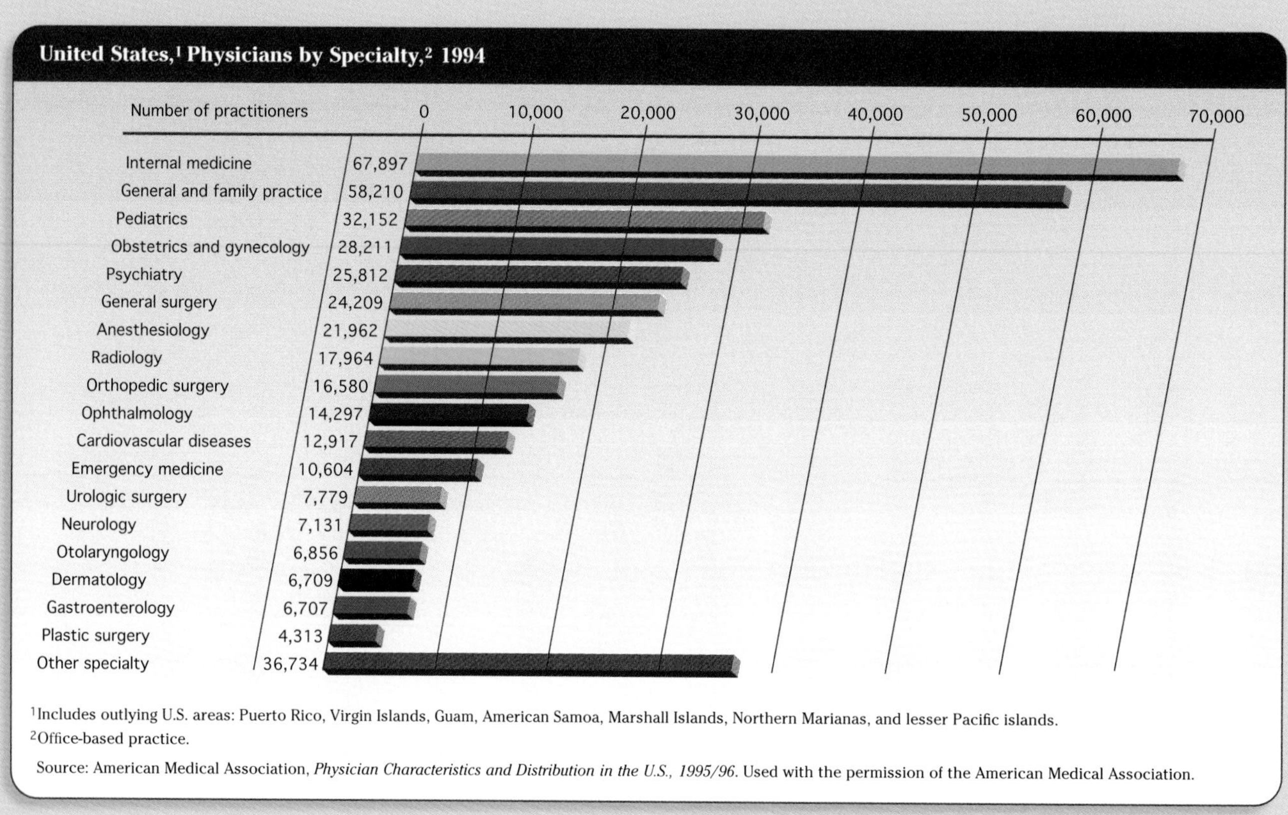

[1]Includes outlying U.S. areas: Puerto Rico, Virgin Islands, Guam, American Samoa, Marshall Islands, Northern Marianas, and lesser Pacific islands.
[2]Office-based practice.

Source: American Medical Association, *Physician Characteristics and Distribution in the U.S., 1995/96*. Used with the permission of the American Medical Association.

United States, AIDS Incidence, Early 1996

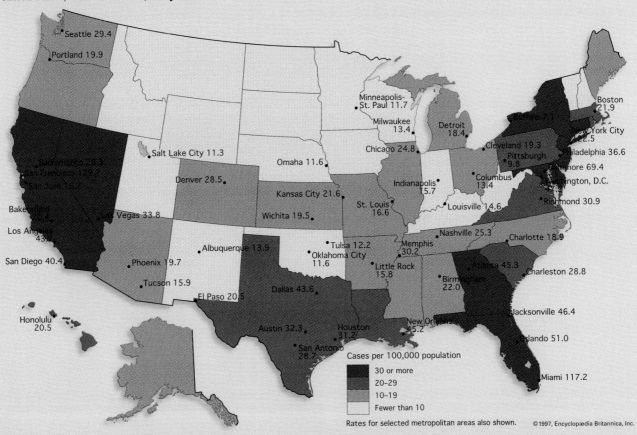

Seattle 29.4
Portland 19.9
Sacramento 28.3
San Francisco 129.7
San Jose 16.7
Bakersfield 20.4
Los Angeles 43.7
San Diego 40.4
Las Vegas 33.8
Phoenix 19.7
Tucson 15.9
Salt Lake City 11.3
Denver 28.5
Albuquerque 13.9
El Paso 20.5
Honolulu 20.5
Omaha 11.6
Kansas City 21.6
Wichita 19.5
Tulsa 12.2
Oklahoma City 11.6
Dallas 43.6
Austin 32.3
San Antonio 28.7
Houston 31.2
Minneapolis-St. Paul 11.7
Milwaukee 13.4
Chicago 24.8
St. Louis 16.6
Little Rock 15.8
Memphis 30.2
New Orleans 45.2
Detroit 18.4
Indianapolis 15.7
Louisville 14.6
Nashville 25.3
Birmingham 22.0
Atlanta 45.3
Cleveland 19.3
Pittsburgh 9.8
Columbus 13.4
Charlotte 18.9
Charleston 28.8
Jacksonville 46.4
Orlando 51.0
Miami 117.2
Buffalo 7.1
Boston 21.9
New York City 22.5
Philadelphia 36.6
Baltimore 69.4
Washington, D.C.
Richmond 30.9

Cases per 100,000 population
30 or more
20–29
10–19
Fewer than 10

Rates for selected metropolitan areas also shown.

United States, Age-Adjusted Death Rates, 14 Causes, 1950–94 (Logarithmic Scale)

Rate per 100,000 U.S. standard million population

400.0
200.0
100.0
80.0
60.0
40.0
20.0
10.0
8.0
6.0
4.0
2.0
1.0
0.8
0.6
0.4
0.2
0.1

1950 1955 1960 1965 1970 1975 1980 1985 1990 1995

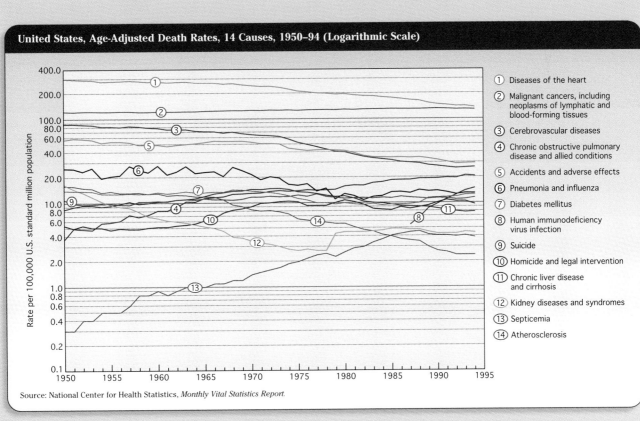

1. Diseases of the heart
2. Malignant cancers, including neoplasms of lymphatic and blood-forming tissues
3. Cerebrovascular diseases
4. Chronic obstructive pulmonary disease and allied conditions
5. Accidents and adverse effects
6. Pneumonia and influenza
7. Diabetes mellitus
8. Human immunodeficiency virus infection
9. Suicide
10. Homicide and legal intervention
11. Chronic liver disease and cirrhosis
12. Kidney diseases and syndromes
13. Septicemia
14. Atherosclerosis

Source: National Center for Health Statistics, *Monthly Vital Statistics Report.*

United States, Personal Injury from Violent Crime

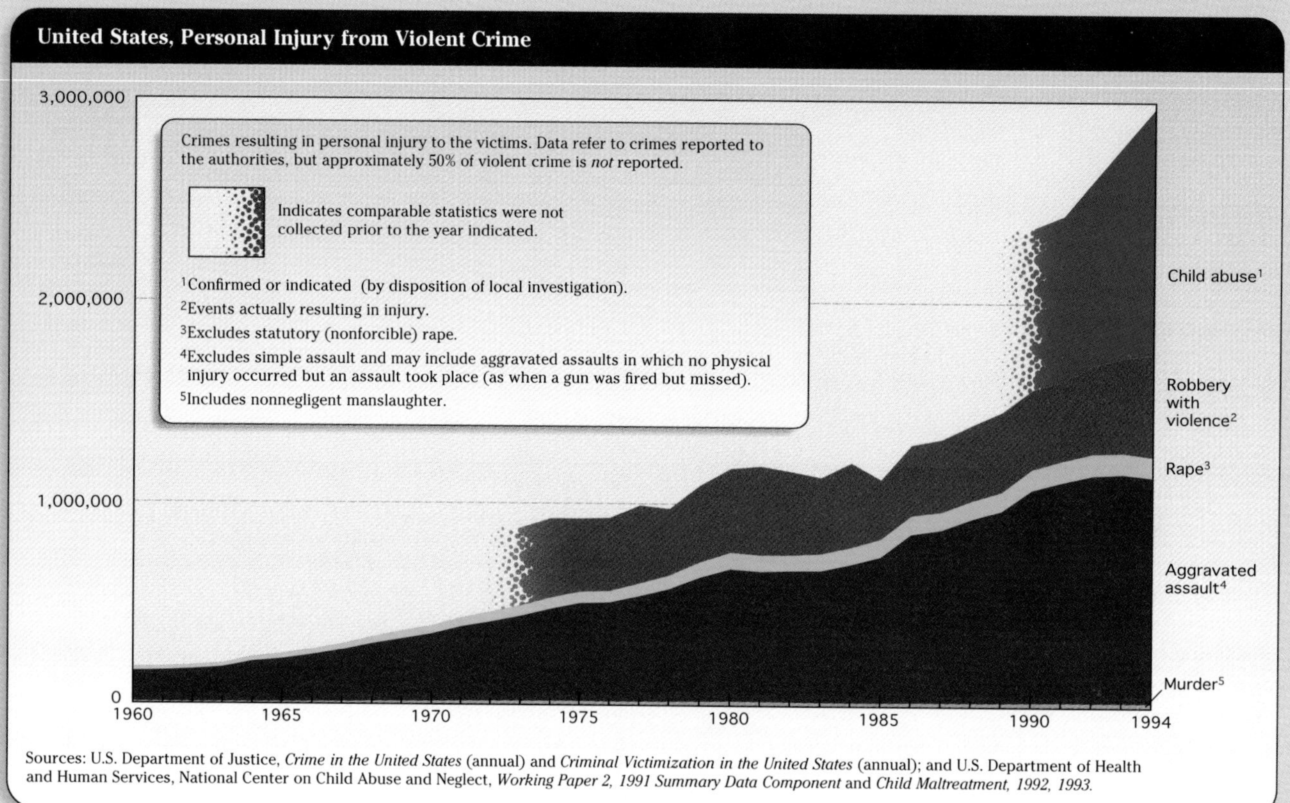

3,000,000
2,000,000
1,000,000

Crimes resulting in personal injury to the victims. Data refer to crimes reported to the authorities, but approximately 50% of violent crime is *not* reported.
Indicates comparable statistics were not collected prior to the year indicated.
1Confirmed or indicated (by disposition of local investigation).
2Events actually resulting in injury.
3Excludes statutory (nonforcible) rape.
4Excludes simple assault and may include aggravated assaults in which no physical injury occurred but an assault took place (as when a gun was fired but missed).
5Includes nonnegligent manslaughter.
Child abuse1
Robbery with violence2
Rape3
Aggravated assault4
Murder5

Sources: U.S. Department of Justice, *Crime in the United States* (annual) and *Criminal Victimization in the United States* (annual); and U.S. Department of Health and Human Services, National Center on Child Abuse and Neglect, *Working Paper 2, 1991 Summary Data Component* and *Child Maltreatment, 1992, 1993.*

United States, Annual Per Capita Food Consumption (in Pounds)

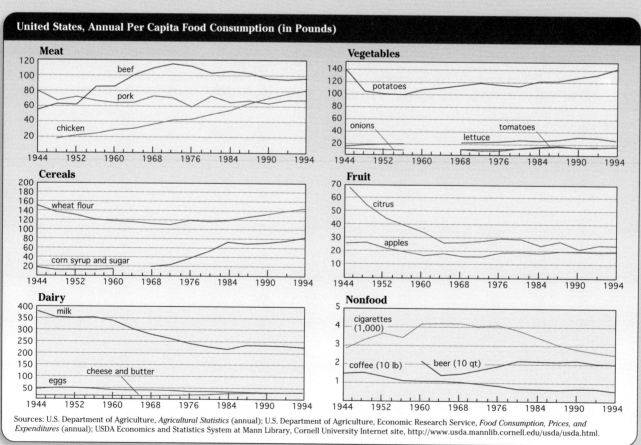

Meat

120 100 80 60 40 20

beef
pork
chicken

1944 1952 1960 1968 1976 1984 1990 1994

Vegetables

140 120 100 80 60 40 20

potatoes
onions
tomatoes
lettuce

1944 1952 1960 1968 1976 1984 1990 1994

Cereals

200 180 160 140 120 100 80 60 40 20

wheat flour
corn syrup and sugar

1944 1952 1960 1968 1976 1984 1990 1994

Fruit

70 60 50 40 30 20 10

citrus
apples

1944 1952 1960 1968 1976 1984 1990 1994

Dairy

400 350 300 250 200 150 100 50

milk
cheese and butter
eggs

1944 1952 1960 1968 1976 1984 1990 1994

Nonfood

5 4 3 2 1

cigarettes (1,000)
coffee (10 lb)
beer (10 qt)

1944 1952 1960 1968 1976 1984 1990 1994

1965
1970
1975
1980
1985

Sources: U.S. Department of Agriculture, *Agricultural Statistics* (annual); U.S. Department of Agriculture, Economic Research Service, *Food Consumption, Prices, and Expenditures* (annual); USDA Economics and Statistics System at Mann Library, Cornell University Internet site, http://www.usda.mannlib.cornell.edu/usda/usda.html.

Contributors to the World of Medicine

Michael A. Allan, M.D.
New Tools for ENT
Department of Otolaryngology Head and Neck Surgery, Kaiser Foundation Hospital; Clinical Assistant Professor, University of Southern California School of Medicine, Los Angeles

Donna C. Bergen, M.D.
Stroke Update
Associate Professor of Neurological Sciences, Rush Medical College, and Senior Attending Neurologist, Rush-Presbyterian-St. Luke's Medical Center, Chicago

Ellen Bernstein
Pedaling with a Passion: A Photo Essay
Editor, *Medical and Health Annual,* Encyclopædia Britannica, Inc., Chicago

Peter D. Blanck, Ph.D., J.D.
Accommodations in the Workplace: Smart Business
Professor of Law and Professor of Psychology at the University of Iowa, Iowa City; Senior Fellow, The Annenberg Washington Program; and member, President's Committee on Employment of Persons with Disabilities

Lester E. Block, D.D.S., M.P.H.
U.S. Health Care Reform: Still on the Critical List
Director of Graduate Studies, Division of Health Management and Policy, School of Public Health, University of Minnesota, Minneapolis

Regina Botting, Ph.D.
Aspirin: Ageless Remedy (coauthor)
Information Scientist, The William Harvey Research Institute, St. Bartholomew's and Royal London School of Medicine and Dentistry, London

Phyllida Brown
NewsCap: *Malaria Update: Don't Forget the Bednet*
Biomedicine Consultant, *New Scientist* magazine; science writer specializing in health, London

Charles M. Clark, Jr., M.D.
Diabetes Update (coauthor)
Professor of Medicine and Pharmacology; Director, Diabetes Research & Training Center; and Codirector, Regenstrief Institute, Indiana University School of Medicine, Indianapolis

Darrell Debowey, M.S.
Angiography: At the Heart of Cardiac Research
Director, Angiography Core Laboratory, Cleveland Clinic Foundation, Cleveland, Ohio

Don C. Des Jarlais, Ph.D.
Needle Exchange—It Works
Director of Research, Chemical Dependency Institute, Beth Israel Medical Center, and Professor of Epidemiology, Albert Einstein College of Medicine, New York City

Alvin N. Eden, M.D.
Toddlers at the Table
Chairman and Director, Department of Pediatrics, Wyckoff Heights Medical Center, Brooklyn, N.Y.; Associate Clinical Professor of Pediatrics, The New York Hospital-Cornell Medical Center, New York City

Weylin G. Eng, O.D.
Focus on Low Vision (coauthor)
Director of Professional Affairs and Associate Clinical Professor, University of California, Berkeley, School of Optometry; formerly Captain, Medical Service Corps, U.S. Navy

Terry D. Etherton, Ph.D.
Fundamentals of Fats (coauthor)
Professor of Animal Nutrition, Pennsylvania State University, University Park

Danielle Foullon
New Drugs Approved by the Food and Drug Administration, January 1995–July 1996
Assistant Managing Editor, F-D-C Reports, Chevy Chase, Md.

Barry A. Franklin, Ph.D.
Heart Smart: To Shovel or Not to Shovel?
Director, Cardiac Rehabilitation and Exercise Laboratories, William Beaumont Hospital, Royal Oak, Mich.; Professor of Physiology, Wayne State University School of Medicine, Detroit, Mich.

M.J. Friedrich
NewsCaps: *Breast Cancer Genes: Insights and Issues; Heart-Stopping News; Cystic Fibrosis: Answers Raise Questions; Gene Therapy: Promise Unfulfilled; Havoc in the Helix; Mapping Human Genes: 3,600—and Counting; Obesity: The Plot Thickens*
Associate Editor, Encyclopædia Britannica, Inc., Chicago

Bruce G. Gellin, M.D., M.P.H.
Immunization Update (coauthor)
NewsCap: *Smallpox Virus: On Death Row*
Medical Officer, Division of Microbiology and Infectious Diseases, National Institute of Allergy and Infectious Diseases, National Institutes of Health, Bethesda, Md.; Assistant Professor, Johns Hopkins University School of Hygiene and Public Health, Department of International Health, Division of Vaccine Sciences, Baltimore, Md.

Katherine I. Gordon
Tobacco and Health: Continuing Saga
NewsCaps: *A Billionaire's Gift to Research; Valor in Oklahoma City; Better Paps; Teens Have a Future with Foster; Do I Dare to Eat a Peach?*
Editorial Coordinator, Encyclopædia Britannica, Inc., Chicago

David Y. Graham, M.D.
Ulcers Update
Chief of Gastroenterology, Veterans Affairs Medical Center, and Professor of Medicine, Baylor College of Medicine, Houston, Texas

Jian-Qiu Han, M.D.
Hepatitis: From A to G (coauthor)
Assistant Professor, Shanghai Institute of Biological Products, and Visiting Scholar, University of Iowa College of Medicine, Iowa City (1993–96)

Robert A. Hatcher, M.D., M.P.H.
Update on Birth Control Pills
Professor of Gynecology and Obstetrics, Emory University School of Medicine, Atlanta, Ga.; senior author, *Contraceptive Technology*

Robert P. Heaney, M.D.
Osteoporosis Update
John A. Creighton University Professor, Creighton University, Omaha, Neb.

James Hennelly
NewsCaps: Visible Woman: View Her Byte by Byte; Iraq's Children: Paying the Price of Politics
Writer/Researcher, Encyclopædia Britannica, Inc., Chicago

Laurence S. Kalkstein, Ph.D.
Global Warming: How Hazardous to Health?
Professor of Climatology, University of Delaware, Newark; Principal Investigator, Climate Change/Health Program, U.S. Environmental Protection Agency

Jane Katz, Ed.D.
Take the Plunge: Swimming for Health
Professor of Health and Physical Education, John Jay College of Criminal Justice of the City University of New York; fitness instructor for members of New York City's police and fire departments; Water Safety Instructor Trainer, American Red Cross; consultant, President's Council on Physical Fitness and Sports; World Masters champion swimmer and winner of numerous awards; and author of many books and a videotape on swimming and aquatic exercise

Penny M. Kris-Etherton, Ph.D., R.D.
Fundamentals of Fats (coauthor)
Distinguished Professor of Nutrition, Pennsylvania State University, University Park; member, Nutrition Committee, American Heart Association

Daniel R. Kuritzkes, M.D.
AIDS Update
Associate Professor of Medicine and Microbiology, Division of Infectious Diseases, University of Colorado Health Sciences Center, Denver

John La Puma, M.D.
Back to the Future
General Internist, Alexian Brothers Medical Center and North Suburban Clinic, Elk Grove, Ill.; demonstrating chef and lecturer, Chicago; and coauthor, *The McGraw-Hill Pocket Guide to Managed Care: Business, Practice, Law, Ethics* (1996)

James W. LeDuc, Ph.D.
Latin America: The New "Hot Zone"
Medical Officer, Division of Emerging and Other Communicable Diseases Surveillance and Control, World Health Organization, Geneva, on assignment from the National Center for Infectious Diseases, Centers for Disease Control and Prevention, Atlanta, Ga.

Michael E. Mahler, M.D.
Parkinson's Disease Update (coauthor)
Associate Professor of Neurology, University of California, Los Angeles, School of Medicine

Robin Marks, M.B.B.S., M.P.H.
Australians Get Smart About the Sun
Professor of Dermatology, University of Melbourne, and Director of Dermatology, St. Vincent's Hospital Melbourne, Fitzroy, Victoria; National Australian Spokesman on Skin Cancer Control for the Australian Cancer Society

Jerry Mason
Death in the 1990s
Freelance writer and photographer, London

Mark Messina, Ph.D.
Soy to the World (coauthor)
Nutrition consultant, Port Townsend, Wash.; coauthor, *The Simple Soybean and Your Health* (1994)

Virginia Kisch Messina, M.P.H., R.D.
Soy to the World (coauthor)
Nutrition consultant, Port Townsend, Wash.; coauthor, *The Simple Soybean and Your Health* (1994)

Tom Michael
NewsCap: Panic in the ER
Assistant Editor, Encyclopædia Britannica, Inc., Chicago

Robert E. Michler, M.D.
Xenotransplantation Considered
Director, Cardiac Transplantation Service, Division of Cardiothoracic Surgery, Columbia-Presbyterian Medical Center, and Associate Professor of Surgery and Director, Transplantation Research Laboratory, Columbia University College of Physicians and Surgeons, New York City

Stephen S. Morse, Ph.D.
Tracking Trouble: Disease Surveillance via the Internet
Assistant Professor, Division of Epidemiology, and Director, Program in Emerging Diseases, Columbia University School of Public Health, New York City; Chair, Steering Committee, ProMED (Program for Monitoring Emerging Diseases) of the Federation of American Scientists

Vikkie A. Mustad, Ph.D.
Fundamentals of Fats (coauthor)
Postdoctoral Fellow, Medical Nutrition Research and Development, Ross Products Division, Abbott Laboratories, Columbus, Ohio; formerly Research Associate, Pennsylvania State University, University Park

Thomas L. Petty, M.D.
Chronic Obstructive Pulmonary Disease: Insights and Advances
Professor of Medicine, University of Colorado Health Sciences Center, and consultant and faculty member, HealthONE Center for Health Sciences Education, Denver; Chairman, National Lung Health Education Program of the National Heart, Lung, and Blood Institute

Ana Priscu, M.D.
Diabetes Update (coauthor)
Endocrinology Fellow, Indiana University School of Medicine, Indianapolis

Regina Rabinovich, M.D., M.P.H.
Immunization Update (coauthor)
Chief, Clinical Studies Section, Division of Microbiology and Infectious Diseases, National Institute of Allergy and Infectious Diseases, National Institutes of Health, Bethesda, Md.

David B. Reuben, M.D.
Parkinson's Disease Update (coauthor)
Chief, Division of Geriatrics, Director, Multicampus Program in Geriatric Medicine and Gerontology, and Associate Professor of Medicine, University of California, Los Angeles, School of Medicine

Wade Roush, Ph.D.
The Genetics of Violence: A Controversial Conference
Reporter/Writer, Boston Bureau, *Science* magazine

Jack Thomas Stapleton, M.D.
Hepatitis: From A to G (coauthor)
Professor of Internal Medicine, University of Iowa College of Medicine, Iowa City

Margretta Madden Styles, R.N., Ed.D.
New Responsibility and Respect for Nurses
President, International Council of Nurses, Geneva; President, American Nurses Credentialing Center, Washington, D.C.

Linda Tomchuck
NewsCaps: Good Reasons to Eat Liver and Legumes; Eat (Vegetables), Drink (Moderately), and Be Healthy; Vitamin A Gets an F; Beta-Carotene: A Dream Deferred; Eating Defensively; Mad Cow Chronology; Score Two for Prevention
Senior Editor, *Medical and Health Annual,* Encyclopædia Britannica, Inc., Chicago

Joseph Turow, Ph.D.
NewsCaps: No Appointment Necessary; Remembering TV's Toughest Surgeon
Professor of Communication, The Annenberg School for Communication of the University of Pennsylvania, Philadelphia

Sir John Vane, D.Sc., F.R.S.
Aspirin: Ageless Remedy (coauthor)
Director General, The William Harvey Research Institute, St. Bartholomew's and Royal London School of Medicine and Dentistry, London

Jeff Wallenfeldt
NewsCaps: Believing in Magic; Jaws V: A Cutting-Edge Discovery; Covering the Costs of What Works; Finding "C" Level; Agent Orange Update; Playing Fair: Drug Testing at the Olympics; Mop That Floor, Tread That Mill; Glaucoma: Lasers Take the Pressure Off
Assistant Editor, Encyclopædia Britannica, Inc., Chicago

Beverly Woodward, Ph.D.
Patient Privacy in a Computerized World
Research Associate in Philosophy and Sociology, Brandeis University, Waltham, Mass.; author of a forthcoming book on medical surveillance

Michael D. Yapko, Ph.D.
Depression Update
Clinical Psychologist and Marriage and Family Therapist in private practice, Solana Beach, Calif.; author, *When Living Hurts* (1988), *Hypnosis and the Treatment of Depressions* (1992), and *Breaking the Patterns of Depression* (1997)

Robert C. Yeager, M.J.
Focus on Low Vision (coauthor)
Senior Editor, Chevron Corp., San Francisco; freelance science writer and book author

Glossary

A

acclimation: *see* acclimatization

acclimatization: adaptation by the body to a new environment, especially to changes in climate, altitude, weather, or temperature—*also called* acclimation

acetylcholine: a neurotransmitter that is released at the synapses of the autonomic nervous system and most neuromuscular junctions

acidosis: a condition usually caused by excessive acid production in the body, resulting in decreased alkalinity in the blood and tissues; symptoms include sweetish breath odor, headache, nausea, vomiting, and visual disturbances

acquired immune deficiency syndrome: *see* AIDS

acquired immunodeficiency syndrome: *see* AIDS

adrenaline: *see* epinephrine

Aedes aegypti: a species of mosquito that acts as a vector for infectious diseases, including yellow fever and dengue—*see also* dengue

aerobic activity: any sustained, moderately strenuous effort (as jogging, bicycling, or walking briskly) carried on at a level of intensity sufficient for the heart and lungs to keep pace with the muscles' increased need for oxygen—*compare* anaerobic activity

aerobic capacity: the maximum amount of oxygen the respiratory system can deliver to the muscles during very strenuous activity

age-related macular degeneration (AMD): *see* macular degeneration

agonist *1:* a chemical substance (as a drug) capable of initiating a reaction or activity by combining with a receptor on a cell; *2:* a muscle that upon contracting is automatically checked and controlled by the simultaneous contraction of an opposing muscle—*compare* antagonist

AIDS (acquired immune deficiency syndrome or **acquired immunodeficiency syndrome):** a disease of the immune system that is caused by infection with HIV and spread through the exchange of blood and other body fluids; symptoms include extreme fatigue, swollen lymph glands, wasting, and susceptibility to life-threatening conditions—*see also* HIV

alga (plural **algae**)**:** a chiefly aquatic green plant or plant-like organism

algal bloom: an excessive accumulation of algae in lakes, ponds, and coastal waters; may be brightly colored; detrimental to aquatic life

allele: any of the different forms of a gene that can occur at a given locus, or site, on a chromosome

allergic rhinitis: a swelling of the nasal passages caused by an allergen, or antigen, (as dust, animal dander, or pollen); symptoms include watery nasal discharge and itching of the nose and eyes

alpha-receptor: any of a group of cellular sites in tissues that are supplied by the sympathetic nervous system and that bind to natural stimulants in the body (as norepinephrine) or drugs in order to evoke "fight-or-flight" sympathetic nerve activity (as vasoconstriction)—*compare* beta-receptor; *see also* sympathetic nervous system; vasoconstriction

alternative medicine: a group of diverse approaches (as acupuncture and chiropractic) to the treatment of disease or pursuit of health that differ from the orthodox medicine taught in medical schools—*see also* complementary medicine

Alzheimer's disease: a degenerative brain disorder of unknown cause usually originating in middle or old age and marked at onset by slight memory loss and behavioral changes; as disease progresses, symptoms include severe memory loss, confusion, restlessness, difficulty with speech and motor skills, and, ultimately, dementia

AMD: *see* macular degeneration

anabolic steroid: any of various usually synthetic hormones that raise metabolism and are sometimes used by athletes to increase muscle mass, although such use is banned by official sports organizations

anaerobic activity: any sudden vigorous action (as sprinting) causing an intense burst of muscle stimulus that inhibits the heart and lungs from supplying the oxygen needed to perform the action and produces an accumulation of lactic acid in the muscles—*compare* aerobic activity; *see also* lactic acid

analgesic: any substance (as a nonsteroidal anti-inflammatory drug) that reduces sensitivity to pain without producing a loss of consciousness—*see also* nonsteroidal anti-inflammatory drug

androgen: any of a group of male sex hormones (as testosterone)—*compare* estrogen; progestogen; *see also* testosterone

anemia: a disorder in which the blood is deficient in red blood cells, in hemoglobin, or in total volume; symptoms include dizziness, fatigue, headache, difficulty in breathing during activity, and pale skin

anencephaly: a neural tube defect in which the brain and spinal cord fail to form, the skull fails to close, and the spinal column remains a groove—*see also* neural tube defect

angina: chest pain usually due to decreased supply of oxygen to the heart muscle and generally associated with a blockage in one or more of the coronary arteries—*also called* angina pectoris

angina pectoris: *see* angina

angioplasty: a procedure used to enlarge the lumen (inner hollow portion) of a partly obstructed artery by passing a catheter through the narrowed area, where the tip of a balloonlike device is inflated—*also called* balloon angioplasty

animal model: an animal similar to humans in its anatomy, physiology, or susceptibility to a pathogen and used in research to obtain results that can be applied in human medicine; also, a condition similar to a human condition or disease that occurs naturally in an animal or can be produced artificially

antagonist *1:* a chemical substance that acts within the body to reduce the normal activity of another substance; *2:* a muscle that contracts with and limits the action of another muscle with which it is paired—*compare* agonist

antibody: any of a large number of proteins that are produced by specialized cells to attack an antigen in an immune response—*also called* immunoglobulin; *see also* antigen

anticholinergic agent: a drug that blocks the action of acetylcholine and reduces muscle spasms; often used to treat Parkinson's disease, especially in early stages or younger patients—*see also* acetylcholine

antigen: any substance (as a toxin, allergen, or enzyme) capable of stimulating an immune response

antioxidant: a substance (as beta-carotene) that inhibits reactions with or promoted by oxygen or peroxides and that protects the body from the effects of free radicals—*see also* free radical

antipsychotic: a powerful drug, often a tranquilizer (as chlorpromazine), used to treat severe mental disorders characterized by a deficient or lost contact with reality; believed to act by blocking dopamine receptors—*also called* neuroleptic

antipyretic: a substance that prevents or alleviates fever

antiseptic: a cleansing agent (as hydrogen peroxide) applied in or on body tissues to prevent infection by inhibiting the growth or action of infectious microorganisms (as bacteria)

apoplexy: *see* stroke

apoptosis: the natural process of cell destruction that initiates an orderly breakdown and elimination of superfluous or defective cells—*also called* programmed cell death

arenavirus: any of a family of viruses usually transmitted to humans by infected wild rodents through contamination of food and personal items or by inhalation of airborne viruses; symptoms of arenavirus infection include fever, rash, malaise, headaches, and muscular pain

assay: a detailed laboratory analysis of a substance (as of a drug) to determine the presence, absence, or quantity of certain components or characteristics of that substance

atherosclerosis: a common condition of the arteries characterized by deposits of cholesterol, fat, and other substances in the inner layer of the arteries; a major cause of angina and heart attacks; often linked to high blood pressure, diabetes, and obesity

atrial fibrillation: a heart condition marked by rapid uncoordinated contractions of the atria, resulting in a lack of synchronicity between the heartbeat and pulse

atrium: a cavity or passage in the body, especially a chamber of the heart that receives blood from the veins to be oxygenated

atrophy: a decrease in size or wasting away of a body part or tissue; also, arrested development or loss of a part or organ incidental to the normal development of an animal or plant

attenuate: to reduce the severity of a disease or virulence of a pathogen

autoimmune disease: a condition (as rheumatoid arthritis) caused by an immune response against the body's own tissues or cells—*see also* immune response; rheumatoid arthritis

autonomic nervous system: a part of the vertebrate nervous system that activates muscular and glandular tissues (as of the stomach and heart) and governs involuntary actions (as digestion and heart rate); made up of the sympathetic and parasympathetic nervous systems—*compare* parasympathetic nervous system; sympathetic nervous system

B

bacillus: any member of the genus *Bacillus,* a group of rod-shaped, spore-forming bacteria some species of which cause disease in humans and animals; also, a rod-shaped bacterium of a genus other than *Bacillus*—*see also* bacteria

bacillus Calmette-Guérin (BCG) vaccine: a vaccine that is used to protect primarily young children at risk of developing tuberculosis but does not prevent most contagious forms of the disease in adults; adverse effects include allergic reactions and the development of tuberculosis—*see also* tuberculosis

bacterium (plural **bacteria**)**:** any of a group of one-celled microorganisms of different shapes (as round or spiral) that are found in soil, water, plants, and animals and may cause infection; the nature, severity, and outcome of the infection depend on the species of bacterium

balloon angioplasty: *see* angioplasty

basal cell carcinoma: a skin cancer involving the innermost cells of the deepest layer of the skin—*compare* malignant melanoma; squamous cell carcinoma

basal ganglion (plural **ganglia**)**:** any of four masses of gray matter (nervous tissue consisting primarily of the nucleus-containing portion of nerve cells) in the brain that control posture and coordination and provide a crucial link in the feedback loop that allows the brain to communicate with the body

BCG vaccine: *see* bacillus Calmette-Guérin vaccine

benign: of a mild type or character, not threatening to health or life; also, not malignant—*compare* malignant

beta-blocker: any of a class of mainly cardiovascular drugs that block the activity of beta-receptors and thereby decrease blood pressure and heart rate

beta-carotene: an antioxidant found in plants, mainly dark green and deep yellow vegetables and fruits (as sweet potatoes, spinach, carrots, pumpkin, and cantaloupe); converted in the body into vitamin A (retinol), an essential vitamin that aids in the prevention of night blindness and promotes healthy hair, teeth, gums, bones, skin, and mucous membranes—*see also* antioxidant

beta-receptor: any of a group of cellular sites in tissues that are supplied by the sympathetic nervous system and that bind to natural substances in the body (as epinephrine) or drugs, which results in an increase in the muscular contraction and beat of the heart and a relaxation of muscles in the bronchi (air passages leading to the lungs), intestines, and blood-vessel walls—*compare* alpha-receptor; *see also* sympathetic nervous system; vasodilation

biopsy: the removal and examination of cells, tissues, or fluids from the living body

birth control: the purposeful control of the number of children born, usually by prevention of conception by any of several methods (as a condom or diaphragm)—*see also* contraception

bismuth: a brittle metallic element often used in the form of a reddish powder; used to treat gastrointestinal disorders

bisphosphonate: any of a group of chemical compounds that suppress the natural process of bone remodeling by interfering with the function of cells that resorb damaged or weakened bone tissue; used to treat osteoporosis and other bone disorders

bloodborne: transmitted through the blood (as an infectious agent)

blood plasma: *see* plasma

bone densitometry: the process of determining the optical or photographic density of bone for the purpose of measuring bone mass

bone marrow: a soft, vascular connective tissue that occupies the cavities of most bones and occurs in two forms: whitish or yellowish marrow made up mostly of fat cells, and reddish marrow containing little fat and producing red blood cells

bradykinesia: an abnormal condition characterized by a slowness of all voluntary movement and speech; often caused by parkinsonism, Parkinson's disease, other nerve disorders, and certain drugs—*see also* parkinsonism; Parkinson's disease

brain stem: the base of the brain, which controls various motor, sense, reflex, and regulatory functions

breakbone fever: *see* dengue

bronchopulmonary dysplasia: a chronic disorder of the lungs and bronchi (air passages leading to the lungs) characterized by tissue inflammation and scarring; typically occurs in infants who have received treatment for respiratory distress syndrome—*see also* respiratory distress syndrome

C

calcium: a silver-white element that is the most common mineral in the human body, found primarily in bones and teeth; critical in the prevention of certain bone diseases (as osteoporosis)

calcium channel blocker: any of a class of drugs that prevent calcium from entering smooth muscle cells (as of the heart) and thereby cause the tissue to relax; mainly used to treat cardiovascular conditions (as angina)

calorie: a unit of measurement expressing the heat-producing or energy-producing value of food once oxidized in the body; *also called* kilocalorie

cancer: a malignant tumor capable of potentially unlimited growth; *also* a diseased condition of the body marked by such tumors; causes include hereditary predisposition, viruses, radiation, smoking, and environmental chemicals—*see also* malignant

carbohydrate: any of various compounds of carbon, hydrogen, and oxygen (as sugars, starches, and celluloses), most of which are formed by green plants and constitute a major class of foods

carcinogen: an agent producing or inciting cancer

cardiac arrest: the temporary or permanent cessation of heartbeat; often caused by myocardial infarction—*see also* myocardial infarction

carotid artery: one of a pair of arteries that supply blood to the head

carotid endarterectomy: a surgical procedure that clears obstructions from the carotid arteries and restores blood flow

cataract: a clouding of the lens of the eye or its surrounding transparent membrane; causes obstruction of the passage of light and may eventually result in blindness; occurs especially in the elderly

catheter: a tubular device for insertion into canals, vessels, or body cavities, usually to permit injection or withdrawal of fluids or to keep a passage open

CD4: a large protein found especially on the surface of T-helper cells that aids them in recognizing foreign antigens and that is the receptor for HIV—*see also* antigen; HIV; T-helper cell

CD4+ lymphocyte: *see* T-helper cell

central nervous system (CNS): the part of the nervous system that consists of the brain and spinal cord, to which sensory impulses are transmitted and from which motor impulses pass; coordinates the activity of the entire nervous system

cerebral hemorrhage: bleeding into the tissue of the brain from a ruptured blood vessel

cerebrovascular accident: *see* stroke

cervix: *1:* the back part of the neck; *2:* the narrow lower or outer end of the uterus—*also called* cervix uteri

cervix uteri: *see* cervix

chemotherapy: the utilization of chemical agents in the treatment of disease;

often associated with cancer treatment

chiropractic: a system of therapy that relies on manipulation and adjustment of body structures (as the spinal column)

cholera: an acute bacterial infection of the small intestine marked by severe diarrhea and vomiting, muscle cramps, and dehydration; usually results from toxic substances produced by the bacterium *Vibrio cholerae*

cholesterol: a fatlike substance manufactured by animal cells, present in body cells and fluids, important in normal physiological processes, and implicated as a factor in atherosclerosis—*see also* atherosclerosis

chondriosome: *see* mitochondrion

clinical: of, relating to, or conducted in or as if in a clinic; involving direct observation and treatment of the living patient; often applied to objective methods (as interviews) used to describe, analyze, evaluate, and classify a patient's symptoms or behavior

clinical trial: a study done to test either an experimental or a standard therapeutic agent (as a drug or vaccine) in consenting humans to determine if the experimental treatment is safe or effective or to compare the effectiveness of different agents; typically, a specific set of criteria is used to determine the end point of the trial for each patient—*see also* end point

cognition: the mental process of knowing, thinking, learning, and judging

colonize: to become established in a particular habitat (as a wound, body system, organ, or tract); usually refers to a mass of microorganisms

complementary medicine: any aspect of alternative medicine that is accepted and practiced by mainstream health professionals—*see also* alternative medicine

complex carbohydrate: a sugar or starch made up of a series of different glucose molecules; usually found in fruits, vegetables, and whole grains—*see also* glucose

compression fracture: a condition in which bone tissue is severed and the bone collapses; occurs most often in a short bone, such as a vertebra—*also called* crush fracture

computed tomography (CT): an imaging technique involving X-rays that produces cross-sectional views of internal bodily structures—*also called* computerized tomography

concordance rate: the percentage of twins who share a particular trait or disorder

congestive heart failure: a condition in which the heart is unable to maintain an adequate circulation of blood to the tissues or to pump out the blood returned to it by the venous circulation

contraception: the deliberate prevention of conception or implantation of a fertilized egg in the uterus—*see also* birth control

contraindication: a condition or symptom that makes a particular treatment or procedure inadvisable

control group: subjects in a clinical trial or an experiment who are treated or followed as a comparison group and who typically do not receive any treatment during the investigation or who receive a standard treatment as opposed to the experimental one

coronary artery: one of a pair of arteries that branch from the aorta (the major artery of the heart), one from the right side and one from the left side, and that feed a system of smaller arteries supplying the heart muscle with blood

crush fracture: *see* compression fracture

CT: *see* computed tomography

culture: the maintenance of cells or microorganisms in a prepared medium for diagnostic, therapeutic, or research purposes

D

dementia: a condition of mental deterioration marked by lethargy, confusion, personality change, and a progressive decline in cognitive function, affecting memory, judgment, and reasoning

dengue: an acute viral infection transmitted by mosquitoes of the genus *Aedes* especially in tropical regions and characterized by fever, rash, and acute head, joint, and muscle pain; the infection clears up within several weeks without treatment—*also called* breakbone fever; dengue fever

dengue fever: *see* dengue

dengue hemorrhagic fever: a sometimes fatal form of dengue that affects mainly children and is characterized by coughing, breathing problems, vomiting, and abdominal pain, followed by severe bleeding, bruises, shock, and sometimes the eventual failure of the circulatory system

deoxyribonucleic acid: *see* DNA

diabetes: *see* diabetes mellitus

diabetes mellitus: a disorder caused by the failure of the pancreas to produce sufficient insulin (the hormone that regulates glucose absorption) or the body's inability to properly utilize the insulin produced; characterized by excessive urine production, large amounts of sugar in the blood and urine, thirst, hunger, and weight loss—*also called* diabetes; *see also* impaired glucose tolerance

digital recording: the process of recording data (as images) in the form of numerical digits or discrete units for later storage or display

diuretic: any of a class of substances that promote the formation and release of urine and are used to lessen the volume of fluid (as water) in the body

DNA (deoxyribonucleic acid): a large molecule that makes up the threadlike structures called chromosomes in the nucleus of a cell and contains the cell's genetic information

dopamine: a neurotransmitter in the brain that is a key link in the synthesis of epinephrine; the lack of this chemical in the brain causes symptoms (as muscular rigidity and slowness of movement) characteristic of Parkinson's disease—*see also* levodopa; Parkinson's disease

double-blind: related to or being an experimental procedure in which the identity of the test and control groups is known to neither the subjects nor the investigators during the course of the study

drug resistance: the ability of infectious microorganisms (as those causing pneumonia or tuberculosis) to survive exposure to therapeutic agents (as drugs) formerly effective against them; the development of such resistance has been attributed to the overuse of antibiotics

duodenum: the beginning of the small intestine, usually the shortest and widest section, which extends from the opening between the stomach and the intestine to the undersurface of the liver

dyslexia: a difficulty in reading, despite normal intelligence and education, marked by a tendency to read and write letters or words in reverse sequences

E

echocardiography: a noninvasive and painless diagnostic procedure that uses high-frequency sound waves to evaluate heart structure and function

electrolyte: any of the ions (as of sodium, potassium, calcium, or sulfate) that in a biological fluid regulate or affect most metabolic processes (as the flow of nutrients into and waste products out of cells)

embolus: a blood clot, large bubble of air, piece of tissue or tumor, or foreign object that travels through the bloodstream until it becomes lodged in a blood vessel

encephalitis: an inflammation of the brain usually caused by a virus transmitted most often by the bite of a mosquito or tick or by direct contact with the infective agent; symptoms include headache, neck pain, vomiting, fever, and nervous system disorders—*see also* spongiform encephalopathy

end point: the stage in a clinical trial at which a patient is removed from treatment owing to one of several predetermined factors (as spread of disease)

endemic: restricted to or prevalent in a particular locality or region

endocrine system: the glands and parts of glands that secrete hormones distributed in the body via the bloodstream, which help to integrate and control metabolic activity; includes especially the pituitary, thyroid, adrenals, ovaries, and testes

endogenous: originating, arising, or produced within the body—*compare* exogenous

endorphin: any of a group of proteins with potent analgesic (pain-blocking) properties that occur naturally in the brain

endoscope: a flexible tube for visualizing the interior of a hollow organ or structure (as the nasal passages or urinary tract)

epidemic: an outbreak of disease affecting many individuals within a population, community, or region at the same time—*compare* epizootic; pandemic

epidemiology: a branch of medical science that involves the study of the incidence, distribution, and control of disease within a population or populations

epinephrine: a colorless crystalline sympathetic-nervous-system-stimulating hormone that is secreted by the inner portion of the adrenal gland and functions as the principal blood-pressure-raising hormone; used medically as a heart stimulant, vasoconstrictor (an agent that narrows blood vessels), and muscle relaxant—*also called* adrenaline; *see also* sympathetic nervous system

epithelial tissue: *see* epithelium

epithelium: the membranous cellular tissue that covers the body's surface and lines most tubes and cavities within the body—*also called* epithelial tissue

epizootic: an outbreak of disease that spreads rapidly through an animal population—*compare* epidemic

equine encephalitis: *see* Venezuelan equine encephalitis

erythrocyte: *see* red blood cell

erythropoietin: a hormone that is formed especially in the kidney and stimulates red blood cell production

estradiol: the most potent natural estrogen

estrogen: any of a group of hormones that aid the development of female secondary sex traits (as breasts); drugs containing natural or synthetic estrogens are used to prevent pregnancy (as in oral contraceptives) and to relieve symptoms of menopause and prevent postmenopausal osteoporosis and heart disease; also used in the treatment of breast cancer—*see also* estradiol; progestogen; progesterone

eugenics: a science concerned with the improvement of hereditary qualities of a breed or race (especially by influencing mating and reproduction)

euthanasia: the act or practice of killing sick or injured individuals, often for reasons of mercy, or of allowing an ill patient to die by taking less-than-complete measures to prolong life

exogenous: introduced from or produced outside the body—*compare* endogenous

F

fatty acid: one of numerous organic (as carbon-based) compounds that are important components of lipids in animals, plants, and microorganisms; some fatty acids essential to human life cannot be synthesized by the body and must be ingested in foods—*see also* lipid

fecal-oral route: a common pathway for transmission of infection in which fecal matter is ingested as a consequence of poor hygiene or inadequate sanitation

fertilization: the union of sperm and egg to form an embryo that has the potential to grow into a fetus

fibrin: a white insoluble protein formed when the blood clots

folate: *see* folic acid

folic acid: a vitamin of the B-complex group that is required for normal production of red blood cells and synthesis of nucleoprotein (protein joined to nucleic acid); major food sources include green leafy vegetables, liver, dry beans, mushrooms, and whole-grain cereals—*also called* folate

free radical: an especially reactive atom or group of atoms that is found in the body and has one or more unpaired electrons—*see also* antioxidant

G

gastritis: an inflammation of the lining of the stomach; symptoms include nausea and vomiting; may be asymptomatic

gene: the physical unit of inheritance that consists of a segment of DNA and carries characteristics from parent to offspring; usually occurs in pairs (alleles); genes regulate the development, growth, and function of body cells and tissues—*see also* DNA

genome: the genetic material of a given individual or species

geriatrics: the branch of medicine that deals with the problems and diseases of old age and aging people

gerontology: the specific study of aging and its phenomena

glaucoma: a generally age-related disease of the eye marked by a progressive increase of the pressure within the eyeball caused by a blockage of the outflow of fluid between the cornea and the lens; usually results in gradual loss of peripheral vision and may progress to loss of central vision

glucose: a simple sugar found in many foods, especially fruits, that is produced by the digestion of carbohydrates and provides the body with energy

glycogen: the major carbohydrate in animal cells; stored chiefly in the liver and, to some extent, in muscle—*see also* carbohydrate

H

HDL: *see* high-density lipoprotein

health maintenance organization (HMO): a public or private organization that provides comprehensive medical care to a group of voluntary subscribers on the basis of a prepaid contract and delivers those services for a fixed, prenegotiated fee—*see also* managed care

heart attack: *see* myocardial infarction

helper T cell: *see* T-helper cell

hematocrit: a measure of the number of red blood cells found in the blood and conveyed as a percentage of the total blood volume—*see also* red blood cell

hemoglobin: the iron-containing pigment occurring in red blood cells that functions in the transport of oxygen from the lungs to tissues of the body and carbon dioxide from the tissues back to the lungs

hemorrhage: a copious discharge of blood from the blood vessels that results in heavy or uncontrollable bleeding

herpes zoster: *see* shingles

herpesvirus: any of a group of viruses that cause several diseases, including chicken pox, shingles, and genital herpes; the group also includes cytomegalovirus, a major cause of infection in AIDS, and the Epstein-Barr virus, the cause of infectious mononucleosis

high blood pressure: *see* hypertension

high-density lipoprotein (HDL): a lipoprotein composed of a high proportion of protein and a low proportion of cholesterol; associated with a decreased probability of atherosclerosis—*compare* low-density lipoprotein; *see also* lipoprotein; atherosclerosis

HIV (human immunodeficiency virus): any of a group of retroviruses that infect and destroy certain immune system cells (as T-helper cells) and ultimately cause AIDS—*see also* AIDS; retrovirus; T-helper cell

HMO: *see* health maintenance organization

homocysteine: an amino acid that is implicated as a factor in atherosclerosis and may function like cholesterol by contributing to the obstruction of the coronary arteries—*see also* atherosclerosis; cholesterol

human immunodeficiency virus: *see* HIV

hyaline membrane disease: *see* respiratory distress syndrome

hypertension: a common, often asymptomatic condition in which the blood pressure (the force exerted by blood against the walls of the vessels) in either arteries or veins is abnormally high; may occur as a complication of a preexisting disorder (as of the kidneys or adrenal glands), pregnancy, or use of oral contraceptives but most often is of unknown cause; risk factors include obesity, cigarette smoking, high sodium level, heredity, and emotional or physical stress—*also called* high blood pressure

hypoglycemia: a condition marked by an abnormal decrease of sugar in the blood; symptoms include weakness, hunger, dizziness, headache, loss of muscle coordination, anxiety, and, if untreated, delirium, coma, and death; typically occurs in people affected with diabetes

idiopathic: of unknown cause

immune response: the body's natural reaction against foreign substances (as infectious agents)

immunocompetent: possessing the capacity to mount a normal immune response—*compare* immunocompromised

immunocompromised: having an impaired or weakened immune system (as by drugs or illness)—*compare* immunocompetent

immunoglobulin: *see* antibody

impaired glucose tolerance: a metabolic condition in which the body is unable to regulate blood sugar; caused by cellular resistance to insulin (the hormone regulating glucose absorption); results in an increased level of glucose in the blood—*see also* diabetes mellitus

incidence: the number of new infections of a disease in a given time period—*compare* prevalence

incubation period: the time between exposure to a disease-causing agent (as a virus) and the onset of symptoms

informed consent: the consent to surgery or to participation in a medical experiment by a patient or subject after learning about the potential benefits and risks of the procedure

inoculate: to introduce into the body, usually by injection, a small amount of a causative agent of disease (as a virus), an antibody, or an antigen in order to treat or prevent disease (as in vaccination); also, to introduce a microorganism into a laboratory culture in order to grow additional microorganisms for study, experimentation, or diagnostic purposes—*see also* culture

intrauterine device (IUD): a metal or plastic device that is inserted into and left in the uterus usually to prevent implantation of a fertilized egg—*see also* birth control

intravenous: situated within, occurring within, or administered via a vein

invasive: involving entry (as by incision) into the living body; also, tending to spread within the body, especially to healthy tissue

ischemia: a reduced blood supply to an organ or tissue, often marked by pain and impairment of function

IUD: *see* intrauterine device

K

Kaposi's sarcoma: a form of skin cancer marked by the development of typically painless red-purple or blue-brown spots or lesions on the surface of the skin; believed to be caused by a virus; occurs especially as an opportunistic infection in AIDS patients, in whom it can affect internal organs (as the lungs and stomach)—*see also* AIDS; opportunistic infection

kilocalorie: *see* calorie

kinesiology: the study of muscular activity and of the anatomy, physiology, and mechanics of body movement

L

lactic acid: an organic acid normally present in tissue; one form, found in muscle and blood, is a product of the anaerobic (occurring in the absence of oxygen) breakdown of glucose and glycogen to energy that takes place during the course of strenuous physical activity; the accumulation of lactic acid in the muscles typically causes cramping—*see also* anaerobic activity; glucose

larva (plural **larvae**)**:** the immature stage in the development of many animals (as butterflies and frogs) that is usually physically quite different from the mature or adult form

LDL: *see* low-density lipoprotein

L-dopa: *see* levodopa

leukocyte: *see* white blood cell

levodopa: a substance that stimulates the production of the neurotransmitter dopamine in the brain and is used in treating Parkinson's disease—*also called* L-dopa; *see also* dopamine; Parkinson's disease

lipid: any of a diverse group of fats or fatlike organic compounds (as cholesterol and triglycerides) that are insoluble in water but soluble in organic solvents; lipids are stored in body tissues and serve as an energy reserve; lipids also play a role in the synthesis of important compounds in the body and are necessary for normal nervous system function; elevated lipid levels are sometimes characteristic of certain diseases (as atherosclerosis)

lipoprotein: any of a group of substances containing both lipid and protein; lipoproteins in the blood function in the transport of cholesterol—*see also* high-density lipoprotein; low-density lipoprotein

low birth weight: a condition in which an infant is born weighing less than 2,500 g (5.5 lb); low-birth-weight babies are at risk for oxygen starvation during labor, low blood sugar after birth, and slow growth during childhood

low-density lipoprotein (LDL): a lipoprotein that is composed of a moderate proportion of protein and a high proportion of cholesterol; associated with an increased risk of atherosclerosis—*compare* high-density lipoprotein; *see also* cholesterol; lipoprotein

lumbar puncture: the introduction of a hollow needle into the fluid-filled area of the lower portion of the vertebral canal (containing the spinal cord) either to withdraw the fluid that circulates in the brain and spinal cord for diagnostic purposes or to inject anesthetic drugs; *also called* spinal tap

lycopene: the red pigment from which tomatoes and some berries and other fruits derive their characteristic color; functions as an antioxidant—*see also* antioxidant

lymphatic system: the group of interrelated body tissues, nodes, vessels, and ducts that produce specialized cells to regulate immunity; also produces a fluid (lymph) containing white blood cells that bathes the cells and circulates through the body via a series of ducts and channels

macrophage: an immune system cell that engulfs and consumes foreign material and debris and that functions in the protection of the body against infection and harmful substances

macular degeneration: a usually progressive, age-related loss of central vision resulting from damage to or breakdown of the macula lutea, the small central area of the retina that allows the sharpest vision—*also called* age-related macular degeneration

magnetic resonance imaging (MRI): a noninvasive diagnostic technique that produces computerized images of internal body tissues and is based on the response of atomic nuclei to a magnetic field induced by radio waves

malaria: an acute or chronic infectious disease caused by parasitic protozoans of the genus *Plasmodium* that are transmitted to humans by the bite of an infected female mosquito; characterized by fever, anemia, chills, and enlargement of the spleen; occurs throughout tropical and subtropical regions of the world—*see also* protozoan

malignant: tending to produce death or deterioration by infiltration into tissue; having an unfavorable prognosis—*compare* benign; *see also* cancer; metastasis

malignant melanoma: an often fatal form of cancer that originates especially in the pigmented cells of the skin but may also develop in the mucous membranes, eyes, or central nervous system and that spreads rapidly to other parts of the body; most often arises from a pigmented mole—*also called* melanoma; *compare* basal cell carcinoma; squamous cell carcinoma

malnutrition: a disorder that is characterized by poor nourishment and that often results from an imbalanced, inadequate, or scanty diet or from defective absorption of nutrients by the body due to disease; usually leads to overall bodily deterioration

managed care: a system that sets policies and procedures for controlling the cost and delivery of health care—*see also* health maintenance organization

maximal heart rate: *see* maximum heart rate

maximum heart rate: the level at which the heart is working to its utmost capacity, measured as the number of heartbeats per minute; determined by the individual's age and physical condition—*also called* maximal heart rate

melanoma: *see* malignant melanoma

menarche: the beginning of the menstrual function, usually marked by the first menstrual period—*compare* menopause

meningitis: a disorder usually resulting from a bacterial or viral infection that causes swelling of the membranes covering the brain and spinal cord (the meninges); symptoms include headache, fever, vomiting, and severe stiffness of the neck; untreated bacterial meningitis may result in convulsions, coma, and death

menopause: the end of a woman's reproductive function, usually marked by the last menstrual period; accompanied by a decline in hormone levels and various symptoms (as hot flashes)—*compare* menarche

meta-analysis: a method of combining data from many experiments or studies to obtain statistical results that represent a synthesis of the data on a specific scientific question

metastasis: the process by which cancer cells spread to sites distant from that of the primary lesion and that results in the development of a similar lesion in a new location in the body

mitochondrion (plural **mitochondria):** a small threadlike structure in a cell that is the primary energy source of the cell—*also called* chondriosome

molecular biology: a branch of biology concerned with studying the molecular basis of inheritance by analyzing the structure and function of DNA and RNA—*see also* DNA; RNA

monounsaturated fat: a derivative of a fatty acid (as oleic acid) in which only one pair of carbon atoms is linked by a double or triple bond; food sources include olive oil and canola oil—*compare* polyunsaturated fat; saturated fat

morbidity: a diseased state or abnormal condition; also, the rate of illness in a specific community or group

mortality: the condition of being subject to death; also, the rate of death in a specific community or group

MRI: *see* magnetic resonance imaging

multi-infarct dementia: a condition resulting from repeated small strokes and characterized by progressive loss of cognitive function similar to that seen in Alzheimer's disease

mutation: an alteration in the genetic material involving either a physical change in chromosomal structure or a biochemical change in the subunits that make up genes—*see also* gene

myocardial infarction: damage to the heart muscle that occurs when one or more of the coronary arteries are blocked and the supply of blood to a portion of the heart muscle is interrupted; may be marked by sudden chest pain, shortness of breath, nausea, loss of consciousness, and sometimes death; risk factors include hypertension, family history of cardiovascular disease, cigarette smoking, obesity, and high blood cholesterol—*also called* heart attack; *see also* cardiac arrest

nerve cell: *see* neuron

neural tube defect: any of a group of congenital defects of the brain and spinal cord caused by abnormal development of the neural tube, the precursor of the brain and spinal cord, during early embryonic life; examples include spina bifida and anencephaly

neuron: the nervous system cell that transmits and receives nerve impulses—*also called* nerve cell

neurotransmitter: a chemical substance (as serotonin) that transports nerve impulses across the synapses, or junctions, between neurons—*see also* serotonin

nonsteroidal anti-inflammatory drug (NSAID): a medication (as aspirin, ibuprofen, naproxen, or ketoprofen) used to relieve pain, stiffness, and inflammation, especially in conditions affecting the muscles, bones, and joints

NSAID: *see* nonsteroidal anti-inflammatory drug

nucleotide: the basic structural unit of DNA and RNA

occlusion: a blockage in a canal, artery, vein, or passageway of the body

onchocerciasis: a tropical disease of the skin and eyes caused by the parasite *Onchocerca volvulus* and transmitted to humans by the bite of the blackfly; symptoms include rash, skin thickening, loss of skin color, and, in chronic untreated cases, blindness—*also called* river blindness

oncogene: a gene possessing the potential to cause a normal cell to become cancerous—*see also* cancer; malignant

opportunistic infection: an infectious disease caused by a microorganism that is usually harmless to an individual with normal immune function; such infections occur in individuals with AIDS or other diseases involving impaired immune response and in persons taking immunosuppressive drugs

oral contraceptive: any of a group of orally administered synthetic hormones used for birth control and for alleviating the symptoms of premenstrual syndrome—*see also* premenstrual syndrome

osteoporosis: a disorder of the bones marked by a loss of normal bone density and a thinning of skeletal tissue causing bone brittleness and an increased risk of fracture; occurs most frequently in postmenopausal women

oxidation: the act or process of combining with oxygen

P

pandemic: a disease occurring globally or over a wide geographic area and affecting an exceptionally high proportion of the population—*compare* epidemic

panic disorder: a mental disorder marked by recurrent unexpected anxiety attacks; symptoms include palpitations, rapid breathing, chest pain, sweating, trembling, and dizziness

parasite: an organism living in, with, or on another organism

parasympathetic nervous system: a part of the autonomic nervous system that induces secretion, increases the tone and contractility of smooth muscle, slows the heart rate, and stimulates digestion; the neurotransmitter acetylcholine is the principal regulator of this system—*compare* autonomic nervous system; sympathetic nervous system; *see also* acetylcholine

parathyroid hormone: a hormone that acts to keep a constant level of calcium in body tissues and that regulates the retention of calcium by bone

parkinsonism: a neurological disorder with symptoms similar to those of Parkinson's disease that occurs especially as a side effect of certain drugs (as antipsychotics) and sometimes as a result of environmental exposure or infectious disease—*see also* Parkinson's disease

Parkinson's disease: a progressive, degenerative neurological disease of unknown cause characterized by tremor, muscle rigidity, shuffling gait, difficulty in initiating and stopping movement, and in some cases dementia; linked to the brain's decreased production of the neurotransmitter dopamine; treated with drugs (as levodopa) that increase the amount of dopamine present in the brain—*see also* dopamine; levodopa; parkinsonism

pathogen: a causative agent of disease

pathogenesis: the origin and development of a disease or disease process

pathophysiology: the physiology of the functional changes that accompany a particular syndrome or disease

PCR: *see* polymerase chain reaction

peripheral vessel: an artery or vein in the systemic circulatory system (the part supplying blood to all areas of the body except the lungs)

PET: *see* positron-emission tomography

placebo: an inert or innocuous substance or treatment used especially in controlled experiments to test the effectiveness of an active substance or treatment

placebo effect: an improvement in a patient's condition that is due not to the specific treatment given but to other factors (as the patient's belief in the treatment's effectiveness)

plaque: *1:* a patch of fatty material deposited on the lining of an artery that can eventually obstruct blood flow; *2:* a sticky film on the teeth that harbors bacteria and is a cause of tooth decay; *3:* a brain lesion that is characteristic of Alzheimer's disease—*see also* Alzheimer's disease

plasma: the fluid part of a liquid (as blood, lymph, or milk) as distinguished from suspended material; blood plasma consists of water and its dissolved constituents (as salts, sugars, fats, proteins, and hormones)—*compare* serum

plasmid: a ring of DNA found in some bacteria that is located outside of and replicates independently from the chromosome; some plasmids enable bacteria to resist antibiotic drugs—*see also* DNA

plasticity: a capacity for being molded or changed, as the brain's ability to learn or relearn following trauma; in the nervous system, the ability of neurons to form new connections to each other following destruction (as by injury) of existing connections

platelet: a small, colorless, disk-shaped component of

the blood that assists in blood clotting by adhering to other platelets and to damaged tissue

PMS: *see* premenstrual syndrome

polymerase chain reaction (PCR): a technique for rapidly synthesizing large quantities of a given segment of DNA—*see also* DNA

polyunsaturated fat: a derivative of a fatty acid (as linoleic acid) in which the carbon atoms are linked by more than one double or triple bond; food sources include vegetable oils (corn, safflower, sunflower, soybean, cottonseed), fish, and fish oils—*compare* monounsaturated fat; saturated fat

positron-emission tomography (PET): a diagnostic imaging technique that detects evidence of collisions between electrons (negatively charged particles) and positrons (positively charged particles) emitted by radioisotopes (radioactive forms of elements) in the body; produces three-dimensional images that reflect and characterize the biochemical activity of tissues

potassium: an essential mineral found in foods (as bananas, meats, and bran) that facilitates muscle contraction and the transmission of nerve impulses, helps regulate fluid balance in cells, and promotes the release of energy from carbohydrates, proteins, and fats

premenstrual syndrome (PMS): a group of symptoms that occur in some women prior to menstruation and that may include emotional instability, irritability, anxiety, depression, fatigue, and abdominal pain

prevalence: the proportion of people in a given population who are infected with a given disease—*compare* incidence

prion: an abnormal form of a protein implicated as the cause of various infectious diseases of the nervous system (as bovine spongiform encephalopathy, also known as mad cow disease); derived from the term *proteinaceous infectious particle*

progestagen: *see* progestogen

progesterone: a female hormone that functions primarily to prepare the uterine lining for implantation of a fertilized egg and during pregnancy to ensure proper function of the placenta; used in synthetic forms as an oral contraceptive, to treat menstrual disorders, and to alleviate some cases of infertility in women

progestin: *see* progestogen

progestogen: any of a group of natural or synthetic hormones with progesterone-like effects—*also spelled* progestagen; *also called* progestin; *compare* androgen; estrogen; *see also* progesterone

programmed cell death: *see* apoptosis

prophylaxis: treatment to prevent the onset or recurrence of disease

prospective study: a research protocol in which subjects who are healthy or untreated are followed from the present into the future and monitored for the development of a particular illness or the effects of a particular treatment—*compare* retrospective study

prostaglandin: any of a group of compounds present in many tissues and organs of the body and having a variety of hormonelike functions (as controlling blood pressure or muscle contraction)

protease inhibitor: any of a group of compounds that slow or interfere with the chemical decomposition of proteins; includes several recently introduced anti-HIV drugs that have shown initial success in reducing the amount of virus in some HIV-infected individuals—*see also* HIV

protein: any of numerous combinations of amino acids that occur naturally in the body and are among the most essential components of living cells and tissues; examples of proteins include enzymes, antibodies, hemoglobin, and some hormones; proteins found in foods (as poultry, milk, fish, eggs, cheese, and nuts) are broken down during digestion into component amino acids, which are absorbed by the body and used by cells to form other proteins essential for normal body function

protozoan: any of a large group of single-celled organisms that are present in almost every habitat; about 30 different kinds are known to cause disease in humans

psychosis: a serious mental disorder (as schizophrenia) characterized by defective or absent contact with reality; often marked by hallucinations or delusions

pulmonary embolism: a potentially fatal blockage of the pulmonary artery (the vessel supplying blood to the lung) or one of its branches in the lung by foreign matter, most often a blood clot originating in a vein of the leg or pelvis; symptoms include labored breathing, chest pain, and shock

R

receptor *1:* a protein molecule on or within a cell that selectively binds to various substances, including hormones, neurotransmitters, drugs, and viruses, and initiates specific cellular activity; *2:* any of the various sensory nerve endings in the skin, deep tissues, viscera, and sense organs (as the eyes or nose) that translate a stimulus into nerve impulses

red blood cell: any of the nonnucleated (lacking a nucleus) hemoglobin-containing cells of the human blood that transport oxygen to the tissues and are responsible for the red color of human blood—*also called* erythrocyte; *compare* white blood cell; *see also* hemoglobin

remission: a period during which the symptoms of a disease abate

remodeling: the cyclical process of bone formation and resorption

respiratory distress syndrome: a common complication in premature newborns in which there is deficient surfactant, a substance that keeps the alveoli (air spaces) of the lungs open; characterized by extremely labored breathing, cyanosis (a bluish tinge to the skin or mucous membranes), and abnormally low levels of oxygen in the blood—*also called* hyaline membrane disease

retrospective study: a research protocol in which individuals who have a particular disorder are compared with unaffected individuals with respect to their previous exposure to a risk factor; also, research in which persons who have taken a particular drug or undergone a particular procedure in the past are compared with untreated individuals with respect to their present condition—*compare* prospective study

retrovirus: any of a group of viruses (as HIV) that carry their genetic blueprint in the form of RNA and, by means of the enzyme reverse transcriptase, use RNA to synthesize DNA (a reversal of the process used by most other viruses and all cellular organisms); retroviruses include numerous tumor-causing viruses—*see also* reverse transcriptase; RNA

reverse transcriptase: an enzyme of a retrovirus that directs the synthesis of DNA from a viral RNA template, a process that is necessary for the genetic material of the virus to be incorporated into the DNA of an infected cell—*see also* retrovirus

Reye's syndrome: a potentially fatal neurological illness of children and young teenagers that usually follows a viral infection (as chicken pox) and has been linked to aspirin use during the infection; symptoms include vomiting, lethargy, irritability, confusion, liver enlargement, seizures, and coma

rheumatoid arthritis: a usually chronic autoimmune disease of the connective tissues; characterized by pain, stiffness, inflammation, swelling, and sometimes deterioration of the joints—*see also* autoimmune disease

ribonucleic acid: *see* RNA

risk factor: a characteristic or circumstance (as an aspect of personal behavior or lifestyle, an environmental exposure, or an inherited trait) associated with an increased likelihood of developing a particular disease or condition

river blindness: *see* onchocerciasis

RNA (ribonucleic acid): a large molecule found in both the cell's nucleus and cytoplasm that plays a major role in the synthesis of protein; in some viruses RNA replaces DNA as a carrier of genetic information

S

saturated fat: a derivative of a fatty acid (as palmitic or myristic acid) in which all the carbon atoms are linked by single bonds and that tends to be solid at room temperature; food sources include beef, butter, cheese, whole milk, and palm and coconut oils—*compare* monounsaturated fat; polyunsaturated fat

screening: testing of a population or group in order to detect a specific disease or calculate its prevalence—*see also* prevalence

seropositive: possessing antibodies against an infectious agent or allergen in the bloodstream; commonly used to mean having antibodies to HIV in the blood—*see also* antibody; HIV; seroprevalence

seroprevalence: the rate of occurrence of an antibody in a given population as reflected in blood tests; commonly used to refer to the rate of HIV infection—*see also* seropositive

serotonin: a natural chemical that constricts blood vessels, inhibits gastric secretion, stimulates smooth muscle, and serves as a neurotransmitter in the central nervous system; thought to be important in numerous neurological and psychiatric conditions

serum *1:* the clear watery fluid that moistens the surface of certain membranes (as the lining of the abdominal cavity) or is exuded when those membranes are inflamed; *2:* the clear yellowish fluid that separates from plasma when it clots—*compare* plasma

severe combined immunodeficiency: a usually fatal hereditary disorder marked by a lack of crucial enzymes (as adenosine deaminase) that are important in fighting infection

shingles: a viral infection of adults that involves acute inflammation of the nerves that supply certain skin areas and produces a painful rash of small, crusting blisters; caused by the herpesvirus *Varicella zoster,* which is usually acquired in childhood as chicken pox—*also called* herpes zoster; *see also* herpesvirus

sodium: an element that functions within the body primarily to regulate fluid balance and preserve the structural integrity and function of body cells

spina bifida: a common neural tube defect present at birth and characterized by an abnormal opening in the bony canal that normally encloses the spinal cord—*see also* neural tube defect

spinal tap: *see* lumbar puncture

spongiform encephalopathy: any of several degenerative disorders of the brain marked by the development of holes that give the brain tissue a porous texture much like that of a sponge

squamous cell carcinoma: a skin cancer arising from the scalelike cells of the outermost layer of the skin; tumors usually occur in areas exposed to strong sunlight over a period of many years—*compare* basal cell carcinoma; malignant melanoma

stem cell: an unspecialized cell capable of giving rise to different types of cells

stenosis: a narrowing or constriction of a bodily passage or orifice

sterilization: *1:* the process by which an individual is rendered incapable of reproduction; *2:* the destruction of all microorganisms in or on an object (as a surgical tool)

steroid: any of a large family of natural and synthetic chemical substances (as hormones, vitamins, and drugs) that are used to enhance the body's natural abilities, build muscle mass, and cure disease—*see also* anabolic steroid

strain: a group of organisms (as subtypes of HIV) sharing or presumed to share similar structure or appearance but often having different physiology

stroke: the sudden diminishment or loss of consciousness, sensation, and voluntary motion caused by a rupture or an obstruction in an artery that supplies blood to the brain; symptoms vary depending on which area of the brain is damaged and include dizziness, numbness, paralysis, impaired speech and vision, and confusion—*also called* cerebrovascular accident; *formerly called* apoplexy

substantia nigra: a layer of pigmented tissue in the midbrain that contains dopamine-producing nerve cells; degeneration of cells of the substantia nigra is one of the major anatomic changes characteristic of Parkinson's disease and parkinsonism—*see also* dopamine; parkinsonism; Parkinson's disease

sympathetic nervous system: the part of the autonomic nervous system that is concerned especially with preparing the body to react to situations of stress or emergency and that induces dilation of airways, sweating, increase in heart rate, relaxation of blood vessels in muscle, and inhibition of digestion; the neurotransmitters epinephrine and norepinephrine are the principal regulators of the system—*compare* autonomic nervous system; parasympathetic nervous system

syringe: a device used to inject fluids into or withdraw them from the body or its cavities; often used to administer drugs or vaccines

T

T-helper cell: a type of immune system cell that recognizes foreign antigens and induces an immune response; usually possesses the CD4 receptor for HIV on its surface and progressively declines in number upon infection with HIV—*also called* CD4+ lymphocyte; helper T-cell; *see also* HIV

TB: *see* tuberculosis

testosterone: a naturally occurring hormone that stimulates the growth and development of male sex organs and masculine characteristics (as facial hair)

thalamus: a structure deep within the brain composed of two walnut-sized masses of nervous tissue that sit near the top of the brain stem and that function as a relay center for sensory information; sensory impulses travel from the thalamus to the cerebral cortex (the outer layer of the brain)

thanatology: the study of death, as well as of the mechanisms used to cope with grief

thrombolytic agent: a substance used to dissolve blood clots

thrombosis: the formation or presence of a clot within a blood vessel—*see also* venous thrombosis

thromboxane: any of several substances that cause constriction of the blood vessels and promote coagulation of the blood

TIA: *see* transient ischemic attack

titer: the concentration of a substance as determined by means of a process that assesses the smallest amount of the substance needed to produce a given effect

total fat: the amount of fat (in grams) listed on nutritional labels of packaged foods; includes the amount of saturated, polyunsaturated, and monounsaturated fat in a serving

trabecula: any of the small strands or rodlike bundles of fibers that provide the framework for a body organ or mass of bone—*also called* trabecular element

trabecular element: *see* trabecula

***trans* fatty acid:** a monounsaturated fatty acid that has a distinctive molecular configuration and is produced as a result of the addition of hydrogen molecules (hydrogenation) to a polyunsaturated fatty acid; food sources include margarine and some shortenings—*see also* monounsaturated fat; polyunsaturated fat

transgenic: having chromosomes into which genes from another species have been incorporated either naturally or artificially

transient ischemic attack (TIA): a brief episode of interrupted blood flow to the brain that may cause blurred vision, slurred speech, fainting, or paralysis; may be a precursor to a stroke—*see also* stroke

triglyceride: any of a group of lipids composed of one molecule of glycerol and three fatty acid molecules; triglycerides serve as energy reserves in fatty tissue and circulate in the blood in the form of lipoproteins—*see also* lipid; lipoprotein

tubal ligation: an operation that renders a female sterile by blocking the tubes through which the egg enters the uterus from the ovaries

tubercle bacillus: the bacterium *Mycobacterium tuberculosis*, which is the usual causative agent of tuberculosis—*see also* tuberculosis

tuberculosis (TB): a usually chronic infectious disease that is caused by the tubercle bacillus or, rarely, by a related bacterium and usually is contracted by breathing in airborne bacteria; typically affects the lungs but can spread to other organs; symptoms include fever, cough, loss of appetite, wasting, and night sweats

ultrasound: a noninvasive and painless diagnostic technique that uses sound waves with frequencies above the audible range to produce a two-dimensional image; often used to examine and measure internal body structures and to detect bodily abnormalities; also used to reduce inflammation and accelerate healing in soft tissues (as muscles)

ultraviolet-A radiation (UVA): the long-wavelength radiation that is situated closest to the visible spectrum and that reaches the Earth's surface most often; responsible for tanning, sunburn, and other skin problems, including aging of the skin; not as damaging to the skin as ultraviolet-B radiation—*compare* ultraviolet-B radiation; *see also* ultraviolet radiation

ultraviolet-B radiation (UVB): the intermediate-wavelength radiation that reaches the Earth's surface only part of the time but when it does is the most damaging to the skin; responsible for sunburn and other skin damage, including cancer—*compare* ultraviolet-A radiation; *see also* ultraviolet radiation

ultraviolet light: *see* ultraviolet radiation

ultraviolet radiation: the radiation adjacent to the violet end of the visible spectrum that has a wavelength shorter than that of visible light and longer than that of X-rays; occurs naturally in sunlight—*also called* ultraviolet light; *see also* ultraviolet-A radiation; ultraviolet-B radiation

uterus: the muscular organ in female mammals that holds, protects, nourishes, and maintains the developing fetus

UVA: *see* ultraviolet-A radiation

UVB: *see* ultraviolet-B radiation

V

vaginal yeast infection: an infection of the female genital tract caused by the single-celled fungus *Candida albicans;* symptoms include a white vaginal discharge, inflammation, and irritation—*see also* yeast infection

vaginitis: an inflammation of the vagina

vasectomy: an operation that renders a male sterile by severing the ducts through which sperm pass from the testes to the prostate gland and other reproductive organs

vasodilation: a widening of the interior diameter of a blood vessel induced naturally by nerve impulses or artificially by drugs that relax smooth muscle

vector: an organism (as an insect or rodent) that acts as a carrier, transmitting a disease-causing agent (as a protozoan) from one organism to another

Venezuelan equine encephalitis: a mosquito-borne viral infection found most commonly in Central and South America, Florida, and Texas; primarily affects horses but can cause a less-severe illness in humans; characterized by inflammation of the nerve tissues of the brain and spinal cord

venous: made up of, carried on by, or occurring in the veins

venous thrombosis: the presence of a blood clot within a vein

vertebral body: the solid central portion of the vertebra that supports the weight of the body

Vibrio cholerae: the comma-shaped bacterium that is the causative agent of cholera in humans—*see also* cholera

viral load: the number of virus particles (as HIV) in a sample of blood plasma; in recent studies of HIV infection, viral load has been used as a marker for disease progression

virus: a disease-causing agent that consists of genetic material (either RNA or DNA) surrounded by a protein coat and, sometimes, an outer envelope composed of lipid and protein; capable of replicating only within a living host cell; more than 200 different viruses are known to cause disease in humans—*see also* retrovirus

visual acuity: the ability of the eye to resolve detail; a measure of the sharpness of vision

vitamin D: any of several compounds necessary for the normal growth of bones and teeth and for the absorption of calcium into the bloodstream; found in such foods as dairy products, fish, and eggs

viviparous: producing live young in the manner of nearly all mammals, many reptiles, and some fish

wasting: an unintended loss of weight and lean body tissue characteristic of many diseases, including cancer, tuberculosis, and AIDS

white blood cell: any of several kinds of white or colorless cells of human blood that function in the immune defense system and tissue repair—*also called* leukocyte; *compare* red blood cell

yeast infection: an infection caused by any of numerous single-celled fungi; can affect the skin, mouth, bloodstream, genitourinary tract, and virtually every organ system—*see also* vaginal yeast infection

yellow fever: a mosquito-borne viral infection, found primarily in tropical and subtropical regions, that is marked by rapid onset of headache, fever, nausea, vomiting, and bleeding; damage to the kidneys and liver may occur; in humans recovery is followed by lifetime immunity

zoonosis (plural **zoonoses):** any disease that can be passed on to humans from a vertebrate animal host; zoonoses include illnesses as diverse as rabies, Lyme disease, and salmonellosis

zooplankton: the minute animal life that floats passively or swims weakly in a body of water

Primary sources: *Merriam-Webster's Medical Desk Dictionary, Encyclopædia Britannica, The Mosby Medical Encyclopedia.* Other sources: "AIDS Medical Glossary," *Treatment Issues* (newsletter of the Gay Men's Health Crisis); *The American Medical Association Encyclopedia of Medicine; Dictionary of Epidemiology; Jane Brody's Nutrition Book; McGraw-Hill Dictionary of Scientific and Technical Terms; The Merck Manual,* 16th edition.

—compiled by Sara Brant, contributing editor, Encyclopædia Britannica, and Joan Narmontas, associate editor, Merriam-Webster, Incorporated.

Index

This is a three-year cumulative index. Index entries to World of Medicine articles in this and previous editions of the *Medical and Health Annual* are set in boldface type, *e.g.*, **AIDS.** Entries to other subjects are set in lightface type, *e.g.*, alcohol. Additional information on any of these subjects is identified with a subheading and indented under the entry heading. The numbers following headings and subheadings indicate the year (boldface) of the edition and the page number (lightface) on which the information appears. The abbreviation *il.* indicates an illustration.

> **AIDS,** *or* acquired immune deficiency syndrome **97**–164; **96**–268; **95**–52, 215
> animal testing **95**–117
> emerging infectious diseases *map* **96**–247
> injecting drug users **97**–171
> mortality and morbidity *table* **96**–250
> new FDA-approved drugs *table* **97**–330; **96**–409
> alcohol
> aspirin interaction **97**–338
> cultural behavior **96**–146

All entry headings are alphabetized word by word. Hyphenated words and words separated by dashes or slashes are treated as two words. When one word differs from another only by the presence of additional characters at the end, the shorter precedes the longer. In inverted names, the words following the comma are considered only after the preceding part of the name has been alphabetized.
Examples:

> Lake
> Lake, Simon
> Lake Charles
> Lakeland

Names beginning with "Mc" and "Mac" are alphabetized as "Mac"; "St." is alphabetized as "Saint."

a

Dark-type numbers refer to the year of the edition, *e.g.,* **97**–264 for the 1997 edition, page 264.

Dark-type numbers refer to the year of the edition, *e.g.,* **97**–264 for the 1997 edition, page 264.

Dark-type numbers refer to the year of the edition, *e.g.,* **97**–264 for the 1997 edition, page 264.

d

Dark-type numbers refer to the year of the edition, *e.g.,* **97**–264 for the 1997 edition, page 264.

Dark-type numbers refer to the year of the edition, *e.g.,* **97**–264 for the 1997 edition, page 264.

f

Dark-type numbers refer to the year of the edition, *e.g.,* **97**–264 for the 1997 edition, page 264.

g

i

Dark-type numbers refer to the year of the edition, *e.g.,* **97**–264 for the 1997 edition, page 264.

j

k

l

n

p

Dark-type numbers refer to the year of the edition, *e.g.*, **97**–264 for the 1997 edition, page 264.

q

r

Dark-type numbers refer to the year of the edition, *e.g.*, **97**–264 for the 1997 edition, page 264.

S

Dark-type numbers refer to the year of the edition, *e.g.,* **97**–264 for the 1997 edition, page 264.

t

u

Dark-type numbers refer to the year of the edition, *e.g.,* **97**–264 for the 1997 edition, page 264.

V

W

x

y

z